"Curly Lambeau was a combination of Paul Brown, Mike Ditka and Bill Belichick. He left a massive imprint on the NFL that remains today—yet there is so much we never knew about him. Thanks to Herb Gould, that all changes now."
—Dan Pompei, senior NFL writer, *The Athletic*

"Curly Lambeau, was a charismatic yet complex personality who helped lay the foundation for one of the greatest stories in sports history, the Green Bay Packers. Herb Gould captures the essence of the man and his time in this outstanding work that takes us back to the roots of the NFL and how we got here."
—Wayne Larrivee, play-by-play radio voice of the Green Bay Packers

"Curly Lambeau was a lot of things to a lot of people: innovator, genius, businessman, charlatan, friend, enemy, teammate. Above all, he was a football guy who changed the game forever. Herb Gould captures everything in this fascinating look at the fascinating man who built the Green Bay Packers and the mighty NFL."
—Rick Telander, sports columnist, *Chicago Sun-Times*

"Who was Earl Louis "Curly" Lambeau? Yes, his name adorns one of America's iconic football stadiums, but who was he? Herb Gould peels back the layers to reveal a complicated man, whose exploits — good and bad — have been lost to the mists of time. Every Green Bay Packers fan should read this book."
— Gary D'Amato, retired sports columnist, *Milwaukee Journal Sentinel*

"Herb Gould employs his usual writer's flair and reporter's thoroughness to delve deep into the life of a sometimes-controversial man who remains a bit of a mystery despite his iconic status in the most unique franchise in professional sports."
—Tom Oates, Wisconsin Sportscast Podcast and retired sports columnist, *Wisconsin State Journal*

# LAMBEAU

*The Epic Life of Earl Louis "Curly" Lambeau,
the Man Who Invented the Green Bay Packers*

By Herb Gould

GONFALON PRESS
Chicago, Illinois

*Copyright 2025, Herb Gould, Gonfalon Press*
*All rights reserved.*
*Manuscript formatting by Fort Raphael Publishing Company*
*Cover graphics by Touchstone Graphic Design*
*Cover Photo: Curly Lambeau stalking the sidelines, Packers vs. Bears, in Green Bay on Sept 28, 1941. Green Bay Press-Gazette/USA TODAY NETWORK via Imagn Images*

ISBN (Print): 9781732665910
ISBN (eBook): 9781732665927

*"When the legend becomes fact, print the legend."*
      . . . The Man Who Shot Liberty Valance

# CONTENTS

## Part One: A Dream Becomes a Reality

| | | |
|---|---|---|
| 1 | *No Love Lost* | 1 |
| 2 | *Early Times* | 7 |
| 3 | *Notre Dame's Long-Lasting Influence* | 13 |
| 4 | *Birth of a Legendary Team* | 25 |
| 5 | *Little City, Big League Football* | 37 |
| 6 | *A Franchise on the Brink* | 43 |
| 7 | *Birth of a Rivalry* | 59 |
| 8 | *The Championship Mystique Begins* | 69 |
| 9 | *On Top of the NFL World* | 81 |
| 10 | *Rockne's Death Hits Hard* | 99 |
| 11 | *The Third Time is Trickier* | 101 |
| 12 | *The Math Doesn't Add Up* | 107 |
| 13 | *Hawaiian Getaway* | 117 |

## Part Two: Fame, Fortune—and a Dark Side

| | | |
|---|---|---|
| 14 | *Falling from Grace in Too Many Ways* | 125 |
| 15 | *Passing Fancy* | 141 |
| 16 | *The Age of Hutson* | 149 |
| 17 | *Out of Bankruptcy, Into Winning* | 159 |
| 18 | *Singing that Title Tune Again* | 165 |
| 19 | *Growing Pains* | 173 |
| 20 | *The Best in the West* | 181 |
| 21 | *World Traveler* | 189 |
| 22 | *Milwaukee Debate Heats Up* | 195 |
| 23 | *A Messy Second Divorce* | 209 |
| 24 | *The Bears Claw Back* | 213 |
| 25 | *First in Flight* | 221 |
| 26 | *Shining Moments as War Clouds Gather* | 229 |
| 27 | *Pearl Harbor and a Near-Shocker* | 233 |
| 28 | *America Goes to War, the NFL Adjusts* | 239 |
| 29 | *Soldiering On* | 245 |
| 30 | *A Last Hurrah* | 249 |

## Part Three: Turmoil in Packerland

| | | |
|---|---|---|
| 31 | An Old Friend Creates a New Enemy | 259 |
| 32 | Battles on Many Fronts | 265 |
| 33 | Changing of the Guard | 271 |
| 34 | A November to Remember | 277 |
| 35 | Another Matrimonial Contract | 281 |
| 36 | From World War to Football War | 287 |
| 37 | Rockwood Becomes Curly's Folly | 289 |
| 38 | AAFC Hits NFL in the Wallet | 295 |
| 39 | Demanding a Thorough Explanation | 299 |
| 40 | A Modern Passing Game? | 303 |
| 41 | Biting the Hand that Feeds Him | 305 |
| 42 | Off the Cuff | 313 |
| 43 | Cardinals Rule | 319 |
| 44 | The Grip Keeps Slipping | 323 |
| 45 | Amid Unrest, Los Angeles Rumors | 325 |
| 46 | Planes and Trains and Jug Girard | 329 |
| 47 | An Extreme Measure Does Not Pay Off | 331 |
| 48 | War and Rumors of Peace | 339 |
| 49 | A New Coaching Staff | 343 |
| 50 | A $50,000 Drive to Save the Packers | 357 |
| 51 | The Great Lambeau Debate | 365 |
| 52 | "Cardinals Prepared to Pay the Highest Salary" | 371 |
| 53 | With Lambeau, "A Hopeless Cause" | 375 |
| 54 | Lambeau in Limbo | 381 |
| 55 | Down Goes Rockwood | 387 |
| 56 | Taking Flight to the Cardinals | 391 |

## Part Four: Life Beyond Green Bay

| | | |
|---|---|---|
| 57 | A New Beginning in the Windy City | 397 |
| 58 | Packer Board Keeps a Tight Grip | 405 |
| 59 | Packers Honor Curly—and Then Beat Him | 407 |
| 60 | Cardinals Debut a Disaster | 413 |
| 61 | Losing Games and Fans | 417 |
| 62 | Pondering Television | 419 |
| 63 | More Front-Office Turmoil | 425 |
| 64 | Cardinal Sins | 431 |

| 65 | Two and Out | 437 |
| 66 | More Wolfner Machinations | 445 |
| 67 | Job Rumors Galore | 449 |
| 68 | Back in the Saddle | 453 |
| 69 | A Second Term in Washington | 471 |
| 70 | No Wife, No Team | 493 |
| 71 | College All-Stars Beckon | 501 |
| 72 | Green Bay Needs a Stadium | 517 |
| 73 | The Second Time is Not a Charm | 523 |
| 74 | The Only Clash of Packers' Two Titans | 529 |
| 75 | Green Bay Builds it. And They Come. | 533 |

## Part Five: From Exile to Retirement

| 76 | Eying a Return | 537 |
| 77 | "Soviet`` Leadership of Packers? | 545 |
| 78 | "We Want Curly!" | 549 |
| 79 | "The Soviet is Dead!" | 557 |
| 80 | Lombardi in the Packers' Sights | 561 |
| 81 | Two Legends, Two Different Paths | 565 |
| 82 | Full Retirement | 567 |
| 83 | Scratching His Coaching Itch | 573 |
| 84 | Admiring Lombardi's Work | 577 |
| 85 | A Plan to Honor Lambeau Meets Resistance | 581 |
| 86 | Burning Down the House—Again | 585 |
| 87 | One Hall of Fame After Another | 593 |
| 88 | Reunion for King Curly and His Knights | 603 |
| 89 | Last Controversy, Last Triumph | 609 |
|    | Epilogue | 615 |
|    | Author's Note | 619 |
|    | Source Notes | 621 |
|    | Index | 665 |

# PART ONE:
# A DREAM BECOMES REALITY

# 1
## *NO LOVE LOST*

In the spring of 1965, Curly Lambeau had not been feeling his usual energetic self. "My stomach just doesn't feel good," he told his fiancé, Mary Jane Van Duyse. But he had gone in for a physical and a doctor had told him he was fine, so he went about his active life.

Summer was approaching in Door County, the Cape-Cod-like peninsula northeast of Green Bay. It was a time for being on the water in his new boat, for playing golf, for enjoying the outdoor paradise that had been his getaway since childhood.

"A bear for exercise," Lambeau worked on the dock near his summer home in Fish Creek, Wisconsin, on Monday, May 31, the *Green Bay Press-Gazette* would note later, curiously using the word *bear*, his storied rival from Chicago. "He wanted it ready for Wednesday when he planned to bring his new boat up from Sturgeon Bay."

On Tuesday, June 1, Lambeau got into his Cadillac, a shiny new red convertible, and put the top down for the 23-mile drive from Fish Creek to Sturgeon Bay, where Mary Jane lived with her parents. Although he was 67 and she was only 32, she had agreed to marry him. She had accepted the ring he gave her, but the engagement was vague. She had understandable reservations and was in no hurry.

"He did give me a ring. I didn't know what to think about it," Mary Jane said many years later. "He gave it to me in church. I said, 'Curly!' I couldn't believe it. It wasn't going to be in my plans or his plans.' He said, 'Just take the ring and use it as a cocktail ring.'"

Curly had been married three times and divorced three times. That was a big concern for Mary Jane. And then there was the age difference. Curly was as old as her father. But he was charming and fun and handsome—and attentive and wealthy. He also was a living legend, the man who had founded the Packers in Green Bay, northeastern Wisconsin's big city, 44 miles down the road from Sturgeon Bay.

The drum majorette in the Packers' Lumberjack Band, she had organized, at Vince Lombardi's request, the team's cheerleading squad. She also appeared on 'Ask Curly Lambeau,' a television show the former coach did briefly when the Packers were in their 1960s glory days. "That's how we really started to get to know each other," Mary Jane said.

Curly, who had arrived early for his dinner date with Mary Jane, found her father, Francis, cutting the grass at their home at 522 Michigan Street in Sturgeon Bay when he arrived. Curly asked to take a turn with the power mower, joking that "I need some exercise." After pushing it a bit, a sweating Lambeau stopped and mopped his face with his handkerchief, saying, "I feel kind of sick."

Swooning and dizzy, Lambeau collapsed. Francis Van Duyse broke his fall as he fell to the ground, laying on the fresh-cut grass.

"I was upstairs getting dressed," Mary Jane said. "I came down the stairs and heard my mother yelling, 'Curly!' He had fallen into my dad's arms and so I ran out the door. My mother called [for an ambulance], and they came right away."

The attempts to revive him failed. Curly Lambeau had succumbed to a massive heart attack.

"It was such a shock," Mary Jane said. "The doctor came and said he couldn't do anything. He said, 'He's gone, Mary. He's gone.'"

He had just had his annual physical a week earlier, said Dick Weisgerber, a close friend and former Packer who owned the C&C Supper Club in Fish Creek, where Lambeau often held court with an Early Times and water. "I saw him just before he went down to the Van Duyses," Weisgerber said. "He was dancing around and feeling fine."

And then, Earl Louis "Curly" Lambeau, who had started the Green Bay Packers when he was just 21 years old, who won six NFL championships over the next three decades, was dead.

He had presided over the most unique franchise in American sports history—a community-owned small-town team that went toe-to-toe with professional giants. He had kept the Packers alive through perils that had claimed many other teams. He had departed during a divisive crisis and had gone through awkward times before becoming comfortable as the Packers' retired patriarch.

And now he was gone. Felled by a massive heart attack at 67.

"Curly Lambeau, Originator of Packers, Dies," the headline said across the top of the *Green Bay Press-Gazette's* front page.

"LAMBEAU, FOUNDER OF PACKERS, DIES," the *Chicago Tribune* emblazoned across the top of its sports page, telling readers a once-despised but respected opponent was gone. In a separate story, Bears owner George Halas, called the death of his rival "a terrible shock," saying, "Without him, pro football simply wouldn't exist as it does today."

The *New York Times* gave Lambeau a full column on its obituary page. "What he's done for Green Bay borders on the miraculous," Tony Canadeo, a Packer star of the 1940s, said in an *Associated Press* story that appeared around the country. "He brought a small town into the big leagues."

\* \* \* \* \* \* \* \*

Three years earlier, in the autumn of 1962, Curly Lambeau had been elected to the Wisconsin Athletic Hall of Fame. He had founded the Packers and guided the team to a prominent place in National Football League history despite nearly impossible hurdles. He also had been the NFL's first 1,000-yard passer and had won six NFL championships as the Packers coach.

After practice one Tuesday, *Green Bay Press-Gazette* sports editor Art Daley asked Vince Lombardi, who already had taken the first giant steps of his own legendary Packer career, to pose for a congratulating photo with Lambeau.

Lombardi said no.

"He flat out refused, shrugging something like, 'I won't do that with him,'" Daley said.

Determined to have a photo of the two Packer legends, Daley prevailed on noted author W.C. Heinz to change the coach's mind. Heinz was in Green Bay working with Lombardi on a book, *Run to Daylight*.

"Well, come Saturday morning, Vince had on his Sunday coat," Daley said, "and after practice he went to the stadium and posed with Curly for what turns out to be a rare photo."

The photo ran the next morning, on Sunday, November 18, 1962, on the front page of the *Press-Gazette*. At a banquet the night before, Lombardi had told 700 Packer fans it was "a distinct honor" to present Lambeau with his Wisconsin Athletic Hall of Fame certificate.

"From the bottom of my heart, this is my greatest thrill," Lambeau had told the crowd at the Elks Club.

And then, Lombardi went back to winning football games. And Lambeau went back to retirement.

Less than three years later, on June 1, 1965, Lambeau died. Daley, who was putting together *The 1965 Packer Yearbook*, decided to take halfback Tom Moore off the cover and use the photo of Lombardi shaking hands with Lambeau.

"Vince was furious," Daley said. "'What do you mean putting me on the cover with him? That's the worst yearbook you ever put out!'"

Lombardi slammed down the telephone and barely spoke to Daley for months.

A year later, Daley bumped into Lombardi at the Oneida Golf and Riding Club, and asked him why he had been so angry about the Lambeau photo.

"In a rare acknowledgement of his oversized ego," Lombardi biographer David Maraniss wrote, "Lombardi answered, 'Let me tell you something. I don't like to have the spotlight taken away from me and my team.'"

Lambeau and Lombardi. They are legendary names for those who worship the Green Bay Packers, a team that has a magnetic attraction in Wisconsin and beyond.

The Packers' history is filled with tales that have the feel of an almost biblical mythology. In that mystical realm, Lambeau looms large as the founder, the man who kept the Packers alive through monsoon-like rain that put the team on the brink of ruin, banishment from the NFL, a lawsuit that drove the team to bankruptcy and a depression that shuttered banks and drove farmers off their land.

Along the way, Lambeau molded a perennial winner by finding standout players who were remarkable people as well as gifted athletes. He was King Arthur and they were his Knights of the Round Table. Except that in this case, the Round Table was a 100-yard rectangle.

Lombardi stands tall as the man who restored the Packer empire and took it to its greatest heights. On his watch, Green Bay had its share of star players. But Lombardi's system also loomed large over the team's success.

Lambeau gave Green Bay the roots of its "Titletown" nickname by winning six championships in 15 years. Lombardi revived it in spectacular fashion.

And yet, these two Packer heroes did not get along. That can happen with great men who are used to being the rulers of their realm.

The accomplishments of Vince Lombardi are well-known.

The achievements of Curly Lambeau, the man who created the Green Bay Packers, are largely forgotten.

The Lambeau name on the home of the Packers obviously goes a long way toward assuring that future Packer fans—and all pro football fans—will at least recognize his name.

That Lambeau Field became a reality despite the behind-the-scenes opposition of Vince Lombardi and the public resistance of some civic leaders including Green Bay Mayor Don Tilleman, was yet another sign of the grass-roots enthusiasm that Green Bay had for its football team.

But it was merely a final improbable chapter in the story of The Man Who Invented the Green Bay Packers.

"This guy did it all. He founded the team. He was a player. The coach. He was the general manager. He won six championships—more than Lombardi. As many as Belichick," former New England Patriots general manager Upton Bell, said in an interview with the author. The son of NFL commissioner Bert Bell, he spent time observing Lambeau behind the curtain. "If people today knew what he did, he'd be up there as the greatest of all time."

And yet, the passage of time does not completely explain why Lambeau's legacy has faded. There is no simple explanation. Because the story of Curly Lambeau is complex. He was a brilliant and innovative sports executive, coach and athlete—a charismatic leader. But he also abused and deceived people who had put their trust in him. And while he was considered charming by women, he also had a troubling history as a womanizer.

Oliver Griese, a huge Packer fan who owned Green Bay restaurants, recalled being out with his future wife, Mary Lou, in the 1930s when they bumped into Lambeau after his first divorce. "We were drinking Budweiser, and I had to go to the toilet so bad," Griese said. "But everyone knew you didn't dare leave your girl alone with Curly."

All of these qualities and character flaws, combined with his reputation as a yarn spinner—an outright liar in many cases—made an enigma. He built the uniquely popular Green Bay Packers—a community-owned team from a small town that won big. But he also burned bridges.

"There was something about Lambeau that was different, something kind of mysterious." said Bell, a precocious football-obsessed youngster who accompanied his father to NFL training camps. "Halas was open. 'Hey Uppie, come on into the meeting.' Halas didn't treat us like kids. You were part of it. Lambeau was friendly, but I always got the feeling that there was something there that I could never figure out. He seemed like a coach, but he also seemed like a CEO. He seemed like a lot of different things."

In fact, Lambeau was a lot of different things. In his prime, no one, not even George Halas, had Lambeau's gift for spotting and developing players. When it came to public relations—to spreading the word about the fledging NFL—Halas was skilled and dedicated, but Lambeau had a gift. Reporters sought him out in a way that made him the NFL's most visible ambassador.

"With Lambeau, his deeds as a player, a coach, an administrator, a founder, I don't think there's anybody that can touch this guy," Upton Bell said. "And yet he's forgotten."

How can that be? That's the mystery of Curly Lambeau. . . . The Man Who Invented the Green Bay Packers.

# 2
## *EARLY TIMES*

Exactly who was Earl Louis "Curly" Lambeau? His name is destined to be long remembered. It adorns one of the most celebrated stadiums in football—in American sports, really. Lambeau Field is a shrine for Packers devotees and an iconic venue for sports fans across the country.

It is the ultimate Frozen Tundra. The site of the legendary Ice Bowl, when the Packers out-dueled the Dallas Cowboys in 1967. The home of the Lambeau Leap. The 100 yards of turf fought for by Vince Lombardi and George Halas, sparring animatedly on the sidelines in fedoras and coats and ties.. The images all bring to mind the specialness of Lambeau Field in Packers and NFL lore.

Lombardi, who won five championships, is remembered through the NFL's championship trophy and the main Green Bay street that runs past Lambeau Field, which has spawned a vibrant community of businesses around it. But there's nothing like a stadium as a memorial. Lombardi clearly understood that. Lambeau, who won six titles, one more than Lombardi, has that.

And yet, ask dedicated Packer fans, even the most rabid of them, what they know about Curly Lambeau and they will usually say, "He started the team. And he won a lot of games." And that's about it.

Both are true. Green Bay had some amateur football teams in 1918, when Lambeau was playing at Notre Dame for a first-year coach named Knute Rockne. The South Side Skidoos, Whales and Bays all claimed to represent the city, which had been home to amateur, and perhaps some semipro, football clubs since 1895. But it wasn't until 1919—when newspaperman George Whitney Calhoun helped Lambeau start a team, promising to deliver the publicity that would make it a success—that Green Bay had its team for the ages: The Packers. While Calhoun's contribution was invaluable, Lambeau was the central figure in the founding of the team, the one who nurtured it and grew it into an NFL stalwart.

Although he's merely remembered today as the name on a stadium, Earl Louis "Curly" Lambeau played a huge role in helping not just Green Bay, but the whole NFL survive its hard-scrabble beginnings. In the 1920s and '30s, when college football ruled, the Green Bay Packers were a coveted opponent that put fannies in the seats at a time when the NFL was scorned by college coaches, other traditionalists and many potential fans. In the '30s, the NFL, like other shaky businesses, struggled to survive the Great Depression. The Packers, who were able to attract fans because of their success and their small-town mystique, were a most welcome visitor in

Chicago, New York and all the big cities of the NFL. Green Bay was the Notre Dame of pro football.

The National Football League began as a loose federation of teams from small towns like Green Bay. As the Cantons and Daytons, and Portsmouths and Pottsvilles dropped off, only one small town remained amid the Chicagos and New Yorks and Detroits and Philadelphias. And that one, Green Bay, was so good at winning football games that the Packers became a special opponent—a valued box-office attraction—for their big-city rivals.

Like Notre Dame, Green Bay was a team from a small Midwestern city that became an attraction around the country because of its football prowess. Perhaps by design, Green Bay even wore blue and gold, the colors Lambeau had worn as a bruising fullback in his lone college season playing for Rockne. Curly was the Packers' Rockne—the NFL's Rockne.

In those days, Lambeau and other NFL founders could only dream of making their brand of football as popular as the college game. In 1925, a crowd of 5,389 turned out to see the Packers host the Chicago Bears, the most attractive opponent, at their new City Stadium home in Green Bay. Meanwhile, 44,000 watched the Wisconsin Badgers play Michigan's Wolverines—"the champions of the West," as their fight song says—at Camp Randall Stadium in Madison that autumn. Even the Thanksgiving Day showdown between Green Bay's East and West high schools attracted a crowd of 7,000, more than the Bears-Packers game.

After a poorly attended game in Detroit in late November of 1926, drew less than 1,000 spectators, the Detroit club, known as the Panthers, was unable to pay the required guarantee. That left Lambeau and his team scrambling for money to pay their way home to Green Bay.

"We had our railroad fare back to Green Bay but we had to pay for a Pullman from Detroit to Chicago and our hotel bill and, last but not least, meal money," Calhoun recalled later. "We were sort of on the spot. A.B. Turnbull was president of the football corporation at that time. We phoned Mr. Turnbull long distance and told him of our plight. Andy wired us $500, which enabled the Packers to get home without the sheriff breathing down our necks."

In their scramble for financial survival, NFL teams were free to make their own schedules. With the Bears-Packers rivalry already a big draw, they regularly played three times a season, with two of the three games played in Chicago and one in Green Bay.

After barely making it home from Detroit after that game on November, 28, 1926, the Packers did not play again until December 19, when they played a second game in Chicago against the Bears, who had made an early trip to Green Bay.

In 1926 and from 1928 to 1933, the Bears played an early game in Green Bay and the Packers came to Chicago twice after that. It was great for Halas' wobbly bottom line, and for the Packers' perennially shaky finances. All because Lambeau had built a team that fans either adored or wanted to beat.

In 1929, when the Packers won the first of three straight NFL titles, they opened the season with five home games and finished with an eight-game road trip that included four games in Chicago, two apiece against the Bears and the Cardinals—Chicago had two NFL teams from 1920 until 1960 — plus an East Coast swing highlighted by a game against the New York Giants. In 1930, they played their final seven on the road. And in 1931, they finished with five straight road games.

That was how Curly Lambeau paid the bills in the early days, when paying the bills was a very serious challenge.

An immensely popular figure in Green Bay, Lambeau supplemented his modest NFL income by selling menswear at Stiefel's in the 1920s, then switched to hustling Massachusetts Life Insurance in 1930. He was especially good at selling insurance. In his 1946 history of the Packers, *Chicago Tribune* sports editor Arch Ward referred to him as "Earl Louis Lambeau, the insurance peddler whose office walls in the Northern Building are decorated with diplomas of merit, attesting his selling acumen." In those early years, Lambeau operated the Packers out of his insurance office because the team didn't have the money for anything other than a small ticket office. In those days, professional football was more of a passion than a business. And when it came to football, Lambeau was filled with passion.

\* \* \* \* \* \* \* \*

Earl Louis Lambeau seems to have led a comfortable childhood. The son of Marcel and Mary Lambeau, he was born on April 9, 1898, the oldest of four children. Lambeau, his two brothers and baby sister grew up on Green Bay's East Side. His father was a contractor and moved his family at least six times before Curly graduated from high school.

Curly's parents were both the children of European immigrants, part of a wave that came to northeastern Wisconsin in the mid-1800s. Mary, whose family was from Belgium or southern France, was born on a farm about 25 miles northeast of Green Bay, in the Town of Union or near there. Marcel was born in Green Bay, where his parents had settled after emigrating from Belgium.

Marcel had a rough-and-tumble childhood. As a boy, he spent more than two years at a state reform school in Waukesha. When he was 15, his father, Victor, also a building contractor, shot his mother, Marie, in the neck in broad daylight in a jealous rage on a Green Bay street corner and then shot himself to death. His mother recovered from her wounds, although it was an incident that must have left emotional scars on their son.

As an adult, Marcel matured and became a successful builder. He built City Stadium, the Packers' home from 1925 to 1956, where Curly's teams rose to prominence, and many other significant Green Bay buildings. Marcel also was briefly a saloonkeeper and the operator of a boarding house. The family took summer vacations to Door County, the popular peninsula northeast of Green Bay that became a lifelong retreat for Curly and thousands escaping the heat of Chicago, Milwaukee and other steamy cities. Eventually, he would own a large home in Fish Creek.

As a youth and as his athletic career progressed, Curly Lambeau was often referred to as "the Belgian" or "the big Belgian" by friends, rivals and sportswriters.. From the time he was very young, though, "Curly" pretty much replaced his given name. Beyond the abundant mane of curls atop his head, Curly was a well-built, confident young man who excelled at sports. As a youngster, he was the leader who would bring a home-made football and organize the games. As a teenager, he grew into a handsome 5-foot-10, 185-pound whirlwind who was faster and stronger than the other boys—and a better passer, runner and kicker.

Beyond his fascination with football, Lambeau was unblinkingly obsessed with women. And they were very much attracted to him. He was married and divorced three times, and hoping to make young Mary Jane Van Duyse his fourth wife at the end of his life.

"Oh, he was very handsome," Mary Jane said. "Dimples. He had dimples to die for."

How many other dalliances he engaged in during his 67 years is impossible to say. But there must have been many.

Corinne Griffith, a silent-film star who had been nominated for an Academy Award before she left Hollywood and married Washington Redskins owner George Preston Marshall, also was among Lambeau's admirers.

"Curly Lambeau," Griffith, the author of 11 books, wrote when Lambeau was in his late 40s, "is six feet tall, 200 perfectly proportioned pounds, no bulges. . . is one of the kindest men I have ever known, though one of the toughest when necessary. . . has blue-gray eyes, derives his nickname from a head of wavy hair and is—to use [Redskins center] Ki Aldrich's vernacular—'a pretty thing.'"

"Among the ladies, he had a very nice personality," Janice Johnston, the wife of Swede Johnston, a 1930s Packer, said. "He had dimples when he would smile and had a little gray in his hair. He was charming."

In heavily Catholic, conservative Green Bay, Lambeau's stormy romantic life would raise a lot of eyebrows. Ultimately, that would not be good for his position as the leader of the Packers.

"Always known as a sharp dresser who was overly concerned with his own appearance, Lambeau often alienated his players with his continual habit of going after women," biographer David Zimmerman wrote, "even when he was still married or the women were married. Single players often complained that they had to compete with him for women when they were on the road or in Green Bay when Lambeau was between marriages. They would try to engage a young woman in conversation at a bar or restaurant, and the next thing they knew, Lambeau appeared. More often than not, he came away with the date—not the player. Lambeau would constantly display an insatiable need to win women's hearts—whether it would be for a more permanent period or for one night—from early life to the end."

As a wide-eyed youngster, football-obsessed Upton Bell had no idea about Curly's personal life. When he learned about it later, "I thought he must be a helluva man. How did he find time to do all this? He was really good looking. I remember that. There was something about this guy, that I could see translated to women and everybody else. Part of the mystery of this person is, all of these elements would be lauded today. People would love it. George Clooney would be in line to play him."

# 3
## *NOTRE DAME'S LONG-LASTING INFLUENCE*

In the fall of 1916, his senior year of high school, Lambeau led Green Bay East to a momentous 7-6 victory over Green Bay West, which had beaten East seven straight times. Lambeau not only starred in that game. He took credit for being the informal coach of that team. "Our coach the year before, Carroll Nelson, didn't come back," Lambeau told *Green Bay Press-Gazette* writer Lee Remmel in a 1962 interview. "A teacher was assigned to coach us, but he had never played football. I was the captain. . . so I went to him and asked him what he wanted us to do. He said, 'I want to read a book on football, go ahead and do what you want to.' So we used the same plays we had the year before."

It was a fun fable about a man destined to become a legendary coach. The only problem was, in 1916, the East coach was Joe Hoeffel, a second-team All-America on Wisconsin's unbeaten 1912 Big Ten champions who also had been an assistant at Nebraska. Would Hoeffel have gone off to read a book while Curly coached? No.

There would be many more fables like that embellishing the life of Lambeau. He probably was the source of many of them.

A talented all-around athlete, Lambeau also excelled at other sports. He competed well on the East track team and was a star for town baseball teams. His high school did not have baseball or basketball teams.

In the 1917 Green Bay East High School yearbook, Lambeau famously and boldly announced, "When I get thru with athletics, I'm going out and conquer the rest of the world." Those words appeared next to his handsome picture. He would not conquer the entire world. But he would, for a fair amount of time, conquer the world he chose.

The English translation of the word French word *lambeau* is "scrap" or "shred." In the plural form, *en lambeaux* means "torn to shreds" or "in tatters." Given that his father and grandfather built buildings, and Curly built a football team, their surname is ironic.

In the complicated life of Curly Lambeau, however, there would be both conquest and rejection. How else to explain so few details being known about a man whose name adorns such a legendary stadium?

As he neared the end of his time at Green Bay East, football remained Lambeau's primary interest. In January of 1917, when he was a high school senior, he had been contacted by Notre Dame coach Jesse Harper. Lambeau had answered in a handwritten note that Notre Dame was the top school on his list.

"But there is one drawback," Lambeau added. "I am not fixed very well financially, and I would like to know what is the best you can do for me."

Harper responded that there were no free rides, but said, "If you are willing to work, I will be very glad to help you. If you are not willing to work and in addition looking for an offer [of an athletic scholarship], I assure you, you will have to consider some other institution."

Not well fixed financially? His father was a builder and head of what was probably a middle-class family. Curly was industrious. It is one of the many mysteries in the life of Lambeau. Was money the issue? Or was Curly trying to negotiate the best deal?

Whether for financial or other considerations, Lambeau failed to reach an agreement to play for Harper. Apparently taking Harper's advice, he headed to Madison and the University of Wisconsin. Lambeau was among four incoming freshmen "stars from last year's strongest high school teams in Wisconsin" headlining the recruiting class reporting to coach Guy Loman in Madison, the *Wisconsin State Journal* reported on September 27, 1917.

"Lambeau's entrance at Madison has been heralded with joy by the university [news]papers. . . the majority of football critics consider the Green Bay boy one of the best gridiron prospects that has ever been turned out of a high school," George Whitney Calhoun gushed in the *Green Bay Press-Gazette* on September 29. "There is little doubt but that he will more than make good with the Badgers."

That never happened, though. In yet another mystery, Lambeau returned to Green Bay after just a few days. Although some Packer histories say he left Madison when freshmen football was canceled, Lambeau never enrolled at Wisconsin and never participated in any Badger football activities there. What caused him to leave is not clear. Given that he seemed to be angling for a deal from Harper at Notre Dame, it's possible that he had a similar experience in Madison. He proved to be a tough negotiator throughout his life.

Despite being expected to become a Badger, Lambeau returned to Green Bay, where he worked at Indian Packing and played one game for the South Side Skidoos, a Green Bay amateur team. Also on that team was Nate

Abrams, a friend and classmate of Lambeau's at East High, where they played football together. Although only 5-foot-4, Abrams was an enthusiastic player. Sparked by a Lambeau pass to Abrams, the Skidoos defeated De Pere 6-0 on October 21, 1917, despite playing with only 10 players. It was De Pere's first home loss.

A few days later, Lambeau showed another talent, performing "several musical numbers" at a Halloween party attended by about 20 of his East High classmates, including Marguerite Van Kessel.

Lambeau and Abrams also led a Green Bay all-star team on Sunday, November 11, 1917, past a team from Marinette, about 50 miles north of Green Bay, in a benefit for the Red Cross that attracted roughly 1,200 spectators to Hagemeister Park. Curly ran for two touchdowns and passed to Abrams for a third in Green Bay's 27-0 victory.

During the winter, Lambeau kept busy by working at Indian Packing, playing recreational sports and participating occasionally in musical shows. He also was keeping his football options open. One would soon develop at Notre Dame. Although no records survive, Lambeau connected with Knute Rockne, who had been named Notre Dame head coach when Harper resigned.

\* \* \* \* \* \* \* \*

The name Jesse Harper is merely a footnote in Notre Dame's football history. The legendary glory belongs to Knute Rockne and some celebrated successors. It's similar to the Green Bay Packers. Its history is steeped in Vince Lombardi while Curly Lambeau is pretty much a name on a stadium.

And yet, they are inextricably linked. Without Lambeau, there would have been no Green Bay Packers for Lombardi to coach to dizzying pro-football heights. Long before that, Harper set the table for Rockne to turn Notre Dame into a perennial force in college football. And Lambeau was at the intersection of all that gridiron achievement.

When Harper resigned as Notre Dame coach on February 9, 1918, it was a move nearly as shocking as ND's 35-13 upset at Army in 1913, Harper's first season at Notre Dame. In that game, Rockne caught passes from Gus Dorais, a native of Chippewa Falls, Wisconsin, and opened football eyes to the potential of the passing game. Harper had compiled a record of 34-5-1 at Notre Dame from 1913 to 1917.

Officially, Harper was needed back at his father-in-law's 30,000-acre cattle ranch in Kansas. His father-in-law had died unexpectedly, leaving a potential empire that included oil wells as well as livestock, and that was certainly a big factor. Beyond that, though Harper told his son years later that he had wearied of "the pressure by the alumni to do nothing but win, win, win. regardless of what you did to the boys, the school or anything else. . . . I had to leave Notre Dame because winning was getting too important there." Harper went on to build an empire that left him joking that "I've crossed Hereford cows with oil wells, and you can't beat that."

Before leaving South Bend, Harper sold Notre Dame officials on promoting Rockne, who had been his valuable assistant since 1914. By the time Harper left, Rockne was virtually a co-coach who handled the bulk of media relations and was immersed in virtually every aspect of the team's operation. "When Rockne needed fatherly advice, he turned to Harper," Notre Dame historian Ken Rappoport wrote. "When Harper needed a Pied Piper, he turned to Rockne."

One of those who answered the Pied Piper's call was Curly Lambeau. He played one last game for the Skidoos on September 15, 1918, leading them to a 13-0 win over De Pere. Then he quickly departed for Notre Dame, eager to play for new head coach Rockne.

College football was a low priority in the fall of 1918 when Lambeau, after being recruited initially by Harper, suited up for Rockne's first Notre Dame team. Not only was the United States, which had entered World War I alongside Britain and France in April of 1917, devoting its unblinking attention to defeating Germany. An influenza pandemic, called the Spanish Flu, was raging. Following a common practice of that era, Rockne may have arranged a campus job for Lambeau. Other accounts dispute this. But Lambeau was always clever when it came to profiting from his athletic ability.

Rockne, unlike his predecessor Jesse Harper, enjoyed the pressure of coaching at the highest level. If that meant making practical arrangements with talented athletes like Curly Lambeau, Rockne did not flinch.

In addition, with so many young men off to war, freshmen were eligible to play at Notre Dame in 1918 following a ruling by the school's commandant of the Student Army Training Corps. That policy, widely used due to the war, gave Lambeau an opportunity to play varsity football immediately, an option that had not been available the previous year at Wisconsin. That might have been enough of a lure.

In those days, the Upper Midwest was fertile recruiting turf for Harper and Rockne. Lambeau lined up at fullback in the same backfield with second-year standout halfback George Gipp, from the Upper Peninsula of Michigan, not far from Green Bay. One of their key blockers, lineman Hunk Anderson, had been brought to Notre Dame from the U.P. by Gipp.

Lambeau quickly established himself as an important player. At 180 pounds, he carried as much weight as Notre Dame's biggest linemen. But he moved quickly enough to be a dual-threat fullback who could run and catch. While Gipp led the elusive speed backs, Lambeau was an inside power runner. Rockne also used Lambeau to kick extra points.

"That big fellow has surprised me," Rockne said of Curly. "He catches on fast and he has filled a big hole for us."

In Notre Dame's first game, on September 28, 1918, in Cleveland, at Case Institute of Technology, which later became Case Western Reserve University, Rockne started his second team, or "shock troops," a favorite practice of his, designed to wear down opponents and preserve his best players. And so, Gipp and Lambeau, who had already ascended to the starting unit, began the game on the sideline.

"Rockne regards these two birds highly," the *Indianapolis Star* reported, "and they are surely more valuable than anything else in connection with the team. It was Rockne's plan to save them. . . . But soon after the struggle started, Rockne discovered that he couldn't get anywhere without Gipp and Lambeau, and so he had to risk his prize performers to stave off defeat." Once on the field, "Gipp and Lambeau tore off sensational gains."

In the second quarter, with the Irish trailing 6-0, Lambeau "crashed through for a score," pulling Notre Dame into a 6-6 tie with the surprisingly strong Case, which was supposed to be a tune-up team. It was the first touchdown of Rockne's storied career as Irish coach. Gipp added a pair of third-quarter touchdowns as Notre Dame pulled away to defeat Case 26-6. Lambeau kicked both of ND's extra points.

The Irish would not play again until November 2 in that truncated 1918 season, which was shortened by the influenza pandemic. Two minor October home games, against Kalamazoo and Washington & Jefferson, were canceled, as was a big November 2 trip to play Army at West Point. An October trip to Nebraska was rescheduled for Thanksgiving Day.

During their October lull, Rockne scrimmaged the varsity against his freshmen. Settled in at fullback with the varsity, Lambeau was described as "a tower of strength in the back field, which is the whole strength of the team."

To fill in the October schedule gap, Rockne arranged for a team of servicemen from Chicago's Municipal Pier (later called Navy Pier) to come to Notre Dame on October 19. "Lambeau shows up well," a subhead in a preview of the game said before the story said, Another man whose work is delighting the fans is Lambeau at full[back]," the story said. "Lambeau is expected to make the Municipal Pier take notice this afternoon."

That did not happen. The game was canceled at the last minute due to influenza concerns.

And so, Rockne's team had yet to prove itself. But Lambeau was clearly considered a key player. "Bahan and Gipp are grand performers," one report said, mentioning the team's halfbacks. "And Lambeau is coming in great strides. . . is developing wonderfully at full[back]."

When the Irish finally traveled to Wabash for their hastily-arranged second game on November 2, they crushed another minor opponent, 67-7. In that game, Rockne, who had been snubbed when he applied for the Wabash head coaching job while a Notre Dame assistant, made his point about the mistake that Wabash had made.

In another twist of fate, Rockne had missed out on another head-coaching job, at Dubuque College, when he lost a coin toss with Gus Dorais, who had thrown the passes that Rockne had famously caught as a Notre Dame player.

"When their playing careers were over at Notre Dame in 1914, Dorais [and Rockne] flipped for the only available coaching job, in Dubuque," Thomas B. Littlewood wrote in his biography of newspaperman Arch Ward, one of the many Notre Dame people who would be so influential in Curly Lambeau's life. "Dorais won the coin toss. . . . Knute Rockne stayed on at Notre Dame to teach chemistry and help Jess Harper coach."

A coin toss? Like Lambeau, Rockne's life contained fable-like incidents. Dorais went on to a long college coaching career. Although Dorais was not at Notre Dame when Lambeau was there, they knew each other and stayed in contact. Dorais helped Curly find future Packers.

The week after pummeling Wabash, Notre Dame squared off against the star-laden Great Lakes Navy team at its Cartier Field home in South

Bend. With Lambeau at fullback for the Irish and George Halas lining up at right end for Great Lakes, this was the first meeting between two future NFL legends. Halas was the *de facto* coach of the team along with two other future Pro Football Hall of Famers, Paddy Driscoll and Jimmy Conzelman. Many years later, as coach of a championship Chicago Cardinals team, Conzelman would administer a couple of the most crushing defeats of Lambeau's Packer career.

"Game Exceedingly Rough, Many Men Being Taken Out," an *Indianapolis Star* headline said, a fitting summation for the first contest between the men who would lead the Packers and the Bears. "The Notre Dame backs put up a wonderful game. . . . Bahan, Gipp, Lambeau and Mohn are names that will be held in honor at the Gold and Blue school for many a day," the article said.

The physical contest ended in a 7-7 tie. It was a rare setback for Great Lakes, which went on to win its final four games and finish an undefeated 6-0-2. In the final triumph, 17-0 against the Mare Island Marines in the Rose Bowl, Halas was named the Most Valuable Player..

A week after the first Lambeau-Halas encounter, the Irish lost 13-7 at Michigan State on November 16 in a driving rain that turned the field into a sea of mud. Their speed bogged down, the frustrated Irish were whistled for holding and roughing penalties that helped Michigan State to the winning touchdown.

At Purdue the next week, Lambeau "split the center of the line as a knife would rip a watermelon" on Notre Dame's first scoring drive, helping the Irish rebound with a 26-6 win. Gipp, despite being battered from the Michigan State game, led Notre Dame on both sides of the ball.

Five days later, Rockne took his team to Lincoln for the rescheduled meeting with Nebraska, on Thursday, November 28. Playing on a slippery field "covered with mud and slush, as a result of a heavy snowfall," the teams battled to a scoreless tie on Thanksgiving Day.

And so, Notre Dame finished its first season under new coach Knute Rockne with a 3-1-2 record, its schedule diminished by the raging Spanish Flu epidemic and its roster reduced by players going off to war.

Taking advantage of freshman eligibility because of World War I, Lambeau had established himself as a talented bruiser at fullback. The *Notre Dame Scholastic* school newspaper predicted that Lambeau would become an important player: "Gipp ran [opponents'] ends at will and Lambeau tore their line to shreds," the *Scholastic* season review said. "With

Rockne as a teacher, 'Curly' has a bright future in his two remaining years of competition."

The football season over, Lambeau also showed talent in the boxing ring. Rockne, who had assumed Jess Harper's dual role as athletic director as well as football coach, staged a two-night "boxing carnival [that] was a howling success." Fighting in the heavyweight division on the second night, Lambeau, listed at 188 pounds, squared off on Friday, December 13, against a 200-pound opponent, Frank Cahill, who had won some bouts in Chicago. A football reserve lineman, Cahill would become a boxing instructor at Notre Dame. He already had won the featured heavyweight bout when Rockne refereed the first night of his "boxing carnival" a week earlier.

"This bout started off like a whirlwind," the *South Bend Tribune* reported, "and after 24 seconds of the first round had gone, Lambeau put a left and right to the face, which floored Cahill. In falling Cahill some way fractured his leg and was unable to continue. He was carried from the arena and Lambeau declared the winner."

With the first semester nearly over, Lambeau seemed to be off to a fine start at Notre Dame athletically. His Notre Dame career, however, was not destined to continue.

The details are murky and confusing, as they often are with Lambeau, who tended to tailor the facts the way he saw fit. But this much is clear: Lambeau was in terrible shape academically. And at some point he apparently developed tonsillitis. The health issue on top of failing classwork pushed his Notre Dame career to a point of no return.

"I find my studies not very easy," he wrote to his high school sweetheart, Marguerite Van Kessel, in early December. "It is much different than in High School. French & Chemistry trouble me more than the others. Everything is done with such great speed that a fellow must be on the alert all the time or he misses something of great importance."

"My three months here were not wasted," Lambeau added, "and I will be benefited by taking this course. I feel I have accumulated considerable knowledge that will help me in the packing game."

He obviously was saying his studies had not gone well. But had they gone so poorly that he would be ineligible to play football? Or even to return to school at all? That is not easy to say.

\* \* \* \* \* \* \* \*

Here's the problem: Earl Louis "Curly" Lambeau was a serial liar and fabricator. While he led a remarkable, colorful and exceptional life, any biography—indeed, any history of the Packers during his 30-year shepherding of the team—is going to contain important moments where the facts are blurry. If George Washington, who, according to the legend, admitted cutting down a cherry tree, could not tell a lie, Curly Lambeau could not tell the truth.

Crossing this minefield of details caused Lee Remmel, the legendary *Green Bay Press-Gazette* writer who had covered Lambeau and became the Packers' official historian, to shelve his plan to write a book about the history of the team. Curly's penchant for making up history about his life and three decades of running the Packers would make the task too daunting.

"He was a congenital liar," Remmel said. "Cripes! He'd lie to your face and you knew he was lying and he'd still lie to your face and make you like it because he was so good at it."

That said, Remmel knew what Lambeau had accomplished: "Jean Nicolet may have discovered Green Bay, but Lambeau put it on the map."

In some straightforward instances, Lambeau's fabrications can be untangled. That is not as easily done when it comes to the details of his early life. This did not seem to bother sportswriters of his era. They wanted to create heroes and tell interesting stories. That is what readers wanted.

This problem was not confined to Lambeau. Some of his most celebrated players—whether through memory lapses or a desire to be at the center of a good anecdote—embellished stories. So did Lambeau's greatest rival, Chicago Bears patriarch George Halas. Like Lambeau, he came up with some doozies that made for great copy, but were not necessarily accurate.

Arch Ward, the trailblazing *Chicago Tribune* sports editor and Notre Dame crony of Lambeau, played along in his 1946 history of the Packers. At that point, they were just fun, harmless details. Many other writers repeated the dubious tales, which gave them credibility. With no way to determine what was accurate, there was no way to argue with Lambeau's recollections.

And so, the precise details of Lambeau's early exit from Notre Dame are not clear. At some point in December, he dropped out of school, Notre Dame records show, without receiving grades or credits for any of the seven classes in which he had enrolled—a full lineup of French, English, Chemistry, Trigonometry, a second Math class, History and Economics.

Despite that, Lambeau mailed a note to Rockne in early January saying he had money troubles: "Dear Rock: It will be hard for me to go back to school as I cannot depend upon receiving money from home, due to ill luck. No doubt all the bunch is back and going to it again. I sure would like to be with them. I wonder if I could obtain a job so as to make things along smooth, if I should return."

Lambeau returned to South Bend in late January, based on two letters he sent to Marguerite. But the tonsillitis derailed any plan he had to post a successful semester academically through final exams. In late January, he wrote to Marguerite that he had spent eight days in the Notre Dame infirmary and had been advised to have his tonsils removed.

In the second letter, Lambeau "said he was looking forward to meeting her in Chicago in June and maybe bringing her to Notre Dame for a visit. On the other hand, he wrote, 'If I could land a big job with a large salary I would hop right on it.'"

Notre Dame historian Murray Sperber said Rockne, who was welcoming back many World War I military veterans to his football team, no longer required Lambeau's services and withdrew the offer of a campus job that served as a scholarship. But that does not seem to be the case. Packer historian Cliff Christl found no evidence that Lambeau had ever been given a campus job. Sperber also mistakenly said Lambeau was at Notre Dame for two years.

Some Packer historians have written that Curly was not interested in continuing his college education at Notre Dame, even though Marguerite and his family urged him to do that. Given his promising football debut at Notre Dame, even if Rockne had not wanted him, Lambeau easily might have found another collegiate opportunity, particularly in that era, when talented players often moved from school to school.

Then again, he already had had a mysterious problem at Wisconsin, which would have been a very viable alternative to Notre Dame. Seemingly on the verge of becoming a Badger in the fall of 1917, he left Madison after just a few days without enrolling or engaging in any football activity. Considering how dedicated he was to playing big time football, missing the 1917 season was very strange.

In angling for favors from Rockne after the 1918 season, Lambeau's timing could not have been worse. Although Curly had been an important contributor in 1918, Rockne was preparing to take the Irish to another level in 1919. The Great War was over. The cloud of the influenza pandemic was lifting. America wanted entertainment like football. And Rockne was poised to provide it.

"The beginning of the 1919 season found things much brighter for Rockne," Harry Stuhldreher, who would become one of Notre Dame's Four Horsemen, wrote in his biography of Rockne. "The boys were returning to Notre Dame from the war to complete their interrupted education. . . . They had gone away schoolboys and returned grown men. They had their bad points but they more than made up for these with the good. They were old enough to understand that every restriction Rockne put on them was for their own benefit."

In that climate, Rockne had little need for a Curly Lambeau. And given his miserable academic record, Lambeau did not seem to have a path forward at Notre Dame even if Rockne had wanted to keep him on the football team.

Years later, Lambeau told longtime Packer writer and historian Lee Remmel that he "developed tonsil trouble about Christmas time." A South Bend doctor "told me they'd have to come out. I went back to school after the holidays but they kept bothering me so I had another exam" with Dr. James J. Robb, a Green Bay physician who told Lambeau "they'd have to come out, but I'd have to wait until the infection cleared up. I stayed around home for quite a while. . . but by this time, I had missed too much school to go back."

In a strange coincidence, Lambeau's backfield mate, George Gipp, had a chronic tonsil problem. Just before returning to South Bend for the start of football practice in 1920, Gipp went to see A.C. Roche, a doctor in the Upper Peninsula town of Calumet. Roche told Gipp the tonsils needed to be removed. Even though that was a simple procedure, Gipp refused, saying, he was afraid of "going under the knife."

In December, Gipp died of a strep throat infection and pneumonia. Martyred at only 25, he was destined to be long remembered when future President Ronald Reagan, playing Gipp in the film *Knute Rockne, All-American*, told Rockne to "Win one for the Gipper" in a melodramatic death-bed scene.

Curly's tonsil issue gave him a ready explanation for failing to complete his academic work—and Lambeau always was adept when it came to explanations. Although it's strange that he and Gipp shared a medical problem, that's a minor mystery in the life of The Man Who Invented the Green Bay Packers.

The bottom line is, Curly Lambeau and college football were not a good fit. Although he was a talented athlete, he did not handle his student responsibilities. Even before his tonsil crisis, his Notre Dame academic record was *en lambeaux*. Before that, he had raised expectations that he would play at the University of Wisconsin, then abruptly left Madison without even enrolling.

And so Lambeau dropped out of school at Notre Dame and returned to Green Bay. When Rockne gathered his team for the start of practice in August of 1919, he listed Lambeau as ineligible. Just like that, after a very strong first year, Curly Lambeau's career at Notre Dame was over.

# 4
## *BIRTH OF A LEGENDARY TEAM*

Like Rockne, Curly was moving on. As the 1919 season approached, Notre Dame was in his rear-view mirror. He simply had other ideas. His relationship with Marguerite was becoming serious. Rather than play college football, he was planning to settle down in Green Bay. And play football in his hometown.

As The Man Who Invented the Green Bay Packers, Lambeau was the pivotal figure of the team, especially at critical moments in its early history, except for a brief stretch in 1920. But he was surrounded in those defining moments by collaborators who made essential contributions.

One of them was Frank Peck, the president of Indian Packing Company, which was part of an ambitious plan to open a stockyards and meat-packing operation in Green Bay. A Massachusetts native, Peck had moved from Providence, Rhode Island, where he had been president of New England Supply, with the idea that Indian Packing would help turn Green Bay into a regional meat-packing center. Indian Packing had hired Curly's father, Marcel, to oversee construction of a meat-packing compound that had four buildings.

When Curly returned from South Bend to Green Bay early in 1919, he landed a job as a shipping clerk at Indian Packing for what he later said was $250 a month. That amount sounds grossly inflated, like many details that Lambeau exaggerated later in his life. He told Arch Ward about that "handsome sum" for Ward's 1946 Packer history. "I thought that was as much money as any man would want in the world, so I went to work," Lambeau told a *Sports Illustrated* reporter in 1962, when he had had many years to embellish a salary that could not be verified.

Regardless of the salary amount, Lambeau seems to have had a reasonably good job at Indian Packing. He also had worked there before he went to Notre Dame. It probably didn't hurt that his father had built the plant—and that Curly was a local football hero.

Lambeau also credited Peck with providing $500 for uniforms and equipment, a generous contribution in an era where that was nearly two months' wages for the average American worker. That amount also was most likely inflated by Lambeau as time went by. George Calhoun, who co-founded the Packers with Lambeau, suggested the contribution was much smaller and that the team had to borrow its other equipment except for about "15 or 16 jerseys" that Indian Packing purchased.

What is indisputable is the importance of Calhoun, who nudged young Lambeau into starting a football team. A Green Bay newspaperman and sports enthusiast, Calhoun was the great-grandson of Daniel Whitney, a an entrepreneur who had founded Green Bay, which was incorporated in 1819.

That's how deep the roots of the Packer legend go. Lambeau's partner in starting the Packers was a descendant of the man who turned a trading post into the city that would spawn the Packers.

Although born in Green Bay in 1890, Calhoun grew up in Buffalo, following the career of his father, a civil engineer who often traveled for work projects. But the family returned regularly to Green Bay, where his mother, Emmeline, had deep roots.

As a youngster in Buffalo, Calhoun not only played baseball, football and hockey; he organized many teams. Calhoun's athletic career was curtailed, either by a severe case of rheumatoid arthritis or a crippling injury playing football at the University of Buffalo. As with Lambeau, there are conflicting accounts of his early years. But that only seemed to fuel his enthusiasm for sports promotion, which led Calhoun into journalism in Buffalo. He then returned to Green Bay in 1915, where he was managing editor of the *Green Bay Review*. Two years later, he became telegraph editor at the *Green Bay Press-Gazette,* where he soon started writing a sports column, "Cal's comments."

And so, it was only natural that Calhoun joined with Lambeau in organizing a football team. *Press-Gazette* sports columnist Val Schneider, a baseball teammate of Lambeau's in the summer of 1919, also was probably involved. Schneider began writing in April 1919 that a new, better-than-ever city football team was in the works.

The precise details of the Packers' first organizational steps are murky. In one account, Calhoun gave Lambeau a nudge during "a chance conversation over a glass of beer," Calhoun's newspaper protege, John Torinus, wrote in *The Packer Legend,* which Torinus described as "more a collection of recollections than a history" of the team that he dedicated to "my mentor, my friend," Calhoun.

"Cal knew Curly well from his playing days at East High," Torinus said. "As a frustrated athlete himself due to a severe case of juvenile arthritis, Cal could sympathize with Lambeau when he told Cal about missing playing football. 'Why not get up a team in Green Bay?' Cal asked. And he added, 'I'll help you put one together, and I'll give you all the publicity you need.' "

Torinus' version raises several red flags, one of them being that Calhoun didn't move to Green Bay until Lambeau's senior year of high school and didn't join the *Press-Gazette* and start writing about sports until after Lambeau graduated from East High.

Jack Rudolph, Green Bay's preeminent 20th century historian, traced the Packers' founding to a chance, street-corner conversation between Calhoun and Lambeau, which is likely much closer to the truth. While no definitive evidence survives, Rudolph, the son of the Packers' 1920 team physician, was dedicated to Green Bay history.

Whatever the prelude, the birth of the Packers can be traced to an organizational meeting on Monday night, August 11, 1919, at the second-floor editorial office of the *Press-Gazette*. A single sentence in the August 13 edition of the newspaper confirmed the meeting without identifying any attendees.

The August 13 story announced the new team's plans in a series of headlines and subheads: "Indian Packing Plant Squad to Represent City' . . . Great Football Eleven in City This Fall" . . . Best State Teams Will Be Seen Here."

"It will be the strongest aggregation of pigskin chasers that has ever been gathered together in this city," the article gushed. It went on to give the last names of 38 potential players. A second meeting would be held on Thursday, August 14, the article said, adding that "It is important that all of the above mentioned players be in attendance."

That next day, a *Press-Gazette* headline announced, "Curly Lambeau Chosen Captain of Footballers." The article said Lambeau had been elected captain at a meeting at the *Press-Gazette* the previous night. "G.W. Calhoun will again manage the eleven this season," the report said. "Providing a suitable opponent can be secured, the Packers will open the season on Sunday, Sept. 14 at Hagemeister park." Nearly 25 potential players attended and the start of practice was set for September 3.

The Packers. There was that nickname—right there at the very beginning. Other team nicknames, including Indians and Bays, would surface—especially when Green Bay's meat packers halted their operations and their sponsor dollars . But only one name would stick.

Football wasn't the only thing on Lambeau's mind as autumn approached in 1919. The day after Lambeau was elected captain, he took out a marriage license on Friday, August 15, 1919. He listed his occupation as shipping clerk.

The Society Page in the *Press-Gazette* carried the announcement that day: "Lambeau-Van Kessel Wedding—The marriage of Miss Marguerite Van Kessel, daughter of Mr. and Mrs. John Van Kessel, to Earl Lambeau, will take place tomorrow morning in St. Francis Xavier cathedral."

The next day, August 16, Curly and Marguerite Van Kessel were married at St. Francis Cathedral. For their honeymoon, Lambeau and his bride, who worked at Stiller's camera and music store, traveled around Wisconsin and Michigan's Upper Peninsula, Lambeau said later, so that he could arrange games for the Packers' inaugural season. Once again, though, his memory grew foggier with time. Calhoun handled the scheduling, which included sending out press releases throughout Wisconsin seeking games.

Even then, it took more than three weeks for the Packers to find an opponent for a first game. After that, most games were scheduled week to week.

On Wednesday, August 27, a notice in the *Press-Gazette* reminded the players to attend an August 29 meeting. and advised general readers that "The football public will see some of the best professional grid teams in Wisconsin in action here this season." With Indian Packing Corporation providing the uniforms, the article said, "the `Packers' will be outfitted in college style."

Finally, at 7 p.m. on Wednesday, September 3, the Packers held their first practice. At that time, it was announced that Willard "Big Bill" Ryan, the Green Bay West High school coach, would do double duty in 1919, also serving as the Packers' coach. How Ryan and Lambeau shared the duties of running the team on the field was not explained in the *Press-Gazette* that season, but captains often exercised as much authority as coaches at that time. And so, it was very possible that this team belonged to its captain, Lambeau, who also was the coach at Green Bay East. The team practiced a field west of the Indian Packing plant. Meanwhile, Calhoun and Lambeau were still trying to lock in an opponent for their September 14 opening game. "Many of the neighboring teams are not anxious to face Green Bay so early in the season," the *Press-Gazette* reported on September 4.

The next day, the newspaper announced that the Packers finally had found an opponent. The North End Athletic Club of Menominee, Michigan, had agreed to play Lambeau's team. Composed of "former college and high school stars," the Menominee team "looks like a championship machine," the *Press-Gazette* noted in its pregame buildup. The truth was, it appears that the North End Athletic Club team was a hastily arranged squad. It was not even the best team from the twin cities of Marinette, Wisconsin and Menominee, Michigan. There is no evidence that a North End Athletic Club even existed before it agreed to this game.

On game day, it was all about the Packers. Before "a record crowd" later estimated at 1,500, Green Bay "walloped" Menominee 53-0 at Hagemeister Park. A rope around the field was all that separated the crowd from the combatants. Calhoun and others passed the hat to raise a little money for Lambeau's fledgling team. Some fans watched from the comfort of their Model Ts.

Accompanying the report on the game the next day was an announcement, "Practice Tonight," a stern reminder that "Coach Ryan wants every man on the Packers squad to report for practice tonight at the plant gridiron, 6:45 o'clock. There is a hard week of drill ahead of the city footballers because Sunday's game with the Marinette all-stars will go a long way towards deciding the semi-pro pigskin championship of this part of the state.."

On Sunday, though, the Marinette Northerners were no match for Lambeau's Packers, who rolled to a 61-0 victory. "At no time during the argument were they within 45 yards of Green Bay's goal line," the *Press-Gazette* reported.

That was pretty typical of the first team that Curly Lambeau put together. Seventeen of the 25 players had gone to either Green Bay East or West High School. Three others had either played at nearby high schools, or not played high school football. They played for the joy of competing. Although the plan was to distribute any proceeds from passing the hat, the cost of equipment not provided, and medical attention that might be needed, was likely to exceed any money they received for playing.

The 1919 Packers outscored their first five opponents 331-6, with the Racine Iroquois ruining the shutout in the fifth game, before Lambeau's team ventured away from Hagemeister Park. The first road game was a trip on October 19 to Ishpeming, Michigan, about 160 miles north of Green Bay. At that time, Michigan's Upper Peninsula, which produced football stars such as Notre Dame heroes George Gipp and Hunk Anderson, was a football hotbed known for producing rough and talented players. And Ishpeming, which ruled Michigan football, was an epicenter.

"The game at Ishpeming was an odd one," Lambeau told *Milwaukee Journal* writer Chuck Johnson many years later for a 1963 history of the Packers. "They had a tough team and on our first three running plays, three of our men went out with broken bones. We never ran again. We passed on every play and beat them 33-0. It was that day we realized the value of the forward pass."

Three players sidelined by broken bones on three consecutive plays? Packer mythology, as told by Curly Lambeau, does not lack for toughness. This is one of the many Packer fables from Lambeau's reign that bring to mind the famous line from the film, *The Man Who Shot Liberty Valance:* "When the legend becomes fact, print the legend."

Ishpeming's newspaper, the *Iron Ore,* credited Lambeau—"the Green Bay captain played a star game."—and said, "The Ishpeming-Negaunee boys are not one bit downhearted because of their defeat as they realize that they were up against as fast an aggregation of stars as had been assembled."

The *Iron Ore* also noted that Lambeau's team "has the support of the Chamber of Commerce of Green Bay, being sort of an advertising feature for the town, and it is plain to see that the players have spent considerable time in practice work."

Ishpeming is just a little town in the Upper Peninsula of Michigan where iron-ore mining once was king, and where rugged miners were once known for playing rugged football. Its main claim to fame these days is Tom

Izzo, who coached the Ishpeming High School basketball team in 1977-78 before going on to a Hall of Fame career at Michigan State.

But in Packer mythology, this village with the alliterative name looms much larger. It is the place where, in an era of pound-the-football-on-the-ground, Curly Lambeau claimed he first realized he could rely on passing.

Fittingly, the name underscores the legend. According to an English-Ojibwe dictionary, Ishpeming comes from the Ojibwe word *ishpiming*, meaning 'in the air,' 'above' or 'on high.'

Even as a child, though, Lambeau claimed he had somehow known a football could be thrown *ishpiming*. In another neat piece of the legend, the inventive Lambeau said he organized neighborhood football games with a ball "born of a discarded salt sack, and stuffed with Green Bay's falling leaves and a modicum of pebbles and sand. . ." Arch Ward wrote in his history of the Packers, "and prophetically taught his mates to pitch it, rather than run with it, as was the custom in the early years. This, of course, was a foretaste of the passing technique which was to become a definite keystone of the Green Bay Packers' offense."

Lambeau also had been shown the value of throwing rather than running by his mentor, Knute Rockne, who had been a passing pioneer as a Notre Dame receiver and coach. Lambeau continued that approach long after Ishpeming. He not only put the ball in the air when he was the Packers passer in the 1920s. He also used it while coaching legendary receivers Johnny Blood and Don Hutson. And talented passers Red Dunn, Arnie Herber and Cecil Isbell.

"I have great respect for Lambeau," said Hutson, who held virtually every NFL receiving record long after he retired in 1945 from his stellar 11-year career. "Fundamentally, he may not have been the finest coach in the world. But he was a motivator and one of the best. And he was a very offensive-minded coach. He put in a lot of offensive plays that people had never seen before, a lot of pass plays that people had never seen before. That was his greatest asset as far as coaching was concerned."

After the Ishpeming road trip, Lambeau's Packers returned home for three more lopsided victories. Their home season finished, they headed north for another fierce battle in Michigan's Upper Peninsula, this time at Stambaugh, home of the Miners, who supposedly had not lost a home game in six years. After a scoreless first half, Lambeau threw two touchdown passes and kicked a field goal to lead Green Bay to a 17-0 victory on November 16.

About 300 Packer fans made the 140-mile trip north to be part of a crowd estimated at 2,500. The excursion was profitable, the *Press-Gazette* reported: "It is roughly estimated that the Green bay delegation which followed the Packers into the wilds of Michigan came back with about $2,000 of Wolverine money."

In that inaugural season, Green Bay would only play three truly organized teams, all of them on the road. The eight teams they played in Green Bay were either hastily organized or unaccomplished squads. The first two serious opponents were the two Upper Peninsula teams. For their third challenge, the Packers traveled to Beloit, on the Illinois border south of Madison. on November 23 to play the oddly named Fairies, who were sponsored by Fairbanks-Morse, an industrial manufacturer of scales, pumps and engines. The Fairies, Lambeau knew, were tougher than their name.

The officiating was even tougher to swallow for the Packer contingent. In what appeared to be the last play of the first half, Beloit was stopped short of the goal line. But Beloit's team manager, serving as one of two timekeepers, overruled the primary timekeeper, saying there were five seconds left, and referee George "Zip" Zabel agreed. The Fairies scored on the next play for a 6-0 lead, but missed the extra point.

The Packers also had to contend with Beloit fans: "Every time the Packers had the ball, the crowd would sweep out on the playing field leaving practically no room for a forward pass and... putting a big check on the Packers' ground gaining machine."

Most infuriatingly, Zabel snuffed Green Bay at the end of the game, barring three apparent touchdowns with phantom penalties. "Capt. Lambeau's team was robbed of victory by Referee Zabel of Beloit," a *Press-Gazette* writer, most likely Calhoun, reported. "This official penalized Green Bay three times after touchdowns, refusing to allow the scores."

And so, the Packers lost 6-0 to the Fairies and finished the 1919 season with a 10-1 record.

Before settling in Beloit, Zabel had pitched for the Chicago Cubs for three years. In his career highlight, he entered a 1915 game with two outs in the first inning, and went on to pitch 18-1/3 innings in a win against Brooklyn. That record for most relief innings pitched in single game is a lock to never be broken.

Shortly after that, Zabel developed arm trouble and wound up landing a job with Fairbanks Morse. He worked there for 32 years, becoming chief metallurgist at the company. But he might be best remembered as the man who handed the Green Bay Packers their first defeat.

"The boys displayed wonderful fighting ability, but it was simply a case of too much Zabel," Packers coach Big Bill Ryan said. "One of the players put it well when he said: 'Beloit had the game won before the teams stepped upon the gridiron.'"

While disappointed and frustrated by the outcome, Calhoun and Lambeau were eager for a rematch. Considering that at least 2,000 fans had watched the first contest, a second game would provide a payday as well as a chance for the Packers to even the score in what was billed as the Wisconsin state championship.

The teams agreed to meet again in Beloit on Sunday, December 7. A special overnight train was arranged for Green Bay fans to make the seven-hour trip to Beloit. There was talk of bringing in a neutral referee from Chicago to avoid the controversy surrounding the first game.

The Packers also announced plans to play a team from neighboring De Pere on November 30. But that game was canceled by a coating of ice on the field.

In the end, the Beloit football team also canceled the rematch due to an ice-covered field. And so, Lambeau and the first Packer team ended the 1919 football season with a record of 10-1.

One event was not canceled, however. The Packers sponsored a Thanksgiving night dance on November 27 at the armory. Vandenberg's "seven-piece jazz orchestra" played from 8:30 p.m. until 1 a.m. This was the kind of get-together that the outgoing Lambeau relished throughout his life. As a young man, he sang and performed at Green Bay shows. At the end of his life, he was interested in a new dance craze, The Twist, popularized by Chubby Checker.

To commemorate that first season, the Packers, urged to report in a *Press-Gazette* announcement, gathered at the packing plant at 1:30 on Sunday, December 7, for a team photo. "After which the uniforms will be checked in," the announcement said. "This will wind up the greatest season of professional football that Green Bay has ever experienced."

Two timeless photos were taken that day of the original Packers in front of the packing plant's old garage in the foreground of the warehouses and along the plant's western property line.

For their efforts, according to the legend handed down by Lambeau to biographer Arch Ward in 1946, "the original Packers collected, at season's end, the magnificent sum of $16.75 each. This, of course, did not include doctors' bills, which, in the cases of men like Lambeau himself, ran toward $75. Yet every player promised he'd be back the next fall. The Packers were on their way."

Maybe the $16.75 is accurate. Or maybe not. Calhoun wrote in 1934 in his first definitive history of the Packers that there was some money left in the kitty to share with the players, but he didn't remember how much. Not surprisingly, Lambeau often changed the amount when he repeated the story over the years. It's possible that Lambeau, who joked much later that he expected the take to be $20, was fashioning a nice yarn for his friend Arch Ward.

\* \* \* \* \* \* \* \*

On the field, the Packers' 1920 season was pretty much a repeat of 1919. They rolled to a 9-1-1 record, beating Beloit 7-0 in Green Bay but losing to the Fairies 14-3 in Beloit.

The other opponents were similar. Ishpeming was not on the schedule, but Stambaugh, another Upper Peninsula stalwart, came to Green Bay twice. Marinette and Menominee again fielded team, along with local squads from Kaukauna and De Pere. The 1920 Packers outscored their opponents 227-21

At the box office, though, Lambeau's football dream made strides in 1920 thanks largely to a local typewriter salesman, Neil Murphy. Before that season started, Murphy was named team president and business manager, essentially replacing Calhoun, and Jack Dalton was named coach, essentially taking over for Lambeau. Dalton, who had played football for Rockne's Notre Dame teammate Gus Dorais at Dubuque College (now Loras), conducted the first team meeting of the season and oversaw the early practices.

Thanks to Murphy's persistence dealing with city officials and G.E. Walter of the Hagemeister Realty Co., a fence was built around the Hagemeister Park field by local contractors Ludolf Hansen and Marcel Lambeau, Curly's father, so the Packers could charge admission and raise money.

When nearly 40 people gathered for a team banquet at DeLair's Cafe on December 14, 1920, everyone involved with the team—22 players and 13 team officials, including a nurse, timekeeper and waterboy—received a check for $276. That was a month's salary for the average American working man in 1920. It came out of an impressive net profit of $6,049.53. In return, the players surprised Murphy by presenting him with "a handsome diamond stick pin."

It certainly helped the bottom line that the Packers played 10 of their 11 games at Hagemeister Park. Their only road game was the trip to Beloit. It was common then for teams to play at home, or wherever they would attract the biggest crowd. Despite their name, the 1921 Decatur Staleys played their final nine games at Cubs Park in Chicago. Renamed the Chicago Bears in 1922, they played eight of their 12 games at Cubs Park.

While working at Indian Packing and running its football team, Lambeau also coached at his alma mater, Green Bay East, in 1919 and 1920. Lambeau would steer East star Jim Crowley to Notre Dame, where he became one of Rockne's legendary "Four Horsemen of Notre Dame." Crowley would go on to coach at Fordham, where Vince Lombardi was one of his Seven Blocks of Granite, a renowned offensive line.

When Lombardi was hired to coach the Packers, the circular way in which Lambeau had mentored Crowley, who had been coached by

Lombardi, who had been hired to revive the franchise Lambeau had started, was another elegant piece of Packer lore. "The threads of the quill of life, so to speak, run in some very strange repetitive patterns," *Look Magazine* sports editor Tim Cohane, toastmaster of a 1962 banquet honoring Lombardi, said while connecting the Lambeau-Crowley-Lombardi dots.

Although Lambeau served officially as captain, rather than coach, from 1919 to 1921, he is credited with being the head coach of those first three Packer teams, probably because coaches Bill Ryan, Jack Dalton and Joe Hoeffel disappeared from the scene after a year and Lambeau was the face of the team's first three decades.

He not only exercised authority as team captain. He put together the roster, pushed for the Packers' entry into the American Professional Football Association and was the driving force in its rapid rise from a semipro town team to a member of the country's first full-fledged nationally organized league. He was not involved in the team's reorganization in 1920, joining it only days before the first game. Others oversaw many aspects of the team, notably the sports-minded Clair brothers, the Acme meatpacking owners. But as the Packers' captain and best player, Lambeau was in the spotlight.

Even at the outset of Lambeau's football career, there was friction. Like many successful coaches, Curly was a strong-willed leader who rubbed some people the wrong way. In that second season, Lambeau again was team captain. Jack Dalton succeeded Big Bill Ryan as coach because Lambeau had said he planned to return to Notre Dame, Dalton's son, Maurice, said in a 2001 interview. Both played in the backfield. They did not get along. Jack Dalton "wasn't too fond of" Lambeau," Maurice Dalton said. Lambeau " was not of the best character. He was a womanizer, a boozer. He wasn't the same type of person as my dad. They were complete opposites, I would say."

Many others would also question Lambeau's behavior during a long, accomplished career that would make him the most successful coach of the NFL's first 30 years. The truth was, he had a complex personality that swung from genius to pettiness.

"The great ones make enemies," said Upton Bell, comparing Lambeau to ground-breaking coach-general manager Paul Brown, who won three NFL championships after taking all four titles in the rival All-America Football Conference. "Everybody hated Paul Brown. Lambeau had that all-encompassing personality. People like that make enemies quickly."

"Everybody hated his guts. But they all respected him," said Packer Hall of Fame member Bud Jorgensen, a team trainer and equipment manager from 1924-1970, the team's longest-serving employee.

There were exceptions. Don Hutson, the greatest receiver and most celebrated Packer of the NFL's first half-century, had a different view. Then again, Lambeau treated players differently—especially his favorite stars.

"I was fortunate in having a creative coach like Curly Lambeau, one who really saw the merits of the passing game at a time when just about no one else did," Hutson told Richard Whittingham for his oral history of the NFL. "He was a stern coach and there was a big gap between Curly and the players. He didn't mingle with them. He was the coach and that was that."

Lambeau's strengths were his eye for football talent, his motivational skills and his game-planning, even if he borrowed from more experienced football minds. Over the years, his record as a winner on the football field became his greatest legacy.

At his best, Lambeau, like his college coach, Rockne, had the charisma to inspire his Packers to the great things they frequently accomplished. He also had a gift for spotting and developing talent.

"He was one of those rare coaches like Paul Brown or Vince Lombardi," said Clarke Hinkle, the Hall of Fame fullback/linebacker whom Lambeau plucked from obscure Bucknell. "He could see things in a ballplayer that other coaches couldn't."

# 5
## *LITTLE CITY, BIG LEAGUE FOOTBALL*

Encouraged by the success of the first two seasons, Curly Lambeau and his dedicated supporter, *Green Bay Press-Gazette* editor-writer George Whitney Calhoun, wanted to broaden the Packers' horizons. They heard about a football league, the American Professional Football Association, that had been organized in Canton, Ohio, in 1920.

They missed the first APFA season and the legendary inaugural meeting organized by Ralph Hay, a 29-year-old Ohio car dealer who owned the Canton Bulldogs. On September 17, 1920, football enthusiasts gathered at Hay's Hupmobile showroom to form the new league. Among them was George Halas, who sat on a running board.

Lambeau and Calhoun were determined not to miss another. Calhoun, who had returned to being *Press-Gazette* sports editor after more than two years as city editor, wrote in a March 19, 1921, column that the new league might want to consider Green Bay as a possible member. "If they needed another spoke in their old wheel," Calhoun said, "they could pick a lot worse football towns than the Bay."

But they faced potentially huge obstacles. Two weeks after the 1920 season ended, the fence and stands at Hagemeister Park had been torn down, leaving Green Bay without a ballpark. That was resolved after several weeks of wrangling when Marcel Lambeau, Curly's father, oversaw the rebuilding of a 2,500-seat wooden ballpark before the start of the city's semipro baseball team's season.

More ominously, the Packers also had lost their sponsor. In late December 1920, Acme Packing of Chicago announced it had purchased Indian Packing. Frank Peck was no longer in charge. Assuming the local leadership of Acme was Indian secretary John M. Clair, who brought in his younger brother, J. Emmett Clair., to assist him

In the spring of 1921, the enterprising Lambeau met with the Clairs. A charming and bold salesman, Curly convinced them to provide more than a check for uniforms and equipment. "During our meeting, my brother John agreed to finance the club, and it would start that year as a professional team," Emmett said in a 1981 family video. Lambeau was aided by the fact that the Clairs loved sports. They had become avid fans of Notre Dame football and Chicago White Sox baseball while growing up on the South Side of Chicago.

On August 26, 1921, the 24-year-old Emmett took a train to Chicago and went to the La Salle Hotel, where the APFA was meeting, to seek a franchise. The next day, the league granted a franchise to the Clair brothers in Green Bay for the APFA's second season. After operating with 14 teams in 1920, the AFPA would jump to 21 teams in 1921.

A $100 franchise had been set by the league a year earlier, but there is no record of Clair paying anything. Years later, Halas said no franchise fees were collected in the early days.

After two years of playing town-ball teams in Wisconsin and Michigan's Upper Peninsula, Lambeau would line up the Packers against opponents from around the Midwest who also were eager to compete in America's first professional football league.

On September 25, 1921, the Green Bay team began its season with a 13-6 victory against a team called the Chicago Boosters. A non-league game, it would not count in the standings of the AFPA. Three more non league games followed. Green Bay routed the Rockford Olympics 49-0 and Chicago Cornell-Hamburgs 40-0 in its next two games. In their fourth game, they defeated the Beloit Fairies 7-0.

After two years as an independent and four warmup games, the Packers would make their debut in the league that would become the NFL a year later. With Curly's father, Marcel, overseeing the hammering and nailing of more than a thousand additional bleacher seats, Hagemeister Park increased to a capacity of 3,600. The Packers' home field was starting to look like a football arena worthy of Green Bay's rising football status.

Meanwhile, Curly was instrumental in building a team that could hold its own against the tougher competition it would face. The most notable talent upgrade was Howard "Cub" Buck, a former University of Wisconsin captain who had been playing for the Canton Bulldogs. The first player that Lambeau acquired with a guaranteed salary, Buck was now a Packer tackle, lured by $75 a game, Arch Ward reported in his 1946 Packer history and Chuck Johnson repeated in his 1961 history. Other accounts said Buck was paid $100 a game, but it might have been another amount. Between foggy memories and the passage of time, one never knew about the salaries Curly paid.

The Packers' coach in 1921 was Joe Hoeffel. Eight years older than Lambeau, Hoeffel had been an All-America at the University of Wisconsin after starring at Lambeau's alma mater, Green Bay East. Hoeffel also had coached Lambeau at East in 1916, his senior season.

In 2001, both Joe Horrigan, then lead historian at the Pro Football Hall of Fame, and Lee Remmel, then director of public relations for the Packers and the team's unofficial historian, admitted to Cliff Christl, then a sportswriter with the *Milwaukee Journal Sentinel,* that the evidence clearly showed the record books had gotten it wrong when they listed Lambeau as the coach in 1921. But their final verdict was that it was too late to do anything about it.

"I don't think there was ever intent to cover that up," Horrigan said. "It just was a sliding over of the facts, so to speak. I don't have any problem with Hoeffel being acknowledged as the coach.

"To Green Bay fans, who know who Lambeau was and know the history of the franchise, this is going to come as a stark revelation. (But) I don't think you are going to get any fight, given sufficient evidence, and I think you've done that."

That said, in those days, coaches were not allowed to communicate with players on the field. Even substitutes entering the game were not allowed to bring instructions from the coach. The captain was very much in charge. Lambeau thus not only was an integral player. He handled all the decision-making on the field during games. That, combined with his role in assembling of the roster, meant he was likely exercising as much authority as Hoeffel and perhaps even more.

In 2004, though, Hoeffel's grandson, Pennsylvania congressman Joe Hoeffel, a Democrat from suburban Philadelphia, argued that his grandfather should be given credit in the record book as the Packers' 1921 coach. A lifelong Eagles fan, Hoeffel raised the issue before the Eagles hosted the Packers in a playoff game in January 2004—a great time for a Philadelphia politician to talk about family pride in football.

"I'm not bitter," said Hoeffel, "I'm not asking the team to do anything. But it would be nice for my dad to have the Packers acknowledge his dad."

Some 80 years later, though, the situation was not going to change. Hoeffel's grandson had raised an interesting but moot point. By then, Curly Lambeau's position was secure. The Man Who Invented the Green Bay Packers would be credited with being their coach, murky details or not.

On October 23, 1921, the Packers played their first APFA game, also at Hagemeister Park, against the Minneapolis Marines. With wooden grandstands and bleachers between the 20-yard lines on both sides of the field, capacity was around 3,500, but attendance at the game reportedly was about 6,000, including spectators crowding around the field where there were no seats.

Green Bay trailed 6-0 in the fourth quarter of a tense match. When a Marines punt returner fumbled, David "Jigger" Hayes, a 5-foot-7, 165-pound Green Bay end, recovered at the Minneapolis 35-yard line. The Packers drove to the 4-yard line, setting up a four-yard scoring run that tied the game. Curly kicked the extra point for a 7-6 Green Bay victory that delighted the crowd.

"Cushions went flying in the air while soaring hats were as thick as Green Bay flies on a July night," Calhoun wrote after sparing no superlatives in the opening of his *Press-Gazette* account. "In the greatest game of football ever seen on a Green Bay gridiron, the Packers celebrated their entrance into the Professional Football league by taking the far famed Minneapolis Marines into camp to the tune of 7 to 6 before a crowd that jammed every corner of the field at Hagemeister park. It was one of those kind of games that will be talked about for years to come. There was just one thrill after another."

Intrigued, another overflow crowd of 6,000 returned on October 30 to see the Packers host the Rock Island Independents. They left disappointed as Green Bay lost 13-3.

But this was a precarious time for an uncertain enterprise like professional football. In a more ominous development than losing a football game, *The Dope Sheet,* the Packers' official program, revealed in its October 30, 1921, edition that "The Acme Packing Company does not own nor financially back the Packer team."

Acme Packing had fallen on hard times. In a little more than two years, what had originally sold as Indian Packing stock had plummeted from $44 when it debuted on July 30, 1919, to 95 cents. The company was $3.5 million in debt, an enormous sum at that time, and in no position to be sponsoring a football team.

And so, by the time the Packers played their second game in the American Professional Football Association, the forerunner of the NFL, they no longer were sponsored by a meat packer.

By 1926, after failed attempts to revive its meatpacking business, most of the 100,000-square-foot business had been purchased by Atlas Warehouse and Cold Storage Company and turned into a storage facility. Used primarily for cheese storage, Atlas flourished under its founder, Emil R. Fischer, an innovator who attracted some of the nation's largest cheesemakers to Atlas. Fischer later became the Packers president in a time of turmoil.

And so, even the plant that gave the Packers their name wound up being involved in the cheese business, which made much more sense than meat packing in the Dairy State.

"There is not a packing company within 100 miles of here," the *New York Times* noted in 1939. "Though the firm which sponsored the original team some twenty years ago has long been out of existence, the nickname has stuck."

There was a city where a team called the Packers would have made perfect sense. Call it a quirk of history. With its Union Stockyards, and its Swift and Armour meat-industry behemoths, Chicago would have been the ideal home of a team called the Packers. Indeed, when the NBA placed a team in Chicago in 1961, it was nicknamed the Packers. At that point, in a city that despised football's Packers, that was not a great idea. The franchise quickly left for Baltimore and is now the Washington Wizards.

Halas made a fine decision when he called his team the Bears. It was a nice tie-in with his Wrigley Field landlords, the Cubs. Football players are bigger than baseball players. And a bear is a great symbol of ferocity. today. At this point, of course, Chicago Packers sounds like heresy.

Green Bay would never approach Chicago or Kansas City in the world of meat packing. But it does have a dominant industry: Turning the region's abundance of timber into paper products. Legendary *New York Times* sports columnist Red Smith, a Green Bay native, enjoyed reminding readers that his hometown was "the toilet paper capital of the world" in a playful way. The city's Convention and Visitors Bureau takes unabashed pride in noting that "the toilet paper capital of the world." is the place where "splinter-free toilet paper" was invented.

The *Press-Gazette* called Lambeau's team "the Packers," which has become one of the best nicknames in sports, right from their humble 1919 beginnings. In 1922, though, when the meat-packing sponsor dollars stopped, it would have made sense for Lambeau and Calhoun not to use "Packers." Calhoun called the team "the Bays" for a while.

"When the packing company folded, Lambeau tried to get rid of the name 'Packers,'" Chuck Johnson wrote after interviewing Lambeau for his 1961 team history. The problem was, Curly told Johnson, Milwaukee sportswriters "kept referring to us as the Packers and the name stuck. Now we're all glad. It's a great name. But we didn't realize it then."

This seems to be another revisionist claim from Lambeau, though—another case where he tailored the facts to make a better story. More likely, he and Calhoun moved away from "Packers" in hopes of playing under a new sponsor's name. That is only conjecture at this point. But Curly, who had a flair for promotion, had to know that "Packers" was a winner.

What would Green Bay's football team be called today if a young Curly Lambeau had gotten a job and sponsorship more appropriate to "the toilet paper capital of the world?" Rollers? Wipers? Papermakers, as the Kimberly High School team near Green Bay is known? It's pretty safe to say it would not be as embraceable as Packers.

Through the years, the nickname "Packers" has become one of the most iconic nicknames in sports. The combination of the name, the team's success and devotion that Packers supporters bestow on their team only adds to this perfect alignment.

As Lambeau once noted, the Green Bay Packers are "a community project and a regional religion."

# 6
## *A FRANCHISE ON THE BRINK*

Joining the fledgling pro league gave Lambeau and his Packers a chance to compete against the best teams in the nation. But it was not a guarantee of survival. Pro football was in its haphazard infancy. Teams came and went in the early days of the NFL. From 1920 through 1934, more than 40 teams played in the league; 24 of them survived for only one or two years.

Joe F. Carr, who was NFL president from 1921 until his death in 1939, made it a priority to follow the business model of Major League Baseball and locate NFL teams in the nation's largest cities. And yet, after seeing Green Bay firsthand in 1922, Carr modified his view.

"Seeing is believing and I take my hat off to Green Bay," said Carr, who doubled as manager of the Columbus Panhandles at that point. "I've heard a lot about Green Bay as a football community and to my estimation, it has more than lived up to all the nice things which have been said about it. I think it is the greatest football town in the country for its size."

Even the mighty Chicago Bears were a hand-to-mouth operation in their early years, if the tales handed down by George Halas are taken as fact. Then again, like Curly Lambeau, Halas knew how to spin a good yarn.

Like Lambeau, Halas seemed born to lead a football team. Both were gifted athletes with a flair for organizing, selling and marketing. But in a way, even Halas had not been as bold as Lambeau. Halas was using his civil engineering degree from the University of Illinois, designing bridges for the Burlington railroad, when the Staley starch company offered him a job and the money to hire players as he started his team. Curly, on the other hand, had a far more daunting path; he had to convince Indian Packing to take a chance.

Then again, Halas was raised in a family that was focused on upward mobility in business and financial affairs. His father died when Halas was a sophomore in high school. Through careful fiscal management, his mother kept the family comfortable. She was even able to provide for her children's college education. Once the shrewd George Halas had his hooks into the Decatur Staleys, he wasn't going to let go.

"Halas' version of history is that he and partner Dutch Sternaman struck out on their own in 1922 with the blessing of Decatur, Illinois, starch producer A.E. Staley, who had bankrolled the team for two years," Dan Daly and Bob O'Donnell, the authors of *The Pro Football Chronicle*, wrote. "Court records indicate, however, that the parting was less than friendly and that Halas and Sternaman may have simply outmaneuvered Staley for control of the team."

In 1921, when Halas claimed a $7 surplus, Daly and O'Connell, wrote, court records later showed "the Staleys turned a $21,600 profit! . . . So much for the dirt-poor picture Halas always painted of that first year in Chicago."

*The Pro Football Chronicle* goes on to detail communications between Staley Company superintendent George Chamberlain, who had hired Halas, and Chicago Cubs president Bill Veeck regarding a lease for the Bears to play in Cubs Park in 1922. When Veeck, whose son became famous as the maverick owner of the Chicago White Sox, told Chamberlain he was negotiating with Halas and Sternaman, Chamberlain backed off, writing, "We have come to the conclusion that our best interest will be served by withdrawing our application for the use of your park for 1922."

These documents, which came to light in a lawsuit filed by two brothers involved in a separate dispute with Halas and Sternaman, show Halas' business savvy, which was far more sophisticated than Curly Lambeau's in terms of starting a football team and turning it into a profitable business. Halas, of course, had the benefit of a degree from Illinois, while Lambeau had not even completed one semester at Notre Dame.

Halas, who said he pestered Cubs manager Frank Chance for a ticket as a youngster, also had gotten an up-close glimpse of professional sports during a brief stint as a New York Yankees outfielder in 1919, when he played in 12 games, registering two hits in 22 at-bats, before an injury snuffed his baseball hopes. The story that Halas' injury opened the door for Babe Ruth to replace him isn't really true. But it's the kind of tale Halas and Lambeau adored.

Far less worldly than Halas, Lambeau had newspaperman Calhoun prodding and helping him pursue a precarious dream. Another young man in Lambeau's shoes might have taken a different path and continued to play college football, which was far more glamorous at that time than pro football. College football stars also used their celebrity status to move into the business world. But as a college athlete, Curly would not have been in charge. And Curly Lambeau liked to be in charge.

\* \* \* \* \* \* \*

Like two of the most important influences in his life, Halas and Rockne, Lambeau had an iron-willed belief in his ability to build a winning football team.

Although Lambeau played only one abbreviated season for Rockne, and spent no more than six months in South Bend, his time at Notre Dame exerted a lifelong influence on him. Like Rockne, Curly was a passing pioneer in an age where bruising football predominated. Like Rockne, Curly cultivated publicity by giving dynamic interviews. And like Rockne, Curly was a skilled and determined negotiator.

In an era where Notre Dame men went on to coach many of the nation's best college teams, Lambeau relied on his network of Notre Dame friends to build his Packer roster. That was especially important before the NFL began in 1936. Don Hutson, signed by Curly a year earlier, played for Alabama coach Frank Thomas, who played for Rockne not long after Lambeau. The bidding war for standouts like Hutson led to the NFL turning to a draft, which was innovative at the time.

Although Rockne—like many college coaches, publicly opposed pro football—Lambeau said the Notre Dame legend encouraged him to give the pro game his best shot. That might or might not have been true. With Curly, one never knew. Publicly, at least, they seemed to have a cordial relationship until Rockne's death in a plane crash in 1931.

In turn, Lambeau helped Rockne by guiding players such as Jim Crowley, of Four Horsemen fame, to South Bend. Lambeau also made important lifelong allies in Notre Dame men who had a gift for promoting sports—*Chicago Tribune* sports editor Arch Ward and *Tribune* writer/NFL publicist George Strickler. Ward, who created the All-Star baseball game and football's College All-Star game, and Strickler, who is credited with planting the "Four Horsemen of Notre Dame" seed in sportswriter Grantland Rice, both had honed their sports-promotion skills while helping Rockne build the Notre Dame brand. Ward and Strickler remained lifelong friends and allies of Lambeau.

And while Halas and Lambeau were bitter enemies when their teams met on the football field, they knew how essential the Bears-Packers rivalry was to the financial success of their franchises and the NFL, especially in its early days. They were competitors during football games, but they were partners in the business of football.

Unlike Halas and Rockne, though, Lambeau did not keep a tight grasp on his football kingdom.

That was partly due to his different circumstances. Green Bay was neither Chicago nor Notre Dame in its potential for financial success. Beyond that, Lambeau did not have the same obsessive dedication to empire building that Rockne and Halas had. His insatiable and mercurial interest in women, and his overall appreciation of the finer things in life, were distractions that Rockne and Halas did not share. And Lambeau's iron-fisted management approach sometimes crossed a line that not even the driven Rockne and Halas breached.

\* \* \* \* \* \* \* \*

Looking back, Curly Lambeau's stewardship kept Green Bay's football team from going the way of Canton, Rock Island, Pottsville and so many other small towns that dotted the early NFL map. George Halas claims he needed to beg and borrow to keep the Bears afloat in Chicago. How daunting was that challenge in Green Bay?

Lambeau had the determination, the charm and the support of many local football enthusiasts to keep the dream of operating a team that could go toe-to-toe with big-city teams and win, on the field and at the ticket office, against tall odds. But the early hurdles were difficult. And for all of his good moves, Lambeau sometimes made missteps that threatened the whole enterprise.

Late in the 1921 season, Curly used at least three Notre Dame players in a game, including Hunk Anderson, the Upper Peninsula friend of George Gipp who had been Lambeau's teammate at Notre Dame in 1918. As punishment, Irish officials barred Anderson, Arthur Garvey and Fred Larson from playing all future sports at the school, the *South Bend Tribune* and *Chicago Tribune* both reported on December 13, 1921.

In Lambeau's defense, his opponent, Racine Legion, used at least one college star to its squad for the contest, Johnny Mohardt, a talented Notre Dame halfback who'd seen limited playing time behind George Gipp. But Mohardt, who had completed four years at Notre Dame, did not play under an assumed name.

Rockne used the incident to denounce professional football. "It is the hope of every lover of clean sport that we can preserve football from the professional and the gambler," he said two weeks after the scandal broke. "If this professional tendency is not curtailed in college, faculties may have to abolish football as an inter-collegiate sport."

That stance had not stopped Rockne from playing for pay for four seasons, from 1914 to 1917, when he was an assistant coach at Notre Dame. Al Nesser, an early professional star for several Ohio teams, said, "Every time we played a game that year [1914], Rockne and Dorais were on the other team."

Although at least one Packer historian incorrectly pointed to a 20-0 loss to the Chicago Staleys at Cubs Park on November 27, the game in which Lambeau used the three Notre Dame players clearly was the 3-3 tie on December 4, 1921, against Racine Legion, an independent team sponsored by an American Legion post. Racine Legion would begin a four-year run in the NFL in 1922.

Although not an APFA league game, the meeting with Racine was an important moneymaker. Billed as the Wisconsin state championship game, it was played at the home of the minor-league baseball Milwaukee Brewers, Athletic Park, which would accommodate a larger crowd and bring a welcome financial windfall.

Lambeau's worst sin in the matter seemed to be timing. On January 28, 1922, the *Canton (Ohio) Evening Repository* carried the headline, "Pro Football Moguls Here Today to Thresh Out Many Problems for Next Season," Right below that story, an *Associated Press* report detailed a scandal in which two Downstate Illinois towns, Taylorville and Carlinville, created an uproar by pitting players from Notre Dame against University of Illinois players, with up to $100,000 wagered on the November 27, 1921, game. Nine Illini players were suspended a day earlier.

Even though the game did not involve APFA teams, college coaches who did not want competition from a pro league were denouncing the APFA as unsavory. To counter the bad publicity, the APFA came down hard on the Packers, revoking their franchise on January 28, 1922, for using Anderson and the other two players.

For Curly Lambeau, this seemed to seriously test his dream of building an enduring Green Bay football club. After just one season, his team had been kicked out of the league. J. Emmett Clair agreed to surrender the Packers' franchise after apologizing to the other owners at the Canton meeting.

On the other hand, Lambeau reapplied for a Green Bay franchise at that same owners meeting—and the *Press-Gazette* reported on January 30 that "one of the [league] officials stated that it was more than probable that Green Bay would continue to hold a berth in the league."

Many Packer historians, perhaps fueled by Lambeau's unreliable assertions, have turned the Packers' return to the NFL after its expulsion into a perilous melodrama. While there were hurdles to be cleared, the *Press-Gazette* seemed confident, based on an interview with a league official, that the Packers would be reinstated in June, without missing any games.

And that's what happened. At the NFL's summer meeting on June 24, Lambeau was readmitted to the league. "One thing is sure," Lambeau said when he returned to Green Bay on June 27. "The football magnates all over the country take these hats off to Green Bay as a football town. Leaders of teams that played here last fall told other members of the organization that our city gave them the best treatment of any around the circuit."

Whereas the Clair brothers, J. Emmett and John, who provided financial backing from their Acme Packing Company, were the official owners of Green Bay's inaugural foray into the AFPA/NFL, the owner of this second Packer entry was Curly Lambeau himself when Green Bay regained its franchise.

The same meeting in Cleveland is officially credited with being the moment when the league changed its name from American Professional Football Association to the National Football League. "The short but groundbreaking discussion to change the name of the organization" was swayed by George Halas, NFL historian Chris Willis wrote in his biography of league president Joe Carr.

"I lacked enthusiasm for our name," Halas wrote in his autobiography. With his baseball background, Halas believed the words "American" and "Association" were minor league, while the word Professional was superfluous. "I proposed we change our name to the National Football League. My fellow members agreed."

The problem with that version is that the *Dayton Daily News* reported on January 29, 1922, that the APFA had voted to become the NFL at its winter meeting in Canton, Ohio. And in the six months before the

NFL supposedly changed its name, the *Associated Press* already was referring to the National Football League in articles published around the nation.

In other words, Curly Lambeau wasn't the only pro-football pioneer who had difficulty keeping dates straight.

\* \* \* \* \* \* \* \*

When Lambeau was cleaning out his desk years later, he proudly held up the franchise certificate he had received from the NFL and joked that the Packers had never reimbursed him for the $50 franchise fee. Which conveniently ignored the fact that the franchise fee had been set at $100—although Halas later joked that the franchise fees were not collected.

There are two other places where Packer mythology strays from what actually happened when Green Bay was kicked out of the league. The first is a tale of intrigue in which Halas, from the evil Chicago Bears empire, supposedly engineered the ousting of Green Bay so that he could sign Hunk Anderson, who went on to a long career as a Bears player and coach. Some Packer histories have advanced the theory that Halas provided the information to the *Chicago Tribune* that Lambeau used the three Notre Dame players to have the Packers expelled from the AFPA, clearing the way for him to sign Anderson.

As evidence, they point to the long delay in allowing Green Bay back into the league after it had been kicked out. Then again, if Green Bay was allowed to rejoin the league a short time after it was kicked out, the point of the banishment—to show the public that the NFL did not tolerate teams using college players—would have been undercut.

In addition, playing in Chicago made perfect sense for Anderson, who continued to live in South Bend while playing for the Bears. During the week, Anderson, who had studied civil engineering, had a full-time job at the Edwards Iron Works, a company headed up by former Irish player Cap Edwards. He also was an unpaid assistant coach for Knute Rockne. That "triple header," as Anderson called it in his memoir, would not have been possible if he had been playing for the Packers instead of the Bears.

Curiously, Anderson said he played against Green Bay in the game that got the Packers kicked out of the NFL. "I accepted an offer to play pro ball in Milwaukee against the Green Bay Packers," adding that "someone 'squealed,' and he and two teammates, were suspended by Notre Dame, which cost Anderson his eligibility on the school's ice hockey, basketball and baseball teams.

Why would Anderson say he played a*gainst* Green Bay when several newspaper accounts clearly identify him as one of the three Notre Dame players who suited up for Lambeau's Packers? At this point, that is difficult to say.

Today, this is all part of Packer lore—that Lambeau would risk his franchise by using three college players against Racine, an American Legion-sponsored team that was not even in the AFPA, and still only manage a 3-3 tie.

Then again, the unofficial Wisconsin state championship—and a big payday—were on the line. Gate receipts reached $5,700 from 5,700 spectators, the *Milwaukee Journal* reported. The Packers' share was 45 percent, about $2,500. It was, Calhoun reported in the *Press-Gazette,* "The biggest crowd that ever witnessed a pigskin argument in the Cream City."

In other words, this was a huge game for the teams, for the financial windfall as well as the bragging rights.

The conspiracy theory that Halas got Green Bay kicked out of the NFL adds fuel to Packers-Bears rivalry. There just isn't any evidence to support it. The illegal-players story was a much bigger deal in the *South Bend Tribune,* which broke the story on December 13, 1921, than in the *Chicago Tribune,* which took credit for getting Green Bay kicked out of the APFA a month later. By then, the *South Bend Tribune,* which had no stake in harming the Packers, was immersed in the fallout from the Taylorville-Carlinville scandal.

* * * * * * * *

Another great tale of Packer mythology is the story of how the Packers got back into the NFL after they were banished for the first six months of 1922. The version told by *Chicago Tribune* sports editor Arch Ward in his 1946 history, *The Green Bay Packers,* and embellished by David Zimmerman in his 2003 biography of Lambeau is a colorful yarn.

In Ward's version, Curly told a friend, Don Murphy, that he had the $50 franchise fee, but no money to get to Canton to apply for the Packers' franchise. Murphy, who later claimed he had inherited $11 million by then from his family of lumber barons, supposedly responded by selling his brand-new, $5,000, cream-colored Marmon roadster to a butcher for $1,500 and accompanying Lambeau to Canton. In return, Lambeau honored Murphy's request to make a token appearance in a Packer game.

It's a fun story, except that the meeting was in Cleveland, not Canton. The franchise fee at the time had been set at $100, not $50. In addition, there is no record of Murphy accompanying Lambeau to Cleveland, and no record of Murphy playing in a Green Bay game in 1922. He had appeared in a game in 1920, though.

Beyond that, the story contains another life-of-Lambeau coincidence. Just as Curly shared a tonsil problem with George Gipp, he shared a Marmon roadster story with Penn quarterback Bert Bell, who would go on to be an important NFL commissioner. In 1919, before Penn played Dartmouth in New York, Bell "bet one of the Dartmouth players that Penn would beat the shit out of them," Bell's son, Upton said in an interview with the author. "My father said, 'If I lose, I'll leave my Marmon roadster in the parking lot with the keys in it.'"

After Dartmouth beat Penn 20-19 on November 8, in front of 30,000 surprised spectators at the Polo Grounds, there was the roadster, keys and all, Upton said: "Nobody believed that but he actually did that. And the guy drove away."

A Marmon, with Ray Harroun behind the wheel, had famously won the first Indianapolis 500 in 1911—aided by the first rear-view mirror. A popular luxury auto, the Marmon was hit hard by the Depression, when it went the way of the NFL's Staten Island Stapletons and Providence Steam Rollers.

A few days later, the *Philadelphia Inquirer*, discussing Penn's upset loss on November 11, said, "Captain Bert Bell is today no longer in possession of a $1,000 touring car, but instead this machine is now burning the roads of New England, so goes the report. For it is whispered that Bert staked her on the game, and when victory faded, so did the bus."

That's a story likely to have made its way through the football grapevine, if not the newspapers, to Green Bay. Like Lambeau, Bell, who had led Penn to the 1917 Rose Bowl, also had professional football designs. He initially planned to field the Stanley Professionals in Philadelphia in 1920. He abandoned that plan, though, staying on as a Penn assistant coach after blaming the 1919 Black Sox gambling scandal with poisoning interest in spectator sports. He had lined up a solid roster, including African-American star Fritz Pollard, who instead led the Akron Pros to the first championship of the American Professional Football Association, which would be renamed the National Football League. Pollard, who coached as well as played, was the NFL's first black coach.

Bell would finally enter the NFL in 1933, as the owner of the Philadelphia franchise, which he named the Eagles in honor the eagle adorning the logo of the National Recovery Act, part of President Franklin Roosevelt's plan to pull America out of the Depression.

In that era, football heroes such as Lambeau and Bell embellished stories, correctly believing they boosted interest in their football teams. Sportswriters, who correctly believed these fables were good for newspaper sales, were happy to play along.

That said, the Marmon roadster fable is the kind of embellished yarn that Lambeau would tell to Arch Ward, who was able to run with it an era where embellished yarns were standard practice for sportswriters.

Forty years later, Lambeau insisted he had gone to Canton to regain his football franchise, even though the league clearly had met in Cleveland. "There's some confusion over exactly where that meeting was held," a *Press-Gazette* story said on the 40th anniversary of the incident. "Curly insists it took place in Canton. Well, Curly was there—he ought to know." The only problem with that is. . . Curly didn't know.

Lambeau biographer David Zimmerman made the situation even more dire, with Lambeau fretting that the re-entry fee would be $1,500 rather than $50. That might have been a reference to the $1,000 guarantee all teams had to deposit as a safeguard against violating league rules and the $500 franchise fee that league president Joe F. Carr had instituted.

There's no question that Murphy helped Lambeau. He attended the January meeting in Canton, where Green Bay lost its franchise, and could have shown enough money to have swayed the owners that Curly would have the financial backing to field a team again in 1922. After all, they were friends who had both appeared in a minstrel show, entitled "Jollies of 1922," put on by the Green Bay Elks Club. It ran for three nights in January, with Lambeau earning praise for his musical numbers. In 1921, Lambeau also had appeared in the Elks' minstrel show at the Orpheum Theater. An April 16 ad for the show identified him as "Earl Lambeau: I Love the Ladies"—and said he was one of "Six Funny End Men Every One an Expert at Cutting Comical Capers."

What is important today, a century later, is that the determination of Curly Lambeau, backed by some football-obsessed Green Bay residents like Murphy, allowed their small town to survive where so many other small towns fell off the pro-football map.

Having survived expulsion, Green Bay played in the newly renamed NFL in the fall of 1922. But the team would encounter another perilous defining moment in the career of Curly Lambeau and the history of the Packers that fall.

The Packers also were undergoing a name change. having lost the financial support of their meatpacker sponsor and not wanting to be identified with it in any way, Calhoun turned to a variety of awkward names in his *Press-Gazette* stories. They became "the Green Bay football club" and "the Green Bay pro footballers," as well as occasionally the "Bays," "Big Blue" and "Blue."

On the field, Green finished with a 4-3-3 record in 1922, good for a tie for seventh place in the 18-team National Football League. But the biggest story was taking place at the sleepy ticket window. Lambeau and Calhoun went into the season counting on good attendance to make their precarious financial situation work. Bad weather and the Bears' refusal to honor an earlier commitment to play in Green Bay pushed the Packers to the brink of financial disaster.

Due to heavy rain, they had a poor turnout for their 3-0 victory over the Columbus Panhandles on November 5. "The playing field looked more like a swimming pool than a gridiron," Calhoun wrote in the *Press-Gazette.*

In a letter to the *Press-Gazette*, undoubtedly written by Calhoun, published on Tuesday, November 7, the "Green Bay football club" said it had lost $1,500 on the poorly attended Columbus game and had fallen into $3,400 debt for the season. The team needed revenue of $3,600 per game "to make ends meet," the letter said, adding that "The club lost by three one-hundredths of an inch the rain insurance which would have covered the loss on the game."

"To continue major football here," the report said, the team would raise ticket prices to $1.65 and $2.20, up from $1.10 and $1.65. Tickets to the "Jollies of 1922" minstrel show had ranged from 50 cents to $1.50. So it was slightly less expensive to hear Curly sing and tell jokes than it was to watch him pass and kick.

Although underwater with debt, Lambeau and Calhoun came up with the $1,500 guarantee due to the Panhandles. That kept the Green Bay football club in the good graces of Joe F. Carr, who at that point was NFL president as well as the Columbus Panhandles.

More bad weather held attendance to an estimated 2,000 at the Packers' next home game, a 13-0 win against the Milwaukee Badgers, on November 26. And yes, Wisconsin had three NFL teams in 1922, when the Racine Legion competed along with Milwaukee and Green Bay. Kenosha would give the state four NFL teams for one season, in 1924. Milwaukee would last for five seasons, Racine for four. Both teams would be gone after 1926, leaving Green Bay as Wisconsin's lone NFL survivor.

After beating Milwaukee, Green Bay received a gut punch from Chicago. George Halas, who had been scheduled to play a season finale in Green Bay on November 30, raised his guarantee demand to $4,000. Even with a reasonable crowd, that would have put the Packers in a deeper financial hole. As it turned out, Halas, who had his own money worries, chose to stay in Chicago and play the crosstown Cardinals, a game that would bring in a much better payday than a trip to Green Bay. And in those days, teams scuffling for survival could change their schedules on the fly.

Although the Bears lost 6-0 to the Cardinals on November 30, that Thanksgiving Day trip to Comiskey Park drew 14,000 fans. The windfall was so attractive that the Bears returned to Comiskey Park on December 10, where they lost again 9-0 to the Cardinals before a crowd of 15,000. The financial gain more than offset the defeats on the field.

Meanwhile, Green Bay settled for scheduling a Thanksgiving Day meeting with the Duluth Kelleys, an independent team that had beaten the Packers 6-2 in Duluth in their September 24 season opener. To help the Packers chip away at their cash shortage, a team of 25 loyal fans organized a Booster Day and ticket-selling campaign, while Calhoun hyped the game as a way for Green Bay football fans could help their team deal with its financial problems so it could return in 1923.

The crisis only got worse, though. When threatening weather made it likely that the Packers would go further into debt if they proceeded with the game, the franchise went through another Washington-crossing-the-Delaware moment—a decision-making time in which the Packers easily could have gone away and not returned. If they played before a sparse crowd, they would need to cover Duluth's guarantee and lose money. If they canceled the game, they would look unprofessional and risk alienating their fans, or even face being booted from the NFL.

On the morning of the game, Lambeau and Calhoun stared out through a window, lamenting the rain that was crushing their hopes of attracting a good crowd. Years later, Lambeau remembered the low moment taking place at the Hagemeister Park armory, where the Packers dressed. Calhoun wrote that it took place at the office of the *Press-Gazette,* but the armory makes more sense.

"Well, Cal, I guess this is it," Lambeau said, according to the legend he handed down to Packers historian Chuck Johnson. "We might as well call off the game. Then we won't have to pay the whole guarantee. There's no use going into debt any farther. We can't even meet the obligations we've got now."

Calhoun decided to call A.B. "Andy" Turnbull, one of the three owners of the *Press-Gazette,* and ask his advice. Lambeau said Turnbull came down to the armory and listened to the sad story. Turnbull's response was "a turning point," Calhoun said, in the Packers' future.

"Play the game," he said. "We'll straighten [the money] out later, somehow."

And so, the team—which Calhoun was calling the Bays in his *Press-Gazette* articles at that point—played, defeating Duluth 10-0 on a dismal day before a meager crowd of 2,000. The win on the field merely added up to more losses on their balance sheet.

Under the headline "Bays Prove Good Mud Horses" in the December 1, 1922, edition of the *Green Bay Press-Gazette,* Calhoun acknowledged that the weather had made a shambles of the team's fundraising plan: "The weather man knocked the 'boost' out of the 'Booster Day' affair and one of the smallest crowds of the season was in attendance. As a result, the club management is deeper in the hole. The rain, which started in the wee hours Thursday morning and continued up until noon, made the gridiron a sloppy playing field and incidentally kept about 2,000 pigskin followers away from the park. At one time it was thought the game would be called off but in order to keep faith with the fans, the management went through with the contest despite a big monetary loss."

Curly scored a third-quarter touchdown to break a scoreless tie. Former Wisconsin Badger star Cub Buck, who had been lured away from the Canton Bulldogs, added a fourth-quarter field goal. Buck, Green Bay's first salaried player, supplemented his Packer income as an assistant coach at Lawrence College in Appleton, where he also was executive director of the Boy Scouts chapter.

For Curly Lambeau, it was a trying time. His goal was to make a living out of football. But his dedication to the business side of football was not nearly at the level of George Halas and his partner, Dutch Sternaman, who were masters at plotting financial strategy as well as offensive and defensive schemes. And even if it had been, the realities of keeping a team afloat in Green Bay, which had more in common with Rock Island, were far more daunting than in a big city like Chicago.

True to his word, Turnbull and local attorney John Kittell stepped up and rallied financial support for Green Bay's foundering team. The two men quickly began building support that would allow the Packers to solve their money problems and keep their franchise going. Two early supporters were Dr. William Webber Kelly, who would become the team's longtime physician, and prominent wholesale grocer Lee Joannes, who would serve as team president for nearly 20 years.

"What a shame it would be if Green Bay had to get along without 'post-graduate' football," Dr. Kelly said in a *Press-Gazette* article written by Calhoun. "Football is a 'man-making' game. . . . We can't get along without it. . . . Our team is keeping Green Bay in the national eye and we want to stay there. We are the smallest city in the league but have a team which right now, I think, is second to none."

With Calhoun drumming up support in the *Press-Gazette,* Kittell presided over a fundraising meeting. Approximately 150 businessmen and football boosters gathered at the Elks Club on Friday, December 8. Kittell also appointed a committee of five, including Joannes and Turnbull, "to take charge of the sale of stock."

The committee eventually decided to sell 1,000 shares of stock at $5 per share. Those who bought five shares for $25 were given a box seat for home games as a bonus. The football-loving citizens of Green Bay bought in and allowed the Packers to continue to exist. And so, despite being conspicuously absent from the stock sale—he hadn't even bought a share of stock—Curly Lambeau had the foundation he needed.

At the league level, the NFL had yanked the franchise from Lambeau's private Green Bay Football Club shortly after the 1922 season, although there was no new ownership group yet to transfer it to. When the 1923 season arrived in September, Curly Lambeau's football dream was becoming a much more stable reality. The club had a new home field and a solid financial base. After scuffling to 3-2-1 and 4-3-3 league records in its first two APFA/NFL seasons, Green Bay was poised to enjoy a breakout year on the field.

In another sign of stability, the nickname "Packers" became firmly entrenched. In 1922, Calhoun had gone out of his way to avoid using the name in his stories, although "Packers" occasionally slipped into them. By the start of the 1923, season, a full-page ad in the *Press-Gazette* announced, "Here We Are Behind the Green Bay Packers. King Football Rules Supreme."

The ad was signed by 18 local businesses, including two jewelry stores, a pair of auto sellers, a flower shop, a dairy, a cafe and a clothes cleaner. Riding this wave of community support, Curly Lambeau was on his way to defying the laws of economics and building a big-time franchise in a small town.

One key business was missing, though. No packers expressed their support for the Packers. There was no meatpacking operation to be found in Green Bay. Only the name had survived. With or without packers, the Packers was a great brand.

While packers had become scarce in the city of the Packers, the name made more sense than, for example, the Lakers, who had brought their nickname from Minneapolis, in the land of lakes, to oceanside Los Angeles. Or the Dodgers, whose Brooklyn fans were trolley dodgers, to L.A., where people had their own vehicles. That said, the Packers, Lakers and Dodgers are among the most iconic team names in sports.

After the full-page ad of support for the Packers came three pages of photos, biographies and commercial endorsements of Lambeau and his players.

Lambeau, readers were told, "drives a Nash Sport... It seems very fitting that a man of such superior judgment in the selection of a football team that we expect will make a wonderful record, should drive a Nash Sport. Green Bay Nash Co."

The Nash Sport was a sign of things to come for The Man Who Invented the Green Bay Packers. Later in life, Lambeau, who liked fancy boats as well as cars, would be known for his flashy Cadillacs.

From a chance meeting with meatpacker Frank Peck that gave the team its name and its first set of jerseys to joining the nation's fledgling but ambitious pro football league, Lambeau and the Packers found themselves on much more solid ground in 1923, their third in the NFL and fifth overall.

The team still had a ballpark problem. Hagemeister Park had been dug up for the construction of Green Bay East High School and replaced by Bellevue Park. Located across the river from Hagemeister Park, Bellevue Park had a capacity of 4,000 in 1924. But fans grumbled that it was too far from town, lacked adequate parking and was more suited for baseball. "It was not a good football field," Calhoun wrote in a 1963 column for the *Press-Gazette*. "One of the end zones was about three yards short and the gates at the park were a bit too wide open."

In another sweeping change, Curly Lambeau, who had officially been the team owner in 1922, had surrendered that authority and responsibility in 1923, when the Green Bay Packers became a community-owned nonprofit team. Lambeau remained very much in charge from a football standpoint. Not being the owner of the team, though, meant there were limits to his power.

For men like George Halas, who went into debt up to his eyeballs to maintain ownership, this would have been anathema.

Curly Lambeau didn't seem to mind. In an NFL where every team, especially tiny Green Bay, was one step ahead of the bill collectors, it wasn't about owning the team. It was about running the team. And making an increasingly good living doing that.

# 7
## *BIRTH OF A RIVALRY*

Green Bay's big break came in late November of 1921, its first season in the APFA. The Packers' 7-1 record, especially their 3-1 mark in league games, had attracted the attention of the Chicago Cardinals, who offered to play them on Sunday, November 20, at Normal Park in Chicago.

But by the end of the 1921 season, very few Packers were living in Green Bay. The team was transitioning from a home-grown team to a roster of players from around the Midwest. Star lineman Cub Buck and coach Joe Hoeffel may have led the recruiting, with Lambeau learning from them and pitching in.

And so, the team gathered in Chicago at midweek for practices conducted by Hoeffel. Oddly enough, a hustling Lambeau, one of the few Packers who lived in Green Bay, did not arrive until Friday. He was coaching Green Bay East, which was preparing for a tough game at Appleton.

The Packers had eagerly accepted a chance to play the Cardinals for a payday and more football glory. Sloshing back and forth on a muddy, puddle-filled field, the teams played a scoreless first half. Lambeau gave Green Bay a 3-0 lead on a field goal early in the third quarter. Cardinals star Paddy Driscoll answered with a late field goal, though, and the game finished in a 3-3 tie.

"One thing is sure, Chicago now knows that Green Bay has a team and what's more loyal fans," the *Press-Gazette* gushed the next day. Although only 2,000 fans attended, that crowd was bolstered by a traveling party from Wisconsin. Many had attended the University of Wisconsin's game at the University of Chicago the day before the pro game.

The Packers' deadlock with the Cardinals prompted a short-notice offer from George Halas to play his Decatur Staleys the following Sunday, November 27, at Cubs Park. Although the agreement was reached on just five days' notice against the undefeated Staleys, the Packers had no qualms.

"Dreams come true," the *Press-Gazette* proclaimed on Wednesday, November 23.

In that same paper, Halas explained why he felt compelled to add the Packers even though the unbeaten Staleys faced a showdown with unbeaten Buffalo on Thanksgiving Day.

"We realize we are biting off quite a chunk in playing the Packers two days after our game with the All-Americans," Halas said, "but the Green Bay team has made such a record on the gridiron this fall that we were forced to meet them before laying claim to the professional championship of the country."

Halas also had two major incentives to play the Packers. The Staleys could use another victory in their battle with Buffalo for the league title. Plus, another game would mean another payday—and Green Bay fans had shown an inclination to travel to Chicago to support their Packers.

Back-to-back games in Chicago? That gave an early indication that small-town Green Bay might succeed where Canton, Portsmouth and Pottsville would fail. That also must have made a big impression on Curly Lambeau.

At that point, he was on his way to emerging as the face of the Green Bay Packers. He was their star player and captain. He would later be credited with being their coach for their first three years in an era where the lines were blurred between the captain, who made all the on-field decisions, and the coach, who ran practices. Lambeau also was taking on a big role in recruiting players.

Through most of the 1920s, though, his day job selling menswear at Stiefel's probably was what paid a lot of his bills. After living in houses at 124 and 106 South Monroe Avenue, Lambeau and Marguerite had moved to a more comfortable home at 630 Grignon Street by 1925 with their son, Donald, who had been born on September 16, 1920. About a mile south of Monroe, the Grignon house was practically across the street from the east bank of the Fox River.

While Lambeau later claimed he had been hired for $250 a month at Indian Packing when he returned from Notre Dame in 1919, meat packing was a failing endeavor in Green Bay. By the early 1920s, he was selling menswear at Stiefel's, which was a good fit for a man with a clothes-horse reputation. In 1922, the Green Bay East High School yearbook ran a photo of Earl L. Lambeau looking very sharp in a coat and tie and identified him as "Football coach and assistant study room supervisor."

During Thanksgiving week, Hoeffel again led Green Bay practices at Loyola Field in Chicago. Lambeau practiced with the team on Thanksgiving Day, a few days before the Packers faced the Staleys, then took advantage of a scouting opportunity. Passing on turkey and family, he tried to gain an edge by watching Buffalo edge the Staleys 7-6 at Cubs Park. And then the brash haberdasher made a bold prediction.

"We'll beat them," Lambeau said. "After giving the Staleys the 'once over,' I feel confident that the Packers will be champions of the middle west, Sunday night. Come on down fans and let's show Chicago that Green Bay is the best little football town in the country."

From very early on, Lambeau was intent on being successful enough to afford the finer things in life. And while pro football initially did not look like a path toward riches, he seemed to have a vision for the potential of his gridiron passion.

And then, on Sunday, November 27, Lambeau and the Packers went into battle at Cubs Park against the team then known as the Decatur Staleys. Although listed as being from Decatur, the Staleys played their last 10 games in 1921 at Cubs Park , after an opening game in Decatur. Even in their inaugural season, 1920, the Staleys had played five of their nine games in Chicago, with two in Decatur and two at Rock Island. In 1922, the Staleys would change their name to the Chicago Bears.

That 1921 meeting between Green Bay and the Staleys/Bears was the first in pro football's most storied rivalry. Lambeau and the Packers lost 20-0 that day. What made it especially memorable, though, was the roughly 500 fans who took a 12:50 a.m. train out of Green Bay the night before the game. "It was a train of sleeping cars with porters and Pullman berths, but nobody slept a wink," Green Bay newspaperman Harold Shannon said later.

Upon arrival in Chicago, the Green Bay contingent marched through the city's downtown, led by a band dressed in lumberjack clothing, an early version of the Lumberjack Band that would become a celebrated component of Packer support. The merry band marched to the Stratford Hotel at Michigan and Jackson, on the southern edge of downtown Chicago, where the Packers had stayed. It then proceeded more than five miles up to Cubs Park on the North Side, an eye-opening spectacle for citizens of the Windy City.

After watching this scene on the streets of Chicago, Frank Halas, a brother of the Bears founder, told newspaperman George Whitney Calhoun, who had helped Lambeau create the Packers, "Holy Cow! There can't be anybody left in Green Bay."

Never mind that the Packers, with Curly Lambeau trying to throw an over-sized sausage of a football, lost 20-0 to the Bears, who featured George Halas trying to catch that over-sized sausage, that day before 7,000, the biggest turnout for a Packer game that year. It also was another good crowd for the Staleys, who averaged just under 6,300 for their nine Cubs Park games.

The defeat left Green Bay with a 3-2-1 record in its first AFPA season. tied for sixth with the Evansville Crimson Giants. The Packers were 7-2-2 overall that year, including four wins and a tie in non league games.

If the football lovers in Green Bay were dedicated enough to travel to Chicago for games, Lambeau's dream of keeping a pro-football team alive in a small Wisconsin town had a chance. And as the 1920s progressed, Lambeau had the ability to do that.

\* \* \* \* \* \* \* \*

Vince Lombardi's 1960s success casts a much larger shadow. But the Packer championship machine that Curly Lambeau created in the late '20s and early '30s established the winning tradition in Green Bay.

"To me, the six championships that Lambeau won were as important and maybe more so than what Lombardi did," Upton Bell said. "They not only kept the franchise alive. A lot of the players that Lombardi molded—and he did do that and did a fantastic job—they were already there. Curly recruited his own people."

This was where Lambeau really started to build the reputation that would land his name on one of the most hallowed sports stadiums in America. With the dedicated support of Green Bay football fans and the businessmen who would put the team's finances on firm ground, Lambeau was free to do what he did best—create a championship football power.

Using his eye for talent to acquire players who could win and leading them with a relentless thirst for success, Lambeau built and prodded the Packers to the upper tier of the fledgling National Football League. For the next 25 years, they would endure only one losing season. Most years, they would be in the hunt to win the NFL championship.

Green Bay's modest home stadium limited the appeal of traveling there for owners of opposing teams in an era where teams could and did gerrymander their schedules to maximize their profits. Even then, NFL football was a wobbly financial enterprise.

The appeal of traveling to Green Bay for opposing players was a different story. It was a city that largely ignored Prohibition, a city overseen by public officials who were often prodded by federal authorities to stop being lax about enforcing the ban on alcohol.

The abundance of alcohol fueled other unsavory activities, including gambling and prostitution, that gave Green Bay a Las-Vegas-like appeal.

"Green Bay in the '20s was the most popular stop in the league," Dan Daly and Bob O'Donnell wrote in *Pro Football Chronicle,* an earthy history of the NFL and its rivals. "Visiting players loved the place. Teams made it a point to schedule several days there. It had a bustling bar scene, and its red-light district in the northeast section was famous."

In one of the many colorful anecdotes involving Johnny Blood, Lambeau's free-spirited Hall of Fame receiver told quarterback Arnie Herber to "throw it in the direction of Mother Pierre's whorehouse." A saloonkeeper as well as a madam, Mother Pierre operated the Green Mill Garden speakeasy. A true story? With Blood, any yarn was possible.

Northeastern Wisconsin was heavily populated by northern Europeans who had no interest in giving up their alcoholic beverages. That made Lambeau's hometown highly attractive to rough-and-tumble football players.

As the 1920s progressed, more wholesome football players found Green Bay's fishing and hunting opportunities attractive. Because teams often stayed in Green Bay before or after playing in Chicago to save on travel expenses, visiting players became familiar with the appeal of the football-crazy town in northeastern Wisconsin.

In other words, while Green Bay eventually became the butt of small-town jokes, its aversion to Prohibition combined with outdoor activities made it an appealing stop for visiting players. Green Bay's attractions, both wholesome and unsavory, also helped Lambeau's efforts to sign the players he wanted.

When it came to playing on the road, the Packers were a coveted opponent. Because of their success, the colorful players Lambeau had assembled and loyal Green Bay fans who traveled, they tended to draw large crowds.

George Halas, who had crushed Lambeau's hopes for a franchise-saving gate when he refused to bring his Bears to Green Bay at the end of the 1922 season unless he received an unworkable $4,000 guarantee, finally brought his team north early in the 1923 season.

In their first trip to Green Bay, the Bears prevailed 3-0 on October 14, 1923, at the Packers' new Bellevue Park home before a crowd of 4,451. Barely a month earlier, on September 17, the first meeting of the Green Bay Football Corporation had been held at the Brown County Courthouse. At that meeting, the Packers officially became a community-owned team. That gave Lambeau the financial structure to advance his football dream.

The rivalry between the Bears and the Packers is rightfully celebrated as one of the fiercest in American sports. The stories of the animosity between their supporters, and the lengths that Halas and Lambeau would go to beat each other, are a legendary part of Packer lore.

And yet, on another level, the Packers and the Bears were very important partners. While Halas originally balked at taking the Bears to Green Bay, he quickly saw the financial light. The teams met three times each season from 1926 to 1933, except for 1927. The Bears would go north early in the season and the Packers would travel to Chicago twice for late-season games that generally attracted big crowds to Wrigley Field. The three-meetings plan was dropped only when the NFL moved to more standardized schedules in the '30s.

Halas wasn't singling out Green Bay when it came to unbalanced scheduling. From 1921 through 1932, the Bears played at home 118 times while going on the road only 45 times. During those years, the Packers played 72 home games and 78 road games against NFL opponents.

The fierceness of the rivalry—and the determination of Lambeau and Halas to prevail—is filled with examples of their venom for each other.

They didn't, for example, speak or shake hands on game day.

"Shake hands?" Lambeau once said. "That would have been a lie. If I lost, I wanted to punch Halas in the nose."

Lambeau levied fines for Packers who spoke to Bears. Both coaches had elaborate schemes for spying on each other's practices. Halas would sign players Lambeau had cut for the sole purpose of gleaning Packer information from them. Packer fans partied loudly near the Bears' rooms at the Northland Hotel the night before they played in Green Bay. The hotel did its part by assigning the Bears to rooms where the noise would have its greatest effect.

And yet, as much as they wanted to beat each other, Halas and Lambeau appreciated each other as business partners. When the NFL gathered for league meetings, they worked together. When speculation surfaced that that the league no longer had room for small-town Green Bay,

Halas was a staunch defender of keeping the Packers right where they had always been.

As Curly Lambeau went about building the Packers into a championship team in the 1920s, the Bears games became more than the keys to success on the field. Those well-attended rivalry showdowns also were the linchpins to financial success.

And with the growing stability of Green Bay's football team, Lambeau, aided by more experienced football men in the Packer organization, was learning how to put together a roster of players who would bring glory to northeastern Wisconsin.

\* \* \* \* \* \* \* \*

That season-ending 20-0 loss to the Staleys/Bears left Green Bay with a league record of 3-2-1 in 1921, its inaugural season as a pro-football league member.

As the 1922 season began, Joe Hoeffel had departed as Packers coach and gone into private business, although he did work as a head linesman for some Packer games that fall.

For the first time, Lambeau was the undisputed coach, although the *Press-Gazette* generally continued to refer to him as "Capt. Lambeau."

Two days before its season opener at Duluth, Lambeau welcomed Charlie Mathys, a 5-7, 165-pound sparkplug from Green Bay West who had played college football at Ripon and Indiana. Mathys, who had a day job in Indiana, had played in 1921 for the Hammond Pros. Although officially a quarterback, Mathys was a prolific receiver as well as passer in that era of multi-purpose backs. He led the NFL with 90 passes caught for 1,506 yards, according to unofficial statistics in *The Pro Football Chronicle.* An arm injury cut his playing career short in 1926, but he served on the Packers' board until 1980.

In early October, Green Bay added another important player, Francis "Jug" Earp, who had been released after two games by the Rock Island Independents after he had a bad game against the Chicago Bears. A center and tackle who was commonly known by his nickname, a shortened version of Juggernaut, Earp was a cousin of lawman Wyatt Earp. Despite Rock Island complaints that he was over-weight and out of shape, Earp went on to play for 11 seasons in Green Bay. The outgoing Earp went on to be the team's director of public relations from 1950 to 1954.

Green Bay followed its non-league opening 6-2 loss at Duluth with three straight losses in the National Football League. It regrouped from there, winning four and tying three to finish with a 4-3-3 record in 1922.

By 1923, the Packers' third season as a league member, Lambeau continued to mature. He had been captain and key player from the team's 1919 inception. In his second season as coach, he was expanding his role as roster builder. A tougher and sharper Green Bay went 7-2-2 that fall, good for third place behind the Canton Bulldogs (11-0-1) and the Bears (9-2-1) in the 20-team NFL. Green Bay's only losses were to the Bears, 3-0 in Green Bay on October 14, and to Racine Legion 24-3 in Green Bay on October 28. The Packers evened things up with a 16-0 win in Racine on November 11.

Heading into the 1924 season, the *Press-Gazette* gushed on Friday, September 5 that "Green Bay's greatest football eleven will start practicing on Sunday." A big reason for optimism was the addition of end Tillie Voss, "one of the greatest wingmen in the game." A premier star in basketball, which was taking early professional steps, he would live up to his billing. He was the Packers' only all-pro in 1924. But in an era where players moved around like gypsies, that would be his only season in Green Bay. Voss changed teams virtually every year in the 1920s. He played for 10 different teams. Lambeau, sensing that constant roster turnover was no way to build a consistent winner, curtailed the practice, finding talented players he could depend on for more than one season. And so, Voss was basically the last of the Green Bay gypsies.

Although he was very much a wide-eyed, eager kid in the Packers' first few years, Lambeau was starting to assume command in 1924. He was 26 years old. He was still an important player, but he now had ideas about shaping a roster. He also was learning how to draw up a playbook, especially a playbook that took advantage of his players' strengths.

On the recruiting front, Lambeau signed Verne Lewellen. who began a nine-year career in 1924 after starring at Nebraska "Signing Lewellen was perhaps Lambeau's best personnel move ever," Cliff Christl, the Packers' official historian, said. "If not for Lewellen, there probably would have been no three-peat from 1929-31. And without a three-peat there may have been no Packers after they went into receivership. The *Press-Gazette* on several occasions referred to Lewellen as the key to those championship teams."

"One of the most underrated players of the two-way era," NFL Films archivist Chris Willis wrote in "The NFL's 60-Minute Men: All-Time Greats of the Two-Way Player Era, 1920-1945" .his 2024 ranking of ironmen who played offense and defense. Willis ranked Lewellen seventh between a pair of Bears greats, No. 6 Bronko Nagurski and No. 8 Sid Luckman. "He is the highest ranked player on this list NOT in the Pro Football Hall of Fame, although he should be," Willis concluded.

Lambeau found Lewellen through his Notre Dame connection, which frequently led him to gifted players. "Sleepy Jim" Crowley, who had played at Green Bay East for Lambeau before becoming one of the Four Horsemen of Notre Dame, urged Lambeau to sign Lewellen after the Nebraska Cornhuskers defeated the Fighting Irish in 1922 and 1923. Those were Notre Dame's only losses during the three-year reign of the Four Horsemen, who went undefeated in 1924, including a 34-6 win over a Lewellen-less Nebraska. The Pittsburgh Pirates also were interested in Lewellen, but an arm injury apparently ended his opportunity to be a Major League pitcher.

Lewellen was widely viewed as the NFL's best punter in a low-scoring era where punting loomed large. Lewellen also was a runner, receiver, passer and defender. His 51 career touchdowns stood as the NFL record until 1941.

Lewellen was just as remarkable off the field. While still playing for the Packers, he was the Brown County district attorney from 1929 to 1933. He later worked in the Packers' front office as general manager (from 1953 to 1959) and business manager (from 1959 to 1967).

In 1927, Lambeau added a pair of former Marquette stars, quarterback Red Dunn and end Lavvie Dilweg. They not only would be two important pieces in Green Bay establishing itself as a perennial power. They also demonstrated Lambeau's skill at identifying talent and putting his finds in position to excel.

Dunn, who played from 1927 to 1931, was acquired in August 1927 from the Chicago Cardinals, whom he had helped to the 1925 NFL title after playing in 1924 for the Milwaukee Badgers. Often compared to Bart Starr because of his field-general skill, Dunn operated much like a T-formation quarterback, taking a short snap behind center. He also was a highly regarded safety on defense. Lambeau named the versatile Dunn as the quarterback on his all-time Packer team.

Like Lewellen, LaVern "Lavvie" Dilweg was a notable lawyer as well as a football standout. A Milwaukee native and Marquette star who is regarded as perhaps the best two-way end of his era—he was named to an 11-man All-NFL team five straight years—Dilweg was a Packer from 1927 to 1934. He declined Lambeau's initial attempt to sign him in 1926, playing for the Milwaukee Badgers that year to finish law school. Dilweg became a law partner of Gerald Clifford, who was instrumental in the Packers' management for decades. Dilweg also served one term as a U.S. congressman during World War II.

Thanks to Lambeau's growing ability to recruit talented players and coach them up, Green Bay posted winning records throughout the 1920s. In 1927, they went 7-2-1 and finished second, their best NFL showing up to that point. Due to some schedule-wrangling with the New York Giants and the Red-Grange-led New York Yankees, the Packers reported a loss of $1,516.37 in 1927. Despite its growing stature on the field, Green Bay was still fighting an uphill battle at the box office.

In 1928, though, a 6-4-3 campaign provided another big breakthrough. For the first time, the Packers reported a moneymaking season, with a net profit of $3,546.70. For all the talent he had put in place, Lambeau would need more standouts to win a championship. And now he had the resources to do that.

# 8
## *THE CHAMPIONSHIP MYSTIQUE BEGINS*

Curly Lambeau often seemed to ignore trends. He put a big-city franchise in a small town. He passed when the rest of the NFL preferred to run. And in the fall of 1929, when America was starting to go over a financial cliff, he was boldly acquiring three standout players who would take the Packers to wondrous success.

"Curly felt the Packers had the makings of a truly great team in the 1929 season," wrote *Chicago Tribune* sports editor Arch Ward, a Lambeau friend who had been Rockne's first publicist at Notre Dame. "Always a perfectionist, the `Belgian' said that the addition of at least three more players in key positions would make them that kind of team. The problem was to find those three. They would have to be experienced men, and no team in the league was going to yield any talented hands willingly."

Ward—who created baseball's All-Star game and the college football All-Star game, and had his hand in many other major sports developments—never lacked a sense of drama. But in this case, the three players Lambeau signed for the 1929 were worthy of the accolades Curly and his new Packer trio received.

In adding tackle Cal Hubbard and guard Mike Michalske, Lambeau gave himself two standouts who anchored the Packers in the trenches. Considering that Hubbard and Michalske excelled on both offense and defense in an era where many two-way players were weaker on one side of the ball, it was like adding four players.

Hubbard had played end rather than tackle on the New York Giants' 1927 NFL champions in his first pro season. A rural Missouri native, Hubbard began his college career at Centenary in Shreveport, Louisiana, before following his coach to Geneva College in Beaver Falls, Pennsylvania. Although he was an immediate success with the Giants, Hubbard didn't like living in New York. After the Giants played in Green Bay in 1928, Hubbard decided that was the place for him.

"He told the team, `Trade me to the Packers or I quit,' " Glenn Swain wrote succinctly in *Packers vs. Bears*. "Cal had decided he liked Green Bay after spending a week there the year before. `We played the Packers in Green Bay and had to play the Bears in Chicago next so we stayed in Green Bay that week to practice. I kind of liked Green Bay.' "

It didn't hurt, of course, that Lambeau was building a powerhouse. And so Hubbard demanded a trade to Green Bay. It was "a difficult pill to swallow. . . a terrible loss for the [Giants] club," Wellington Mara biographer Carlo DeVito wrote.

Hubbard reportedly played at up to 270 pounds, which was huge in an era where 200-pound linemen were the norm. Beyond that, he had rare quickness that Lambeau sometimes took advantage of by turning Hubbard into a ferocious linebacker.

That said, as time went on, Hubbard came to dislike his new coach. And he didn't mince words about his feelings for Lambeau, saying, "They won't be able to find six men to bury the so and so. He was a hard driver, but he got the job done."

A year before joining the Packers, Hubbard began moonlighting in the off-season as a minor-league baseball umpire. In 1936, when his NFL career was winding down, Hubbard became an American League umpire. He umpired until 1951, when a hunting accident impaired his vision. Known for refining the way umpires worked, he then became a supervisor of umpires until 1969. He is the only man elected to both the Pro Football Hall of Fame and the Baseball Hall of Fame.

Michalske, a guard who had played fullback at Penn State, came to Green Bay from the New York Yankees, a team created in 1926 for Red Grange by his manager, C.C. Pyle. When the Yankees folded after the 1928 season, Michalske became available and Lambeau signed him.

Not as big as Hubbard, the 6-foot, 210-pound Michalske relied on great quickness and anticipation. He also was a gifted tackler who had an innate sense for making good decisions. He would be a Packer from 1929 to 1937, with a timeout in 1936 to coach at Lafayette College, and be a member of the second NFL Hall of Fame class.

By acquiring Hubbard and Michalske, Lambeau showed his eye for bruisers along with his flair for the passing game.

The most memorable member of Lambeau's 1929 signing trio, though, was Johnny Blood, an all-around back who had an exceptional ability to turn a game around with one play. Lewellen was more clutch. He had 49 runs of 10 yards or more, while Blood had 26, but Blood was more dangerous on any given play because he was faster.

The many-layered Blood was a Falstaff-like character right out of Shakespeare, whom he could and did quote.

"Wild. Handsome. Unpredictable," wrote *Milwaukee Journal* sportswriter Oliver Kuechle, who gave Blood his Vagabond Halfback nickname, a tribute to the five NFL teams and two colleges he played for, and his penchant for traveling in the box cars of freight trains because he was short of funds. "As big-hearted as they come and as wasteful both of himself, with the wonderful physique nature gave him, and of his goods. And a great athlete. He could be one with the riff-raff in a waterfront bar one day, then recite Keats, Shelley or Shakespeare by the hour in different company the next. He could drop a pass thrown right in his hands and then get one that nobody else could."

Born John McNally into a relatively wealthy family in New Richmond, Wisconsin, he was searching for an alias with a friend when they were on their way to play for a Minneapolis semi-pro team, the East 26th Liberties, while retaining their college eligibility. They passed a theater marquee displaying the name of the Rudolph Valentino silent film, *Blood and Sand*. Given the timing, it's possible that *Blood and Sand,* which had debuted earlier, merely appeared on the marquee of a later Valentino film. With Johnny Blood, one never knew.

Turning to his friend, Ralph Hanson, who was riding on the back of his motorcycle, McNally said, "That's it. I'll be Blood and you'll be Sand."

The name stuck—to the point where Cliff Christl, the esteemed official historian of the Packers, defended calling him Johnny Blood, not Johnny "Blood" McNally. "I've never seen the name McNally attached to his name in any [Packers] publications or in any NFL game summary. . . . the bottom line is: He was Johnny Blood in his football life until the day he died."

The 6-foot-1, 190-pound Blood played for the Packers from 1929 to 1936, except for 1934, when Lambeau, fed up with his antics, sold him to Pittsburgh. Lambeau had suspended Blood with three games remaining in the 1933 season, when he showed up for practice either hung over or still drunk.

Blood worked his way back into Lambeau's favor in the pre-season of 1935, by playing for the Chippewa Falls Marines and La Crosse Old Style Lagers in exhibition games against the Packers. With Don Hutson making his debut as a Packer that year, Lambeau had given himself two of the best receivers in early NFL history.

Although they remained lifelong friends, the Lambeau-Blood relationship was tempestuous.

"He fined Blood plenty of times," Hutson, who was a rookie in 1935, said in a videotaped interview at the Packers Hall of Fame website. "The first year I was there, Blood played five games and hadn't had any checks at all—and owed the club $200 to $300."

Blood's lax approach to rules wasn't the only reason for his on-again, off-again relationship with Lambeau. They sometimes competed for women. And Blood's free-spirited charm put him in competition with Curly for the spotlight—in newspaper coverage and public speaking, where Blood excelled, as well as with women.

"That's one reason I developed a reputation as a clutch player," Blood said of his complicated relationship; with Lambeau."A lot of times, Curly would only use me when he really needed a big play."

When Blood returned in 1935, Lambeau only used him grudgingly, which left fans clamoring for Curly to put him in. "The fans really liked me —hell, I'd probably had a drink with every one of them," Blood said. "But that also caused problems with Curly. His ego had really gotten swollen by this time; he thought he *was* football in Green Bay, and I think he was kind of jealous of me."

Another important addition Lambeau made for the 1929 Packers was Bo Molenda, a fullback he acquired from C.C. Pyle's New York Yankees on November 22, 1928, near the end of the season. If Molenda had been acquired after the 1928 season, historians might have talked about the four difference-makers Lambeau acquired for Green Bay's 1929 championship run.

"Packer football stock climbed a notch or two when Bo Molenda, one of the best fullbacks in the National Football League, joined the Big Bay Blues," the *Appleton Post-Crescent* reported on November, 24, 1928. "In college, Molenda was a star at Michigan. With Molenda in the fold the Packer squad is beginning to figure on a national championship. A big, powerful fullback like Molenda rounds out the Bay machine to a nicety."

Although the article carried no byline, it bears the imprint of Calhoun, who wrote Packer reports and distributed them to newspapers to spread the team's reach. The piece ran under a dateline from Atlantic City, New Jersey, where Green Bay practiced between games against the New York Giants and Pottsville Maroons. In Atlantic City, Curly and his players presumably could find entertaining ways involving bootleg alcohol, female companionship and general carousing to spend their evenings.

When Lambeau brought Blood, Hubbard and Michalske to Green Bay for the 1929 season, he had the pieces in place for one of the most dominant seasons the NFL had ever seen, or would ever see. This was Lambeau at his best—building a brilliant roster and then coaching it to glory.

It is why students of the NFL like Upton Bell believe Lambeau's contributions rival Lombardi's. Although Curly operated in a largely forgotten, simpler time, that does not diminish his skill at building a team. That's especially true considering that he was competing against teams in America's largest cities, which had more reasons to be successful.

The Packers breezed through a pre-season 14-0 win over the independent Portsmouth Spartans. Although largely forgotten now, Portsmouth was a powerhouse. It would join the NFL in 1930, face the Chicago Bears in a memorable 1932 NFL championship game and become the Detroit Lions in 1934.

Green Bay then handled the Dayton Triangles 9-0 in its 1929 NFL opener. That set the stage for Green Bay's first meeting with the Chicago Bears. The night before the game, Curly Lambeau's wife, Marguerite, awoke to find his pillow case covered with Xs and Os that he had drawn that night. Running out of room, he had used the sheet. Whether Curly came up with this likely fable or Marguerite also had a vivid imagination is not clear. Then again, Curly was known to jot down plays at odd moments.

Lambeau need not have fretted that much. His Packer squad thrashed the Bears 23-0 on September 29 before a record crowd of 13,000 at a jammed City Stadium. Scalpers were reported to be charging $10 for $1 bleacher seats to see the Packers have their way with the Bears. "It was a great game for the Packers and our congratulations are in order," George Halas said. "That 23 to 0 licking was the worst the Bears have ever suffered, but look out when you come to Chicago in November."

The brave words had a hollow ring. The Bears were in turmoil. Halas and his co-owner, Dutch Sternaman, were not seeing eye-to-eye about their football team. It was a rift that would not be settled until Halas bought out Sternaman.

When the Packers traveled to Chicago on November 10, they shut out the Bears again, 14-0. The third meeting, the season-ender in Chicago in December 8, would be a third Green Bay shutout, 25-0. After that, Halas stepped down as coach for three years as he and Sternaman sorted out their differences.

After thrashing the Bears in their second game, the exuberant Packers turned their attention to Chicago's other team, the Cardinals, who were coming to Green Bay next. It was a strange but then-common front-loaded schedule for the Packers. Fearful of bad-weather games that would have put a damper on ticket sales, Green Bay played its first five league games at home in 1929 home before finishing with eight games on the road.

In their third home game, the Packers didn't muster their best effort against the Cardinals, but prevailed 9-2 on October 6 before a crowd of 6,000 at City Stadium. Green Bay did catch a break. Cardinals star Ernie Nevers was starting the second game of a doubleheader that day for the San Francisco Missions, a Pacific Coast League team that was wrapping up its regular season at Seattle. Nevers, who had grown up in Superior, Wisconsin, had been a standout for football coach Pop Warner at Stanford after his family moved to California.

"Ernie Nevers' farewell was indeed brief," the *San Francisco Examiner* reported on October. 7, 1929. After giving up a home run, a double and a single in the bottom of the first, he was replaced on the mound. "Nevers left immediately to join the Chicago Cardinals, a professional football team, which he will lead."

Nevers fared much better at football. Later that fall, on November 28, 1929, he scored all 40 points, including six rushing touchdowns, in a 40-6 rout of the Bears, setting records still in place nearly a century later.

Meanwhile, the Packers, after improving to 3-0 against the Cardinals, braced for a meeting with the Frankford Yellow Jackets, who also were 3-0. The Yellow Jackets, from the Frankford neighborhood of

Philadelphia, had won four of the previous five meetings with Green Bay. They had won the NFL championship in 1926 and had finished second in 1928.

"We have a lot of old scores to settle with the Frankford Yellowjackets," Lambeau said at the top of the *Press-Gazette's* preview on Friday, October 11. "And it's a good bet that some of them are going to be evened next Sunday."

Two days later, Lambeau's 1929 squad fulfilled Curly's prediction, beating Frankford 14-2 on October 13 before a crowd of 9,000 at Green Bay's City Stadium. The Packers were led by Lewellen, who threw an early 46-yard touchdown to Eddie Kotal. Lewellen also showed a gifted leg, *Press-Gazette* writer Arthur W. Bystrom noted: "Some great punting by Lewellen, the Packers' plunging district attorney, did a lot to keep the play deep in Frankford territory."

After taking down the Minneapolis Redjackets 24-0 on October 20 in their final home game the following week, the Packers led the NFL with a 5-0 record. In those five wins, Lambeau's team had outscored its opponents 79-4. The New York Giants (3-0-1) were the only other unbeaten team.

Its 1929 home schedule completed, Green Bay survived its first four road games, winning at Minneapolis and in Chicago three times, once against the Bears and twice against the Cardinals. That is not a misprint. The Packers played six of their 13 games against the Bears and the Cardinals that year. In an era where teams made their own schedules, playing more games in Chicago produced more ticket revenue for Green Bay and its Windy City rivals.

That set up a showdown on November 24 in New York between the unbeaten Packers, who had won their first nine games, and the undefeated Giants, who had notched eight wins and a tie. A crowd of 25,000 turned out at the Polo Grounds to see if the Giants could clear a critical hurdle in their bid to win a second NFL championship in three years. The New York fans left disappointed as the Packers rolled to a 20-6 victory.

"The hard-running, hard-fighting Green Bay Packers punctured the bubble of Giant invincibility yesterday by trampling rough-shod over the hitherto unbeaten New Yorkers," Arthur J. Daley wrote in the *New York Times* the next day. "The Packers had weapons that the local outfit couldn't match. They had a magnificent kicker in Lewellen, whose zooming 60 and 70-yard punts with a wet, sodden ball ever kept the Wisconsin eleven in scoring territory; they had a line of 200-pounders, a line that outcharged and outrushed the highly touted New York forwards; they had a fast, deceptive attack with a set of backs running viciously from well-screened formations behind wall-like interference."

This was Curly Lambeau at his best. He had assembled a championship roster, coached it to a dominating win over an unbeaten team

—and had done it in New York City, where his team's excellence would draw the greatest notice. Remarkably, the Packers played without Red Dunn and Eddie Kotal, who were both injured. That left Lewellen filling in at quarterback. Due to the injury crisis, 10 Packers played 60 minutes and the 11th played 59.

This was a game that put Green Bay on the national map. All things considered, even today, nearly a century later, it rivals the Ice Bowl as the biggest win in franchise history. In Green Bay, the *Press-Gazette* called it "one of the greatest football games ever played" and said, "No event in many years has brought so much pleasure and satisfaction to Green Bay."

Playing a key role in the win was fullback Bo Molenda. who scored a touchdown and kicked two extra points, outshining his former Michigan teammate, Giants quarterback Benny Friedman, regarded as the NFL's best passer. " 'Bull' Molenda never looked better in a Packer uniform," Calhoun wrote in his account, which ran under a giant black banner headline the next day on the front page of the *Press-Gazette* that said, "PACKERS BEAT GIANTS, 20-6."

Calhoun also reported that "Veteran New York Newspaper men. . . said that no team has ever received the 'flowery' ink bestowed upon Green Bay. . . . One 'new[s] hound' expressed his opinion that the Packers of 1929 was the greatest eleven in football history, college, professional or otherwise."

Four days after the big win in New York, the Packers lined up on Thanksgiving Day in the Philadelphia neighborhood of Frankford against their Yellow Jackets. For all the celebrating, Lambeau no doubt reminded his players that this also was a critical contest for Green Bay (10-0), which led the Giants (8-1-1) and Frankford (9-2-3) by thin margins. New York, which would play two more league games than Green Bay, could sneak into the title if each team ended up with one loss.

And given the opportunities in Atlantic City, where the team worked out between games, Curly needed to keep Packers like Johnny Blood focused on football.

As it turned out, a crowd of 8,500 at Frankford Stadium saw the Yellow Jackets give the Packers a tough challenge. Even before the game began, Philadelphia's famous hecklers were in action. "Green Bay never played before a more hostile audience," Calhoun reported on November 29. "From the moment the Bays stepped on the field until the final whistle blew and a near fight developed, these Frankforders were on Capt. Lambeau and his men nearly everywhere. Some of the sideline coaches went to the heights of sarcasm to express their views and the players on the bench had to stand plenty with a smile."

When the game ended in a scoreless tie, the scene was a curious one. The Frankford side celebrated, even though the tie pretty much eliminated the Yellow Jackets' chances of winning the league title.

Meanwhile, the Packers, who had remained atop the NFL, which did not include ties in those days when calculating its championship standings, left the field angry. On the brink of scoring, they felt robbed when the officials ruled that time had run out.

"The Packer players were hot under the collar at the close of the game as they figured that they had been 'gyped' [sic] in the time," Calhoun reported. "Every one of the players are willing to bet their season's salary that there was at least four minutes to go. However, the umpire blew his cold whistle and that was all there was to it. Lewellen just a few plays previous had asked about the time and was informed there was seven minutes to go. Then after Kotal had grabbed a pass and skipped to the 9 yard line, just as the Packers started to line up for another pass, the whistle tooted and the drive was over."

While disappointed, Lambeau and his players moved on. Three days after their Thanksgiving Day win in Philadelphia, Green Bay won 25-0 in Providence, Rhode Island, on Sunday, December 1.

The Packers finished their season a week later, beating the struggling Bears in another 25-0 blowout before a meager crowd of 6,000 at Wrigley Field. In three games against the Bears, Green Bay had won three times by a combined 62-0. With Halas and Sternamen clashing, the Bears limped to a 4-9-2 finish—their only losing season in their first 25 years. To ease the tension, George Halas gave up the coaching reins for three years.

Lambeau had led the Packers to their first NFL title in 1929 in convincing style. They not only posted a record of 12-0-1. They outscored their opponents, 198-22, allowing only three touchdowns and two safeties all season while scoring 29 touchdowns—14 rushing, 12 receiving, two on interception returns and one punt return.

When the Packers returned to Green Bay the night after their final win in Chicago, they were greeted by a mob of 20,000. "No warriors returning victorious from a great battle ever received an ovation such as was accorded the Green Bay players," the *Press-Gazette* reported on its December 10, 1929, front page. "Thousands of persons were everywhere, lining the streets, on tops of roofs and box cars, in windows hoping to get a glimpse of the players. . . It mattered little to them that they were jammed together like bits of sand on a desert for weren't they among the privileged few who were first to see the champions."

Despite freezing weather, the celebrants began the greetings with red fuses five miles south of the Chicago & Northwestern depot. Packer fans lined the tracks and stood on buildings. When the train neared the station, it slowed to a crawl to allow jubilant greeters to get out of the way.

The next night, each player was given a watch and $220 at a victory dinner held at the Beaumont Hotel, the money collected by the *Green Bay Press-Gazette.*

"I was given two of the greatest thrills of my life last night and tonight by the welcome tendered by Green Bay fans," Lambeau told the gathering of 400 at the banquet. "Other teams that won the championship always finished in the second division the following year, but we are going to do our best to break that precedent. And if the fans are behind us, we think we can do it."

Despite all the congratulating and celebrating, the Packers' season was not over. To pick up a few dollars, Lambeau had scheduled a post-season barnstorming game in Memphis on Sunday, December 15, against the independent Tigers. If Curly had expected the Tigers, who had been bolstered by the addition of several top NFL players, merely to be satisfied by the payday from a crowd of 8,000, the biggest in their history, he had miscalculated.

In unseasonably balmy weather, Memphis humiliated the Packers 20-6. "Undefeated in fourteen engagements in the National Pro league, the Packers had their spotless slate smeared dull of Memphis mud by the Tigers, and they could not understand it at all," *Memphis Commercial-Appeal* sports editor John Caldwell wrote in a report published by the *Press-Gazette* on December 16, 1929.

Gnashing his teeth at league headquarters in Columbus, Ohio, NFL president Joe F. Carr could not have agreed more. With Green Bay planning another barnstorming game in Portsmouth, Ohio, "In late 1929, Carr struck a deal with the independent Portsmouth Spartans, who were refused entrance into the NFL earlier that year, to allow them to join the league if they stopped plans to play the NFL-champion Green Bay Packers," historian Craig R. Coenen wrote. "The Packers had just come off a loss to the independent Memphis Tigers and, from a public-relations standpoint, the NFL could not accept another embarrassing defeat."

And yet, owners could not resist the income from barnstorming in the lean years of the 1920s and '30s. "In 1934 alone, the Chicago Bears grossed nearly 50 percent of the revenue needed for season-long operating expenses from a barnstorming tour," Coenen said. It wasn't until after the 1939 season that the league banned all postseason barnstorming.

While the Packers' loss in Memphis was a barnstorming embarrassment to NFL president Carr. there was an explanation for it. Longtime Packers trainer Bud Jorgensen remembered it as an All-Star game against a team loaded with talented NFL players.. "Bud recalls when the Packers played in the first-ever All-Star game in 1929," John Torinus wrote in *The Packer Legend.*

In that account, Jorgensen—whose duties included packing Ma Kline's moonshine for road trips—said Blood got into the moonshine even before the team changed trains in Chicago on its way to Memphis. "Blood had taken a knife and cut the vein in his wrist and he was dipping his finger in the blood and had painted a sign which read: `I am the famous Johnny Blood.' And to make matters worse, he was parading the sign up and down the passenger cars."

Lambeau, who had a well-deserved reputation for blaming others when life did not go his way, unloaded a diatribe of excuses when the Packers reached Chicago on their way home. He blamed the hot weather. injuries, the officials and a loaded Memphis team that had bulked up with several NFL players.

"The weather was the greatest handicap," he said. "Before the players took the field they were perspiring and before the game ended they were so weakened they could barely run. The temperature was 77 and the crowd at the game sat in their shirt-sleeves. The Southerners seemed to thrive on the hot weather."

That was not all. On a roll, Lambeau said the fierce Tigers added injuries to insult against his Packers. Not only did he hate to lose. The strangeness of the undefeated NFL champions being roughed up by an independent team carried a far-reaching sting. It's no wonder that Jorgensen remembered the opponent as an All-Star team rather than the Memphis Tigers.

"The game yesterday was the roughest we have ever played," Lambeau said. "We were weakened in the first quarter by injuries. McCrary broke his collar bone before the game was three minutes old. Dilweg was knocked unconscious after playing five minutes. Bowdoin suffered a dislocated knee and Lidberg's nose was broken. Every man on the team got into the game because we had so many casualties. Blood should never have gone in, but he did because we had no one else to send in. His arm is far from right and he was handicapped greatly in handling the ball and tackling."

The officiating "left much to be desired," Lambeau added. "Jim Durfee, National league official, was sent down by President Joe Carr to officiate, but Memphis refused to let him work and used four of their own officials. We lost many yards on penalties that never should have been executed and they came at a time when we seemed to be on our way to a score."

For all the lamenting about the weather and the officials, the explanation that rang truest was Memphis' beefed up roster, which included five NFL players: Ken Strong and Doug Wycoff, two All-America backfield stars from the Staten Island Stapletons; Jess Tinsley and Jake Williams, a pair of tackles from the Chicago Cardinals and Joe Kopcha, a Chicago Bears guard.

"The Tigers were loaded for this game and every man played hard," said Lambeau, mentioning that quintet plus two more, Larry Bettencourt, an All-America center from St. Mary's College in California, and Al Moore, the "Dixie Flash" from Mississippi.

For all of his excuses, Lambeau finished by saying, "However, the Packers feel that they can beat them. And every man on the squad is willing to go back to Memphis Christmas day and play them for nothing."

Of course, Lambeau knew Green Bay would have gotten another nice payday with a Christmas rematch. But the Packers would not have that opportunity. Next on the docket for the Tigers were the Chicago Bears, who were traveling to Memphis for the second time that season. The Bears had won 39-19 on November 23, but only after scoring three late touchdowns against the Tigers, who were owned by Piggly Wiggly founder Clarence Saunders, who had gone bankrupt with Piggly Wiggly in a bizarre Wall Street short-sell scheme but had made another fortune by opening a 1,000-store chain of Sole Owner stores. The name Sole Owner was Saunders' tweak of the Wall Street men who had muscled him out.

Three star Packers—halfback Johnny Blood and tackles Cal Hubbard and Bill Kern—stayed behind to play for Memphis, which also kept Bears regular Joe Kopcha for the game against Halas' team. A Bear playing against the Bears? That was the power of Memphis money.

Memphis also knocked off the Bears, 16-6, on December 22, giving it back-to-back wins against the NFL champion and one of its original franchises. The Tigers truly were an All-Star team. But the paychecks Lambeau and Halas received made their defeats worthwhile.

After Memphis beat the undefeated NFL champion Packers and won its rematch with the Bears, Memphis owner Saunders boasted that the Tigers were the nation's best pro team.

Rejecting NFL overtures to join the league because he disliked road games, he announced a plan to build a 60,000-seat stadium in time for the 1930 season. The Great Depression hit his grocery empire hard, crushing that grand plan. By the time the 1930 football season arrived, Saunders— who had pioneered self-service grocery shopping at a time when a clerk would assemble a customer's order— was bankrupt. Other owners began operating the Tigers on a smaller scale.

While Halas and his co-owner, Dutch Sternaman, enjoyed the payday from their Memphis foray, NFL president Carr was not pleased. He disliked barnstorming, which was not good for the NFL's shaky reputation, he believed—with good reason. Pro football already was under attack from college coaches, who argued that playing for school pride delivered a far better version of the game than mercenaries ever could.

The reality was, even supposedly stronger franchises like the Bears and Packers were hand-to-mouth operations that needed the revenue they could generate from barnstorming games. Halas and Lambeau were simply trying to be good businessmen. By the late 1930s, the league settled on an alternative to barnstorming games against non-league teams. NFL teams began playing each other around the country—especially in the pre-season, when many of their home fields were occupied by major-league baseball teams.

# 9
## *ON TOP OF THE NFL WORLD*

As the 1930 season approached, Curly Lambeau was at a pinnacle. He was the toast of not only his hometown, but the professional-football world. His Packer team had gone through a magical 1929 season, winning the NFL championship with an unbeaten record. And Green Bay was poised for continued success.

Curly's business-management responsibilities were eased greatly by the Packers' board of directors, which was attending to the nitty-gritty of guiding a community-owned football team through the rigors of selling tickets and balancing the books while America grappled with a crippling depression.

Fortunately for Lambeau and his football team, Green Bay was not feeling the weight of the Depression as heavily as most of the nation. It was a paper-making capital. It was the largest cheese-producing center in the world. Paper goods and cheese did not feel the pinch of the depression as severely as many other industries. In addition, moving those goods meant Green Bay's three railroads also were less subject to America's economic downturn.

"The reason the economy of Green Bay wasn't hurt as severely as other parts of the country is because it was based on basic needs," said Mary Jane Herber, head of the local history department of Green Bay's Brown County Library. "When you're dealing with an economy that produced food —cheese, milk, vegetable canning—and also an economy where they're producing toilet paper, hand paper, that's a whole different thing. And then railroads were the primary mover of product in this country until after the Second World War."

Although it's difficult at this point to imagine the words "Green Bay" followed by anything besides "Packers," a nickname based on paper or cheese would have been more logical.

And while the 1930s would bring major financial challenges to the Packers, life was good for Lambeau as the decade began. His success on the field gave him virtual *carte blanche* among the team's executives as well as an adoring Packer fan base. His celebrity made his insurance business a nice supplement to his football income. And as he prepared the Packers for a second straight NFL title in 1930, he had a winning team in place.

This was in stark contrast to the situation of Lambeau's key rival, George Halas. Although Halas did a fine job of burying that memory, he had co-owned the Bears in their early years with a 50/50 partner, his former Illini teammate Dutch Sternaman. By 1930, their relationship had become strained to the breaking point.

Unlike Lambeau, who was free to focus on football in a community that had rallied around its football team, Halas and Sternaman were owners of a promising but still risky enterprise in a city that had yet to embrace pro football wholeheartedly.

In Green Bay, the Packers were a civic treasure. In Chicago, the Bears competed with many other sports teams and a variety of entertainment options. The major-league Cubs and White Sox ruled. In football, the Bears were overshadowed by the University of Chicago, Northwestern, Notre Dame and Illinois. They also had a crosstown NFL rival, the Chicago Cardinals. To be successful as a business, the Bears needed to win. But Halas and Sternaman had serious disagreements regarding how to go about that. In 1929, the tension contributed to a dismal 4-9-2 record.

"We had two offenses," one of the 1929 Bears said. "One devised by Halas, the other by Sternaman. Nobody knew what to expect. Men ran into each other."

Their compromise was for Halas to step down as coach. In his place, they hired Ralph Jones, an innovator from Lake Forest College who had been an assistant football coach and head basketball coach at Illinois when Halas and Sternaman played for the Illini. Halas also retired as a player.

Jones—a key developer of the man-in-motion T formation that would transform the NFL offenses—would quickly put the Bears back in the thick of the NFL championship picture. The 1929 slip would be an anomaly, one of only two losing records for the Bears between 1920 and 1951.

For Halas, though, the financial road would remain bumpy. His disagreements with Sternaman, on top of the Depression's impact on the Bears and his myriad other businesses, would see to that.

\* \* \* \* \* \* \* \*

Lambeau's Green Bay juggernaut picked up in 1930 where it left off in 1929. In their first four games, all at home, the Packers shut out the Cardinals 14-0 and the Bears 7-0, then took down the Giants 14-7 and Frankford 27-12. They also drew good crowds, by Green Bay standards—starting with 8,000 spectators for the Cardinals, followed by 10,000 who watched the too-close-for-comfort defeat of the Bears under their new coach, Ralph Jones.

The October 5 game against the Giants, a rematch of the Packers' most important win in their 1929 championship march, topped that. A crowd of more than 11,000 squeezed into City Stadium. The Green Bay partisans saw a tight match in which Johnny Blood broke a 7-7 tie in the fourth quarter. Catching a short pass from Red Dunn, "Blood straight armed [Tiny] Feather, New York fullback, in his dash to the goal and swept past Benny Friedman like a locomotive going by a tiny town to score."

At 6-feet, 197 pounds, Tiny Feather wasn't all that tiny by 1930 NFL standards. If *Press-Gazette* writer Arthur W. Bystrom didn't make that clear, he no doubt delighted readers with his dismissal of Friedman, who was arguably the league's best passer but not an exceptional defender in an era where players played both ways.

In a measure of how pro football was perceived even in Packer-crazy Green Bay, the *Press-Gazette's* top story on its front page that morning was an account of the fifth game of the World Series, where the Philadelphia A's took a 3-2 lead on the St. Louis Cardinals. Under the banner, "FOXX HOMER UPSETS CARDS," the newspaper gave nearly three of its eight front-page columns to the play-by-play of a 2-0 baseball game. That front page failed to even mention the Packers' important victory over the Giants. In Green Bay. But that was standard procedure in America at that time. Major League baseball was king. NFL football was still a fledgling enterprise overshadowed by college football as well as baseball.

The Packers and Giants had been thrilled a year earlier to draw 25,000 to the Polo Grounds. A week later, 80,000 would watch Curly's college team, Notre Dame, defeat Army 7-0 at Yankee Stadium. And a week before the Packers-Giants showdown, Lambeau's mentor, Knute Rockne, and his Fighting Irish had edged Southern California 13-12 in front of 112,000 spectators in Chicago's Soldier Field.

Pro football was making small strides. It still had a long way to go.

On Sunday, November 2, 1930, the Packers wrapped up their six-game home schedule with a 47-13 win over the Portsmouth Spartans. They were 7-0, but had played only one game outside of Green Bay, a quick trip to Minneapolis to beat the struggling Minneapolis Red Jackets.

In the second half of the season, there would be no more home games. Having learned early lessons about the perils of trying to attract a football crowd when the weather turned ugly in Green Bay, the Packers embarked on a seven-game road gauntlet that would include three games in Chicago—two against the Bears and one with the Cardinals.

Long before the NFL's popularity had soared so high that Lambeau Field was a weather-proof destination, Lambeau the man wanted no part of bad-weather games in Green Bay if he could avoid them. Attendance-crushing foul weather had nearly snuffed Lambeau's Packer dream before it had hatched. No fan of Lambeau Field weather, Lambeau would spend as much of his winter in California as he could.

To accommodate fans traveling to Chicago's Wrigley Field for the November 9 game against the Bears, St. Mary's Catholic Church scheduled a 5 a.m. mass. "The service will be short," the *Press-Gazette* informed readers, "and will be over in plenty of time for those who attend it to make the train." For those who wanted to travel before the 6:30 a.m. departure, the

Chicago & Northwestern Railway advertised an opportunity to "Go with the Lumberjack Band" on a 12:30 a.m. train.

With Election Day only one day away, an ad ran next to the November 3 account of the Packers' win over Portsmouth urging voters to re-elect Packer hero Verne Lewellen as district attorney. Two days after running for Green Bay's first two touchdowns against Portsmouth and passing for its final score, Lewellen was re-elected as Brown County district attorney as a Republican. It was an office he had first assumed in 1928, when he defeated teammate Lavvie Dilweg, a Democrat, in an All-Packer district-attorney race. In 1930, Dilweg tried to unseat a state assemblyman and lost again.

To bolster his squad for the tough string of road games, Curly announced on the Monday before the Bears game that he had purchased three players from Minneapolis—Orin Pape, an all-conference halfback from Iowa; Kenneth Haycraft, an all-American end from Minnesota, and Chief Franta, a guard from St. Thomas. But they were mere blips on the roster. Haycraft lasted one game. Pape and Franta lasted two.

By contrast, the Giants made a major addition, signing Red Cagle, who had been a star running back at Army, to a three-year contract at $20,000 a year, a boggling NFL salary at that time. Cagle had just finished his first and only season as head coach at Mississippi State, which went 2-7.

Once again, the game was expected to decide the NFL championship. Green Bay stood atop the 11-team league with a 7-0 record, one game ahead of second-place New York (8-1). But everything was precarious. In those days, the league championship was awarded by winning percentage, with no championship game. New York, which played more games, would be the NFL champion if the Giants and Packers each had one loss.

Green Bay began its 1930 road excursion with a challenging game against the fifth-place Bears (4-3-1), who were a fast-improving team. Learning from their new coach, Ralph Jones, the Bears had won three of their previous four games.

The weather was pleasant in Chicago on Sunday, November 9, 1930. It was a dry day in which the temperature would reach the mid-60s at Wrigley Field, which had changed its name from Cubs Park in 1927 to honor Cubs owner William Wrigley Jr. A crowd of 25,000, the NFL'a largest at that point that season, turned out to see the second of three meetings between the two Midwestern powers.

The Packers had won the first game 7-0 in Green Bay on September 28 before a City Stadium crowd of 10,000, more than a quarter of the population of Green Bay. Even including Packer fans from surrounding communities, that was a notable show of support.

At least 3,000 Packer fans traveled to Chicago from Green Bay, which had a population of 37,407 in 1930. In rough figures, nearly 8 percent of the city had gone to Chicago for a football game. It's no wonder that while George Halas hated to lose to Curly Lambeau, he loved to play against him. If 8 percent of Chicago—population 3,376,438 in 1930—had attended a football game, Halas would have needed a stadium that could accommodate a throng of 270,000.

Presiding over all of this was Lambeau. Even a man with a modest ego could not be faulted for feeling he had created something significant. And Lambeau was not a man with a modest ego. Knowing he had spawned a phenomenon must have made him feel powerful. As the years went on, that sense of power and entitlement would become problematic.

The Packer team that took the field against the Bears was a confident squad that had a 19-game unbeaten streak and had not lost since 1928. Like coach Lambeau, who was becoming a legend in northeastern Wisconsin and beyond, many Packer players also were well on their way to becoming mythological figures in Green Bay football lore. The Bears also had their share of stars who would be long remembered.

In that game, Verne Lewellen, perhaps the most overlooked star of the NFL's early days, strutted his stuff in Green Bay's nail-biting 13-12 win. The newly re-elected Brown County district attorney threw a 17-yard pass to Johnny Blood and caught a 21-yard pass from Red Dunn for the Packers' two touchdowns. In a duel between two celebrated NFL heroes, Blood out-wrestled Bears defender Red Grange for Green Bay's first touchdown. "Blood took the ball out of Red Grange's hands and fell over the goal line for a touchdown as Red tackled him," Art Bystrom told his *Green Bay Press-Gazette* readers the next morning.

Chris Willis, the author and NFL Films archivist, picked Lewellen as the NFL's retroactive MVP for 1930. Although the NFL didn't start naming an official MVP until 1938, Willis named Lewellen in 1929 as well as 1930. He was the Packers' leading scorer that season as well as their second leading rusher (behind Molenda) and second leading passer (after Dunn). Lewellen had 911 total yards to Blood's 538. When Blood was honored as a charter member of the Pro Football Hall of Fame in 1963, Blood said, "Verne Lewellen should have been in there in front of me and [Cal] Hubbard."

The real battle was in the trenches, former Chicago Cardinals lineman Wilfrid Smith told *Chicago Tribune* readers the next morning. "The intensity of the struggle was communicated to the thousands in the stands. There was a continuous thunder of applause during the second half," said Smith, who went on to be the *Tribune's* sports editor.

Victory in hand, Lambeau and his Packers boarded one of the trains crowded with the thousands of fans who had descended on Chicago and headed home to Green Bay.

The stay would be brief. The following Sunday, the Packers returned to Chicago to play the Cardinals on November 16, 1930. Before a crowd of 17,000 at Comiskey Park, Green Bay lost 13-6. The defeat, which halted the Packers' 22-game unbeaten streak, was their first loss since a 2-0 defeat at Frankford nearly two years earlier on Thanksgiving Day, November 29, 1928.

Leading the Cardinals, who evened their record at 5-5-2, was Ernie Nevers. The NFL's second-biggest attraction after Red Grange, Nevers had scored all 40 points in a 40-6 rout of the Bears the previous year.

The Cardinals' coach as well as their star, Nevers passed for their first touchdown and ran for their second in their upset of the Packers. His inspired play also fired up the rest of the team. "Ernie Nevers had his players on a fighting edge and they rose to their highest peak of the season, both on offense and defense," Art Bystrom told his *Green Bay Press-Gazette* readers the next morning. *Chicago Tribune* writer Wilfrid Smith agreed, saying, "His direction of the Cardinal attack showed no fault. And his mates played as a unit, seldom yielding on defense."

Lambeau and his disappointed Packers assumed the defeat left them trailing the New York Giants. But while they were cleaning up at their nearby hotel before traveling back to Green Bay, they received a big surprise.

"Gloom was knee deep on the fifth floor of the Del Prado hotel, Chicago, about 4:45 Sunday afternoon as the Packer players were shedding their uniforms after taking it on the chin for the first time since Thanksgiving Day 1928," the *Green Bay Press-Gazette* reported on Monday, November, 17, 1930. "There wasn't much being said. Finally, one of the gridders spoke up saying: 'Call the *Trib* and see how bad the Giants whipped the Bears.' Somebody replied with the request, and when the party on the telephone said, 'What', loud enough to be heard back in Green Bay, those in the room began jumping around like mad men. '12-0 Bears' was the joyous flash. The news spread like wildfire around the fifth floor thanks to a 'Paul Revere' Packer who dashed through the ball in his shirt tail yelling, 'Bears 12, Giants 0.' "

The Bears' win was not a fluke. They would go on to win their four remaining games. New coach Ralph Jones' T formation and overall leadership had begun to take hold, and the Bears were well on their way to challenging the Packers as the premier NFL team in the West, if not the entire league.

In a tribute to what Lambeau had assembled, though, Green Bay still reigned.

"The Packers have represented perfection in professional football for so long they have become a measuring rule for the game," the *Tribune's* Smith noted, to give his readers a gauge on the importance of the Cardinals' upset.

The Packers' next game, in New York against the Giants, now loomed as a major showdown. Far from dwelling on the Cardinals setback, Lambeau dug in, determined to have his players ready for that challenge.

Shaking off the disappointment of losing to the Bears, Lambeau turned his attention to the Packers' upcoming Eastern swing, in which they would play three games in eight days. After facing the Giants in New York on Sunday, November 23, they would play the Frankford Yellow Jackets in Philadelphia on Thanksgiving Day, November 27, and the Staten Island Stapletons in New York on November 30. After that, they would have two games remaining on the seven straight road games that finished their season: A third match with the Bears at Wrigley Field on December 7 and a trip to Portsmouth, Ohio, on December 14.

But no game loomed larger than the game with the Giants. At 8-1, Green Bay could not afford a loss to New York (10-2) in a league that chose its champion based on winning percentage. The Giants, who planned to play 17 games, three more than the Packers, would be the champions if both teams had two losses.

Noting that the Giants game "will probably decide possession of the National league bunting for 1930," the *Press-Gazette* said the Packers went through "an extra long session [on Tuesday], as Coach Lambeau is determined to have the club right on edge for the skirmish with Benny Friedman, Red Cagle and other Giants."

The team planned to depart for New York on Thursday, the Green Bay newspaper said in its detailed account of the Packers' trip: "The workout Thursday will be started earlier than usual to give the squad time to attend the Rotary club luncheon and enable Bud Jorgensen [to have] a few extra minutes to pack the half dozen property trunks for the eastern invasion." For such a long and important trip, those trunks, no doubt, included Ma Kline's moonshine.

"The Bays will leave over the Milwaukee Road early Thursday afternoon for Chicago, then the special Pullman car will be attached to a Pennsylvania train for Gotham," the *Press-Gazette* reported. "On arriving in New York, the team will headquarter at the Lincoln hotel, Times Square. There will be a practice Saturday morning at the Dewitt Clinton high school stadium. On Monday after the game with the Giants, the Packers will head for Atlantic City where they will stay until late Wednesday, when they will depart for Philadelphia. The game with the Yellowjackets is scheduled for Thursday afternoon (Thanksgiving Day). Since 1925, Green Bay has been the Turkey Day gridiron attraction in the Philadelphia suburb."

A special Pullman car for the Packers' trip to New York? Just 11 years from the hard-scrabble beginnings of his football team, Curly Lambeau already was showing a flair for the luxurious upside that the NFL would one day embrace. And for personal comfort.

Lambeau also had become a lightning rod, A.W. Bystrom wrote in a *Press-Gazette* column four days before the showdown with the Giants: "When the team wins, the players are praised and Capt. Lambeau is regarded as a master coach. But when the team loses, the men are a bunch of bums and the coach the biggest bum of all."

Bystrom went on to lecture Lambeau's critics, saying, "We wonder if there is another man in Green Bay who could have done what Curly has done. . . mold [players] into a machine that won 22 out of 24 games. We can't think of anyone who could handle that job as Curly has done it."

Perhaps it was a way of bracing Packer fans if their team came up short—a way of reminding them how much Lambeau had accomplished. The *Press-Gazette* was unflagging in its support of the Packers and their leader. The whole city was unabashed in building up the Packers, who were regarded as a civic treasure.

Lambeau cultivated publicity in Green Bay and wherever the Packers traveled. Halas also recognized the value of media attention, especially when it came to the *Chicago Tribune,* which embraced the NFL as a way to sell newspapers on Mondays. Both men knew how to provide copy, how to manage their message, in an era where reaching their fans through the sports pages was essential to selling tickets.

New York sports fans became nearly as giddy for the Giants-Packers showdown as football followers were back in Green Bay. A crowd of 40,000 turned out on Sunday, November 23, 1930, at the Polo Grounds, the *New York Times* reported. It was the biggest turnout for an NFL game since the Red Grange mania at the end of the 1925 season. And this was different. The thousands who packed stadiums to see Grange were lured by the novelty of a thrilling individual. This throng had turned out to see a championship showdown.

The New York fans were rewarded with a 13-6 victory that left Lambeau and his players bruised and disappointed on multiple fronts.

Among the complaints mentioned derisively by Lambeau's Packer co-founder, *Press-Gazette* writer George Whitney Calhoun: The Packers were whistled for 72 yards in penalties to the Giants' 10. The most critical was a 17-yard half-the-distance walkoff against Red Dunn, who "took a punch at referee Tommy Hughitt." Upset at being tackled around the head as he slid out of bounds, Dunn got up and started arguing with the Giants tackler. When Hughitt came over, Calhoun said, quoting "a Packer spokesman," Dunn "told the referee several things, making stiff arm thrusts in the direction of the referee." One of the thrusts apparently came too close, in the judgment of Hughitt.

Calhoun, in his clearly partisan report, told *Press-Gazette* readers that Hughitt and his three associates "seemed to spend the majority of their time watching the yellow-sweatered Packers. Possibly this color was a bit easier on the eyes than the dirty maroon of the Giants. Anyway, their decisions certainly seemed to be off-color."

Penalties aside, the Packers won the statistical battle even though they lost the game, the *New York Times* noted: "The champions registered fifteen first downs against eight for the Giants. The Giants' ground game gained 172 yards against 160 for the Packers, though the overhead [passing] efforts of the champions showed 138 yards profit, while the Giant aerials totaled only 67 yards." In other words, Green Bay gained 299 yards to New York's 239.

Adding injury to insult, the Packers came out of the game banged up. Halfbacks Lewellen and Blood, left end Dilweg and center Earp "are far from being in the best of shape," reported the *Press-Gazette,* expressing concern about the quick turnaround for Thursday's Thanksgiving Day game against Frankford in Philadelphia. Packers end Tom Nash was ruled out by "a tender nose," the product of a collision with newly signed Giants back Red Cagle, who was knocked out of the game by the hit but returned after being treated for a cut on his face.

Lambeau and the Packers also were left to lament the terms of their financial agreement with the Giants. To entice the New York team to play in Green Bay, the Packers had offered a flat $9,000 guarantee without the usual percentage of the gate. They then asked for the same deal when the two teams met in New York, never imagining a throng of 40,000 and a $60,000 bonanza. That meant the Giants cleared $51,000 from the game in New York while the Packers cleared $8,000 when the Giants played before 13,000 in Green Bay in October.

Lambeau did enjoy a silver lining. Even without the lucrative percentage, Green Bay did well financially in its trip to New York. Because the Packers had, like Notre Dame, become a very attractive team that conjured David-and-Goliath imagery, they regularly drew large crowds against the most important big-city teams. From 1929 to 1931, Green Bay appeared in three of the NFL's six largest crowds.

Another major reason why Green Bay survived when other small cities such as Pottsville and Portsmouth that fielded successful teams failed appeared in the *Press-Gazette* while the Packers were on their three-game eastern trip. "Green Bay Unemployed Total But 5.3 Pct." a front-page headline reported on November 29, 1930, followed by this subhead: "Situation Here Far Better Than in Rest of Wisconsin." A 5 percent unemployment rate was amazing at a time when joblessness peaked at 25 percent in the early 1930s nationally. Thanks to its paper industry, cheese processing and the rail freight that those businesses required, Green Bay was in a better position to support its beloved football team.

The report came two days after the Packers halted their two-game losing streak with a 25-7 Thanksgiving Day win in Philadelphia against the Frankford Yellow Jackets. Hit hard by the Depression, Frankford would be out of the NFL a year later. Meanwhile, in New York, the Staten Island Stapletons shocked the Giants, giving Green Bay's championship hopes a big boost.

Green Bay posted a 37-7 win on Staten Island on Sunday, November 30, against the Stapletons, who would end their four-year NFL run in 1932. When the Brooklyn Dodgers took down the Giants by another 7-6 score that same day, Lambeau's Packers (10-2) held a surprising lead on the Giants (11-4). The Packers' quest for a second straight NFL title, which had been in doubt a week earlier after their loss to the Giants, now looked very promising.

Before heading to Chicago, Curly took his team back on Monday to Atlantic City, where he liked to stay between East Coast games, for a few days to prepare for their next adventure, another game at Wrigley Field against the Bears. In keeping with his first-class style, Lambeau also liked the comfort and diversions of Atlantic City, which was a popular vacation spot.

"The grinders are going in strong for the salt water baths here at the Morton hotel as the three games in eight days were a tough race on some of the 60-minute men and the steaming ocean water is helping a lot in washing away aches and bruises," Calhoun reported in the *Press-Gazette* on December 2, 1930.

Before the Packers left New York, though, Johnny Blood acted out one of the more memorable scenes in his drama-filled life. Impatient when his request for ice was not handled quickly at the team's Lincoln Hotel, Blood took a cab to an ice house and brought back a 100-pound block to the hotel, Calhoun wrote.

In the days before refrigerators, ice blocks were a familiar commodity. Red Grange, the most renowned football player of the era, had acquired his Wheaton Iceman nickname by delivering ice in his suburban Chicago hometown. Blood might have realized that his ice antic would bring Grange to mind.

"At the entrance, he pulled a Red Grange by hoisting the chunk to his shoulder and parading it through the lobby to the elevator and then up to his room on the twelfth floor," Calhoun told *Press-Gazette* readers. Blood was followed by hotel managers and staff, who found that "Blood had deposited the ice in the bath tub and he was having all the cold water he wanted. The situation was amusing to everybody except Johnny who voiced a complaint to the Lincoln 'army' that their boast about service was all bunk."

Although Calhoun reported that the incident took place at noon on Monday, the need for ice would have been greater on Sunday night—to be used with something stronger than water. Virtually every retelling of the Johnny Blood-Ice Block Fable has the ice being used for alcoholic drinks, which were illegal during Prohibition and not something Calhoun would be likely to put in his newspaper.

Clarke Hinkle told a version of the Johnny-Blood-ice-block story in which the ice was used for liquor. Hinkle's recollection was that the Packers returned to their hotel in their uniforms because Lambeau thought the dressing rooms at the Polo Grounds were not clean. They had lost the game, which didn't help matters.

"Some of the guys had a few bottles with them for after the game," Hinkle told Richard Whittingham in his oral history of the NFL, *What A Game They Played*. "Johnny Blood was one of them and he decided to have a drink while he was taking his uniform off, but he wanted some ice. So he called the desk and asked them to bring some ice up for his drinks. It never came. . . . Johnny got about half-stoned, and he got mad, took a shower, and got dressed. We were all sitting in the lobby by this time and Johnny Blood comes down, goes past us and out onto 57th Street, and that's the last we saw of him for about an hour. We were still sitting there when in comes Johnny Blood, with a 100-pound cake of ice on his shoulder. Right through the lobby of the Victoria Hotel he went with it—everybody stopping to stare at him—right into the elevator and up to his room. He put the 100-pound cake of ice into his bathtub, turned the water on, and then called everybody in the hotel and told them come and have a glass of ice water in his room. Hell, we'd all get drunk after a game in those days. Lambeau would say, 'The lid's off, boys, but stay out of jail.'"

This is another one of those stories where it is difficult to determine the Packer mythology from what actually happened. Because in 1930, when Calhoun put the story of Johnny Blood and the Ice Block in the *Press-Gazette*, Hinkle was a junior in college at Bucknell. It is very possible, though, that Hinkle was hanging out with the Packers. For three straight years, in 1929-31, Bucknell played Fordham in New York the day before Green Bay faced the Giants.

Hinkle said the Giants invited him and Bucknell's line coach to be their guests at the 1931 game against the Packers. "I was more impressed with the Packers than the Giants," Hinkle recalled, "so during the second half we went over and sat on their bench." Hinkle had hoped to meet Lambeau, he said, but Curly was in a foul mood because the Packers lost that day. After Hinkle starred in the East-West All-Star game in San Francisco several weeks later, Lambeau would offer Hinkle a contract.

Did Hinkle hang out with the Packers and witness Johnny Blood's ice-block melodrama? Did Hinkle merely appropriate the story after hearing about it? Did Blood go out for ice more than once? Difficult to say at this point. But clearly, Hinkle, who became a Packer for the ages, bought into the Green Bay lore that developed in Lambeau's three decades there.

"One thing I do remember about that [1931 Packers-Giants] game," Hinkle added. "I was impressed by... Cal Hubbard. He stood about 6 feet 5 inches and weighed maybe 250 pounds. I thought I might be better off playing on his side than playing against him."

And before the NFL began its draft in 1936, Hinkle could do that. Players were free to choose which team they wanted to play for.

Like many coaches of that era, Lambeau, who was fond of relaxing with a bourbon and water, had no problem with his players enjoying a few drinks after a game. It was later in the week that the Packers founder demanded discipline. When Blood first joined the Packers, Lambeau, knowing Blood's reputation for carousing, came up with an innovative effort to keep him sober.

"In my negotiations with Curly Lambeau, I asked for $100 a game," Blood told a *Sports Illustrated* writer many years later. "He came back with an offer of $110 a game, providing I would initial a clause in the contract forbidding any drinking after Tuesday of each week. I countered with an offer to take the $100 I had proposed and drink through Wednesday. Curly agreed."

How much of that was fact and how much was just a good after-dinner story? A thread of truth probably became whole cloth as Lambeau and his players, encouraged by sportswriters who craved a good yarn, embellished.

Blood and Hinkle had active imaginations. Don Hutson, the low-keyed and brilliant pass receiver, also played along, or simply didn't remember accurately. They mainly were harmless embellishments that quenched the relentless thirst of football fans, especially Packer fans. Under Lambeau, the Packers had a mystical popularity. Green Bay was, after all, the Notre Dame of professional football. A legendary team needed stories that lived up to its gridiron appeal—even if the details weren't completely accurate.

Blood's background needed little embellishment. He was born and raised in New Richmond, Wisconsin, about 40 miles east of Minneapolis, Minnesota. His mother was a former schoolteacher and accomplished rider of horses. His father, who also had attended college, was the manager of a flour mill and had played on the town baseball team. From them, he had acquired a dedication to literature and a passion for athletics. Somewhere along the way, he also developed a thirst for alcohol and a dare-devil bravado.

Blood got along better with Lambeau than most Packers. He not only was eloquent and charming. He had rare talent. He was tall and fast and a clutch performer. When he was focused on winning a football game, no one was likely to outplay him. Despite his antics, Lambeau entrusted him with calling the Packers' plays on the field.

Lambeau's strict side didn't bother the free-spirited Blood as much as other Packers. Blood just did his thing, which was often influenced by alcohol. He had very little interest in hanging on to money. He was more interested in free-spirited adventures.

"I got along pretty well with Curly, for a while anyway," Blood said. "I was one of the only ones who did. Most didn't like him at all. But for the first three or four years, he put up with me and my antics. I think I was one of the few who could get the best of him. He had a hard time keeping up with me."

Although Blood and Lambeau sometimes competed for the same women, Lambeau valued the way Blood could catch a football and run with it. From 1920 to 1934, Blood led the NFL with 2,429 pass receiving yards, according to the 1994 edition of The Football Encyclopedia. He also was ninth in NFL punting, although he was the Packers' primary punter only once in his seven seasons with them. When he retired in 1938, he held the league record with 31 career interceptions, according to The Football Encyclopedia. He also was ninth in NFL punting. In other words, for all of his crazy and often self-destructive behavior, Blood was an elite player, which was acknowledged by his inclusion in the Pro Football Hall of Fame's inaugural class.

"The Packers had a lot of great players, but until [Don] Hutson came along, Johnny Blood was the one guy who could beat you with one big play," Chicago Bears founder George Halas said.

Another member of the Hall of Fame's inaugural class, lineman Cal Hubbard, quickly came to dislike Lambeau. A small-town guy, Hubbard had come to Green Bay from New York for the lifestyle, not the coach.

"To be frank, Curly really didn't know all that much about football," the outspoken Hubbard told Johnny Blood's biographer, Ralph Hickok. "After all, he spent just that one year at Notre Dame—how much did he learn? Most of us knew more because we spent more time learning, four years of college and then, for most of us, some professional experience, too. Why, sometimes Curly would design a new play, draw it up on the blackboard, and we just knew it wouldn't work the way he drew it. He'd have impossible blocking assignments, or the play would just take too long to develop. The defense would mess it up before it going. And we'd have to tell him that, and one of the veterans would go right up to the blackboard and change it around. Most of the time, Johnny Blood was the spokesman because he was always ready to speak up to Curly, or anybody."

Hubbard valued coaching so much that he changed schools to follow his college coach, Bo McMillin, from Centenary in Shreveport, Louisiana, to Geneva in Beaver Falls, Pennsylvania. McMillin went on to a coaching career that included long runs at Kansas State and Indiana plus quick stops with the NFL's Detroit Lions and Philadelphia Eagles. When the opportunity arose, he attended Packers games to watch Hubbard, who was only five years younger than him.

While Hubbard didn't mince words, Blood diplomatically said Lambeau was receptive to the players' suggestions. "As Cal said, I was the spokesman," Blood told Hickok. "I'd go up and get the chalk, and then we'd all kind of talk about it, in a group discussion, and we'd keep working on it until we got it right."

The third member of Lambeau's talented trio of 1929 signees, lineman Mike Michalske, also credited Lambeau with being open to his players' suggestions: "Curly was willing to learn from us. He really learned football from his players and, after a few years, I think he knew as much as any coach in the league. He just had to have that learning experience for a while."

Not only did some Packers have football experience that Lambeau could not match. Although Curly was the boss, he was their contemporary—only two years older than Hubbard, and five years older than Blood and Michalske. As mature football players, they would only allow the mercurial Lambeau to go so far.

"I remember a deal once where Michalske and Hubbard backed him against the wall one time over some money or something," recalled former Packer board member Howie Levitas, who became involved with the team in 1928 as a water boy. "They literally backed him against the wall in the dressing room."

Although similar episodes took place throughout Lambeau's coaching career, they seemed to be quickly forgotten when it came time to play football. That was especially true in the early days, when NFL players were used to payday chicanery. When Lambeau continued to withhold pay later in his career, the tactic was far less successful. By then, though, many of Lambeau's old-school techniques had become ineffective.

Another talent Lambeau possessed was a knack for bringing in players who were self-motivated to succeed in areas beyond merely playing football. After a stellar NFL career, Hubbard became one of the most influential Major League umpires of his era. Michalske went on to a long coaching career, including a five-year run as Iowa State's head coach.

Even Blood had a brief stint as head coach in 1937 and 1938 of the Pittsburgh Pirates, who would be renamed the Steelers in 1940. Blood had a splashy debut in Pittsburgh. In the fourth quarter of the 1937 opening game, his first game as head coach, he returned a kickoff 92 yards for a touchdown. That broke a 14-14 tie and helped the Pirates to a 27-14 victory over Philadelphia.

In the end, though, Blood's NFL coaching experience would not go well. He resigned after Pittsburgh lost its 1939 season opener to the Bears 32-0. Blood was 7-25-1 as the Pirates coach.

In later years, a sobered-up Blood returned to St. John's to finish his college degree in 1949. He was 45. Blood stayed on to teach history and economics at St. John's. At 50, he enrolled in a master's degree program at the University of Minnesota. Along the way, he wrote a 150-page treatise, *Spend Yourself Rich*, with a unique take on economics.

He also coached the St. John's football team for three years, from 1950 to 1952, compiling a modest 13-9-1 record. When he was fired, apparently for being too stern a taskmaster, he advised his successor, John Gagliardi, not to take the job because "Nobody can win at St. John's." On that count, Blood could not have been more wrong. Gagliardi coached for 60 seasons (1953 to 2012) at St. John's, winning 465 games and four national championships. With 489 wins, including the four years he coached before arriving at St. John's, Gagliardi had won more games than any other college football coach.

While Pittsburgh did not have a talented roster, Blood's lack of maturity certainly contributed to his lack of success as an NFL coach. After a 14-14 exhibition tie against the L.A. Bulldogs—a talented independent team that had two wins and two ties in five games against NFL teams in 1938—at Gilmore Stadium in Los Angeles on November 13, 1938, Blood, apparently enjoying California, failed to travel back east with his team. When he showed up at the Bulldogs' next game in Los Angeles on November 20, he was asked in the press box why he wasn't with his Pirates. He replied that Pittsburgh had an open date. Then he was shown a score of Pittsburgh's game against the Philadelphia Eagles in Huntington, West Virginia, that day.

"I was going to fire him," Pittsburgh owner Art Rooney later said. "But the players loved him. So I told him, 'John, you have to make the games.'" In the long run, Rooney realized that Blood's passion and knowledge of football were not enough to overcome his quirky, immature behavior. "As one of our veterans once said," Rooney explained, "'This is the only team I've been on where the players worry about the coach instead of the other way around.'"

Having quenched their thirst with the help of Blood's ice block after their 1930 loss to the Giants in New York, the Packers headed off to Atlantic City for practice and relaxation, then occupied a Pullman car on a train bound for Chicago. The Packers, needing a win to clinch their second straight NFL title, had won seven straight games against the Bears since the teams had tied 12-12 on September 30, 1928.

A clinching win was not a given. The new Chicago coach, Ralph Jones, aided by rookie fullback Bronko Nagurski, had turned around the sagging Bears. With Nagurski making big plays on both sides of the ball, the Bears smacked Green Bay 21-0 before a crowd of 22,000 at Wrigley Field. The Bears not only beat the Packers at their own passing game, as Luke Johnsos caught touchdowns of 21 and 30 yards from first-year Bears quarterback Carl Brumbaugh. Another Bears rookie, Dick Nesbitt, added a final 41-yard touchdown run against banged up Green Bay. The Bears also intercepted six Packer passes and recovered a Green Bay fumble as Green Bay completed only 4 of its 19 passes.

The defeat left the Packers 10-3, but still in first place ahead of the Giants, who were 13-4. Lambeau's squad had one game left, at Portsmouth, where it needed a win or a tie to earn its second straight NFL title. The Packers returned to Green Bay after the Bears game for a few days of practice before heading to Portsmouth, an industrial town on the Ohio River 100 miles east of Cincinnati.

Before a crowd of 4,500 that included NFL president Joe F. Carr, the bruised and road-weary Packers scratched out a 6-6 tie. That gave Green Bay (10-3-1, .769) a minuscule four-percentage-point edge over the Giants (13-4, .765). But in a league that featured very different schedules and awarded its championship by winning percentage, with ties not included—and a league that had not yet discovered the allure of a championship game—that was all the Packers needed.

With that second championship, Curly Lambeau added to his growing legend. The Packers returned to another heroes' welcome, greeted by thousands when their train reached Green Bay at 8:30 Monday night. Red flares again lit up the way from De Pere into Green Bay.

The champions then made their way to the Columbus Community Club for a short presentation. Nearly half of the 3,000 people at the Northwestern railroad station squeezed into the auditorium, where team president Dr. W.W. Kelly presided at the post-season pep rally.

"Dr. Kelly said 'Curly' is entitled to the respect and admiration of all lovers of football in Green Bay and that he is responsible for the fact that Green Bay has a football team capable of winning national championships," the *Press-Gazette* said, adding this salute from Kelly: "Myself and the other cigar store coaches often abuse him. And we sometimes forget to praise him when he is most deserving of praise."

Years later, Dr. Kelly joined with Calhoun, team legal counsel Gerald Clifford and Lee Joannes, who served as the Packers president from 1930 to 1947, in opposition to Lambeau. "We took all the grief and criticism when things were going tough," Joannes said after Lambeau's Green Bay tenure had ended. "And Lambeau took credit for things when the going was good."

The next night, a crowd of 295 attended a victory banquet at the Beaumont Hotel, where the Packer players each were given $200 checks from a $4,500 fund raised by donations from Packers fans. In promoting the fund, the *Green Bay Press-Gazette* stressed in a front-page article that, "The money is being raised with the understanding that if the Packers lose to Portsmouth, thereby forfeiting the championship to the New York Giants, the donations will be returned to the donors, and the presentation of the fund will not be made."

Not that the Packers needed any more incentive. But in an era where the average salary was barely $100 a game, a $200 bonus was a serious matter.

Then again, in a little more than 10 years, Lambeau had brought Green Bay football a long way. In 12 seasons, his Packers had gone from passing a hat for players to receive what he recalled as being less than $17 per player to earning a decent living. . . for playing football.

Curly received a silver loving cup, a gift of the team's corporation, from *Press-Gazette* publisher A.B. "Andy" Turnbull, who had breathed financial life into a failing franchise in 1922. Turnbull, the *Press-Gazette* reported, "paid a glowing tribute to Coach Lambeau's ability and cited instances in which he had set aside personal advancement to insure a winning team. . . . Curly responded with a tribute to Mr. Turnbull in which he characterized the first [team] president as 'the all-time, all-American quarterback of the Packers.' He also expressed the appreciation of the team for the cooperation of the management and pointed out that the board of directors of the corporation had given freely of its time and effort, without remuneration, to bring football to the place it now holds in the community and to advance the Packers to a place of prominence nationally."

All was good in Packerland—especially for Curly Lambeau. He was the toast of his hometown. As the coach of back-to-back NFL champions, he commanded the respect of the sports world. With the support of a fan base that adored his team and community leadership that eased the business pressure on his shoulders. And perhaps best of all, Lambeau had assembled a team that was well-positioned to continue to set the pace in the National Football League as it moved into its second decade. For Curly Lambeau, life was good.

# 10
## *ROCKNE'S DEATH HITS HARD*

Lambeau's Packers were on top of their world during the winter and spring of 1931. To pick up a few dollars, Wuert Engelmann, Johnny Blood and Mike Michalske put together a Packer basketball team that played teams from Milwaukee to Sturgeon Bay. Engelmann, a 6-foot-3 halfback who had played college basketball at South Dakota State, was manager of the basketball team.

Lambeau, meanwhile, continued to look for talent that would help Green Bay in its quest for a third straight NFL title. One player he dialed in on was end Milt Gantenbein, who had been a University of Wisconsin standout. With money tight for NFL teams in 1931, though, Lambeau issued a subtle request for assistance.

"According to [Lambeau], Gantenbein is a good prospect and probably will be with the team if he can find work," the *Press-Gazette* reported. "Gantenbein being does not want to confine his activities to professional football as he extensively plans for a future in business."

In other words, Curly was saying, it would benefit the Packers if someone could give Gantenbein a job that would supplement his limited football income. Lambeau eventually signed the 6-foot, 199-pound Gantenbein, who became an outstanding defensive end as well as a superb blocker and tight-end-style receiver.

Helping Packer players find outside jobs was standard procedure for Lambeau. "Without question, the Packers' jobs program helped Curly Lambeau recruit players to Green Bay," Packer historian Cliff Christl wrote in a December 28, 2023, article at the team's website.

"We now have an employment committee and are taking in the whole state in our search for positions," Lambeau told Green Bay Kiwanis Club members on June 26, 1939. "Wisconsin as a whole has adopted the Packers and is taking a personal interest in the men. High salaries paid by some of the other teams is one of our problems. If we can give the employment of men full consideration, we can help win the battle."

Throughout his Packer career, Lambeau emphasized the importance of helping Packers find jobs outside of football. That continued long after Lambeau was gone. "The people of Green Bay threw out their welcome mats to the Packers players when they landed in town," Christl said, "and [job assistance] played a critical role in the team's survival."

That spring of 1931 also brought a tragic reality check for Lambeau. On March 31, his Notre Dame coach and mentor, Knute Rockne, was among the eight people killed in a Kansas plane crash. Rockne was on his way to

Hollywood to assist with the production of a film, *The Spirit of Notre Dame*. Rockne was just 43 years old. Lambeau was devastated.

"Rock's death made me stop and think," Lambeau said he later told a friend. "Life is short. You should live it to the hilt while you're here."

Already inclined to adopt that philosophy, Lambeau tended to embrace that view as he grew older—and not always with great results.

Rockne had always surrounded himself with popular public figures—from sports heroes Babe Ruth and boxer Jack Dempsey to flashy New York Mayor Jimmy Walker. Lambeau was proud to be in that group, and followed Rockne's example by moving easily in a celebrity-filled world.

Like many prominent college coaches—including Michigan's Fielding Yost, Illinois' Bob Zuppke and Chicago's Amos Alonzo Stagg—Rockne was frequently critical of pro football. A big part of their concern was probably a fear that pro football would encroach on the college game, which dominated the sport.

Privately, though, Lambeau said Rockne encouraged him, telling him, "Keep it up, boy. You're on to something big." At least that was the way Lambeau remembered it. Exactly how much mentoring Curly received from Rockne is not known. What is clear is that Lambeau was influenced heavily by Rockne.

"Although Knute Rockne is dead, he will still inspire Notre Dame football teams for years to come," Lambeau said after the plane crash. "Rockne went the limit for a loyal friend or player. . . . I have been away from Notre Dame since the spring of 1919 but any time I ever went back to the school or elsewhere I met him, Rockne was always ready to give me a welcome hand. . . . He was the finest kind of a friend and man."

Lambeau had sent Green Bay high school star Jim Crowley to Notre Dame, where he became one of the famed Four Horsemen. Long after Rockne's death, Lambeau relied on the Notre Dame/Rockne network to find talented players and to build the Packer franchise throughout the country.

It was no coincidence that the Green Bay Packers became the Notre Dame of the NFL. They were a pair of little Midwestern teams that were able to humble football giants. Lambeau, who had learned from Rockne, was the link.

# 11
## *THE THIRD TIME IS TRICKIER*

With their formidable roster intact, the Packers began the 1931 season where they left off the previous season, winning their first nine games.

Since the beginning of the 1929 season, they had won 31 of their 36 games. As they prepared to play Ernie Nevers and his Chicago Cardinals at Wrigley Field on November 15, a strange topic popped up.

A group of influential Chicagoans asked Lambeau if the Packers would be willing to play Notre Dame. Curly's response: The Packers would welcome playing against the Fighting Irish "any time after Dec. 7."

The game never happened. But it was part of an ongoing debate about how top NFL teams would fare against top college teams in an era where the pros played second fiddle to the vastly more popular college men.

The main topic that week focused on whether the Cardinals, who had ended Green Bay's 23-game unbeaten streak in 1930, could again stop the mighty Packers. Lambeau's men had started a new nine-game winning streak.

Although the Cardinals were just 2-3, the Packers had made "Remember last year" their focal point in practice. They had already beaten the Cardinals 26-7 in Green Bay, but Nevers now had the Cardinals playing better. They had won their last two games.

"Chicago Cards expecting to upset Packers," a *Press-Gazette* headline blared on November 11, 1931, the Wednesday before the game.

"Cards Expect Line to Stop Packer Backs," a *Chicago Tribune* headline said two days later.

Adding to the pre-game hype, the newspapermen were pointing out that a Green Bay loss and a Portsmouth win over struggling Cleveland would allow the Spartans to close to within half a game of the Packers. Clearly, Lambeau would have Green Bay primed to bring its best.

In the midst of all this preparation, Nevers took the Cardinals to Michigan on the Wednesday for an exhibition. They smoked the Grand Rapids Maroons 36-0 before a crowd of 3,000, then quickly returned home.

Despite the pre-game hype, only 9,000 spectators were lured to Wrigley Field to see if the Cardinals could stop the mighty Packers again.

Meanwhile, 15,000 turned out at Chicago Stadium to watch the Blackhawks battle the New York Americans to a 1-1 tie in the National Hockey League.

The show at Wrigley Field was a case of Nevers again. Led by their sensational star player-coach, the Cardinals defeated Green Bay 21-13, ending the Packers' nine-game winning streak. Green Bay had only lost four games in three years. Two losses had come against Nevers and the Cardinals.

The All-American from Stanford threw two touchdown passes, kicked all three extra points and was a whirlwind on defense. "Ernie Nevers, the big blond Viking from the West Coast, rose to great heights to mire the Packers in the mud at Wrigley Field and stopped their 1931 winning streak after nine straight," Arthur W. Bystrom wrote, summing up things in the *Press-Gazette on* November. 16, 1931.

In a key consolation for Packer fans, the Milwaukee Road pushed back its Train No. 9 for 15 minutes, from 5:05 p.m. to 5:20 p.m. With the game expected to end at 4:40 p.m., Packer fans would have 40 minutes to get to Union Station to catch their train home. Refreshments would be abundant on the northbound train.

After regrouping at home for a few days, the Packers departed for a three-game eastern swing. Playing in front of 35,000, the biggest NFL crowd of the season, they defeated the New York Giants on November 22 in the Polo Grounds. That same afternoon, the Cardinals did Green Bay a huge favor, defeating Portsmouth 20-19. That gave Green Bay (10-1) a two-game lead on the second-place Spartans (10-3).

The Packers added two more wins, beating Providence 38-7 on Thanksgiving Day and the Brooklyn Dodgers 7-0 on Sunday, November 29, at Ebbets Field. Green Bay's third win in eight days gave it a record of 12-1 —and seemingly its third straight NFL championship. A final game in Chicago against the Bears would not be able to take that away, win or lose.

"PACKERS CAPTURE THIRD GRID TITLE," the *Press-Gazette* announced with its biggest front-page headline. Its sports page blazed an even bigger banner, "PACKERS CLINCH NATIONAL CHAMPIONSHIP."

The only snag was. . . in the Ohio River town of Portsmouth, the Spartans saw a way that they could still nudge past the Packers.

If Green Bay lost to the Bears, it would be 12-2, one game ahead of Portsmouth, which was 11-3. And the Spartans and their supporters wanted the Packers to show up for a December 13 showdown in Portsmouth that had been tentatively scheduled between the two teams. They had not played yet.

And so, Lambeau faced a different challenge to secure the 1931 championship. To win a third straight title, he needed to *avoid* playing a game. If this felt strange to a competitor who had always been determined to play football, The Man Who Invented the Green Bay Packers made it sound very natural in his public comments.

It could only have happened that way in an NFL that was still trying to figure out a lot of things—especially how to organize itself.

At the league's schedule meeting the previous summer, Lambeau and Spartans president Harry Snyder said, "Let's make the December 13 contest a 'tentative game' because of the prospect of bad weather in December," author Chris Willis wrote in his biography of NFL president Joe Carr. "The Spartans' management put the game on its schedule. . . but Lambeau. . . didn't put it on the original schedule that [the Packers] released."

In other words, bad weather would probably lead to a lousy crowd. No one wanted to bother with a financially risky game. A game for the NFL championship might have been a monetary success. But that apparently wasn't considered when both sides agreed to make the game tentative.

Before heading off to Chicago, Lambeau said he would only think about taking the Packers to Portsmouth if they defeated the Bears. A win in Chicago would assure that a final game against the Spartans was merely an exhibition that would not affect the NFL championship.

"We do not plan to put our title in jeopardy," Lambeau said before the Packers went to Chicago. "But if the Packers defeat the Chicago Bears, thereby clinching the pennant, we may follow through with a game against Portsmouth Dec. 13."

Lambeau said he wouldn't risk the NFL championship because his team was not healthy: "I don't know a man not on the squad, including myself, who hasn't a cold or doesn't feel as though the grippe was bothering him."

And then the ailing Packers went to Chicago and lost 7-6 to the Bears before a crowd of 18,000 shivering fans at Wrigley Field "on a field made slippery by frost and thaw with a cold wind driving off Lake Michigan across the gridiron."

Portsmouth coach Potsy Clark and team president Harry Snyder, who were at the Packers' loss to the Bears, pressed their demand for Green

Bay to play the Spartans. If the Spartans, who had defeated the Bears 3-0 a week earlier, could beat the Packers in that 'tentative' game, the teams would have identical 12-3 records. That would give Portsmouth the championship based on the most-recent-winner precedent.

"I don't see how a team can claim the pennant when they have not played all the teams in the league," Clark argued. "I think Mr. Carr has overstepped his authority. . . . The Packers didn't finish the season and if a pennant is to be awarded it should go to the Spartans. I think my boys are entitled to gold footballs and not the Wisconsin eleven."

Before champions received gaudy rings, NFL president Carr handed out gold footballs. And after watching the Bears beat the Packers, Clark and Snyder were determined to force Lambeau and Packers president Lee Joannes to come to Portsmouth and play for the gold footballs.

"Several weeks ago when it seemed that we might keep pace with the Packers, they wanted to play us," Snyder said after noting that Green Bay had the right to call off the tentative game. "Now, however, when we can tie for the title by beating the Packers, they will not give us that opportunity, although the game is a sellout."

Lambeau and Joannes steadfastly refused to play a game for the championship with a battered roster. And NFL president Carr stood by his decision that the Packers were under no obligation to go to Portsmouth, saying, "The Green Bay-Portsmouth arrangement was made after the regular schedule had been drawn up" and adding that he "had no power to force Green Bay to play the game."

In Green Bay, the *Press-Gazette* ran a pensive photo of Lambeau, arms akimbo, under the headline, "Leads Packers to Third Title," but did not quote him or Joannes. Clearly defensive, the Green Bay newspaper said the team "had nothing to be ashamed of in this upset and the Packers possess a third straight championship. So what more can one ask?"

Unabashed in defending Lambeau and the Packers, the *Press-Gazette* went on to say the Spartans "refused to book Green Bay earlier in the year at Green Bay but now with everything to gain and nothing to lose sought the battle." What the dispute really pointed out was the need for the league to be the final voice in scheduling. That would not happen until 1935.

The *Portsmouth Times* also took up the cause in an editorial, saying, "In refusing to come to Portsmouth, the Green Bay Packers have revealed that they are more anxious about the safety of a paper championship than they are about the future of the National League. . . . The present Portsmouth-Green Bay mixup appears to be an indication of the loose way in which the National League is operated. . . . President Carr would do well to take a firmer grasp on his official duties."

Joannes gave this explanation to the *Chicago Tribune*: "Green Bay never signed a contract to meet Portsmouth next Sunday. The whole proposition was verbal and tentative. Our boys have played 14 games this fall and we believe they have had enough football. The game with the Bears concluded our schedule."

And so, Green Bay, turning aside the howling in Portsmouth, secured its third straight championship. Nearly a century later, Lambeau's three titles in 1929-31 remain tied for the NFL record with the 1965-67 Packer teams coached by Vince Lombardi.

These disputes were the rule rather than the exception in the early days of the NFL.

The Buffalo All-Americans cried foul when the Chicago Staleys were awarded the 1921 championship even though the teams had identical 9-1 records in that era where ties were tossed out. Chicago and Buffalo had split their two meetings, but the Staleys won the later game, which was the tie-breaker. And no one seemed to grasp that a rubber game would have been a cash windfall, which would have been huge for those struggling franchises.

In 1925, the Chicago Cardinals' title was disputed by the Pottsville Maroons, who argued after finishing 10-2 that the Cardinals—who were 11-2, with one tie—had nudged ahead of them by notching a tainted 58-0 rout against a Milwaukee Badgers team that used four high-school players.

League president Carr, seeming to agree with Pottsville's complaint, basically drove the Badgers out of the league by fining the team and ordering its owner to sell. But Carr stopped short of throwing out the Cardinals' tainted win. Once again, no one seemed to realize how much sense a playoff game would have made. And how many dollars.

And so, the dispute between Lambeau's Packers and the Portsmouth Spartans for the 1931 NFL championship was nothing new. If Lambeau was forced to win the title with debating points as well as hard-fought football victories—well, that was life in the NFL in its early days. Carr was earnest and dedicated. But in a league still groping around to establish its rules and procedures, the bespectacled league leader kept his vision practical and pragmatic.

The reluctance of Curly and Packers president Joannes to risk the NFL championship in Portsmouth was very logical: Green Bay could win the championship by not playing a tentatively scheduled game—or risk the title in a difficult road contest with a banged-up roster.

The refusal to play a league game did not stop Packer players, lured by an offer of $100 a game, from participating in two barnstorming games the following weekend. Insisting that these games were not sanctioned by the team, Joannes did not allow the players to use any team equipment or the Packer name.

Calling themselves the Green Bay Pros Team, the players defeated the Milwaukee Ische Radio Stars 44-0 in Milwaukee on Saturday and the Fort Atkinson Blackhawks 21-2 in Janesville on Sunday before a total of 7,500 fans. They played without an exhausted Lambeau, who spent a couple of days in St. Mary's Hospital with "a severe cold," the *Press-Gazette* reported.

All things considered, the players probably earned more for the two exhibition games than they would have if Green Bay had traveled to Portsmouth. The Packers also authorized a bonus of $100 for each player as a reward for their championship season.

But the citizens of Green Bay did not engage in the celebrations that accompanied their first two championship. Packer fans either understood that their team had backed into the 1931 NFL title. Or else they were getting accustomed to the Packers' success. The Depression also might have weighed heavily.

# 12
## *THE MATH DOESN'T ADD UP*

In 1932, though, despite the exceptional group of players he had assembled, Lambeau's Packers were not all that different from the rest of the National Football League. Every team was trying to attract enough spectators to survive.

As the 1932 season approached, the NFL was feeling the effects of the Great Depression along with the rest of the nation. Unemployment was approaching 25 percent, a grim threshold it would soon cross. In November, the United States would elect Franklin D. Roosevelt its new President amid growing unrest with Herbert Hoover's inability to reverse an economic downturn that was devastating the nation and the world.

The NFL had shrunk from 10 teams to eight. Frankford, Cleveland and Providence were gone. But thanks to president Carr's enterprise, a new franchise had been established in Boston, with George Preston Marshall as its principal owner. Marshall had grown his flourishing chain of Washington, D.C., laundries with showmanship. Now he planned to put some flash into the no-frills game of pro football.

In 1932, the Packers returned the core of a squad that had won three straight championships. And Curly Lambeau, at the peak of his football mastery, continued to bolster his roster to stay on top. The key acquisition for his 1932 Packers was Clarke Hinkle, a fullback/linebacker who had played at relatively obscure Bucknell. In those days before the term linebacker became common, Lambeau called him a two-way fullback.

He had gone largely unnoticed among NFL teams. But Lambeau was familiar with Hinkle, who had played in the Bucknell-Fordham game in New York the day before the Packers played the Giants there. He would be inducted into the NFL Hall of Fame's second class in 1964. Any list of Lambeau's greatest players would either start with Hinkle or include him among the top three.

Lambeau liked to mix his taste for relaxing in California in the winter with spotting talent at the Rose Bowl and the East-West game, an all-star event that benefitted the Shriners' hospitals for children. Lambeau zeroed in on Hinkle, who led the East to a 6-0 victory with 21 rushes for 62 yards on a sloppy field at Kezar Stadium in San Francisco. "The mud was terrible," the *San Francisco Examiner* told readers on January 2, 1932. "All players, covered with liquid earth after the first fifteen minutes, looked alike."

An hour after the game, Hinkle said he was back in his hotel room, having a drink with his roommate, Jim McMurray, an All-America from Pitt. "There was a knock on the door and there was Curly Lambeau with a contract in his hands," Hinkle said. "So I signed a contract, $125 a game."

Michigan star Bill Hewitt told Lambeau he would like to be a Packer, too, and offered to play for $90 a game, Hinkle said: "But Lambeau wasn't interested in him." Instead, the spurned Hewitt, who played without a helmet until they were required in 1939 and went by the nickname "Stinky," went on to a Hall of Fame career with the Bears.

That assumes, of course, that Hinkle's recollection of the Hewitt story is not one of those fables that were common in that era of the NFL, especially with the Packers. Even Hewitt was quick to admit he hadn't played up to his potential at the University of Michigan or even in high school at Bay City, Michigan.

But that was life in the NFL during the Great Depression. Even the Packers, who seemed to be all right financially thanks to the team's success and community support, had to mind their budget. The Packers lost $6,732 in 1931, their biggest loss in history, and would lose $6,052 in 1932. They would not turn a profit again until 1937.

To ease the burden on their fans in the midst of a national economic crisis, the Packers dropped their season tickets from $25 to $20 for box seats and from $15 to $10 for grandstand seats. They also lowered their prices for single-game tickets, dropping seats between the 30-yard lines from $2 to $1.50. Other grandstand tickets were priced at $1.25, $1 and 50 cents, leaving Green Bay with the lowest ticket prices in the NFL.

To cope with the decline in ticket revenue, Lambeau also reduced his players' salaries. He sent out a form letter with the contracts he mailed to players. "Due to present conditions and anticipating a drop in attendance at the game this fall, we have adjusted salaries," Lambeau began in an August 1, 1932, letter to Mike Michalske, a first-team All-Pro in each of the previous five seasons. "All clubs in the league have reduced salaries and we feel that the amount stated in your contract is very fair. . . . Players that have not signed by August 10 will be placed on our suspension list." Across the top of the letter were two ominous handwritten words: "Be careful."

Stars like Red Grange and Ernie Nevers helped the bottom line. But even before the Wall Street stock-market crash in October, 1929, life was hardscrabble in the NFL. After peaking with 22 teams in 1926, the league cut back to 12 teams. Even that list included a few wobbly small-town teams like the Pottsville Maroons and Dayton Triangles.

By 1932, five of the league's eight teams would be located in Chicago, which had the Bears and Cardinals, and New York, where the Giants, Brooklyn Dodgers and Staten Island Stapletons played. Boston had its expansion Braves. That left only two small-market teams, the Packers and the Portsmouth Spartans, who would move to Detroit in two seasons. Only Green Bay would survive.

Strange as it may sound, although the Depression imposed many burdens, it helped Lambeau, Halas and the league's other executives build attractive rosters while keeping their payrolls manageable. "The Depression sent a lot of boys into professional football who would've had other jobs in good times," said Ken Strong, a star fullback for the New York Giants in the '30s.

In this climate, Lambeau had and other NFL team managers had leverage as well as tight budgets. By sending out form letters to his players, even stars like Mike Michalske, he was essentially saying, " take it or leave it," confident that they would take it.

Lambeau's rival, George Halas, took an even tougher stand. "In 1934, midway through the season," rookie guard Danny Fortmann said, "Halas told his players that they would have to take a fifty percent cut or the franchise would be shut down." Despite that bluster, Halas made at least $50,000 that season. That said, Fortmann, who went on to a Hall of Fame career, became a very loyal supporter of Halas, who allowed him to miss countless practices so Fortmann could attend medical school. After football, Fortmann worked as a surgeon in Burbank, California, and was the Los Angeles Rams' team physician from 1947 to 1963.

\* \* \* \* \* \* \* \*

Besides contending for championships, Lambeau and Halas led the league in dramatic tales about steering their teams around the brink of ruin. Lambeau may have more of these stories. But when it comes to moments of crisis, Halas was no slacker. For both men, the legends have become fact to the point where separating them is difficult.

After the Packers were thrown out of the NFL following the 1921 season, Lambeau needed to scramble to regain entry into the NFL in 1922, only to see Green Bay's foundering franchise facing bankruptcy a year later, but saved by an infusion of community funds. And Lambeau, who was more dedicated to the line of scrimmage than the bottom line, would face more moments of crisis that threatened his survival and the Packers' very existence.

Meanwhile, in Chicago, Halas was staring at another do-or-die situation in the summer of 1932. He had broken away from the Staley starch company after the 1921 season, either with A.E. Staley's blessing, as Halas said, or by out-maneuvering Staley, as legal documents show.

As previously noted, after Halas and his partner, Dutch Sternaman, began arranging a lease to play in Wrigley Field without the knowledge of Staley officials, the company chose to give up the football team it had hired Halas to form.

When Halas and Sternaman began to clash to the point where they could no long co-exist, Halas agreed to buy out Sternaman, who needed cash to hold onto his other businesses. That deal set up a storyline that would have made a fine Hollywood melodrama. The only thing missing was a sinister mortgage holder fondling his mustache.

For sheer drama, it rivaled the debunked story of Lambeau saving the Packers when a friend sold his Marmon roadster to provide the money needed for Green Bay to be reinstated in the NFL. In another common trait, Halas and Lambeau were masters at telling tales that showed their determination. And while the essential fact of survival was certainly true, the details of how they got there are bound to raise eyebrows.

Halas' tale of separation from Sternaman went like this: In 1931, he agreed to pay Sternaman $38,000, with an initial payment of $25,000 and the remaining $13,000 to follow in two payments. After making a payment of $6,000, Halas needed to come up with a final payment of $7,000 by July 31, 1932. Halas, who had only about $2,000 on hand, was able to talk Sternaman into an extension until August 9. After that, Sternaman's lawyer warned, the Bears' stock would be put up for public auction.

Halas was desperate. He already had borrowed from several people and couldn't think of anyone. "No one could help me," he said in his autobiography. "At noon I would lose my Bears."

At 11 a.m. on August 9, Halas said, C.K. Anderson, president of the First National Bank of Antioch, Illinois, near the Wisconsin border, called and offered to loan Halas the $5,000. Anderson had met Halas a few years earlier, when they had worked together on a real estate deal. Halas said he beat the noon deadline by 10 minutes.

The details of this survival story make for marvelous drama. Sternaman had owned rental apartments and a gas station. Halas had invested in real estate and the stock market. Both men were reeling from the Depression, desperately trying to keep their finances in order. And then, all of a sudden, a banker Halas had known but hadn't thought to contact called him out of the blue to save the day. If his football career had gone bust, Halas could have written Hollywood scripts.

Beyond their many skills when it came to playing, coaching and putting together a football team, Halas and Lambeau also shared another trait: Both were dedicated to and skilled at publicity.

Halas' tales of the Bears' struggle for survival are metropolitan versions of the stories about how Lambeau and his loyal supporters kept the small-town Packers in business. The little community-owned team is more compelling. But Halas knew how to paint an underdog picture, too. And he realized the value of it. The key difference was that Halas owned the Bears while Lambeau did not own the Packers. In the end, that difference proved to be monumental.

When the 1932 season began, Green Bay looked like it would steamroll to its fourth NFL title. Lambeau's squad went unbeaten in its first nine games, playing the Bears to a scoreless tie in its second game and winning the rest. Even a 6-0 upset loss to the struggling New York Giants at the Polo Grounds on November 20 seemed to be merely a bump in the road. The Packers (8-1-1) still had a big lead in games-won over Portsmouth (5-1-3) and the third-place Bears (3-1-5).

But 1932 was a year filled with danger for Curly and his Packers.

Green Bay bounced back with wins at Brooklyn and Staten Island. But then the Packers, who were finishing their season with seven straight road games, traveled to Portsmouth. The talented Spartans, still angry that the Packers had refused to risk the 1931 championship by playing them, drilled Green Bay 19-0.

When the Packers lost their final game to the Bears 9-0 in Chicago, they finished with a record of 10-3-1. By modern calculations, they still would have wrapped up their fourth straight title, ahead of the Bears, who were 6-1-6, and Portsmouth, which was 6-1-4.

If ties had been counted as half-a-win and half-a-loss, Chicago would have been 9-4 and Portsmouth 8-3 for won-lost percentage purposes. And the 10-3-1 Packers would have been the NFL's 1932 champions.

"By any ordinary method of accounting, we won the championship," Johnny Blood said years later. Blood, a true man for all seasons, wrote an economic treatise, *Spend Yourself Rich*, that he completed in 1940 at the Winnebago State Mental Hospital, where he had gone to "get dried out."

While interesting, Blood's views on classical economics did not become widely appreciated. But his take on the simple mathematics of determining the NFL's champion was spot-on, even if it got no further than his proposed economic policy.

The problem was, 1932 was not modern times. Ordinary methods of accounting were not being used. With ties thrown out rather counting as half a loss and half a win, the Bears and Portsmouth both were 6-1 (.857). The Packers' 10-3 (.769) did not measure up. And never mind that the Packers won four more games.

And so, by that fuzzy math, Green Bay missed out on a fourth straight NFL title despite having four more wins than any other team. With three in a row, Lambeau must settle for being tied with Vince Lombardi for consecutive NFL titles.

A 10-win team finishing third behind a pair of teams that had only six regular-season wins? That disappointment left Lambeau thinking forward—and reaching a conclusion that was decades ahead of its time: Ties need to be settled.

"The fans hate tie games and so do the players," Lambeau told the *Indianapolis News* on December 7, 1932. Under Lambeau's proposal, each team would be given an opportunity to score from the 10 yardline. "[Each team] keeps the ball until [it] scores or loses possession by a fumble, intercepted pass, incomplete pass in the end zone, but never on downs. . . . The team that scores in the fewest number of plays wins the game."

Lambeau expressed confidence that the plan would be adopted by the NFL for the 1933 season. "The idea of an extra quarter never will be brought into pro football," he said, "because that would require too much time and might not settle the matter."

When the NFL finally did turn to overtime for regular-season games in 1974, it did use an extra quarter. In 1996, though, college football adopted an overtime where teams started with the ball at the 25 yardline in an effort to break the tie quickly.

It was another case where Lambeau expressed an idea that was ahead of its time.

* * * * * * * *

To break their regular-season tie, the Bears and Spartans met in a playoff. And what a playoff it was. With Chicago snowed under and Bears fans unlikely to embrace an Ice Bowl at Wrigley Field in those simpler times, the game was played indoors at the Chicago Stadium on an 80-yard field with all kinds of bizarre rules adjustments and controversies. It was a gimmick Halas had used in a December 15, 1930, exhibition game against the Chicago Cardinals with encouraging attendance results. A crowd of 10,000 watched the Bears beat the Cardinals 9-7. Proceeds of the game were given to the Illinois governor's fund for the unemployed.

In modern times, Green Bay fans celebrate tundra-like weather, bundling up and enjoying what they consider a home-field advantage as part of their wintry birthright. But the success of the 1932 indoor NFL championship in attracting a full house to the Chicago Stadium did not go unnoticed. Packers founder Lambeau shared NFL president Joe F. Carr's enthusiasm for indoor football.

By 1943, Lambeau foresaw a domed future for the NFL after World War II. "Curly Lambeau predicts that within five years after peace is declared pro football owners will begin building roofs over the stadia to eliminate the weather hazard, only remaining obstacle to pro grid prosperity," *United Press* columnist Jack Cuddy reported on October 30, 1943. "He explained that most pro tickets are sold on the day of the game, whereas most seats for college games are sold in advance." The prediction appeared in the *Green Bay Press-Gazette* under the headline, "Curly Provides a New Idea; Build Roofs over Grid Stadia."

Beyond his passion for warm-weather California in the winter, Lambeau was recalling how poor weather left the Packers scrambling for survival in their early years—and how poor weather continued to adversely affect attendance throughout his career.

It is another of those Packer ironies: If Lambeau had realized his vision, football would not have been played on the frozen tundra of

Lambeau Field. Instead, Packer players would have been making their Lambeau Leaps in a climate-controlled dome.

* * * * * * * *

Even before the Bears and Spartans met at Chicago Stadium, the first NFL championship game in 1932—an unofficial title game needed as a tiebreaker—was shaping up as a strange affair. Portsmouth's best player, Dutch Clark, was unable to play. He had returned to his alma mater, Colorado College, where he was head basketball coach. And the school's athletic director denied his request to delay his arrival on campus in order to play in the NFL's first championship game.

It is not a stretch to think Clark's absence was a game-changer. Clark had led the NFL with 581 rushing yards and 55 points scored in 1932, his second straight season as the league's first-team All-Pro quarterback.

The Bears won 9-0 despite the protests of the Spartans, who argued that the game-winning fourth-quarter touchdown pass—a two-yard jump pass from Bronko Nagurski to Red Grange—was launched closer than five yards behind the scrimmage line. Seeing the possibilities, the NFL responded by changing its rules the next season to allow passes to be thrown from anywhere behind the line of scrimmage. The capacity crowd of 11,198 at the Stadium had wanted action. That moment of controversy had given the crowd what it wanted.

That was not the only scoring-oriented rule introduced in 1933 after the Chicago Bears won the NFL championship in 1932 despite not scoring in their first four games. After opening with three scoreless ties, they had lost 2-0 to Green Bay. But that was about to change in a big way.

League president Joe F. Carr and team officials realized the NFL needed more offense to attract fans. In addition to allowing passes from anywhere behind the line of scrimmage, the league introduced another rule used at its first indoor game and first playoff: Rather than spotting the ball very close to the sideline after an out-of-bounds play, hash marks were set down 10 yards from the sideline so that the next play could be an attacking effort, rather than a wasted down that moved the ball away from the sideline. And in another move to increase scoring, goal posts were moved to the goal line from the back of the end zone.

The huge turnout despite wintry conditions in Chicago also opened the eyes of the NFL to the possibilities of making the post-season championship playoff a regular thing. It had only happened in 1932 because the Bears and Portsmouth had played to a pair of ties during the regular season, which wiped out the tiebreaker that gave the title to the team that had won the most recent game. In 1933, the NFL changed to two divisions. From that point on, the league would have a championship game.

Any change that opened up football for offense was welcomed by Curly Lambeau, who had been an early advocate for passing and scoring. "Curly did not care about [defense]," said Buckets Goldenberg, a Green Bay star in 1933-45 who was named to the NFL's 1930s all-decade team. "He always figured if they got 100, we would just get 101. I think if we had played the Little Sisters of the Poor, they would have scored on us. Curly remembered the 6-3 games of the past and knew the fans wanted to see scoring, so he stressed the wide-open game."

The Packers certainly could have used more offense in their crushing 19-0 loss at Portsmouth on December 4, 1932. Road-weary—they had not played at home since October 30—nursing injuries and colds, Lambeau's men were thoroughly outplayed. Dutch Clark led the Spartans, running eight yards for one touchdown, throwing a 27-yard pass for another, kicking their only extra point and handling the punting.

While Green Bay's regular season ended on that sour note, an incredible post-season adventure lay ahead.

# 13
## *HAWAIIAN GETAWAY*

The Packers' Portsmouth disaster did produce one positive. While shivering in the early-winter cold that gripped Ohio, Johnny Blood decided that the Packers should make a barnstorming junket to Hawaii.

Blood apparently got the idea for the 1932 Hawaii trip from his former Duluth Eskimos teammate, Ernie Nevers, who told him he had received offers from Hawaii to bring a team to Honolulu. Nevers, though, wanted to confine his barnstorming to California. In 1926 and '27, the two years when Nevers and Blood were teammates, Duluth played 22 of its 23 games on the road, so Nevers could be forgiven if he was still road-weary.

To get the ball rolling, Blood sent a telegram to the sports editor of the *Honolulu Star-Bulletin,* "asking if anyone would be interested in bringing the Packers over for post-season play," Ralph Hickok wrote in *Vagabond Halfback,* a fascinating biography of Blood in which he quotes the colorful Packer star extensively.

Blood's recollection was that he received a telegram advising him to contact Scotty Schuman, a prominent Honolulu car dealer and sports enthusiast. The Honolulu Quarterback Club still gives out a Scotty Schuman Award to honor someone who brings "great recognition to sports in Hawaii."

However, the promoting of the Packers' trip seems to have quickly fallen on the shoulders of John Ashman Beaven, a Hawaii Sports Hall of Fame member who built Honolulu Stadium in 1925. Whether from Schuman or Beaven or some other islander, Blood received a telegram in reply, asking how much of a guarantee Green Bay would require.

Blood took the telegram to Lambeau, who did some quick calculating and said the Packers would need $9,000 plus expenses to play two games in Hawaii. Blood wired back that the team wanted $10,000, believing that would give him some negotiating room. Much to his surprise, another telegram arrived from Honolulu, agreeing to the amount.

The players initially planned to go without Lambeau, but their fair-weather coach objected to that. "Curly said, `You can't go and use the Green Bay Packer name unless I go along,' " fullback Clarke Hinkle said in the 1983 documentary Grandstand Franchise. `We had to give him $1,000 as a guarantee to do that.' "

And so, Lambeau, Blood and the rest of the Packers had a very serious offer to spend Christmas in Hawaii. Blood apparently initiated the Hawaii telegrams while shivering in Columbus, Ohio, where the Packers stayed and practiced before going to Portsmouth.

During the early discussions, everyone assumed that Green Bay would be barnstorming to Hawaii after winning its fourth straight NFL title. Despite the defeat in Portsmouth, it was decided that Green Bay was popular enough for their Honolulu trip to go on. Even though the Packers had been denied another championship, they still had four more wins than any other team. Another Packer loss in their season finale in Chicago, however, might torpedo the trip.

"If the Bears treat the national champions as roughly as did the Portsmouth Spartans, the long tour probably will not be taken," the *Press-Gazette* reported on Wednesday, December 7.

The Bears did indeed treat the Packers roughly, beating them 9-0 at Wrigley Field on Sunday, December 11, before a meager crowd of 5,000. Chicagoans were understandably scared off by brutal winter conditions. The game was played in a swirling snowstorm amid 25-degree temperatures. And with Green Bay out of the championship race, Packer fans understandably decided not to trek to Chicago.

The weather remained so poor in Chicago that George Halas feared the economic consequences of asking fans to shiver in a frigid Wrigley Field. That set up the decision to play the NFL's first championship game indoors at Chicago Stadium.

It's no wonder that Lambeau embraced Blood's idea of a Hawaiian junket. Although post-season tours generally were taken by champions rather than also-rans, prominent Packers board member Andy Turnbull said that would not be a deal-breaker: "The Packers are the team with the reputation." Which was true. Green Bay also was the team with 10 wins, four more than Chicago's Bears or Portsmouth.

In the end, the chance to realize Johnny Blood's dream of escaping winter and making a few dollars proved irresistible. Lambeau led a contingent of 17 Packers out of Green Bay on Tuesday, December 13. They took a train bound for Chicago, then caught another for Los Angeles, where they boarded a ship for the six-day voyage to Hawaii.

It was almost a contingent of 16 Packers instead of 17. Johnny Blood, who had a knack for making things interesting, arrived at the station late and discovered that the train had already pulled out.

"John was going out with an entertainer at a Green Bay night club," Hickok wrote "They were driving to the railroad depot in her car and John insists they were going to make the train. But he was driving too fast and a policeman stopped them. By the time John explained who he was and where he was going, they couldn't make it."

Presumably driving too fast again, Blood raced ahead of the train and forced it to stop by parking on the tracks. "John kissed his girlfriend goodbye and climbed aboard while she drove away," Hickok wrote.

At least that's how the story has been handed down.

"I could see Lambeau wasn't happy," Blood said, "but he didn't say anything. Nobody did. I was pretty popular because I'd set up the Hawaii trip." His teammates even drank to Blood when a friend of his boarded their train in Tucson with "several gallons of moonshine."

Eight days after leaving Green Bay, the Packers finally arrived in Honolulu on December 21 after a liquid-refreshed voyage aboard the *S.S. Mariposa,* which was not subject to Prohibition when cruising in international waters.

Stepping off the ship in their coats and ties, per Curly Lambeau's look-sharp dress code, the Packers posed for a group shot with leis around their necks, then headed off for a practice, accompanied by a squad of photographers.

"To the tune of strumming ukuleles and accompanied by a blast of newspaper publicity, the Green Bay Packers left the *S.S. Mariposa,*" Johnny Blood wrote under a dateline of HONOLULU, T.H., for Territorial Hawaii. A true jack of all trades, the accomplished Blood—who had written for his college paper and worked as a stereotyper at the *Minneapolis Tribune,* which was owned by his uncle—filed regular reports for the *Green Bay Press-Gazette,* which did not send a correspondent on the trip.

"Within an hour after they left the ship, the former national champions put their days of idleness on the ocean strictly behind them, and jogged out upon a convenient field for a stiff practice," Blood reported. "The weather is unbelievable. The temperature registers 70, and after today's workout, the squad went for a swim off Waikiki beach. They then returned to the Hotel Moana, where the best of accommodations were obtained."

That was the way Lambeau liked to travel.

"The Green Bay eleven," the *Honolulu Advertiser* noted in its December 22, 1932, report on the Packers' arrival, "is known throughout the country as 'the pro team with the college spirit.'"

Calling Lambeau's men "two and a quarter tons of the greatest beef known to football," the *Advertiser* said the Packers had arrived to meet "the Warrior Alums of Kamehameha, senior league champions, on December 26, and McKinley Alumni, runners-up in the senior circuit, on January 2."

To entice spectators, Beaven took out P.T. Barnum-like newspaper ads for "the greatest game you'll ever see—don't miss it!" and kept ticket prices low, even by Depression standards. There were 4,800 seats available at 55 cents, 6,000 seats at $1.10 and 1,800 seats at $1.65, plus 2,300 students seats at 25 cents.

In its December 24 edition, the *Press-Gazette* noted in an unbylined report from Honolulu that the Hawaiian players "never wear shoes while playing, but the Packers have flatly refused to join them, preferring to wear the heavy cleated shoes worn by continental football teams."

To accommodate Packer fans back home, WHBY radio arranged to broadcast a play-by-play report. Details were telephoned from Honolulu Stadium to a local RCA office, which radioed them to San Francisco, where they were relayed by telegraph to Green Bay. Because of the lag, the broadcast began at 9 p.m. in Green Bay, half an hour after the 8:30 p.m. kickoff. The game began at 2:30 p.m. Hawaii time.

The broadcast was sponsored by the *Press-Gazette* and Walker's Cleaners and Tailors—and arranged by Lambeau, who never missed a trick in those days, and the sports editor of the *Honolulu Star-Bulletin*.

Green Bay fell behind 7-0 early after yielding a long touchdown pass, but wound up winning 19-13 in a surprisingly competitive game before a crowd of 13,262 at Honolulu Stadium. Whether the game was close because the Packers were rusty or not interested in pounding on their welcoming hosts, or because the Hawaiians were more adept than Green Bay anticipated, they put on a good show. And that, after all, was the point of an exhibition game—not stepping on barefoot toes.

"In spite of heat, humidity and hospitality of gracious Hawaiians," Johnny Blood reported in his *Press-Gazette* dispatch, "Green Bay's Packers defeated. . . the University of Hawaii alumni team, better known as the Kamehameha university stars."

The Hawaiians passed for 220 yards to Green Bay's 183, Blood said, adding, "For those who like figures," the Packers had 277 rushing yards while holding the Hawaiians to just 19 rushing yards.

"The contest was about the best that has been seen on a local gridiron," Don Watson told *Star-Bulletin* readers. "The score does not matter—the fact remains that a great football game was played and the fans were satisfied."

The people back in frozen Green Bay also were pleased to follow the Packers' progress through the relayed radio play-by-play.

"Word came back from Green Bay that at no time during the game did the *Press-Gazette* receive the reports more than minutes after the play was run in Honolulu," the *Honolulu Star-Bulletin* reported on Wednesday, December 28. "The play by play was broadcast by a radio station in Green Bay, so that the folks throughout that part of the country, all of whom are staunch backers of the Packers, would get prompt service on the report of the game."

There was one wistful downside, the *Star-Bulletin* added: "Coach Lambeau says the Wisconsin folks were probably envious of the Packers when the wire was received stating that the temperature here during the game was between 75 and 80 degrees. He says it was probably below freezing with snow on the ground in Wisconsin."

The Lambeau name may adorn a stadium famous for hosting football games in the fiercest of winter weather. But Curly once again eagerly basked in the sun, avoiding the frozen tundra of Wisconsin whenever he could.

In the week between their Hawaiian games, the Packers vowed to put on a better show. But they were concerned about their depth, especially after Johnny Blood's status was in question due to an injury. Although the *Honolulu Star-Bulletin* had mentioned "star performer" Verne Lewellen in mid-December to promote the game, Lewellen did not make the trip. That was a big blow to Green Bay's depth. Although Lewellen did join the team after Hawaii for its barnstorming games in California, he was winding down his last season of football. No longer the Brown County district attorney, Lewellen had decided to concentrate on his law practice.

Lambeau, who had stopped playing in 1928, practiced and said he planned to suit up for the second game, against the McKinley Alumni. "Lambeau, former Notre Dame star and coach of the Green Bay Packers, will see action during the game," the *Star-Bulletin* reported on December 31. "Lambeau stepped into the lineup Friday after John Blood, one of the Packers two quarterbacks, pulled a tendon in his leg during practice."

As it turned out, Blood recovered. That allowed Lambeau, who was 34 years old, to stick to coaching as the Packers rolled to a 32-0 victory. But "the Mick Alumni team," as it was known in the *Honolulu Star-Bulletin,* took pride in the fact that the score was only 6-0 at the half.

Were Lambeau and his Packers going easy again to keep things entertaining? Hard to say. But Green Bay's second game in Hawaii was an artistic and financial success, witnessed by more than 18,000, including 17,764 paying customers.

"The largest crowd ever to attend a football game in Hawaii. . . took advantage of popular prices to see the world's greatest football team, the Green Bay Packers, smother the McKinley Alumni eleven, 32-0," the *Star-Bulletin* reported on January 3, 1933.

The huge turnout, the *Star-Bulletin* added, "contributed greatly to the smile J. Ashman Beaven wore all afternoon. And why shouldn't he? In the face of terrible odds, with the old 'bugaboo' depression staring him in the face, with a bunch of 'I told you sos' advising him, in the face of many financial experts telling him it can't be done, 'Bev' went ahead and did it! Three cheers for Bev!!!"

Attracting more than 30,000 spectators to their two games, the Packers turned Johnny Blood's daydream about spending Christmas in Hawaii into a very real success. A longshot telegram to a Honolulu sports editor allowed Blood to dodge a big chunk of Midwestern winter while putting some money in the pockets of the Packers and promoter Beaven. And it gave Honolulu sports fans and newspapers a fine diversion.

The following winter, Beaven would lure baseball stars Babe Ruth, Lou Gehrig, Jimmy Foxx and other major leaguers to Honolulu for gala exhibition games. Lambeau once again was a trendsetter. The Packers were in Honolulu nearly a month, played two football games and one basketball game—and were treated like royalty.

Years later, the 1966 game between the Bears and the Packers at Lambeau Field would be the first professional football game to be televised live in Hawaii. Exposure like that contributed to the Packers continuing their Notre-Dame-like national appeal.

Although the Packers played the second of their two Hawaiian games on January 2, 1933, they were not finished with their fun in the sun.

With the first of two California barnstorming games not scheduled until January 22, Green Bay did not depart for San Francisco until January 11.

In the meantime, the Packers put on a football demonstration on January 6. One basketball game, scheduled for Thursday, January 5, against the Luke Field Fliers at the University of Hawaii gym, fell through. But on Monday, January 9, the Packers beat "a team of local professionals" 35-30 in basketball before a capacity crowd of 800 at the Palama Arena.

Blood, who returned from a "flying visit to Kauai" on Saturday, January 7, didn't play after sustaining a knee injury in practice. Blood and quarterback Arnie "Flash" Herber had been listed as the Packer forwards, with halfback Wuert Englemann at center and tailback Hank Bruder and guard Mike Michalske at the guards.

Blocking back Roger Grove, who had been an All-America in both football and basketball at Michigan State, led Green Bay with 13 points. The Hawaiian team included many players who had played at mainland universities.

Two days later, on January 11, Lambeau and his Packers boarded the *S.S. Maui* and went to San Francisco, arriving on January 17. In the Bay Area, Green Bay began practicing for its two barnstorming games in California.

The Packers' first game on the mainland did not go well on the field. Even though Lambeau had bolstered his roster—and the game's box-office appeal—by adding an aging Red Grange, Green Bay lost 13-6 on Sunday, January 22, 1933, to a group of Pacific Coast all-stars led by Green Bay nemesis Ernie Nevers. The charity contest at Kezar Stadium in San Francisco was a success at the box office, where it attracted a crowd of 30,000.

"Nevers Again," a *Press-Gazette* subhead said. The former Stanford and Chicago Cardinals star, who had succeeded Grange as the NFL's top attraction, threw two touchdowns, kicked an extra point and intercepted two Green Bay passes. Grange, near the end of his career, had joined the Packers for the game to earn a few dollars.

"The Galloping Ghost" also picked up a new appreciation for Johnny Blood, his barnstorming roommate. "Great receiver and there never was any better runner in the open field than Johnny," Grange said. "Quick as a rabbit. He was a character, though."

Grange witnessed one of Blood's many bloodlettings when a girl asked for a postgame autograph: "He said, `Sure,' then cut himself on the wrist, took her pencil and signed her program in blood. It took a couple of stitches to close it up. . . He also was one of the smartest persons I ever met. He could talk with anybody about literature and poetry and he could recite Shakespeare and practically every poet who ever lived. He liked that almost as much as he did raising a little hell."

The phrase "drink responsibly" came along far too late for Johnny Blood.

Green Bay bounced back in the final game of its winter tour, defeating a team of former USC and UCLA standouts 19-6 at the "other" Wrigley Field, in Los Angeles, on Saturday, February 4, 1933, before a crowd of about 10,000. An *Associated Press* photo of "screen actress" Merna Kennedy sitting between a sharply dressed Curly Lambeau and a leather-helmeted Red Grange, made its way around the nation. If the photo raised eyebrows among some proper Green Bay residents, that would not be surprising. Then again, some insiders might not have been surprised at all.

Given that Kennedy, sometimes identified as Myrna rather than Merna, announced her engagement two months later to director Busby Berkeley, Kennedy's public appearance with Lambeau and Grange might have merely been good publicity for her. Her latest film, "Laughter in Hell," a prison film with Pat O'Brien, had just come out.

A Kankakee, Illinois native, Kennedy was best known for "The Circus," a 1928 silent film she made with Charlie Chaplin. She retired in 1934 after marrying Berkeley. It was a marriage that lasted only one year. She died in 1944 at only 36, four days after marrying an army sergeant.

In a bylined *Press-Gazette* report on the following Tuesday, Blood said most of the Packers began "the long trek back to Wisconsin" on Saturday after the game, including Curly Lambeau, who was due to arrive in Green Bay on Tuesday night.

"Only Johnny Blood, who plans to return to Honolulu, and Nate Barrager, whose home is near [Los Angeles], remained" in L.A., Blood noted.

For Barrager, a Packer center who played at USC, to remain on the West Coast made perfect sense.

And for Blood to return to carousing in Honolulu. . . well, that made perfect sense, too.

# PART TWO:
# FAME, FORTUNE—AND A DARK SIDE

## 14
### *FALLING FROM GRACE IN TOO MANY WAYS*

In 1932, a trip from Wisconsin to Hawaii was an epic adventure. The symbolic line that Curly Lambeau crossed in his life on that journey also was vast. A football hero in his hometown, Lambeau made a decision on that trip that would change the fabric of his life. For all of his accomplishments, he was still searching for more. It was a quest that would become more and more burdensome.

Lambeau finally resurfaced in Green Bay 10 days after the Packers' final California game. Interviewed by the *Green Bay Press-Gazette* on Tuesday, February 14, 1933, the Packers' leader said, "It was the greatest trip I've ever taken. All the boys had a wonderful time and we believe we did a great deal to help the professional sport."

Including the eastern swing that began in early November, the Packers had been gone three months, except for a brief return to Green Bay before they departed for Hawaii. The *Press-Gazette* said the Packers traveled approximately 20,000 miles and called it "the longest road tour ever taken by a football club."

The players "never lacked for entertainment," Lambeau told the Green Bay newspaper, "either on the islands or in California; Honolulu hosts had something arranged for every night in the week."

That was certainly the case for Curly. During the cruise from Los Angeles to Honolulu, Roger Grove "saw this girl and he falls in love," Herm Schneidman, who played for the Packers from 1935 to 1939, told Cliff Christl in a 2001 interview. "He starts talking to her and another player comes over and he sort of fell for her. To end the argument, Lambeau took her and ended up marrying her."

The young woman, identified as Billie Copeland, was a 24-year-old who had won the Miss California pageant five years earlier. Before she was able to compete in the 1927 Miss America pageant in Atlantic City, however, she was disqualified. She had appeared in a Hollywood revue before the state pageant, violating a rule that barred contestants with stage, screen or professional modeling experience.

Copeland was traveling to Hawaii with her mother and older sister on the same ship as the Packers when Lambeau charmed her away from his players.

"This gal was a starlet," Patricia Vandeveld, a close friend of Lambeau's wife, Marguerite, told Christl in a 2011 interview. "Two of the players got in a fight over her, and Curly stepped in to break up the fight and walked off with the girl. He came home from that and asked Marguerite for a divorce. She was shocked."

And so, Curly returned to Green Bay in February 1933 and told Marguerite he wanted a divorce. They had been married in August 1919, and had one child. their son, Donald, who had been born in 1920.

A devout Catholic for whom divorce was virtually unthinkable, Marguerite, did not file for divorce until more than a year later. On May 18, 1934, the *Press-Gazette* reported in a terse item that she had been granted "temporary alimony of $100 a month and custody of their son, Donald, until the divorce has been granted. . . . it is reported she will charge cruel and inhuman treatment."

Curly finally married Copeland on June 26, 1935, in Waukegan, Illinois. "Grid Coach Weds Sun-Kissed Beauty," the *Waukegan News-Sun* reported. After obtaining their marriage license at the Lake County clerk's office, they were married by Justice of the Peace Henry J. Wallenwein. "The coach of the famous football team gave his age as 37 and his home as Green Bay, Wis. The bride said she was 26 years old. She was `Miss California' in 1927." Returning to Green Bay, they lived at Grace Manor, a luxury apartment building on Monroe Avenue near downtown.

If Marguerite, who died at 102 in 2001, carried hard feelings toward Lambeau, there is no record of her speaking negatively about him. She never remarried, in accordance with her Catholic faith. She dated an architect who wanted to marry her, "but she just wouldn't give up her religion," said Mrs. Vandeveld, who worked for years with Marguerite selling clothes at the H.C. Prange department store. They became so close that Marguerite called her "Daughter."

Marguerite even voiced understanding for Lambeau's wandering eye.

"She said it wasn't really his fault," Mrs. Vandeveld said. "Women used to call him all the time. . . She listened in a few times. She was amazed at how the women would call him and ask to meet for a drink or something. Even people she knew real well."

At some private level, though, it would not be surprising if Marguerite held feelings of deep disappointment.

When Lambeau asked for the divorce, the Packers had just completed a three-month odyssey that included seven straight road games at the end of their NFL season, plus the long trip to Hawaii and California. Since early November, they had been in Green Bay only sparingly.

Extensive travel was a growing pattern in Curly Lambeau's life, which would see him spend more and more time in California, scouting for players at the East-West Shrine all-star game in San Francisco and the Rose Bowl—and extending his West Coast stays whenever possible. He also was making glamorous new friends in California while escaping harsh Wisconsin winters.

\* \* \* \* \* \* \* \*

The 1932 NFL title had eluded Green Bay even though it won four more games than the Chicago Bears and Portsmouth Spartans, who wound up playing for the championship. A fourth straight title, which would belong to Green Bay if the now-accepted method for using ties had been in place, would have given Lambeau a monumental accomplishment unlikely to be reached by any future NFL coach.

Even without the fourth championship, Lambeau stands on high ground. The only team that has matched Green Bay's three titles in 1929-31 is the 1965-67 run of the Packers under Vince Lombardi.

In 1929-32, Green Bay had an overall record of 44-7-3, far outdistancing the runner-up Giants (37-17-4) and third-place Bears (28-19-9).

Curly Lambeau was at the pinnacle. He had conquered the football world. There would be more glory. But things would change. The championships would be more business-like, and ultimately, success would become elusive.

And when he came home from Hawaii and divorced his high-school sweetheart for a glamorous new wife, the whole direction of his life seemed to change. A man who seemingly had everything basically announced that it was not enough.

From that point, the innocence was lost. The youthful dream of creating a football franchise—of becoming an adored hometown hero—suddenly had a different spin. Curly Lambeau was still adored by many for his dazzling Packer creation. But now there was something more mercenary and more hedonistic about his life. In Green Bay, that changed the way some people started to view him.

In the 1930s, Lambeau "was introduced in night clubs in New York like Bill Tilden and Jack Dempsey," *Press-Gazette* sportswriter Lee Remmel said, mentioning the celebrity tennis and boxing champions. "That was the so-called Golden Age of Sport, and Curly became a national figure."

Back home in northeastern Wisconsin, where Lambeau's divorce was accompanied by an increased awareness of his dalliances, his celebrity now included baggage. Also important for his legacy, the Packers would undergo significant change. The Depression era would create obstacles that would threaten the team's existence. And when the franchise adapted, it would be more stable—but also more business-like. And Lambeau, whether he knew it or not, would have less of a hold on the reins.

After the dominant run from 1929 to 1932, Lambeau would rely more on the support of dedicated businessmen to keep pro football alive in his hometown. He would reward that support by building more championship teams. But Curly Lambeau would change, too. There had been an innocence to the way the Packers started, and the way they climbed to the top.

They would rise again. But things would be different for the Packers. They also would be different for Lambeau. On the field. And especially in his personal life.

\* \* \* \* \* \* \* \*

Today, Lambeau Field presides over a Packer-centric section of Green Bay that is Disney-like in its dedication to the Green and Gold. All manner of enterprises pledging allegiance to the team that Curly Lambeau created in 1919 occupy prominent places along Lombardi Avenue.

A few miles away, "the picturesque courtyard at the Birthplace Home of Curly Lambeau is available for parties, meetings and other informal gatherings, " the lambeauhouse.com website notes. Lambeau House, which is operated by a charitable foundation that benefits Nicolet School, also is "available on a limited basis for overnight stays."

Highlighted by the major thoroughfare of Lombardi Avenue, no fewer than 14 Green Bay streets are named for Packers. Eight, including Tony Canadeo Run, Bart Starr Road, Holmgren Way, Brett Favre Pass—are near Lambeau Field. In June of 2020, Green Bay residents were greeted with the grim news of a high-speed traffic accident that claimed the lives of three family members at the corner of Lombardi Avenue and Bart Starr Road. Chicagoans need not worry about a similar tragedy at the corner of Halas Road and Payton Drive. There is no corner of Halas Road and Payton Drive.

There is a Lambeau Street. But it's more of a frontage road where Interstate 41 crosses Mason Street, about three miles northwest of Lambeau Field.

With all of these Packer monuments, it's difficult to imagine how precarious the Packers' survival was at crucial junctures. One of those moments came during the depths of the Depression.

While Lambeau was rearranging his personal life—trading in one wife for another—during the winter of 1933, the Packers received a devastating financial blow that threatened their existence.

At a game two years earlier, while the Packers were cruising past the Brooklyn Dodgers 32-6 on September 20, 1931, at City Stadium, one of the 7,000 fans in attendance, Willard Bent, "fell from the bleachers. . . and broke two vertebrae in his back." Bent's younger brother, Gordon, who owned the largest sporting goods store in Green Bay, had outfitted the original Packers team in 1919. In 1922, Gordon had been one of the 204 original stockholders in the Green Bay Football Corporation and among the 38 businessmen chosen to sell stock in the club.

In contrast to his successful brother, Willard Bent, 54, was a ne'er-do-well—"an alcoholic with a sixth-grade education, a heart condition and an advanced case of syphilis [who] had no teeth," as Mark Beech summed up court testimony in *The People's Team,* his Packer history. And perhaps worst of all, for Willard and the Packers, he had no pull from his brother in terms of obtaining a better seat location.

On September 20, 1931, Bent was sitting in the top row of the wooden bleachers that Curly's father, Marcel, had built. During an important play, he stood up with the crowd around him to watch. "Somehow the plank serving as his seat came loose. When Bent sat back down, there was nothing under him. He fell about 12 feet."

His spine fractured, Bent spent 53 days in a body cast. In September of 1932, he sued the Packers for $20,000, claiming he was "permanently crippled" and blaming unsafe conditions at City Stadium.

When the case went to trial in late February of 1933, the Packers' legal team initially tried to argue the club was not liable because the city owned the stadium. The defense also maintained that Bent was negligent and that his health problems were his own fault. "We will concede that if we could have put him in a hammock and given him a nurse to hold his hand, it might have been safer," Packers attorney Gerald Clifford said. Clifford was assisted by young attorney Lavvie Dilweg, who was nearing the end of a standout nine-year career as a Packers end.

To illustrate their point, the Packers' legal team had Curly's father, Marcel Lambeau, build a section of grandstand in the rotunda of the courthouse.

On February 28, the jury deliberated for five hours and awarded Bent $4,989.73 for medical bills, lost wages, and pain and suffering. It reduced its initial finding of $5,544.14 by 10 percent due to Bent's negligence.

Ordinarily, the Packers' liability insurance would have covered the claim and the team would have moved on. But this is where another epic moment in Packer mythology intervened. In another test of the team from little Green Bay, the team's insurer, Southern Surety Company of New York, had gone bankrupt on March 22, 1932.

In the middle of the Great Depression, an unexpected setback of less than $5,000 pushed a precariously-funded community-owned football team to the brink. With liabilities of more than $10,000, the team went into receivership on August 15, 1933.

"When Judge Henry Graass walked into my office... and told me he had appointed me receiver of the Packer corporation, he handed me $76.18 in cash—and judgments and unpaid bills amounting to over $15,000," said Frank Jonet, a Green Bay accountant who had at one time been the office manager of the Indian Packing Company.

Team president Lee Joannes sought to reassure fans that while the Packers had encountered financial turbulence, the team was here to stay. "The Green Bay Football corporation is solvent," Joannes said, noting that the bankruptcy of the team's longtime insurance provider left the Packers temporarily unable to pay their bills "because of two very unprofitable years of operations, due not only to business conditions, but unfavorable weather.... The Packer team, an institution in Green Bay, has brought more advertising to this city, and for that matter to Wisconsin, than any other medium. In these days of stress and uncertainty, the club... needs more than ever the support of all the loyal fans in this community.... While we realize that many will have to stretch a point to buy tickets this year... it seems certain that the club will be a strong contender for national championship honors, and there will be plenty of thrills and excitement for the fans this fall. Let us all get behind this marvelous club and secure the continuance of professional football in Green Bay."

While the trial was playing out, Lambeau was in Pittsburgh on February 25 and 26, 1933, at a special NFL meeting called to adopt rules changes designed to open up the game to more scoring.

George Preston Marshall, the flamboyant owner who had just finished his first NFL season, led the push for scoring. Marshall's legacy as the founding owner of the Washington Redskins is now shredded by his disgraceful racism. In his day, though, he was a strong-willed showman with a P.T. Barnum-like flair. He had built up his Palace Laundry by luring customers with employees in attractive uniforms at artfully decorated facilities. A newspaper ad cleverly featured a blank page with a small message at the bottom: "This space was cleaned by the Palace Laundry and Dry Cleaning Company."

"Gentlemen, it's about time we realized that we're not only in the football business," Marshall told the gathering at the Fort Pitt Hotel. "We're also in the entertainment business. If the colleges want to louse up their game with bad rules, let 'em. We don't have to follow suit. The hell with the colleges. We should do what's best for us. I say we should adopt rules that will give the pros a spectacular individuality and national significance. Face it, we're in show business. If people don't buy tickets, we'll have no business at all."

Always maneuvering, Marshall had moved his expansion Boston Braves from Braves Field to Fenway Park and renamed them the Redskins, which neatly connected them with their new landlords, the Red Sox, by color while still keeping the Indian imagery that Marshall favored. After three years in Boston, Marshall would move the Redskins to Washington, where his laundry business was located.

Having grown his Palace Laundry empire with a sense of drama, he would do the same in the NFL. He ordered Sammy Baugh, his sensational quarterback prospect, to arrive from Texas in cowboy gear befitting a gunslinger. He had his players wear Indian headgear to drum up publicity. And he outfitted a band for halftime entertainment, an unfamiliar frill in pro football at the time. Marshall also put together strong football teams. The Redskins, along with the New York Giants, would become the league's Eastern anchors, balancing out with the Bears and the Packers in the Midwest.

Enthusiastic for ideas that would attract spectators in the depths of the Depression, NFL owners announced three major changes. In 1933, the goal posts would be moved from the back of the end zone to the goal line. The football would be spotted no closer than 10 yards from the sideline for the next play. In addition, forward passes would be permitted from anywhere behind the line of scrimmage. Previously, passes had to be thrown five yards behind the line.

Lambeau, appointed with George Halas to draft the wording of the changes, welcomed them enthusiastically.

"The new rules are made to order for the Packers," said Lambeau, who had been the league's first 1,000-yard passer at a time where most teams disdained passing. "I expect to see our men take to the new rules like a duck to water, and the fans can rest assured that the ball will be in the air most of the time. . . . Teams inclined to use the open style of play will prove more sensational this season than the clubs that have been playing a more conservative game."

On his way back to Green Bay from the NFL meeting in Pittsburgh, Curly stopped off in Chicago on Monday, February 27, to see the opening night of a "tournament of [boxing] champions" at the Chicago Stadium that included four young men from Green Bay among its 321 entrants. "After seeing the bouts, he said he'd stick to football," the *Press-Gazette* reported.

On July 9, 1933, anticipating that Pennsylvania's blue-law ban on Sunday sports would be lifted, the NFL approved three new franchises in Pittsburgh, Philadelphia and Cincinnati at its meeting at the Blackstone Hotel in Chicago. The next day, Marshall made yet another innovative proposal: Divide the 10-team NFL into two divisions—Boston, Brooklyn, New York, Philadelphia and Pittsburgh in the East, with the Chicago Bears and Cardinals, Cincinnati, Green Bay and Portsmouth in the West.

The league's owners adopted the change, which would allow the league to have an annual championship game between the two division winners. That not only would curtail debates about who deserved the league's championship. It also would create a money-making contest that also would end the season with a publicity flourish.

Lambeau was not in favor of splitting the league into divisions. Perhaps he was reluctant to risk a one-game playoff for the championship. Although Green Bay had won three of the previous four titles, and narrowly missed winning a fourth, December was by far the Packers' worst month. They were 0-4-1 in December in 1930-32, despite an overall record of 32-8-2 those years.

But Lambeau said he still liked the Packers' chances: "The league should be stronger than ever this year, as every club is ready to spend money to put great teams on the field. We still are rated as the team to beat to win the championship, so every club will be gunning for us again. We have an attractive schedule as all the teams want to play Green Bay as they realize we are one of the best drawing cards on the circuit."

Unfortunately for Green Bay rooters, Lambeau's optimism proved to be inaccurate. The club would remain in receivership for 17 months, limiting Lambeau to a bare-bones player payroll. Attendance, which had been declining, continued to go low as a result of Depression economics and the Packers' struggles on the football field.

In addition, Lambeau was in personal limbo. He had asked Marguerite for a divorce after returning in February 1933 from the Packers' Hawaiian barnstorming adventure. The divorce decree was not granted until May 22, 1934—by the same busy judge, Henry Graass, who had presided over the Willard Bent lawsuit that pushed the Packers into receivership.

Adding to Lambeau's problems, the Chicago Bears had gained momentum. In 1932, they had sneaked past the Packers and won the NFL championship even though they had won four fewer regular-season games. Ralph Jones, who had been a compromise coach when the Bears co-owners, Halas and Sternaman, were squabbling, had introduced innovations, including putting the quarterback directly under center and spreading out the offensive line to help open running holes.

Jones, who had been Halas' varsity basketball coach as well as an assistant football coach at Illinois, also benefitted greatly from the arrival of Bears legend Bronko Nagurski, from International Falls, Minnesota, by way of the University of Minnesota.

Although the Bears had defeated Portsmouth in the NFL's inaugural championship game in 1932, they changed coaches. Despite a successful three-year run, Jones was replaced by Halas, who claimed he needed to save on Jones' coaching salary because the Bears had lost $18,000 in their 1932 championship season. Having completed his buyout of Sternaman, Halas was free to operate the Bears as he saw fit. Jones returned to Lake Forest College.

In the first 1933 meeting between the two great rivals, Lambeau received a bitter taste of where Green Bay's season was headed. Leading 7-0 with five minutes to go, the Packers gave up two touchdowns and lost 14-7 on September 24.

"Outplayed and outfought by the Packers for practically four full quarters and apparently hopelessly beaten by the count of 7 to 0, the Bears suddenly came to life in the last five minutes," Howard Roberts told *Chicago Daily News* readers on September 25

Leading the Bears' miracle comeback was Bill Hewitt, whose offer to play for Green Bay had been turned down by Lambeau. Hewitt threw a 46-yard touchdown to Luke Johnsos for the first Bears touchdown. Hewitt then blocked a Packer punt and returned it five yards for the winning score.

The loss left the Packers, who had tied Marshall's Boston Redskins 7-7 in their opening game, winless as they prepared to host the stout New York Giants in their third game. Desperate to increase revenue, Packers president Lee Joannes, who had loaned the club $6,000 to keep it afloat, moved the game to Milwaukee. This first game outside of Green Bay fueled speculation that the team, under pressure from the NFL, would move to Milwaukee.

A crowd of 12,467 showed up at Athletic Park, where the Packers failed to impress. Playing another sloppy game, they lost the ball on a fumble and an interception and fell behind 10-0. Johnny Blood caught a 30-yard touchdown pass from Bob Monnett in the fourth quarter. But that was as far as Green Bay got.

"The once mighty Green Bay Packers slipped deeper into the depths of the National Football League standings Sunday when they were humbled by the New York Giants 10-7," the *Associated Press* account began the next day, spoiling Lambeau's breakfast.

The defeat left Green Bay 0-2-1, its worst start in five years. Even the fiercely loyal *Green Bay Press-Gazette* said the Packers "played one of their worst games, offensively, in many years."

The Packers' losing ways clearly didn't help their attendance prospects for their three remaining games in Green Bay. With unbeaten Portsmouth (3-0) coming to town and a steady downpour adding to the prospects for a miserable football day, only a few thousand fans dug into their depression-addled wallets on October 8.

But Lambeau's squad, fed up with losing, erupted, "smothering the hitherto undefeated Portsmouth eleven by a score of 17 to 0," Art Bystrom wrote in the *Press-Gazette.* "Playing in a driving rain which seemed to wash them clean of the mistakes and lethargy of their previous games, the Green Bay players showed a brave crowd of 4,000 that fumbling, missing signals and listless tackling is not their regular style."

The weather let up only slightly the following Sunday. Was it any wonder that Lambeau envisioned a day when football would be played in the climate-controlled comfort of a dome? Only 4,000 braved a slow, drizzling rain on October 15 to see the Packers rout the Pittsburgh Pirates 47-0. Only 3,007 fans turned out for a 35-9 win over the Philadelphia Eagles. That added up to only 12,007 fans for three straight games in Green Bay. Depression or not, the Packers would be on shaky financial ground if that pattern continued.

To keep his payroll down, Lambeau cut three players after the loss to the Giants in Milwaukee. He also placed two injured players on the suspended list and said he would cut two more players when the injured Packers were able to return.

Its record evened at 2-2-1, Green Bay headed to Chicago for the second of its three meetings with the Bears. Although Halas' team was a perfect 4-0, Lambeau brought a confident Packer squad to Wrigley Field, Green Bay led 7-0 with four minutes to go, but the Bears rallied to win 10-7. For the second time that season, the Packers had blown a late lead and fallen to the Bears.

The weather was cool and dry on October 29, 1933, when the Packers wrapped up their home schedule at City Stadium against the Philadelphia Eagles. But only 3,007 loyal souls turned out, adding to Lambeau's money worries. He couldn't even blame foul weather. "Sunday was a fine day with a minimum of 47 degrees, which made it nice for football, driving or outing among the autumn woods," the *Press-Gazette's* weather report noted the next day.

Their home season completed, the Packers started packing for their final six games, all of them on the road. They were 3-3-1 and in a distant third place behind the unbeaten Bears (6-0) and Portsmouth (5-1). But after the Packers defeated the Chicago Cardinals 14-6 at Wrigley Field despite myriad injuries, Lambeau was hopeful that they could still win NFL's Western Division. Not only did Green Bay have a game remaining against each of them. Portsmouth and the Bears still had a pair of games left against each other.

The bubble burst quickly, though. Green Bay lost 7-0 to the Spartans in Portsmouth on November 12. Their faint hopes of winning the 1933 championship gone, the Packers then headed off to Boston. Banged up and no longer a contender, Green Bay lost 20-7 to "George Marshall's high priced gridders," as Calhoun called them in the *Press-Gazette.*

It's no wonder that finances were on the minds of Calhoun and Lambeau. Back in Green Bay, Willard Bent's attorney went to court to try and grab $1,500 that the Packers had received from the Bears. In 1932, when George Halas had his own money problems and couldn't pay the

Packers their guarantee for a game in Chicago, team president Lee Joannes had taken an IOU note for the $1,500.

When Halas paid off the note in 1933, Bent's attorney said the money should go to Bent, who had won a $5,000 judgment after he fell from the bleachers at a Packer game. Packers attorney Jerry Clifford argued that the transaction was between Joannes and the Bears, and did not affect the Green Bay football team's underwater finances. Judge Henry Graass allowed the Packers' receivership protection to stand.

Meanwhile, the Packers, having lost at Portsmouth and Boston, moved on to New York, where they would face the Eastern Division leading Giants. With a record of 4-5-1, Lambeau was feeling the strain of a disappointing season amid injuries and the team's perilous financial situation. Green Bay had no chance of sneaking past the Bears and Portsmouth in the NFL's new Western Division. It was not a happy time for Lambeau, who had grown accustomed to winning.

After capturing three titles in four years and narrowly missing a fourth straight, Green Bay was in danger of losing more games than it won. That surprising downturn kept the publicity spotlight on the Packers. Like Notre Dame, Green Bay's football over-achievers remained a fascinating subject, win or lose—especially in the media capital of America.

Curly was up to the task. On Sunday morning, November 26, 1933, amid a sports section jam-packed with college football—the dominant form of the sport at that time—the *New York Times* devoted its only sports column to the struggling Packers. "A couple of years ago the Green Bay Packers were the rulers of the professional gridiron," columnist John Kieran began. "Now the Wisconsin wanderers are down in the swamp. It was no wonder that Coach Curly Lambeau was playing the part of the Knight of the Rueful Countenance as he strolled down Broadway."

Kieran's playful column mixed self-deprecating quotes from Lambeau with gentle needles of Green Bay's total immersion in football.

"I don't like to be hauling alibis out for inspection," Lambeau was quoted as saying, "but rub out two fumbles and we'd be right up with the league leaders, yes, sir! We lost to the Chicago Bears twice when we were leading with less than four minutes to play. A fumble did it each time—plumb ruined us. Now where are we? Don't answer; I can't bear it."

It was true. If those two Bears games had ended four minutes sooner, Green Bay would have been 6-3-1 instead of 4-5-1 and Chicago would have been 4-4-1 instead of 6-2-1. But Lambeau knew that was the way the football bounced.

Kieran then addressed Green Bay's fall from grace, setting up a Lambeau response with a series of questions alluding to the city's trust and loyalty in its football team: "How was the town of Green Bay bearing up under the loss of five football games by the once proud Packers? A successful season for the Packers was a plank in the political platform out there. Wasn't the team a municipal institution of some kind? An eleemosynary institution, in fact?"

If Lambeau didn't know that *eleemosynary* was a fancy word for charitable, he did a good job of rolling with the friendly jab at his hometown and his football team. He even joked about the American Legion Post in Green Bay being the beneficiary of the Packers' non-profit community organization.

"Not quite that bad," Lambeau replied. "We still give our profits to the American Legion—even when we don't have profits. We lost money for the first time last year, so we took a chunk out of the reserve fund and gave it to the Legion. That's why we're the only football team in the country that sells its tickets without a tax—our home games, I mean. The town is bearing up all right. We'll be back up there again next year."

Kieran's response: "In that case the captain of the team probably will run for Mayor and win by a landslide. Isn't it the custom for Green Bay to put its football players into municipal offices? A couple of years ago they were here with a justice of the peace in the back field, a Sheriff's officer at guard and a leading attorney leading the interference."

Lambeau shrugged off the kidding reference to, among others, retired Packers star Verne Lewellen, a two-term Brown County district attorney who had left the team after the 1932 season.

"We ran out of municipal officers," Lambeau told Kieran. "They got a little bit old for this game. That Lewellen was a great kicker, wasn't he? But we had to get younger players."

With a light but relentless touch, Kieran then asked Lambeau if the Packers were still using "the Notre Dame style of play," a reference to the Notre Dame Box backfield formation. This was a loaded question because the Fighting Irish were wrapping up a 3-5-1 season, the first losing campaign in Notre Dame history—in the same year the Packers were enduring their first losing season.

" 'Sure,' " said Mr. Lambeau, a former Notre Dame player himself. 'Why not? It's been going all right about everywhere this season except at Notre Dame—and Green Bay.' "

Ironically, the Fighting Irish were coached that year by Hunk Anderson, in his third and final season at Notre Dame. Hired after Rockne's shocking death in a plane crash, Anderson would blame his inability to win on school officials who cut back on scholarships. Anderson, one of the college players that Lambeau had used illegally when Green Bay was tossed out of the NFL, had played for the Bears and would coach them when Halas was in the Navy during World War II.

All in all, Kieran's Packer column was a good pro-football beacon in a sea of college football results. Lambeau was happy to play along with

Kieran's light needling; the important thing was the spotlight it put on the Packers and the NFL. He was fine with being portrayed as the simple coach from the football-obsessed little town who was selling his sport in the sophisticated big city. With his playful answers, the Green Bay coach had shown his flair for publicity, which in turn would translate at the box office. Lambeau's rival, George Halas, had a similar talent for selling pro football, which was not initially an easy sell. But Lambeau was unrivaled when it came to charming writers.

"Curly enjoyed the limelight and felt at ease with the media," Steve Cameron wrote in *The Packers!* "The more, the merrier. He relished those early, history-making trips to New York City and likely would have been a television dandy if he'd come along later."

Not only was Lambeau a natural at publicity. He also had a gifted tutor in George Whitney Calhoun, the newspaperman who co-founded the Packers, guiding a 21-year-old Curly through the rigors of starting a football team.

From the first kickoff in 1919 until his death in 1963, Calhoun never missed a home game. And he was a road-trip regular in the early decades, filing detailed stories of the games and their buildups and aftermaths back to Green Bay.

Calhoun's other great contribution was his gift for publicity. "Unlike run-of-the-[mill] publicity men, who haunt newspaper offices, Cal used the system of making the sports writers come to him," Jack Rudolph, a *Press-Gazette* colleague and Green Bay historian wrote after Calhoun died. "Cal would get a hotel room, fill the bathtub with ice and beer and then call the papers to let the sports writers know where he was. They all came flocking, too. . . . Most of the resulting ink went to [Curly], but Cal didn't mind. In fact, he preferred it that way."

On a crisp late-fall day, a crowd of 17,000 showed up at the Polo Grounds to see the division-leading Giants, headed for the NFL's inaugural championship game, defeat the struggling Packers 17-6 on November 26, 1933. An 85-yard interception return for a touchdown gave New York an early lead. Only a late touchdown kept the Packers from being shut out.

Two years earlier, Green Bay had drawn 35,000 to the Polo Grounds. But that was when the Packers, pro football's answer to Notre Dame, were on their way to a third straight NFL championship. Now the proud team from northeastern Wisconsin had lost its fierceness.

All was not well with Lambeau's football team. Conspicuously absent was Johnny Blood. Even though the Packers' roster was diminished by injury, Curly had suspended his star receiver for "breaking training rules" the day before the Giants game.

Always clever with words, Blood, who found drinking irresistible, downplayed his hangovers by saying, "Alcohol rarely hangs onto me." In this case, though, it was clinging tightly.

The trouble started on Friday night. When a millionaire's wife from Green Bay had called on Friday night and asked him to meet her at the Stork Club, Blood said, he had maturely turned her down to be ready for the Giants game. But then, two nurses who were Packer fans had knocked on his door. Unable to resist, he and his roommate let them in and ordered drinks sent up to their room.

"We didn't call them groupies, of course, but there were a lot of them around, even then," Blood told his biographer, Ralph Hickok. "Girls and women who liked athletes. . . . [The two nurses] were young, and they were attractive, and they knew the Packers were in town."

At practice that Saturday, Blood was either hung over or still drunk. "Curly gave me kind of a funny look. . . I guess it showed," Blood said. "Then, when I tried to punt, I missed the ball completely and fell flat on my ass. Curly sent me back to the hotel."

When Lambeau returned to the hotel, he summoned Blood and told him he had been cut. That shaved a few dollars off the Packers' payroll. Blood recouped some spending money by playing for a semi-pro team in Paterson, New Jersey. Two weeks later, Lambeau allowed Blood to rejoin the team for Green Bay's final game, in Chicago against the Bears. That enabled him to retain the rights to Blood. Lambeau then sold Blood to the Pittsburgh Pirates before the 1934 season. "This way, he got some money for me," Blood said.

That was one of many cost-cutting measures taken by Lambeau. Declining Curly's salary offer, all-pro end Tom Nash had refused to play in 1933, and was sold to Brooklyn on October 10, 1933. "Nash was a holdout from the Packers—sub rosa, it was contract trouble—and his release was bought by Brooklyn for the staggering sum of $1,500," the *Brooklyn Eagle* reported. The newspaper considered that a small price to pay for "the greatest end in pro football."

After suspending Blood, Lambeau released Wuert Engelmann and Jesse Quatse, leaving the Packers with only 17 healthy players for their Thanksgiving Day game against the Staten Island Stapletons, who had left the NFL but were still operating as a talented independent team. Added to the injured list was standout lineman Cal Hubbard, who had fractured his left thumb and forefinger against the Giants.

Like Blood, Hubbard, who had been named to the All-NFL teams in 1932 and 1933, would not return for the next season. In 1934, with Lambeau still battling payroll problems, Hubbard took a job as an assistant coach at Texas A&M while continuing to umpire minor-league baseball in the off-season. Hubbard rejoined the Packers in 1935. The following year, he became an American League umpire. While he played football briefly for the Giants and Pittsburgh in 1936, umpiring became the top priority for the only man inducted into both the Baseball and Pro Football Halls of Fame.

Not surprisingly, all the stress took a toll on Lambeau. Fearing appendicitis when he felt acute abdominal pain after the loss to the Giants, Lambeau went to see a doctor. "The attending physician calmed some of the fears by discounting the appendix attack," Calhoun told *Press-Gazette* readers. "It is a stomach disorder brought on by nervousness and Lambeau has been placed on a strict diet with some sure cure powders thrown in to hasten a quick recovery."

Green Bay and its coach recovered well enough to handle the Stapletons 21-0 on Thanksgiving and take down the Philadelphia Eagles 10-0 on December 3 before moving on to a 7-6 loss to the Bears in Chicago on December 10. The Packers wrapped up their disappointing season with a 21-0 barnstorming win over the St. Louis Gunners that attracted a crowd of 15,080 in St. Louis on December 17, 1933.

Swept by the Bears in their three meetings, the Packers watched from the sidelines as Chicago, the Western Division champion, defeated the Eastern champion New York Giants, 23-21, in the NFL's first title game under the division format. A crowd of 26,000 turned out at Wrigley Field on December 17, a welcome payday for pro football teams trying to survive the Depression.

Two days before the Packer-less NFL title game, the *Press-Gazette* sports section ran a wistful headline, "Eight Minutes, Six Inches, Keep Packers from Crown." It detailed how Green Bay had blown late leads in two games against the Bears, and barely missed a game-changing touchdown in the other—losing all three games to their big-city rivals.

The article listed the standings if the Packers had won those games: Green Bay 8-4-1, Chicago 7-5-1 rather than the way they turned out: Chicago 10-2-1, Green Bay 5-7-1.

"Scratching those spectacular rallies from the books, and eliminating last week's tight margin, the Packers would have won all three games with the Bears," the piece concluded.

The 1934 season, the Packers' second under the constraints of receivership, would only bring more frustration, though.

# 15
## *PASSING FANCY*

From the very beginning, Lambeau had been a passing pioneer. As the NFL's first 1,000-yard passer, he threw the football himself for his earliest teams.

"Lambeau was one of the greatest passers of all time," Fritz Gavin, a center on the first two Packer teams, said. "No matter where you were he could hit you. He could hit a dime at 40 yards."

That seems to be the exaggeration of an adoring teammate. In the leather-helmet days of 1924, when Lambeau completed 75 of 179 for 1,094 yards, he only completed only 42 percent of his passes, according to unofficial statistics in *The Football Encyclopedia*.

Passing was haphazard in the NFL's first decade. It had not emerged as a reliable and important part of the game. The over-sized football was difficult to throw and catch. And the records indicate that Lambeau also threw 29 interceptions. In those days, interceptions were common, which was why many teams were reluctant to throw.

It's no wonder, then, that the Chicago Bears, who finished second in 1924, attempted only 30 passes, completing only 10 for 58 yards, with no touchdowns and three interceptions. No passing statistics are available for the NFL champion Cleveland Bulldogs.

Lambeau threw for the third-most passing yards in the NFL in the 1920s. He appeared in 76 of the Packers' 87 NFL games from 1921 to 1928, and made his final playing appearance in one 1929 game. Halas also wrapped up his playing career in 1928.

His 1,000-yard effort helped Green Bay to a 7-4 record in 1924, sixth in the 18-team league. The Bulldogs, who had moved from Canton to Cleveland (7-1-1), edged the Bears (6-1-4) and their 58-yard passing game.

That said, Lambeau is not remembered as an exceptional passer. His legacy is as a coach who designed an innovative passing scheme that featured outstanding passers and receivers. Some of his earliest player acquisitions show that he knew the value of the players in the trenches. But he also knew the value of flashy skill players. His eye for talent is a big reason his name is on the historic home of the Packers today.

A key player in the Packers' formative years, Lambeau played primarily at right halfback in an era where the four backs tended to specialize in their strengths, whether running, throwing, blocking, receiving or kicking. Right halfback tended to be the most prominent passing position in the Notre Dame Box, although Lambeau modified that as the years went on, depending on the strengths of his players.

As Lambeau, who had been the team's main star in 1919 and 1920, transitioned from player-coach to strictly coaching, he always had at least one dependable passer. In 1922, Charlie Mathys, the former Green Bay West high school star who had played in college at Ripon and Indiana, joined the Packers. Mathys threw seven touchdown passes in 1925, including the game-winner in the Packers' first victory over the Bears. He also caught 90 passes for 1,506 yards in the 1920s, the most in the NFL.

When Mathys suffered a career-ending arm injury three games into the 1926 season, Lambeau resorted to passing by committee. Lambeau led the way, but he knew that had to change.

To fill the void, he acquired Red Dunn, Milwaukee native who had been a Marquette standout. Playing for the Milwaukee Badgers in 1924, he had been the NFL's second most productive passer, completing 36 of 73 (49 percent) for 565 yards with four touchdowns and eight interceptions. In 1925, he moved on to the Chicago Cardinals, throwing nine touchdown passes to help the Paddy-Driscoll-led Cardinals win the NFL title.

After slipping to a 5-6-1 record in 1926, the Cardinals were revamping their team and sold him to Lambeau. "Paid $250 for him but that was a lot of money in those days," Curly told the *Press-Gazette* when Dunn died of a heart attack at 55 on January 15, 1957. "He gave us our first championship [in 1929] and he was the best quarterback in the league during his last three years." Dunn retired after the 1931 season, returning to Milwaukee to become Marquette's freshman football coach.

For some teams, replacing a player of Dunn's stature would have created a problem. In another example of Lambeau's gift for spotting talent, the Packers already had their next great passer on the team.

Arnie Herber was more than a future Pro Football Hall of Famer who became, in the words of Packer historian Cliff Christl, "pro football's first great long-ball passer." Like Lambeau, he was a hometown Green Bay hero who became a prominent NFL star after a brief college career.

After leading Green Bay West to a 24-1-1 record—*Milwaukee Sentinel* sports editor Stoney McGlynn called Herber "the greatest high school player in the nation."—Herber enrolled at Wisconsin in the fall of 1928 and was captain of the freshman team.

Before the start of the 1929 season, though, he was ruled academically ineligible. He wound up in Denver playing at Regis College, a small Jesuit school that briefly tried to play big-time college football. In another similarity to Lambeau, Herber had married while young. With a newborn daughter, he returned to school at Wisconsin in February of 1930, but soon flunked out. "The brevity of his stay at Wisconsin was predicted by all who knew anything of his interest in studies," his high school teammate, Miles McMillin, wrote after Herber died of stomach cancer in 1969. McMillin, who became publisher of the *Capital Times* in Madison, also noted that he had "never seen [an athlete] on whom nature had showered so many of its gifts."

Returning to Green Bay, Herber became "a handyman around the Packers clubhouse" and Lambeau eventually signed him. Even then, he was bullied by teammates who called him "Dummy." Lambeau said he put a halt to that by telling his team, "Lay off the `Dummy.' . . . This kid is going to win with us." Curly even went to the extreme of cutting star fullback Bo Molenda because he continued to harass Herber, the *Milwaukee Journal* reported.

Lambeau signed the 5-11, 200-pound Herber on August 9, 1930. A month later, he was starting at quarterback ahead of Dunn in the Packers' only pre-season game, a 46-0 rout on September 14 of the Oshkosh All-Stars. Herber also started Green Bay's first two regular-season games. In the season opener, he threw a 50-yard touchdown as the Packers beat the Chicago Cardinals 14-0. But in their next game, Herber played only sparingly. Dunn regained the quarterback job and stayed there the rest of the season. Herber remained a backup in 1931, when Green Bay won its third straight NFL title.

In 1932, though, with Dunn gone, Lambeau made Herber the Packers' primary passer. He was still only 22 years old. Although regarded as a quarterback historically because he was a passer, Herber actually lined up at right halfback in the trusty Notre Dame Box that Curly had modified after learning it from Knute Rockne.

While the Packers narrowly missed winning their fourth straight NFL championship in 1932, Herber established himself as an offensive force. In the first year where official statistics were kept, Herber led the NFL in virtually every passing category: touchdowns, passing yards, passing yards per game, completions and attempts.

Along with the rest of the Packers, Herber had a frustrating season in 1933, when the bankruptcy-burdened Packers slumped to a 5-7-1 record. Despite the new NFL rule that allowed passing from anywhere behind the line of scrimmage, rather than five yards back, Herber threw 12 interceptions with only three touchdown passes. The previous year, he had thrown nine touchdowns and nine interceptions, according to Pro Football Reference statistics.

In addition, Herber's season ended prematurely on an ominous note. After apparently having too much to drink, he rammed his car into a truck four days before the Packers' final game against the Bears and missed the trip to Chicago. He lost a lot of blood from a gash on his forehead, badly injured his right forearm and dislocated his right hip. "With proper care," Dr. Kelly, the Packers' physician, said, "the halfback might be able to play football again next season."

That proved to be accurate. In 1934, Herber led the NFL in virtually every passing statistic for the second time in three years. But Herber's passing was not enough. After a disappointing 5-7-1 record in 1933, the Packers had gone an unsatisfying 7-6 in 1934. Green Bay did not have enough talent around Herber, especially at receiver. That left the Packers a distant third behind the arch-rival Chicago Bears (13-0) and Detroit Lions (10-3), who had moved from Portsmouth.

Especially troubling, Green Bay lost both meetings with the Bears, 10-6 and 27-14, as Chicago rolled to its unbeaten regular season. In the 1934 championship game, the Bears were a heavy favorite to defeat the Giants in New York. The Bears had led 10-3 at halftime on a slippery field coated with frozen rain. Switching to basketball sneakers that were hastily borrowed from Manhattan College, the Giants had stormed back in the second half to stun the Bears 30-13.

Meanwhile, in Green Bay, a fan base that had enjoyed three straight titles in 1929-31 and a narrow miss in 1932 was growing restless, And pointing fingers at Curly Lambeau.

"Green Bay wolves have started to nip at Curley Lambeau's heels," Oliver Kuechle wrote in the *Milwaukee Journal* on December 2, 1934. "They don't like the way Lambeau has handled the team this fall. They think the Packers should have done more."

Kuechle, a lifelong friend and defender of Lambeau, then gave a patient and detailed explanation—that the Bears, Lions and New York Giants, who had won the East with an 8-5 record, simply had more talent and better depth. And they were the only teams that had finished ahead of Green Bay.

"The Packers stand just about where they belong," Kuechle said. "That more hasn't been done certainly shouldn't be laid at Lambeau's doorstep."

A day later, Lambeau spoke up, saying, "Only one team can be said to have had it over us in the 1934 season—the Chicago Bears." As proof, he pointed to Green Bay splitting its games against the Giants and Lions. Losing two out of three to the Chicago Cardinals was "disappointing. Both [losses], however, were played in mud. As the leading passing club in the league, you can imagine what a muddy field does to spoil our offense."

Saying he planned to add two ends, two guards, a center and two backs, Lambeau said, "If we show as much improvement next year as we did in 1934 over last year, we'll be a contender for the title from the opening whistle to the final gun."

To do that, Lambeau would need more money to pay players. Where would that money come from? In 1934, the Portsmouth Spartans had moved to Detroit, where they became the Lions. The nickname change gave Detroit the football Lions and baseball Tigers, a combination similar to the Bears-Cubs stance Halas had taken in Chicago.

With Portsmouth gone, Green Bay was the smallest city in the NFL, which was following baseball's big-city model. Every other NFL team played in a major-league city—a city with a big-league baseball team and stadium. In another sign of danger for Green Bay, the Packers played two 1934 games in Milwaukee, increasing speculation that they would relocate to Wisconsin's largest city.

But even that brought mixed results. After drawing 11,000 to State Fair Park for an early-season 20-6 win over the New York Giants, Lambeau's team attracted only 3,000 spectators on November 18 to see a 9-0 loss to the Chicago Cardinals, who failed to provide attendance help even though Chicago was as close to Milwaukee as Green Bay.

Once again, Lambeau's original vision of presiding over major-league football in his minor-league-sized hometown seemed to be on the verge of collapse. But once again, his supporters had decided to come to his rescue.

On December 14, 1934, team president Lee Joannes announced another stock sale. "Green Bay is not going to lose the Packers!" the first paragraph of the top story on the front page of the *Press-Gazette* told its readers.

After a rousing speech by Joannes, 25 business and industrial leaders voted to raise $10,000. "You have been invited here tonight to decide whether the Packer football team shall be retained here, or whether you want to throw it overboard," Joannes said, noting that the $5,000 Bent judgment, coupled with the insurance-company bankruptcy, had put the team in a tough but survivable situation. "Green Bay is the smallest town in the NFL, but with careful management and a comparatively low overhead, we have been able to compete with such cities as New York, Chicago, Boston, Philadelphia, Brooklyn and Detroit, and up until a year ago keep going without a deficit," Joannes said. "As a matter of fact over the last twelve years the club has made money, enough to build the City Stadium, which represents a permanent investment of more than $20,000, all paid for by professional football. However, the club did not make any profits this year due to the fact that the team—handicapped by weather, injuries and lack of sufficient first class material—did not make such a good showing and was not as good a drawing card as in previous years."

Jonet, the court-appointed receiver, then laid out the deficit: "The operation of the Packer football team has entered the realm of big business. This year receipts totaled $99,586.01, a sizable sum. Our total disbursements and unpaid bills are $102,992,33."

With $10,000, Joannes said, "We can settle all the claims against the club and once more be in a position to go ahead and give Green Bay a good ball club."

For the Packer president, that amount was literally a small price to pay considering the return the community received. "Do you think it is worthwhile to attempt to do this, or do you want to pass the whole thing up?" he asked his audience. "Personally, in view of the worth of the team to Green Bay as an advertising medium and as an entertainment feature during the fall, I think it would be a crime to let the Packers leave Green Bay without trying to do something about it. I am confident that if we once cleaned up these liabilities and built up our team to the 1929 or 1930 standard we could keep our head above water for many years to come."

Other cities, notably Portsmouth and Pottsville, had tried the community-ownership approach, but had failed to remain solvent because of the crushing weight of the economic depression on their local economies. Anchored by depression-resistant businesses like paper making, cheese distribution and railroad work, Green Bay remained in better shape than many other areas. That meant the community was able to come up with the support the Packers needed to survive.

With the dedicated leadership provided by wholesale grocer/team president Joannes, accountant Jonet, attorney Clifford, newspapermen Calhoun and Turnbull and team physician Kelly, Curly Lambeau was surrounded by men committed to giving him the financial means to keep the team in business. Rescued by the $10,000 fundraising drive, the Packers emerged from their 17 months in receivership with the January 29, 1935, formation of Green Bay Packers Inc.

Signing the Articles of Incorporation that day were attorney Gerald Clifford, team president Joannes and team physician Dr. Kelly, a former team president. Along with *Press-Gazette* publisher Andrew Turnbull, they were a group that Lambeau called " 'the Four Horsemen' of the Packer Corporation," a quartet that refused to let the Green Bay Packers go the way of Canton, Rock Island, Pottsville and so many other small-town pro football franchises.

Lambeau's friend, *Chicago Tribune* sports editor Arch Ward, later would add Curly's name to a group he called "the Hungry Five" in a tribute to their relentless pursuit of finding the dollars to keep football alive in Green Bay. The Packers' rich tradition is filled with nicknames and other evocative words and phrase that give the team's history its legendary feel.

Like George Halas in Chicago, Lambeau was the face and driving force of the team. To the outside world, the Packers belonged to Lambeau just as much as the Bears belonged to Halas. Where they were different was in team finances. Halas handled the money and relentlessly guarded his ownership and control of his team. Lacking an owner's reins, Lambeau was supported by a legion of dedicated men who guided the Packers through their financial ups and downs. Curly's control depended on that support. Without it, Green Bay's football team would not have survived.

Responding to the $10,000 fundraising campaign, businesses and citizens pledged nearly $11,900, team president Joannes announced at the January 29, 1935, meeting. The newly formed Green Bay Packers Inc. called for 600 shares to be issued at $25 a share, or $15,000 if fully subscribed. That fundraising—combined with negotiations in which creditors had agreed to accept $6,700 for claims totaling $12,322—would leave the club with about $3,500 heading into the 1935 season. Joannes called for additional stock purchases to raise that figure to $5,000 and give the team a sound financial base.

In return, Lambeau, the man at the top of the Packer pyramid, provided the football leadership required to again make the team a winner that would inspire Green Bay to support its football team. Lambeau had planted the Packer seed. The people of Green Bay had helped him grow it until the Packers had become an essential part of the city.

Lambeau did not have to wrestle with nearly as many business details as George Halas and the other men who ran NFL teams. That freed him up to do what he did best—find players and coach them into an entertaining championship contender.

Green Bay responded to the threat to its football team's survival, coming up with the money that allowed Lambeau to start restoring the Packers to their glory days in 1935. And Lambeau responded by finding a player who would give Green Bay more championships—and set the stage for the entire NFL to ramp up its glamour and appeal.

# 16
## *THE AGE OF HUTSON*

A list of all the outstanding players that Curly Lambeau found and developed would be lengthy—and filled with exceptional characters who accomplished amazing deeds.

No one would rank higher, though, than Don Hutson. A standout receiver, Hutson was Jerry Rice before Jerry Rice. He revolutionized pass-catching and became a very solid defensive back in the Iron-Man Era. When Hutson retired in 1945, he held 19 NFL records, including virtually every receiving record. Hutson was named to the NFL all-pro team, which had only 11 members in an era where players played on both offense and defense, nine times in his 11 seasons. In 1941 and 1942, he was named the league's Most Valuable Player, a stunning achievement for a receiver. Hutson also would have been the 1943 MVP if one more voter had put him first and Sid Luckman second, instead of the other way around.

Hutson excelled with brilliant speed, which he used cleverly, and deceptive route-running. Although he was from Pine Bluff, Arkansas, Hutson was known as the Alabama Antelope, a tribute to the fame he reached while playing in college for Alabama's Crimson Tide.

As a Green Bay Packer, Hutson continued to excel, dominating football games in a way that no pass-catcher had done before him. In the many decades since he retired in 1945, few receivers have approached his impact.

In a 1944 article for *Collier's Magazine* entitled "The Wizard of Green Bay," Arthur Daley, who was the sports columnist at the *New York Times* for 32 years, spared no hyperbole in describing Lambeau's greatest player.

"I just concede him two touchdowns a game, and hope our boys can score more." George Halas told Daley, no doubt recalling a game in which Hutson caught two touchdowns in the final 2½ minutes to beat the Bears 17-14 during his rookie season.

"Although he is a 190-pound six-footer," Daley said, "Don gives the impression of frailty. He wears practically no padding and looks like a little boy when he gets out on the field with the hulking brutes who man the line. But that is only his first deception. His second is speed."

No question, Hutson was exceptionally fast. Daley credited him with covering 100 yards "in 9.6 seconds or thereabouts. . . not too far away from world-record time," to win the Southeastern Conference championship. Prominent NFL writer Peter King told the *Green Bay Press-Gazette* in 1994 that Hutson's time had been 9.5 seconds, and that he had done that between innings of an Alabama baseball game.

Packer historian Cliff Christl's research showed, however, that Hutson finished fourth at the meet, which was won by a Tulane runner with a time of 9.8 seconds. Hutson never won an SEC event, Christl said, but finished second in the 220-yard dash as a senior.

As with so many tales from the Packers' past, the story was embellished over time. But it does not diminish the fact that Hutson was exceptionally fast. That speed, in combination with his pioneering route-running style, made him a receiver who set a new standard in the NFL.

Daley also used a description that would now be considered appallingly racist, but is notable because, coming from a prominent *New York Times* writer, it gives an idea of how different America was in 1944.

"As he runs, he looks like the laziest white child ever produced by the State of Alabama," Daley wrote. "He shuffles along with less effort and far less concern than a commuter dashing for the 5:15. Finally he seems to attain his maximum rate of speed. . . . Hutson [also] is a master of the dead pan and an artist of the feint. Never does his expression change as he's about to catch a pass. His arms suddenly go up and he has the ball. And when he feints—mammy!"

Another Bunyan-esque tale of Hutson's brilliant speed came from his 1930s teammate, Clarke Hinkle, who said he saw Hutson "literally fake Beattie Feathers of the Bears out of his shoes. They had to call a timeout so he could put them back on."

But first, of course, Lambeau had to find and sign Hutson, the receiver who would take NFL passing to dazzling heights, winning games for Green Bay and changing the way the pro game was played. And the way the Alabama Antelope became a Green Bay Packer was another story where separating the myth from the fact is not easily done.

\* \* \* \* \* \* \* \*

While Packer backers were bustling about in wintry Green Bay in December of 1934, trying to reach their goal of raising 10,000 franchise-saving dollars, Curly Lambeau was in California, which became his turf when Green Bay started to freeze over. Frequently seen with Hollywood starlets, Lambeau no doubt was enjoying himself. Divorced from Marguerite the previous May, Lambeau might have been enjoying life with Susan Johnson/Billie John Copeland, whom he would marry in June. Or given his wandering eye, he might have been busier.

"Like the sailors, he had a lady in every place that the Green Bay Packers played football," said Lyla Hoyt, the daughter-in-law of the woman who would become Lambeau's third wife. On postseason scouting trips, Lambeau had even more time to relax.

One thing was certain. He was mixing pleasure with important business—scouting for the next crop of Packers. Lambeau tended to spend most of his time at the East-West Shrine all-star game in San Francisco, which had more pro prospects. But he also kept an eye on the Rose Bowl, which was close to Hollywood nightlife.

At that time, college football towered over pro football in popularity. And the Rose Bowl, by far college football's biggest event, was the Super Bowl in those days. A second post-season bowl, the fledging Sugar Bowl, would debut on January 1, 1935, the same day Hutson rocked the Rose Bowl. But in the world of team sports, only the World Series was bigger than the Rose Bowl, which surpassed even the World Series as the biggest single-day sporting event. A record crowd had bought more than 84,000 tickets to see Hutson, one of Alabama's three All-Americans, face Stanford, which also had three All-Americans. In an era before platooning, the game featured six of the nation's 11 consensus All-Americans.

It was a dream matchup, one of the most anticipated and memorable games of that era. Stanford (9-0-1) had allowed only two touchdowns all season. Alabama had cruised to a 9-0 record to earn its fourth trip to Pasadena in 10 years. It was a time before the Deep South became known for outstanding college football. The Crimson Tide was changing that—especially with its Rose Bowl appearances. A relatively small school, Alabama had become a southern version of Notre Dame, a team that would travel far and wide, and beat top opponents despite featuring under-sized players.

Hired by Alabama in part for his Notre Dame connection, Tide coach Frank Thomas had played quarterback for Knute Rockne, who reportedly had called Thomas the smartest player he had ever coached. Alabama president Mike Denny wanted a coach "with knowledge of the

Knute Rockne system to turn the Crimson Tide into the Fighting Irish of the South," Bear Bryant biographer Allen Barra wrote.

Thomas, who arrived at Notre Dame shortly after Lambeau, was among the many members of Curly's Irish scouting network. That connection gave Lambeau the leeway to concentrate on the East-West game, and rely on Thomas' recommendations for the two Pasadena participants.

A few games into his senior season at Notre Dame in 1922, Thomas had lost the starting quarterback job to Harry Stuhldreher, who joined fellow sophomores Jim Crowley, Don Miller and Elmer Layden to form the Four Horsemen of Notre Dame, one of the most celebrated nicknames in football. At the 1935 Rose Bowl, Alabama was achieving its goal of Notre-Dame-like publicity. Its practices were attracting so much media attention that assistant coach Hank Crisp, angry that his receivers could not run their pass routes, offered a $2 bounty to the first receiver who knocked down a sportswriter. In that competition, Hutson, a lean and swift end, was no match for Alabama's other end, the aggressive and sturdily-built Paul "Bear" Bryant, who also happened to be Hutson's close friend. Ends had not yet been broken into subsets, but Hutson basically was a wide receiver and Bryant a tight end.

While both were from Arkansas, Hutson and Bryant were different in many ways—as different as their nicknames. Hutson, the Alabama Antelope, was known for his speed and grace. Bryant had gotten his nickname for wrestling a bear when he was barely a teenager, lured by the promise of a dollar for every minute he could stay in the ring with the bear.

Bryant, who had grown up dirt-poor, used his size, strength and feisty approach throughout his playing career. Relentless in his attention to detail, he would become a successor to Rockne as the greatest college football coach of his era, winning six national championships between 1961 and 1979.

Hutson, who had enjoyed a comfortable childhood, combined his exceptional speed with shrewd route-running and remarkable hands to become a great football player. Off the field, he was a gifted businessman who opened a popular bar/bowling alley in Green Bay and later became a very successful Wisconsin car dealer. Bryant, who probably would have been a low-paid journeyman in the NFL, opted immediately for coaching. Hutson, meanwhile, was a sought-after commodity, especially to a coach with vision like Curly Lambeau.

Although very different in personality and career paths, Hutson and Bryant remained close lifelong friends. Many years later, Bryant told his Alabama quarterback Scott Hunter, who became a Packer, a story about visiting Hutson in Green Bay, most likely in the fall of 1936.

On his way back to Alabama, Bryant said he had hitched a ride with Lambeau, who was going to Chicago to do a radio show with George Halas. Coming out of Milwaukee, a young state trooper stopped Lambeau for speeding. When Curly tried to bribe him with a $10 bill, the trooper started to arrest him and a scuffle broke out between the two. Two Milwaukee police officers arrived and convinced the trooper to let Lambeau go.

"Coach Bryant said Lambeau's expensive suit and silk tie were all askew and it was a funny sight," Hunter said in an interview years later.

In a sign of how football changed over the years, Bryant, perhaps recalling the Lambeau incident, devised a way in which he never had to worry about speeding. When he had become a coaching legend at Alabama, he would put his signature houndstooth hat on the back window. That alone stopped ticket-writing troopers in their tracks. "The affection of Alabama state troopers for Bryant bordered on the mystical," Bryant biographer Allen Barra wrote.

Expert opinions of the 1935 Rose Bowl seemed to favor the Crimson Tide against Stanford, but only slightly in an era where teams from different parts of the country were difficult to compare.

Under sunny skies and basking in temperatures in the 70s, a crowd of 84,474 watched as Stanford took an early 7-0 lead after an Alabama fumble. From there, though, the Crimson Tide erupted, notching three touchdowns and a field goal in the second quarter for a 22-7 halftime lead. Alabama went on to win 29-13.

Hutson caught touchdown passes of 54 and 59 yards. Tide quarterback Dixie Howell—who ran for 111 yards, passed for 164 yards passing and punted six times for an average of almost 44 yards—was named the game's Most Valuable Player.

Lambeau was in San Francisco on New Year's Day, watching the West beat the East 19-13 before a crowd of 65,000 at Kezar Stadium. But he gave a rundown of Alabama's pro prospects in a telegram he sent back to the *Press-Gazette* in Green Bay on January 2.

"I talked to Frank Thomas, coach of the Alabama team, over the telephone after his team whipped Stanford yesterday," Lambeau reported, "and he says that he has three good prospects for professional football.

They are [Bill] Lee at tackle, Hutson, an end, and [Charles] Marr, a guard." Marr and Hutson had been high school teammates in Pine Bluff, Arkansas. In a subsequent report, Lambeau explained that Howell, "although a good passer, is not considered a good prospect for the professional ranks, because of his size and lack of weight." Howell, who was listed at 5-foot-10, 164 pounds, played briefly for the Washington Redskins, but concentrated mainly on coaching, and wound up as head coach at Arizona State and Idaho.

As Hutson became one of the NFL's most glamorous players, the always inventive, always accommodating Lambeau came up with more and more fantastic yarns about his Alabama Antelope. And Hutson not only played along; he added to the hyperbole.

Lambeau, as a coach who also was sending information to the *Press-Gazette,* easily could have been admitted to Alabama's practices, which were open to sportswriters. But Hutson made it sound special, saying, "Thomas would let him in [to practice] because they were old friends."

With the Rose Bowl kicking off in Pasadena at 2:15, fifteen minutes after the East-West started in San Francisco, Lambeau, who was at the East-West game, did not claim he saw Hutson shred Stanford's pass defense. And Lambeau's telegrams back to the *Press-Gazette* from San Francisco indicate that it would have been impossible for him to even see Hutson practice in Los Angeles before the Rose Bowl.

But that didn't stop them from spinning interesting fables for sportswriters as Hutson become the NFL's biggest star. Both men handed down dubious tales to illustrate Lambeau's determination.

"Finding the gates locked" when he went to practice one day, "Lambeau climbed the fence and tore his new suit," Glenn Swain wrote in his history of the Packers-Bears rivalry. "Police then tried to eject Lambeau but a Notre Dame alumnus intervened. . . . `When I saw [Hutson] cut. . . I knew I had to have him. I hadn't seen anybody cut like that since Grange. . . . That's why I broke my neck to get him.' "

The imagery demonstrates the importance of Hutson: Former menswear salesman Curly, a dedicated clothes horse, ruining a fancy suit scrambling over a fence to check out Hutson. The only problem is, Lambeau was in San Francisco when Hutson was practicing in Los Angeles. It has all the trappings of another fictional anecdote concocted by

Lambeau and repeated eagerly by sportswriters who liked entertaining yarns..

How Hutson wound up in Green Bay is another one of those fable-like turning points in Lambeau's 30-year Packer reign, one of the many stories that make Packer lore so dramatic and irresistible. There may be plenty of fiction mixed in with the facts. But they certainly are very entertaining tales.

Skeptics wondered if Hutson's lean frame would be sturdy enough to hold up playing both ways, which was then mandatory in the physical NFL. But after Hutson's spectacular Rose Bowl performance, he was on the radar of many teams. That was a great situation for Hutson. Having conveniently finished his Alabama career one year before the NFL draft began, he said, "I was the equivalent of a free agent." The bidding war for Hutson fresh in their minds, NFL owners would soon adopt a player draft.

Even before Hutson grabbed the spotlight in Pasadena, Brooklyn Dodgers co-owner Shipwreck Kelly had visited Tuscaloosa. "I promised him I'd sign with Brooklyn if he matched any offer I got from another team," Hutson said. "When I got back from the Rose Bowl, I began hearing from all the teams." As the bidding went up, it came down to the Dodgers and the Packers. "Each time Curly would make an offer, I'd wire Shipwreck and he would match it."

When Lambeau's offer reached $300 a game, Hutson said, Kelly did not reply. After about a week, Hutson signed the contract Lambeau had sent. Right after he put it in the mail, Kelly resurfaced, saying he had been on vacation in Florida. Kelly told Hutson, "Sign a contract with me, too, and let me worry about it."

Both contracts supposedly arrived at the Columbus, Ohio, office of NFL president Joe F. Carr on the same morning. The 8:30 a.m. postmark on Lambeau's package was 17 minutes earlier than Kelly's 8:47 postmark. "Carr decided that the only fair method of settling this issue was to award Hutson to the team that had mailed their contract first," Carr biographer Chris Willis wrote.

That's the story that has been handed down. It's a great piece of Packer lore, but far more fiction than fact. It might have stemmed from Hutson's Alabama teammate, All-America tackle Bill Lee, who signed with Lambeau after he had signed with Kelly's Brooklyn team. In his third season in Brooklyn, Lee was acquired by Lambeau in a trade and played for Green Bay in parts of seven seasons.

There is no evidence that Hutson signed two contracts, but he and Lambeau seemed to enjoy telling the story. The more they told it, the higher the salary amounts seemed to go—and the more true it all seemed.

"Unfortunately, through the lens of history, Lambeau's account of Hutson's signing, like so many others propagated by him, was nothing more than a ragbag of tall tales, half-truths and outright lies," Packer historian Cliff Christl concluded.

Fact or fiction, it is fitting that Hutson, one of the greatest players to wear a Packer jersey, wound up in Green Bay. And Lambeau's ability to identify and acquire Hutson, who was a key reason Curly added three more championships, shows why Lambeau, for all of his quirks, was an exceptional NFL leader who could coach, motivate and recruit.

As it turned out, Hutson said, "It was probably the biggest break I ever got in football. The reason is that Brooklyn was a grind-it-out team. . . but at Green Bay, they had a real good passer in Arnie Herber, and Lambeau was a very pass-oriented coach. . . . it was obviously a real break for me to end up there."

That's an understatement. Then again, if Hutson had gone to Brooklyn, either the Dodgers might have built a passing game around him —or traded him to a team that would have known how to take advantage of Hutson's skills. To this day, Hutson and Jerry Rice remain the most dominant receivers in NFL history.

The only pass-catcher to win back-to-back league MVP honors, Hutson revolutionized the passing game the way Babe Ruth opened up the home run as a game-changing weapon. Like Ruth, Hutson not only led his league. He lapped the field, going far beyond any other receiver of the NFL's first 25 years. And he did it with a style that, *Time Magazine* said, "began to take on the glamour of baseball's Babe Ruth."

In another indicator that Lambeau knew how much Hutson would elevate his team, the Packers coach said he came up with an elaborate subterfuge to conceal Hutson's salary. It makes a great statement about Hutson's worth—and Lambeau's dedication to keeping his payroll low. George Halas, by the way, also resorted to chicanery that left his players earning fewer dollars. So did many other NFL money managers in those days.

The problem—or fun part, depending on your point of view—with the Hutson gambit is that, through the years, Hutson changed the amount he was paid in this legendary tale. Like Curly, he apparently saw no harm in a little hyperbole if it made a better story.

In the 1970 oral history, *The Game That Was*, Hutson told interviewer Myron Cope, "I was making $175, so every week I would get two checks, one for $100 and the other for $75." That jibes with Hutson's NFL personnel file, which indicates that he received $175 a game.

However, in perhaps the best remembered version—the one that most Packer chroniclers handed down, Hutson told Richard Whittingham in the 1984 oral history, *What a Game They Played*: "When I got to Green Bay, Curly told me he didn't want the other players or anybody to else for that matter to know how much I was earning. Well, there were two banks in Green Bay in those years and the Packers had an account in each. So, to keep it a secret, I got two checks after each game, $150 each, and each was drawn on a different bank up there."

Hutson actually signed with Green Bay for $175 a game, not $300, on February 19, 1935, his personnel file at the NFL office shows.

With Hutson was receiving two checks, Lambeau could pull out a Hutson pay stub when negotiating with other players. In an era before agents, where a player went back-and-forth with a Lambeau or a Halas, pulling out the contract showing that a team's superstar was making $75 or $100 rather than $175 was a very effective way to keep player salaries low.

The plan had a drawback, though for Hutson. He didn't necessarily know what his teammates were paid, either. In 1939, for example, second-year passer Cecil Isbell was paid $7,100, while Hutson's salary was $5,075. Isbell was one of the NFL's best passers from the moment he arrived in Green Bay from Purdue. So it's possible that while Hutson was deceiving his teammates, Lambeau was misleading the NFL's premier receiver.

\* \* \* \* \* \* \* \*

It is no coincidence that while Lambeau was maneuvering to add Hutson, a group he called " 'the Four Horsemen' of the Packer Corporation" was putting the football team back on firm financial ground. Hutson was signed a month after the club, rescued by the $10,000 fundraising drive, emerged from its 17 months in receivership with the January 25, 1935, formation of Green Bay Packers Inc.

Signing the Articles of Incorporation that day were attorney Gerald Clifford, team president Joannes and team physician Dr. Kelly, a former team president. *Press-Gazette* publisher Andrew Turnbull was also among Lambeau's Four Horsemen of Green Bay. With the addition of Lambeau himself, that group would acquire the nickname of the Hungry Five, a tribute to their relentless pursuit of finding the dollars to keep a football team in Green Bay. The Packers' rich tradition is filled with nicknames and other evocative words that give the team's history its legendary feel.

The nicknames are well deserved. Thanks to the dedication of men like Joannes, Clifford, Kelly and Turnbull, after two shaky restricted-payroll seasons in 1933 and 1934, Curly Lambeau again had the tools to put together a top-notch NFL contender.

# 17
## *OUT OF BANKRUPTCY, INTO WINNING*

Many stars were aligning for Curly Lambeau in 1935. The year began with him reeling in Don Hutson. On June 26, he married Susan Johnson/Billie John Copeland, the former Miss California he had met on the voyage to Hawaii after the 1932 season, in a civil ceremony in Waukegan, Illinois.

And then, freed from severe budget constraints by the fundraising drive that brought the Packers new financial stability, Lambeau went about adding other players who would help Green Bay compete in the NFL's challenging Western Division.

Lambeau also put the Packers in Green and Gold in 1935 for the first time. A sharp dresser and accomplished menswear salesman, Lambeau designed the uniforms himself. Their jerseys were kelly green, accented by old gold numbers and sleeves, and old-gold pants with green socks. Previously, Green Bay uniforms had featured the navy and gold of Lambeau's college team, Notre Dame. Lambeau would bring back the navy-and-gold combination in 1937.

The Packers' new financial stability also enabled Lambeau to take the Packers to their first out-of-town training camp. In 1935, he moved preseason workouts 135 miles northwest of Green Bay to Pinewood Lodge on Lake Thompson, near Rhinelander, Wisconsin. Twice a day, they rode a bus into town to practice on a high-school field.

Curly's idea, of course, was that his players would be completely focused on football and healthy North Woods pursuits like fishing and taking chilly dips in Lake Thompson. "The setup is ideal for training purposes, as there's nothing the Packers can do which isn't good for them," the *Press-Gazette* reported on August 26. "Equipment for playing shuffleboard, horseshoes, croquet and other resort sports is available, there are boats and canoes, and several varieties of diving standards for those inclined toward aquatic activities."

What this training camp lacked—carousing—didn't seem to bother the Packers, who arrived in camp August 24 and stayed only one week. Whether there was contraband beer and whisky stashed somewhere is not known. But it wouldn't be surprising.

Green Bay then played four exhibition games in nine days against nearby local teams. The Packers were paid modest guarantees, typically $300. And the local squads borrowed players to give the Packers their best shot. Which Lambeau appreciated.

On Saturday, August 31, Curly took his team to Merrill, Wisconsin, for a game against the Merrill Foxes. Two nights later, Green Bay played the Chippewa Falls Marines in Chippewa Falls. They played again on Wednesday night in Stevens Point before wrapping up their pre-season slate in Green Bay against the La Crosse Old Style Lagers on Sunday, September 8.

Although Hutson topped the list of Green Bay newcomers for 1935, he missed most of the Packers' training camp. He was playing for the College All-Stars, who faced the NFL champion Chicago Bears at Soldier Field on August 29. The game, which annually gave pro football a needed spotlight, drew a crowd of 77,450, more spectators than the 73,100 Green Bay would draw for its seven regular-season home games.

On a rainy night in Chicago, Hutson put the All-Stars, who trailed 3-0 in the fourth quarter, in position for a game-winning touchdown on an endaround. That 17-yard gain gave the collegians a first-and-goal at the 8 yard line. But the drive stalled there. On fourth down from the 16, Hutson tried another endaround but was stopped again at the 8. A late safety gave the Bears a 5-0 victory.

Lambeau also added a pair of collegiate linemen for the 1935 season. In mid-February, he announced the signing of Buster Maddox, from Kansas State, and Ernie Smith, from USC, two All-Americans who were expected to shore up the left-tackle spot. Maddox made only a token contribution. Smith played four years, earning all-pro honors in his second season.

For his most important additions, though, Lambeau brought back two Packer legends, Johnny Blood and Cal Hubbard. Bulked-up financially by the stock sale, Lambeau could bolster his roster.

Blood had been cut by Lambeau in December of 1933, when he showed up for practice so hung over, or perhaps still drunk, that he whiffed on a punt, falling in a heap to the ground. Lambeau had reclaimed Blood, and then—still hamstrung by receivership—sold him to Pittsburgh to make a few dollars.

Hampered by injuries, Blood had played sparingly in 1934 for the Pirates, who would become the Steelers in a 1940 renaming contest. Before the 1935 season started, Blood had talked Pirates owner Art Rooney into releasing him so he could try to return to the Packers.

Showing his usual flair for drama, Blood made his comeback playing *against* the Packers in two Wisconsin towns known for brewing beer. Playing in the hometown of the Leinenkugel brewery with the Chippewa Falls Marines on September 2, Blood "was much in the limelight." Trying to impress Lambeau, Blood quarterbacked Chippewa Falls, which trailed by only 3-0 at the half before losing 22-0. Shaking off a couple of early fumbles, Blood made a 31-yard run in the second half. Six days later, Blood was in the backfield of the La Crosse Old Style Lagers, who were routed 49-0 by the Packers in Green Bay on Sunday, September 8.

The next day, Lambeau relented and let Blood rejoin the Packers, who were preparing to open their NFL season on September 15 against the Chicago Cardinals. Beyond showing that he still could play, Blood was aided by a spate of injuries in the Green Bay backfield. And Lambeau had more payroll leeway thanks to the Packers' latest stock sale.

Cal Hubbard, who had been an assistant coach at Texas A&M in 1934 despite being an all-NFL standout at Green Bay the previous three years, rejoined the team in mid-September after finishing his season as an International League umpire.

"Cal Hubbard, 265 pounds of beef whose absence left a gaping hole in the Green Bay Packer line of 1934, was back in uniform today," the *Press-Gazette* reported on September 12, three days before the Packers' opening game against the Chicago Cardinals. "Hubbard arrived late yesterday in time to attend a chicken dinner given for the squad by the directors" at the Beaumont Hotel.

Even with Blood and Hubbard back, the Packers came up short, 7-6, in their season opener against the Cardinals. Due to lingering injuries, passer Arnie Herber and running backs Clarke Hinkle, George Sauer and Roger Grove made only token appearances.

Always positive, the *Green Bay Press-Gazette* headline on the game said, "Packers Hold Cardinal Team to One-Point Win," explaining that "The Packers were terribly handicapped by the absence of several of their best blocking and running backs." The *Press-Gazette* described Johnny Blood as "a very active performer." But not active enough to overcome the Packers' long injured list.

Hutson, who was under the radar after spending most of the preseason with the College All-Star team, had an inauspicious NFL debut in the second quarter against the Cardinals, with no catches and one rush for no gain. With Herber, who was intercepted on his lone attempt, "scarcely able to stand" due to injury, throwing a deep pass to Hutson was not an option.

The next week, though, when the Bears came to Green Bay, Lambeau, aided by a healthier Herber, knew exactly how to make the most of his new offensive weapon.

Hutson's debut sounds like one of those embellished fables that Lambeau loved to embrace. Except that in this case, it was a true tale of Packer glory.

After the Bears kicked off, the Packers started at their own 17 yardline. On the second play of the game, Lambeau had Johnny Blood line up on one side and Hutson on the other.

When a streaking Blood attracted the attention of the Bears defense, Hutson also took off. Herber dropped back to the 4 yardline. Using one of the best long-distance arms of the NFL's early days, Herber launched "a bullet-like forward pass [that] exploded from [his] hand." A streaking Hutson reeled in an 83-yard bomb for a touchdown.

"Thirteen thousand fans, overtaxing the small high school stadium, had hardly settled back from seeing Arnie Herber return the opening kickoff 17 yards," Lambeau's friend, George Strickler, wrote in the *Chicago Tribune* the next day. "Blame for the defeat will rest largely with [Beattie] Feathers, regarded as one of the fastest men in the league. Standing in midfield he waited for Hutson to race up to him and allowed the end, the fastest man on the squad of 43 All-American college men [at the College All-Star game] last month, to get past him."

The rest of the game reverted to a typical early-days NFL quagmire. With no further scoring, Green Bay won 7-0 on Hutson's dramatic first catch, the first touchdown of his magical career.

That was it. On the first play from scrimmage against the arch-rival Bears, Don Hutson caught an 83-yard touchdown pass for the only score of the game. That was the first of 488 catches for 7,991 yards, the first of 99 touchdown receptions, in his storied 11-year career.

Hutson continued to torment the Bears on October 27, in his first trip to Chicago. In another stranger-than fiction performance, Hutson and the Packers trailed the Bears 14-3 with 2½ minutes left. Many of the 29,386 spectators had already started heading out of Wrigley Field. But Hutson and Herber connected on a 69-yard touchdown. They then combined on a four-yard scoring pass after Green Bay recovered a Bears fumble to notch a dramatic 17-14 win.

Hutson wound up with six touchdown catches in 1935, his first NFL season, tied for the league lead in an era where running was still the main tool of NFL offenses. Although he had only 18 catches while playing in nine games, his 46.7 receiving yards per game topped the league.

No player would prove to be more important in Curly Lambeau's 31-year career than Don Hutson. Cases can be made for other Packers, notably Verne Lewellen and Clarke Hinkle. Lewellen excelled at punting in an era where punting was critical. And Hinkle was a standout fullback/linebacker. But Hutson gave Green Bay offensive separation—and his glamorous contribution helped sell professional football when it needed selling.

The arrival of Hutson in Green Bay marked the beginning of a new resurgence for the Packers. With Lambeau taking full advantage of Hutson's ability, the team would add more championships. Green Bay would find relative economic stability. And a maturing NFL would tweak its game to make it more attractive—and distinctive.

College football still ruled. Pro football still faced a struggle for survival. The fact that the College All-Star game attracted more fans (77,450) than the Packers drew in their seven home games (73,100) made that point. But the NFL, bolstered by the electrifying receiver that Lambeau had unleashed, was making progress.

The Western Division race was a tight one in 1935. All four teams—the Lions, Packers, Bears and Cardinals—all would wind up within a game of each other. Despite winning two of three meetings with the Lions, who finished 7-3-2, and winning more games, the Packers (8-4) finished second under the old rule in which ties were thrown out. Under the modern calculation, Green Bay would have tied Detroit for the West.

But the Detroit-Green Bay rivalry set up an opportunity for the two teams to help themselves to another good payday after the 1935 season. Combining his dedication to wintering on the West Coast with his football business, Lambeau scheduled a pair of attractive barnstorming games in California.

On January 19, 1936, more than 20,000 saw Green Bay register a 24-14 win at Kezar Stadium in San Francisco over "the Coast All-Stars," a team organized by Chicago Cardinals player/coach Milan Creighton.

In the Packers' main West Coast event, more than 20,000 filled Gilmore Stadium in Los Angeles a week later for their fourth meeting with the Lions. Even though it was merely an exhibition, Lambeau and Detroit coach Potsy Clark hyped the game by sparring verbally.

"Those paunchy Packers got two decisions over us as a result of breaks," Clark said, blaming some sand that the Packers used at City Field to bog down Detroit runners for one of the losses. "The Lions are the National champions and they'll prove it Sunday."

"My team," Lambeau replied, "beat them twice, and can do it again. The Lions are a good team, but the Packers are better."

Exhibition or not, Detroit validated its NFL title in the fourth meeting, beating Green Bay 10-3 on January 26 on an 84-yard touchdown run by Ace Gutowski.

All things considered, the 1935 season was very promising for the Packers. They had won more games than the NFL champion Lions. They had learned to take advantage of their new offensive weapon, game-altering rookie receiver Don Hutson. Using a new infusion of community funds, they had emerged from receivership and were on sound financial ground.

The Packers were positioned to reach new heights. Curly Lambeau was already calculating exactly how to do that.

# 18
## *SINGING THAT TITLE TUNE AGAIN*

When Hutson arrived in Green Bay in 1935, Lambeau had assembled the greatest passing attack in the early decades of the NFL, with Herber throwing to Hutson and Johnny Blood. The NFL conveniently had gone to a slimmer, easier-to-throw football. More passing meant more passing, more scoring and more fans.

The Herber Legend is rich with details. Although built like Curly with a muscled but agile body, Herber had an unusual throwing style. "Herber had a peculiar way of holding the ball," biographer Don Smith noted. "Handicapped by short fingers, he put his thumb over the laces to prevent the ball from wobbling and to assure plenty of spiraling action. Arnie's passes quickly became noted for two qualities: distance and accuracy."

In 1936, after coming up short the previous four seasons, Lambeau had Green Bay focused on a fourth NFL title. That bubble seemed to burst quickly, however. In the Packers' second game, the Chicago Bears smacked them 30-3 on September 20 before a record crowd of 14,312 at City Stadium.

"Get the wrapping paper ready to go," Irv Kupcinet told *Chicago Times* readers the next day. If the Bears keep that up, he said. "you can wrap up that National Football League championship and deliver [it] to Mr. George Halas."

Mr. Curly Lambeau wasn't conceding anything though. "Despite our defeat at the hands of the Bears, we will win a lot of ballgames this year. The one-sided win by the Bears may have been a good thing for us. . . . Over-confidence is always followed by off-color play."

From that setback, Green Bay did not lose another game. Reeling off nine straight wins, Green Bay finished 10-1-1, beating the Bears (9-3) to win the Western Division.

That put Green Bay in the 1936 NFL championship game, the first official playoff game in Packer history. It was the Eastern Division winner's turn to host the title game, which alternated each season. But Boston Redskins owner George Preston Marshall, frustrated by the lack of support from Boston fans and media, asked permission to move the game to New York's Polo Grounds, and NFL president Joe Carr agreed. For the next season, Marshall would transfer the Redskins to Washington, where he owned a large laundry business.

Before a New York crowd that was more curious than partisan, Arnie Herber delivered on Lambeau's prediction that his homegrown passer would be a winner. Faking a handoff to Clarke Hinkle, Herber threw a 48-yard touchdown to Hutson for Green Bay's first touchdown.

Leading 7-6 in the third quarter, Herber completed a long pass to Johnny Blood that put the Packers inside the Redskins 10 yardline. He then threw an eight-yard touchdown to his other accomplished receiver, Milt Gantenbein, who gave Green Bay a tight-end-like presence.

Green Bay then added a late rushing touchdown to seal a 21-6 victory, giving Lambeau his fourth NFL championship in Green Bay's 16 years in the league.

On the day before the championship game, Lambeau took time out to participate in the second NFL draft. Drafting last because Green Bay had the best record in the nine-team league, Lambeau selected Ed Jankowski, a University of Wisconsin fullback and Milwaukee native. Jankowski played in Green Bay for five years. The other notable among the Packers' 11 picks was Minnesota quarterback Bud Wilkinson. Lambeau's third-round pick, Wilkinson passed on the NFL, and went into coaching. In the 1950s, he led Oklahoma to three national championships and a 47-game winning streak.

With his fourth NFL championship, Curly Lambeau solidified his position as a premier football coach and leader. George Halas was the only other man in that discussion. At that point, Halas had won three NFL titles (in 1921, 1932 and 1933). As the Bears owner and a driven businessman, Halas had found a path to keeping his team successful financially and competitively in the midst of a depression that threatened a sport that had been struggling to find stability even before the economic downturn. But if the NFL had a public face for its most successful team builder, it was the flamboyant Lambeau. Halas was skilled at cultivating media attention; Lambeau was a magnet for it.

"Curly himself became the best-known figure in football," biographer Stuart Stotts wrote. "Curly was featured on magazine covers and in sports articles. Although no longer a player, he was in great shape. He was always confident and self-assured. He loved to talk with reporters.... Curly Lambeau was always interesting to watch at a game. He strutted up and down the sidelines, shouting, cursing and gesturing... He enjoyed the attention that came from winning."

Lambeau's short temper and fierce competitiveness sometimes made his sideline routine as dramatic as the game he was coaching.

" 'Why do I get so excited?' a player once asked the Bombastic Belgian. 'I think better when I get excited,' " Lambeau explained in *Pro Football's Hall of Fame*, a set of profiles of the inaugural set of Hall of Fame inductees written by *New York Times* writer Arthur Daley.

And yet, the complex Lambeau was a strange combination of personality traits. While adored by women as well as newspapermen, his own players never found him to their liking.

"I don't think Curly Lambeau had a friend in the world as far as football players were concerned. Yet all of them respected him as they respect Lombardi," Clarke Hinkle, a standout Packer in the 1930s, said after Vince Lombardi had restored Green Bay to glory.

As an example, Daley, the *New York Times'* authority on pro football, described the snarling reaction when Lambeau told four players who had missed practice that they were fined $500. "Write out the checks," Lambeau told the players, Daley reported, adding that Lambeau "even read their minds," telling the players that he intended to cash the checks before they could stop payment.

"If you cash my check, I'll kill you," replied a player that Daley described as a "mastodonic lineman." The most logical Packer answering that description would be Cal Hubbard, a giant who rarely minced words, especially when it came to his dislike of Lambeau.

"It won't do you any good," said Curly. "It would merely cost you another $500."

That particular story is the kind of playful hyperbole that athletes and sportswriters engaged in during that era. It was good publicity for the athletes, good copy for sportswriters and entertaining for readers. It didn't hold up under the harsh light of "true story." But this type of anecdote did give insight into Lambeau's many clashes with his players.

Another unconfirmed, perhaps-apocryphal tale from Daley's profile described Lambeau's last appearance as a player. According to Daley, Lambeau, furious at the Packers' passing ineptitude, put himself into the game, saying, "I'll show you fellows how to throw passes."

Hubbard, according to Daley, "offered a happy solution" to his teammates, instructing them to "open the gates on Curly." When the ball was snapped to Lambeau, the "Packer blockers all stepped aside and admitted a swarm of enemy tacklers. They virtually hammered Lambeau underground. Curly... cast a reproachful glance at his grinning hired hands and limped to the sidelines. He never played again."

Daley said the incident took place in 1930. Lambeau's last appearance in an NFL game was in 1929, when he only played in one game. It's possible that it happened in practice, even though that neither jibes with Daley's account nor makes the story nearly as dramatic.

Wanting to see The Man Who Invented the Green Bay Packers play football for one last time, the crowd at the Packers' final 1929 home game had chanted for him during a 24-0 rout of the Minneapolis Redjackets on October 20. The 31-year-old Lambeau had declined, saying afterward that he already had used 18 players, the NFL limit for games.

Lambeau's last documented appearance as a player in an NFL game came a month later, on November 17, 1929, in the Packers' 12-0 win over the Chicago Cardinals at Comiskey Park. A crowd of 15,000, the Cardinals' largest home crowd since 1925, turned out, the *Chicago Tribune* reported.

Lambeau entered the game in the second quarter, when he came in for Herdis McCrary at right halfback, which was often the passing position in Lambeau's version of the Notre Dame Box. McCrary had been sidelined by a pulled leg muscle.

"Curly got into the game for the first time this season," the *Press-Gazette* reported. "Lambeau did some excellent passing, but was forced to retire when he cracked a rib blocking a Cardinal man out of a play. It was like old-times to see Curly heaving the ball. He threw one pass of 50 yards to [Tom] Nash, but it slipped out of the end's hands... Lambeau can still pass with the best of them, and that includes Benny Friedman of the New York Giants."

That was the last time that Curly played in a regular-season game. And it seems to have been an emergency situation rather than a teaching moment. Then again, Lambeau was injured on his last NFL play. Whether that was the play in which his players allowed him to get clobbered, it seems very likely that they did abandon him, as Daley wrote, somewhere at the end of his playing career.

But Lambeau's players also appreciated playing for The Man Who Invented the Green Bay Packers. If he got under their skin with his mercurial ways, he also put together a roster of winning talent and pushed it hard to win. If Lambeau pinched pennies on salaries, every NFL team did in the 1930s. And Lambeau at least extended his love of the finer things in life to his players, who enjoyed traveling first-class.

"Just too bad that the Cardinals traded me to Green Bay!" tackle Lou Gordon shouted sarcastically into a microphone when the Packers were greeted by a throng of 10,000 on Monday, December 14, 1936, the day after they defeated the Boston Redskins in New York for the NFL championship.

Gordon's playful needling came from the heart. The 6-foot-5, 224-pound tackle was born in Chicago, played at the University of Illinois, began his career with the Cardinals and ended it with the Bears. But before that final season with George Halas, Gordon played on a championship team—and that was special, even if it meant that he had to go to Green Bay to do it.

Relaxing after the Packers' day-long train ride back from New York and enthusiastic welcome in Green Bay, Lambeau lavished praise on his players.

"Every man was working all the time," he said. "Can you imagine an extended professional trip during which every man was in bed every night at 11:30, and no player broke training so far as to take a glass of beer? We had it. These Packers, the new champions, are as fine a squad of men as ever represented any city. They have been marvelous—not only on the football field, when they came back from a crushing defeat to win the national title, but in their everyday relations toward their work, their coaches and the city they represent."

The crushing defeat that Curly mentioned had come in the Packers' second game, the 30-3 loss to the Bears on September 20. After that, Green Bay had won nine straight, then settled for a scoreless tie in Chicago against the Cardinals after clinching the Western Division title.

The final six games had come during another Green Bay road odyssey. The 1936 Packers finished with seven straight road games—to Chicago, Boston, Brooklyn, New York, Detroit and Chicago again before the NFL championship game in New York.

Lambeau's assertion that no Packer had so much as a glass of beer during a six-week road trip is a little hard to swallow. It's difficult to imagine Johnny Blood going without alcohol for days, let alone weeks. But that was the way Lambeau unabashedly handled media relations. As Hugh Brown, who covered the NFL for the *Philadelphia Bulletin,* once put it, Curly was "a facile yarn-spinner."

Lambeau tended toward high praise for winning, with harsh criticism for losing. But the key fact was unquestioned. He had the 1936

Packers at the top of their game in the march to their first NFL championship since 1931.

The citizens of Green Bay, who might have taken the Packers' third straight title for granted in 1931, celebrated giddily when the Packers won the 1936 championship. Dipping deep into its black-ink stockpile, the *Press-Gazette* ran giant headlines usually reserved for declarations of war and peace on Monday and Tuesday, December 14 and 15.

"WELCOME PACKERS TONIGHT," the front-page banner said on Monday, followed by "PACKERS AGAIN REIGN AS CHAMPIONS" on the sports page.

The next day was more of the same: "10,000 FANS GREET PACKERS" and "WELCOME GREEN BAY GRID CHAMPIONS."

When the Packers' Milwaukee Road train arrived at 10:15 p.m. on Monday, they were welcomed by "the lurid light" of hundreds of red flares along the tracks from De Pere into the city, where 10,000 fans were eager to see and hear their heroes. Floodlights and loudspeakers were set up for the celebration.

Among those in the Packer party were Clarke Hinkle and his new bride, Emilie Cobden, from Larchmont, New York. Married in a 7:30 p.m. ceremony on Sunday night hours after the Packers defeated Boston, they boarded the train for Green Bay with the rest of the team.

The main event was a victory dinner to be attended by about 1,000 celebrants, plus another 500 who watched from the balcony, at the Columbus Club on Wednesday night. Tickets had become so scarce that the Lions Club, which organized the gala, urged Packer fans to be wary of scalpers and counterfeit tickets.

"Eagerness to see the league's champions became so great that scalpers were reported to be getting $2 and more for the $1.50 ticket. Members of the Lions committee warned against scalpers and also against the purchasing of fake tickets," the *Press-Gazette* said solemnly on December 14.

Seven additional gas stoves were brought in to cook the 600 pounds of tenderloins that fed the hungry Packer fans. The gala lasted five hours, with former Packer Lavvie Dilweg serving as master of ceremonies. Defeated twice when he ran for district attorney and state assembly while he was a player, Dilweg would finally be elected to to the U.S. House of Representatives in 1942. Among the long list of speakers was Curly's old

Notre Dame friend, *Chicago Tribune* sports editor Arch Ward, who formally invited Green Bay to face the College All-Stars at Soldier Field in Chicago.

Packer fans everywhere were eager for more football. And Curly Lambeau already had those wheels turning. Even if many of them would be sitting beside their radios in wintry Wisconsin, Lambeau was sorting out an extensive series of warm-weather games to be played in January.

Their fourth NFL championship sewn up, the Packers acknowledged that their 10-1-1 season had left them physically and mentally drained. But their work was not finished. To cash in on their championship status, Lambeau booked a series of exhibition games.

"I like to play football, but it got so it wasn't fun any more," said all-pro end Milt Gantenbein, the Packers' captain. "We are glad it's over. I would just as soon play a few games now and really feel that I could get some kick out of it—win, lose or draw."

Winning the NFL championship was nice. But using that title to make some money on a barnstorming tour was irresistible. And these games would not be as pressure-filled as the march to the championship.

Lambeau booked Green Bay to play in Denver on New Year's Day, followed by some games in California and a game in New Orleans. The schedule was subject to change, Curly said, "if the Packers accept a bid to go to Honolulu for a January game."

The New Orleans and Hawaii excursions did not materialize. But with the stamp of its NFL championship as a lure, Green Bay did go on a five-game post-season barnstorming tour as Lambeau combined his passion for Packers football with his love of escaping to California in the winter.

On New Year's Day, the Packers posted a 21-13 win in Denver over the Brooklyn Dodgers, who stepped in when the plan for a combined Detroit Lions/Chicago Cardinals squad fell through. Green Bay then continued to the West Coast. On January 10, it defeated the Salinas Iceberg Packers, who were billed as "West coast champions," in a 47-7 rout before a meager 2,500 fans at rainy Kezar Stadium in San Francisco.

Lambeau and his Green Bay Packers then settled in at Los Angeles, where they played for three straight Sundays. After defeating an independent team, the L.A. Bulldogs, 49-0, Green Bay squared off twice against George Halas and the Chicago Bears, playing to a 20-20 tie on Christmas Eve before beating the Bears 17-14 on New Year's Eve.

While in California, Lambeau arranged for the Packers to make a short film at the MGM movie studio. During the filming, Herber provided one of the many stranger-than-fiction moments from the legend of King Curly and his Knights in Shiny Shoulder Pads.

Asked to break a six-foot-by-six-foot pane of glass from 60 yards, Herber was given a practice throw before the cameras rolled. "Herber busted the glass with that throw, much to the chagrin of the film crew who had to find a replacement pane."

The film, *Pigskin Champions*, would have its world premiere at the Orpheum Theater in Green Bay on Friday, August 13, the day before the Packers began training camp for their 1937 season. In this case, the grumbles in his hometown that Curly had "gone Hollywood" were literally true. But at a time when NFL teams craved publicity, Lambeau knew how to capture the spotlight.

* * * * * * * *

Between their Hollywood film debut and feverishly hawking tickets to their first appearance against the College All Stars, the Packers' buildup to the 1937 season was many-faceted.

That was especially true because Johnny Blood, Green Bay's talented but unpredictable receiver, was about to embark on an unlikely new chapter, as Pittsburgh's player-coach. The Pirates job was open because the previous coach, Joe Bach, had left to coach Niagara University.

Blood went to Pittsburgh only after the NFL rejected his application to start a team in Minneapolis. On his way out of Green Bay, Blood was fined $100 on July 8 after being arrested for drunken driving. For modern coaches, that might have been a dealbreaker. For Blood, it was neither a problem nor unusual.

In another measure of how college stars regarded the NFL, Bud Wilkinson, a quarterback/defensive guard who had helped Minnesota win three straight national championships in 1934-36, had snubbed Lambeau, who had drafted him 29th overall. After playing against the Packers in the 1937 College All-Star Game, he would spend a year working at his father's mortgage company, then begin his coaching career as Syracuse's line coach and go on to win three national championships at Oklahoma. Pro football apparently was not all that interesting to him.

# 19
## *GROWING PAINS*

With the lights at Soldier Field shining bright, Lambeau was intent on having the Packers look their best when they opened their 1937 season against the College All-Stars in Chicago on Wednesday, September 1.

The College All-Star game was far more than an exhibition game that raised money for charity. Inspired by baseball's All-Star game, it annually attracted more than 75,000 to Soldier Field in Chicago, the largest NFL crowd of the season. As the first football game of the year, it was like a pre-season Super Bowl. It added spice to the debate over which brand of football was better. Sportswriters from around the nation descended on Chicago, giving the game the attention of a World Series or Kentucky Derby.

In other words, it was the kind of game that Curly Lambeau relished. In the first three contests, the NFL had won one game and tied two. Not wanting to be the first to stumble, and knowing the talent of the college team, he conducted a tough training camp. Some wondered if he had pushed too hard. Even Lambeau hinted at that.

"Our practice last night was the finest we've ever had," Lambeau said as Green Bay boarded a train to Chicago the day before the game. "But it's hard to tell what the men are thinking about. They do not seem to have their minds on the game. I am worried."

A crowd of 84,560 turned out to see the fourth annual meeting between the NFL champion and the cream of the college football crop. For its six home games that season, Green Bay would draw a total of 82,332. It was no wonder this was no mere exhibition to Lambeau.

Curly not only had drilled his Packers hard in training camp. He had designed fancy new myrtle-green uniforms, with gold lettering. Always on top of publicity, he even posed for a *Press-Gazette* photo unveiling the green jerseys on the day after St. Patrick's Day. After relying on Notre-Dame-like blue, with white or gold accents, in its early years, Green Bay had first worn a kelly green in 1935. This myrtle-green shade was darker.

"With these attractive jerseys will be worn gold helmets, gold pants and myrtle green socks. Jerseys and pants will be of jockey satin," Lambeau told the newspaper.

Somewhere along the way, though, Lambeau and his players seem to have discovered that jockey satin would be a sweat-absorbing nightmare on a hot and muggy night. And so, another fact-defying mystery in the life of Curly Lambeau was born.

With a forecast calling for a temperature approaching 80 degrees with 80 percent humidity for the 7:20 p.m. kickoff at Soldier Field,

Lambeau had given himself a backup wardrobe plan. When the Packers left for Chicago the day before the game, they brought along "a new set of lightweight green jerseys," a special order from the Wilson Brothers shirt factory in Chicago, the *Press-Gazette* reported. If the weather was as hot as the forecast, "The men will change into them from their dripping uniforms at the intermission."

It was a steamy night. And despite their preparations, the Packers wilted. They lost 6-0 before a crowd of 84,560. Before the largest College All-Star crowd, Green Bay became the first NFL team to lose to the college men.

The All Stars, coached by Gus Dorais, the Chippewa Falls, Wisconsin, native who had thrown to end Knute Rockne when Notre Dame began shocking the college football world with its passing offense, defeated the Packers on Sammy Baugh's 47-yard touchdown to LSU star Gaynell Tinsley.

Although the Packers had a big statistical edge—piling up 343 yards to the All-Stars' 185—a shoulder injury knocked their passer, Arnie Herber, out of the game in the third quarter. That gave the offensive edge to the All Stars and their quarterback, Baugh, who would move past Herber that season to become the NFL's dominant passer in 1937 and beyond.

"We lost the game on the three yard line on third down in the second quarter," Lambeau said. "It was the first time in three seasons that we have gotten down there and failed to score."

Although the heat was the same for both teams, Green Bay seemed to feel it more.

"It was 100 degrees," said Packers fullback Clarke Hinkle, recalling the heat of the night in Green Bay's sopping uniforms years later. "When the game was over, I found I'd lost 25 pounds."

That was probably another Packer-lore exaggeration, but it made the point. A newspaper account at the time reported that Hinkle "lost 16 pounds, going in at 205 and coming out at 189," while "Lou Gordon, giant tackle of the Packers, lost the most weight, going into the game at 232 pounds and coming out of it at 215."

Lambeau and his players could point to their soaked jerseys in the heat. They could lean on the loss of Herber, and their failure to score on the goal line. The real culprit, however, might have been Lambeau driving his team too hard in training camp because of the importance of this All-Star showcase game.

The usually sympathetic *Press-Gazette* cast a harsh light on the Packers' failure, saying, "The winning team played the better ball. Statistics favored the Packers, but nobody ever won a ball game on statistics. The keen mental edge which Coach E.L. Lambeau had been seeking all week never arrived, and when the Packers began play in the first period, they looked like a beaten team."

In a further humiliation for the Packers, it was the first time in four tries that the collegians had defeated the NFL champs in the College All-Star game.

"They were outhustled and outrun by the All Stars," John Walter told *Press-Gazette* readers, "but they might have won even at that, had not Arnold Herber, who was matching Baugh pass for pass, received a painful shoulder injury and gone to the bench in the third period. The importance of Herber to the club never was seen more clearly."

Lambeau, whose byline appeared on a sidebar in the *Milwaukee Journal,* said the Green Bay loss was due to All-Star hero Baugh, "the greatest passer we have ever faced," and the way Dorais prepared the All-Stars.

But he also said, "I never felt so sorry for one of my teams as I did for this one and the scene in the dressing room between halves was something I shall never forget. It was up around 118 or 120 [degrees] in the small, poorly ventilated room when the boys came in dripping wet and all fagged out, and for the first time I didn't have the heart to bawl anybody out."

Down through the years, the satin jerseys became the culprit, even though the Packers had given themselves another jersey option. Reading between the lines, Lambeau's intense training camp seems to have been a major factor. In later years, he would become known for not running physically intense training camps.

\* \* \* \* \* \* \* \*

The loss was a tough one for Lambeau, who was not a good loser. His excitement at the opportunity to showcase his team against the College All Stars not only didn't work out. When Herber's injury lingered, so did the defeats. The Packers started their season with a pair of losses to the visiting Chicago Cardinals 14-7 on September 12 and the Bears 14-2 on September 19 as their signature passing game struggled.

An open date on September 26 meant that Green Bay, the reigning NFL champion, would still be looking for its first win as the calendar turn to October. The loss to the College All-Stars was a national disappointment. The losses to the Bears and the Cardinals dug a hole that would leave Green Bay chasing the Bears all season.

Although Lambeau's legacy is anchored in Green Bay's three straight titles from 1929 to 1931, the four-year stretch from 1936 to 1939 is another example of his exceptional skill at assembling and coaching a dominant team. If he had not been held back by the financial constraints of a bankruptcy during the Depression, Lambeau might have put together an uninterrupted decade of success.

When the Packers failed to reach the 1937 NFL championship game —their only miss from 1936 to 1939—a different issue seems to have held him back. As the 1937 season began, Curly Lambeau must have been a very distracted man.

Lambeau and his second wife, Sue, the former California beauty queen who had been known as Billie John Copeland when they had marred two years earlier, had separated on September 11, the day before Green Bay's season opener, divorce records would show later. Troubles must have been building during that summer, when Lambeau was pushing his Packers hard in training camp.

At the time of the separation, Sue was approximately five months pregnant. Lambeau initially claimed he was not the father, which proved to be yet another Lambeau falsehood. He clearly did not welcome the pregnancy. It might even have surprised him. Susan apparently had been the one who left the house when they separated.

A few months earlier, Lambeau had purchased and renovated a cottage on the northeast outskirts of Green Bay, near the Riviera, a popular supper club, on property that is now part of the Wisconsin-Green Bay campus. They planned to live there 10 months a year, Lambeau said, although that was probably a stretch for his Packer constituency, given his love for California and dislike for the cold weather of Wisconsin.

On Friday night, September 24, Lambeau said he had gone into the city after starting "a grate fire." Returning home at 9:30, he found the house very warm and opened a window, turned on the radio and had fallen asleep in a chair. Less than 10 minutes later, he said, he woke up in a smoke-filled room to find the whole living room in flames. He rushed out the back door, breaking the lock to escape. A neighbor helped him get his cars out of the garage.

By the time the Preble fire department arrived, the whole house was engulfed in flames, which shot up 100 feet in the air, burning about 20 nearby trees. The house was a total loss, including many mementos—photos and trophies—of Lambeau's Packer successes. The fire, "traceable to a defect in the chimney," burned from 10 p.m. until 5 a.m. Pumping water from Green Bay, the firemen managed to keep sparks from igniting nearby cottages.

"Coach Lambeau had left only the suit he was wearing," the *Green Bay Press-Gazette* reported. The damage was estimated at $10,000 to $15,000, "partly covered by insurance." Given that Lambeau continued to be a successful insurance salesman while coaching the Packers, it is reasonable to assume he had written a good policy for himself.

And so, in a span of two weeks, Lambeau had separated from his pregnant wife, fled from his burning house and lost the first two games of the 1937 season. Heading into the College All-Star game on September 1, he had been basking in glory. By October 1, his football team and personal life seemed to be in shambles.

\* \* \* \* \* \* \* \*

And so, the 1937 Packers were a shocking oddity: As the reigning NFL champions, they lost their first three games. What was also strange: Even though Green Bay would have the league's most productive offense in 1937 for the second straight year, it scored just one touchdown while losing to the College All-Stars, the Cardinals and the Bears.

On top of his broken marriage and burned-down house, Lambeau was dealing with the shoulder injury to Arnie Herber. Desperate for passing help, Lambeau had signed quarterback Ed Smith the day after the opening loss to the Cardinals. But that had been more of a headline-making Hail Mary than a meaningful acquisition. Hailed as a savior who had been "the East's greatest forward passer" at NYU in 1935. Smith "had obtained his release from the Redskins" and was out of football. He wound up throwing two passes while in Green Bay. One was incomplete, the other was intercepted.

After missing the two opening losses of 1937 with his shoulder injury, Herber played briefly in Green Bay's third game at Detroit on October 3, contributing a couple of timely quick-kick punts in a 26-6 victory over the Lions. His shoulder was healed sufficiently for him to throw the ball a bit the following week, when he helped the Packers overwhelm the Cardinals 34-13 in Milwaukee. Herber passed four times, completing one, a 12-yard touchdown pass to end Milt Gantenbein.

Herber threw two more touchdown passes the following week, both to Don Hutson, as the Packers swamped the Cleveland Rams, who were in their first NFL season, by a 35-10 count. With that win, Lambeau's Packers improved to 3-2, but were chasing the unbeaten Bears (4-0), who looked like they were going to be hard to catch.

Playing like the NFL's defending champions, the Packers continued to roll. After winning two more games, they took a 5-2 record into Chicago. They won their sixth straight game there, defeating the Bears 24-14 on November 7 before a feverish crowd of 44,977 at Wrigley Field. Halas' team still had a slight lead, with a 5-1-1 record to Green Bay's 6-2.

Green Bay added a seventh straight win, crushing the Philadelphia Eagles 37-7 in Milwaukee on November 14. After the game, Bert Bell, the Eagles' Halas-like owner-general manager-coach, said he and Pittsburgh coach Johnny Blood tried to come up with an Eastern Division All-Star team that could beat the Packers. "Out of the entire 125 players on Eastern club rolls, there is no such team. . . . it wouldn't have a chance," Bell said.

Next up was a trip to New York to face the Giants, who were dueling the Redskins for the Eastern Division title. It was a must-win game for both teams, and both teams took that phrase very seriously.

"Fists flew, two players were fired for fighting, Referee Thorp and Umpire Savage were mobbed and manhandled and a last period riot flared at the Polo Grounds yesterday," *New York Daily News* writer Harry Forbes reported on Monday, November 22, "as the Giants stopped a seven-game Green Bay winning streak with a 10-0 victory, before 38,965 blood-thirsty fans."

"This was easily the best game of the season," Arthur J. Daley concluded in the *New York Times* after opening with a fierce description: "Playing with a fury and inspiration found almost exclusively in the most moss-bound of traditional college games, the New York Giants upset the dreaded Green Bay Packers, 10 to 0, in a thrill-packed battle at the Polo Grounds yesterday."

*New York Daily News* columnist Jimmy Powers also celebrated the intense brutality mustered by the Packers and the Giants: "Cops on field. Fists banging into ribs. Split lips, cheekbones laid open. Our Giants and Green Bays played the most savage game seen at the Polo Grounds. This brutal exhibition may happen again. I hope."

The bottom line was, the Giants stayed neck and neck with the Redskins in the Eastern Division. And the Packers sank out of contention in the West. With only one game left at Washington, Green Bay could not catch Halas' Bears. The 0-2 start weighed heavily.

While the Packers prepared for their final game, Lambeau took his players on a visit to the Justice Department, where they were greeted by FBI director J. Edgar Hoover. Green Bay players also visited Ford's Theater, where Lincoln had been shot, and took in the view from the top of the Washington Monument. They also were on hand to see Uncle Ray Steele out-wrestle Alec Kobler.

On Sunday, though, the Packers saw nothing but Redskins. After Vice President John Nance Garner—surrounded by several Bethesda-Chevy Chase Chamber of Commerce beauties— tossed out the first football, a crowd of 30,000 paid $34,000, a record take for Redskins owner George Preston Marshall, to see Washington take down the Packers 14-6.

For Lambeau, the season ended the way it started, with a loss to Sammy Baugh, who had become a Redskins sensation after leading the College All-Stars past the Packers. "That sinister character of the gridiron known as Slingin' Sam Baugh bobbed up once more to confront the Green Bay Packers," the *Press-Gazette* reported.

Completing a storybook rookie season, Baugh led Washington past the Giants in New York and the Bears in Chicago to give the Redskins their first NFL championship in their first season in the nation's capital. A year earlier, as the Boston Redskins, they had lost the NFL championship game to Lambeau's Packers.

In an indication of how important the Packers and Bears were to their fans and their financial stability, a crowd of 44,977 had jammed Wrigley Field to see Green Bay beat the Bears 24-14 on November 7. When the Bears lost to the Redskins in the NFL championship game on December 12, only 15,878 spectators showed up at Wrigley Field.

Although the Packers came home with pair of losses, they were greeted by nearly 1,000 cheering fans when they arrived home on the Milwaukee Road Chippewa at 4:40 p.m. on Monday. Green Bay Motors provided Packards that took the Packers to the Northland Hotel. Lambeau rode in the first car with three of his players. The fire chief's red vehicle had its sirens blaring and private autos accompanied the procession as Green Bay loyally showed its support for a team that finished with seven wins and four losses, tied for second with Detroit.

Lambeau gently directed the blame for the season-ending losses to the Giants and Redskins at his players. "It's not fair to say that the team was not giving its best efforts on the Eastern trip," he said. "Some of the men never fought harder, never tried harder, never played harder, but there were a few who didn't seem to be 'putting out' in New York and Washington. They didn't seem to have their minds on football. There was too much sight-seeing, too many friends around to entertain them. Understand me, there was not a bit of dissipating. The squad behaved perfectly. But there were too many things happening to take their minds off their games."

Curly acknowledged that the Packers dug a big hole with their 0-2 start: "We put ourselves at a terrific disadvantage right at the start by losing those two first games. We then were in a position where we had to win every remaining game on our schedule."

Rather than blaming the shoulder injury that sidelined Arnie Herber in the second half against the College All Stars and kept him out for two more games, Lambeau pointed to the attitude of some Packers, and said he wouldn't allow that to happen again.

"Some of our best-known players will report next year with instructions to prove their worth before they resume their regular positions with the squad," he said. "The men did not report with the proper mental attitude. They lacked the determination to win so important to a football team, and doubly important in a professional league, where the teams are all tough and most of them are evenly matched. Our team did not regain the proper attitude until it had suffered three defeats—by the College All Stars, the Chicago Cardinals and the Bears. We should have defeated the All Stars and the Cardinals, and we should have given the Bears a much better battle than we did."

Left unsaid was the wrenching personal turmoil that undoubtedly took a toll on Lambeau. During Green Bay's miserable start, he separated from his wife and lost virtually all of his personal belongings in a fire that burned his home to the ground.

# 20
## THE BEST IN THE WEST

For all of the bluster about his players' attitude, Lambeau addressed one of Green Bay's tangible 1937 shortcomings a couple of weeks later. At the 1938 NFL draft at the Sherman House in Chicago on December 12, he selected Cecil Isbell, a passer from Purdue, with the seventh pick in the draft. That move not only gave him passing depth. It gave him his throwing star of the future.

Once again, Lambeau showed his knack for spotting talent. Of the six players taken before Isbell, only one, Hall of Fame center Alex Wojciechowicz, went on to a better NFL career. And Isbell would have been a lock for the NFL Hall of Fame if he hadn't quit playing early to return to Purdue as a coach. Some Hall of Fame experts believe his spectacular five-year career is still Hall-worthy even though it was brief.

With Isbell, Herber and Bob Monnett, a solid passer from Michigan State, on his roster, Lambeau had the potent passing offense he wanted. They combined for 20 touchdown passes in 1938, five more than any other team, and Green Bay led the league with 20.3 points per game.

The 1938 season featured tight races in both divisions. When the Packers went to Detroit and beat the Lions 28-7 on November 13, they led the West with an 8-2 record. Detroit (5-3) was one game behind in the loss column. Green Bay had one game left, in New York against the East-leading Giants (6-2), who were being chased by the Redskins (5-2-2).

The win at Detroit came with a big cost for the Packers, though. Don Hutson, who led the NFL in receiving yards and touchdown catches, injured a knee. Without the league's premier receiver, Green Bay was bottled up 15-3 by the Giants before a crowd of 48,279 at the Polo Grounds on November 20, 1938. Their season completed, Green Bay (8-3) would need to wait and see if Detroit (6-3) could win its final two games and force a Western Division playoff.

After they "heard with disgust" that the Lions had defeated the Bears 14-7 on Thanksgiving Day, the Packers started preparing for a playoff meeting with the Lions. Detroit only needed to beat Philadelphia, which had muddled to a 4-6 record, on December 4 to tie the Packers.

If a playoff was needed, Lambeau said the game should be played in Milwaukee on December 11. "I have only one voice in the matter,"

Lambeau said, "but I am definitely in favor of Milwaukee for a playoff if one is necessary. I am opposed to playing in Detroit again and I think Detroit is opposed to playing in Green Bay. A neutral field should be picked. Milwaukee looks like the best place."

Milwaukee a neutral field in a game between Green Bay and Detroit? Lambeau drew on his years as a salesmen of menswear and insurance to promote that shaky idea.

"The biggest obstacle to Milwaukee as a site is the relatively limited seating capacity of State Fair park," the *Milwaukee Journal* noted. "At tops, the field here can accommodate only 22,000 fans. Briggs stadium in Detroit can seat close to 50,000 and City stadium in Green Bay 27,000."

Meanwhile, in Detroit, Lions general manager Bud Shaver announced on the same day that that if there was a playoff game, it would be held in Detroit on December 11. Shaver added that Packers president Lee Joannes had agreed to that, but Joannes denied any such agreement. The key opinion, if the game was needed, would rest with NFL president Joe F. Carr.

Noting that the Packers had completed their regular season with challenging back-to-back meetings against Detroit and New York, the *Green Bay Press-Gazette* said, "Now, it appears likely they'll have to face the same two opponents again, on consecutive weekends" to win the NFL championship. And they would need to do it in weather that was less favorable to their passing attack, the newspaper added ominously.

But there was a surprise for Green Bay fans. Led by Bill "Stinky" Hewitt, the future Hall of Famer that Lambeau had declined to sign, the Eagles knocked off the Lions 21-7 in Detroit on December 4. On Philadelphia's first touchdown, Hewitt caught a pass and cleverly lateraled to Joe Carter, who ran 52 yards for the score. Hewitt later caught a 25-yard touchdown pass. And played stellar defense.

A Bay City, Michigan, native, Hewitt was the only University of Michigan player in the NFL that year, the *Detroit Free Press* noted. Hewitt had started his pro career with the Bears, but was traded to the Eagles after announcing his retirement. He decided to play when Eagles owner/coach Bert Bell doubled his salary from $100 to $200 a game.

The Eagles' upset win gave Green Bay the Western Division title and put the Packers into the NFL championship game against the Giants. It was the East's turn to host, so the Packers would be playing in New York for the second straight game.

With a tip of the cap to Hewitt, who was famous for playing without a helmet, the Packers prepared to go back to New York and try to win their second NFL title in three years. Even with a three-week layoff between games, Hutson, who had not played in a month, remained bothered by a knee that was "still too sore and weak to permit him to pivot or cut," George Strickler wrote in the *Chicago Tribune* the day before the game. "The Packers' outlook is dismal," Strickler concluded, perhaps presenting the concerns of Lambeau, his Notre Dame crony.

Fulfilling those low expectations, Hutson caught no passes as the Packers lost 23-17 to the Giants before 48,120 at the Polo Grounds, the NFL's largest crowd for a playoff game. Green Bay's star receiver played briefly in the second quarter, then returned at the end of the game. He gained 10 yards on a lateral but "a last desperate pass attempt... failed," the *Press-Gazette* said.

Two days before the game, Lambeau made the move that would cut down greatly on the wear-and-tear that Hutson faced in future seasons. Acquiring another player that showed his sharp eye, Lambeau selected Larry Craig, a powerful defensive end from South Carolina.

When the NFL draft was conveniently held at the New Yorker Hotel on December 9 two days before the championship game, Lambeau was able to snatch the under-the-radar Craig in the sixth round, with the 49th overall pick. The unheralded Craig came to Green Bay through Lambeau's productive Notre Dame network. He had played at South Carolina for Rex Enright, who was a fullback/linebacker for Curly's Packers in 1926 and 1927 after playing at Notre Dame.

Craig not only was an asset at defensive end who could be used as a blocking back on offense. With Craig at end on defense, 6-foot-3, 183-pound Hutson, the lightest end in the NFL, was freed up to play defensive back, where his speed made him an important contributor rather than a fragile liability. Combined with the upgrade that Craig provided upfront, the Packers' defense improved significantly at two positions.

Despite the conclusions and evidence that the Giants had been the superior team, Lambeau blustered after the championship game that the Packers had been robbed by head linesman Larry Conover. In the postgame gloom, Lambeau said his complaint would be backed up by game film. Leaning on game film was a novel crutch in 1938 that would become a coaching cliche.

Decades before the introduction of replay, Lambeau had the vision to see its value. It wouldn't reverse any calls in 1938, but the Packers coach believed it would at least make him sound like a victim, rather than a whiner.

"I don't want to say this in the form of an alibi," Lambeau said, "but in my opinion Conover was definitely wrong when, in the second period, he ruled Tuffy Leeman's pass to Len Barnum complete. Moving pictures of the play will prove that Barnum fumbled immediately, the ball going out of bounds, and that the receiver had not held it long enough to establish possession. Since that play led to a Giant touchdown, Conover's decision hurt us plenty."

Continuing, Lambeau pointed to anther Conover gaffe: "Late in the last quarter, Herber threw a first down pass to Gantenbein and Conover called Gantenbein an ineligible receiver. How he arrived at such a conclusion is beyond me, because [Bernie] Scherer, our other end, was at least a yard behind the line of scrimmage. As a result, instead of us being in possession in Giant territory, New York took over in our zone. The movies will prove that I'm right about this play, too. There is nothing that can be done about it now, but it just isn't fair for us to lose a game on account of incompetent officiating. That's my sincere opinion."

Back in Green Bay, Lambeau was still railing about the mistakes of Conover, who had become a referee after playing for Penn State and the Canton Bulldogs. "Two decisions by Conover, the official, were completely wrong and we are going to have a showdown on it. The Giants are champions, of course, and nothing can be done about it, but something must be done about incompetent officiating."

Stepping off the Milwaukee Road Chippewa train that brought the Packers back to Green Bay on Tuesday night, December 13, Lambeau continued to rant: "We're not going to take this sitting down. We had that championship taken away from from us, and the boys didn't deserve it."

True to his word, Lambeau would campaign for better officiating at NFL meetings at the Congress Hotel in Chicago in February.

"Such rapid strides have been made in professional football in the past few years that the game has passed the officials," Lambeau said. "It is partly the league's fault. Officials were not given a chance to keep up with the speedy progress of the game." Lambeau urged pay increases for officials, to be accompanied by rigorous mental and physical exams before the season. Beyond written rules and eye exams, Lambeau said "all

National league officials should be able to run 60 yards in 10 seconds or less." He also urged that officials should work in teams that are designated before the season began.

Lambeau's promise that game film would prove his point took a hit, however, when a portion of the fourth quarter was not on the film, possibly because "the darkness . . . made it difficult for pictures to be taken prior to the turning on of the floodlights." A disappointed Lambeau said he had asked Fox Movietone "to make a complete picture of the game. . . to use for lecture material. . . and for scouting purposes."

Despite the gap, Packer fans filled the Orpheum Theater on Thursday to watch the film that was available and to hear Lambeau and several of his players go over a diagram of the disputed play, explaining why Milt Gantenbein had shifted properly, making him an eligible receiver whose critical pass reception should have been allowed.

Film or not, wronged or not, Lambeau faced the fact that the New York Giants were the NFL champions. He would soon immerse himself in his goal of putting Green Bay on top of the NFL in 1939.

\* \* \* \* \* \* \* \*

Lambeau kept a busy, almost frantic pace during the 1938-39 offseason.

After waging his very public campaign in Green Bay about the officiating mistakes that cost the Packers the 1938 championship in New York, the Packer leader departed soon for California, his annual escape from wintry northeastern Wisconsin.

Lambeau Field may celebrate cold weather. The man whose name is on the stadium, however, had no interest in shivering.

The NFL draft had changed the way he added college players. That was especially true because the NFL liked to hold its draft at the championship-game site in mid-December, which meant that Lambeau's scouting missions to the East-West All-Star game and Rose Bowl were ill-timed. By then he already owned exclusive rights to his draft picks. And talented prospects rarely slipped through the extensive draft.

Lambeau's notable selections in the 1939 draft were No. 2 pick Charley Brock, a linebacker/center from Nebraska, and No. 6 pick Larry Craig, the defensive end/blocking back from South Carolina who would change Hutson's football life. Brock and Craig both would end up in the Packers Hall of Fame.

Actively seeking free-agent signees as well as draft picks, Lambeau satisfied his wanderlust by deciding that he needed to "personally contact all prospects before offering them contracts. In the past many men were signed without our seeing them, and often we were disappointed when they reported. Often the weight was off as much as 20 pounds." That also helped justify his California forays.

Reporting back to the *Green Bay Press-Gazette* in a telegram from Los Angeles on January 16, 1939, Lambeau said he had signed UCLA tackle Slats Wynick to a free-agent contract. "I personally contacted six players in the last two weeks out here," he said, "and this boy was the only one who looked good enough to sign."

Although the NFL draft had diminished the importance of California scouting, Lambeau remained dedicated to pursuing prospects in warm weather and around the nation. He left Los Angeles on January 16 to contact players at St. Mary's and Santa Clara in "the start of a recruiting trip which will cover about 7,000 miles and end in Green Bay early in February."

In Lincoln, Nebraska, Curly signed his No. 2 draft pick, Brock. Before that, though, Lambeau went to Santa Clara to sign fullback Bill Aunther and Houston to sign Rice end Frank Steen. Neither of them lasted long in Green Bay. It was a lot of traveling for free agents, but Lambeau didn't seem to mind.

After signing Brock on January 31, Lambeau had planned to drive on to Green Bay the next day. But a blizzard forced him to stop in Iowa City. On February 3, the *Press-Gazette* reported that "Lambeau was back at his desk today, following an 8,700-mile motor trip."

That mileage figure seems a little high. But his journey was still a massive undertaking, given the automobiles and road conditions of the late 1930s. Even with stops that the *Press-Gazette* mentioned, if Lambeau had gone from Green Bay to Los Angeles and then on to Santa Clara, Tucson, Houston and Omaha before returning to Green Bay, he would have traveled about a boggling 6,000 miles.

Although Wynick never played a down for Green Bay or any other NFL team, that was not a big deal. Then and now, NFL teams routinely bring in many free agents who advance no further than training camp.

Every so often, though, a gem emerges from the free-agent signees. And the relentless Lambeau found one of those when he signed end Harry Jacunski, who had been among the Seven Blocks of Granite at Fordham. Jacunski's talent was well-known, but he had gone undrafted in December after announcing that he didn't plan to play pro football. Unable to find a suitable job, Jacunski changed his mind about football and accepted Lambeau's offer.

It might have helped Lambeau that Jacunski had been coached at Fordham by "Sleepy Jim" Crowley, the former Green Bay East star that Curly had steered to Notre Dame, where he became one of the Four Horsemen. Jacunski became a starter at Fordham in 1937, a year after his teammate, right guard Vince Lombardi, began building the "Seven Blocks" reputation.

It also might have helped that as a free agent, Jacunski was able to go to Green Bay, which was a coveted place to play. Whatever the reason, Curly knew Jacunski would be a good addition.

"We were misinformed concerning Jacunski's size," Lambeau said after returning from what the *Green Bay Press-Gazette* called "an eastern material hunt" on May 10, 1939. "He is much larger than we expected him to be, reversing the usual trend. We heard the Fordham end was six feet tall and weighed around 188, but he goes two inches over six feet and hits the scales at 203."

Jacunski played on the 1939 College All-Star team before joining the Packers. Persuaded to turn pro by Lambeau, Jacunski would go on to a six-year career at Green Bay and end up in the Packers Hall of Fame. He also would be an assistant coach for 33 years at Yale, in his home state of Connecticut.

"We were good," Jacunski said of his Packer years. "Although we only made about $100 a game, the Packers took care of us. We had a team doctor and a trainer. Money was tight. We had to buy our own shoes. I always felt it was just a job."

# 21
## *WORLD TRAVELER*

One thing seems clear. In his second year of being separated from his second wife, Curly Lambeau was more energized than ever for wide-ranging travel. In a way, this was the first time he had been free to see as many women as he wanted without deception.

He had married his first wife, Marguerite, on August 16, 1919. While married to her, he had become involved with Copeland in December of 1932, when the Packers sailed to Hawaii. Finally divorced from Marguerite on May 22, 1934, Lambeau married Copeland on June 26, 1935. They were separated in September 1937 and finally were granted a divorce on March 25, 1940.

Married, separated or divorced, Lambeau never seemed to lack for female companions. Handsome, charismatic and often treated like a movie star when seen in public, especially at night clubs, Lambeau also "had a way with women," said Lyla Hoyt, the daughter-in-law of Grace Garland, who would become Lambeau's third wife. "Like the sailors, he had a lady in every place that the Green Bay Packers played football."

Lambeau clearly enjoyed life on the road. As the most high-profile coach in the NFL, he was a major American celebrity. "Goodness! Curly would walk into Toots Shor's restaurant in New York in those days and he was treated like Napoleon coming home with the Russian flag," former Packer board member and *Press-Gazette* publisher Dan Beisel told Cliff Christl in a 2001 interview.

Divorce implications aside, this was the first time he had not needed to hide his romantic escapades from a wife. Perhaps his initial period of estrangement from Copeland during the winter of 1937-38, had shown him that he needed to spend even more offseason time away from Green Bay, where his pursuit of women was more difficult to conceal. Or maybe, having turned 40 on April 9, 1938, and barely coming up short of guiding the Packers to the 1938 NFL championship, he was having a midlife crisis that renewed his energy for building the best possible Packers roster—and seeing the world.

Whatever the case, beyond his lengthy automobile trip to the West Coast, Lambeau had even more elaborate travel plans before his Packers gathered for training camp in August of 1939.

In late February, only a few weeks after returning from California, Lambeau set out to scout and sign more prospects in the Midwest and on the East Coast. And then, saying he wanted to "forget about football for a while," he boarded the *Normandie* in New York on March 3 for a curiously timed vacation to Europe, which was about to be engulfed in World War II. He would not return to Green Bay until late April.

But first, Lambeau rolled up his sleeves and stumped hard for referee reform at the NFL meetings in Chicago. Arriving on February 8, the day before the four-day meeting began, Lambeau outlined his proposal, which included a pay raise for officials and an extensive pre-season meeting in which they would be educated and tested on the rules, especially controversial rules and rules changes.

Other team executives embraced the idea. At the NFL's pre-season meeting in Pittsburgh on July 22-23, thanks to Lambeau's proposal, officials heard an extensive rules seminar followed by two written tests. They also underwent physical checkups, including 50-yard and 100-yard dashes. "Every whistle toter seeking to work league games [was] ordered to report for [the] lengthy ordeal,"

Although Lambeau's initial public flogging of Larry Conover seemed to indicate he wanted Conover fired, that apparently was not the case. Conover continued his work as an NFL head linesman until his death on August 4, 1945, of an exertion-related heart attack. The former Penn State football star, who had been a lifeguard in his hometown of Atlantic City for 28 years. died after running half a mile and trying to revive a boy who had drowned. Conover was 51.

After the NFL's February meeting in Chicago, Lambeau returned briefly to Green Bay, but quickly departed for Minneapolis, where he signed a pair of his Minnesota Gopher draft choices, first-round fullback Larry Buhler on February 18, and 20th-round tackle Charlie Schultz on February 20. Both would play sparingly for the Packers for three years.

On February 23, Curly left Green Bay. On the way to sailing from New York, he signed his 19th-round pick, Michigan lineman Jack Brennan, in Chicago. Moving on to Pittsburgh, he completed an agreement with Pirates owner Art Rooney and his coach, Johnny Blood, to play a preseason night game in Green Bay on August 25.

In keeping with Lambeau's jam-packed 1939, that meeting would turn into "the only doubleheader in NFL history." A game between the rookies would be followed by a matchup of the teams' regulars. Each game was condensed to 40 minutes.

While in New York, Lambeau found time to visit with John Kieran, the *New York Times* columnist who regularly turned out playful columns about "the big boss of the Green Bay Monsters. . . the squad that was finally subdued by Stout Steve Owen and his jolly Giants in the play-off game for the national paid post-graduate championship late last Fall."

This piece was not about football, Kieran quickly announced in a quote from Lambeau.

"Alone at last!" said Curly. "No tackles need apply. . . . I'm on the loose now and off for England. . . . Just a vacation. And all alone. No football team this time. . . . I'm not carrying diagrams of plays in my pocket now. I've got the map of London instead."

Playing along, Kieran expressed disbelief that Lambeau would leave the Packers permanently: "Why, Curly Lambeau was Mr. Green Bay himself in a football sweater. Even if he tried to break loose, somebody would force a law through the Wisconsin Legislature to keep him in his place."

Kieran advised Lambeau to check out the Grand National, "the greatest horse race in the world." Curly eagerly agreed.

Lambeau also said he had stopped by at Fordham, where his son, Don, had played on the freshman team the previous autumn. "A little fellow, weighs only 224 now," Lambeau told Kieran. "But he's only 18. He may pick up weight. Between us, if he does I'll choke him. Or maybe [Fordham coach Jim] Crowley will."

Following in his father's footsteps, Donald had been a star fullback at Green Bay East. Donald played freshman football at Fordham in 1938. Heavier than his father but not as quick or as agile, he never earned a varsity letter.

Donald would enlist in the Army in 1941. Assigned to duty as a surveyor in advance of construction crews in New Guinea, he became seriously ill, running a high fever from scrub typhus. After recovering, Donald finished his service in the Philippines. Awarded a a Bronze Star and Purple Heart, he was discharged on October 27, 1945, He returned to Green Bay in time to watch from the bench as the Packers defeated the Chicago Cardinals 33-14 the next day.

After some banter about the NFL, Kieran wrapped up the column with Lambeau planning to check out a rugby match: "They tell me there's some great kickers there. I might bring one back."

Kieran finished by approving of that idea, saying, "A Green Bay Monster with an English accent would be a fetching novelty in pro football."

With that, Lambeau set sail on March 3 for a six-week tour of Europe that included stops in England, France, Belgium, the Netherlands, Italy and Germany.

Toward the end of his trip, Lambeau received the news that his father, Marcel, had died of a heart attack on April 11 at 8:30 p.m. at his home at 625 Pine Street in Green Bay. Marcel Lambeau was 62.

The *Press-Gazette* called him a "prominent contractor" in its front-page obituary the next day. The buildings he had worked on included "the Allouez and Whitney schools, the North Side Community club, Green Bay Labor temple and the plant of the Indian Packing company, made famous by its sponsorship of the team organized by his son. When the Packers became a Green Bay institution, it was Lambeau who built the first stands at City stadium." Marcel also had been Green Bay's first building inspector and a one-term city councilman, his obituary noted.

The funeral was held on Saturday, April 15, with burial at Allouez Cemetery. Curly did not make it back to Green Bay until April 18. "E.L. Lambeau, coach of the Green Bay Packers, returned to the city last night after an extended European tour, prepared to concentrate on the serious business of shaping up his 1939 professional football team," the *Press-Gazette* reported on April 19, with this sympathetic note. "Curly missed by only a few days the funeral of his father Marcel Lambeau who died unexpectedly during his son's absence."

Sharing his European adventure with Green Bay, Curly described the trip at a Lions Club luncheon at the Beaumont Hotel on April 24. Under the headline, "Berlin Gay With Little Talk of War, Lambeau Says," Curly told his audience, "Only the soldiers in Germany and Italy remind one of war in those countries today."

On the front page, however, the citizens of Green Bay were informed that a British ambassador was given "the runaround" in Berlin when he tried to meet with senior Nazi officials. A second front-page story said Britain was planning to start a compulsory military draft and was planning an increase of $3.15 billion in defense spending, a staggering sum.

Lambeau did tell the Lions Club that soldiers were seen almost everywhere in Italy and Germany, adding that the Italian soldiers "appeared better drilled" than those in Germany.

"I expected all huskies in the German army," Lambeau said, "but half of them were timid looking kids. All except the soldiers guarding Hitler's home, and they were really big boys."

After noting "that the German people were unable to get such foodstuffs as butter and fruit. . . Lambeau concluded his talk with the observation that if an American citizen becomes dissatisfied with life here, all that is necessary is to plant him in Europe and due to the lower standard of living there, he will soon appreciate this country."

That said, Lambeau "didn't think there would be a war in Europe if the nations can hold out for a month or two and have 'an honest understanding.'"

Curly proved to be a far better judge of gridiron battles than actual warfare. In less than five months, on September 1, World War II would begin.

\* \* \* \* \* \* \* \*

The NFL's leadership received a jolt when league president Joe F. Carr died of a heart attack on May 20, 1939. He was 59. A former newspaperman and owner of the Columbus Panhandles, Carr had been NFL president since 1921. In his 18 years, he had molded the NFL from a loose federation of small-town teams into a prominent major league. And he had done it without the far-reaching power that baseball commissioner Kenesaw Mountain Landis possessed.

"Having enjoyed a fine relationship with Joe Carr since 1921, I was shocked deeply to hear of his death," said Lambeau, who joined the rest of the league's owners and executives in Columbus, Ohio, on May 24 for the funeral. "He was completely honest, always fair and the National league has been fortunate to have him as its president."

"The loss of Mr. Carr is irreparable," George Halas said. "Pro football's remarkable growth and popularity today. . . is due entirely to Mr. Carr's fair and impartial administration of its affairs and his steadfast belief in the game."

Carr had been pragmatic when it came to the Packers, a stance that proved beneficial to the team and the league in the long run. After kicking

Green Bay out of the NFL after the 1921 season for using college players, Carr had reinstated Lambeau's franchise during the same off-season. And while Carr, who wanted the NFL to stick to major cities, had initially questioned whether Green Bay deserved to remain, he came around to being a Packer advocate. The city's support, combined with the Packers' ability to draw big crowds on the road, overcame Carr's skepticism.

# 22
## *MILWAUKEE DEBATE HEATS UP*

Intent on fielding a championship team in 1939, Lambeau had been diligently signing draft picks and free agents since January. He energetically continued his quest for players throughout the summer. He opened training camp began in Green Bay on August 5 with his largest pre-season roster. When everyone arrived, 55 players would be competing for the 30 player slots that NFL teams were allowed in 1939.

Meanwhile, Johnny Blood, the improbable coach of the Pittsburgh Pirates, began drilling his players on August 6 in Two Rivers, Wisconsin, just 40 miles south of Green Bay on Lake Michigan. Some credited Blood, who saw the virtues of training camp in milder climates, with starting a trend. Other teams that had headed north to beat the heat included the NFL champion New York Giants, who trained in Superior, Wisconsin, before taking on the College All-Stars in Chicago. Next to Superior, the Chicago Cardinals stayed cool in Duluth, Minnesota. And the Washington Redskins traveled west to Spokane, Washington. The Bears held their camp for the sixth straight season in Delafield, Wisconsin, west of Milwaukee.

"John 'Blood' McNally, head coach of the Pirates, pioneered the idea of moving National league teams northward for training purposes," an unbylined story out of Chicago told *Green Bay Press-Gazette* readers. "A year ago, McNally predicted that league teams eventually would be forced to train in the north as a logical solution of the perplexing heat problem."

To further insulate against the heat and to make it easier for fans to attend, the Packers and Pirates scheduled their exhibition doubleheader at night. The idea was to get the longest possible look at prospects who were trying to make the team. To keep things moving, the two games were shortened to 40 minutes, so the crowd would see 80 minutes of football, instead of the 60 minutes for a traditional game. The doubleheader, the *Press-Gazette* said, "will give the fans an ante-season grid show on a scale never before attempted."

On an ideal night where the temperature stayed in the mid-60s, the teams battled to a 7-7 tie in the first game before 9,416 fans at City Stadium. With their deeper and more talented roster, the Packers defeated the worn-down Pirates 17-7 in the second game. Using an innovation that would become standard procedure in the modern NFL, Lambeau and Blood agreed to free substitution so they could see their players in as many situations as possible.

"Both coaches were trying out their men with almost reckless abandon, never once attempting to field a team that had experience as a unit," Stoney McGlynn told his *Milwaukee Sentinel* readers.

On September 1, as Lambeau took his Packers to Texas for a high-profile exhibition, his conclusion from his European tour in the spring that war would not break out proved to be false. When Germany invaded Poland, Britain and France joined the fight. The United States would not become involved for more than two years. Until then, Lambeau would be immersed in trying to win football games and help the NFL grow.

Curly wanted to have his team whipped into good shape for its only other pre-season game, an ambitious trip to Dallas to play "the Southwest College All-Stars" in a Labor Day contest on Monday night, September 4. In the wake of the success of the College All-Star game in Chicago, pre-season contests pitting pro teams against college all-star squads had popped up in many cities.

The Dallas college team, led by Baylor's Billy Patterson and TCU's Davey O'Brien, was expected to be very competitive. Despite 106-degree heat, Lambeau put his team through a two-hour workout on Saturday, September 2.

"Lambeau regards it as an even stiffer test for a pro team than the All-Star contest at Chicago," the *Press-Gazette* reported, "for the players are elected by merit by the coaches themselves, a hand-picked group instead of one picked by popular vote which is often influenced more by publicity than ability."

The Packers opened a 31-6 halftime lead, then held on for a 31-20 win in the Cotton Bowl before 20,000 sweltering fans in what the *Milwaukee Journal* described as "oppressive heat." Clarke Hinkle claimed he lost 30 pounds that night, even more than the 25 pounds he said he had shed when the Packers played in the Chicago All-Star game two years earlier.

Green Bay's Dallas contest was one of eight games that pitted college all-star teams against NFL squads, a concept that had mushroomed beyond the original game in Chicago. Topping the 1939 list were the Chicago game, which drew a crowd of 81,456 to see the Giants win 9-0, and an Eastern All-Star game in nearly 40,000 fans saw the Giants prevail again 10-0 at the Polo Grounds in New York. The 20,000 at the Packers game in Dallas came next. College All-Stars also played against pro teams in Philadelphia (Eagles), Cleveland (Rams), St. Louis (AFL Gunners), Boston (Washington Redskins) and Providence (New York Giants).

After the game, Lambeau caught a plane to Chicago, and then took a train to Green Bay. He arrived on Wednesday. His players arrived at 10:10 p.m. that night after going by train all the way from Texas.

That still left them with 10 days to prepare for their season opener against the Chicago Cardinals. Green Bay would play its first six games in Wisconsin and finish with five road games in its 11-game schedule. Knowing it would be a long season, Lambeau gave his players a few days off. When practice resumed on Saturday, September 9, the team went through a predictably erratic workout. It was what he expected, Lambeau said, " following the hard game in Texas and the long train ride."

For all of Lambeau's roster building, Green Bay did not begin its 1939 regular season looking like an unbeatable force. The Packers opened a 14-0 lead, then held on for a 14-10 win over the Chicago Cardinals on September 17 in their opening game, leaving northeastern Wisconsin football followers wondering if Curly had a championship-worthy squad.

The real test would come a week later in Green Bay's second game against the Chicago Bears. George Halas, who was among the 11,792 at City Stadium, was not lulled that the Cardinals had nearly beaten Green Bay. Because the Bears had won their opener on Friday, Halas led a contingent of seven Bears players to Green Bay to scout the Packers.

Among the seven Bears were quarterback Sid Luckman and running back Bill Osmanski, a pair of rookies who had been among the top six picks in the 1939 draft. Osmanski would lead the NFL in rushing that fall. Luckman, who was drafted second overall by Pittsburgh and traded to the Bears in a shrewd maneuver by George Halas, would become the first great T-formation quarterback.

"Despite the fact the Cardinals completely outplayed the Pack in the second half of Sunday's game," Irv Kupcinet told *Chicago Times* readers, "Green Bay still showed signs of living up to advance notices, which have pegged the 1939 Packers as the greatest machine in a long line of great Packer grid machines.

Kupcinet was a busy man that day. After serving as head linesman on the officiating crew, he had taken off his striped shirt to write an account of the game. The Cardinals staged "a second-half rally, in which their line completely took charge of the vaunted Packer attack, [but lost] 14-10, with the Red Birds coming up fast on the outside," Kupcinet said. Although having a newspaperman double as an official created multiple conflicts of interests—a writer paid by the league would hardly write unfavorably about the league—the situation was common in the early days of both pro and college football.

"As the Packers looked considerably short of excellent in their opening clash with the Cardinals, Lambeau has ordered a strenuous work program for this week, designed to whip his forces into first class battle formation before the Bears invade City stadium," the *Press-Gazette* said, adding this comment from Curly. "Our team was not entirely off. Some of them played fine football, but the team as a whole must improve vastly before it will be ready for the Bears."

Green Bay had a miserable start against the Bears, who led 13-0 at halftime on a 16-yard run by Osmanski and a seven-yard run by quarterback Bernie Masterson.

In the third quarter, though, Green Bay erupted. Cecil Isbell ran 11 yards and Clarke Hinkle plunged one yard to give the Packers a 14-13 lead. When Bears returner Dick Schweidler muffed a punt and the ball rolled into the end zone, rookie center Tom Greenfield, Lambeau's 15th-round pick from Arizona, recovered it to put Green Bay ahead 21-13. The Packers then held the Bears to a field goal in the fourth quarter for a 21-16 win before 19,192 at City Stadium on September 24..

Kupcinet credited a Lambeau halftime speech that was worthy of his college coach, Knute Rockne, with inspiring the Packers. "Rising to oratorical heights, [Lambeau] delivered an old-fashioned, rip-snorting pep talk," he wrote in the *Chicago Times* the next day. "Out came the Green Bays for the second half with fire in their eyes, determination written (in code, of course, to stymie spies) on their faces." That was a reference to Halas and Lambeau being obsessed with spies uncovering their plans.

The Packers stood 2-0. But they had needed all of Curly's off-season roster machinations to squeak past their two Chicago rivals in their first two games. Skeptical Green Bay fans, who had left a few thousand seats unsold for the Bears game, were even slower to buy tickets for the next game, against the Cleveland Rams.

Even though the Rams had lost all four meetings with Green Bay in their first two years in the NFL, Curly sounded the alarm, saying, "We can't let down against anyone. Any time you ease up in this league, you take a licking. The Rams are a much improved ball club over their last year's team, which was good enough to beat the Chicago Bears twice."

The ploy didn't work. Neither the Packers nor their fans got excited about playing Cleveland. Only 9,888 tickets were sold at City Stadium. The Packers' smallest crowd of the season winced through a 27-24 Green Bay loss. The sportswriters who covered the game "were unanimous in declaring that the team's attitude was listless, sluggish and in no sense indicative of a prospective championship," the *Press-Gazette* said in an unbylined story.

Lambeau's former star, Johnny Blood, was having an even worse time in Pittsburgh. The day after the Bears whipped his Pirates 32-0, Blood quit as their coach. The Pirates were 0-3, and had scored only seven points. Blood was 6-19 in his two-plus seasons as an NFL coach. Assistant coach Walt Kiesling, another former Packer whom Blood had brought to Pittsburgh, moved up to head coach. Blood's resignation came on the first anniversary of the Pirates' last win, a 13-10 upset of the Giants in New York.

Blood's greatest legacy as a coach was convincing Byron "Whizzer" White to play for the Pirates in 1938 and delay heading off to England on a Rhodes scholarship.

They became lifelong friends. White presented Blood when he was inducted into the Pro Football Hall of Fame in 1963. Blood attended a White House reception in 1962, when President John F. Kennedy appointed White to the Supreme Court. Blood already knew President Kennedy, who came from a football-obsessed family. They had met when Kennedy was campaigning in Wisconsin, where JFK told Blood, "Your name was a household word in our family."

Johnny Blood's friend remained on the Supreme Court until 1993, when he was succeeded by Ruth Bader Ginsburg.

While Blood was departing Pittsburgh, the Packers were treating their loss to Cleveland as a wakeup call. The *Green Bay Press-Gazette*, taking its cue from Lambeau, noted that the Packers had been in a similar situation in 1936, when they were drubbed 30-3 in an early game by the Bears, but bounced back to win the NFL title. "Lambeau is hoping that the Cleveland triumph will serve as a proper spur," the newspaper said, adding that ticket sales were going well for Green Bay's next game, in Milwaukee against the Chicago Cardinals. "If the weather breaks properly, the Packers will in no sense be alone when they face the Cardinals."

A crowd of 18,965, the largest to see the Packers play in Milwaukee, turned out at State Fair Park on October 8 for the Cardinals game. They were rewarded with a 27-20 win that included two long touchdowns. Hutson caught a 92-yard pass from Arnie Herber to start the Green Bay scoring. After the Packers stopped the Cardinals with a goal-line stand in the third quarter, Andy Uram, sprung by the blocking of Clarke Hinkle and Larry Craig, went around right end for a 95-yard touchdown run that put the Packers ahead 21-0. Green Bay then held on for a 27-20 win.

The Packers then added two more solid victories. They handed Detroit its first loss of the season with a dominant 26-7 win in front of 22,558 at a sold-out City Stadium on October 22, their final 1939 game in Green Bay. That left the teams tied for first place with 4-1 records.

A week later, Green Bay took down another unbeaten team, defeating the Washington Redskins 24-14 on October 29 before 24,308 at State Fair Park in suburban Milwaukee. With that, Green Bay wrapped up its home schedule. Lambeau and the Packers would play their final five games on the road, where they drew their three biggest crowds of the season..

Next up was the kind of game that made Curly Lambeau and George Halas such great business partners as well as fierce rivals. A crowd of 40,537 jammed Wrigley Field on November 5 to see the Packers, tied for the Western Division lead at 5-1 with Detroit, take on the Bears, who had fallen to 4-3 in a 10-0 loss to the Lions the previous week.

With their backs to the wall, the Bears knocked off the Packers 30-27 in what the *Green Bay Press-Gazette* called a "savage game." There were six lead changes in a back-and-forth game that saw the Packers pass for more than 300 yards but manage only 54 rushing yards.

"Players came to blows on the field. Fans fought in the stands," the *Chicago Tribune* reported. "With only six minutes to play, three freshmen in professional football—Bill Osmanski, Bob MacLeod and Sid Luckman—combined on a 75-yard drive to score the winning touchdown."

With four road games left to play, the Packers (5-2) were in second place, sandwiched between Detroit (6-1) and the Bears (5-3). While disappointed by the wrenching loss to the Bears, Lambeau kept an even keel publicly.

"We can't lose a single ball game from here on. If we win them all, we know we'll be in," he said, refusing to comment on the possibility of a Western division playoff. "We're going to think about each game as it comes, and forget about the championship."

Green Bay reeled off wins at Philadelphia, Brooklyn and Cleveland, then went to Detroit needing a win in their final game to avoid a playoff with the Bears for the Western Division title. The game, played before 30,699 fans at Briggs Stadium, "was a surging battle, fought through mud and water under sodden skies," *Press-Gazette* sportswriter John Walter wrote.

After trailing 7-3 at halftime, Green Bay was able to grind out a 12-7 win. By winning their final four games, the Packers earned a slot in the NFL championship game against the Eastern Division champion New York Giants.

"Green Bay's Packers rose up out of the mud of Briggs Stadium in the second half to beat back a stubborn Detroit Lion team and win the western division championship of the National Football League," Curly

Lambeau's Notre Dame friend, George Strickler, wrote in the *Chicago Tribune* on December 4.

A 25-yard field goal by Tiny Engebetsen gave the Packers their only first-half points. Buford "Baby" Ray blocked a third-quarter punt to set up Green Bay's safety. In the fourth quarter, Clarke Hinkle scored the winning touchdown from two inches out on a daring fourth-down call.

The Packers, in their Notre Dame box, all shifted to the right before the snap, which went directly to fullback Hinkle in what future generations would call a wildcat snap. While all the Packers ran to the right, Hinkle went left, "bucking headlong into [Detroit] tackle Ray George. His charge moved both George and the ball over the goal for the touchdown," Strickler reported.

The nail-biting victory in Detroit allowed Green Bay to win the West with a 9-2 record, one game ahead of the 8-3 Bears, who had been hoping for a tie that would have forced a Green Bay-Chicago playoff. The Lions, who had been the frontrunner at 6-1, lost their final four games to finish third at 6-5.

The excitement in Green Bay at winning the West was overshadowed, however, by the scramble for tickets to the championship game against the New York Giants. Packer fans in Green Bay were outraged that the game had been moved to West Allis, outside Milwaukee, where Wisconsin State Fair Park could hold a crowd of 32,000, which was 10,000 more ticket buyers than Green Bay's City Stadium.

"As Curly Lambeau's men went through preparations today for the big game the crowds in every hotel lobby, tavern and inn had but one topic of conversation. One faction is up in arms because the contest will be held in Milwaukee, 120 miles from here," the *New York Times* reported from Green Bay. "This group maintains that the classic belongs here, though the local stadium can accommodate only 22,000 spectators."

Even with more than 32,000 tickets available in Milwaukee, Wisconsin Governor Julius Heil and Illinois Governor Henry Horner were unable to buy tickets, the *Times* reported. That situation was resolved by gametime. But the frenzy generated ticket revenue of nearly $85,000, an NFL post-season record.

The mania was so great that Packers president Lee Joannes warned people to watch out for 1,500 fake tickets. He urged fans not to buy from strangers, adding that the Packers would give a $250 reward to anyone who provided evidence leading to the conviction of ticket counterfeiters. Some angry Green Bay area grocers who bought products from Joannes' wholesale business reportedly told Joannes truck drivers to sell their groceries to Milwaukee.

It was league officials, not the Packers' front office, who were behind the move to Milwaukee, historian Craig Coenen wrote in his comprehensive economic history of the NFL.

"When the NFL forced the Packers to play the 1939 championship game in Milwaukee, Green Bay citizens resented the action and were quite vocal in their opposition because it threatened their claim to the team," Coenen said.

The Packers, who as a community-owned team were always preoccupied with staying solvent, showed no sign of resisting the move. More likely, they were on board with it.

Intent on beating the Giants, Lambeau stayed out of the Green Bay-Milwaukee debate. But judging from his later views that the Packers needed to move to Milwaukee or another large city to survive, he realized the need to play games like the 1939 championship game somewhere larger than Green Bay's City Stadium. Whether forced by the NFL or not, Joannes and the Packer board of directors also agreed with that economic reality.

Even by hastily adding 6,000 seats, State Fair Park (32,000) was the second-smallest football arena in the NFL, barely larger than Washington's Griffith Stadium (30,600).

Weighing in on the revolt on its editorial page, the *Green Bay Press-Gazette* defended the decision to play in Milwaukee with a lengthy editorial.

"The strong resentment aroused in Green Bay and vicinity over the decision of the Green Bay management to hold the championship playoff in Milwaukee is perhaps the most natural thing in the world in a community where the pride in the team is so intense that about 99 percent of the citizens would regard any slight of the team as a personal affront," the editorial said solemnly. "Indeed the *Press-Gazette* would be one of the first to fight for the game for Green Bay if it were to consider only what might be called the matter of sentiment. There are, however, practical considerations to the question which must be recognized, and these when fairly weighed seem to dictate another view of the situation. . . It is evident that Green Bay cannot today support a full six-game league schedule. The Packer management in transferring two games to Milwaukee turned those two game from definite financial losers to nice profit makers for the Packers and Green Bay. As a result . . the National league officials were fully justified in designating it a Green Bay home field and demanding that the playoff be held there.

"The Packers cannot relinquish Milwaukee," the editorial continued, "as a home field for a part of its schedule without endangering its financial stability, and indeed the entire football program. The people of Green Bay should go along with the management of the Packers, not blindly and without criticism, but at least to the point of acknowledging that the present management has guided the destinies of the Packers through the good years and the bad ones. . . .the members of the board of directors are directly interested in the welfare of Green Bay and further that they are better informed on the needs of the club than others. Perhaps the day will come when Green Bay can have a championship game. No one would welcome that time more than the *Press-Gazette*. But until we have the facilities it would be extremely unwise to demand the game for Green Bay as a sop to our civic pride, and enforce an unfair condition on the other teams of the league, if we are to expect them to be fair with us."

It was a debate that would go on for years. If anything, speculation that the Packers needed to leave Green Bay would mount as the NFL became a bigger business. The issue would not be settled until 1956, when the voters of Green Bay were faced with a bond issue to finance an NFL-caliber stadium. Before the stadium that eventually would carry his name was built, Lambeau himself would be among those who believed the Packers needed to relocate.

*New York Journal-American* sports editor Bill Corum, one of the most prominent sportswriters in the East, fanned the debate by derisively insisting that the Packers had outgrown Green Bay. The NFL, he said, "must soon strengthen its membership. Great as Green Bay is as a team, loyal as the fans of the little town are, it can't go on indefinitely being a big league city. It isn't."

Even Milwaukee's State Fair Park was not adequate, *Milwaukee Sentinel* columnist Stoney McGlynn said, calling for a stadium that could hold at least 40,000 to be built. "A county stadium that would seat 40,000 fans would not be large enough. And the need for such a stadium will be here next year, the year after and the year after and for as many years as one Earl (Curly) Lambeau has anything to do with the Packers. The Packers are no longer just a Green Bay institution. They are a Wisconsin institution. They draw from all over Wisconsin. They play some of their games in Milwaukee each year. They have built up a clientele that wants the best—and is getting it. Under Curly Lambeau the Packers have won four league championships and seven western crowns in 11 seasons. It can't be luck. It must rest somewhere and if the coaches are to be blamed for the losing teams then they must be credited for the victorious ones. As long as the Bays have Curly they'll have a football club that will be up there. And as long as they are up there the need for a larger stadium will always be with us."

When Milwaukee County Stadium finally opened in 1953, the Braves moved to Milwaukee from Boston. Lured by even an greater financial future, they left for Atlanta in 1965. The Packers, meanwhile, played two to four home games there from 1953 until 1994.

Putting aside their outrage, about 11,000 Packer fans, almost a third of Green Bay's population, traveled from the Green Bay area to Milwaukee for the 1939 championship game against New York.

They were among the crowd of 32,279 that squeezed into State Fair Park on December 10, 1939, to see Lambeau guide the Packers to a 27-0 victory. It was the fifth title in 20 years for Curly since he had started the Green Bay football franchise.

No other NFL team had won more than three titles over that span. In two decades, Lambeau not only had defied the rules of sports business by creating a franchise that could survive in a small town. He had built the most successful team in the league.

"When I get thru with athletics, I'm going out and conquer the rest of the world," he had brashly stated in his high school yearbook. Considering that athletics was his world, Lambeau had made good on his vow.

The $703.97 that each Packer received for winning the championship was a windfall for Lambeau's players. Only a few stars—notably Cecil Isbell ($7,100), Clarke Hinkle ($5,110), Don Hutson ($5,075) and Charley Brock ($3,147)—had salaries of more than $3,000

For Dick Weisgerber, whose salary of $1,780 was at the lower end of the team, the championship bonus brought his earnings to $2,483.97, a 40 percent increase. Over the years, the impact became even higher in his mind. "My dad used to say he made $500 for the season and $500 for winning the championship, so he doubled his salary," Weisgerber's son, Rich, said in a 2023 interview with the author. Although Dick Weisgerber exaggerated the numbers a bit, the point was valid. In 1939, when the average family income in America was $1,231, an extra $700 meant a lot.

The clamor for a stadium in Milwaukee picked up momentum as a result of the 1939 championship game. The day after the game, a Milwaukee alderman, T.R. Froemming, chairman of a special stadium committee created by the city council, announced a meeting would be held on Tuesday to discuss building a municipal stadium.

A blustery day featuring 25 mile-per-hour gusts left many sportswriters, especially big-city writers, fearful that their hastily-built wooden press box would be lifted up and taken to Oz like Dorothy's Kansas home. The press box "trembled and swayed continuously and it appeared that at any moment the whole thing would crash. When finally the men descended one remarked: 'We're lucky to be alive,' and all agreed."

But they put aside their fears and reported glowingly on Green Bay's dominant performance.

"While a whistling wind swept down from the north, Green Bay—blazing hot as few football teams ever have been—rode the icy blasts to victory," Arthur Daley wrote in the *New York Times*. "Everything clicked for Curly Lambeau's beautifully drilled [team]."

Gracious to the extreme, Giants owner Tim Mara jokingly told Lambeau, "The only thing I regret is that we didn't lose to Washington last Sunday. Then Washington would have been here to take this beating."

Celebrating at the team's Milwaukee hotel after the game, Lambeau proudly proclaimed that "There wasn't a team in the world that could have beaten our club today. . . Everything worked to perfection. . . . We certainly are not that much better than they [are]. But our boys were out to avenge that beating of last year. They had keyed themselves as few teams were keyed."

After the disappointment of losing the 1938 NFL championship game to the Giants, Lambeau certainly had dedicated himself to winning in 1939. And after a frenzied offseason of roster building, he had shown the right amount of patience and prodding to get to this pinnacle.

Lambeau and his Packers had come a long way. If he had imagined this kind of success when he opted to stay in Green Bay in 1919 rather than return to Notre Dame, he had a very large imagination.

Green Bay's fifth NFL championship was secure. Whether the little city in northeastern Wisconsin could keep its Packers was a question that would continue to simmer, though. A week before the Giants had lost in Milwaukee, they had played before 62,404 fans who had jammed the Polo Grounds to see New York defeat the Redskins 9-7 on December 3, 1939, for the Eastern Division championship. The NFL's popularity was booming. Playing in larger stadiums was critical to the sport's growth.

That didn't necessarily rule out Green Bay, though. Giants owner Tim Mara and the Bears' George Halas, who appreciated the crowds the Packers attracted, both came to Green Bay's defense.

"If the question of the Green Bay franchise ever arises," Mara said, "we'll be there to bat for them. If Green Bay ever needs us, we'll give them our full support."

While Halas was obsessed with defeating the Packers on the field, the Bears leader was also determined to see Green Bay keep the football team he loved to beat. "Let Mr. Corum confine his activities to Times

Square," Halas said. "Green Bay will retain its franchise as long as I have anything to say about it." It was a statement Halas would back up whenever the question came up, including the trip he made to Green Bay in 1956 to stump vigorously for Green Bay voters to approve building the stadium that would become Lambeau Field.

When Lambeau and his Packers made the quick 120-mile trip back to Green Bay on Monday from Milwaukee, they received a championship welcome home. A crowd of 10,000 gathered to greet their train. The Lumberjack band played *Go You Packers* and *On Wisconsin,* but the songs were drowned out by the cheering throng. The celebration continued with a jammed reception at the Northland Hotel.

To celebrate the 1939 championship, the Packers were honored by 1,500 of their supporters at a Victory Banquet at the Columbus Club, where they were presented with gold watches. Only four of the team's 30 players did not attend. Three of the four—Harry Jacunski, Paul Kell and Cecil Isbell—were absent because they were "on their way to be married."

Curly's longtime Notre Dame friend, *Chicago Tribune* sports editor Arch Ward, attended the banquet and formally invited the Packers to kick off the NFL season at the 1940 College All-Star game.

The 1939 season was not over yet, though. As the league champion, Green Bay qualified for the second annual Pro Bowl, a January game that pitted the league champion against an NFL All-Star team in Los Angeles. That gave Lambeau another reason to dodge the Midwestern winter with his annual California scouting trip and vacation.

Lambeau and the Packers left Green Bay on December 22 for Los Angeles, where Curly had arranged for the team to be based at the Riviera Country Club. Lambeau and assistant coach Red Smith played golf on Christmas in a match against Don Hutson and tackle Bill Lee, who had been teammates at Alabama. Beginning on December 26, the Packers practiced from 10 a.m. to noon on a polo field next to Riviera, then played golf in the afternoon.

In another indication that Lambeau was approaching the game differently, he announced on December 29 that he would start eight first-year players. That said, he and the All-Star team coach, New York Giants head coach Steve Owen, tossed barbs and boasts to build up interest in the game. And Lambeau later revealed a plan to put his veterans on the field when the rookies started to tire.

"We have. . . a team that has played together as a unit," Lambeau said. "Every man knows exactly what to do when the occasion arises. I can't believe any gathering of All-Stars, no matter who they are, can beat the top essential of football—which is team play, rhythm."

Owen had a ready reply, saying, "No one has to tell me anything about Curly Lambeau's Green Bay Packers. . . . They had too much power and speed for my Giants when we met at Milwaukee. But this game on Sunday here is entirely different. I have the pick of the league—outside of the Packers."

As the game approached, a steady rain forced the teams to curtail their practices. When the rain continued, the game was pushed back a week, from January 7 to January 14, to allow the Packers and the All-Stars to put on a better show. And to ensure the kind of weather that would fill 18,000-seat Gilmore Stadium.

Although the Packers were a 9-to-5 betting favorite in a world before point spreads, the postponement was said to be an advantage for the All-Stars, who would have an extra week to mesh as a unit.

When game day dawned, Lambeau's competitive juices were flowing. Exhibition game or not, he wanted to win. Showing his skill at preparing a team, he shrugged off his low-keyed approach and guided Green Bay to a 16-7 victory "although opposed by probably the greatest collection of talent ever to grace a single line-up," the *Los Angeles Times* said under the headline, "Packers Smash Way to Pro Bowl Grid Victory."

Many of Lambeau's best players didn't start. But when they got into the game, they finished. With the Packers leading 6-0 late in the second quarter, Ed Jankowski stopped an All-Stars drive with an interception at the Packer 8 yardline. Don Hutson caught a pass from Cecil Isbell that went for 92 yards and gave Green Bay a comfortable 13-0 lead. The All Stars' tiny hero, 5-foot-7, 151-pound Davey O'Brien, threw a touchdown pass that cut the lead to 13-7 in the third quarter. But the Packers bottled up the All Stars the rest of the way.

"It was just like a spring practice game for a college team," Lambeau said afterward, "and it did us a lot of good. The game enables us to get complete information about some of the boys who had little chance to show their stuff during the past season. Of the 28 men who took part in the game, 26 showed a desire to win. Two didn't. It is good for us to know who they are. They are not good enough to be Packers and will be replaced."

Lambeau noted that first-year players "played a little more than 50 percent of the game."

That was the way Curly rolled. He had given his players a mix of practice time and relaxing time. This was, in the end, an exhibition game.

But results counted. And he had calculated how best to evaluate his young players while still putting together a successful effort.

Departing from his usual lengthy stay in California, Lambeau boarded the Santa Fe Chief for the long train ride back to Green Bay. Curly arrived on Wednesday, January 17. "Arnold Herber, who is driving Lambeau's car home, along with Joe Laws and Ed Jankowski, is expected back by Saturday," the *Press-Gazette* reported. Given Herber's driving record, Lambeau showed great faith in his quarterback.

Before heading out to sign players, Lambeau said the Packers would need to step up their game if they planned to win the 1940 championship: "We know that we must be 15 percent better than our opposition to repeat for the title. When you're the champion, they're all set for you, and the margin of victory or defeat depends on the attitude of your players."

Well aware that no team had gone on to win the NFL championship after appearing in the College All Star game since it began in 1934, Lambeau already was priming his team to become the first team to repeat as NFL champion since the Bears in 1932 and 1933.

Lambeau also was basking in the adoration that came with being NFL champion. Nearly 500 people attended a dinner on February 13, 1940, in Madison, Wisconsin, where he showed a film from the championship rout of the Giants.

"I can't put you on the spot because you had a pretty good season," *Wisconsin State Journal* columnist Roundy Coughlin, who emceed the event, told his pal Lambeau. Replied Curly, "You wouldn't catch me down here if I'd had a bad season." Coughlin, a golfing friend of Lambeau's, came back by saying, "If you'd had a poor season I wouldn't have asked you." The crowd of Packer fans enjoyed the Curly-Roundy banter as well as the meal and the film session.

During the spring, Lambeau went about his usual business of traveling around the Midwest signing players and formulating his roster plans.

# 23
## *A MESSY SECOND DIVORCE*

While Lambeau was steering the Packers to their fifth championship in the fall of 1939, his second marriage was headed for a rocky end. In October, 1939, his estranged wife, Sue, returned from California to Green Bay, to either reconcile with Lambeau or, more likely, to fulfill the residency requirement for filing for divorce in Wisconsin. Known earlier as Billie Sue Copeland Lambeau, she had become Sue Lambeau.

Married on June 26, 1935, they had separated two years later, on September 11, 1937. Four months after that, on January 13, 1938, Sue had given birth in Los Angeles to a son, whom she named Earl Louis Lambeau II.

On March 25, 1940, Curly and Sue Lambeau were granted a divorce in the Green Bay courtroom of Henry Graass, who was pretty much the official judge of the Green Bay Packers. Before the Lambeau divorce, he had presided over the team's 1933 bankruptcy hearing and the 1932 lawsuit filed by Willard Bent after he fell out of the bleachers at City Field during a Packer game.

Under the terms of the agreement, Mrs. Lambeau was to receive $6,750, plus $25 a month for child support "for the care of a child, two years old last January." From the settlement, she had to pay $975 for living expenses she had incurred after moving to Green Bay the previous October. That was necessary for her to obtain the divorce.

Curly "alleged that incompatibility made it impossible for the two to live together," the *Press-Gazette* reported. "Mrs. Lambeau charged that her husband refused to live with her, and refused to recognize her as his wife." By reaching a divorce agreement, the Lambeaus avoided a jury trial, which had been scheduled for April. That would have been lurid and sensational—and unthinkable to Lambeau, who took great care with his public image.

If Lambeau has not been given his proper place as a key founding father of the National Football League, his personal life may be a reason. And his 1940 divorce is a tale filled with sad details. Lambeau's treatment of his second wife and the son he refused to acknowledge paint a grim picture.

There is also a conspiracy theory—that Lambeau kicked Arnie Herber off the Packers for aiding Sue Lambeau.

"Herber ran into [Lambeau's] wife downtown," Herm Sehneidman, a Packer from 1935 to 1939, told team historian Cliff Christl. "She said, 'I'm not supposed to be in town. He kicked me out and told all the hotels not to let me in.' So [Herber] took her home and let her stay with [him] and his wife. Lambeau found out about it and [cut] him."

The problem is, the conspiracy theory doesn't match the timeline. Herber was cut on September 9, 1941, about 18 months after the Lambeau divorce was granted on March 25, 1940. A possible explanation for the time gap is that Susan had returned to Green Bay to seek child support. It's also possible that there was an element of lingering vindictiveness. Lambeau was not above doing that. Most likely, though, he was ready to move on to his next great passer, Cecil Isbell, who would quickly become one of the NFL's most productive quarterbacks. In 1940, Isbell also was Green Bay's second-leading rusher.

Herber was slowed by a drinking problem that contributed to his weight problem. Early in training camp, he weighed 212 pounds despite a contract that called for him to be no more than 200 pounds at weekly weigh-ins on Saturdays during the regular season. Although Herber had shed the required pounds as the season neared, he no longer was running effectively or throwing as well as Isbell, who had emerged as a premier passer, a player at the elite level of Sammy Baugh and Sid Luckman.

Hard feelings or not, while Lambeau's decision to cut Herber made football sense. Isbell had become the Packers' most productive passer. Although listed as a tailback in the Notre Dame Box offense that Lambeau favored, Lambeau often tinkered with that offense. Wherever Isbell lined up, he was the passer. He had steadily increased his production in his first three years, moving ahead of Herber in 1940. Isbell not only was improving his passing. He was a productive rusher, while Herber was a liability as a ballcarrier.

That said, by cutting Herber five days before Green Bay opened its 1941 season at home against Detroit, Lambeau made a shocking move. Home-grown passing hero Herber had played on four of Green Bay's five NFL championship teams, and had done his best work from 1932-36. Although he had yielded the primary passing role to Isbell, he was only 30 years and could still throw. He also was a popular local hero.

The Herbers may have irritated Lambeau by helping Sue Lambeau. But either way, Herber had become expendable. In a minor effort to soften the blow, Lambeau announced that Herber had been offered a job as an assistant coach with Green Bay's minor-league affiliate, the Long Island Indians. It was an offer that Herber refused.

Regardless of the exact circumstances, the nasty details of Lambeau's divorce from Susan/Billie Sue are another example of unsavory behavior by the man whose name is memorialized on one of the most iconic sports venues in America.

Ironically, while Lambeau had nothing to do with his second son, Earl Louis Lambeau II became a successful sports promoter after changing his name. He started using the name Earl Louis Duryea after his mother remarried a man by that name. He kept the Duryea name even after his mother and stepfather divorced.

After spending some early years in Los Angeles and Chicago, Duryea was a three-sport letterman in football, basketball and track at Hillside High School in Michigan. After attending the University of Michigan and serving in the Navy, Duryea followed in his biological father's footsteps and went on to a career in sports management. While serving as president of the Harlem Globetrotters in the 1980s, Duryea was credited with bolstering their box-office appeal by increasing the talent base and cutting back on their pranks and jokes.

Duryea told Cliff Christl during a 2008 interview that he had no relationship with his father. "I don't remember Curly," he said. "As far as I know, I didn't have an association with him."

# 24
## THE BEARS CLAW BACK

His divorce completed, Lambeau turned his attention to the 1940 football season. In late May, his old Notre Dame friend, *Chicago Tribune* sportswriter George Strickler, came up to Green Bay, to prepare for the College All-Star game. As the 1939 NFL champion, Green Bay would open the football season against the All-Stars in Chicago on August 29.

While Lambeau was single again in the spring of 1940, he was pleased to help Strickler have a memorable wedding. Strickler and Amy McKay were married on Friday, May 31, 1940, aboard Curly's power cruiser, *Lazy,* in Menominee, Michigan, on the Wisconsin border about 55 miles north of Green Bay. The Rev. Gilbert G. Curtis, pastor of an Episcopal church in Menominee, performed the ceremony, which was witnessed by Lambeau and Miss Delores Tustison of Green Bay and attended by some Menominee residents.

The group then cruised across Green Bay, stopping in "Door County ports" for the rest of the holiday weekend. In addition, "Strickler and Lambeau worked on publicity material for the Packer-College All Star football game at Chicago Aug. 29."

In an effort to add depth to his running game, Lambeau signed Beattie Feathers, who had set an NFL rushing record as a Bears rookie in 1934, when be became the first player to rush for more than 1,000 yards. Lambeau hoped a "change of scenery" would help Feathers, who had been hobbled by injury, but that didn't happen. Feathers rushed just four times for 19 yards before leaving pro football. In Green Bay, Feathers remained best remembered as the Bears defensive back who got burned on Don Hutson's first NFL touchdown catch.

When the Packers gathered for a kickoff breakfast at the Northland Hotel on August 10 to start training camp for the 1940 season, 40 players were present. Three veterans were expected to join the team soon. Also missing the opening of camp were five rookies who were members of the College All Star team that would face the Packers on August 29 in Chicago. Strickler, still working on publicity material for the All Star game, attended the kickoff breakfast, and reported that ticket sales were "terrific" for the game, sponsored by *Chicago Tribune* Charities.

The All Stars' coach, Iowa's Eddie Anderson, and Curly had been teammates at Notre Dame in 1918 before Anderson went on to a distinguished coaching career at DePaul, Holy Cross and Iowa. Anderson had been chosen to coach the All Stars in voting by football fans. The 1940 season would be his second at Iowa, which he had guided to a 6-1-1 record in 1939. When the Packers had been upset 6-0 in the 1937 All-Star game,

Lambeau also had coached against another fellow Notre Dame alum, Gus Dorais, who steered prospects to Lambeau, including future standout Tony Canadeo.

The coaching tree of the martyred Knute Rockne seemingly had endless branches. That was a very big help to Lambeau, who enjoyed the scouting benefits of his Notre Dame network.

Nile Kinnick, the Heisman Trophy winner who had led the Hawkeyes, also would face the Packers after receiving more votes for the All Star team than any other player. Snubbing a lucrative $1,000-a-game offer from the NFL's Brooklyn Dodgers, Kinnick chose to remain in Iowa City in the fall of 1940 to attend law school. The grandson of a former Iowa governor, Kinnick seemed destined for a career in politics, but was killed in a U.S. Navy training-flight crash in 1943. Like Lambeau, Kinnick's legacy lives on in bricks and mortar. Iowa's football stadium bears his name.

Although the All Star game would not affect Green Bay's hopes of winning a second straight championship, Lambeau had plenty of reasons to have his Packers primed to play well.

Attracting a crowd of more than 80,000 and massive publicity, the All Star game was important to the perception of the NFL champion in particular, and the league in general. The first six games were deadlocked at two wins, two losses and two ties. Having lost to the All Stars in 1937, Lambeau wanted to make sure the Packers atoned with a win in their second appearance.

Despite rainy weather that limited practice time for four days before the game—or perhaps because they had fresh legs—the Packers and the All Stars came out and put on a show for the 84,567 who squeezed into Soldier Field on August 29, 1940. The game, which raised $150,000 for Chicago charities, began with a bang and continued to be a rare touchdown-filled contest. After an early interception of a Cecil Isbell pass, the All-Stars took a 7-0 lead. USC quarterback Ambrose "Ambling Amby" Schindler, the hero of the Trojans' 1940 Rose Bowl win, ran six yards to give the All-Stars their first score. Green Bay answered quickly, tying the game on a 79-yard touchdown from Isbell to end Don Hutson. After an All-Star turnover, Isbell connected with end Carl Mulleneaux on a 26-yard pass.

Green Bay led 14-7 in a first quarter that delighted a crowd that often watched entire games to see three touchdowns. The pace continued to be action-packed. With less than eight minutes to play, Schindler's second rushing touchdown closed the Packers' lead to 35-28.

When the game ended, Lambeau and his Packers had emerged with a 45-28 victory in the 1940 College All-Star game. In scoring 73 points, the Packers and the All-Stars erupted for nearly as many points as the 78 scored in the first six All-Star games combined. Isbell threw three touchdown passes and Herber threw two. Hutson caught three of their touchdown passes.

"We expected the All-Stars to score and we expected to score," Lambeau said. "But I did not dare hope that we would click so well in such an important game so early in the season."

While Schindler, the most valuable All-Star, was a Green Bay draft pick, he never played pro football. Lambeau had taken him in the 13th round, apparently aware that Schindler wasn't interested. Schindler went on to the stability of a long career as a high-school and community-college coach in the Los Angeles area. Although he never played for the Wizard of Green Bay, Schindler did work as a stunt double for Jack Haley, who played the Tin Man, during the filming of *The Wizard of Oz.*

Another West Coast All-Star who impressed the Packers was UCLA back Kenny Washington. After Washington bowled him over at the goal line, Green Bay guard Buckets Goldenberg "termed the dusky UCLA star the finest man on the college squad," Strickler reported in the *Chicago Tribune.*

George Halas was so impressed that he kept Washington in Chicago for three weeks while he tried to convince other NFL executives, notably his segregationist friend, Redskins owner, George Preston Marshall, to allow him to integrate the league.

That day would have to wait. As *Time Magazine* noted, "Super-Stars Schindler and Kinnick have spurned all offers to play pro football. Schindler has taken a job coaching football at a California high school. Kinnick, grandson of onetime Governor George Clarke of Iowa, prefers to study law. Another of last week's college stars whom football fans will probably see no more is kinky-haired Kenny Washington. Considered by West Coast fans the most brilliant player in the U.S. last year, Washington cannot play major-league pro football because he is a Negro."

A teammate of Jackie Robinson at UCLA, Washington became the first black player to sign an NFL contract after World War II. In 1946, he joined the Los Angeles Rams, who were required to integrate to be able to play in the L.A. Coliseum.

It appears that Lambeau never knowingly put an African-American in a Packer uniform. Long after Lambeau was gone, though, it was revealed that lineman Walter Jean, also known as Walt LeJeune, appeared in 19 games for the Packers during the 1925 and '26 seasons. Although DNA testing later revealed that Jean was half-black, he passed for Caucasian in an era where discrimination was the way of life.

An Ohio native, Jean divided his later years between Florida and Jacksonport, Wisconsin, on the Door County peninsula where Lambeau vacationed. In the early 1950s, Jean hosted annual Packer get-togethers at his cottage in Jacksonport, about 60 miles northeast of Green Bay.

"Curly Lambeau would come over. Johnny Blood," next-door neighbor Bob Schutt, who observed the partying as a wide-eyed teenager, told Packer historian Cliff Christl. "I never went over. I looked through the bushes when they were giving it hell. He probably had 10, 15 people over here. I remember it twice. It was Packers, all Packers." Although Schutt said his mother wondered if Jean was black, he said he never gave it much though. But given that era, it would not be surprising if Jean continued to pass for being white.

After the win over the 1940 All-Stars on a Thursday night in Chicago, Lambeau had scheduled an interesting pre-season game against the Sammy-Baugh-led Washington Redskins the following Monday, which was Labor Day, in Milwaukee. While the Packers and Bears were the glamour teams in the West, the Redskins' rivalry with the New York Giants anchored the NFL's Eastern Division .

It was a matchup against Sammy Baugh, the premier passer in the NFL, that gave Lambeau's Packers another nice pre-season attraction. The Redskins had drawn a crowd of 24,308 to Wisconsin State Fair Park the previous year, Green Bay's largest regular-season crowd in Milwaukee up to that point. When 14,978 paid their way into State Fair Park on Labor Day, 1940, Lambeau had arranged another good payday.

Curly also used the game to prepare his team for the 1940 season. He "ran the risk of giving his young material a thorough test under big league fire at State fair park here Monday afternoon, and the experiment was a howling success," *Press-Gazette* sports editor John Walter wrote. "With most of the men who carried the burden against the College All-Stars last Thursday sitting under wraps for much of the playing time, the Packers walloped the Washington Redskins, 28 to 20, in an exhibition contest and made it look easy. The veterans did the scoring, but it was the younger players who wrestled with the Redskins most of the afternoon."

While Walter also noted that "On the debit side of the ledger was the undeniable fact that the Packers looked terrible on pass defense," Baugh did that to a lot of teams that year. Washington would lead the NFL in virtually every passing category as well as scoring that season.

Green Bay then opened its 1940 season on September 15 with a modest 27-20 win over Philadelphia before a modest crowd of 11,657 Packer fans at City Stadium.

When the hated Chicago Bears came to Green Bay the following week, though, 22,557 squeezed into City Stadium. It was the largest crowd ever to witness a football game in Green Bay.

What they saw was a game that turned ugly. George Halas had methodically been building a powerhouse. The previous year, he had drafted Bill Osmanski, who led the NFL in rushing in 1939, and passer Sid Luckman, the prototype for the modern quarterback. In 1940, he added two more future Hall-of-Fame stars, center/linebacker Bulldog Turner, who was as tough as his name, and George McAfee, a wispy back who was generously listed at 6-feet and 178 pounds.

A shrewd trader in those days, Halas had sent veteran tackles Russ Thompson and Milt Trost to Philadelphia for the elusive McAfee, who had been the second pick in the 1940 draft. In 1939, Halas also had acquired Luckman with the second pick, acquired from Pittsburgh as part of the compensation for Eggs Manske, a durable end who had been an All-American at Northwestern. Halas' draft maneuvers were especially irritating to many other NFL team leaders. He even figured out a way to reacquire Manske for the 1940 season.

On that autumn Sunday, Green Bay found out what Halas had built. After the Packers took an early 3-0 lead, McAfee returned the ensuing kickoff 93 yards for a touchdown. Osmanski added a short touchdown run to give the Bears a 14-3 halftime lead. When Ray Nolting returned the second-half kickoff 97 yards, the Bears held a commanding 21-3 lead. A 35-yard touchdown catch by Don Hutson gave the Packers a glimmer of hope at 21-10 in the third quarter. McAfee answered with an eight-yard touchdown pass to Ken Kavanaugh and added a nine-yard scoring run in the fourth quarter that gave the Bears a 34-10 lead.

When the game ended, a stunned Packer crowd sat in disbelief. The Bears had crushed the defending NFL champions 41-10 on September 22, 1940. It was the most points the Packers had ever allowed—and their largest margin of defeat in a home game since Lambeau had created the Packers in 1919. An early-days 31-0 loss to the Pottsville Maroons on November. 26, 1925, had come by the same margin, but it did not compare. In 1925, Green Bay was a fledgling pro team, not the league's defending champion. And that defeat had come on the road, not in front of the shocked hometown fans.

For Lambeau, his players and their legion of dedicated fans, it was a demoralizing collapse on virtually every front. Knowing the Packers had a whole season ahead of them, though, Curly put on a calm public face.

"Despite the size of the score, we are not in the least alarmed concerning the future, and we do not think that the margin between the teams is anywhere near as bad as pictured," he said, adding that at least one player missed an assignment on one of every three plays. "We have no one to blame but ourselves for the loss. We must know all our assignments and execute them in every game or we shall not deserve to be champions. Every mistake made Sunday can be corrected. You will remember that in the playoff against the New York Giants last fall the team played an entire afternoon without a single man missing a single assignment. That's the type of ball the Packers can play, and must play to retain their championship."

Lambeau also pointed out that in 1936, the Packers bounced back from an early 30-3 loss to the Bears and won the NFL championship.

Later in the season, Lambeau attributed the Bears' shellacking to cockiness. "They really murdered us," he said. "Tell you why. We had won the All-Star game and we had beaten the Washington Redskins in an exhibition game. We got all swelled up. We needed bigger headguards than anybody makes for humans. We were ripe and ready to be knocked off—and they really knocked us off."

Just three days later, on Wednesday, September 25, Green Bay got right back in the race. The Bears, playing an unusual midweek game, were upset 21-7 at Comiskey Park by the Chicago Cardinals. Whether it was an emotional letdown, the quick turnaround, the Bears' ambitious scheduling of six pre-season games or the surprising fire of the Cardinals' rookie-laden roster, the Bears joined the Packers with a 1-1 record.

Lambeau took his lone assistant, Red Smith, along with end Don Hutson and tackle Bill Lee to Chicago to scout the Cardinals, who would line up against the Packers in Milwaukee on Sunday. "Best Cardinals team I have seen in years," Lambeau told the *Press-Gazette*. "Marshall Goldberg looks wonderful. He ran around end for one touchdown so fast the Bears didn't know what was happening."

Beyond the Cardinals' strong play, Lambeau was concerned about having his team mentally ready. "Our problem is. . . to keep those who gave us their best from getting discouraged, and at the same time correct the mistakes of those who made them. I'm sold on our boys. There are [simply] some who don't seem to realize the seriousness of our loss. We are allowed a squad of 33 men, but if necessary we would not hesitate to reduce it to 28 or 30 men if that meant keeping only the men with the proper mental attitudes."

The night before the Cardinals game, Curly arranged for his team to see a showing in Milwaukee of *Knute Rockne, All-American,* the Hollywood movie about Lambeau's Notre Dame mentor, played by Pat O'Brien, and Lambeau's backfield mate, George Gipp, played by Ronald Reagan.

The next day, the Packers went out and knocked off the Cardinals 31-6 on September 29, 1940, in Wisconsin State Fair Park before a good turnout of 20,234. The short turnaround hurt the Cardinals, just as it had hurt the Bears coming off their win in Green Bay. Every Western Division had one loss, setting up an interesting race.

Green Bay stumbled only one more time before its rematch with the Bears in Chicago on November 3. That left the Packers with a 4-2 record, one game behind the 5-1 Bears, in position to tie for first place with a victory. Anticipating a great showdown, a record crowd of 45,434 fans jammed into Wrigley Field. The Bears flexed their muscle in a 14-7 win that gave them a 6-1 record, two games ahead of Green Bay (4-3).

The Bears' hero was Bob Swisher—a 5-foot-11, 163-pound free agent from Northwestern. "In the lengthening shadows of a magnificent

Indian summer afternoon," the *Chicago Tribune* reported, Swisher broke up three touchdown-pass opportunities in the end zone "with as near a perfect demonstration of covering the elusive Don Hutson as anyone of the overflow crowd in Wrigley Field ever expects to see."

Not all was lost for Green Bay, though. The Bears reopened the door to the Packers' plans for a second straight NFL title when they lost 17-14 in Detroit while Green Bay was beating the Cardinals in Chicago.

That meant the Packers (5-3) were still only one game behind the Bears (6-2), who faced a challenging trip to Washington to play the East Division leading Redskins (7-1) and their standout passer, Sammy Baugh. Meanwhile, Green Bay also would travel east to play in New York. The Giants (4-3-1), who had lost to the Packers in the 1939 championship game, were having a frustrating season. But they figured to be ornery after being shut out 13-0 at home by the Cleveland Rams.

# 25
## *FIRST IN FLIGHT*

Always innovating, Lambeau decided that the Packers would be the first NFL team to travel by air. Considering that the Yankees, the first baseball team to travel regularly by air, didn't start flying routinely until 1946, the Packers were trailblazers in professional-sports air travel.

In the modern world where teams fly everywhere, and where headphone-wearing athletes can travel without ever really having to notice that they have gone anywhere, it's easy to overlook the step Curly Lambeau took by putting his Packers on a pair of DC-3s in 1940. The Cincinnati Reds had flown once in 1934 to Chicago. But in a sports world where teams didn't fly regularly until the mid-1940s after World War II, Curly Lambeau was an airborne pathfinder.

Given the high winds and below-freezing temperatures in Green Bay, Lambeau must have been even more excited about his decision to leave northeastern Wisconsin on Thursday morning, November 14, 1940, for the Packers' game against the Giants in New York on Sunday, November 17, 1940.

Green Bay's airport, Austin Straubel Field, would not open until 1947 and would not have regular airline service until 1948. And so, the Packers took their familiar Milwaukee Road train trip to Chicago, then boarded a pair of United Mainliner DC-3s for the flight to New York.

When the Douglas DC-3 debuted in 1935, it revolutionized passenger air travel. Before that, "a flight from New York to Los Angeles was a grueling ordeal, typically requiring 25 hours, more than one airline, at least two changes of planes and as many as 15 stops or so. Now, a single plane could cross the country, usually stopping only three times to refuel."

Even Orville Wright, who was to airplanes what Lambeau was to the Green Bay Packers, was dazzled. "They tell me that [the DC-3] is so sound-proof that the passengers can talk to each other without shouting," Wright told reporter Douglas Ingells when TWA opened a route in Dayton, Ohio. "This is a wonderful improvement. Noise is something that we always knew would have to be eliminated in order to get people to fly. Somehow it is associated with fear."

The DC-3 could accommodate up to 28 passengers and needed fewer ground stops for refueling. Its cruising speed was just 207 m.p.h. and routes were limited. But it was right in the wheelhouse of Curly Lambeau, who was known for putting the football in the air. Now his whole team would be airborne.

After leaving Green Bay by train at 7 a.m. Thursday, the Packers were scheduled to depart from Chicago at 12:30 p.m. and arrive at LaGuardia in New York four hours later.

At Chicago's Municipal Airport, which would be renamed Midway in 1949, the Packer traveling party posed for a gaggle of photographers on the tarmac. "One photographer wanted a picture of Cecil Isbell throwing a pass to Don Hutson," the *Press-Gazette* reported. "No football being available, Isbell "threw" a stewardess, Roberta Shilbach by name, and the pass was a complete success. Then a football turned up, and Miss Schilbach booted a couple of trial kickoffs for publicity purposes with Isbell holding the ball. By this time, the Packers were chilled thoroughly, and they piled into the planes." Judging from the photo that appeared in the newspaper, Isbell seemed to be on the verge of handing off a smiling Miss Schilbach to Hutson rather than passing her. Which was probably a better idea, from the standpoint of air safety.

"The men who make the wheels turn in the NFL will have their eyes on the Green Bay Packers," the *Press-Gazette* said. "If the experiment of flying to a scheduled contest turns out favorably. . . many weary hours on the train will be saved. The Packers will have pioneered in a new development for the National league, just as they have pioneered in a score of other movements since the circuit was formed in 1921. And it is very probable that the National loop again will follow the leader, shooting its game-bound hordes into the sky next season for more. . . out-of-town dates."

The planes departed 25 minutes apart, with 21 passengers on each flight. Due to the weight that the two DC-3s were carrying, they made a refueling stop in Cleveland. While there, United officials expressed concern about fog in New York that was limiting the number of landings. Because it was possible that the Packer planes would be unable to land, Lambeau decided that his team would proceed by train.

"The ponderous Packers of Green Bay, more than four tons of muscular manhood, left Chicago aboard two chartered planes. . . but bad flying weather forced a landing at Cleveland," *New York Times* writer Arthur Daley said. "Present plans call for the Packers to practice at the North Meadow at Central Park, but this cannot be guaranteed. The secretive

Coach Curly Lambeau has a habit of announcing plans for one thing and doing something else. Rain, however, might interfere seriously."

Between the wind and cold in Green Bay, rain in New York, their travel schedule and media obligations on Friday, the Packers were left with just one good practice opportunity, on Saturday. But the Giants, who were hobbled by injuries, had their own problems.

Lambeau placed a high value on making the media rounds. He visited the office of New York *Times* sports columnist John Kieran, who regularly wrote a witty column about Lambeau when the Packers were in New York. Curly also was interviewed on Friday night on Red Barber's Mutual System national radio sports program, which could be heard in Green Bay via WGN from Chicago.

Under the headline "The Master of the Eleemosynary Monsters," Kieran poked fun at Green Bay's nonprofit status with the use of *eleemosynary,* a synonym for *charitable* that would appear in big type in only the most sophisticated of newspapers. "That's what they are by Federal law and judicial ruling. Eleemosynary Monsters, beneficial blockers, charitable kickers, tax-free tacklers," Kieran wrote, adding that "profits for the Green Bay season. . . go to the American Legion. . . for charitable purposes."

Feigning indignation that Kieran's colleague Daley had called him secretive, Curly told Kieran, "Who said I hid my team, practiced in secret places and never let anyone know what hotel we were stopping at? Secret practice? Know where we practice every time we hit New York? In Central Park! Is there any place more public than that?"

Kieran referred to Curly as "M'sieu Lambeau," a reference to his French-speaking Belgian ancestors. But he did allow him to pontificate on why the Packers would overtake the Bears.

"We haven't hit our peak," Lambeau said. "We're coming along. I believe the Bears hit their peak and are on the way down. . . . If we can catch them now, they'll never shake us off."

Sunday, November 17, was Green Bay's chance.

The problem was, when Packer running back Larry Buhler fielded the opening kickoff, he was smacked around by swarming Giants at the 20 yard line. New York recovered the fumbled ball at the 6 yard line, then scored a quick touchdown and made it stick.

Like Buhler, the Packers never knew what hit them and lost 7-3.

Green Bay dominated the statistics, notching 16 first downs to the Giants' five and rushing for 132 yards to New York's 95 while passing for 95 yards to New York's 25. But the Packers, who went without a touchdown for the first time in 22 games, had four turnovers, while New York had only one.

And that's how Lambeau's team muffed a great chance to pull into a tie with the Bears, who also lost 7-3 in Washington that day. That pretty much ended Green Bay's hopes of winning a second straight NFL championship in 1940.

The Packers "were both chagrined and bewildered at their failure to defeat an admittedly inferior team of New York Giants," John Walter told readers in Green Bay. The explanation from New York analysts was that the Giants, with some key players sidelined by injury, decided to play a stout defensive battle after scoring their early touchdown. And they made it work, bottling up a Green Bay offense that averaged 21.6 points a game.

In an odd twist, the Giants were eliminated from the Eastern Division race despite their win, while Green Bay retained its fading hopes of winning the West even though it had lost. The truth was, the Bears, who had beaten the Packers twice, had shown they were the better team.

Disappointed by the loss, Green Bay continued its pioneering air-travel trip by flying from New York back to Chicago—with a refueling stop in Cleveland—on Monday.

"Yesterday the Packers ate breakfast at the Hotel New Yorker on Eighth avenue; had their lunch aboard two United Airliners 10,000 feet above the state of Indiana; and dined as their Milwaukee Road special coach was wheeling north through Wisconsin," John Walter told *Press-Gazette* readers. The return leg of their air Odyssey was as smooth as silk. There wasn't a bump in the sky all the way from New York to Chicago, making more converts for this most modern method of moving a football club."

Taking off from LaGuardia, they had a magnificent view of the New York skyline and the Statue of Liberty as their DC-3s, which had taken off to the east, turned and headed back toward Chicago. After a hot lunch, "There was another treat. . . . two by two the men were allowed to go forward and watch the pilot and second officer at work behind the plane's giant instrument panel. There also were duplicate earphones, so that the Packers were permitted to listen in on radio conversations between the planes and the airports."

At the time, Lambeau's airborne idea seemed visionary. "You can sneer, if you like, at the action moving the Packers around by plane," Walter wrote. "You can whine, 'What's the hurry?' But the fact remains that. . . you're bucking progress. . . . Before two years pass every football squad which can afford it will be traveling. . . by airplane."

Encouraged by the New York experiment, Curly arranged for the Packers to fly to their next game, at Detroit. Once again, they took a 7 a.m. train to Chicago. From there, they flew to Detroit in time to practice there, "which they would miss if they made the Chicago-Detroit trip by rail."

For the return to Green Bay, the team planned to fly to Chicago right after the game, "in time to grab the 7:25 [p.m.] Milwaukee Road train for home. This will mean an arrival [in Green Bay] at 11:50 p.m. Sunday, and the Packers will be able to start work Monday for their final regular schedule game of the season at Cleveland."

If there were any notions that air travel had anything to do with Green Bay's loss in New York, the Packers dispatched that idea in Detroit, where they swatted a very capable Lions team 50-7. They then flew back to Chicago, arriving in Green Bay by rail late Sunday night.

"None of the nervousness which attended the Packers' first flight was evident over the weekend," Packer fans learned from the *Press-Gazette*. "The players now are experienced air travelers, and practically all of them think it's a great idea. They loll back in their seats on the planes, gaze idly at the clouds or landscape, and talk wisely of altitudes, land speed and air speed, and meteorological conditions."

The only grumbling came from 6-foot-6, 249-pound tackle Buford "Baby" Ray. After noticing on the New York trip that "the stewardesses always started serving the meals from the stern of the ship," Ray had taken a seat in the last row for the flight to Detroit. The problem was, Lambeau overheard Ray talking about his strategy and asked "the stewardess to start service from the front of the plane. To Baby's expressed rage, this policy was followed, and he was the last Packer to get his fodder. On the return trip he sat in the middle of the plane."

\* \* \* \* \* \* \* \*

Despite the threat of wintry weather, Lambeau followed the same routine for Green Bay's final game. Flying from Chicago to Cleveland, the Packers played out the string by rallying for a 13-13 tie with the Rams before a dedicated crowd of 16,249 on the frozen tundra of Municipal Stadium on December 1. Down 13-3, the Packers scored 10 fourth-quarter points, missing their opportunity to win when Clarke Hinkle, who had already made two field goals, missed a third try in the final seconds.

And so, Green Bay ended its 1940 season with a whimper. If the Packers had not been upset at New York, they would have been determined to win at Cleveland. Instead of finishing 6-4-1, wins in those two final games would have given them an 8-3 record, the same as the Bears. That would have set up a Western Division playoff.

Then again, the Bears had already beaten Green Bay twice. And the Bears were peaking. Big-time.

As the Western champions, the Bears traveled to Washington for the NFL championship game. An overflow crowd of 35,331 would squeeze into Griffith Stadium, where the Redskins were tenants of baseball's Washington Senators.

It was a big improvement from 1925. Exactly 15 years earlier, when Red Grange had been introduced to President Calvin Coolidge as a member of the Chicago Bears, Coolidge had said, "Glad to meet you, young man. I always did like animal acts."

Now everyone in Washington knew the Bears as a football team.

Despite the Bears' 7-3 loss to the Redskins three weeks earlier, Bears end Ken Kavanaugh said gamblers favored the Bears by 21 points in their title-game rematch. Injuries to a pair of key Washington defensive stars outweighed the fact that the Redskins had recently beaten the Bears on November 17.

After that game, the Bears bemoaned the officiating that gave them eight penalties for 80 yards. Noting that the NFL had a statistic for "yards lost by penalties," *Chicago Tribune* writer George Strickler said, "By the end of the season it may be necessary to insert a companions line, 'Games lost by penalties,' to complete the record on the Chicago Bears."

Amid the grumbling about penalties from Chicago, Washington owner George Preston Marshall had replied that "The Bears are a bunch of crybabies. They're frontrunners. They can't take defeat…The Bears are quitters."

Halas, who saw a fine motivational opportunity, "plastered all the stories on the locker room bulletin board," Bears end Ken Kavanaugh said.

Whipped up to a feverish pitch by Halas' reminders, the Bears crushed the Redskins by an astonishing 73-0 score that pro football had never seen—and, barring the unfathomable, will never be seen again.

It was a day in which everything went the Bears' way. Wide open on the Bears' 4-yard line, Washington receiver Charley Malone dropped a Sammy Baugh pass that would have tied the game at 7-7. Asked if tying the game early would have made a difference, Baugh reportedly said, "Yes. It would have been 73-7 instead of 73-0." Whether he actually said that or whether it was the work of an enterprising sports scribe, the remark pretty much summed up the day.

The Bears' dominance was not lost on Lambeau, One year removed from the 1939 championship, he knew he had his work cut out for him. George Halas had assembled a juggernaut.

# 26
## *SHINING MOMENTS AS WAR CLOUDS GATHER*

In 1941, the United States was on the verge of plunging into World War II with all its might. Before global battle dimmed the lights on recreation, though, American sports fans were treated to a marvelous year.

In baseball, Joe DiMaggio went on a 56-game hitting streak. Ted Williams batted .406, the last hitter to break the .400 barrier. In the National League, the Brooklyn Dodgers were awakening from a 21-year slumber that would transform them from legendary losers into a perennial power. Whirlaway won the Triple Crown in horse racing. Joe Louis knocked out Billy Conn in the 13th round of an epic heavyweight title defense.

While the baseball season headed toward a climax, the Bears and the Packers prepared to duel for control of the NFL. In the eight seasons since the league had adopted a championship game, either Chicago or Green Bay had played in seven, with each team winning the title twice.

The 1941 season promised to be no different. The Packers had three players—Don Hutson, Clarke Hinkle and Tony Canadeo—who would wind up in the NFL Hall of Fame. A fourth, Cecil Isbell, would top Sammy Baugh and Sid Luckman in passing yards, touchdowns and completions. The Bears were anchored by four future Hall-of-Fame stars—Luckman, Bulldog Turner, Joe Stydahar and Danny Fortmann..

During training camp, a confident Curly Lambeau said he believed the Packers had found the missing ingredient. "We really seem to have something this year that we lacked last season," he said. "The squad has spirit, it works with real enthusiasm. A team isn't great unless it tackles the job with the proper mental attitude."

The question was, Would the Packers' improvement be enough to muzzle the surging Bears?

While Green Bay opened the 1941 season with a pair of easy victories over Detroit and Cleveland, Chicago capped a six-game preseason schedule with three games on the East Coast. Halas, not content with the spotlight from a boggling crowd 98,203 that saw the Bears beat the College All-Stars 37-13 in Soldier Field, was always on the prowl for exhibition revenue.

And so, when the Bears began their 1941 regular season with a trip to Green Bay, the Packers already had played and won two league games.

Eager to see the Bears humbled, a crowd of 24,876 squeezed into City Stadium on September 28, 1941. On that same day, Red Sox hitting legend Ted Williams turned down an offer to sit out and preserve his .3995 batting average, which would have rounded up to .400. Playing in a doubleheader against the A's in Philadelphia, he had six hits in eight at-bats to finish the season at .406.

The throng of Packer fans left City Stadium disappointed. Green Bay led 17-15 in the third quarter, but the Bears toughened up and scratched out a 25-17 victory. Virtually everyone who saw the game credited the Bears' win to dominating the line of scrimmage. Everyone except George Halas. "It was finesse, nothing more, that beat the Packers today," Halas said while holding court after the game in Room 707 of the Northland Hotel. "Our power wasn't any better than the Packers'. But we did come through when it counted. I'd like to have some of Curly's boys on my club. We could use them."

Beyond some vague vows that the outcome would be different when the teams met in Chicago on November 2, Lambeau and his players were not quoted directly in either the *Press-Gazette* or the *Chicago Tribune*.

The Bears proceeded to crush their next four opponents—the Rams, Cardinals, Steelers and Lions—by a whopping 184-35 count. The Packers also won their next four games, but two of them were by a combined four points.

And so, Green Bay took a 6-1 record into Chicago for the rematch against the 5-0 Bears. It was no wonder that 46,844 fans jammed their way into Wrigley Field to see if the Packers could stop the unstoppable Bears.

With Isbell running for one touchdown and passing for another, Green Bay opened a 16-0 lead after three quarters and then held on for a nail-biting 16-14 win over the Bears, who had won 15 straight games—including seven exhibitions—since their last defeat, on November 17, 1940, nearly a year earlier.

The Packers mounted intense pressure that limited the Bears' vaunted T-formation to only nine completions in 32 passing attempts. Meanwhile, Isbell and runner Clarke Hinkle took advantage of a Chicago defense that was overplaying dangerous receiver Don Hutson.

Lambeau explained the key to victory to *Chicago Tribune* writer James Costin, who reported the next day:

" 'The game was a setup for us, psychologically,' Curly said while being pounded joyously on the back in the Packers' dressing room. 'They had beaten us four times in a row and had taken the championship away from us. Our players kept reading, day after day, about the Bears being the wonder team—the unbeatable team. We read where they had, not one team, but three teams. We knew the Bears were reading that stuff, too. We hoped they believed it—we didn't. We knew that they could be beaten, but it would take the best football we—or anybody—could play to do it. And with that in mind, we got ready for 'em.'"

The upset required more than a fired-up Packer roster, though, Lambeau told Costin. "We built up a special defense to stop their power and passing," Lambeau admitted. While it was obvious that Green Bay had stacked its line with five, six and even seven defenders at times, Lambeau believed Halas and his Bears still hadn't figured that out.

"Not one word about defense!" he shouted to his players when a Chicago reporter asked for details on the Green Bay defense. "Not one word about what we did on defense today."

And so, Lambeau, often credited with being a brilliant offensive strategist and a skilled motivator, had overseen a baffling defensive scheme. It was a stretch, however, for Lambeau to think the talented Bears would not figure out an answer to his defensive maneuvering, no matter how clever.

The game was a bonanza for Halas, ticket scalpers and car-parkers —just about anyone who had a financial interest in the game. Ace Gutowsky, the recently retired Detroit Lions rushing star, said he paid $4 a ticket for a pair of $2.50 upper-grandstand tickets. Police reported the arrests of 11 scalpers. Meanwhile, a gas station operator doubled his parking price to $1.50 per automobile. And with the standing-room-only crowd spilling onto the turf around the field, the gate was estimated at more than $100,000.

Adding even more drama, a game that looked safely in Green Bay's hands for three quarters turned into a narrow escape for the Packers, who saw their 16-0 fourth-quarter lead shrink to 16-14. Unable to get the timeout his team was frantically motioning for in the final seconds, Halas rushed the field afterward to argue with the officials after being denied a desperate chance for a long field goal.

"They're a great ball club," the Bears coach and owner said afterward. "But just a little break here or there...would have won the game for us."

Halas declined to talk about the referees' refusal to give the Bears a final timeout. But Bears co-captain George Musso said referee Heintz, who didn't realize Musso was a captain, said only a captain could ask for a timeout. Even so, the Bears, who were at the Green Bay 40 yardline, would have needed to convert a very long field goal to pull out a 17-16 win.

"We got cocky in the fourth quarter; very careless, in fact," Lambeau said. "Being the great team that they are, the Bears took advantage of our mistakes and came right back with two touchdowns which made it a ballgame that was one for the books. They are still a great team—one of the best of all time—but I think we are better, and I also think we proved it this afternoon."

# 27
## *PEARL HARBOR AND A NEAR-SHOCKER*

On December 7, 1941, Lambeau took his entire team to the South Side of Chicago to watch the Bears play the Cardinals. Green Bay had completed its season a week earlier with a win in Washington that gave it a 10-1 record.

Anticipating that the Bears, who were 9-1, would beat the Cardinals and force a Western Division playoff with Green Bay, Lambeau wanted his players to see the Bears for themselves. And so, the Packers boarded a 7 a.m. train out of Green Bay and booked a return that would bring them back home by midnight. To keep his men comfortable, Lambeau chartered two parlor cars and a diner. "They will have all three meals on the train," the *Press-Gazette* noted.

In the unlikely event that the Cardinals upset the Bears, the excursion would have been unnecessary. Green Bay would win the Western Division and host the Eastern Division champion New York Giants in the NFL title game.

If, as Lambeau and the NFL watching world expected, the heavily favored Bears prevailed, Green Bay and Chicago would meet at Wrigley Field on December 14 to determine the Western Division champion. The Bears had won a coin toss for home field if a playoff was required.

Sitting in the upper deck at Comiskey Park before the Bears-Cardinals game, Lambeau emphatically denied George Halas' charge that Lambeau had stationed spies in apartment buildings overlooking Wrigley Field during Bears' practices and had fed the information to the Washington Redskins before a recent game in Chicago.

"That was the most absurd thing Halas ever said," Lambeau said. "Our scout arrived in Chicago on Saturday and went by on Sunday to see Ray Flaherty, Washington's coach, only an hour before the game. That's pretty late for turning over plays, isn't it? I've never been that hard up for information on the Bears and if I ever do come to that sort of thing, I'll just get out of the business."

Wearing a jaunty trench coat and with an over-sized set of field glasses around his neck, Lambeau seemed dressed for espionage. And from the upper deck of Comiskey Park, he liked what he saw. The undermanned

Cardinals, who had been hammered by the Bears 53-7 on October 12, came out with a stout start, jumping on the Bears for an early 14-0 lead.

With the Cardinals leading 17-14 at halftime, some even more startling news reached the South Side of Chicago. The Japanese had launched a devastating attack on Pearl Harbor. "They announced it over the loudspeaker," Bears quarterback Sid Luckman said. "It was a tremendous shock to everybody in the stadium. The teams just didn't have the same emotions, knowing our country had just been attacked."

"I didn't know what to do," Halas said. "We decided the game should go on. Very few people left."

The Bears pulled ahead 21-17, but the Cardinals took a 24-21 lead early in the fourth quarter.

"A crowd of 18,879 sat in amazement as an embattled bunch of Cardinals, led by Marshall Goldberg and Ray Mallouf and featuring a hard-charging line, outplayed the Bears and threatened to knock the champions right out of the title picture," Howard Roberts reported in the *Chicago Daily News* on December 8.

Looking down from end-zone seats in cavernous Comiskey Park, Lambeau and his players started believing they could avoid another showdown with the Bears.

"The Packers, huddled in great coats in the upper deck, were whooping lustily as they envisioned a clear claim to the western crown," Roberts said.

But then the bubble burst for the Cardinals—and the Packers. Goldberg left the game with an injury. And then a pass-interference call against the Cardinals set up a 39-yard touchdown catch by George McAfee that gave the Bears a 28-24 lead. McAfee added a 70-yard scoring run as the Bears rallied for a 34-24 win.

"The Bears, like the Yankees, will knock another team's brains out if given so much as one break," Roberts said.

Their hopes of going directly to an NFL championship meeting with the New York Giants crushed, the Packers headed back to Green Bay. Their stay would be short. They would be back in Chicago by the end of the week for their third meeting with the Bears to decide the Western Division champion.

Perhaps needing a diversion from the hash reality that America had been thrust into World War II by Japan's attack on Pearl Harbor, football fans stormed the Bears' two ticket outlets on Monday morning and snapped up every available seat for the playoff game between Halas' Bears and Lambeau's Packers, which would be played on Sunday, December 14, at Wrigley Field. Halas said 11,700 tickets were sent to Wisconsin. That was not enough. "On Lambeau's desk are a number of slightly indignant wires from his Wisconsin constituents who were unable to obtain tickets. He estimates that requests for at least 10,000 tickets could not be filled."

To remain available for troop movements, the North Western railroad initially planned no special fares or trains to Chicago. But even with a higher fare of $7.51, demand among Packer fans was so great that a Green Bay tavern sponsored a special train for Packer fans.

The players also were having difficulty trying to keep their focus on football. Before practice Tuesday, "the Bears were taking turns venting their wrath on the Japanese when Bob Swisher quietly cut in with: 'Me, I hate Don Hutson!'"

"The Packers," Bears quarterback Sid Luckman said, "tricked us once this season with their seven-man line but they are not going to do it this time."

Amid boastful predictions that the Bears would crush the Packers, Lambeau said, "They really do have a chance of winning, even by 40 points. But don't forget—we have [just] as excellent a chance of trimming them by that kind of score."

Lambeau also disputed the opinion that Green Bay's hopes rest on "three old men"—Hutson, Isbell and Hinkle—who had a combined 21 years of NFL football under their belts. "Without this trio. . . the Packers wouldn't have any business in the league," *Chicago Sun* columnist Tom Siler wrote.

Age wasn't really the point. Considering that Hutson, 28, was the NFL's premier receiver, that Isbell, 26, had the best passing year in the league statistically and that Hinkle, 32, a bruising runner, led the NFL in kicking and was among its best running backs, Lambeau had assembled a trio capable of winning at the highest level.

The Packers' problem was, so had George Halas. In speedy runner George McAfee, fullback/linebacker Norm Standlee and fullback Bill Osmanski, Chicago had three of the NFL's top six rushers in 1941. The Bears averaged 44 yards more than No. 2 Brooklyn. The Packers were third, but averaged 1.1 fewer yards per carry (3.3) than the Bears (4.4).

Although Isbell was the league's most productive passer that year, the Bears also led the NFL in passing offense, with nearly 25 more passing yards per game. While Isbell was effective in Lambeau's increasingly antiquated Notre Dame Box, Sid Luckman was emerging as the prototype for the modern NFL quarterback.

Halas' powerhouse averaged 36 points a game, nearly two touchdowns more than the runner-up Packers' 23.5 points per game. And while the Bears were allowing a few more points, they led the NFL in stopping the run. The Bears defense had a host of dedicated players, including future Hall of Famers Bulldog Turner, Joe Stydahar and Danny Fortmann.

Sunday, December 14, 1941, dawned cold in Chicago and stayed that way. Although temperatures that began in the teens nudged into the mid-20s by mid-afternoon, a northwest wind was gusting up to 17 m.p.h. The chill in the air, combined with widespread reports of a sellout, actually backfired for scalpers. Very few potential buyers showed up looking for tickets. Prices came down shortly before kickoff, and the crowd of 43,425 wound up being slightly smaller than the 46,484 who saw Green Bay shock the unbeaten Bears 16-14 on November 2.

That said, this game still attracted a throng eager to see the first divisional playoff game in NFL history. Anticipating a tough contest, NFL leaders even came up with the league's first overtime plan. In case of a tie, the teams would remain on the field during a three-minute break and then they would begin "a second game." The first team to score would win. This would be the first game that would use, if necessary, the format that came to be known as "sudden death."

Adding to the massive buildup for the Bears-Packers playoff showdown, many wondered if, due to World War II, this would be the last meeting between the two venerable NFL franchises for the foreseeable future. There was considerable speculation that organized sports activity would be shelved as the United States dedicated itself to fighting.

President Franklin D. Roosevelt, who had been a talented and active athlete before being confined by polio, eventually decided that sports should continue as a morale booster. But with able-bodied men trading their shoulder pads and baseball gloves for rifles and tanks, halting sports during the war was a real possibility.

In many ways, the 1941 Western Division playoff was the end of an era for Lambeau against Halas. Never again would Curly line up against his longtime rival with a championship-caliber team.

Halas, who had been disappointed at not being sent overseas when he was in the Navy in World War I, would go off to the Navy five games into the 1942 season. Lambeau would continue to guide the Packers. By the time Halas returned to coaching in 1946, though, Lambeau no longer would be presiding over a powerhouse in Green Bay.

The Packers got off to another good start in the 1941 playoff, taking a 7-0 lead after Bears returner Hugh Gallarneau fumbled the opening kickoff, allowing Green Bay to score on a 19-yard drive. Gallarneau also fumbled the next kickoff, but the Bears recovered, only to lose the ball again when Norm Standlee fumbled at the Bears 35 yardline.

From there, the pendulum swung. Chicago blocked Clarke Hinkle's field goal. When Hinkle punted soon after that, Gallarneau handled it cleanly at the 18 yardline—and went 82 yards for the first Bears touchdown. A missed extra point kept Green Bay on top 7-6, but in the second quarter, the Bears erupted. After a short field-goal drive for a 9-7 lead, Chicago recovered the second of two Green Bay fumbles. That set up a 12-yard Bears touchdown drive. Chicago added two more touchdowns in its 24-point second quarter. Leading 30-7 at the half, the Bears rolled on to a 33-14 victory.

Seeing the bright side, the *Press-Gazette* pointed out that the Packers won the second half 7-3. Lambeau was in no mood for that kind of balm; the Packers had been crushed in the first half: "Let's not alibi. Let's take it. The team wasn't fighting, and they made a lot of mistakes."

The following week, the Bears finished the job, whipping the New York Giants 37-9 to win the 1941 NFL championship. Despite an unseasonably warm 54-degree day, only 13,341 fans showed up at Wrigley Field. It was the smallest crowd to attend an NFL title game.

More than 43,000 to see the Packers-Bears playoff game in daunting weather? And 30,000 fewer fans to see the Giants-Bears championship game on a relatively balmy day? The contrast was another testament to the appeal of the rivalry that Curly Lambeau and George Halas had created.

"You just can't get the Packers out of your hair, even when they're not playing," Irv Kupcinet wrote in the *Chicago Times* the next day. "The Giants, following in the wake of the Packers, were anti-climactic. The fans, like the Bears, rose to emotional heights for the Green Bays and any game that followed even though it was for the National Football League championship, was bound to suffer by comparison."

# 28
## *AMERICA GOES TO WAR, THE NFL ADJUSTS*

Amid fears that the Japanese could attack the West Coast, football adjusted. The Rose Bowl was moved to Durham, North Carolina, where Duke played host to Oregon State. The East-West Shrine game shifted from San Francisco to Tulane Stadium in New Orleans. And so, Lambeau went to New Orleans to ring in 1942 while scouting future Packers at the Sugar Bowl between Missouri and Fordham and at the Shrine all-star contest, which was played on January 3, two days after the Sugar Bowl.

Returning home to Wisconsin, Lambeau weighed in on the appropriateness of sports in wartime. Stumping for wartime football at a banquet for high school players on January 23 in Wausau, he said, "Football players should make good soldiers, because fundamentally football and war have many tactical maneuvers in common." Because of football's value in training, the sport should be expanded rather than curtailed during the war, Lambeau told 60 Wausau high school athletes and more than 200 parents and friends at the annual Victory banquet given by the Drug Store Coaches association at the Wausau Elks Club.

Despite Green Bay's 10-2 season, "The final playoff defeat by the Bears spoiled it all," Lambeau said. He then explained why a draft-rule change would help the Packers close the gap on the Bears. The day after Halas' team demolished Washington 73-0 in the 1940 championship game, the league had adopted a rule barring the sale or trade of draft picks for one year unless every other NFL team approved the deal. That was aimed at the Bears, who had acquired eleven No. 1 picks in five years. The Eagles and Steelers regularly traded their top picks to Chicago for veteran talent. By acquiring Sid Luckman and Norm Standlee from Pittsburgh, and George McAfee from Philadelphia, Lambeau said, Halas had done an endaround on attempts to keep competitive balance in the league.

"But that is enough for 1941," Lambeau said. "We, too, are building. Naturally, we will lose many men who are going into the armed forces, but we are combing the country for material and I can promise a representative Packer team for next fall. Outside of the 20 men on our league draft list, we have 60 fine college prospects in mind. Of these we estimate that about 40 will be lost to the army and navy. But the remaining 20, plus the men on our list and our veterans, should give us a fine squad."

Lambeau finally did escape to California shortly after his Wausau remarks. After several weeks on the West Coast, he headed to New York for NFL meetings on March 26-28, 1942, at the Hotel Commodore. At the meeting, rosters were reduced from 33 to 27 players because so many players and prospects would be in military service. Team officials agreed to schedule exhibition games against service teams. With smaller rosters, they also discussed easing their substitution rules to create their best units on offense and defense..

Like major-league baseball, pro football would be a very different game during World War II. Struggling to find athletes, most teams were not nearly of the same caliber as their pre-war squads. The Bears and the Packers would continue to dominate the NFL West, as would the Redskins and the Giants in the East. But the talent level would not be the same.

By the time the 1942 pre-season arrived, Lambeau was ready to plunge back into football. Undeterred by wartime travel restrictions, he arranged exhibition games against the Brooklyn Dodgers at Ebbets Field and against the Washington Redskins at Memorial Stadium in Baltimore.

Because he wanted to scout the Bears against the College All-Stars in Chicago on Friday, August 28, Lambeau planned to miss the game against the Dodgers. So did Don Hutson, who was in Chicago to receive his MVP award for the 1941season.

Lambeau's absence did not stop *New York Times* columnist John Kieran—who also was a regular on the very popular *Information Please!* radio quiz show—from gently needling Curly while providing some invaluable publicity.

After detailing a Packer press release that listed the 15 Green Bay players who now were in military uniform, Kieran said, "Lambeau needn't come around looking for sympathy as long as he has Don Hutson and somebody to throw him a football when the game is on. But probably Curly was looking for justice rather than sympathy. If this is justice, he has it."

As it turned out, the Brooklyn game was postponed a day due to weather—and perhaps to entice more fans to attend. That enabled Lambeau and Hutson to get to New York, where Hutson lived up to Kieran's high praise.

Trailing 16-7 before a Sunday afternoon crowd of 9,874 at Ebbets Field, Green Bay rallied. After running for a one-yard touchdown, Isbell threw a two-yard touchdown to Hutson with four minutes left, nudging the Packers past Brooklyn 21-16.

Hutson "could pick your pocket while you were running a 100-yard dash, and you'd never know it," Dodger halfback Dean McAdams said after Hutson had denied Brooklyn of a credibility-building win.

The Packers then moved on to Baltimore, which was hoping for a strong turnout to build support for landing a pro football team at Green Bay's exhibition game against the Washington Redskins on Monday, September 7.

Before the game, Lambeau joined Redskins owner George Preston Marshall and *Chicago Tribune* sports editor Arch Ward at the inaugural luncheon of the Downtown Quarterbacks of Baltimore. Ward "named

Lambeau, Marshall and [George] Halas as the three men who had contributed most toward bringing the pro league to its present point."

After Lambeau praised Baltimore as a good sports town, Marshall echoed that view. While the NFL would not consider any expansion during wartime, the Redskins owner said, "Baltimore very definitely would be considered as a likely location" when the NFL added teams. In the meantime, Marshall said he was very interested in having the Redskins play more pre-season games there, or even moving a league game to Baltimore.

That night, more than 50,000 spectators, including 10,000 military guests of Marshall, saw the Redskins break a 7-7 fourth-quarter tie with three touchdowns to post a 28-7 win over the Packers. A week later, 45,000 fans turned out at Baltimore's Municipal Stadium on September 16 to see the Eastern Army All-Stars defeat the Brooklyn Dodgers 13-7.

World War II was putting America to work. After scuffling through the Depression, Americans had defense-job money to spend. And they were interested in the kind of entertainment that football provided. Although finding capable players was a challenge in wartime, the NFL, which had struggled for survival, now found itself on better financial ground. It was ground that soon would be coveted by other sports-minded businessmen.

The Packers headed home to prepare for their September 13 exhibition against the Western Army All-Stars in Milwaukee. Coached by the legendary Wallace Wade, who had turned Alabama into a powerhouse before doing the same at Duke, the Western Army team had defeated the Detroit Lions 12-0 on Wednesday, September 9.

Lambeau used the Lions' loss to motivate his Packer team, which he thought "lacked fight" against Washington, and to sell tickets. A crowd of 20,000 saw the Packers, who trailed 7-6 at halftime, erupt for 23 points in the third quarter and go on to a lively 36-21 win over the Western Army All-Stars at Marquette Stadium in Milwaukee. The benefit game raised $40,000 for the Army Emergency Relief Fund.

After that, Green Bay had two weeks to prepare for its 1942 season opener against the Bears. Even though it was the first game, both sides realized that it would go a long way toward deciding the Western Division. The Rams, Cardinals and Lions figured to be no match for the Bears or Packers.

The flood of NFL players going into military service changed the league in a huge way. A total of 638 NFL people—including players, coaches, management—served in the war. By March of 1944, 68 percent of the 347 players who had been on NFL rosters in 1941 were in the military, Lambeau's friend, George Strickler, who had left the *Chicago Tribune* to become the NFL's publicity director, calculated.

In Green Bay, 16 of the 33 players from the 1941 team were claimed by the military for the 1942 season. And 19 of the 20 players Lambeau selected in the 1942 NFL draft were unavailable, claimed for fighting duty.

To help keep his roster stocked, Lambeau secured defense-work jobs that would shelter his players from military service. The Packers coach contacted officials at Green Bay defense plants and Sturgeon Bay shipyards about jobs for players and adjusted his practice times to accommodate their defense work. That gave the Packers an advantage, Lambeau said, on big-city teams that needed to hold their training camps out of town. Even teams that were able to train in big cities faced difficult commutes, whereas Green Bay players were able to walk to many defense jobs. Fullback Ted Fritsch and guard Sherwood Fries did that while working at the Green Bay Food Company.

The manpower shortage was so great that the Steelers combined with the Eagles in 1943 to form the Steagles. In 1944. the Steelers combined with the Cardinals, forming a Card-Pitts team so feeble it became known as the Carpets. The 1943 Cleveland Rams and 1945 Brooklyn Dodgers simply shut down.

The league's depression-era anchors—the Bears and Packers in the West and the Redskins and Giants in the East—also weathered World War II the best. In 1942-45, they secured seven of eight title-game berths.

After the Western Army All-Stars fundraiser, Lambeau turned his attention to the season-opening game against the Bears. Knowing that Chicago again would be Green Bay's chief obstacle, Lambeau left no competitive edge to chance.

Under the headline, "No Malted Milks for Packers, Coach Says," Lambeau said he wanted to improve his team's conditioning, which he had not liked against the Western All-Stars. "We'll have to stress our diet," he said. "Some of the boys are drinking too many malted milks between meals. That extra weight is slowing us down."

Before a crowd of 20,007 at City Stadium, Green Bay got off to a good start and led the Bears 21-13 at halftime of the season opener. In the third quarter, a pair of rushing touchdowns gave the Bears a 27-21 lead. Don Hutson's second touchdown catch from Cecil Isbell put Green Bay back on top 28-27 heading into the fourth quarter.

Milk shakes or not, the Bears were the better team in the fourth quarter. They scored 17 unanswered points and notched a 44-28 victory. It was the most points Green Bay had ever allowed the Bears, another sign that the Bears' T formation was the future while the Packers' Notre Dame Box was the past.

"The Packers," Lambeau said afterward, "made the Bears look like a good ball team with their lack of fight at crucial moments."

The two touchdown catches by Hutson, who had been the NFL's Most Valuable Player in 1941, were the beginning of another epic season. He wound up catching 17 TDs, more than twice as many as the next NFL receiver and the same number of touchdown catches as the next three receivers combined. Hutson's NFL-leading 1,211 receiving yards and 110.1 yards per game both more than doubled runner-up Ray "Scooter" McLean's numbers. Hutson also had 74 catches; the next closest receiver had 27. Hutson would be named the league's Most Valuable Player for a second straight season in 1942, and narrowly miss a third MVP award in 1943, when he was edged by Sid Luckman.

By the time the Packers started getting ready for the rematch in Chicago, it was apparent the game would settle the Western Division struggle. Green Bay was 6-1. The Bears were 7-0.

Having failed to beat the Bears by banning milkshakes, Lambeau turned his attention to a more adult beverage: "Beer will be $50 a glass for Green Bay players this week," assistant coach Red Smith told the Packers after they beat the Rams in Cleveland on the Sunday before their Chicago trip. "Other violations of strict training will cost on a comparable basis. That's straight from the Belgian's mouth."

By game day, interest in the rematch bordered on an obsession. A crowd of 42,787 squeezed into Wrigley Field on Sunday, November 15. And "Chief Usher Andy Frain estimated that another 15,000 to 20,000 were turned away."

Halas, who had left the Bears after their fifth game to join the Navy, ran up a $40 phone bill to receive a full post-game report in Norman, Oklahoma. The Bears owner talked with co-coaches Hunk Anderson and Luke Johnsos, who were in charge while Halas patriotically took steps to head overseas after being disappointed at not leaving the United States while in the Navy during World War I. Lambeau, meanwhile, did not share Halas' passion for military service.

It was a joyous phone call. The Bears throttled the Packers 38-7, turning the showdown into a rout. Hutson, who had sprained his right ankle a week earlier in Cleveland, had not practiced all week. Still hobbled, he managed a meaningless touchdown catch only after Chicago led 38-0. Passer Cecil Isbell also played on a heavily taped ankle.

The Bears jumped out to an early 14-0 lead on a pair of gift touchdowns. Bulldog Turner returned a fumble 42 yards and Luckman scored on a 54-yard interception return. Less than two minutes before halftime, Green Bay failed on a fourth-down pass attempt from its own 30 yardline, setting up the Bears for a 21-0 halftime lead.

"We had to gamble," Lambeau said.

At a football luncheon on Tuesday, November 17, Luckman had a quick response when a fan suggested that the Bears allowed Green Bay to score their late touchdown so that Isbell and Hutson could keep their scoring streak alive. "Listen, pal, get this straight," Luckman said. "The Chicago Bears don't give anybody anything."

Lambeau, who had kept a tight lid on the Hutson and Isbell ankle problems the previous week, played the injury card as Green Bay prepared to face the Giants in New York, listing 13 Packers with varying physical ailments.

Not that it mattered. Unable to catch the Bears for the Western Division title, Green Bay left New York with a 21-21 tie, then slipped past the Eagles and Steelers in its final two games to finish 8-2-1.

The Bears, pursuing their third straight NFL title, wound up a perfect 11-0. Their season was spoiled, however, by a 14-6 loss to the Redskins in the 1942 NFL championship game. At least Lambeau could take comfort in knowing that his 1929-31 Packers remained the only team to win three straight titles.

# 29
## *SOLDIERING ON*

As America's involvement in World War II enveloped the nation in 1943, the NFL considered shutting down. Talented players were in short supply. Travel restrictions further complicated matters. Weighing most heavily, though, was the fact that most teams anticipated significant financial losses due to the restrictions.

"It is fairly well established that a half-dozen teams in the circuit would be very happy if Commissioner Elmer Layden's advisers prevailed upon him to skip the whole thing for the duration [of the war]," *Chicago Sun* columnist Warren Brown wrote when NFL owners gathered at the Palmer House in Chicago on April 6, 1943.

Amid these obstacles, the Packers' board voted on April 1, 1943, to allow the team's executive committee to decide whether Green Bay would field a team.

Lambeau, vice-president of Green Bay's nine-man executive committee, was adamant: The NFL should play. If the league shut down and tried to resume after the war, he believed, it would need to rebuild its connection with its fans, an important consideration because rival leagues were certain to challenge the NFL after World War II.

Having learned to be creative in roster building in 1942, Lambeau said, finding players in 1943 would not be as difficult: "We had our big problem last year. . . . We got over that hurdle and managed to have a pretty fair team." The solution, he said, was to delve back into the past and find capable players who were not in the military. "A football player might be a trifle rusty after a two or three year layoff, but he'll come back quicker than you think. . . . It's up to us to find 'em."

Playing on was an easier decision for Lambeau. He was skilled at finding players. He also was adept at lining up defense jobs for players—which was a simpler task in Green Bay, where the Packers were a civic treasure. An autumn without the Packers would be a barren time. And while Lambeau acted like an owner, the bottom line did not affect his bank account. That risk belonged to the Packers' community ownership rather than him.

Joining Lambeau in pressing for the NFL to play on was Redskins owner George Preston Marshall. Unlike George Halas, Art Rooney and the

Maras—owners for whom football was the primary business—Marshall had a laundry empire that was flourishing in wartime Washington. Like Lambeau, Marshall also feared the consequences of shutting down.

Heading into the NFL's early-April meeting in Chicago, the teams were pretty evenly divided on whether to play in 1943. The undecided Halas, on leave from the Navy, arrived in Chicago as the key vote. Lambeau and Marshall, the main proponents of playing on, urged the Bears owner to keep the league open for business, even if it meant a temporary financial setback.

"If we fold, we're likely to destroy a league that we've been building for more than twenty years," Marshall argued. "It would be like trying to warm up an old soufflé. The Redskins won't fold. We're going to continue even if it means that we have a four-team league consisting of Giants, Lions, Packers and Redskins."

"Marshall's arguments swung Halas into line," Halas biographer George Vass wrote.

Most teams wanted to reduce rosters from 33 players to as low as 20 or 22. Halas, on a 14-day leave from the Navy, said teams "could get by with as few as 20 players, while 22 would be a really safe quota," the *Chicago Sun* reported on April 6, 1943. The coaches of the Eagles, Cardinals and Rams agreed with Halas.

Lambeau disagreed, saying, 25 was the bare minimum. "I wouldn't want to try operating with any less than that," he said. "I feel sure we can get that many. After all, there are 25,000 boys with collegiate football experience available out of the last five senior classes. I think one percent of that will be available."

Lambeau prevailed. In another major move, the league permitted the Cleveland Rams to not operate in 1943. The remaining nine teams divided the Rams' players. During the Rams dispersal draft, Halas and Lambeau jousted verbally. As Halas complained that the Packers' roster was "so much better fortified than the other clubs that they constituted a menace to the league," Lambeau "developed a slow burn that gave him the appearance of a well-done lobster," Francis J. Powers reported in the *Chicago Daily News* on April 10, 1943.

Halas led the chuckles when Lambeau pulled No. 9 for the draft, which meant he would have the ninth selection in a blind draw for Rams players. Considering that there were only nine teams in the league, the Man Who Invented the Green Bay Packers must have been cursing his luck.

Miraculously, Lambeau still managed to draw the player he had coveted, Chet Adams, one of the best tackles in the league. "A huge grin split Curly's face as his eyes searched for George Halas."

\* \* \* \* \* \* \* \*

Although few observers seemed to realize it at the time, NFL officials also approved at their 1943 Chicago meeting a change that would transform professional football: Free substitution was adopted as a war-time concession to smaller rosters.

"The league made this change reluctantly, feeling it would work to the advantage of 'specialty' players such as Green Bay's Don Hutson," the *Chicago Daily Times* noted on April 8, 1943. To Lambeau, it only made sense to let stars do what they did best. To some, it was a temporary measure. To Lambeau, who was always interested in innovations that would expand the NFL's appeal, it was the future of the sport. Fans wanted to see stars shine. That was the way to grow the league's audience.

"Lambeau believes the rule will change the entire strategy of the game," Art Daley told *Press-Gazette* readers under the headline, "Free 'Subbing' May Revolutionize Pro Football."

"In future years. . . coaches will employ two teams, one for defense and the other for offense," Daley wrote, explaining a then-radical concept. "Coaches are always confronted with players who have certain weaknesses on offense or defense, but free substitution will give the pilots an opportunity to put their best players—defensively or offensively—on the field at the same time."

Allowing coaches to put their best offensive and defensive players on the field as a unit, Lambeau said, would result in a better brand of football. It not only would showcase the most talented players. It would boost the game's spectator appeal. It seems obvious now. But once again, it took men like Curly, who foresaw the future, to advance the game of football.

In baseball, having specialists on offense and defense would have been unthinkable—and baseball ruled the spectator-sports world. In football, having separate units became a key that allowed football to challenge baseball's popularity.

That was far off, however, for the NFL in 1943. As late as mid-June, Lambeau and others were predicting that only six teams would operate in

1943. The league finally settled on an eight-team circuit. Not only would the Cleveland Rams sit out. The Steelers and Eagles would combine into one team.

To comply with wartime travel limitations, the NFL, after a marathon 16-hour session on June 21 at the Blackstone Hotel in Chicago, came up with a 10-game schedule. Lambeau agreed to a schedule that gave the Packers only four home games—two in Green Bay and two in Milwaukee.

On the plus side, the Packers' four biggest crowds would come on the road. While their best home crowds were under 24,000 due to the smallest stadium in the NFL, they attracted crowds of more than 40,000 in New York, Chicago and Detroit, and nearly 35,000 turned out in Philadelphia.

Green Bay's popularity as a road attraction propped up its challenged wartime finances. Lambeau's team continued to be the Notre Dame of the NFL, the team from the little town that played big time football.

On the field, though, the 1943 season turned out to be more of the same frustration that Lambeau had known in the previous two autumns.

Green Bay went 25-5-2 from 1941 to 1943. Ordinarily, five losses in three years would lead to joy and championships. The problem was, all five losses came against the Bears. The Packers' 1-5-1 record against the Bears made all the difference those three years. The Bears lost only twice, posting a 29-2-1 record in 1941-43. They added two NFL championships and narrowly missed a third, upset by Washington 14-6 in the 1942 championship game.

The Packers managed a 21-21 tie in their 1943 opener with the Bears, their only true obstacle in the Western Division. But they lost 33-7 to the Redskins in Milwaukee and 21-7 to the Bears in Chicago and wound up with a 7-2-1 record.

That left Lambeau's Packers one game behind the Bears (8-1-1), who defeated Washington for the NFL championship. It was the Bears' third title in four years.

"We had a good enough team to win but those two defeats, plus injuries and a lack of spirit put us where we are today." Lambeau said in his post-season analysis. That pretty much summed things up.

# 30
## *A LAST HURRAH*

In the summer of 1944, Lambeau went about the business of putting together a Green Bay roster that could overcome the powerhouse Bears. It ended up being an interesting mix of young players and veterans who had somehow not entered the military.

After a modest 14-7 win against the Brooklyn Tigers in Milwaukee, the Packers turned their attention to a pivotal game against the Bears in Green Bay. Before a crowd of 24,362 at City Stadium, the two historic rivals put on a hyper-active show in which the Packers opened a 28-0 second-quarter lead, gave it all back and then broke a 28-28 tie in the fourth quarter with a pair of late touchdowns for a 42-28 win.

"We've lost too many ballplayers," said Luke Johnsos, who was sharing the Chicago coaching duties with Hunk Anderson while George Halas served in the Navy. "There are too many freshman backs in there. The Packers have a strong club, and there's no substitute for experience against them."

Always searching for an edge, Lambeau coached from the press box, relaying strategy by telephone hookup to assistant coach George Trafton, who had been despised in Green Bay when he was a fierce Bears player. Johnsos also sat upstairs, talking to Anderson on the sideline.

The victory was only the Packers' second win in 11 meetings with the Bears, and their first in Green Bay against the Bears since 1939. Intent on winning their first NFL championship in five years, the Packers continued to roll. They took a 6-0 record into Chicago for their second meeting with the Bears on November 5, 1944.

Meanwhile, the Bears were a modest 2-2-1. They had followed up their loss at Green Bay with a surprising loss at Cleveland to a Rams team that had sat out the 1943 season.

Green Bay still had its magic when it came to attracting a crowd. The 45,553 spectators who squeezed into Wrigley Field that day was the second biggest crowd in the NFL in 1944, to be exceeded only by the 56,481 that would flock to the Polo Grounds two weeks later to see the Packers play the Giants.

At halftime, when the Bears led 7-0, Lambeau was so bothered by the Packers' performance that he abandoned his press-box perch and coached from the sideline in the second half.

That did not change the momentum. After scoring the only touchdown of the first half on a one-yard run, Ensign Sid Luckman, on leave from the Merchant Marines, added a pair of touchdown passes in the second half as the Bears took down the unbeaten Packers 21-0.

It was the first time Green Bay had been shut out in 73 games, since a rain-swept 2-0 loss to the Bears on September 18, 1938 at a soggy City Stadium. The Packers still held a one-game lead on the Bears, their closest rival for the Western Division.

But Lambeau and his Packers still faced obstacles on the field. And off of it.

\* \* \* \* \* \* \* \*

Curly Lambeau's 30-year reign as the leader of the Packers and a key figure in the entire NFL was marked by curious controversies as well as dynamic success. The final stages of the 1944 season provided both.

In a strange wartime setting, a crowd of 56,481, the NFL's biggest of the season, squeezed into the Polo Grounds on November 19, 1944, to see the NFL's two best teams. This meeting between the 7-1 Packers and the 4-1-1 Giants matched two good candidates to meet again in the championship game.

At quarterback for New York was Green Bay native Arnie Herber, who had been cut by Lambeau in 1941. At the time, Lambeau had said Herber, who always battled a weight problem, was no longer mobile enough to play for the Packers.

Although Herber, 34, directed the NFL's worst passing offense, the Giants had a stiff defense and a good running game. With the wartime shortage of capable players, Herber was adequate enough for a team that shut out five of its 10 opponents. Given that Lambeau had booted him from his hometown team, Herber did not lack for motivation.

Enjoying a moment of revenge, Herber threw a 36-yard touchdown in the second quarter. Meanwhile, the Giants' imposing defense intercepted five Packer passes as New York rolled to a 24-0 win even though Green Bay had twice as many first downs and 26 more yards. The touchdown pass was Herber's only completion in six attempts.

In another curious twist, despite being shut out for the second time in three games, Green Bay clinched the Western Division title as the Bears lost at Detroit 41-21.

The hero in this battle between war-depleted rosters was Giants back Howie Livingston, an obscure rookie who had served in the Navy after playing football at Fullerton (California) Junior College. Built like lanky Don Hutson, the 6-1, 183-pound Livingston smothered the Packer star. He even scored New York's first touchdown with a 34-yard interception return.

"The Giants are always tough," said Lambeau. "And don't be surprised if we have to take 'em on again in the playoff. It's beginning to shape up. . . . No, I didn't play Hutson in the last quarter. What was the use in using him up in that kind of game?"

With that, the Packers, who had given up air travel due to wartime constraints, boarded a train for the long trip home. When they got off the Milwaukee Road Chippewa in Green Bay late Monday afternoon, they were greeted by controversy rather than a throng of welcoming Packer fans celebrating Green Bay's first division championship in five years.

From the very beginning, one of Curly Lambeau's greatest strengths was his skill at attracting and managing publicity. That talent was essential to the success of fledging sports enterprises. But toward the end of his 30-year reign with the Packers, Lambeau increasingly had problems with the wrong kind of publicity. This was one of those moments. Winning smoothed over the bumps this time. That would not always be the case.

After their return to Green Bay, Lambeau and Hutson angrily denied a prominent report claiming that Hutson and Green Bay's former passing star, Cecil Isbell, "were not even on speaking terms [in 1942] the last season they played together." If true, that would have helped explain why Isbell did not return in 1943 after leading the NFL in touchdown passes and passing yardage the previous two seasons.

Then again, Isbell's return to his alma mater, Purdue, made sense in many ways. He earned more money as the Boilermakers assistant coach and his wife's family lived nearby. The decision looked even better when Isbell became the Boilermakers' head coach after one season as an assistant.

Lambeau blamed his former longtime assistant coach, Red Smith, who had moved on to the New York Giants in 1944 after eight seasons as Lambeau's senior assistant coach. The article, a profile of Hutson entitled "The Wizard of Green Bay" that appeared in the November 25, 1944, issue of *Collier's* Magazine, was written by *New York Times* sportswriter Arthur Daley, one of the most prominent NFL writers of the league's early decades. Although Lambeau said Daley had told him that Red Smith was the source, Daley denied that.

Coach Red Smith is not to be confused with Green Bay's most famous Red Smith, who became perhaps the best sports columnist of his generation. Like Lambeau, both Red Smiths went to Notre Dame. And further, *Green Bay Press-Gazette* sports editor Art Daley was not related to New York writer Arthur Daley, except that they both moved in Curly Lambeau's gridiron world.

"I am thoroughly burned up about it," Lambeau told the *Press-Gazette*. "As a matter of fact, Isbell and Hutson are the best of friends and there is no truth to the statement that they were not on speaking terms. Don has visited Isbell's home and just this year sat on the Purdue bench at the Michigan game at Isbell's invitation."

In the same article, Hutson said he was "dumbfounded" when he read the article. When he called Daley, Hutson said, "Daley was all apologies about it but he could have asked Isbell, me or hundreds of others whether what he had written was true. I can't understand why he would do that without checking the truth of the statements first."

Reached in Lafayette, Indiana, by the *Press-Gazette*, Isbell also insisted that he and Hutson "never had any trouble and I think that we got a pretty rotten deal. I am very unhappy about the whole thing and I feel that Daley owes both Hutson and me an apology. We never had any differences. In fact, not even a minor squabble. We always tried to help each other out. I can truthfully say that we never had an argument. It seems to me that Daley should have checked with at least one of us to find out if what he wrote was true."

One thing seemed clear. Lambeau and Smith had had a serious falling-out. "Red Smith made trouble for us when he was here," Curly said, "and we attempted to protect him. But when he violates the first principle of sportsmanship by giving out deliberate falsehoods, it is time to call a halt."

Coach Smith, who was from Kaukauna, near Green Bay, was a popular northeastern Wisconsin native. Like Lambeau, he had played for Rockne at Notre Dame before moving on to the Packers in 1927. The Red Smith Banquet, first held in Appleton in 1965, continues his memory by honoring sports figures and raising money for youth sports.

Smith also had played baseball, appearing in one game for the New York Giants in 1927 before beginning a long career as a minor-league coach and manager.

When Smith resigned on December 16, 1943, Lambeau said it was because he preferred to have a year-round assistant and Smith was unwilling to give up baseball coaching. That did not ring true, though. Smith had been a baseball coach or manager throughout his eight years as a Packer assistant.

When Smith left the Packers, he also was a coach for the Milwaukee Brewers, a AAA minor-league team managed by Charlie Grimm and owned by Bill Veeck. When Grimm was hired to manage the Chicago Cubs during the 1944 season, Smith stayed in Milwaukee to assist Grimm's successor, Casey Stengel. Grimm brought Smith up to the Cubs as a coach in 1945, when the Cubs won the National League pennant. He was a Cubs coach until 1949, when Grimm resigned.

One possible explanation: With his baseball spotlight, Red Smith was shining a little too brightly for Lambeau.

In departing from the Packers, Smith played along with Lambeau, publicly leaving on polite terms. "Because of the fine treatment I have been accorded," Smith said, "I shall always consider Green Bay my home."

By late February, Smith had been hired as line coach of football's New York Giants, for whom he had played in 1930 and 1931. Clearly, there were ill feelings between him and Lambeau.

Responding to Lambeau's accusations, Smith denied that he had been the source for the alleged Hutson-Isbell feud and produced a letter from Arthur Daley, who refused to identify Smith as his source. "Little boys always come home to cry," Smith told the *Press-Gazette* after the Giants had whipped the Packers 24-0 in New York on November 19, 1944, "and this time it is the coach and not the players."

When Lambeau continued to insist that Smith had fed Daley false information about Packer turmoil, Daley said he never told Lambeau that: "I told him that I had talked to many persons and had picked up considerable information throughout the many years I had covered professional football. Apparently, Curly chose to jump to conclusions he wanted to jump at. According to all traditions of the craft, newspapermen never reveal their sources of information."

Not only is the life of Curly Lambeau filled with tangled intrigues. The alleged Hutson-Isbell rift added another layer of mystery to the career of Isbell. When he abruptly walked away from playing in Green Bay on July 15, 1943, to take a job as an assistant coach at Purdue, he was coming off of two spectacular seasons. Hall of Famers Sid Luckman and Sammy Baugh are far better remembered, and rightfully so because of their longetivy. But in 1941 and '42, Isbell led the NFL in nearly every passing statistic. With Isbell throwing to Hutson, Lambeau easily might have added another NFL title or two.

Isbell seemed destined for the Hall of Fame as one of the best passers of the NFL's first 50 years if he had continued to play. But he only played five seasons after Lambeau drafted him seventh overall in 1938, abruptly walking away at the top of his game. Isbell once explained his early retirement by saying he had seen Lambeau cut star players when their skills had diminished and saying, "I vowed that it would never happen to me. I'd quit before they came around to tell me."

But that didn't ring true to *Green Bay Press-Gazette* writer Art Daley, who believed Isbell's wife talked him into a decision he regretted for the rest of his life. Isbell's wife was from Lafayette, Indiana, and her family had strong Purdue ties, Daley told Packer historian Cliff Christl. "I think [he regretted it] because he took up drinking like crazy."

Lambeau tried to talk Isbell into returning for the 1944 season. But Purdue elevated him to head coach of the Boilermakers that season—forcing Lambeau to make do with Irv Comp, who led the NFL in passing yards (1,159) but also had the most interceptions (21) in 1944.

With Green Bay preparing to take on the Giants in New York for the 1944 NFL championship, *United Press* columnist Jack Cuddy chose to shine a national light on the Smith-Lambeau dispute.

Noting that Lambeau "attributes a portion of his outfit's success this season to the fact that Red Smith is no longer their line mentor," Cuddy countered that by mentioning that New York coach Steve Owen "believes that Smith has been worth his weight in gold." For emphasis, Cuddy described the 5-foot-10, 230-pound Smith as "truck-like."

Smith declined to joust in public with Curly, saying, "I cannot recall having any difficulty with [Lambeau] or with the Packer club. I will break down and confess, however, that I hope we beat the hell outta them Sunday." Cuddy said Wisconsin sportswriters told him that Lambeau and Smith had been "at loggerheads . . . for most of Smith's tenure" with the Packers—and that Smith's relatives in Kaukauna urged Smith to resign and stop taking abuse from Lambeau.

And so Lambeau entered a game that could give him his sixth NFL championship against a team that featured two people with deep revenge motives to beat The Man Who Invented the Green Bay Packers: Giants line coach Smith and Giants quarterback Arnie Herber.

Before Green Bay's 24-0 regular-season loss in New York, Lambeau had taken the Packers to practice at Bear Mountain, an idyllic spot near the Hudson River about 50 miles north of New York City where the Giants held their pre-season training camp.

Lambeau wanted no part of Bear Mountain again—because of weather and especially because he said an anonymous caller had tipped him that the Giants had spied on Green Bay's practices. Lambeau insisted he was skeptical: "We don't do that in this league. . . . we don't spy on practices. It could have been, [though]."

It was classic Curly. He and George Halas regularly denied spying, even though there was ample evidence that both of them had regularly hired men to do that. Now Lambeau was bringing up spying with the Giants, but cleverly avoiding turning it into an accusation.

"It was possible," Don Hutson said. "They were shifting to meet those new plays of ours. . . and we haven't run them off against any other team in the league this year."

Before the rematch in the NFL championship game, the Packers did not take any chances. To eliminate more espionage, and to get out of the four inches of snow that had blanketed Green Bay, Lambeau took his team to Charlottesville, Virginia, home of the University of Virginia Cavaliers, who were coached by former Marquette coach Frank Murray, who had coached former Packer stars Lavvie Dilweg and Red Dunn at the Milwaukee school.

In one-game situations like that, Lambeau always seemed to be at his best, whether he was deploying his team in an unexpected way, motivating his players or exploiting an opponent's weakness. In the 1944 NFL championship game against the Giants, he used a combination of those ingredients.

It also helped that the Giants were a worn-out and beat-up team. The well-rested Packers had closed their season with a 35-20 win in Chicago against the combined Cardinals-Steelers squad on November 26. That season-ending loss left the hapless Card-Pitts, or "Carpets," with an imperfect 10 losses and no wins in their only season.

The Giants, meanwhile, went on to play two more games after that, both of them against Washington, on December 3 and 10. While the Packers were going deer hunting and playing gin rummy, New York needed to win twice to nudge past the Redskins, who had been favored to win their third straight Eastern Division title, and the Philadelphia Eagles, who had taken flight with the arrival of rookie running back Steve Van Buren.

The Giants won both games, 16-13 in New York and 31-0 in Washington. In the process, though, they lost the effectiveness of "Bazooka" Bill Paschal, the best power runner in the league, to a badly sprained ankle. The hobbled Paschal tried to play against Green Bay, but he was not the same bruiser who led the NFL in rushing yards and touchdowns in 1943 and 1944. He rushed twice for just three yards against the Packers.

Meanwhile, when Green Bay had the ball, Lambeau employed a new role for his dynamic receiver, Hutson: Decoy. The still brilliant Hutson, who was narrowly edged by Sid Luckman in voting for his third straight NFL Most Valuable Player honor, caught only two passes. But the Packers ran for 163 yards against a banged-up Giants defense that had only been yielding 100 rushing yards per game.

Green Bay fullback Ted Fritsch gave Green Bay a 7-0 lead in the second quarter on a one-yard score, only the sixth rushing touchdown New York had allowed in 11 games. Still in the second quarter, Fritsch caught a 28-yard touchdown from Irv Comp when the Giants secondary focused on Hutson. That expanded the Packers' lead to 14-0.

"Ted and I talked about that play without telling Hutson," Comp told the *Milwaukee Journal* in 1978. "Near the end [of his career], Hutson had a tendency to loaf a little if a pass wasn't supposed to go to him. Since he didn't know he wasn't the primary receiver, he ran a crossing pattern and took both the defensive back and a linebacker with him. Fritsch ran a [flare] pattern into the left flat and he was all alone."

New York finally scored in the fourth quarter, closing the gap to 14-7. But the Packers held on, disappointing a crowd of 46,015 that had turned out hoping to see Green Bay lose in the Polo Grounds for the second time in four weeks.

Exulting in their championship, the exuberant Packers gathered around Lambeau and hoisted him up onto their shoulders for a locker-room photo that captured a coach and his players in unbridled joy.

Sports accomplishments during World War II carry reduced weight for a good reason. Because so many accomplished athletes were in the military, the caliber of play was tainted. But that did not diminish the satisfaction that championships brought to those who were able to win.

The title was the sixth for Lambeau and his Packers, the most in the first 25 seasons of the NFL, one more than the Chicago Bears. Thanks to the leadership of Lambeau and the dedicated support of Green Bay businessmen and football fans, the league's last small town not only had survived. It had flourished to the point of being the NFL's most successful franchise in championships and wins—and widespread affection.

As the Packers celebrated before the long ride back to northeastern Wisconsin, it was difficult to foresee that Lambeau's run of glory was about to come to a troubled and surprising conclusion.

A crowd of nearly 1,500 fans braved single-digit temperatures to welcome back the Packers to Green Bay at 10:20 p.m. on Monday night after their 24-hour train ride from New York. But the aftermath of Green Bay's sixth NFL championship had a different feel to it.

Rather than speech-making at the Milwaukee Road station, there were merely cheers, handshakes and slaps on the back. And Packers president Lee Joannes announced that the traditional Victory Dinner would be postponed until August, when the team gathered for the start of the 1945 season. Many players had gone directly home from New York. And Curly Lambeau and his new line coach, former Bears terror George Trafton, had remained in New York for a league meeting to address the threat of the rival All-America Football Conference.

First order of business was NFL commissioner Elmer Layden's announcement that any NFL player who played for another league would be barred from playing in the NFL for five years. The AAFC already had started signing college players, including Angelo Bertelli, the Heisman Trophy winner from Notre Dame, and Bill Daley, an All-America fullback from Minnesota. It would sign many more.

Curly Lambeau (back row, third from left) scored the first touchdown for new coach Knute Rockne (far left). Also on the 1918 Notre Dame team were George Gipp (on Lambeau's left) and Hunk Anderson (second row, far right), who would be a longtime Lambeau friend and rival. *University of Notre Dame Archives*

Always the man in the middle, a beaming Lambeau clutches a football as the 1919 Packers mark their inaugural season with a team photo outside Indian Packing Co. *Green Bay Press-Gazette/USA TODAY NETWORK via Imagn Images*

Lambeau was a passing pioneer in the 1920s NFL, despite slippery footing and a fat football. *AP Images*

Crusty newspaperman George Whitney Calhoun (right) made a monumental contribution to birthing and nurturing the Packers.
*Neville Public Museum*

Johnny Blood's arrival in Green Bay in 1929 helped trigger the first of three straight championships.
*Neville Public Museum*

A leather-helmeted Red Grange made headlines by announcing he would retire after a 1933 barnstorming appearance with the Packers in Los Angeles. But tongues were wagging in Green Bay when Curly Lambeau was seen seated next to actress Merna Kennedy. *AP Images*

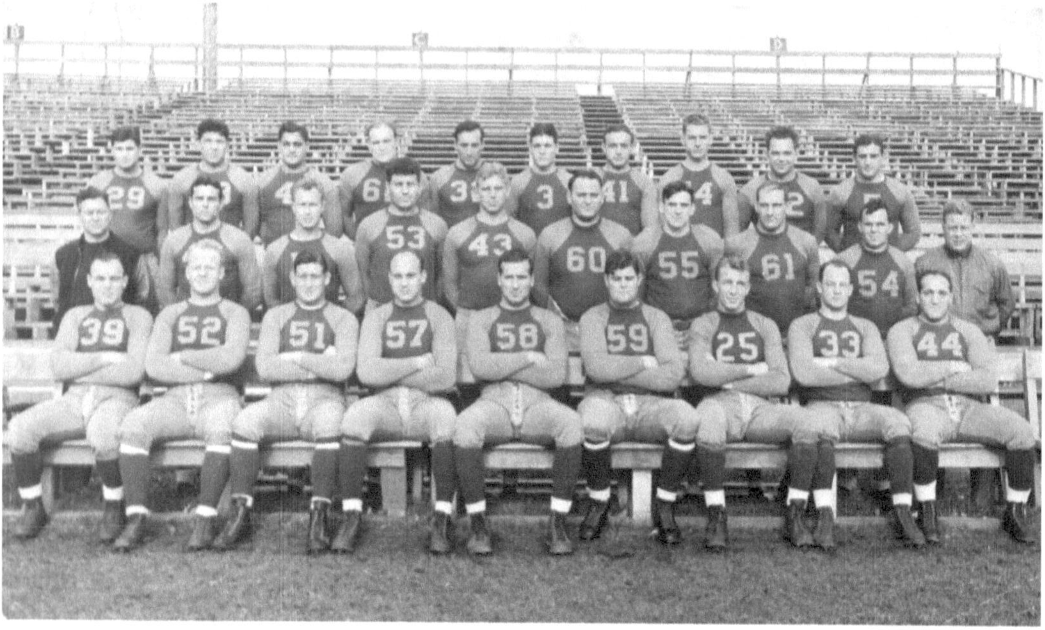

The 1936 Packers won Green Bay's fourth NFL title. It was their first topped off by a championship game victory. *Neville Public Museum*

Curly Lambeau could be a stern taskmaster when in coaching mode. *Neville Public Museum*

Lambeau and some of his 1930s stalwarts: Arnie Herber, Mike Michalske, Lambeau, assistant coach Red Smith, Milt Gantenbein and Hank Bruder. *Neville Public Museum*

Don Hutson cradles an armful of footballs, one for each NFL record he held. *Neville Public Museum*

On Pearl Harbor Day, December 7, 1941, Curly Lambeau was sitting in the upper deck at Comiskey Park, using binoculars to watch the Bears play the Cardinals. Huddling next to him are Baby Ray and Joe Laws, who were Packers although they resembled mobsters. *Chicago Sun-Times*

Curly and his Packers celebrate after beating the Giants in New York to win the 1944 NFL championship. *AP Images*

With snow on the ground for another important Packer moment, Lambeau and a group of Packer heroes participate in a benefit scrimmage on Thanksgiving Day in 1949 to raise $50,000 for a desperate franchise. Standing (from left): Fee Klaus, Herb Nichols, Curly Lambeau, Jug Earp, Lavvie Dilweg, Verne Lewellen and Johnny Blood. Kneeling (from left): Charley Brock, Don Hutson, Arnie Herber and Joe Laws. *Green Bay Press-Gazette/USA TODAY NETWORK via Imagn Images*

George Halas welcomes Lambeau to Chicago at a baseball dinner on Feb 2, 1950, a month after Cardinals president Ray Benningsen (center) hired Lambeau to coach Chicago's ``other'' NFL team. *Chicago Sun-Times*

Lambeau and Charley Trippi, the backfield star who did not always see eye to eye with his coach. *Chicago Sun-Times*

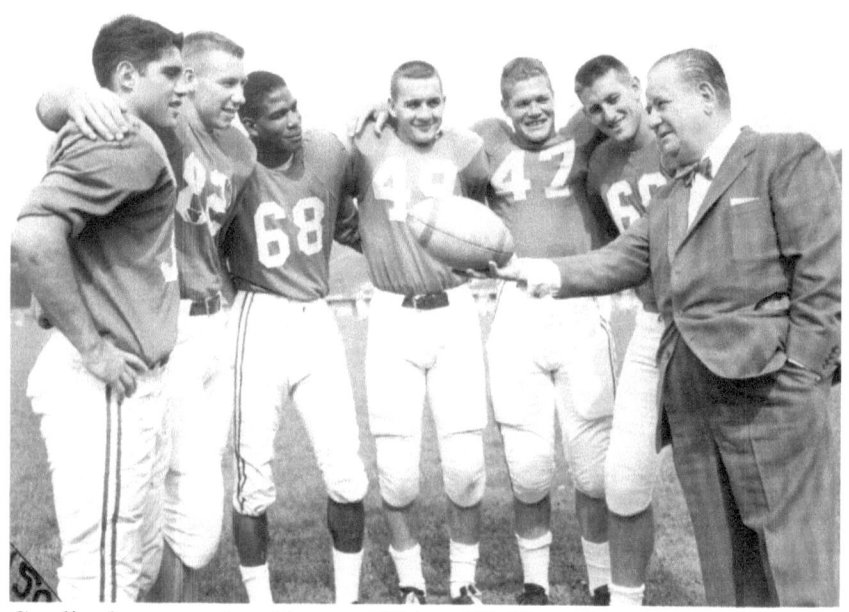

Cardinals managing director Walter Wolfner shows some post-Lambeau Cardinals who holds the football. just as he did with Curly. *Chicago Sun-Times*

With Lambeau gone, a relaxed Wolfner jokes with star Ollie Matson and Cardinals president Charles W. Bidwill Jr. *Chicago Sun-Times*

George Halas leads the Bears during their 1963 NFL championship win over the Giants. A decade after his longtime rival Lambeau had coached his last game, Papa Bear was notching his last title. *Chicago Sun-Times*

After initially saying no, Vince Lombardi agreed to pose for a photo with Curly Lambeau in 1962 at the stadium that would become Lambeau Field.
*Green Bay Press-Gazette/USA TODAY NETWORK via Imagn Images*

Mary Jane Van Duyse and Curly Lambeau. *Van Duyse family.*

Curly and the five Packers who joined him in the Pro Football Hall of Fame were honored at a dinner in Green Bay on April 26, 1965. Five weeks later, Lambeau would be dead. Left to right: Mike Michalske, Don Hutson, Curly Lambeau, Cal Hubbard, Clarke Hinkle and Johnny Blood. *Green Bay Press-Gazette/USA TODAY NETWORK via Imagn Images*

# PART THREE: TURMOIL IN PACKERLAND

## 31
### *AN OLD FRIEND CREATES A NEW ENEMY*

World War II continued to present many obstacles for professional sports, notably finding capable athletes and managing travel restrictions. But having seen how popular the National Football League had become, other sportsmen wanted in on the action.

Ironically, the greatest threat to the NFL would come from a man who had been a great friend and supporter of George Halas and Curly Lambeau It was a threat that would have disastrous consequences for Curly.

The man was Arch Ward, who came from the same Notre Dame/Rockne football huddle that had spawned Lambeau. Ward had been a student in 1915-16 at Dubuque College, where Notre Dame passing hero Gus Dorais was the football coach. Dorais had won a coin toss for the job with his receiver, Knute Rockne, who stayed on at Notre Dame as an assistant coach and chemistry instructor. Unless, of course, that is one of those fables created by the collusion of sportswriters and athletes.

After serving in World War I, Dorais would return to Notre Dame as baseball coach. He also would serve as an assistant to Rockne, who had become head football coach. How would things have turned out if Rockne had won the coin toss and become Dubuque's football coach? The world will never know.

Ward had left Dubuque College, which would later be renamed Loras College, where he had displayed a gift for publicity, to become sports editor of the *Dubuque Telegraph Herald*. With Notre Dame eager to spread the word about its football program, Dorais made Ward an offer: "Rockne would arrange for Archie's enrollment as a [Notre Dame] student if Archie would be Rockne's publicity assistant." Ward accepted. "He would be taking his place in the formation of one of sports' enduring legends—the Rockne Era at Notre Dame."

When Ward advanced to sports editor of the *Chicago Tribune*, he helped his friend, George Halas, attract fans to the Bears. It was a good partnership for Ward, who needed the fresh headlines that Sunday football provided for his Monday newspaper. As a sports visionary, Ward had gone on to create baseball's All-Star game in 1933 as a one-time event that would promote Chicago's World's Fair. It proved so popular that baseball commissioner Kenesaw Mountain Landis made it a cherished mid-summer moment.

A year later, to promote the second year of the World's Fair, Ward created the College All-Star game, in which the best college players took on the NFL champion. The game, a benefit for Tribune Charities, annually attracted the biggest crowds the NFL enjoyed each year. There is evidence that George Halas prodded Ward to give professional football this bonanza.

In 1941, NFL owners changed their leadership title from president to commissioner and approached Ward about becoming the NFL's first commissioner. Longtime league president Joe Carr, who had shaped the league for nearly two decades, had died two years earlier. His successor, NFL secretary-treasurer Carl Storck, was not dynamic enough for NFL owners, who were eager to grow their sport through Ward's deft touch for publicity and marketing.

Although Ward was offered a top-dollar salary of $25,000 and free rein, he declined the offer. Ward was a promoter who preferred to operate from the throne of a powerful newspaper. In his place, he convinced NFL leaders to hire one of Notre Dame's legendary Four Horsemen, Elmer Layden, another branch from the Rockne tree.

Not long after that, Ward approached the NFL leadership with a proposal. Actor Don Ameche, who had been a student at Dubuque College after Ward and was one of Ward's many entertainer friends, wanted to secure an NFL franchise in Los Angeles. With the financial backing of many other actors and celebrities, Ameche proposed to have the team play initially in Buffalo, then move to the West Coast when wartime travel restrictions were lifted.

"So Ward agreed to use his clout with the NFL owners" to get the deal done, Ward biographer Thomas B. Littlewood wrote.

There were problems, though. Washington owner George Preston Marshall raised the legitimate question about travel to the West Coast, which required at least an 11-hour flight from the East Coast. More importantly, other NFL owners already were eying Los Angeles. Halas had agreed to help Chicago Cardinals owner Charlie Bidwill move his team to L.A. after the war. Cleveland Rams owner Dan Reeves had the same idea. Never mind the long flight. Everyone wanted in on the West Coast market.

Beyond that, with their league becoming an attractive commodity after years of struggle, NFL owners were not keen on sharing the wealth through expansion.

"We owners were a tight little group," Halas wrote in his autobiography. "We had gone through a lot together. . . . we perhaps were too unresponsive to newcomers wanting to join our League. . . . But we liked things the way they were. . . . Looking back, I can see our closed door was certain sooner or later to produce trouble for us."

While not a team owner, Lambeau enjoyed the power and prestige of an owner at NFL meetings. An important owner, actually. He was a charismatic, visionary leader and a winner—and his status as a Green Bay vice-president made him a powerful voice. Whether everyone foresaw the trouble that Halas mentioned, Lambeau and Packers president Lee Joannes might not have fully grasped its implications for their Green Bay franchise. Other upstarts had tried to challenge the NFL and failed. Unlike the others, though, this rival would prove to have a good plan—and the deep pockets to make it work.

The trouble came in the form of Arch Ward, who was furious at NFL owners for turning down his proposal to place a team in Los Angeles.

"Arch could not bring himself to believe that the same men who had pleaded with him to be their commissioner a short time earlier would refuse his request for immediate West Coast expansion. But that is exactly what they did." Littlewood wrote. "If the National Football League would not expand after the war—which its owners clearly indicated they had no intention of doing—then Arch Ward would organize a new league."

The disagreement fractured the relationship between Halas and Ward, who had been so close that they took their families on outings together. "The breach between the two men would never be healed. They would never be friends again," Littlewood wrote.

"The rival league spoiled their friendship," Halas' daughter, Virginia McCaskey, said. "That was such a sad development."

In the summer of 1944, while Lambeau was assembling the roster that would give him his last taste of NFL glory, the development that would weigh heavily on his future was taking place.

On June 4, two days before the D-Day invasion by Allied troops in Normandy, several "men of millionaire incomes" met in St. Louis and took the first steps to form a new professional football league. The meeting was called by Ward, who had carefully assembled these deep-pockets sports enthusiasts. Snubbed by the NFL after he had rejected its offer to be commissioner, he now was laying the groundwork for a rival that would end up costing the NFL a fortune in the bidding war for players.

Although a close friend of Lambeau, Ward now was pushing Lambeau's Packers into a place they could not afford to be.

Ward would write an engaging history of the Green Bay Packers that would be published in 1946. This tribute to Earl Louis "Curly" Lambeau would debut in the same year that the All-America Football Conference began play. At the same time that Ward was celebrating Lambeau, Ward's AAFC would present Lambeau with a monumental challenge to the survival of his Green Bay Packers.

As 1944 turned the page to 1945, Lambeau was unable to make his annual New Year's pilgrimage to California to scout players at the Shrine college all-star game and the Rose Bowl. There was simply too much going on.

On Monday, December 18, the day after Green Bay defeated the Giants for its 1944 championship, NFL owners and team leaders held a special session at the Commodore Hotel in New York to address the threat of the All-America Football Conference raiding its rosters.

Commissioner Elmer Layden announced that players who jumped to the new league would be barred from playing in the NFL for five years. Knowing that would not be a sufficient deterrent, some NFL teams "began signing as many players as possible as quickly as possible in an effort to combat the menace to its prosperity" posed by the AAFC, the *United Press* reported from the NFL's New York meeting.

Meanwhile, War Mobilization Director James F. Byrnes, who wanted more athletes in the military, began questioning how men could be unfit for the military but able to play professional sports. Layden replied that many players worked in defense jobs and defended professional football because it "provided recreation and relaxation" for defense workers and servicemen. But NFL teams were caught in a tightening vice when it came to filling out their rosters.

In another problem that the NFL faced, after operating as the Card-Pitts in 1944, the Chicago Cardinals and Pittsburgh Steelers had decided to field separate teams in 1945. If a 12th franchise was not granted, an 11-team NFL would face awkward scheduling problems.

Amid that cauldron of controversies, the NFL was scheduled to hold its 1945 player draft at its annual winter meeting in Chicago on January 9-12.

"There's plenty to do before that meeting," said Lambeau, who arrived back in Green Bay from the 1944 championship game after his players because of the New York league meeting, "and besides we have to start thinking about the All-Star game next August. . . . The championship game is over. Our boys did a swell job, but we can't afford to rest on past laurels. The draft will be held at the January meeting, and we'll have to do gobs of work before then to get our list in shape."

On January 10, the date set for the draft, Lambeau and the other three members of the league's executive committee abruptly suggested that the NFL postpone its draft and other business until its spring meeting in April in New York. The adjournment was approved by all but one club. Calling the adjournment illegal, Redskins owner George Preston Marshall stomped out of the meeting and retreated to the sportswriters' press room, saying, "They acted in violation of our constitution."

By April, Lambeau and the rest of the NFL's leadership would have another controversy to sort out. Dan Topping, owner of the NFL's Brooklyn team, had become a co-owner of baseball's New York Yankees on January 26. Now he wanted to move his Brooklyn NFL football team into Yankee Stadium. That move was opposed by the Giants, who played in the Polo Grounds, just across the Harlem River from Yankee Stadium.

## 32
## *BATTLES ON MANY FRONTS*

That was not enough intrigue for Curly, though. On January 27, he announced the hiring of Steelers head coach Walt Kiesling as a third Packers assistant coach. This was surprising because Lambeau, who had only recently started having two important assistants, already employed George Trafton and Don Hutson. The Packers had just won the 1944 championship, in which Trafton, in his first season in Green Bay, had been credited with elevating the team's line play. Meanwhile, Hutson was serving as a player-coach near the end of his legendary career, and would stay on as an assistant in 1946 after wrapping up his playing career in 1945.

It was a strange move for Kiesling as well as Lambeau. Kiesling had played briefly for the Packers in 1935 and '36 at the end of a 14-year Hall of Fame career, but left for Pittsburgh in 1937 to be a player-coach on the staff of his friend, Johnny Blood. When Blood quit three games into the 1939 season, Kiesling became the Steelers head coach. He had held that job for six seasons when Lambeau hired him away to be a Green Bay assistant. Kiesling apparently had been persuaded by Lambeau to return to Green Bay during the NFL winter meetings in Chicago in January.

The situation became more clear a month later. On February 22, Lambeau announced that Trafton would not be returning. Trafton only had a one-year contract for 1944, Lambeau said, adding that he told Trafton he was being dismissed before he hired Kiesling but had kept it quiet to help his chances of landing another job. "If times were normal we would have more than three coaches on our staff and undoubtedly would have kept George as a fourth member," Lambeau said. "I think a great deal of his ability and am sorry that circumstances are such that he is leaving us."

It was the publicity-conscious Lambeau doing his usual job of spinning a story. But it didn't ring true. Like another capable assistant, Red Smith, who had left Green Bay, signs pointed toward Lambeau firing Trafton because he was either getting too much credit for Green Bay's success or making too many suggestions about strategy. Or just generally wearing out his welcome with the increasingly temperamental Lambeau.

Like Red Smith before him, Trafton played along, telling the *Press-Gazette* that he enjoyed living in Green Bay and had made many friends since arriving in August to begin his coaching duty. "I am happy that the football season was a terrific success," Trafton said, "and I take a great deal of pride in the fact that the Packer line had a great share in winning the championship. I have nothing but respect for all the linemen, who did all that was asked of them on every occasion.'"

His former boss, Lambeau, was conspicuously absent from Trafton's exit remarks.

Far from mellowing as he aged, Curly Lambeau had become increasingly demanding and Machiavellian. His methods had always had a tough edge. A degree of that was necessary in a still-emerging sport like professional football. But now Lambeau was using less charm and more iron fist. In addition, Lambeau was on the verge of losing his coaching edge. For more than two decades, he had been a winner and an innovator. Soon there would be whispers that the game had passed him by.

Trafton said he planned to remain in Green Bay "for some time since he has paid a year's rent for an apartment and because of the condition of his wife who is expecting a baby in March." At the age of 51, two years older than Lambeau, Trafton became a father for the first time on March 16, 1945, when his third wife gave birth to a daughter, Bliss, at Bellin Memorial Hospital in Green Bay.

Before there was a Dick Butkus, Trafton brought a Butkus-like combination of fierceness and talent to the NFL's early days. A Chicago native who trained boxers and operated a boxing gym there, Trafton had been knocked out in 1930 by future world champion Primo Carnera. Red Grange once called Trafton "the toughest, meanest, most ornery critter alive." In the *Press-Gazette,* the 6-foot-2, 230-pound former lineman was routinely referred to as George "Brute" Trafton.

Trafton was yet another link in the Notre Dame-Packers-Bears chain that was so defining to Curly Lambeau's football life. He played center on the Fighting Irish's undefeated national championship team in 1919, a year after Lambeau's season at Notre Dame. Moving on to the Decatur Staleys in 1920, the NFL's inaugural season, Trafton continued to be a brilliant player for an astounding 13 years, earning entry into the second Pro Football Hall of Fame class in 1964.

In 1920, when Decatur played a particularly rough game against the Rock Island Independents, Trafton enraged Rock Island fans by knocking out one player, who required 19 stitches in his head and a cast for a broken wrist, and shoving another Independent into a fence and breaking his leg. When the Staleys departed for their train ride home after the brutal scoreless tie, Halas gave Decatur's share of the gate, $3,000, to Trafton for safekeeping, saying, "If we did encounter obstreperous Rock Island fans, I would run for the money, but Trafton would run for his life." At least that's the legend handed down by Halas in his autobiography.

The Trafton tales must have been appreciated by Lambeau, who said he gained an early appreciation for passing when three Packers received broken bones on three straight running plays at Ishpeming in 1919. At this distance, it's virtually impossible to determine how many Rock Island bones George Trafton actually broke. Like Curly Lambeau, George Halas was a skilled yarn-spinner who knew how to generate interest in his football.

Trafton's mother also played a key role in the survival of the Bears. In 1931, when Halas was desperate for money to pay off his partner, Dutch Sternaman, Mrs. Trafton loaned Halas $20,000 to help provide the $38,000 Sternaman wanted. "Some years later. . . Mrs. Trafton thought I should make her son George coach," Halas said. "We held a stockholders' meeting. She was outvoted." Halas said he then bought Mrs. Trafton's stock for $40,000.

Unlike Red Grange, Bronko Nagurski and other football pioneers who shaped the Bears, Trafton has been largely forgotten. But he was an exceptional player and talented coach. After helping Green Bay to the NFL championship in 1944, Trafton was hired as line coach of the Cleveland Rams, who won the NFL championship in 1945, giving him his second straight title. He remained with the Rams for several years before coaching the Winnipeg Blue Bombers to a Grey Cup appearance, the Canadian Football League's Super Bowl.

Firing Trafton was not the first questionable decision Lambeau made after winning his sixth NFL championship. And there would be an increasing number of separations in the late 1940s from men who had helped him win. At a time when Lambeau needed all the help he could get, he was pushing away people who could have helped.

After announcing on January 27 that he had hired Kiesling, Lambeau finally was able to head for his beloved California. He turned up in Los Angeles a few days later on what the *Los Angeles Times* described as "a combined vacation and business trip—hoping to sign whatever players of ability happen to be running around loose."

His first order of business on January 30 was to conduct a wide-ranging press conference that appeared in the *Los Angeles Times* and was conveyed around the nation via *United Press* writer Gene Friedman. Lambeau was accompanied by his close friend, key Packers board member Andrew Turnbull, the *Press-Gazette* co-owner who had saved Green Bay's franchise from early extinction in 1922 by organizing the first community stock sale. Introducing Turnbull in Los Angeles, Lambeau told reporters, "Andy took me out of the gutter."

Lambeau predicted the NFL would find enough players to play football in 1945 amid concerns that the government quest for able-bodied men might might make that impossible.

"The war comes first, of course, but I think we'll be able to operate next fall," Lambeau said. "All of our [Green Bay] players worked in war plants last season, They practiced during their leisure time and we were still able to get in as much practice as we used to before the war."

Lambeau also described the prospect of a rival football league as "a swell thing. . . . I think it would help professional football. But it has to be a good league. . . . Air travel would help another league. I like to travel by air. We did [it for] two years before the war and only the war keeps us from doing it now."

A rival league a swell thing? In a *United Press* report that was sent around the nation? This would not be the first time a sunny Lambeau prediction failed to come true. And this almost certainly was Curly trying to downplay a major problem. But he wasn't the only NFL executive who publicly under-estimated the threat of the All-America Football Conference.

Clearly, there was more going on for Lambeau in California than the Packers coach/vice-president wanted people to know. The grumbles that Curly had "gone Hollywood" were growing louder around Green Bay —especially with a war going on. On the plus side, the Packers were the reigning NFL champions, a great balm for any unrest.

By February 20, Lambeau was back in Green Bay, working on the NFL draft, which had been pushed back to April 8 in New York. "The Packer coach did not say who the players were that he interviewed, preferring to keep that information under his hat until such time as it can be presented at a league meeting. While on the Pacific coast, he met Carl Mulleneaux, former Packer end now in the Navy." Mulleneaux, a Packer from 1938 to 1941 who was named to the NFL All-Star team in 1939 and 1940, would appear in five games for Green Bay in 1945 and one in 1946.

When Lambeau headed to New York in early April, there was a lot more on the table than the draft. That was especially true because only a dozen of the more than 300 draftees were expected to be available while World War II was going on. Then again, the war was going well. Germany would be defeated in May, and Japan also was on its heels. In the United States, football men were preparing for a post-war sports boom.

To head off the dispute between Brooklyn Tigers owner Dan Topping, who wanted to play in Yankee Stadium after buying the baseball Yankees, and the Mara family, which did not want another NFL team across the river from their Giants, a temporary solution was found. The Brooklyn team would combine with the NFL's Boston Yanks for the 1945 season. That team would play in Boston, with one game at Yankee Stadium against the Giants. The NFL would be a 10-team league that fall, with a plan to expand to 12 teams in 1946.

Meanwhile, Lambeau said he drafted players that he expected to be available for the 1945 season. It didn't work out that way; many of them would not arrive until 1946, if they played in Green Bay at all.

Curly also expressed his unhappiness with an NFL draft system that punished successful teams. The draft, he believed, hurt the NFL's appeal by diminishing its best teams—which turned the league's turnstiles.

"Curly Lambeau fears the NFL is making a serious mistake by giving the weaker teams top choices in the player draft each year," a *Chicago Tribune* article reported after the draft. "There are only about a half dozen big name graduating college stars each normal year," Lambeau said. "Therefore, only six teams will get a key player. So your leading clubs—the Bears, Redskins, Giants, and Packers—are deprived, year after year, of a chance at these outstanding boys. Sam Baugh of the Redskins and Sid Luckman of the Bears aren't getting any younger. We've lost Cecil Isbell. The Giants have no one whose name is a box office wallop. My point is that here you have a system working against the teams which have been the backbone of the league. I believe the order of selection should be rotated each year. It's all right trying to build up the weak sisters, but not to hold back the stronger teams."

If it had been adopted, Lambeau's plan would have benefitted his Packers while undermining a basic intent of the draft—to help losing teams improve. Although cleverly phrased, it was a self-serving argument that didn't go anywhere.

On May 23, 1945, Lambeau returned to Green Bay after yet another scouting trip to California. There were no magic player pipelines on the West Coast, though. Packer fans keeping score at home probably chalked up this western visit to another example of how Curly had "gone Hollywood."

By the time NFL leaders gathered in New York in early June, two proposed rival leagues had dissolved before they had gotten very far. Both had apparently learned that the Giants had agreed to allow Topping's NFL team to play in Yankee Stadium in 1946.

Red Grange resigned on June 1, 1945, as president of the U.S. Football League, warning that soaring player salaries were a major problem. "I would not advise anybody to start in pro football right now," Grange said, saying he had never taken a USFL dime and adding that he would stick with his insurance business. The same day, Trans-America League founder Chick Meehan, a former Syracuse head coach, also abandoned his plan for a new league. "With [Yankee] Stadium, I had plenty of ammunition," Meehan said. "Without it, I just had a conversation."

But the main threat to the NFL, the All-America Football Conference, continued to build momentum. And Arch Ward's millionaires had the bank accounts to make Ward's NFL friends pay for snubbing him.

Although not interested in beginning play before World War II ended, the AAFC already had been signing players who were in the military. It saw the Japanese surrender in August of 1945 as a green light to make 1946 its first season. "It probably will take three to six months before all our players return from service," AAFC organizer Arch Ward said. "By next August, then, the teams will be fully organized and we should be all set to get down to business."

The war clouds had broken up in Europe and Asia. The prospect of a battle with the AAFC now was hanging over every move made by Lambeau and the other NFL coaches and general managers. And Lambeau entered this conflict short on the most important weapon—money for soaring player salaries.

# 33
## *CHANGING OF THE GUARD*

Green Bay opened its 1945 training camp amid a celebration of the Packers' 25th year in the National Football League. Lambeau, who organized the team in 1919 and guided it into the NFL in 1921, was in the spotlight of a "Silver Anniversary Year" dinner attended by 300 at the Beaumont Hotel.

Honored with "a large engraved plaque" for outstanding service to the community, Lambeau recounted the early trials and hurdles the team had to overcome before it went on to win a league-leading six NFL championships.

Club president Lee Joannes recited the grassroots history of the community-owned Packers, including the 114 individuals and businesses that bought nonprofit stock at $25 a share in 1933. "This assured football for Green Bay," Joannes said, adding that speculation that the team would be moved to Milwaukee "is the most remote idea any of us has."

Moving the Packers out of Green Bay, however, would become a very real possibility as the NFL was staggered by the battle with the AAFC. Even The Man Who Invented the Green Bay Packers would come to some conclusions that were feared by football fans in his hometown.

The plaque was presented to Lambeau by Dr. W.W. Kelly, the team physician for 23 years. Kelly paid tribute to how Lambeau guided the Packers' rise "from Hagemeister park to the Polo Grounds," to a record of 192-75-21 and six NFL titles in its 24 seasons. "He described how the team was first sponsored by the long defunct Acme Packing company and how the players split a postseason financial melon that gave each gridder $16.50, or $1.50 per game for the 11-game campaign. It was through 'Lambeau's courage and determination that the team moved into big time circles,' Dr. Kelly said, adding the hope that the Packer coach will continue in that capacity many more years."

What Dr. Kelly didn't say was that he stepped down after only one glorious year, the 1929 championship season, as Packers president, apparently because he found Lambeau difficult to deal with. The public story was that Kelly resigned because he needed to concentrate on being president of the Green Bay Board of Education.

Dr. Kelly also failed to mention that he would not be the Packers' team physician in 1945, a position he had held for 23 years. Lambeau had replaced him in one of the many moves that would alienate some of his oldest and most dedicated supporters.

As the NFL headed into its first post-war season, the spotlight was on Lambeau and his Packers. The league's defending champions handled their first assignment, defeating the College All-Stars 19-7 on August 30, 1945, before a crowd of 92,753 at Soldier Field in Chicago. And if that crowd was inflated by Arch Ward ticket giveaways, a practice that became common at future All-Star games, the paid attendance still was remarkably high.

Two weeks later, a crowd of 90,218 saw Green Bay play the Philadelphia Eagles in an exhibition game on September 13, 1945, at Shibe Park, the longtime home of baseball's Philadelphia Phillies. The game was sponsored by *Philadelphia Inquirer* Charities, following the lead of *Chicago Tribune* Charities in the College All-Star game. And while some saw the Packers' 28-21 loss to the Eagles as a sign of future offensive problems, the huge turnout softened the blow.

After they played the Pittsburgh Steelers in Hershey, Pennsylvania, on September 19, Lambeau took the Packers to Washington for an exhibition against the Redskins on September 23.

"I'm going to present Curly Lambeau with some kind of an award when the Packers play the Redskins in Washington," Redskins owner George Preston Marshall said. "He's done one of the great all-time jobs in either college or professional football in coaching the Packers so successfully over a 25 year span."

Green Bay lost all three of the Eastern pre-season games, falling to the Steelers 12-8 and the Redskins 21-7 after losing to the Eagles. These games were more about making some money and checking out prospects than wins and losses. But they also were an indicator. And Lambeau and Packer fans much preferred to win.

Don Hutson, who had been talking retirement for years, had not played in any of the three Eastern exhibitions, but had traveled with the team as an assistant coach. Hutson had been the hero of the 19-7 win over the College All-Stars. He returned an interception 85 yards for the clinching touchdown, and kicked a field goal and two extra points.

After the 1944 championship season, Hutson had said, "If I ever play on the field again, I'll jump off the Empire State building." He had made an exception for the College All-Star game. The result of that game mattered. But he finally seemed to be serious about retiring after announcing he was finished playing football each year since 1942. A talented entrepreneur, he had opened the popular Playdium bar and bowling alley in Green Bay in 1943. He also owned a car dealership and had other business interests, Hutson genuinely looked forward to life after football.

The Bears weren't buying Hutson's retirement vow, though. Especially not Bears co-coach Luke Johnsos, who was sharing the coaching duties with Hunk Anderson until Papa Bear Halas returned from naval duty.

"The Packers are playing possum on us," Johnsos said on Tuesday, September 25, as the Bears prepared for their season opener at Green Bay on Sunday. "Don't kid yourself. Those Packers are laying for us, just like they always do. And don't you believe that Don Hutson won't play. You'll see old No. 14 on the field next Sunday."

To be ready, the Bears were working on two defensive game plans —one with Hutson, one without him—at their St. Joseph's College training camp in Rensselaer, Indiana. "I wish we were sure that Don wouldn't play," Johnsos said. "That would simplify our task of preparing for the Packers."

Lambeau and Hutson kept the Bears guessing. It was a minor distraction, but the kind of opportunity Lambeau could not resist—a chance for pre-game headlines and speculation that just might mess with an opponent's head.

While Curly closed Green Bay's practices, Hutson opened the door for playing one more game. "I meant my retirement to stick," he said. "A couple of things came up on our trip east, though, and this Bears game is so all-important in our plans for the season, that maybe I'll have to play. Just this one. We're going to have a pretty good team again later. Maybe I can help in this spot because it means so much. But maybe things will straighten out in the next day or two that I won't have to play. We probably won't know until Saturday."

Lambeau went along with the charade, saying Hutson, who was supposed to be merely a non-playing coach this fall, had not looked good in practice: "His 'dogs' barked all over the place as he ran and I wonder whether in such condition he would be any help to us. We'll have to wait until he works out a couple more times, and even then, it will be entirely up to him."

On Saturday, Hutson announced that he would play. By this point, Lambeau had added another layer to his mind game with the Bears—

although the Bears, who expected to see Hutson, were more concerned about the actual game than any mind game.

On Sunday, Hutson caught three passes for 83 yards and kicked four extra points against Chicago. And the Bears' focus on Hutson opened up Green Bay's running game, which accounted for all four touchdowns and 198 of the Packers' 292 yards, that spelled the difference in their 31-21 win over the Bears.

"It was old man Hutson," Johnsos said afterward. "I hope the fifth time he retires, he means it."

The next week, Hutson's supposed retirement was exposed as mere deception. He caught four touchdowns as Green Bay routed the up-and-coming Detroit Lions 57-21 in Milwaukee. That set the stage for a showdown with the suddenly potent Cleveland Rams, who had shut out the Cardinals and the Bears in their first two games.

Led by first-year quarterback Bob Waterfield, who would become a premier NFL passer, the Rams defeated the Packers in Green Bay 27-14 on October 14, 1945, before a disappointed home crowd of 24,607 at City Stadium.

"The Big Four reign is over," Cleveland general manager Chili Walsh said, predicting that the Packers, Bears, Giants and Redskins no longer would dominate the NFL. "Cleveland and Detroit are breaking through in the Western division and Philadelphia and Boston are coming up in the east and it's the best thing that ever happened in the National league. It hasn't been good for the league at all to have that supremacy."

Walsh's brother, Rams coach Adam Walsh, excitedly said, "This is the first time in the history of the National League that a team has defeated the Bears and Packers on successive Sundays."

Also enjoying the moment was Rams line coach George Trafton, who said he was "delighted" to defeat the Packers a year after being dumped by Lambeau despite helping lead Green Bay to the NFL title.

Lambeau pointed his usual fingers, saying, "Bad officiating and our own mistakes beat us. I don't like to appear to alibi, but you can't have poor officiating and make costly mistakes and expect to beat a good club like the Rams."

Green Bay bounced back in its next two games, handling the struggling Boston Yanks and Chicago Cardinals. But when the Packers traveled to Chicago for their rematch against the Bears, they blew an early

14-0 lead and lost 28-24 before a raucous crowd of 45,527 at Wrigley Field on November 4, 1945.

It was the first win for the struggling Bears, who had lost their first five games while an absent Halas wound down his Navy service. The upset defeat left the Packers 4-2, a game behind the division-leading Rams and Lions, who were both 5-1—and delivering on Chili Walsh's predictions that Cleveland and Detroit would overtake the Western Division's traditional powers.

The clinching disaster came a week later, when the Packers traveled to Cleveland and lost 20-7 on November 11. On a rainy day next to Lake Erie, the Rams' Fred Gehrke ran past the Packers for two spectacular touchdowns of 72 and 42 yards in the first quarter. When Green Bay responded with a 75-yard touchdown pass from Irv Comp to Clyde Goodnight, the Rams answered with an 84-yard touchdown from Waterfield to Jim Benton.

After that four-touchdown first quarter, there was no more scoring. Also in that tumultuous first quarter, a section of temporary bleachers at League Park collapsed, dumping 300 to 400 spectators from their perches, and injuring more than 30 spectators among the crowd of 28,686.

The back-to-back losses to the Bears and Rams on the first two Sundays in November effectively ended Green Bay's 1945 championship plans.

Lambeau again blamed his players. "We have a good ball club and the boys want to win," he said, "but they aren't willing to make the personal sacrifices necessary to achieve victory. They have too many outside interests. It's too bad for those who are putting forth every effort." Lambeau vowed to crack down: "We've gone through these periods of stress and strain before. It's nothing new. But it will not be tolerated. While we're where we deserve to be right now, 100 percent attention to football will be the rule from now on in. Or else."

There were two problems with that analysis. Lambeau's best player, Hutson, was operating businesses that demanded his attention. If forced to choose, he easily might have retired from football. In addition, the teams that were beating the Packers were simply more talented. And they were turning increasingly to the T formation that the Bears had pioneered, while Lambeau stubbornly stuck to his dated Notre Dame Box.

Walt Kiesling, the former Steelers head coach that Lambeau had hired as his line coach to replace George Trafton, also weighed in. "We've got to have spirit from the water boy up," said Kiesling, pointing to missed assignments against Trafton's new team, the Rams.

With Green Bay no longer in the championship hunt, Lambeau cut three players while adding fullback Chuck Sample, a Green Bay native who had mustered out of the Army. The moves saved a few payroll dollars.

Lambeau also announced a rigorous practice plan for the final three games "because we don't want to wind up in the second division for the first time in our history."

Green Bay won its next two games, but lost 14-3 in its final game at Detroit. That enabled the Lions (7-3) to edge the Packers (6-4) for second place in the Western Division behind West champion Cleveland (9-1).

Also leaving the Packers was Charles "Buckets" Goldenberg. Hobbled by a season-ending foot injury, Goldenberg announced his retirement in mid-November after the Rams game in Cleveland. He had played in 120 NFL games.

In his 13th season, Goldenberg, 35, was another of the last links to Lambeau's final three NFL titles. The only players who had appeared in more NFL games at that point were Packers legend Johnny Blood (137) and Giants center/linebacker Mel Hein (167). Goldenberg, who had played at Wisconsin, would return to Milwaukee, where he operated the popular Pappy's restaurant.

Also winding down was Hutson, who had joined the Packers in 1935. The linchpin to bringing three NFL championships to Green Bay would play in the Packers' remaining three games and then finally end his epic career. That departure alone assured that Green Bay would have a very different football team in the future.

# 34
## *A NOVEMBER TO REMEMBER*

The month of November 1945 proved to be a momentous one in the life of Curly Lambeau. Four days after the defeat in Cleveland sealed Green Bay's fate for that season, the team's executive committee showed its continuing faith in the The Man Who Invented the Green Bay Packers by giving him a five-year contract extension through the 1949 season.

The contract reportedly was worth $25,000 a year. From 1940 to 1945, Lambeau had been paid $10,000. From 1937 to 1939, his salary had been $7,500.

How did Lambeau negotiate a $15,000 raise when he had been making $10,000? In many ways, he was the most prominent professional football coach in America. He had won the most games and the most championships, the last one coming only one year earlier. He also was a huge celebrity—a charismatic man with a salesman's flair for garnering attention. He coached the team. He sold the tickets. He truly was the Green Bay Packers in just about every way.

With the NFL looking forward to post-war prosperity, the men who oversaw the nation's only community-owned team looked to Lambeau to lead the Packers to financial success as well as victories. In addition, the people of Green Bay believed Lambeau gave the city its best chance for a small town to keep its football team in a metropolitan league.

Without Curly, the pressure would be turned up to relocate the Packers in a larger city. And with the AAFC challenging the NFL, that pressure was building. Green Bay's population was less than 50,000; teams in the biggest cities were putting more than 50,000 people into their stadiums.

In short, Lambeau had a track record—and bargaining power, especially with the post-war boom expected in spectator sports. He was, as many people said, the Green Bay Packers. As long as the team was doing well, Curly would do well.

And so, the executive board showed its faith in him by giving him a fancy new five-year contract in November of 1945. In discussing his new $25,000-a-year deal, Lambeau dismissed speculation that the Packers would need to move to a bigger city as "ridiculous."

In major professional sports, the small towns all had lost their teams to big cities. Only Green Bay had kept its team. At some point within the next few years, Lambeau would conclude that the Packers would fare better if they were privately owned and in a bigger market. Perhaps he had already concluded that. In the fall of 1945, though, his public opinion was that the Packers were not going anywhere.

"There have been rumors in the past about the Packers moving out of Green Bay. I don't have the power to move them, and, even if I did have the power, I would never do it," Lambeau said. "I was born in and have lived in Green Bay all my life and I have no intention of moving. My home is here and will always be here. I don't plan on being away from the city any more than I have during the last five years."

Perhaps knowing that his winter escapades were a hot topic among Packer fans, Lambeau stressed that overseeing the team required him to travel extensively to scout and sign players, and to stay on top of the rapidly changing pro-football business.

"If we did not work the year round our team would be seriously handicapped," Lambeau said. "There is a constant fight for players which requires personal contacts with those involved. Not only that, but I have had a constant battle in our league meetings to maintain our rights to a full home schedule and any other benefits the rules allow."

Lambeau vowed to prevent the Packers from becoming "a traveling team" due to their appeal around the league. That was a battle, he said, that required 100 percent support from Packer fans. "When we don't get the cooperation of everyone, it works a hardship on us," he said, adding that a stadium expansion would be required as well as ticket-buying.

There were precedents for "traveling teams," but even in 1945, they were ancient. The Duluth Eskimos, a barnstorming group led by Ernie Nevers, played only one home game in two seasons (1926-27), when they went 6-5-3 and 1-8. And Halas' Decatur Staleys only played two league games in Decatur in 1920 and only one there in 1921 before changing their name to the Chicago Bears. They played five of their eight games in Chicago in 1920 and 10 of 11 games there in 1921.

But that was long before the NFL had matured into a true major league. In the early days, small-town teams did whatever was needed to survive. In the 1940s, a barnstorming Packer team no longer would fit in.

Lambeau also laid out his goal for the 1946 Packers in the first year of his new five-year contract: "Our problem now is to weed out the spiritless players and replace them with men who have a desire to win. When Green Bay doesn't have a winner, it will be practically impossible to stay in the league of which we are one of the original members."

He also praised the men who had given him this five-year vote of confidence. "To date, the executive committee and I have always worked in harmony. They've been generous in giving me the right to vote and I appreciate it. I shall always strive 100 percent to protect the interests of the Packers."

At that point, no one knew how perilous the future would be for the Packers. Very soon, though, the challenge of maintaining a small-town team in the big-city environment of the post-war NFL would threaten the survival of the Green Bay franchise. Making matters worse, Curly Lambeau's clashes with the team's leadership would become a major problem, one that his publicity skills could not hide.

Another question also loomed large: Would Lambeau be able to keep up with the dramatic changes the NFL was going through after World War II?

# 35
## *ANOTHER MATRIMONIAL CONTRACT*

Yet another momentous development in the life of Curly Lambeau in November of 1945 became public from an odd source—gossip columnist Louella Parsons. The day after the Packers lost to the Bears, Curly remained in Chicago to address the Monday Quarterbacks at the Morrison Hotel, where he responded to Parsons' report that he had married Grace Garland in July.

Lambeau's life had been filled with contradictions for a long time. On one hand, he was a charismatic and brilliant coach, an NFL pioneer who had become a celebrity by guiding a pro team with Notre-Dame-like appeal. He was the most successful coach of the league's first quarter-century, achieving things that keep him ranked among professional football's most accomplished mentors to this day.

On the other hand, his relationships with his players and the Green Bay businessmen who oversaw the Packers were becoming increasingly strained and tempestuous. And with his marriage to Grace Garland, Lambeau crossed another line in a personal life that had become increasingly unsavory in they eyes of conservative Green Bay. He had wed a well-traveled California beauty.

"Grace met Curly at the Roosevelt Hotel [in Los Angeles]," said her daughter-in-law, Lyla Hoyt, who was married to Grace's son, Warren Hoyt, from her first marriage. "She kept a room there all the time, for when she was in town. . . shopping or out for the night. . . . After they married, Curly moved out to the Malibu house."

It was the third marriage for Lambeau, the fourth for Grace, an attractive brunette who had once aspired to a movie career. A former Miss Cleveland, she had married at 19 and moved to Hollywood with her first husband, reportedly encouraged by movie mogul Sam Goldwyn.

Although she listed her age as 45 on their marriage certificate, Grace was 51, four years older than Lambeau. She said it was her third marriage, while Curly said it was his second. Both were one wedding short of the truth. A Cleveland native, Grace had also claimed incorrectly to have been born in Buffalo.

Grace gave her residence as the Malibu beach house built by her second husband, who also had owned a mansion in Los Angeles. Lambeau said he lived at the Roosevelt Hotel in Hollywood.

When asked in Chicago about the Louella Parsons report, Lambeau said they had gotten married on Friday, July 13, "to prove we're not superstitious." They had taken out their marriage license in Santa Monica on Friday the 13th, but were married on Monday, July 16, by Judge Thurmond Clark in Los Angeles. By Lambeau standards, that was only a mild stretch of the truth.

Lambeau said he preferred to let the bride "tell the romantic details." Before moving back to football talk, he said, "We had hoped to keep the news a secret until after the football season, but she called me early today and said a columnist had published the news."

The biggest headline Lambeau generated that day, however, was calling Cecil Isbell the greatest passer of all-time. Isbell had finished his five-year Packer career in 1942. In 1945, he was in his second season as head coach at Purdue, his alma mater.

"Isbell was a master at any range, short, medium or long ones. He could throw soft passes, bullet ones or feathery lobs," Lambeau said. "He's the best with Sid Luckman of the Bears a close second and Sammy Baugh a long third." Isbell, who also addressed the Monday Quarterbacks that day, must have been beaming, if not blushing,

Of great interest in Chicago, Lambeau predicted that Detroit would beat the Bears in their meeting Sunday because the Bears would have a letdown after their emotional win over the Packers. Although Bears tackle Lee Artoe received a broken jaw and a swollen right eye, Lambeau claimed Packers Pete Tinsley and Clyde Goodnight, who were ejected from the game, were merely answering the Bears' roughness. "We tried to retaliate and some of our players were thrown out," Lambeau said. "We're not very clever at that sort of stuff."

In a sense, Lambeau and Grace were a matched pair. They not only had long, complicated matrimonial histories. Both had also had relatively normal first marriages that lasted more than a decade. Their subsequent spouses were far more curious. After a nearly 20-year marriage to first husband Warren Hoyt, who was a salesman, Grace had moved on to the son of a California tycoon and a Hollywood director. Meanwhile, Curly, after a 15-year first union with his high school sweetheart, had married a pair of beauty queens.

Born Grace Nicholls in Cleveland in 1894, she had married Warren E. Hoyt, a salesman, in 1913, in Ohio when she was 19. They had a son, Warren Jr., and were together for nearly 20 years and were living in Los Angeles. They apparently were separated, but not divorced, when Grace married businessman William Garland Jr., whose father had made a fortune in railroads and real estate, on August 30, 1932.

After five weeks of marriage, Grace left Garland and filed for divorce in November. From there, things got really complicated. Saying Garland was worth $3 million, she asked for $1,500 a month in alimony, plus $500 for her unborn child. She said she was accustomed to living "in sumptuous style with servants caring for a large mansion in the city and a $40,000 beach home in Malibu," the *Los Angeles Times* reported on November 23, 1932.

The marriage was annulled on December 14, 1932, at Garland's request on the grounds that Grace was still married to Hoyt. They remarried, though, on February 1, 1933, and moved into Garland's Malibu beach house, at 22368 Pacific Coast Highway. On May 19, Garland gave birth to a daughter, Jane Mary Garland.

Garland died on July 25, 1940, of cirrhosis of the liver. He was 48. Within five months, Grace married her Malibu neighbor, Gregory La Cava, a Hollywood producer/director whose credits included *My Man Godfrey* (1936) and *Stage Door* (1937), two films for which he received Academy Award nominations for best director.

By 1940, when La Cava secretly married Grace in Las Vegas on December 2, 1940, his film work was dropping precipitously. They divorced on June 15, 1944, after a bitter legal battle in which he accused her of marrying him for his money. Grace countered by alleging cruel treatment.

Thirteen months later, she married Curly Lambeau on July 16, 1945. Although her divorces were sordidly public, Grace had a curious penchant for keeping her marriages secret. Grace and Lambeau finally were outed by Louella Parsons in November. "How do they keep those things secret?" *Associated Press* Hollywood correspondent Bob Thomas wondered while reporting the four-month-old marriage in his national column.

For the first few years, their marriage seemed to be the union of a perfect couple. In photographs, a confident or cocky Curly Lambeau is often seen with an adoring, beautiful Grace on his arm.

\* \* \* \* \* \* \* \*

Two weeks after Green Bay wrapped up a 6-4 season with a 14-3 loss at Detroit on December 2, 1945, newlywed Lambeau was back in Southern California, driving on Wilshire Boulevard in Beverly Hills with *Los Angeles Times* columnist Braven Dyer. They were on their way to a Pacific Coast Football League game between the Los Angeles Bulldogs and the Hollywood Bears, basking in the sun while listening to the Rams-Washington NFL championship game—which was being played in minus-2 degrees in Cleveland.

"This is the way to enjoy that game," Lambeau said. "I imagine everybody in the Cleveland park is half-frozen." A disappointing crowd of 32,178 had braved the elements at cavernous Cleveland Municipal Stadium, which was prone to frigid gusts from nearby Lake Erie. By 1946, the Rams would share Curly's sun-worshipping and move to Los Angeles—a move that Rams owner Dan Reeves was allowed to make after he threatened to fold his team.

Lambeau remained in California through New Year's—to scout the Rose Bowl and enjoy life with Grace. In early January, he began the long train ride to New York, where the NFL would conduct its 1946 draft and make plans to deal with the All America Football Conference threat. He did not stop in Green Bay. But while changing trains in Chicago, he gave a telephone interview to the *Press-Gazette* to share his draft thoughts with Packer fans.

\* \* \* \* \* \* \* \*

Returning to Southern California after the NFL draft and a quick stop in Green Bay, Lambeau and Grace were invited to dinner at the Beverly Hills home of Corinne Griffith, the former silent-film star who had married George Preston Marshall, the influential and mercurial owner of the Redskins.

Griffith, who received a Best Actress nomination in 1929, went on to write 11 books. Her childhood memoir about growing up in Texarkana, Texas, *Papa's Delicate Condition,* was made into a 1963 comedy starring Jackie Gleason. It featured the Academy-Award-winning song, "Call Me Irresponsible." She also would write the lyrics to *Hail to the Redskins,* the rousing team fight song tainted by Indian imagery that would become politically incorrect.

A friend and an admirer of Lambeau, Griffith described him in her 1947 memoir, *My Life With the Redskins,* as "six feet tall, 200 perfectly proportioned pounds, no bulges" and "a pretty thing."

After dinner, Marshall excused himself to get some background material for a trade he wanted to discuss and Grace left to powder her nose, leaving Corinne and Curly alone for a few moments. She detailed what followed in her Redskins book this way:

*"Curly was gazing into the fire when he said, `Corinne, I think I'm the happiest man in the world.' I didn't answer, it was one of those tiny, tight moments in which one must be very still. He was talking half to himself, half to me. `You know this football world is a man's world. It's fierce, exciting, blood and thunder; it's men, men all day, day in and day out. . . but days have a habit of getting over with and it's pretty lonesome coming home alone night after night. Oh, I don't mean I haven't friends, wonderful ones, but you're still alone—you know what I mean.' "*

*"Yes, I know. I've had some of those nights since George and I have been married. Don't let Grace have too many of them."*

*"I won't," Lambeau replied. "I wouldn't do anything on earth to spoil this."*

They sat quietly for a while.

The moment was broken by the sound of quick footsteps.

*"Whose gorgeous footsteps do I hear?" Lambeau said.*

*"Are you out of your mind?" Marshall said, entering the room. "What's happened to the great Green Bay coach? Has he gone soft? . . . Now, Curly, let's get down to business. . . . Who have you got good enough to trade for [Cecil] Cece Hare?"*

For Lambeau, it was a rare candid glimpse into his personal life. If he experienced extreme loneliness at the end of the day, that was far from his public persona as a man.

\* \* \* \* \* \* \* \*

Several months later, Lambeau wound up buying Hare, a blocking back who had played with Packers star Tony Canadeo at Gonzaga before the war, from the Redskins in late July. But then, a few days before Green

Bay's regular-season opener with the Bears, he sold Hare on Tuesday, September 24, to the New York Giants, Washington's big rival.

The private moment with Corinne Griffith showed a relaxed and personal side to Lambeau. That would become increasingly rare for The Man Who Invented the Green Bay Packers.

# 36
## *FROM WORLD WAR TO FOOTBALL WAR*

The 1945-46 off-season was an especially busy one for Lambeau. He would be 48 years old in April as he prepared for his 28th Packer season. Not only was he adjusting to married life, which was complicated by the fact that Grace was very much a California woman who would only reluctantly endure Green Bay. With World War II over, Lambeau also was in the trenches as the NFL's war with the AAFC began to heat up in earnest. A money-draining battle with a rival league created monumental challenges for the budget-conscious Packers.

Feeling the need for a tough and aggressive commissioner in the battle with the AAFC, NFL owners hired hardliner Bert Bell on January 12 to replace low-keyed Elmer Layden. A co-founder of the Philadelphia Eagles in 1933, Bell was now co-owner of the Steelers. He would sell his Steelers interest and then go about the business of being a commissioner who took a very tough stand against the AAFC. The next day, NFL clubs approved Reeves' plan to move his Cleveland Rams to Los Angeles and go head-to-head against the AAFC Los Angeles Dons.

The NFL held its 1946 draft in New York on January 14. Officially, it kept the names of selections private, fearing the AAFC would swoop in and sign its most coveted players. Lambeau broke the embargo, though, revealing that his top pick was Johnny Stryzkalski, a Milwaukee native who had played on an Army All-Star team after one standout season at Marquette.

Two days later, on January 16, the Cleveland Browns announced they had signed Stryzkalski. As it turned out, he wound up with the San Francisco 49ers, who already held his rights. Stryzkalski went on to be a very productive running back during a seven-year career with the 49ers. He was one of many Green Bay prospects who wound up playing in the AAFC, where wealthy owners easily outbid the tight-budget Packers.

Back in Green Bay in late January, Lambeau said the Packers had a reserve list of 192 potential players in anticipation of roster competition with the AAFC. He added that Green Bay would not "go so far out of line so as to endanger" the survival of the franchise.

He also said he was pleased to have a working agreement with San Diego, in the minor Pacific Coast League, to develop talent for the Packers.

Included in the deal: Green Bay would pick the San Diego coach to assure that prospects learned the Green Bay system. A California affiliate conveniently gave Lambeau another reason to be on the West Coast.

The AAFC went after Green Bay veterans as well as draft picks. In April 1946, star fullback Ted Fritsch accepted a reported $15,000 contract from the Cleveland Browns. Rejected by the military due to a perforated eardrum, Fritsch had led the Packers in rushing the previous two years.

"I can hardly believe it," Lambeau said when reached in California by telephone. "The last word I had from Ted was that he had received an offer from Cleveland and that he definitely was not interested in playing football for anyone but the Packers."

Fritsch's mother refused to accept the decision. Reached in Spencer, Wisconsin, 134 miles west of Green Bay, she said she felt "just terrible about it" and wanted Fritsch to "stick with Curly." Her son was working construction in North Dakota, but she said she planned to "have a long talk with Ted when he returns." She and her husband never missed Packer games played in the Midwest, she added.

After reporting to the Browns' training camp, Fritsch pulled out and returned to Green Bay on August 10, where Lambeau signed him to a Packer contract. "I just made a mistake, that's all," said Fritsch, who would go on to a legendary career as a high school coach in Green Bay after his Packer Hall of Fame career.

The *Associated Press* reported Frisch's return as the first trade between the National Football League and the new All-America Conference," quoting Paul Brown as saying the Browns had agreed to release Fritsch as part of a three-way agreement in which the Packers would compensate the Rams for two players who were joining the Browns. Insisting that the Browns had released Fritsch, Lambeau denied that he had agreed to a trade with the AAFC, which would have been a strict violation of the NFL's refusal to recognize the upstart AAFC.

"We're not making any deals with the All-America boys," NFL commissioner Bert Bell said, although it clearly looked like Lambeau had worked something out with Brown.

Lambeau and the men who helped him keep the Packers solvent had been through many financial challenges. Navigating Green Bay through the expensive war with the AAFC would be as difficult as any of them.

# 37
## *ROCKWOOD BECOMES CURLY'S FOLLY*

Before World War II, pro football had been a relatively small-time operation. College football and major-league baseball dwarfed the pro-football league that Curly Lambeau and George Halas were trying to build.

The NFL had moved beyond the early struggles for survival that had claimed every small-town team except for Green Bay. But in 1939, when Lambeau won his fifth NFL title, only three of the Packers' big-city rivals—the Bears, Giants and Redskins—were well-run, financially-sound opponents who were consistent championship threats.

In 1944, when Lambeau jockeyed Green Bay to its sixth NFL championship, the NFL was a wartime shell, kept alive for morale and continuity purposes by diehard football men.

After World War II, the sports landscape changed dramatically. Pro football was becoming a big business. The AAFC's challenge to the NFL inflated salaries wildly for both sides. Wealthy owners of the new league were prepared to lose money by paying a premium for player salaries.

For Lambeau, operating on the tight budget of a community-owned team, that was a whole new ballgame. He had kept his payroll under control by cajoling players who had no other football option. So had the rest of the NFL. In the Depression economy of the 1930s, their job options outside football also were limited.

Unlike Halas, who always had an eye on the bottom line as the owner of the Bears, Lambeau spent freely when he was in the mood to do so. Because, unlike Halas, Lambeau's bank account was not one and the same with his team's bank account.

Lambeau wanted a reasonable budget. But he also wanted to run the Packers like a modern sports franchise, where expenses were not always the first priority. And increasingly, Curly Lambeau liked the finer things in life. For his Packers—and especially for himself.

They traveled in style—enjoying Pullman coaches and staying in first-class hotels. Between East Coast games, they often practiced in Atlantic City, a popular resort at that time. The Packers had gone on a unique barnstorming trip to Hawaii in 1932. In 1940, they were the first NFL team to fly to a road game, and really, the first professional team in any sport to fly regularly.

In the spring of 1946, Lambeau engineered another move that was ahead of its time... the purchase of Rockwood Lodge, a dedicated training facility 15 miles northeast of the city of Green Bay on a bluff above the Green Bay waters where Lambeau liked to cruise in his power boat. Now known as Bay Shore Park, a popular Brown County campground, it once was a Lambeau innovation.

"I've always had my mind on a training table combined with training headquarters for Packer players and Rockwood Lodge is a natural," Lambeau said. The purchase "fulfilled a dream of many years for Lambeau," the *Press-Gazette* noted.

Rockwood Lodge was a cathedral-like limestone building with a rustic knotty pine interior. It included a dining room that could seat at least 40 comfortably and a lounge where more than 100 could relax in "davenports and easy chairs. . . . A small stage at one end of the lounge. . . makes it an ideal place for programs."

At Lambeau's urging, the Packers' board of directors voted unanimously on May 24, 1946, to spend $32,000 for the 53-acre property. The plan was for the team to practice and stay there. Another $8,000 would be used for improvements to the property. In June, the board also voted to spend $17,500 on five pre-fabricated cottages for Lambeau and married players. Single players would stay in the main lodge, which had some single rooms and a dormitory. Players who already had homes in Green Bay were allowed to stay in town.

The main building had been built in 1937 by the Norbertine Fathers as a pastoral getaway for the members of their Columbus Community Club in downtown Green Bay. But the Catholic order found the ambitious retreat financially unworkable and closed it during World War II, when gas rationing made it an impractical destination. In 1944, it was bought by restaurateur Fred DeMeuse, who wanted to open a supper club there.

When that plan did not go well, the Packers purchased Rockwood Lodge from DeMeuse. The concept sounded good when Lambeau sold the idea to the team's board of directors. Like most of the United States, Green Bay was facing a housing shortage as G.I.s returned from World War II. Rockwood would provide a much-needed place for the team's players to stay. In addition, Lambeau felt that, being isolated 15 miles out of town, his players would concentrate on football, enhancing the team's chances for success.

"I loved Rockwood Lodge," receiver Clyde Goodnight, who lived there four years, said. "I was single at the time and I thought it was a great innovation. Curly, as far as I know, was the first football coach to have a place where guys could stay. It didn't cost us anything. Good food, a good place to live. It was great. It wasn't anything plush, but nice. I could save several hundred dollars because I didn't have any expenses. The guys enjoyed it."

Upton Bell, who later would become a super-scout for the Baltimore Colts and general manager of the New England Patriots, went to Rockwood Lodge in 1947 while touring training camps with his father, NFL commissioner Bert Bell.

"All the other camps I'd gone to—the Bears camp, All-Star camp, Cardinals, Eagles, Steelers camps—seemed to be at a college," Bell said. "Curly's was at a motel, on the water. I remember saying to my brother and my father, 'This doesn't feel like training camp. It feels like staying in a hotel.' The whole thing felt completely different, other worldly to me, compared to all the training camps I was at before."

But problems arose in Lambeau's vision. Major problems. And the team's board members began to question their decision to go along with this expansive Lambeau project.

"It seemed like a hell of an idea," said Dick Wildung, a standout Green Bay tackle in 1946-1953. "But there was not one foot of black dirt over rock. It was tough on players. Many of them got shin splints. I got shin splints and I had never had them in my life. In 1947, we finally went to town to practice."

The problem was, Rockwood Lodge stood on the thin soil of the Niagara Escarpment, a stony ledge that stretches in an arc on the northern edge of the Great Lakes from Niagara Falls to Wisconsin. The peninsula northeast of Green Bay is basically a rocky finger jutting into Lake Michigan, with a light dusting of dirt over the rock. Lambeau was no geologist. There was no suitable practice ground on the Rockwood Lodge property.

"It was built on a cliff and I don't think the dirt was more than six inches over that granite rock," said Ward Cuff, a veteran who played in Green Bay in 1947 after spending most of his career with the Giants. "Everybody had bad legs. Shin splints, stuff like that. They realized it was a bad place for a practice field."

Very soon after the Packers began their 1946 training camp at Rockwood on August 12, Lambeau moved their rigorous morning practice to City Field in Green Bay. Players were developing leg problems on the hard ground at Rockwood—which quickly became Curly's Folly.

"The Rockwood Lodge purchase began to anger Packer Executive Committee members. . . when it was found that there was such a shallow cover of topsoil on the practice field that players very quickly came down with shin splints, sore feet and other maladies," wrote John Torinus, a sportswriting protege of Packers co-founder George Whitney Calhoun who became executive editor of the *Press-Gazette* and a member of the team's board and executive committee.

Another major problem was the soaring costs incurred at Rockwood.

With the team isolated outside of town, the Packers organization took on the responsibility of providing all meals. That was no small assignment, feeding a hungry football team. At the start of training camp in 1946, the 50 players on the roster weighed in at 10,704½ pounds, the *Press-Gazette* noted. From 306-pound Tiny Cross to 161-pound Jimmy Richardson, the Packers averaged 214 pounds. "Curly Lambeau," the paper said, "has the biggest baby in the world on his hands."

It was a hungry baby. The Packers' food bill totaled more than $8,000 at Rockwood Lodge in 1946, not including an additional $6,000 in other restaurant expenses.

Another costly problem that stuck in the craw of Packer board members: Lambeau had given his new wife, Grace, the assignment of redecorating the main building at Rockwood Lodge as well as the Lambeau's cottage. And he apparently had not assigned a reasonable budget.

"Grace had threatened to join that other league," Curly joked, saying he eventually signed her and adding that "She'll work free of charge." That was not completely accurate. Grace ran up a big bill with Marshall Field's, the Chicago department store she hired to do the decorating.

"Expenses for equipping and decorating the lodge began to mount," Torinus said. At one meeting, the team's executive committee "threatened to resign over the bills which were being presented by Lambeau for decorating the cottage that he and his wife were occupying."

To put the financial drain of Rockwood Lodge in perspective, the Packers showed a profit of $24,000 in 1945, and less than $4,000 in 1946. By 1948, Green Bay would lose more than $35,000, a staggering sum for a nonprofit operation that left many Packer board members and Green Bay citizens questioning Lambeau. An expense like Rockwood Lodge of more than $40,000, plus increased operating costs for food and transportation, created a huge burden.

Far into the future, every NFL team would own its own practice facility, which would have many of the components of Rockwood Lodge: a training table and meeting areas as well as a practice field.

In the late 1940s, though, a dedicated practice facility was an extravagance for NFL teams trying to fight off the challenge of a well-financed rival league. That was especially true for the community-owned Green Bay Packers, who operated on a tight budget.

For Curly Lambeau, despite his status as the winningest and most celebrated coach in the NFL, there was more trouble ahead.

# 38
## *AAFC HITS NFL IN THE WALLET*

In April of 1945, when All-America Football Conference leaders announced that they would like to meet with NFL officials to discuss a cooperative arrangement that would put the two leagues on equal footing, NFL commissioner Elmer Layden had responded with a haughty taunt.

"All I know of new leagues is what I read in the newspapers," Layden said. "There is nothing for the National Football League to talk about as far as new leagues are concerned, until someone gets a football and plays a game."

Despite Lambeau's brash statement that a rival football league would be "a swell thing," NFL officials must have realized that a second league would be a serious threat to their financial health. With a collection of wealthy owners carefully recruited by *Chicago Tribune* sports editor Arch Ward, AAFC teams were willing to pay inflated player salaries.

The bidding war for players strained even top NFL franchises such as the Bears and Giants. For their owners, George Halas and the Mara family, football was their main business, not an expensive toy. For Lambeau and community-owned Green Bay, which operated on a tenuous shoestring budget, war with another league posed a barely sustainable threat.

The AAFC struck another huge blow when Dan Topping, owner of the NFL's Brooklyn Tigers, dropped out of the NFL. Topping, who had become a co-owner of the New York Yankees baseball team in January of 1945, had bided his time during the 1945 football season, when his in-limbo Brooklyn franchise combined with Boston.

For 1946, he wanted his NFL team to play in his newly acquired Yankee Stadium. Ebbets Field was no longer an option for Topping's Tigers. Branch Rickey, general manager of the baseball Dodgers, had put together a football Dodgers team for the All-America Football Conference that would play in Ebbets Field.

The AAFC also gave Topping leverage. Weary of wrangling with Giants owner Tim Mara and his sons, who were dictating schedule terms that Topping found unacceptable, he simply dropped out of the NFL and joined the new league on December 5, 1945.

Answering Layden's dismissive remark that the AAFC should "get a football" before the NFL considered recognizing the new league, AAFC commissioner Crowley fired back at long-ago Notre Dame teammate, "Well, we've got a football—and now we've also got the New York Yankees."

The war between the NFL and the AAFC was on.

Don Hutson, the Packers' recently retired receiving legend, "predicted failure for the All-America Conference in a radio interview. He said the new professional football circuit didn't have enough money back of it," Henry J. McCormick, sports editor of the *Wisconsin State Journal* in Madison, reported.

That prompted Jimmy Powers, the influential columnist of the *New York Daily News*, to fire back that "Hutson told the folks a big fib when he said the All-America Conference would flop because it didn't have enough money behind it. Any one of three owners in the All-America Conference could buy the whole town of Green Bay."

McCormick then disputed Powers' contention, saying the wealthiest AAFC owners "would probably run out of money before they had bought even a small section of Green Bay. New York sportswriters' ideas of real estate values must still be influenced by the fact that all of Manhattan Island was originally purchased for $24." McCormick further dismissed Powers' pro-AAFC view because his New York paper was owned by the same family that owned the *Chicago Tribune*, "which took such a prominent part in organizing the All-America Conference." That was a reference to *Tribune* sports editor Arch Ward.

There was no disputing, though, that the AAFC had owners who were wealthy enough to challenge the NFL—and they were showing a willingness to dip into their deep pockets.

"The National League is no league at all. It's a racket," Topping, who had switched to the AAFC from the NFL, told a *Collier's Magazine* writer. "I ought to know. I was one of the six stooges for the Big Four until I got some brains and pulled out."

In a measure of what Curly Lambeau had built, Topping lumped the small-town Packers with three NFL heavyweights—the Bears, Giants and Redskins—in the Big Four. The war with the AAFC would poke large holes in that notion.

Topping, heir to a vast fortune that had started with the American Can Company, added one more millionaire to the AAFC's already imposing list of owners. In Los Angeles, Arch Ward paired his friend and fellow Dubuque college alum, actor Don Ameche, and other Hollywood entertainers with Chicago racetrack owner Ben Lindheimer. Ward also had recruited trucking executive John Keeshin for his Chicago Rockets franchise and lumber executive Tony Morabito for the San Francisco 49ers.

For Cleveland, Ward brought in owner Arthur "Mickey" McBride, who owned a variety of businesses, notably Cleveland's largest taxicab company. Ward then convinced former Ohio State coach Paul Brown, who had coached the Great Lakes Navy team near Chicago, and Northwestern quarterback Otto Graham to sign on with the Cleveland team, named the Browns after its coach. And so, "the meek-looking sports editor from Chicago produced the owner, the head coach. . . and the star quarterback" of the Browns, who would achieve legendary success. In another lasting flourish, McBride hid the Browns' extra players as drivers at his cab company, giving birth to the phrase "Taxi Squad."

In a bit of irony, Ward, who had convinced the NFL to hire one of Notre Dame's four Horsemen, Layden, when he turned down their offer to be commissioner, installed another Horseman, "Sleepy Jim" Crowley, as AAFC commissioner. Crowley, the former Green Bay East star that Lambeau had steered to Knute Rockne, now was leading the league that would push his hometown Packers to the brink of extinction—and put his mentor, Curly Lambeau, in a most precarious position.

# 39
## *DEMANDING A THOROUGH EXPLANATION*

After orchestrating the hoopla surrounding the Rockwood Lodge purchase in late May of 1946, Lambeau and Grace headed back to California for an extended stay. Six weeks later, the *Press-Gazette* reported on July 12 that "Coach Curly Lambeau returned to his Northern building headquarters today following a scouting tour and vacation on the west coast. The Packer pilot plunged into a desk loaded with football data and prepared to clear things away for the opening of practice at Rockwood lodge a month from today."

A mountain of challenges sat on that desk. Beyond organizing Rockwood Lodge, he had lost his top draft pick, running back Johnny Strzykalski, to the AAFC. Legendary receiver Don Hutson, who had finally stood firm on his annual vow to retire, was now merely the Packers' backfield coach. And Hutson's expanding business interests were his primary concern.

Lambeau also faced increasing scrutiny, if not downright ridicule, for clinging to the antiquated Notre Dame Box. In 1946, the Packers and the Pittsburgh Steelers were the last NFL holdouts who had not switched to the T formation or a close variation.

Perhaps in response, Lambeau explained the Notre Dame Box in the January/February 1946 issue of *True Sport,* which featured this headline on its cover: " `Curley' Lambeau coach of the WORLD'S CHAMPION professional FOOTBALL TEAM diagrams a series of plays that should win for any High School Team."

High school team? That didn't exactly convey a dazzling message.

No matter what offense Green Bay used, the real problem was that Lambeau no longer had the talent edge to win. Not only had the NFL draft limited his ability to out-scout other teams for players. After 25 years, he had lost a step in his hunger for roster building. But the biggest problem was the rival AAFC raising the price of players.

In a strange twist, Lambeau's old friend Arch Ward, the driving force behind the AAFC, brought out a book celebrating the history of the Packers in October 1946—at the exact time when Ward's rival league was threatening to remove all the romance from Green Bay's football team.

Lambeau's biggest personnel problem was the absence of a gifted thrower. From the time he had founded the Packers in 1919 until Cecil Isbell retired in 1942, Lambeau had nearly always had a premier passer. After Isbell, Green Bay struggled to find a standout passer.

Thanks to the aerial emphasis of Lambeau, who had been the NFL's first 1,000-yard passer, the Packers had pioneered the passing game after joining the NFL in 1921. From 1934 to 1943, Green Bay had led the league in passing yards five times, finished second four times and third once. After Isbell's surprising early retirement, the Bears, with Sid Luckman, and the Redskins, with Sammy Baugh, moved ahead of Green Bay, which fell to an unprecedented fourth and fifth in 1944 and 1945.

Propped up by Hutson, the league's best receiver, and playing against war-depleted teams, Green Bay's lack of a standout passer had not been a major issue. In 1944, the Packers had managed to win the NFL championship with Irv Comp doing the passing, thank to a strong running game, a solid defense and an NFL that was limping along with platoons of its top players in the military. Comp led the league with 1,159 passing yards, but he also led the NFL with 21 interceptions. In his seven years (1943-1949) with Green Bay, Comp threw 28 touchdowns, but was intercepted 52 times. Which was obviously not the way Lambeau liked to throw the ball. At least Comp, who was a ball-hawking defender, picked off 34 enemy passes.

In 1946, though, against a muscled-up NFL throwing out of the T formation, the Packers' substandard passing game tumbled all the way to 10th—last in the league.

Knowing he didn't have the thrower or the receivers to compete, Lambeau abandoned his aerial preference and let talented runners Tony Canadeo and Ted Fritsch pound the ball. Green Bay led the NFL in rushing yards that year. But that was somewhat misleading. Green Bay's 3.2 yards per carry was tied for sixth.

Lambeau's adaptability translated to a 6-1 record in 1946 against everyone not named the Bears or the Rams. The problem was, the Packers lost both meetings with the Bears, who were surging in Halas' return from war duty. Green Bay also dropped a pair to the defending NFL champions Rams, who were enjoying their first season in Los Angeles after moving from Cleveland. That left the Packers with a disappointing 6-5 record.

A determined defense that allowed 14.3 points a game, second in the NFL, helped. But all in all, it was a troubling start to post-war football for Curly Lambeau and his Packers.

The 1946 campaign was especially unsatisfying because the Packers lost their first two games. After falling to the Bears 30-7 in Green Bay and to the Rams 21-17 in Milwaukee, the Packers were 0-2—and in desperation mode the rest of the way.

The loss to the Rams was especially maddening to Lambeau, who angrily insisted that L.A.'s game-winning one-yard touchdown had come after the clock had run out. If referee Bill Downes had not mistakenly and egregiously called a timeout with less than 10 seconds left, Curly argued, the game would have been over and Green Bay would have won 17-14.

"I am demanding a thorough explanation of the referee's timeout," Lambeau said. Along with being a passing pioneer and scouting pathfinder, Curly was an innovator in insisting that his team had been robbed. To underscore his angry protest with NFL commissioner Bert Bell, Lambeau cited the rulebook, showed game films and incited the *Green Bay Press-Gazette* to carry the Packers' banner.

Downes, who refereed NFL games for 34 years, refused to engage with a full-throttle Lambeau, who rushed the field demanding that the touchdown be disallowed. The short version came out later: Downes stopped the clock because the Packers were lollygagging—taking too much time in getting up after stopping Bob Waterfield's quarterback sneak.

"The most courageous guy on the football field at State Fair park Sunday afternoon was not one of the trained behemoths in pads and a helmet," the *Milwaukee Journal* noted sympathetically. "The most courageous guy was a little fellow with a gaudy red striped shirt and a white baseball cap by the name of Bill Downes."

In a further bit of irony, after grounding Curly's 1946 Packers, Downes went on to become aviation commissioner for the city of Chicago, overseeing O'Hare and Midway airports.

Green Bay reeled off three wins in a row to stay in the hunt at 3-2. But the Packers came up short in their rematch with the Bears, losing a defensive battle 10-7 before a crowd of 46,321, the largest to see a pro football game in Chicago.

Although Green Bay was 3-3 and in fourth place behind the front-running Bears (4-1-1), Rams (3-2-1) and Cardinals (4-3), Lambeau insisted that the Packers could still win the West, saying he expected the division champion to have three losses. Lambeau wasn't off by much. The Bears finished 8-2-1 to win the West, with Green Bay (6-5) tied for third with the Cardinals.

The Packers finished their season against the Rams in Los Angeles. Despite attracting a crowd of 46,000, the largest to see a pro football game in L.A., the trip was another exercise in frustration for Lambeau.

Not only did Green Bay come up short 38-17 in its battle for second place. Lambeau was unable to remain in California. After enjoying a couple of days of sunshine, he departed for New York, where the NFL draft would be held on December 16, a day after the Bears defeated the Giants 24-14 in the NFL championship game before 58,346 at the Polo Grounds.

The Bears' win was one final disappointment for Green Bay in 1946. It gave them their seventh NFL championship, nudging them one title ahead of Green Bay. Lambeau still owned the league record for coaching championships, though. Halas had only been the Bears coach for five of their titles.

All in all, the man known as Papa Bear was making a triumphant return from World War II. And that was not a good situation for The Man Who Invented the Green Bay Packers.

# 40
## *A MODERN PASSING GAME?*

The day after the Bears romped in the Polo Grounds, the NFL conducted its 1947 draft at the Commodore Hotel in New York. With the Packers' passing game floundering, Lambeau used his first pick in the 1947 draft to take lefthanded quarterback Ernie Case, who had returned from World War II bomber-pilot duty to lead UCLA to the 1947 Rose Bowl.

Back in Green Bay, Lambeau announced on January 11, 1947, that he would install a V formation. Finally forsaking the Notre Dame Box, Curly believed the V, which was a variation of the T, would propel the Packers into a modern passing attack.

Lambeau, who had vowed at the draft to bolster his passing game, further backed that up on January 24 by acquiring "Indian Jack" Jacobs from the Redskins. Jacobs, from the Muskogee (Creek) nation who had been a star quarterback and punter at the University of Oklahoma, fit neatly into the Indian imagery of Curly's old friend, Washington owner George Preston Marshall. But not, apparently, into Marshall's football plan.

Lambeau and Marshall struck the deal at the NFL's winter meetings in Chicago. "They had been dickering since last December," Art Daley noted in the *Press-Gazette*.

With Sammy Baugh still a premier passer, Jacobs had not been destined to play a lot in Washington. Lambeau acquired him for Bob "Bomber" Nussbaumer, a halfback who would become Baugh's favorite receiver in 1947, catching 47 passes.

The key difference between the T formation and the V that Lambeau preferred: In the T, the quarterback lined up under center. In the V, the quarterback lined up to the side of the center, who could still make a direct snap to the fullback or halfback as well as the quarterback.

The main point, as stated in the *Press-Gazette:* "Coach Curly Lambeau believes he will have the material next fall to make this shift over to his modernized quick-opening formation which is a variation of the 'T.'"

*Material* had become a major issue for Lambeau in the AAFC bidding war. His new plan took another hit when Case, his top draft pick, chose to sign a three-year contract on February 11 with the AAFC's new Baltimore Colts franchise, which had moved north after one murky season in Miami.

The misfire on Case also carried a personal insult for Curly. Case would be playing for Isbell, the former Green Bay star who had been among the NFL's best passers when he retired prematurely in 1942. "The acquisition of Case follows smack-dab on the heels of Cece Isbell's hiring as head coach of the Miami-transferred outfit," the *Los Angeles Times* noted.

In 1947, when Isbell was 32, his passing rivals Sid Luckman and Sammy Baugh were 31 and 33. Luckman would play for four more years. Baugh would play for six more years. Meanwhile, Lambeau would still be searching for his next great passer—and that would have major implications for him and the Packers.

Although Case had set passing records at UCLA the previous fall, it's not likely that he would have solved Green Bay's passing problems. In Baltimore, he threw only 11 passes. He was edged out by Bud Schwenk, who led the AAFC in interceptions as the Colts struggled to a 2-11-1 record. As a Chicago Cardinal, Schwenk had previously led the NFL with 27 interceptions in 11 games. And yet, Isbell preferred Schwenk to Case.

In addition, Lambeau no longer had Hutson reeling in fancy catches. In his first year of retirement, the NFL's premier receiver now was merely a Packer assistant coach when he was not managing his growing business empire. The receiving duties fell to Clyde Goodnight and Nolan Luhn, who had been college teammates at Tulsa.

In his relentless quest for innovation, Lambeau ordered uniforms made of lightweight nylon. "Each Packer now will lug only eight pounds of uniform, from five to seven pounds less than a year ago," the *Press-Gazette* reported. He also flipped the Packer color scheme, emphasizing the gold instead of the blue in Green Bay's blue-and-gold uniforms. Lambeau had put Green Bay in green and gold only briefly. In his three decades as the Packers leader, he mainly stuck to blue and white, or blue and gold, the primary colors of his old school, Notre Dame.

A new offensive scheme. New uniforms. After two years of third-place finishes, a restless Curly Lambeau was determined to shake up his Packers in 1947.

There were far bigger changes on the horizon. With football success not up to the Packers' high standards, the behind-the-scenes maneuvering was about to reach a new crescendo in 1947.

# 41
## *BITING THE HAND THAT FEEDS HIM*

Since the Packers' 1919 beginning, Lambeau had done it all. He had started the team and had been a valuable player. He had coached the team, built the roster, humbled the big-city teams and charmed the sports world. He had enlisted the loyal support of an entire city, region and state. They were Curly's Packers in virtually every way.

He had sold the team to Green Bay football fans with his personality and his ability to produce winning teams. And then he had done the same on a national level, helping the NFL rise in popularity as much as any man with his flair for publicity and innovation. Among the earliest owners and coaches, only George Halas played the kind of role that Curly Lambeau played in the rise of professional football.

Lambeau's problem was, unlike Halas, he was not an owner. That shielded him from financial risk and, in some ways, responsibility. But it also left him more vulnerable.

Through the Packers' success and his charismatic style, he had become a celebrity—a pro football version of his college coach, Knute Rockne. By the late 1940s, however, Lambeau gradually had moved away from his roots. He was spending more and more time in California, distancing himself from his Green Bay constituents. And as the NFL was changing into a more complex enterprise, Lambeau remained stuck in his ways.

While Halas became fascinated with the intricacies of the T formation and hired coaches who knew how to implement it, Lambeau had clung to the Notre Dame Box before turning to the V formation. While Halas learned to manipulate the NFL draft after it was adopted in 1936 by trading veterans for top picks, Lambeau, who had excelled at scouting talented players, had seen that strength diminished by the draft.

In addition, while Halas, and other owners who are remembered as founding NFL fathers, carefully managed the financial side of their franchises, Lambeau seemed to be paying less and less attention to balancing the budget. His vision for the NFL's future was remarkable. That said, his inability to recognize that the Green Bay Packers had not arrived yet at that rosy future was a dangerous flaw.

He would mind his player payroll, even use excessive fines to keep his players motivated. But he spent lavishly on things that were ahead of their time. First-class travel and Rockwood Lodge were good ideas. But they also were especially perilous in Green Bay, a low-revenue franchise with a small stadium. An owner like Halas always watched his finances first.

That was understandable, in a way. The Man Who Invented the Green Bay Packers was supported from the very beginning by football-minded businessmen who took care of many bottom-line issues for Lambeau. They tended to put up with Curly's excesses. But that was becoming an increasingly untenable situation.

And then, Lambeau overstepped by alienating the very men who had supported him. Once a model of unity, the Green Bay Packers were becoming a house divided.

Before the 1945 season, he had quietly removed Dr. W. Webber Kelly as team physician, a position Kelly had held since 1921, without even the courtesy of a face-to-face meeting. A longtime board member, Kelly had had differences with Lambeau before. The dismissal turned him into a determined opponent.

A year after being ousted, Dr. Kelly was the M.C. for a halftime event honoring the original 1919 Packers and an all-time Green Bay team. A talented speaker with a fine sense of humor, Kelly skillfully went through the whole program without mentioning Lambeau's name once.

After removing Kelly, Lambeau then dumped Packers co-founder George Whitney Calhoun, the Green Bay newspaperman and Packer publicist who had been at his side every step of the way. Calhoun had encouraged a 21-year-old Curly to start a football team, had poured all of his energy into generating the publicity needed to make the team a success. Basically a co-founder, Calhoun had been essential to the rise of Lambeau and his football team since its inception.

On March 24, 1947, Calhoun was going about his business at the *Green Bay Press-Gazette* when he read on the *Associated Press* teletype that George Strickler had been hired as the Packers' "assistant general manager and vice-president of public relations." The hiring would not affect Calhoun, Lambeau was quoted as saying.

Calhoun could not have disagreed more. "He was a bitter enemy of Lambeau from that day forward," Calhoun's protege, John Torinus, wrote in *The Packer Legend.*

Calhoun resigned from his position as the Packers' publicity man, which had been a voluntary labor of love. "I know it would be impossible for me to function with Lambeau's Strickler," Calhoun said in a letter of resignation to board president Lee Joannes. "Rather than let him completely cut my throat, I am beating him to the punch and filing my resignation with you."

Even after that, Calhoun continued to maintain historical files on the Packers that were valued highly by the creators of the Pro Football Hall of Fame as well as NFL researchers.

Lambeau and Calhoun, who had arranged the first organizational meetings of the Packers in 1919, never patched up their differences. "I hope to live so I can piss on his grave," Calhoun told his *Press-Gazette* colleague, sportswriter Lee Remmel. Calhoun never got that chance. He died at 73 on December 6, 1963, about 18 months before Lambeau.

George Halas sent a floral arrangement in the shape of a goal post to Calhoun's funeral. Several former Packers attended. Curly Lambeau was not among them.

Even if Lambeau somehow believed he had valid reasons for firing Kelly and Calhoun—that they were too old, that he was putting better men in those jobs—the rough handling turned two longtime Lambeau supporters into bitter enemies. And they weren't the only ones. In the summer of 1947, another major Lambeau ally had had enough. Lee Joannes, who had been team president since 1930, resigned that post. Whether forced out by Lambeau or simply weary of Lambeau's regal ways, Joannes was gone.

Initially a dedicated believer in Lambeau's ability to field a winning team, Joannes joined the alienated friends who now had concluded that Lambeau's leadership was no longer tolerable. Between fiscal mismanagement, failing to keep the team competitive, acting irresponsibly toward people around him and not putting in the time necessary to be successful, Lambeau had shaken the faith of an alarming number of key supporters.

Because of Lambeau's public popularity, and because he had founded and steered the franchise so remarkably for three decades, jettisoning him was a complex, almost unthinkable matter. Packer fans saw a charismatic, home-grown leader who had won six championships. And even insiders who saw the flawed leadership must have wondered about Packers without Lambeau.

When the team lost its edge on the field, Lambeau's cold personnel moves and questionable business decisions started isolating him further. Joannes claimed that other projects made it impossible for him to continue as Packers president. Insiders knew Joannes no longer wanted to butt heads with Lambeau. By that point, Joannes wouldn't even mention Lambeau by name, preferring to call him "the man in the gray suit."

The new Packers president was Emil R. Fischer, a longtime board member who had agreed to take on the difficult task of managing Curly Lambeau. Fischer knew Joannes and Lambeau well, and had gotten along with both. He still might have under-estimated the difficulty of the task he had accepted.

Fischer was the founder of the Atlas Cold Storage Company, a cheese-warehousing enterprise. A brilliant businessman, Fischer had convinced major cheesemakers, including Kraft, to make Green Bay a key distribution center, with Atlas serving as a critical link to Wisconsin dairy farms.

Atlas occupied the buildings of the Indian Packing Company, which had given the Packers their nickname and their jerseys before being bought by the failed Acme Packing. Neither Indian nor Acme packing were destined to survive.

There would be no packers in Green Bay. Only Packers.

But cheese and paper were northeastern Wisconsin's bread and butter. And in his business travels, Fischer had seen how the Packers' football success could raise Green Bay's profile. As a result, Fischer had become a member of the team's executive committee, and had replaced Joannes as president on July 25, 1947. That was a most difficult time for the team, leaving Fischer with the unenviable challenges of managing the dissatisfaction with Lambeau and trying to keep the team in Green Bay.

Another key board member had become disenchanted with Lambeau: Attorney Gerald C. Clifford, who had regularly charted the franchise through dangerous legal waters. Clifford viewed Lambeau's handling of the team's finances as reckless. And he took a dim view of the way Lambeau had treated Kelly and Calhoun, men who had poured their energetic hearts into the Green Bay Packers.

In the summer of 1947, Lambeau was in no position to maneuver around Clifford, the attorney who was antagonized by Lambeau's imperial ways and budget disasters. Without Clifford's legal skill, the Packers' improbable survival as a small-town franchise would have been doubtful.

And with his intimate knowledge of Lambeau's transgressions, Clifford also had become Curly's loudest critic.

Clifford, Joannes and Kelly were three members of a group of Packer supporters that gained notoriety as "The Hungry Five," a nickname coined by Arch Ward. The other two were *Press-Gazette* owner/publisher Andrew Turnbull and Lambeau himself.

There has been debate about who deserves to be included in Green Bay's Hungry Five. Lambeau, for example, is so unique that it can be argued that he stands alone. And certainly, no one was hungrier for the Packers to succeed than publicist/co-founder Calhoun. Treasurer/accountant Frank Jonet and attorney John Kittell, who is credited with drafting the first documents that created the Packers' nonprofit, community-own status, also made critical contributions.

But there is no question that with Clifford, Joannes, Kelly and Calhoun aligning against Lambeau in 1947, The Man Who Invented the Green Bay Packers faced a powerful armada.

\* \* \* \* \* \* \* \*

Among the Hungry Five, only Turnbull, who had saved the team from financial ruin in 1922, remained aligned with Lambeau. Turnbull tried to arrange a truce that would allow Lambeau to retain the authority to operate the franchise while satisfying his many critics.

"While no longer as enthusiastic in backing Lambeau as he had been in earlier days, [Turnbull] nevertheless sought to keep peace and to bring the warring factions back together," *Milwaukee Journal* sports writer Chuck Johnson wrote in his 1961 history of the Packers. "That proved impossible. Besides variance of opinion on matters of policy, Lambeau and his antagonists had personal differences."

In this frosty and troubled climate, the Packers underwent a major reorganization. At the July 25, 1947, stockholders meeting at the courthouse, Fischer replaced Joannes as team president. Lambeau was re-elected as vice-president and Frank Jonet was retained as secretary-treasurer. Jonet had been the court-appointed receiver who helped guide the Packers out of bankruptcy in 1932.

The stockholders then approved Clifford's motion to increase the board of directors from 22 to 25 members, and increase the executive committee from nine to 12.

Of critical importance, the team's executive committee decided on July 28 to place the power to oversee various aspects of the Packers' operations in the hands of sub-committees. Lambeau would now need approval to make moves he had previously been making unfettered.

"Each sub-committee is empowered to act on normal routine matters," the *Press-Gazette* reported. "Problems or matters of unusual importance will be acted upon by the entire executive committee."

The announced reason was that the job of running the Packers had become too big for one man. Behind the scenes, Lambeau had lost the confidence that had been placed in him—especially when it came to dealing with the budget crisis caused by the war with the AAFC.

Initially, Lambeau kept his objections to himself. But he undoubtedly was angered by the changes. They limited his power. His grip on the Packers was becoming more and more tenuous.

Amid the turmoil, Curly Lambeau turned to what he had always done best. He dedicated his efforts to winning. There was no better way to answer his critics than by guiding the Packers to a seventh NFL championship.

Despite all of his roster juggling and all of the organizational turmoil and the soaring player payroll, Lambeau mustered a fast start in 1947. The Packers beat the Bears 29-20 in their opener by rushing for 236 yards and intercepting five passes. The next week, they built a 17-0 lead with another powerful running game, then held on for a 17-14 win over the L.A. Rams before 31,613 in Milwaukee.

With the Chicago Cardinals coming to Green Bay the next week for a showdown of the Western Division's two remaining unbeaten teams, a record crowd of 25,502 squeezed into City Stadium.

Trailing 14-3 in the third quarter, the Packers closed to 14-10 on a 70-yard drive capped by Tony Canadeo's seven-yard run. They knocked on the door to another touchdown three times, but came up short each time and lost 14-10 to the Cardinals.

Despite the grumbling about Lambeau's personnel and scheme, Green Bay had come close. It had not been enough against what would turn out to be the most glorious team in the Cardinals' long history. But the Packers were still potent.

Afterward, Cardinals coach Jimmy Conzelman had high praise for Lambeau. They had first squared off as pros in 1921, when Conzelman was player/coach of the Rock Island Independents while Lambeau was doing that same double duty in Green Bay's first NFL season. Even before that, they had lined up as opposing players in 1918, when Lambeau was at Notre Dame and Conzelman was on the same Great Lakes service team with Halas.

"The Packers have a great ball club," Conzelman said. "Curly has done something I or no other coach has ever seen. He has combined the quick opening of the T formation with the power of the single wing—and he's done a magnificent job.... With his personnel, he'll just wear out a lot of ball clubs this year.... Curly works his 5-4 [defense] better than any coach I know of. And he has the courage to stick with it when he had his ears nearly kicked off by the Bears here last fall and it has paid big dividends. It worked beautifully against our running game."

That high praise did not give comfort to Lambeau, who was "bitterly disappointed. We lost because we didn't execute our plays properly. There was too much carelessness and not enough deception. You can't win from a team like the Cardinals with faulty execution."

Lambeau vowed to change the result when the Packers traveled to Chicago on November 16, saying, "The Cardinals were a better ball club than we were today—but they won't be when we face them in Chicago."

# 42
## *OFF THE CUFF*

Curly Lambeau's 30-year Packer reign contains a pantheon of heroes. . . Don Hutson, Johnny Blood, Clarke Hinkle and Arnie Herber easily come to mind. And there are so many more. The list of outstanding players who helped Lambeau turn Green Bay into a football marvel would be a long one.

Ward Cuff is not one of them. In many ways, though, he played a critical role in Lambeau's Packer reign.

Cuff spent the bulk of his 11-year career with the New York Giants, where he excelled as a runner, receiver, blocker, defensive back and place-kicker. A Minnesota native, Cuff had been a blocking back at Marquette, which was led to the first Cotton Bowl in 1937 by quarterback Ray Buivid and the Guepe twins, Art and Al.

Lambeau planned to pick Cuff in the fourth round of the 1937 NFL draft. But New York coach Steve Owen, drafting five slots ahead of Curly, got to Cuff first. At least that was Curly's story after a Marquette player became a valuable Giant.

In the 1938 NFL championship, Cuff frustrated Lambeau again. With the Packers trailing 23-17 in the fourth quarter, Green Bay end Wayland Becker caught a long pass at the Giants 20 yardline, intent on scoring. Cuff hit Becker so hard that he fumbled and the Giants recovered, preserving their 23-17 victory.

"Ward Cuff is Hero of Win for Giants," the headline above an account by *United Press* writer Henry Super said, noting that Cuff made "the tackle of the game." Cuff also kicked a field goal and two extra points. That was the first time Cuff knocked Lambeau and his Packers out of a championship opportunity. It would not be the last.

After playing in New York for nine productive years, Cuff asked to be released from his Giants contract so that he could finish his career close to Milwaukee. With three children of school age and his business interests there, he no longer wanted to relocate his family during the football season. In an attempt to keep him out of Green Bay, the *Press-Gazette* reported—most likely, based on information from Curly—the Giants traded Cuff to the Chicago Cardinals in 1946.

In April 1947, Lambeau finally bought a 35-year-old Cuff from the Cardinals, who had become comfortable with having second-year fullback Pat Harder, a Milwaukee native who had played at the University of Wisconsin, do their place-kicking.

By the time Cuff reached Green Bay, he was valued primarily for his kicking. The premier place-kicker of his era, Cuff converted 155 of 162 extra points and led the NFL in made field goals four times, including 1947. Only the legendary Lou Groza, with five, has led the league more times than Cuff.

But it was the ones that got away in 1947 that make him such an important figure in the life of Curly Lambeau.

\* \* \* \* \* \* \* \*

After the disappointing loss to the Cardinals in their third game, the Packers got back on track, defeating the Redskins in Milwaukee and the Lions in Green Bay. In 1947, while playing their first six games at home, they alternated between Green Bay and the Milwaukee suburb of West Allis to take advantage of the larger capacity of State Fair Park.

Before heading to Chicago for back-to-back games against the Bears and Cardinals, Green Bay played its final home game in Milwaukee on November 2 against the Steelers, who led the East Division.

In a sloppy, penalty-filled performance, the Packers missed a chance to keep pace with the West-leading Cardinals. And they did it in a most frustrating way, losing by one point to Pittsburgh after quarterback Jack Jacobs was tackled in the end zone for a safety. That fourth-quarter safety left Green Bay trailing 18-10. Jacobs bounced back, throwing a 27-yard touchdown. Cuff kicked the extra point—the NFL did not allow two-point conversions until 1994—but that saddled the Packers with an 18-17 loss.

"We lost our own ball game. Our penalties were big factors, and we gave them all but three points with our miscues and those same penalties," said Lambeau, described as "in a black mood" by *Press-Gazette* writer Lee Remmel. "Nevertheless, we must give Pittsburgh credit for playing 60 minutes of good, tough ball. Pittsburgh deserved to win. . . . But one thing you can be sure of. You will see a different Packer club at Chicago next Sunday."

Riding the Milwaukee Road back to Green Bay, Lambeau kept muttering, "One measly point," as he pondered strategy for the Bears with assistant Walt Kiesling.

Instead of being tied for first with the 5-1 Cardinals, the Packers were tied for second with the 4-2 Bears. Lambeau knew he had a championship-caliber team—the type of team he needed to answer his restless Green Bay critics. He also knew that the loser of Sunday's game against the Bears would see its championship hopes fade dramatically.

On November 9, an eager crowd of 46,112 squeezed into a chilly, wind-swept Wrigley Field to see the Bears and Packers. What they saw was a hard-hitting contest in which the Packers lost four fumbles but won the turnover battle by recovering five fumbles and intercepting four passes.

What they didn't see was a game-tying 29-yard field goal. With 12 seconds left, defensive back Noah "Moon" Mullins blocked that last kick by Cuff, the veteran Lambeau had been counting on. A 5-foot-11, 182-pound defender from Kentucky, Mullins broke free thanks to a fierce hit by Ed Sprinkle on Bob Forte.

"Three or four times this year I've missed blocking kicks because the ball had passed under my arms," Mullins said. "This time I kept my left arm down against my side and the ball smacked right against my elbow. If my arm had been up—the way people usually try to block kicks—the ball would have gone through."

That gave the Bears a 20-17 victory. For the second straight week, Lambeau saw a game slip through his fingers.

"We played a very good game physically. . . But we made too many mental mistakes—a lot of little A-B-C errors," Lambeau said. "Jack Jacobs wasn't his normal self. It was not because he didn't want to be—but because he couldn't be. His father died Friday, . . . He couldn't help but feel it. He left by plane immediately after the game for Oklahoma."

Cuff's missed game-tying field goal stood out. But there were plenty of other reasons that the Packers, who had led 10-0 in the second quarter, missed their chance to sweep the Bears for the first time in 12 years. Green Bay failed to score on two golden opportunities—from the Bears 7 yardline in the second quarter and from the 2 in the third period.

Among his laments, Lambeau had a legitimate gripe. At a time when the chicanery between him and George Halas was peaking, the phone line between the press box and the Green Bay bench went dead, costing the Packers the guidance of assistant coach Walt Kiesling, who had made the long trek upstairs. An innocent mistake? The Packers weren't buying that. The telephone outage affected their substitutions and their play-calling.

The press-box view was especially important in Wrigley Field because both teams were on the same sideline, which often left them farther from the line of scrimmage. "Two of our marches failed because we couldn't get our substitutes in there fast enough. They had to run 80 yards to reach the play in both cases. We didn't know what yard line it was or what plays to use because of that. But I'm not alibiing. We should have won anyway."

Despite falling two games behind the Cardinals, Lambeau vowed that, "We're not through yet. The team that wins the title will lose three games—and we're through losing. We're going to win all our games from now on—or we'll operate below the player limit."

Publicly, at least, Lambeau did not take Cuff to task. A blocked kick isn't necessarily the kicker's fault. It can be a breakdown in the blocking.

But inside, Lambeau must have been sizzling. He had acquired Cuff, who was a perfect 30 for 30 on extra points that season, for moments like that. And while Cuff converted only 7 of 16 in an era where field goals were risky business, he tied for the league in most field-goals made. And yet, with that miss, the week in between the Bears and Cardinals games could not have been an easy one for Lambeau's Packers—especially Cuff.

"I was warned before I went to Green Bay that Curly was tough to play for," said Cuff, who had gotten an earful from Don Hutson when they went to Europe on a USO Tour during World War II. "Even a guy like Don Hutson had problems with Curly, although not severe problems."

With compelling reasons to be near Milwaukee, Cuff decided to play for Lambeau in what turned out to be a very difficult year.

"A lot of the players didn't like Curly and there was pretty good reason for it. He was taking their money, trying to date their wives. I'll tell you he was bad," Cuff said. "He was a son of a bitch in every way you can think of. He was kind of crude and a schemer and a womanizer. I don't know how the hell he kept his job as long as he did."

And so, the Packers returned to Green Bay after their tough loss to the Bears intent on regrouping the following Sunday against Chicago's other team, the Cardinals.

Cuff was not optimistic about Lambeau's strategic ability or his leadership skills. The Man Who Invented the Green Bay Packers had been an offensive innovator earlier in his career. He had shown the NFL what a passing game could do, and then had gotten the most out of Hutson, who is still arguably the most accomplished receiver in NFL history.

By 1947, Cuff said, Lambeau "was terrible. He [had] lost it by the time I played for him. He had that old Notre Dame Box that he played. Hell, you could defense the [damned] offense he had and almost have three guys on the field without an assignment. He pulled both guards, either way, sometimes both guards and a tackle. There was no way they could keep those guys from busting through the line at that time. So Curly was having a problem. And every time, hell, he didn't blame him[self], he blamed the players."

For all the chatter about Lambeau installing a variation of the T formation in 1947, Cuff said, there were still many vestiges of the Notre Dame Box: "That's the only kind of football Curly knew. It was far outdated." After playing the T formation in college, all of Curly's new players "had to learn the signals, the positions, all over again. And [Curly's offense] was easy to defend."

Cuff's complaints were not merely sour grapes. A skilled football strategist, he had invented *Ward Cuff's Football Game* after his rookie year with the Giants, who retired his No. 14 jersey after he left the team. After finishing his playing career, Cuff coached Green Bay Central Catholic High School to a 23-4-2 in four seasons and went on to be an assistant coach at Oregon State.

Evidently, he did not learn much from the mercurial Lambeau, who divided Green Bay's place-kicking between Cuff and Ted Fritsch, who had kicked a 50-yard field goal against the Bears, the third longest field goal the NFL had seen at that point. Cuff was 7 for 16 and Fritsch was six for 13 on field goals in 1947. And while Lambeau seemed to favor Cuff for shorter attempts, "There was no rhyme or reason for it," Cuff said. "It was [whoever] Curly sent in to kick it. You didn't ask him any questions because he was unreasonable to deal with."

There had been complaints about Lambeau for most of his coaching career. Cal Hubbard, a key member of the three-time NFL champions in 1929-31, had been a vocal critic. But after World War II, the gripes seemed to ring more true. Other coaches were taking football strategy to new heights, far beyond Lambeau's playbook. Players had more options and were more mature. In that context, Lambeau's scheming and cajoling was less effective—and more frustrating for him and everyone around him.

# 43
## *CARDINALS RULE*

Although no longer on top of his coaching game, Lambeau had assembled a very competitive Packer team in 1947. He believed it was championship-worthy, which added to his frustration. As it headed to Chicago for the second straight Sunday, Green Bay had lost three games by a total of eight points and was a disappointing 4-3, two games behind the 6-1 Cardinals and one game behind the 5-2 Bears.

Green Bay still had an outside chance of catching the Cardinals, who would play four challenging road games after finishing their home schedule against the Packers. That said, Lambeau's hope of answering the unrest in Green Bay with a seventh championship was looking dimmer.

The Packers' season had taken a difficult turn. But they still had a solid running game and a stout defense—and Lambeau had them prepared for another strong effort. Making good on Curly's vow to atone for losing to the Cardinals in Green Bay, the Packers led 20-7 with 12 minutes to play.

A crowd of 40,086 at Comiskey Park looked on with disappointment. This was the last home game for the Cardinals, who still faced trips to Washington, New York and Philadelphia, plus a game against the Bears at Wrigley Field. A loss to Green Bay would have left the Cards tied with the Bears at 6-2, and kept the Packers in the hunt at 5-3 for the Western Division title.

But the Cardinals had two things going for them. One was that their Million Dollar Backfield—quarterback Paul Christman, fullback Pat Harder, and halfbacks Charley Trippi, Elmer Angsman and Marshall Goldberg—was not finished. The Million Dollar nickname was an exaggeration, although the unprecedented $100,000 that owner Charlie Bidwill paid Trippi seemed boggling in that era, regardless of the number of zeroes. Their other nickname—Dream Backfield—was not in dispute.

The other Cardinal virtue against the Packers that day? Lady Luck. Everyone pointed to it—from Cardinals coach Jimmy Conzelman to Chicago sportswriters to the Packers themselves.

After Green Bay went ahead 20-7 against the sloppy Cardinals, Christman, who had been having a bad day, led a 57-yard, nine-play drive capped by a one-yard plunge from Harder. Harder then kicked the extra point, cutting Green Bay's lead to 20-14.

A Milwaukee native who had played at the University of Wisconsin, Harder was exactly the kind of player Lambeau would have signed in the pre-draft era. After the Cardinals took Harder second overall in the 1944 draft, Lambeau, selecting seventh, settled for Merv Pregulman, a Michigan offensive lineman who played in Green Bay in 1946 after serving in the Navy. Lambeau then traded Pregulman to Detroit. He played three more years in the NFL before becoming a millionaire businessman.

Trailing 20-14, the Cardinals quickly got the ball back. Starting at their own 34 yardline, they moved into Packer territory. When Mal Kutner fumbled after catching a pass from Christman, Green Bay had a chance to stop the drive. But Billy Dewell recovered for the Cardinals at the Packers' 23 yardline and Kutner followed with a 23-yard touchdown catch.

When Harder added another extra point, the Cardinals led 21-20. Urged on by an intense Lambeau, Green Bay remained determined. Taking the ball at the Packers 27 yardline with 75 seconds left, Jacobs completed three passes to Luhn. That gave Green Bay a first down at the Cardinals' 15 yardline.

After calling a timeout with 35 seconds left to talk things over, Lambeau sent in Cuff to attempt a 23-yard field goal that would give Green Bay a final-minute lead.

Cuff's kick sailed wide left.

That miss ended the Packers' hopes of sneaking back into the 1947 NFL championship race. But really, it ended so much more. Never again would Curly Lambeau mount a real challenge for another title.

For The Man Who Invented the Green Bay Packers, it was the end of an era.

Whether anyone realized it at that point, Lambeau would never have a team good enough to win a championship again. His tactics were not keeping up, his ability to build a roster was too limited by the AAFC war—and he could only push his players so far with his intimidating style.

Judging by the way he reacted, Lambeau might have grasped what had slipped away that blustery, gray day at Comiskey Park.

As soon as a furious Lambeau spotted him, Cuff said, "The first thing he said to me was, 'You missed that field goal on purpose,' because I played for the Cardinals the year before. He yelled right in my face. I said, 'You better shut your mouth or you won't get off the field.'"

For the third straight Sunday, Green Bay had lost in agonizing style. Three losses by a total of five points left the Packers with a 4-4 record—on the outside looking in at the 7-1 Cardinals and the 6-2 Bears.

"I've never in the history of football heard of a team losing games like that," Cardinals coach Conzelman said.

"We have got a good club, but we have not played championship ball," said Lambeau, trying to contain his anger at some of his players. "That's why we are where we are today. . . . We have some who have been playing championship ball, but too many of them haven't been. There have been some important missed assignments—those that were missed in the clutch and put us where we are today. We could just as well be on top right now, if some of us had been thinking football all season long."

After *Chicago Daily News* writer Harry Sheer made his obligatory rounds in the Cardinals dressing room, he went to the Packers' room, hoping to catch a lingering Lambeau.

"Seen Curly?" he asked.

"He's gone," one player snarled, "and if I were you. . . I wouldn't ask him any questions. . . even if you do find him."

Although there was a lot of talk about the Cardinals' luck, one member of their outstanding line, which played a huge role in the success of the Million Dollar Backfield, pointed to something more substantial.

"We knew," [said] tackle Chet Bulger, who just about earned all-league honors yesterday, "that Cuff always misses under pressure. And when he saw Blackburn, Apolskis and Colhouer roaring in on him, he looked up. That's all there was to it."

Some wondered why Curly hadn't gone with Ted Fritsch, who already had kicked field goals of 35 and 45 yards. Then again, Fritsch also had missed two shorter first-half field goals that day.

"The answer: Cuff is supposed to be more talented from shorter distances," Joe Agrella told his *Chicago Times* readers.

Lambeau was not finished with Cuff.

"He kept my check," Cuff said. "He tried to fine me a whole game's salary."

After the season ended, Cuff said, he confronted Lambeau. "I got him in his office . . . and said, 'OK, Curly, pay up or else you go out the window.' " Under that threat, Lambeau ordered a check made out to Cuff.

And that was the way Cuff ended his accomplished 11-year NFL career.

## 44
### *THE GRIP KEEPS SLIPPING*

Knowing how important the Packers were to Green Bay, the *Press-Gazette* sports staff was relentlessly loyal to Lambeau and his football team. However, the newspaper did publish the occasional critical letter to the editor, especially when it touched on a controversy.

Lambeau's decision to let Ward Cuff attempt to make the game-winning field against the Cardinals rather than Ted Fritsch was one of those controversies.

"Why didn't Lambeau leave Fritsch in, in that crucial moment? . . . Lambeau lost the game last Sunday with the Bears by the same mistake. . . sending in Cuff after Fritsch had made a 50-yard field goal earlier in the game. . . . We have the players and all we need is a new coach." The letter was signed by *A disappointed Allouez Packer fan.*

Allouez, on Green Bay's southern border, was not the only Fox Valley community trying to process the defeat. The thoughts of *Disappointed in Allouez* prompted rebuttals, including a letter from *A Packer Fan* who had met people from all over the country while in the military. "Upon mentioning that I was from Green Bay, the conversation usually turned to the Green Bay Packers and not to the cheese or paper industry. . . The people of Green Bay owe a great deal to Mr. Lambeau for the caliber of the teams that he has turned out. I think it is about time to give a few slaps on the back instead of the numerous kicks in the pants to a man that has helped put Green Bay on the map."

That same day, *A Personally Interested Fan* defended Lambeau by saying, "no one is perfect, everyone makes mistakes at one time or another. . . . I don't think it is right to continually criticize the coach and the players."

And yet, that is exactly what was going on. That's what frustrated sports fans do. For the third straight year, the Packers had come up short in the Western Division, and been shut out of another National Football League championship. For the first time since Lambeau created a football phenomenon a quarter-century earlier, doubt was mounting about his ability to produce a winner.

On the *Press-Gazette's* sports page, Art Daley explained that Lambeau let Cuff attempt the final 23-yard field goal because "It was his usual procedure—Fritsch for long and Cuff for shorts." Each had made six field goals.

To be precise, Daley crunched the numbers: "Fritsch got off kicks of 21, 23, 35, 44, 49 and 50 yards this league season for an average of 37 yards while Cuff made kicks of 13, 14, 15, 28, 28 and 39 yards for an average of 22.8 yards."

Two of Fritsch's field goals had come from 21 and 23 yards while Cuff had kicked from as far as 39 yards. Which didn't exactly fit into the Long and Short Theory. Cuff's explanation, that "There was no rhyme or reason for it," made more sense.

What was not debatable: Green Bay was 4-4, with four losses by a mere nine points. Packer fans were restless. And Lambeau was trying not to boil over.

"We should have won them all. As it is, all we wind up with is ulcers," Lambeau told New York-based *United Press* columnist Oscar Fraley under the headline, *Lambeau's No. 1 Draft Choice. Fraley Suggests a Psychiatrist*.

Remembering that clever quotes meant good publicity, Lambeau described Cuff as "a guy who has kicked 60 a day without missing since the Revolutionary War, it seems, and who always has had ice water in his veins." When Fraley suggested that the Packers would have been better off if they had taken a 15-yard penalty and let Fritsch kick, Curly replied, "If we had to do it over, we probably would."

It helped that sportswriters like Daley and Fraley tried to soften the blow of Green Bay's disappointment. Fraley even reminded readers that Lambeau "played for the Fighting Irish on the same team with the legendary George Gipp."

But that didn't change the fact that the Packers were struggling—and that the grumbles about Curly were gaining momentum. As usual, Lambeau deflected the blame by pointing at his players, telling the *Milwaukee Sentinel,* "You can't miss assignments, touchdown passes or kicks in key spots and still get over the hump in close ballgames."

Years later, Cuff gave insight into another part of the Packers' problem: "The thing that I couldn't understand in Green Bay was that the kickers never practiced kicking during the week. I never practiced kicking field goals when I was in Green Bay. In New York, we had practiced it every day."

That was not the sign of a coach on top of his game.

# 45
## *AMID UNREST, LOS ANGELES RUMORS*

Beyond staring at another disappointing season, Lambeau was wrestling with myriad other issues. Topping the list: Green Bay Packers Inc. was awash in red ink.

As the Packers prepared to finish up their 1947 lament with a coast-to-coast road trip to New York, Los Angeles, Detroit and Philadelphia, Lambeau cut a few corners.

He dropped end Johnny Kovatch, putting Green Bay at 33 players, one under the roster limit, and trimmed an inactive player, fullback Bob McDougal. Although of minor budget importance, the moves showed the impact of the salary war with the AAFC. The Packer player payroll had soared from $201,917 in 1946 to $276,000 in 1947. That was a much bigger financial strain than Rockwood Lodge, but Green Bay's ambitious training facility also was an expensive burden.

Adding to the Packers' problems, they had to abandon plans to fly on portions of their arduous season-ending road trip when all DC-6s, including President Harry Truman's official plane, were grounded by a mysterious problem that had caused fires on two of the 52-passenger airliners. Under their new itinerary, the Packers would depart New York by train at 6:30 p.m. on Sunday after playing the Giants and arrive in Los Angeles at 8:45 a.m. Wednesday.

Feeling down—and out of the championship chase—Green Bay was fit to be tied. And that's what happened at the Polo Grounds. Trailing the winless Giants 24-10, the Packers needed a pair of late touchdown passes to salvage a 24-24 standoff.

Despite their cross-country railroad odyssey, the Packers proceeded to defeat the Rams 30-10 in Los Angeles. Traipsing back to Detroit, they beat the Lions 35-14. Moving on to Philadelphia for their final game, the Packers lost 28-14 to the Eagles. That win set up a playoff between Philadelphia and Pittsburgh for the Eastern Division title. The Eagles would win that game and lose in the NFL championship to the Cardinals.

Green Bay finished the season 6-5-1, behind the Cardinals (9-3) and the Bears (8-4), in third place for the third straight year. Except for a brief decline in 1933-34 when the team was dealing with bankruptcy, it was the worst stretch since Lambeau had created the Packer mystique more than a quarter-century earlier.

The maddening part was that the Packers' first four losses had come by a mere nine points, including three losses by just five points in three straight November games.

Meanwhile, Curly wound up loudly denying a rumor that he was headed to the Los Angeles Dons, in the rival AAFC. If true, he would be betraying not just Green Bay, but the entire NFL. It was no wonder that Lambeau said it wasn't so.

"Watch for a N.F.L. coach (Curly Lambeau) to jump to the A.A.C. and join the Dons," *Los Angeles Times* columnist Braven Dyer, a Lambeau confidant, said in an odds-and-ends column on Tuesday, December 16, 1947. Why did he identify Lambeau between parentheses? At least that made more sense than calling him "a N.F.L. coach," rather than *an* NFL coach.

"It is based on unfounded facts," Lambeau said, noting that the speculation started after "a New York newspaper reported that I was being placed on probation in Green Bay. Immediately, football people contacted me and asked me about my plans for 1948. From their connection with me, the rumors spread further. No offers of any kind were made to me."

After Lambeau's denial, however, Hy Turkin told *New York Daily News* readers, "the Los Angeles Dons apparently will fill their coaching gap by raiding one of the bulwarks of the rival NFL, Curly Lambeau."

Adding to the mystery, L.A. Dons president Ben Lindheimer, who owned the Arlington Park racetrack in suburban Chicago, declined to deny reports that Lambeau would be the Dons' coach in 1948. Lindheimer, in New York for the AAFC player draft, said the Dons were considering four candidates for their coaching job. "Three have applied for the post, but we have had no contact with the fourth," Lindheimer said. "Asked whether No. 4 was Lambeau, Lindheimer "would rather not say."

Lindheimer's non-denial sent a message heard around the nation—that The Man Who Invented the Green Bay Packers might be heading west. A key part of the intrigue: Would Lambeau take a chance on the upstart league to coach in Los Angeles? Or was he merely using the Dons as leverage to solidify his increasingly shaky situation in his hometown?

In Green Bay, where there were plenty of grumbles about how much time Lambeau spent at his new wife's Malibu home, Curly taking a job in Southern California sounded very logical.

In an apparent effort to downplay the speculation, Packers president Emil Fischer responded by saying, "Why, we in Green Bay wouldn't know how to act if Curly wasn't coaching the team. And I don't think the team would either." Commenting on a report that Lambeau had been "on probation" in 1947, Fischer said, "Curly Lambeau will be coach of the Green Bay Packers just as long as he wants to be and we hope that is for the rest of his coaching career."

As it turned out, Curly's denial was not the whole truth. Behind-the-scenes maneuvering involving Lambeau, the Dons and the Packers would become clear two years later. Lambeau had reached a secret agreement with Lindheimer to coach the Dons, *Los Angeles Examiner* columnist Vincent X. Flaherty revealed later.

"How do I know Lambeau wanted to coach the Dons?" Flaherty wrote. "I contacted him for Lindheimer when Lambeau said he was 'very much interested.' I drove him to Lindheimer's home in Beverly Hills where the two of them hit it off great from the start. What happened when he got back to Green Bay is something only Curly and the Green Bay board of directors can answer."

On some levels, it made sense for Lambeau to take the Dons job. He not only relished spending time with Grace at their Malibu home. He also had big concerns about having the financial resources to keep the Packers competitive amid the soaring salaries created by the NFL-AAFC war.

Did he really intend to begin coaching in Los Angeles in 1948? Or was he just using Lindheiemer's offer as leverage in Green Bay?

"He agreed to terms and sought one stipulation, which was granted," Flaherty claimed. "He wanted to break the news gently to the people back in Green Bay. So Lambeau. . . returned to Green Bay, where he met with the club's board of directors. He told them he was leaving and that parting was such sweet sorrow and so forth, and, in a long distance phone call to Lindheimer in Los Angeles, even repeated his assurances that everything was all set for his switch to the Coast. However, the Green Bay board of directors got together, gave Lambeau a boost in salary and the whole picture was changed right there. Lambeau stayed on at Green Bay, forgetting all about his verbal agreement with Lindheimer—proving once again that football coaches are worse than women when it comes to changing their minds."

The scenario was eerily similar to one that played out with Lambeau's college coach and mentor, Knute Rockne. In December, 1925,

Rockne agreed to coach at Columbia. Rockne had even signed a three-year contract at $25,000 a year. In the end, though, he merely used Columbia to get what he wanted from Notre Dame.

The Lambeau-L.A. Dons leverage scenario would have made more sense two years earlier, when Lambeau secured his big five-year contract shortly before the Dons began their battle of Los Angeles with the Rams. In 1947, the Packers board actually was reining in Lambeau's power. The bottom line, though, is that in the late 1940s, Lambeau and the team's citizen executives were clashing increasingly—and Lambeau was becoming increasingly restless.

Lambeau would continue as Green Bay's coach and general manager, with authority to cast the franchise's vote on all league matters. Even while the L.A. Dons rumors were swirling, Lambeau was listed in the *New York Daily News* among "the NFL owners" who were "tiring of the added financial burdens imposed by the 'war' between the two loops." While Boston owner Ted Collins and Philadelphia owner Alex Thompson were bristling at the expansive conflict, the report said, "Lambeau, one of the founders of the NFL, has hinted that peace would be welcome."

The only individual in a comparable position to Lambeau was the Bears' George Halas. And Halas had occasionally moved away from his various roles as coach, general manager and chief executive. He had stepped down as coach for three years during the jockeying with his partner, Dutch Sternaman, and had been absent for four years while serving in the Navy.

There was one big difference, though. Halas was a chief executive/general manager/coach who owned his team; Lambeau did not own the Packers. They were community-owned. For all of his authority, Lambeau was subject to the consent of the team's executive committee and board of directors.

To stay in power, Lambeau could give himself leverage by fielding a competitive team and by keeping the team in good financial shape. When those two things were not happening in the late 1940s, he could resort to threats to jump to another team. But that would only be effective for so long. Problems were mounting between the men who oversaw Green Bay Packers Inc. and The Man Who Invented the Green Bay Packers.

## 46
### *PLANES AND TRAINS AND JUG GIRARD*

Lambeau did not have time to dwell on the disappointment of close losses in 1947 for very long. Five days after the Packers' season-ending loss to the Eagles in Philadelphia, the 1948 NFL draft was held in Pittsburgh on December 19.

With the seventh pick overall, Lambeau selected Earl "Jug" Girard, who seemed to be a natural for the Packers. A native of Marinette, Wisconsin, on the Michigan border 50 miles north of Green Bay, Girard had starred at Wisconsin in 1944, then returned from two years in the Army to lead the Badgers again in 1947. At Wisconsin, he was coached by Harry Stuhldreher, one of Notre Dame's famous Four Horsemen. An all-around talent who was considered an excellent passer, Girard was a homegrown star who appeared to fill a glaring Packer need.

But it wasn't that simple. The AAFC New York Yankees had taken a flier on Girard in the 27th round and offered him a $7,500 contract for 1948. With that, Yankee owner Dan Topping's deep pockets put the penny-pinching Packers in a bind. Beyond football, Girard was a talented third baseman who had attracted the interest of the Cubs and the Indians. And baseball's financial upside was far greater than football for athletes in those days.

After the draft, Lambeau and Grace headed off to California for Christmas, "but what a trip he had!" gossip columnist Dorothy Morris reported in the *Topanga Journal and Malibu Monitor* on December 26. "Flying from the east the weather got bad and they couldn't land in Chicago so they came down in a cornfield. . . . They were stuck there for hours with no food and no heat (and Malibu looks mighty, mighty good to him.)"

After a brief Christmas break, Lambeau went up to San Francisco for a week of observing the players in the East-West Shrine All-Star game. Considering that he was a close friend of East coach Bernie Bierman and West coach Andy Kerr, Art Daley told *Press-Gazette* readers, "Don't be surprised if the Packers' novel defense pops up on one of the squads." Daley described it as "sort of a cone-shaped affair (5-3-2-1) with the ice cream end facing the opposing line."

Returning to Green Bay from California, Lambeau was scheduled to meet on January 9 at his Northern Building office with Girard, who had promised not to sign his AAFC Yankees contract until he heard Curly's offer.

Girard didn't show up. Later that day, a report out of Marinette said Girard would sign with the Yankees. Driving up to Marinette a few days later, Lambeau made his pitch, which continued when he boarded the Chicago & North Western's 400 train with Girard, who was on his way to California to play in an All-Star game.

Girard agreed to sign with Green Bay for $8,000 as the train rolled through Peshtigo. But he was a couple of weeks short of his 21st birthday, so the signing was not valid. Girard's mother, Ann, claiming the Yankees had raised their offer to $10,000, refused to authorize her son's Packer contract.

Racing back to the West Coast after an NFL meeting in New York, Lambeau finally convinced Girard to join the Packers for $10,000. "As a bonus for signing, Girard was to be Lambeau's guest on the West Coast for three weeks," the *Press-Gazette* reported.

By landing Girard, a homegrown hero, Lambeau had won the headline battle. He had shown that Green Bay could outbid the AAFC for a player it wanted. Whether Girard would live up to the hype and help Lambeau win on the football field remained to be seen.

# 47
## *AN EXTREME MEASURE DOES NOT PAY OFF*

As Lambeau prepared the Packers for 1948, they again faced a tough road. The Cardinals were the defending NFL champions. The Bears, who had finished a close second in the West after winning the NFL title in 1946, also looked strong. To vault ahead of the two Chicago teams would be a major challenge. Everyone in Green Bay realized that.

But there was reason to believe Lambeau's Packers could be successful. Green Bay won its three pre-season games against the Giants, Steelers and Redskins by a combined 59-7. In its NFL opener, it had added a 31-0 rout of the struggling Boston Yanks on Friday night, September 17, before a meager crowd of 15,443 at Fenway Park. But that was all merely a warmup.

"Set your watches back two hours, everybody. Set 'em back to our time—Bear time," Lambeau announced as his Packers boarded a plane in Boston the next day for the trip back to Green Bay.

A curious, hopeful and eager crowd of 25,546 Packers fans gathered at City Stadium to see the 59th meeting between the Bears and Green Bay. They left downcast. Fueled by six Packer turnovers, the Bears crushed Green Bay 45-7, the most lopsided score in their fierce rivalry.

"We are not as good as we showed today," Bears leader George Halas insisted afterward. "What happened today has nothing to do with the real ability of the Green Bay football team. Those first two touchdowns were lucky breaks. And we were just fortunate enough to be able to carry on from there."

Lambeau was far less expansive. Entering the Packers' dressing room, he said, "Meeting tomorrow at eleven," as his players grimly took off their shoulder pads. Heading into his office, Lambeau and assistants Walt Kiesling, Bo Molenda and Don Hutson "smoked in silence" for a few minutes.

An NFL coach and his assistants puffing on cigarettes after a tough loss? That's an image from the distant past. Lambeau then told reporters, "We played a very poor ball game. But we're a lot better team than we showed today. That's all I've got to say."

He undoubtedly had more to say to his club that week. The objective was clear for the Packers and their fans: They needed to redeem themselves against the Lions. On Thursday, Lambeau emphasized the point by practicing for 80 minutes in a steady downpour.

The Packers responded by handling Detroit 33-21 before a crowd of 21,403 at City Stadium, 4,000 fewer than had shown up for the Bear game. Against the unimposing Lions, it was not an overwhelming performance.

But it set the stage for Green Bay's next game, in Milwaukee against the Cardinals. The 1947 defending champions had lost to the Bears 28-17 in a raucous Monday night showdown attended by more than 52,000 at Comiskey Park. The Cardinals would not be interested in losing a second straight game.

Although the underdog, Green Bay looked capable enough. A record crowd of 34,369, the largest ever for a pro football game in Wisconsin, elbowed its way into State Fair Park in West Allis, outside Milwaukee. The Packers put up a good battle, scoring a fourth-quarter touchdown to trail 14-7 after being stifled in the first three quarters. But they lost 17-7 to a better team that would come close to winning its second straight NFL title.

A 72-yard rushing touchdown by Elmer Angsman and a 45-yard punt return for a touchdown by Charley Trippi provided the Cardinals with a pair of big plays. The Cardinals were not at their best. They had lost quarterback Paul Christman to a broken hand in their previous game. They were still shocked by the heart attack that had killed 27-year-old tackle Stan Mauldin two weeks earlier. Before the game, equipment man/trainer Dutch Kriznecky also had a heart attack and was rushed to the hospital. He was well enough to return to Chicago with the team, but that was after the team had received an emotional jolt.

The Packers made their share of mistakes against the distracted Cardinals. With Ward Cuff now retired, Green Bay kicker Ted Fritsch had missed a pair of first-half field goals. Apparently fired up, the Packers also were whistled for 12 penalties that cost them 140 yards. In the end, the Cardinals prevailed by rushing for 320 yards against an over-matched opponent.

Lambeau went ballistic after the game, which left the Packers 2-2 and chasing the unbeaten Bears and one-loss Cardinals and Rams. In his mind, this game had been a must-win. The only explanation for defeat was a lack of effort by his players.

"I'm not feeling bad. I'm mad!" Lambeau ranted afterward, vowing that "Salary adjustments will be made until we begin to play the brand of ball we're capable of. I never have been so disappointed in my life. There was a decided lack of spirit today. This can't be applied, of course, to all 35 of them because we had a half a dozen boys out there who had it—but that isn't enough. We always have had a reputation for spirit. We haven't shown it once this year. But we're going to correct this situation this week—or else. . . . The boys are getting good salaries and they're content. For that reason, there's got to be a penalty for losing."

On Monday, Lambeau announced that he had docked every Packer 50 percent of his salary that week. Withholding half of the paycheck of every player? After a game where the Packers had been down 14-7 in the fourth quarter against the NFL's defending champion?

For all of Curly's forward-thinking ideas, this was a draconian and archaic response.

"The Cardinals were league champions and they'd barely beaten us on two long plays," said Bob Forte, a captain and linebacker who was a Packer in 1946-53. "Curly told us we'd been fined half a game's salary. 'For indifferent play,' Curly said. We couldn't believe it,"

Lambeau also cut halfback Bruce Smith, the All-America from Minnesota who had been limited by injuries. "The slightest bump has knocked him out of play," the loyal *Press-Gazette* said. Smith said he planned to return to his sporting goods business in Northfield, Minnesota. After dabbling with the Giants, though, Smith eventually landed on the Rams for the final eight games of 1948.

After reviewing the Cardinals game film for the fifth time—apparently his own little form of punishment—on Wednesday night, Lambeau said, "The fines stick." He added, though, that he might relent on the withheld pay after he reviewed Green Bay's upcoming game against the Rams.

Fair punishment or not, the Packers responded to Lambeau's salary docking and shut out the high-scoring Rams 16-0 for the first time since they had moved to Los Angeles in 1946. Green Bay intercepted a boggling seven passes by flashy Bob Waterfield and shut down the L.A. running game.

Despite his players' impressive performance, Lambeau remained noncommittal about returning the money he had withheld.

It was an extreme and old-school maneuver. Even in the '40s, pro football had progressed far enough to make it difficult to imagine fining an entire NFL team half of its salary for "spiritless performance." A 10-point loss to the NFL champion Cardinals? Lambeau's fury was hard to fathom. And a grave miscalculation.

"Morale was at an all-time low," Forte said. " Some of the guys wanted to quit right then." One player literally had packed his car, Forte said, but teammates talked him out of leaving. The Packers were 3-2; it felt like 3-20.

But that was Lambeau as he neared the end of his Packer reign. He had often coached with emotional and extreme tactics. Increasingly isolated and losing the respect of his players for clinging to antiquated offensive principles and trying to get results by intimidation, Lambeau was losing his grip on his players—and his ability to be a successful coach.

Even after they shut out the Rams, Lambeau did not pay his players the money that they were due. By failing to reward them for winning their next game, he paid the extreme price of losing his players.

"We thought we'd get the money if we played well the next week against the Rams," Tony Canadeo said. "Well, we did, shut them out 16-0, but we didn't get the money from Curly. After that we all were twice as mad and everything went downhill from there. We didn't win another game all year, lost seven straight. After the season, Lambeau gave us back the money, though."

That was too little, too late. Whether Lambeau genuinely thought that docking his players would translate into wins, or whether he had the Packers' troubled finances in mind, the decision was a colossal mistake.

With that pay withholding, Lambeau crossed another point of no return in his unique Packers career. In 1947, a loss to the Cardinals had halted his last chance to bring another title to Green Bay. And in 1948, another loss to the Cardinals triggered the salary rift with his players that ended his ability to field a team with any hope of competing.

The number of loyal Packer fans who were starting to question Lambeau's ability was growing. Curly's enemies on the Packer board were paying close attention.

From there, Green Bay slipped into an unbreakable downward spiral, losing to the Washington Redskins 23-7 in Milwaukee before 13,433, more than 20,000 fewer fans than had turned out for the Cardinals loss in which Lambeau docked his players.

Green Bay then lost 24-20 in Detroit to the previously winless Lions and was crushed 38-7 in Pittsburgh by a Steelers team that had only won twice in six games. That fueled a "Get Lambeau" movement by Packer fans and some former players. Publicly, the team's directors paid no attention.

With the Packers preparing for their rematch with the Bears in Chicago, Lambeau's detractors might have figured the time was right for open rebellion. Green Bay was in a frustrating three-game tailspin, while the Bears, who had already whipped the Packers 45-7 in Green Bay, were 6-1 and tied with the Cardinals for the Western Division lead.

In that dark hour, though, the Packers forgot their differences with their coach and their struggles on the field to play an inspired game. Their determination to beat the Bears even outweighed their anger at Lambeau for cutting their pay in half.

In the end, though, that only made the day more frustrating. Green Bay lost 7-6 on November 14, 1948, before a crowd of 48,113 at Wrigley Field. "Veterans like Tony Canadeo and Bob Forte sobbed unashamedly as they plodded off the field," Lee Remmel told *Press-Gazette* readers. "Some of the others were close to tears and those that weren't able to give vent to their emotions were bowed and grim."

Lambeau could find no fault with a team that had played a fierce game, only to be undone by a missed extra point and a blocked field goal. "The way our boys played today, they deserved to win," Lambeau said, gently lamenting a slight Irv Comp stumble on the Bears' lone touchdown pass. "When you play that hard, you deserve to win. . . . I feel bad because the boys deserved to win the ball game.. The score should have been 10-7. . . . It's what it is. All in all, I was very well satisfied with our defense. It was too bad Comp slipped, but that couldn't be helped."

An unnamed Packer said a Lambeau tirade in the dressing-room gloom after the loss to the Steelers had helped stoke Green Bay's fiery game against the Bears. "I don't care if we have only 24 men left to play against the Bears," Lambeau said, threatening to fire any player who didn't perform in practice.

In a demonstration of Green Bay's love for its Packers, a large crowd had shown up at the Chicago & North Western station on Saturday to encourage their struggling team. In an even more passionate embrace, an estimated 3,000 fans turned out at 10 p.m. on Sunday night to welcome home their devastated heroes.

"Green Bay fans don't forget the Packers when they play the kind of football they played today," longtime trainer Bud Jorgensen said.

The determined effort against the Bears kindled hopes that Green Bay (3-6) would win its final three games to finish with a 6-6 record.

First up was a game in Milwaukee against the struggling New York Giants, who were 2-6. Despite all of the positive feelings about Green Bay's effort against the Bears, only 12,639 fans were curious enough to show up at Wisconsin State Fair Park on November 21, 1948, to see the Packers and the Giants.

In a shocking turnaround, New York crushed the Packers 49-3, scoring seven unanswered touchdowns after Green Bay led 3-0 in the second quarter. Never had the adage about a team leaving everything on the field seemed more appropriate to explain the Packers' empty performance a week after their gut-wrenching loss to the Bears.

Lambeau, who had been consoling after the loss in Chicago, erupted in a fury after the Giants debacle.

"We've tried everything to bring this team along after looking bad, and nothing has worked," he said. "We've tried driving, easing up, fining. Now we're through. The exhibition this afternoon was as sad a thing as I have ever seen. It made up my mind. A lot of these boys still have a lot of football left, I know. They showed it early in the season and they showed it again against the Chicago Bears a week ago. But they just refuse to play it for us, or at least consistently. As things are now they suffer in the long run and so do we. A change of scenery will probably help a lot of them. We will have to rebuild."

To emphasize his point, Lambeau announced that he was cutting end Ted Cremer, a mid-season acquisition from Detroit, and added that 15 or 16 more Packers would be gone as soon as the season ended. "There may be even more," he said.

After a restless night in Milwaukee, Lambeau and his Packers boarded a TWA Constellation for their six-hour-and-40-minute flight to Burbank, California, then transferred to the Ojai Valley Inn, a luxury resort hotel 80 miles from L.A. that featured a golf course, a swimming pool and 70-degree temperatures.

Amid these splendid surroundings, Lambeau issued another ominous warning. Speaking under "a hot sun," Lambeau told his floundering team, "Naturally our main thought is on the next game but I'm not forgetting 1949. We don't want anyone on this club who doesn't want to win or who doesn't give a damn whether he wins or loses, though he may give his best on half of the games. We will never tolerate another year like this one."

The season took another wrong turn, though, on Saturday, when the Packers headed to Los Angeles. A truck hauling their gear caught fire, destroying $4,000 in uniforms and equipment, including 12 uniforms and two dozen warmup coats. A lighted cigarette thrown from a passing car was blamed.

The next day, 10 Packers wore uniforms cobbled together with items obtained from the Rams and other local teams and stores. Once the game began, though, the Rams were not as kind. They atoned for their 16-0 loss in Green Bay in October with a 24-10 win on November 28.

Considering that the Rams had spent a week practicing at Maxwelton Braes, a resort in Door County, 80 miles northeast of Green Bay, before losing to the Packers, the concept of practicing in plush surroundings was not a path to success in the series.

Returning to the Midwest for its final game of 1948, Green Bay was pounded by the Cardinals 42-7 on December 5 in Chicago. The Packers completed only one of their 15 passing attempts, and that completion came in the waning minutes of the rout.

That ended "the most disastrous season in history," as the *Chicago Tribune* put it, for the Packers—and for Lambeau, the only leader they had ever known. Green Bay finished with three wins and nine losses.

Only once before, when they went 5-7-1 in 1933, had the Packers lost more games than they won. In 1933, Green Bay was battling bankruptcy and the Depression. In 1948, it was fighting a losing a battle for players with the AAFC.

"All they need is a few additions and they'd go places," Cardinals coach Jimmy Conzelman said afterward, trying to be sympathetic.
Hesitating after lighting a cigarette, Conzelman added, "I don't like to say anything but, if the Packers got a little better passing, they'd be a much better ball club."

A little better? Actually, Green Bay needed to be a lot better at throwing the ball. It finished ninth in passing out of 10 teams in 1948. And it was dead-last in team offense. Even if the Packers had not quit on their pay-withholding coach, the passing game would have sputtered.

The larger problem, though, was that more and more people in Green Bay were wondering if The Man Who Invented the Green Bay Packers was still the right man to lead the Packers.

Lambeau, however, was already digging in to turn around the Packers' sinking fortunes in 1949.

"Although extremely disappointing and aggravating, the situation is not exactly a new one for the Packers," he said. "We faced it before— in 1933 and 1934—and came back to win championships in 1936 and 1939 and a divisional title in 1938. We corrected it then and we can and will correct it now. . . . We know what held us back and we are going to correct it. It will just take hard work and some sound thinking."

Lambeau took the first step by reaching agreement in mid-December with his top draft pick, Stan Heath, who led the nation in passing at Nevada in 1948, for $15,000. Only a year before, he had given a then-pricy $10,000 contract to Jug Girard. The cost of doing business in professional football continued to soar.

Green Bay had selected Heath fifth overall at a secret draft meeting in Pittsburgh on November 15, 1948. The formal NFL draft was held a month later, on December 21, in Philadelphia.

At that gathering, a group of AAFC owners met with NFL officials in an effort to end the war that was draining both sides financially. They got close to an agreement in which the most attractive AAFC teams would join the NFL, but the deal fell through when the AAFC insisted that Baltimore be allowed to enter the NFL along with Cleveland and San Francisco.

A huge problem for the Packers was that Lambeau had lost his gift for coming up with talent. He still had not found a successor to his last great passer, Cecil Isbell, who had left Green Bay in 1942. For six years, Lambeau had been on a quest for a premier passer. In 1949, with the pressure on him to answer his critics, he had lined up three candidates to restore the Packers' feeble passing game.

After the season ended, Lambeau finally paid his players what they were owed: The 50 percent of their paychecks for the 17-7 loss to the Cardinals in Milwaukee. It was one of his worst moves.

# 48
## *WAR AND RUMORS OF PEACE*

By late December, Lambeau and Grace were back in California, where Lambeau now had a wider choice of bowl games to attend. With the 1949 draft already completed, he was merely checking out players he already had chosen. But Lambeau never passed up an excuse to be on the West Coast. Meanwhile, assistant Don Hutson went to the Sugar Bowl, centrally located between his Arkansas roots and his Alabama college days. And Packers president Emil Fischer, who wintered in South Florida, kept an eye on the Orange Bowl.

Adding to the draft intrigue, Green Bay had only revealed the names of three of its 25 draft picks, a common practice as warring NFL and AAFC teams tried to keep their plans secret.

Lambeau's top pick, Heath, was going to lead Nevada against Villanova in the Harbor Bowl at San Diego. His fourth-round pick, Utah fullback Bob Summerhays, was playing in the East-West Shrine Game in San Francisco. And because 22 draft picks remained secret, it was possible that other Packer selections would be playing in the Rose Bowl between Northwestern and Cal.

Lambeau announced on January 4, 1949, that Heath was officially signed. He had mailed in his contract from San Diego, where Villanova roughed up Heath and Nevada 27-7 on New Year's Day. At least Lambeau could feel good about his third-round pick, Villanova defensive tackle Lou Ferry.

"I think Stan will have a good season with us," Lambeau said, adding some extremely high praise. "He seems to me to be a combination of one of our great passers, Cecil Isbell, and the Los Angeles Rams' Bob Waterfield."

Lambeau planned to give Heath every opportunity to be his starting quarterback next season. "The veteran Packer coach was not satisfied with the passing of Indian Jack Jacobs, nor Jack's understudies, Irv Comp and Perry Moss, last fall," the *Press-Gazette* reported.

The 6-foot-1 Heath was from Milwaukee, where his father, Mickey, had played for and managed the minor-league Brewers baseball team. Heath played at Wisconsin for one season, then transferred to Nevada after flunking out at Madison.

As it turned out, mentioning Heath in the same breath with Isbell and Waterfield was wishful thinking.

"Heath could throw the ball," said former Rams head coach Bob Snyder, the Packers backfield coach in 1949. "He could throw any pass in football," Snyder said. Heath's problem was between the ears: "He was a rascal. He was his own man."

The third announced draftee, Michigan center Dan Dworsky, who was taken in the second round, already had played in the North-South game on Christmas Day in Miami. He wound up playing for the AAFC Los Angeles Dons.

Green Bay was not the only football team reeling under the weight of the expensive war for players. On January 10, sources said Dan Topping planned to fold his New York Yankees AAFC franchise—an unmistakable sign that the NFL-AAFC battle could not continue for long. Despite his huge bankroll in the nation's largest city, Topping had grown weary of the financial drain.

To end the costly war, Philadelphia Eagles owner Alexis Thompson, a 37-year-old millionaire sportsman and entrepreneur, laid out a plan in the November 1948 issue of *Sport* Magazine to absorb a few AAFC teams into a 12-team NFL. Under Thompson's plan, the NFL would abandon Green Bay because "visiting teams take a licking at Green Bay due to the small population and small stadium."

Lambeau fired back by listing the gate receipts for several Packer home games and saying, "Over half of the clubs in either professional league cannot equal these figures. . . . I don't think Thompson knows what he's talking about; he hasn't attended a league meeting in four years; he's not equipped to speak for or about the other clubs in our league."

Of far greater importance, NFL commissioner Bert Bell and influential Chicago Bears owner George Halas led a long list of league executives who were stout supporters of keeping a team in Green Bay. "There will always be a Green Bay in professional football," Bell said.

What everyone agreed on was the need for the pro football war to end. When NFL leaders held their winter meetings in Chicago in mid-January 1949, the two warring sides met informally amid rumors of compromise plans in which two to four AAFC would join the NFL. The Cleveland Browns and San Francisco 49ers were considered locks. The question was, would Baltimore and Buffalo be admitted?

Making light of the AAFC rumor mill, Lambeau posed for a photo in the *Chicago Tribune* that showed him holding a phone to his ear while four other NFL leaders cupped their ears under a headline, "Carrying Out the `Secret' Theme."

Speculation flared up, though, when Lambeau and Halas "hustled out of the meeting rooms and disappeared into an elevator. They did not return for the morning session but were present when the meetings resumed in the afternoon," the *Press-Gazette's* Art Daley reported. "Since Lambeau and Halas rarely, if ever, engage in player trades, it was assumed that something concerning the other league was cooking."

"Sooner or later, the top two clubs in the All-America conference will join the NFL," Lambeau said, summing up the hardline stance of the senior league. There would be no mass merger.

The peace speculation proved to be a false alarm. That scenario would have to wait. Unwilling to accept those terms, the AAFC resolved to continue on its own in 1949 with a seven-team league, including a combined Brooklyn-New York Yankees franchise.

# 49
## *NEW COACHING STAFF—AND OTHER MANEUVERS*

Overshadowed by all the merger talk was the NFL's permanent adoption of a free substitution rule, which had been used during World War II. Previously, only three players could enter the game unless there was a timeout. "Now we can concentrate on two complete offensive and defensive units," said Lambeau, who strongly supported the change.

In a curious Packer development, assistant coach Walt Kiesling arrived in Chicago for the meetings on Tuesday, January 18, only to be told there was no room reserved for him at the Blackstone. The hotel's staff found him lodging at the Stevens Hotel. Three days later, Lambeau, in another clumsy firing, announced that Kiesling would not return for a fifth season on the Packers' coaching staff.

Kiesling, who had quit as the Steelers head coach to be a Green Bay assistant, went back to Pittsburgh as line coach. He would be on the Steelers' staff from 1949 until 1956, the last three years as head coach. After resigning due to poor health. Kiesling remained in the Steeler organization until 1961. Having started as a player with the Duluth Eskimos in 1926, Kiesling had seen it all in pro football.

Backfield coach Bo Molenda and ends coach Don Hutson would not return, either. Molenda ended up as an assistant on the Chicago Hornets AAFC team; Hutson happily left football to concentrate on his expanding business interests, including a Hudson Motors dealership and the popular Playdium bowling alley and bar.

In their place, Lambeau, who still knew how to put together a football team, hired three talented assistants: Charley Brock (defense), Bob Snyder (backfield) and Tom Stidham (line).

Brock, who had been a standout Packer center/linebacker, returned to Green Bay after one year as a college coach at Nebraska-Omaha. A future Packer Hall of Fame member, Brock had been a top-notch blocker on offense with a knack for interceptions on defense. He also had a Green Bay pedigree.

Snyder, who had played sparingly on three NFL championship teams with the Bears while backing up Sid Luckman at quarterback, had been the Rams head coach in 1947, but resigned early in 1948 due to an ulcer condition. A T-formation expert, Snyder was credited with developing Rams quarterback Bob Waterfield into a star. Snyder finished the 1948 season as a USC assistant when his ulcer improved.

New line coach Stidham had been a head coach at Oklahoma and Marquette for nine years. He had had a good four-year run as Oklahoma coach, where he coached Packer quarterback Jack Jacobs, before coaching Marquette for five years. He had been an assistant with the AAFC Baltimore Colts for two years when Lambeau hired him.

Did they know what they were getting themselves into? Going to work for a frustrated legend like Curly Lambeau in 1949 was risky business. Then again, all three were moving up in the coaching world. They were joining a proud franchise. And trying to help Curly Lambeau, the winningest coach in NFL history, get back on track was a risk worth taking.

"It will be a pleasure working with Curly and I'm going to enjoy working with this lad, Stan Heath," Snyder said. Without irony.

Snyder also explained why he was leaving Southern California to become an NFL assistant again after being the Rams head coach. "What the heck, it's coaching. And I'll not have all that pressure that caused all those ulcers. I'll be getting for four months' work with no pressure on me within $2,000 of what the Rams gave me for a year-'round job as head coach. That ain't bad."

No pressure? Working for a volatile, embattled Curly Lambeau? That was an interesting take.

Facing a pivotal year, Lambeau had assembled "the finest coaching staff in Green Bay's history," *Los Angeles Times* sportswriter Frank Finch said in his "Scouting the Pros" column. That would help matters. But it would only go so far. With the AAFC war still raging, Lambeau was struggling to build a competitive roster. Between the twin trends of Green Bay losing games and losing money, those who wanted to remove The Man Who Invented the Green Bay Packers were gaining momentum.

Lambeau's angry vow to cut a dozen or more players right after the season turned out be a blustery tirade. Lambeau had threatened the mass exodus after the Packers were embarrassed 49-3 in Milwaukee by the struggling New York Giants in November.

Instead, Lambeau had overhauled his coaching staff rather than his roster. Under the headline, "Same Brawn but New Brains Seems to be Packer Outlook," an *Associated Press* report published on February 3, 1949, in Appleton, Wisconsin, and around the country said. "As of today, the 1948 squad roster remains intact. The coaching department is another story."

After the NFL meeting in Chicago, he returned to the Malibu beach home built by Grace's late husband, William Garland. But even half a continent could not keep Lambeau from the problems and intrigues that the Packers were facing. Among them, he regularly refuted rumors that the team would leave Green Bay for Milwaukee or another large city.

"That is not true," Lambeau said, also denying a report that the Packers "had to borrow a lot of money and were bad off financially. We never borrowed a dime in our lives. . . . The Packers positively will not leave Green Bay. We have been in Green Bay since the league began and we will still be in Green Bay many years from now."

The denial of money problems was Lambeau spinning the truth. The Packers not only had gone through a bankruptcy. They operated on a tight budget that depended on the support of businessmen and football fans to endure though difficult times. And the failure to end the NFL-AAFC battle for players was straining every team in both leagues.

Even the Chicago Bears, one of the few teams in either league to show a profit during the AAFC rivalry, were not immune. That became apparent when the *Chicago Tribune* announced on March 14, 1949, that the Bears' annual trip to Green Bay would be shifted to Milwaukee, which could accommodate 10,000 more spectators than City Stadium in Green Bay.

"Additional revenue is obviously the reason behind moving the game," the *Tribune* said. "Increased operating expenses, including skyrocketing of player salaries, have made City Stadium's seating inadequate in comparison to other big league gridiron arenas which accommodate from 50,000 to 100,000."

The presumptuous announcement seemed to have come from George Halas, undoubtedly eying a revenue boost for his Bears. Although a loyal supporter of keeping a franchise in Green Bay, Halas' support had certain limits. And moving the Bears game to Milwaukee would be a financial win for both clubs, as far as he was concerned.

Reached in Hollywood, California, "where he was in conference with A.B. Turnbull, a member of the Packer executive committee," Lambeau emphatically said the Packer-Bear game would remain in Green Bay. "The Packers have never entertained the thought of taking the Bear game out of Green Bay. . . . Halas has been trying to shift the game to Milwaukee."

After speaking with Lambeau, *Press-Gazette* sports editor Art Daley took the ball and ran, saying, "The very backbone of the Packers in the National league would be at stake if this game would be removed from Green Bay. . . . you can bet that the Packers would go down fighting to the last drop of blood to keep the game in City stadium!"

Although Lambeau insisted publicly that the Packers were on sound financial ground, the ledger showed a different story. The Packers had lost more than $35,000 in 1948. Without private ownership to weather the losses, the football team was in financial straits. Again. Complicating matters, fans accustomed to having a winning team were not buying as many tickets.

In another apparent effort to rally support for the sagging franchise, a Green Bay Packer Alumni Club was organized in February. If this was not the idea of Lambeau and his close friend, Packer publicity chief George Strickler, it certainly had their full blessing. Coming off their 3-9 season, the worst in team history, the Packers needed all the positive energy they could muster to counter an increasingly restless fan base..

"We are organizing chiefly as a cooperative, a group to promote rather than tear down the Packers," said Fee Klaus, a Packer center from 1920 to 1924. About 20 former Packers attended the inaugural meeting at the Silver Rail Restaurant and Bar. Also there was Strickler, most likely to give Lambeau, who was in California, an encouraging report.

All was not harmony, though. Two former players who were at the meeting, Ken Keuper and Chuck Tollefson, would file suit against the Packers that spring, claiming they were owed back pay.

Lambeau returned to Green Bay "from his winter home in California" on Friday, April 1, 1949, and was back at his desk in the Northern Building the next day, preparing for his first meeting with his new coaching staff the following Monday.

At the staff meeting, new backfield coach Bob Snyder, the T formation expert, was charged with polishing the Wing T, the modified T formation with a wingback that Lambeau preferred. Lambeau wanted defensive backs coach Charley Brock to emphasize playing with intensity and coming up with turnovers.

Continuing his public-relations awareness, Lambeau said City Stadium would be made available for the North-South High School football game if that state all-star contest did not interfere with the Packers' schedule. The game, which had previously been held in Madison, was played at City Stadium on Saturday, August 27, while the Packers were on an eastern trip for exhibitions against the Giants and the Steelers.

Lambeau and his staff also got together with the new Green Bay Packer Alumni club on Monday, April 4, at the Silver Rail. In a show of the alumni club's position, former Packer president Lee Joannes attended the alumni gathering. So did another Lambeau friend-turned-enemy, former publicist George Whitney Calhoun, who had basically co-founded the Packers with Lambeau.

Alumni club president Fee Klaus presented Lambeau with a gift: A bear trap. The gift was obviously given with the team of Papa Bear George Halas in mind. Considering Lambeau's gloomy hat trick of fewer wins, declining revenue and plummeting popularity, it probably should have come with a Handle With Care warning.

After meeting with his new assistant coaches, sending out player contracts and making the public-relations rounds in April, Lambeau quickly returned to California. He had been in Green Bay for about one week.

On Thursday, April 7, 1949, Lambeau was relaxing at his Malibu home when he and his stepdaughter, Jane Garland, thought they saw a plane go down shortly after midnight in the Pacific off Malibu pier. They called police, sparking a search by "Sheriff's fliers, Coast Guard patrols and lifeguards [who] spent the early morning hours scanning the ocean surface under the flickering light of aerial flares... But Capt. Sewell Griggers of the Sheriff's aero detail said an intensive search of a 10-mile-long area off the pier failed to show any sign of wreckage."

What was going on? Had Curly, celebrating his return to California, had too much to drink? Had Jane, who later would battle schizophrenia, convinced Lambeau she had seen something strange? Was there an actual UFO or merely some misleading lights on a boat? At this point, there's no way to know. But Curly and Jane had given Captain Griggers and the other searchers a long night.

In June, the Packers brought their offices under one roof at 349 South Washington Street, across from the Milwaukee Road depot. The team's ticket office moved there from the Legion building on Walnut Street. And Lambeau gave up his old office at the Northern Building, where he had operated his insurance business as well as his football team.

On July 16, Lambeau returned to Green Bay, making a quick stop in Chicago on his way back from California. That gave him a couple of weeks to prepare for his 31st season of guiding the Packers. Training camp was scheduled to open on August 1.

Before training camp began, Lambeau mounted a determined effort to boost the Packers on the field and at the ticket window by trying to acquire former Wisconsin and Michigan college star Elroy "Crazy Legs" Hirsch.

A 25-year-old Wausau, Wisconsin, native who was enthusiastic about playing in Green Bay, Hirsch had originally opted to play in Chicago because, he said, it was close to his wholesale food business in Milwaukee. He would have been a perfect fit in Green Bay. Not only was he a local hero who would help attendance. Originally an elusive halfback, he would switch to end and become a star receiver, where the Packers needed help.

Claiming the AAFC Chicago Rockets had breached his contract by failing to pay him a required bonus, Hirsch gained his release. But the NFL Rams held his rights. When Lambeau was unable to acquire him, Hirsch signed with the Rams.

"Elroy Hirsch's decision to play with the Rams, after he first said he would play nowhere except in Green Bay because of his business in this state, made Lambeau wince," the *Milwaukee Journal* said on the eve of the Packers' 1949 training camp, when Hirsch signed with the Rams. The choice, though, was between the Rams and quitting football. The Packers were not an option.

"Hirsch is undoubtedly one of the greatest broken field runners in the game today," Rams coach Clark Shaughnessy said. "With the type of support we will be able to give him, Hirsch should be the sensation of the coming year."

Their Hirsch hopes dashed, the Packers opened their fourth training camp at Rockwood Lodge, minus eight unsigned players. However, the *Press-Gazette* noted, "Only Jay Rhodemyre is considered in the 'serious' class since he's still making up his mind whether to play or remain in the refrigeration engineering business."

Rhodemyre, a center/linebacker who was the Most Valuable Player at the 1948 College All-Star game, finally came to terms on August 20. Lambeau apparently played hardball with his top returning center, who decided to put the refrigeration engineering business on ice. Rhodemyre played at Kentucky for coach Bear Bryant, Hutson's good friend and former Alabama teammate.

The Green Bay Packer Alumni association followed up on its goal of supporting the team by forming a Green Bay Men's Quarterback Club. Membership in the club was limited to 750, the size of the Vocational School auditorium, where the group planned to meet on Thursday evenings to watch film of the previous Packer game, with coaches providing commentary. It quickly had 750 members, with 350 more applicants unable to join.

Something was clearly on the minds of Lambeau and the football fans involved with the team's community ownership: Coming off the worst season in their history, and facing a growing financial crisis, the Packers needed all the help they could muster to sell tickets.

On the bright side: While the Packers were desperate for financial stability as well as wins, Packer fans were desperate for all things Packers.

Beyond the alumni association and the Quarterback Club, a group of civic-minded football enthusiasts known as the Minute Men had been organized to help rally support for the Packers. More than 5,000 Packer fans turned out at City Stadium on Friday, August 19, to show their support. The pep rally was the first for a professional team, the *Press-Gazette* claimed, adding that the alumni association also was a first. Green Bay's reputation as the professional team with college spirit was richly deserved.

The next night, 18,785 turned out to see Green Bay's first pre-season game—a good crowd but slightly under the goal of 20,000 for a team in need of every dollar it could muster. What they saw was not encouraging. The Packers were humbled 35-0 by the Philadelphia Eagles, who had won their first NFL title in 1948. They would make it back-to-back championships in 1949.

Quarterback Jack Jacobs took the worst of it. "He was smeared six times trying to pass as his protection folded like paper dolls," *Press-Gazette* writer Art Daley said. Backfield coach Snyder said, "Never in my 14 years in the National league have I ever seen a quarterback take a beating like Jack Jacobs did from the Eagles."

During the rout, Snyder said he asked Jacobs late in the game, "Are you sure you can still take that beating?" Jack said, "I can take it as long as they dish it out."

Harder to take, Jacobs said, were the Packer fans who rode him relentlessly. Weeping in the dressing room after the game, Jacobs said, "I didn't mind [the pounding from the Eagles.] It was the booing that hurt."

Knowing his club was over-matched, Lambeau took the thrashing in stride—in his public comments, at least.

"We played a team in midseason form," Lambeau said, crediting the Eagles' early training camp and their 38-0 cruise past the College All-Stars. "And, of course, we were missing Tony Canadeo, [Lou] Ferry, Larry Craig and Jay Rhodemyre, fellows who would have helped us a lot. . . . But we'll be a lot better ball club. . . . You'll see a different ball club Sept. 25 [in the season opener against the Bears]."

The Packers did not deliver on that promise. They battled, and trailed by a mere 3-0 in the fourth quarter. But the Bears got a pair of long touchdown passes from Johnny Lujack and pulled away for a 17-0 win over their fierce rivals, disappointing a crowd of 25,571 at City Stadium.

Afterward, speaking in "a smoke-filled room" at the Northland Hotel, Halas was gracious in victory, saying, "Had the Packers scored 17 points and the Bears none, it wouldn't have surprised me. . . . I can see where this Packer team is going to give a great account of themselves. They did a splendid job."

Outwardly, Lambeau also remained even-tempered, telling his team, "This is only one game. Your effort out there today was all right and if you keep it up, you're going to win a lot of ball games. . . . When a ball club tried like this one did today, we [coaches] won't criticize."

That evening, though, The Man Who Invented the Green Bay Packers showed obvious signs of strain. The once-unflappable leader and football hero now was beginning to behave strangely.

Many years later, Roger Skaletski, a 17-year-old busboy, told Packer historian Cliff Christl about delivering dinner to Lambeau in his large suite on the top floor of the Hotel Northland after the Bears loss. Also dining were five other guests: "a female companion—not his wife, Grace—along with his sister Beatrice, her husband Francis Evrard, and a third couple."

Skaletski said he accidentally spilled a small amount of gravy on Lambeau's mashed potatoes. "I didn't spill much, but enough along with the 17-0 defeat for him to make me take it all back," Skaletski told Christl. "He made me take all six meals down and bring up six new ones, including the silver coffee pot. When I got back up. . . he didn't apologize or say thank you. . . . before Curly reached in his pocket and handed me a dime tip, he took the gravy and poured it over his potatoes. Everything was charged to the Packers."

That was merely the beginning of a turmoil-filled week. The next day, Lambeau met privately at 5 p.m. Monday with the team's executive committee at the Northland Hotel and informed them that he was turning over the coaching of the team to his three assistants. Lambeau said he planned to concentrate on rebuilding the team.

On Tuesday, Lambeau cut two veterans: center Bob Flowers and receiver Clyde Goodnight. Flowers, who was 32 and no longer a capable player, retired. But Goodnight had been the Packers' best receiver in the three years since Hutson retired. With the moves, Lambeau trimmed his payroll. But Goodnight was quickly signed by Washington, where he had two more productive seasons.

For the next few days, Green Bay focused on the upcoming game against the Los Angeles Rams and their newest star, Elroy Hirsch. With a win, the Packers could even their record at 1-1 and be in the hunt for the Western Division. After the frustrations of close losses the previous year, optimistic Green Bay fans expected to have a solid team.

On Friday, Lambeau dropped the bombshell. In his 31st season, Lambeau no longer would be at the helm on gameday. He was turning over the team to his three assistants so that he could concentrate on his duties as vice-president and general manager of the club.

"Under this arrangement I feel I can do the ball club more good," Lambeau said. "The duties of major club officers, especially the head coach and general manager, have increased so much in recent seasons that it is impossible for one man to do justice to three positions. I have three of the outstanding assistants in football and I know they can carry on the field operations successfully, leaving me to do what must be done to get Green Bay back in the championship class. My one aim is to have a solid, spirited organization from the water boy on up and to build the Packers into a championship club again. And that is exactly what we intend to do under this new arrangement."

Spirit from the water boy on up? That was a phrase used a few years earlier by Walt Kiesling, the assistant coach Curly had dumped.

Despite Lambeau's noble explanation, his abrupt and startling pronouncement created confusion, rather than charting a new course.

"Curly Lambeau, founder of the Green Bay Packers and only head coach in the club's 30 year history, has stepped down, or taken a leave—which interpretation is correct still is a matter of conjecture," the *Milwaukee Sentinel* said.

The official front-office explanation was that "Lambeau is stepping down as head coach for the time being," which left the door open for him to return as coach. "Curly did not step down as head coach," said George Strickler, Lambeau's friend and publicity man. "He merely handed the field operations over to the three assistant coaches. That is nothing new. The

Chicago Cardinals have a two-man staff and the Bears for many years have had a similar arrangement, with George Halas in charge of all operations."

Those situations were very different, though. The Bears merely used co-coaches when Halas was serving in the Navy. And the Cardinals had co-coaches because of an indecisive front office. Lambeau had concocted his co-coaches diversion to distance himself from a losing team and its heckling fans, who had reduced quarterback Jack Jacobs to tears at an exhibition game.

Lambeau also was under intense pressure to keep a tight lid on the team's budget at a time when pro-football salaries were soaring. It was a vice from which there was no escape. Lambeau, who was used to winning, and doing it on his own terms, was desperate to find a way out. But turning the team over to his assistants was more subterfuge than solution.

"It was a complete surprise to the executive committee," Packers president Emil R. Fischer said. "But Curly feels he can be of greater service to the club under present circumstances and we, therefore, were in no position to demur. After all it must be remembered that Curly has been coaching for 30 years in the toughest football league in America and I think all of us realized that, some day, the way the business has grown, there must come a time when he would have to delegate some of his duties. We feel he could not have picked three better men than Snyder, Stidham and Brock to put his plan into effect."

Or three more surprised men. "Lambeau [came] in and said, 'You're all head coaches. I'll never coach again,' " Snyder recalled. "What he did was divide the squad. We were like a damn fly in a windstorm."

That was a far cry from the low-pressure pleasure Snyder had anticipated when Lambeau hired him. But no one could have known that Curly was losing his grip in so many ways at the same time.

Elevating one assistant to head coach would have made more sense. Snyder had been an NFL head coach, Stidham had had a good run as a college head coach and Brock was a leader with impeccable Packer roots. But that was not on Lambeau's agenda. Maintaining his authority trumped the challenge of fielding a successful team—which wasn't very likely to happen, no matter what Lambeau did.

In a strange twist, by not naming one assistant as head coach, Lambeau, who was bristling at the committee oversight that had reduced his power, had now installed a similarly cumbersome committee of coaches.

Two days after Lambeau's shocking announcement, the Packers were torn apart by the Rams 48-7 on October 2 before 24,308 numbed fans at Green Bay's City Stadium. It was the Packers' worst defeat on the team's home turf. Only a late touchdown, set up by a determined Ted Fritsch, spared Green Bay from "their worst licking anywhere," as *Press-Gazette* writer Art Daley put it.

The Packers' 49-3 loss to the Giants in Milwaukee in 1948 remained the most lopsided in their 31-year, 333-game NFL history. Another 1948 loss, 45-7 in the home opener against the Bears, had been eclipsed as the worst loss in Green Bay, though. Including the 42-7 debacle against the Cardinals in Chicago that ended the 1948 season, the Packers had been humiliated three times in their previous five games.

That could explain, but not excuse, why Lambeau behaved badly to a Northland Hotel busboy.

The next week, the Packers took out their frustrations on the New York Bulldogs 19-0 at the Polo Grounds on Friday night, October 7, 1949. Only 5,099 were on hand to support the Bulldogs, a struggling, short-lived franchise owned by Ted Collins, the manager of singer Kate Smith, known for her brassy version of God Bless America. The win halted the Packers' nine-game losing streak since their last regular-season win against the Rams on October 17, 1948.

"Get out the band, Green Bay. The Packers won their first NFL game in nearly a year by defeating a spunky litter of New York Bulldogs," Daley told Green Bay readers in his version of a Bronx cheer.

When Daley had been hired at the *Press-Gazette* in 1941, Turnbull had told him, "Just remember: Don't say anything real bad about our team because if we lose 'em, we'll never get 'em back."

Staying positive was not an easy task in Curly Lambeau's 31st season. When Green Bay completed nine of its 30 passes against the Bulldogs—a dubious achievement—it made huge strides from its first two games, when it completed only 4 of 33, including an ugly 0 for 13 against the Bears.

"The Packers came out with something virtually strange—a passing attack," Daley wrote.

Fritsch made a pair of field goals, but missed four others in what was a chippy game. "Tempers flared thruout [*Tribune* owner Robert McCormick had mandated phonetic spelling for words such as ``throughout," an apparent consonant-saving move] the game, and roughness penalties against both teams were numerous," *Chicago Tribune* writer Edward Prell said in his brief account.

Far removed from angry Packer fans back in northeastern Wisconsin, Lambeau safely watched most of the game from the Packers bench, occasionally patting a player on the back or conferring with his assistant coaches, who remained in charge officially. Unofficially, Lambeau "was involved in all of the meetings and on the practice field," said rookie tackle Lou Ferry, who later was head coach at Villanova, his alma mater.

That afternoon, Lambeau had taken a timeout from lurking over the Packers to watch the Yankees beat the Dodgers 4-3 at Ebbets Field in the third game of the World Series. He and his wife, Grace, were accompanied by Daley and Green Bay businessman Frank Cowles.

Playing at night after a World Series game in Brooklyn certainly contributed to the poor attendance. The Giants, the Polo Grounds' other football tenant, were fortunate enough, or smart enough, to play in Washington that weekend. Then again, the Bulldogs and the Packers already were tracking to be among the NFL's worst teams that year. Fans needed no excuse to shun that showdown.

Back in Green Bay, Lambeau did some roster shuffling. He trimmed defensive end Don Wells and halfback Ed Smith, and signed end Steve Pritko and tackle Glen Johnson. He also signed Jack Kirby, a halfback who had "led USC to their surprise tie with Notre Dame" in 1948.

By mid-October, Lambeau had made good on his vow to overhaul his roster after the disappointment of 1948. A year later, 16 veterans were gone. But there was no indication that the team had been improved. Changing the players had not changed the disappointing results.

The Packers now prepared for "a must-win" against the banged-up Cardinals in Milwaukee. While it was true that Green Bay, at 1-2, could not afford another loss if it intended to stay within range of the Rams and the Bears, it was not clear that the Packers were ready to handle the Cardinals, injuries or not.

To encourage Packer fans to make the trip—1,000 were expected to drive down from Green Bay—"But why not 5,000 or 6,000!" Daley wrote in a column, accompanied by a map and driving directions. "The route, which eliminates travel through the congested part of Beer town, can be covered in two and a half or three hours. Incidentally, the detoured section of Highway 57 below Plymouth is now open and the new blacktop stretch is in excellent shape."

That helped lure a crowd of 18,464 to Wisconsin State Fair Park, a decent turnout but far below the 34,369 who had watched the two teams play in Milwaukee the previous year. Green Bay was not up to the challenge. With four interceptions and two lost fumbles, the mistake-prone Packers lost 39-17 to the Cardinals on October 16.

Lambeau and his sagging team then headed west to play the unbeaten Rams. While Lambeau was in Los Angeles, the team's executive committee held its weekly meeting on Wednesday, October 19, and voted to cut the team payroll by $3,500 a game for the rest of the season. Team president Fischer was charged with calling Lambeau and informing him of the decision.

On that Sunday, October 23, the Rams improved to 5-0 with a 35-7 cruise past the Packers. Casting aside the three gift touchdowns the Rams received after Green Bay fumbles, assistant coach Bob Snyder said the

Packers "actually played their best game of the season." Lambeau, who was not in the post-game dressing room, did not weigh in on that subject.

Returning to Green Bay, Lambeau ventured to the Quarterback Club and defended his three co-coaches. Ordinarily "a co-coaching setup is unsatisfactory, [but] our three coaches, Tom Stidham, Bob Snyder and Charley Brock, have been working smoothly and there is no reason for making a change this season," Lambeau, who was described as Packer Advisory Coach, was quoted as saying.

Lambeau attended the next executive committee meeting on Wednesday, October 26. An involved discussion of the team's financial problems became heated and the meeting was adjourned. Lambeau was finding this civilian oversight increasingly difficult to swallow. To the executive board, however, it was the only way to keep the team from financial collapse.

Two days later, the executive committee reconvened at noon on Friday, October 28. Lambeau presented his recommendations, which included trimming "all operating expenses to the bone." He added, though, that he opposed cutting players or selling Rockwood Lodge, two suggestions that had been under consideration..

The committee voted to limit salaries to $24,500 for the rest of the season, in place of its plan for a $3,500-per-week payroll. Clearly, frustrations were mounting. The weekly committee meetings were necessary, but increasingly irksome for Lambeau, who was used to having complete authority.

On Sunday, October 30, Green Bay notched its second victory, beating the struggling Lions 16-14 in a battle of teams that had lost four of their first five games. Detroit botched multiple chances to beat the Packers, the last coming with less than three minutes to play, when Wild Bill Dudley missed a potential game-winning field goal. It was Dudley's fourth missed field goal of the game.

Of greater concern, only 6,177 customers had paid their way into Wisconsin State Fair Park in suburban Milwaukee. When the Packers were not playing well, football fans in Wisconsin's biggest city were not interested. Declining ticket revenue only made the Packers' money problems more acute.

The next day, Monday, October 31, the executive committee met at noon and called a meeting of the 25 members of the board of directors for that night at the Brown County Courthouse. At that meeting, president Fischer stressed that Green Bay was not alone; many teams were in financial straits. Finance committee chairman H.G. Wintgens then laid out a revised budget.

Then Jerry Clifford, the attorney who had become one of Lambeau's harshest critics, proposed that a committee be formed to analyze the team's issues, especially the financial crisis. A seven-member committee was formed, including two former team presidents, Joannes and Kelly, who, like Clifford, had come to believe that an unfettered Lambeau would bring the Packers to ruin.

Another Clifford proposal, which called for Fischer or his proxy to be the only Packer representatives able to vote on behalf of the team at league meetings, also was passed. For the first time since he had steered Green Bay into the NFL, Lambeau no longer was empowered to vote on league matters. One of the most influential voices in the league, Lambeau was frequently described as an owner. His views on rules, scheduling, guarantees, expansion—anything that mattered—had carried a lot of weight.

For a man used to being a prominent leader as well as a decision-maker, losing the authority to represent his team must have been difficult to accept.

# 50
## *A $50,000 DRIVE TO SAVE THE PACKERS*

Encouraged by the Quarterback Club, thousands of Packer fans gathered at the Chicago & North Western railroad depot on Saturday morning to give their heroes a sendoff for their trip to Chicago to play the Bears at Wrigley Field on November 6, 1949.

Green Bay was a 14½-point underdog, courtesy of the point spread, which had been devised and popularized in the 1940s by Charles K. McNeil, a former prep-school math teacher who had graduated from the University of Chicago. While working later as a securities analyst at a Chicago bank, McNeil opened a bookmaking operation to supplement his income. Before McNeil, football wagering had used odds—along the lines of 2 to 1 that the Bears would beat the Packers. McNeil's point spread proved irresistible, and helped fuel the surge in interest in the NFL. And so, an alum of the University of Chicago, which had dropped college football because of rising professionalism, provided the gambling system that helped the NFL become a national obsession.

At Wrigley Field, the 3,000 Packer fans who had ventured south were drowned out in the crowd of 47,218 at Wrigley Field. The Bears covered the 14½ points, winning 24-3 despite 95 rushing yards from Tony Canadeo, the Chicago native who had had found a home in Green Bay.

Undeterred, 500 Packer rooters were on hand when the team arrived back in Green Bay at the Milwaukee Road station at 12:40 a.m. that night. A group of fans hoisted a protesting Canadeo up on their shoulders.

Imagine the reception if Green Bay had won. This was the phenomenon that Curly Lambeau had nurtured through three decades, supported by a football-obsessed community.

But fast-moving events were threatening to bring down all that Lambeau had built.

On Monday, November 14, a day after Green Bay lost its next game 30-10 to the New York Giants before 20,151 loyalists at City Stadium, the *Press-Gazette* announced the depths of the problem.

"Open $50,000 Drive to Save Packers," the main headline on the front page said. Fischer told a breakfast meeting of 100 "Packer Backers" at the Northland Hotel that the club was staring at a possible loss of $90,000 that season. With $50,000 from a fund drive, improved attendance at its remaining games and some other maneuvering, he said, the team had a chance to break even.

"The future of the Packers rests on this drive," said executive committee member Bill Servotte, the general manager of a paper company.

The franchise that Lambeau had started was at a crossroads similar to 1923 and 1933, when the Packers needed community fund-raising drives to survive. Without another determined financial recovery plan, Green Bay's football team would be bankrupt—and likely end up in a new city.

"There is danger of losing the Packers if [our] goal is not reached," Fischer said. "Our losses last year amounted to $33,000, but we [had] resources to cover it."

Although many Packer fans pointed to the extravagant Rockwood Lodge purchase that Lambeau had engineered, the key issue was soaring player salaries. In 1945, the last year before the All-America Conference began play, only one Packer, Don Hutson, earned more than $5,900. And Hutson, who was paid $11,950, was a legendary receiver who had the leverage of being content with retiring from football to manage his growing business empire. By 1948, five Packers were paid at least $10,000.

Lambeau, referred to as Green Bay's "advisory coach" since he had dramatically handed over the day-to-day reins to his three assistants following the season-opening loss to the Bears, spoke first at the breakfast meeting. Although under fire for the team's losing ways on the field, The Man Who Invented the Packers remained the face and heart of the club.

"It would not be necessary to hold a meeting of this kind if things were normal," he said, blaming the competition for players with the AAFC with causing salaries to soar "entirely out of line. A well-known coach in the other circuit came into Green Bay in 1946 and offered to double the salaries of every Packer player."

Every Packer? That claim seems far-fetched, yet another example of Lambeau's unabashed penchant for inventing facts that suited his agenda. That said, there was no question that the rival league was driving up salaries in a way that threatened to devastate Lambeau's wobbly team.

A proponent of the negotiated peace that had nearly happened a year earlier, Lambeau predicted an NFL-AAFC accord would come soon: "Too many of the rich owners in the other circuit are fed up with taking tremendous losses and are anxious to get out of the game." In other words, if Green Bay could just weather this current crisis, the franchise soon would be on solid financial ground again.

The cornerstone of the drive would be a Thanksgiving Day intrasquad All-Star game, with Jug Girard quarterbacking the veterans and Stan Heath leading the younger players.

The period from November 14, when the crisis was made public, until November 25, when the All-Star fundraising game was played, was basically Ten Days that Shook Green Bay. Nearly every morning, representatives of the 500 volunteer Packer Backers crowded into the office of fundraising chairman Jerry Atkinson, general merchandise manager at Prange's department store, to plot strategy for that day.

A *Press-Gazette* photo showed 14 men crowded around Atkinson's desk, which was covered with papers and coffee cups. The attendees included Lambeau, Fischer, team treasurer Frank Jonet and *Press-Gazette* sports editor Art Daley.

In addition to hawking tickets, the volunteers collected merchandise to be given away at the game. The items included everything from motor oil to haircuts, from lumber to a refrigerator. Cases of beer came from Miller High Life, Meister Brau, Budweiser, Blatz and Oconto breweries or distributors. An abundance of cheese, sausages, a bologna basket, steak dinners and turkeys also were donated to entice football fans to support the strapped Packers. Roughly 1,000 merchandise items would be distributed, the *Press-Gazette* noted.

Despite this determined effort, the fundraising total stood at $31,116 on Tuesday, November 22, two days before the benefit game, $18,884 short of its goal. And even if the goal of $50,000 was reached, the Packers were still facing a projected deficit of up to $40,000 beyond that. Ticket sales for Green Bay's three remaining road games would play a large role in the final tally. And the prospects for those games, against the Cardinals in Chicago and at Washington and Detroit, were not promising.

Even more ominously, the rift between the anti-Lambeau faction and supporters of the Man Who Invented the Green Bay Packers was becoming alarmingly public.

On Monday, November 21, the day after the Steelers roughed up the Packers 30-7 in Milwaukee before a meager turnout of 5,483, *Milwaukee Journal* columnist Oliver E. Kuechle reported that "a determined attempt" to oust Lambeau as general manager of the team would be made at that night's executive committee meeting at the Northland Hotel. Among the complaints, the *Journal* said, "The anti-faction. . . has questioned Lambeau's choice of George Strickler as director of publicity, Lambeau's move to play some games each year in Milwaukee and Lambeau's expansion moves, including the purchase of Rockwood lodge near Green Bay as a club base."

After the meeting, club president Emil Fischer, in a lengthy telegram to the *Associated Press,* issued a denial of the report, saying, "The matter of asking Curly to resign has never been discussed by the executive committee or any member of it." He did acknowledge, though, that "cognizance was taken of press reports to the effect that Curly Lambeau was being asked to resign."

Lambeau also knocked down the report, telling the *United Press* that "The rumors about my resignation are absolutely untrue and without foundation." Lambeau, the story noted, "piloted the Green Bay Packers from a makeshift sandlot team through six National Football League championships."

Official denials did not make the story go away, though. Nor did the reports directly address the question of whether Lambeau would continue to be in charge of the Packers for the 32nd straight season. The Lambeau Question was creating a civil war in Green Bay.

On November 21, the *Press-Gazette* sports page reported that the Packer fundraising drive was barely halfway to its $50,000 goal and urging, "If you are a loyal Packer fan, not to wait for someone to call but please contact the ticket office."

Meanwhile, on its back page, next to some obituaries, the *Press-Gazette* ran a brief account of the *Milwaukee Journal* report that an effort would be made to remove Lambeau. A small second story ran under the headline, "Lambeau Declines to Comment on Story," but added, "Lambeau, however, told friends Saturday night that he planned to leave the Packers. He also said he had no plans for the future. . . . Also over the weekend, Lambeau said he intended to be on the field coaching every game next year."

Either Curly was leaving. Or he was coming back strong. Which was it to be?

Lambeau might have been wielding the threat to leave. Or he might have genuinely been planning to get out of Green Bay if his power to run the Packers the way he saw fit was not restored.

Although Lambeau had become a controversial, even divisive, figure in Green Bay, he was still the most successful coach in the first three decades of the National Football League. He might be an attractive leader in another city. Three years earlier, he had apparently used interest from the Los Angeles Dons to negotiate a new deal with the Packers. Would he change teams this time around?

The obvious assumption would be that he intended to be coaching the Packers. Lambeau *was* the Packers. Always had been. Then again, with his five-year Green Bay contract expiring on December 31, and with reports swirling that his Packer future was in doubt, the obvious assumption was not necessarily accurate.

On November 22, *Milwaukee Journal* columnist Oliver E. Kuechle reiterated that despite the denials, the Monday night executive committee meeting was called to discuss "the growing factional strife within the organization. The fans in Green Bay all know about it. The fans elsewhere in the state know all about it. The battle lines, while not always clear in the beginning, are now certainly well drawn: Lambeau and the anti-Lambeau. Either Curly Lambeau, who organized the Packers in 1919 and who kept them in the forefront of professional football for more than a quarter of a century, remains and his policies prevail, or he does not remain. It is futile to try concealment."

Kuechle, a proud Lambeau supporter and confidant, then laid out the battle lines in detail. The anti-Lambeaus were led by Dr. Kelly, attorney Clifford and former club president Joannes, three-fifths of the so-called Hungry Five, who had at one time been Lambeau's biggest supporters.

"The differences among them developed gradually," Kuechle wrote. "Dr. Kelly was deposed by Lambeau as club physician because of his age and because he no longer cared to make trips with the club. He is in his seventies. He was succeeded by Dr. Henry Atkinson. Lee Joannes was deposed as club president, under pressure, but still was able to keep Lambeau from the job, which Lambeau wanted. Emil Fischer was elected as a compromise. Clifford, a very close friend of Kelly, remained on the executive committee but with less authority or influence."

The other two members of the Hungry Five were Lambeau himself, and his friend and supporter, Andy Turnbull, who remained in Lambeau's corner, but who had no official role after resigning from the executive committee and the board of directors, and had retired in California.

Standing by his report that Monday's meeting had been called by the anti-Lambeau faction to try and oust the team's founder, Kuechle laid out the complaint in detail: Lambeau had put the team on the brink of bankruptcy by spending too much on Rockwood Lodge, had alienated longtime Packer officials by bringing in publicity director George Strickler, had alienated the community by pushing for games in Milwaukee and had further eroded his support by commanding a big salary while spending more and more time in California.

The showdown over Lambeau, the *Journal* reported, "was laid over until after the season. The Packers have three games left."

Against this backdrop of a hard-to-conceal civil war over the future leadership of the team, both sides maintained a public front of harmony to rally financial support for the Thanksgiving Day intrasquad fundraiser.

It was eerily reminiscent of another crossroads in the life of the Packers, America's only enduring publicly owned sports franchise. Like the 1922 game against the Duluth Kelleys, this benefit scrimmage shaped up as crucial to the Green Bay team's financial survival. And like that Duluth game, foul weather threatened to ruin it all.

Is it any wonder that Curly Lambeau favored the endless good weather of California, and the vast ticket-buying potential in big-city Milwaukee?

In the saga of The Man Who Invented the Green Bay Packers, the 1949 Thanksgiving benefit scrimmage was another historic moment. This was far more than an exhibition to allow Green Bay football fans to dip into their wallets and save their team. For Curly Lambeau and his Packers, this was potentially a Last Supper.

Thanksgiving Day, 1949, dawned cold and snowy in Green Bay, with temperatures in the 20s. Just as in 1922, it was another foul-weather test of the mettle of all but the most faithful football fans—and their heroes.

"The ground was frozen solid and a half inch coating of snow made it buttery," Art Daley said in the *Press-Gazette* the next day. "The footing was treacherous but the athletes responded with many long pass plays and runs."

Capturing the moment is a photo of King Curly surrounded by 10 of the knights who helped him slay NFL dragons on the way to his six NFL championships. Some are in full uniform, from leather helmets right down to football cleats. Some are looking right at the camera. Most are wearing wide grins, including Johnny Blood, Verne Lewellen and Lavvie Dilweg. A kneeling Don Hutson, who has neither a helmet nor a football jersey, has been caught looking away.

Lambeau, who also is looking away from the camera, has a helmet on under his thick glasses, but wears a leather-sleeved letterman's jacket. Hands in his pockets, he too wears a wide grin.

Behind these Packer legends, who are posed on a snowy football field, is a low bleachers holding hearty football fans. It is a memory captured one year after Milwaukee station WTMJ began airing Packer games on television. But it has the timeless feel of a moment from the early days, when a young Lambeau organized a football team for the joy of it—with only a glimmer of how big the Green Bay Packers might become.

Despite the wintry weather, 15,000 Packer fans bundled up and gathered at City Stadium to help save their football team—to see their football heroes and perhaps go home with a bologna bag or some motor oil.

By gameday, a 1930 Chevrolet sedan also had been added to the giveaway items.

Five future Pro Football Hall of Famers were on the field: Lambeau, Hutson, Blood, Herber and Canadeo. Hutson kicked some extra points during the game, in which the Girard Blues defeated the Heath Golds 35-31. At this point, Green Bay's uniforms were still the Blue and Gold of Lambeau's Notre Dame. The now familiar Green and Gold had yet to become the Packers' permanent color scheme.

A dozen members of the original 1919 Packers were on hand. Two of them, end Herb Nichols and center Fee Klaus, were in uniform. During halftime exhibition, Lambeau threw a few passes to Nichols, "but they were, pardonably, a bit rusty and no pass was completed until advent of the next group, which included Johnny Blood. F.L. (Jug) Earp, Verne Lewellen and Lavvie Dilweg," Lee Remmel noted in the *Press-Gazette*.

When it was time for Herber to throw to Hutson, the two Packer heroes delighted the crowd by re-enacting Hutson's famous touchdown catch in his first NFL game against the Bears. Lining up against a Beattie Feathers stand-in, Hutson wheeled past the Bears defender.

For levity, the Packers' Lumberjack band warmed up the crowd by playing, "In the Good Old Summertime."

Best of all for the Packer organization and its supporters, Jerry Atkinson, chairman of the Packer Backers fundraising effort, announced that the campaign had reached its goal of $50,000, including $42,174 in cash and $7,826 in pledges.

Team president Emil Fischer gave his "heartfelt thanks to our many fans for their generous support." The money raised "does not put the Packers in the black but it certainly will go a long ways in reducing our deficit," Fischer said.

*Milwaukee Sentinel* columnist Lloyd Larson put the fundraising achievement in perspective this way: "That was more than a great job those enthusiastic folks in Green Bay did for the Packers. It was miraculous. Just think what they did: Raised about $50,000 in a whirlwind 10 day campaign climaxed by the Thanksgiving day football carnival headlined by an intrasquad game! I doubt that anything like it could have been accomplished in any other community in the nation, large or small. . . . This unbelievable display of loyal backing might even serve as the super pep talk for Sunday's return game with the Cards in Chicago's Comiskey Park. No team ever had a greater incentive—a greater debt to the community it represents."

This was a tribute not only to the dedication of Packer fans. It also was a living, breathing testament to what Curly Lambeau had built—a football team that could generate the loyalty and purpose of a community.

To further inspire the team when it got to Chicago, Lambeau abandoned his plan to let his assistants do the coaching and gave a pregame pep talk in the Packers' dressing room. "We have had some unpleasant situations. . . ." he began. "You all have heard about them. . . . I think the stories going around Green Bay are highly exaggerated, but, nevertheless, it's still a bad situation. For that reason, now is a good time to find out who are our athletes and go out and win the ball game for the good fans of Green Bay. We expect everybody to do their best and we're going out to win this game. If we don't win, and everybody puts out to the best of his ability, that's all we can ask. Let's see some viciousness out there. This is a good day to get vicious—rock 'em and sock 'em all day. . . . I'd like you to go out and win this ball game for the good fans of Green Bay."

It lacked the emotion of "Win one for The Gipper." Unlike his mentor Rockne, Lambeau was unable to lift his team with words. Green Bay trailed by a shocking 34-0 in the second quarter. The Packers responded with 21 points to trail 34-21 at halftime, when Lambeau tried another pep talk: "We know we can score and that we can win. All we need is two touchdowns and we'll be ahead. And what's two touchdowns? All we've got to do is keep this fire and we'll score and they won't be able to."

There was no storybook ending, though. Green Bay did not score again, and lost 41-21. The "Win one for the Packer backers" locker-room speech had not provided Rockne-like magic. With two games to go, the Packers were 2-8, tied for last place in the Western Division with Detroit.

# 51

## *THE GREAT LAMBEAU DEBATE*

As Green Bay lost for the eighth time in 10 games, Lambeau watched grimly from the sideline—his lonely despair captured by a *Chicago Tribune* photographer: "smoke rises lazily. . . cigaret droops. . . dejection etched on a man's face." read the caption of the photo, which showed Lambeau staring blankly, his fedora pulled low over his glasses, his double-breasted overcoat buttoned up over a necktie.

Back in Green Bay after the disappointing trip to Comiskey Park, the Packers faced an even harsher reality. When Lambeau downplayed the troubles that the franchise was facing, that was pure deception. The Packers' situation was dire—from the financial crisis to the angry bickering about Lambeau.

When the Packers' board of directors met on Wednesday, November 30, everything was on the table. At the top of the list was the future of Lambeau, whose contract would expire on December 31. His opponents had compiled a long list of reasons for wanting him gone.

The complaints: He had steered the franchise to the brink of bankruptcy, hastened by Rockwood Lodge, an expensive purchase that was a burden to maintain. He was spending too much time in California instead of taking care of business in Green Bay. He had alienated many of the men who had supported him through thick and thin. And he no longer was fielding a winning team. That not only made the financial crisis even worse. It left him defenseless against the litany of other complaints.

Lambeau also wanted the air cleared. To make the club successful again, he wanted his authority to run the team restored. And despite all the opposition lined up against him, Lambeau had two key points on his side.

There was still great community support for The Man Who Invented the Green Bay Packers. Without him, selling tickets would be even more problematic. His biggest trump card, though, was a belief that he was critical to keeping the Packers in Green Bay.

"If Curly Lambeau is retained," Oliver Kuechle said in the *Milwaukee Journal,*, "Green Bay undoubtedly will continue in the National league. The league has always had a friendly feeling toward him. It has recognized his service since the league's inception, has valued his counsel and has gone along with him, although it has not infrequently chafed at the presence of so small a community in a major league."

On the other hand, Kuechle continued, "If Lambeau is fired, the National league may well apply pressure to have the franchise moved. There have been little hints of this. It might take time, but it could be done."

A Lambeau supporter, Kuechle was not merely stating an argument for keeping Lambeau. He was raising a very legitimate concern. Without Curly, external forces might take away Green Bay's football team.

The key to ending the war between the NFL and the AAFC was the AAFC's insistence that three clubs be admitted to the NFL Cleveland and San Francisco were locks; the AAFC wanted a third franchise, either Buffalo or Baltimore, to be admitted. But that would mean an unwieldy 13-team NFL.

If Green Bay, which had been ridiculed as too small to have a major-league team, went away, the NFL-AAFC conflict, which had exhausted both sides financially, would be much easier to resolve. With Lambeau and his NFL influence gone, Green Bay might be gone, too.

That was the perceived dilemma. It was a risk, however, that lawyer Clifford, Dr. Kelly and newspaperman Calhoun were determined to take. If Lambeau was allowed to spend, they believed, the Packers would be strangled by a money crisis.

While they were marshaling their forces to dethrone him, Lambeau was digging in to defend himself. He not only was lining up board members; he was lobbying for more power to restore Green Bay as an NFL champion.

The team's board of directors convened at 7:40 p.m. on Wednesday, November 30, at the Brown County Courthouse, with 21 of 25 board members present. To ease the scrutiny the board would face if it ousted Lambeau, the trio of Clifford, Kelly and Calhoun asked for a secret ballot on the question of whether to give Lambeau a two-year extension.

The motion was defeated 12-9, with board president Fischer voting for the secret ballot proposed by the anti-Lambeau faction. Former president Joannes voted against the secret ballot, siding in effect, with Curly. That provoked a gasp from Clifford, who apparently had expected Joannes to help remove Lambeau. Even though Joannes, one of the most influential men in Packers history, had come to question Lambeau's leadership, the consequences of a Lambeau-less franchise weighed heavily for him.

The meeting went on for nearly four hours. News reporters, broadcasters and dedicated Packer fans gathered outside the first-floor room heard shouting and heated exchanges. Some even watched through a glass door.

When the meeting was officially adjourned at 11:40 p.m., the two-year extension for Lambeau had been approved 18-3. Clifford, Kelly and Calhoun—the team's lawyer, doctor and co-founder—cast the dissenting votes.

The board also approved a plan to issue $200,000 in stock "to not only increase the working capital of the corporation but also to permit broadening of the base of ownership in the Packer football team—to be more truly representative of the people interested in the Packers. [Unlike the smaller stock issuance in 1934] This will enable everyone in Packerland, who desires, to become an owner in the Packer team."

The board also stated that contrary to reports of a "hot session," the meeting was conducted in a "most businesslike fashion."

Terms of Lambeau's extension were not disclosed, but the board did announce that Lambeau would return to his head-coaching duties. He had officially been "advisory coach" after he had decided to turn over the team to his three assistants on September 30.

The day after the showdown, Lambeau declared that there was "complete harmony in the organization for the first time in four years." Fischer agreed, pointing to the overwhelming approval Lambeau had received from the board for a contract extension.

"All major points in connection with our operation and my contract were settled on the floor," Lambeau said, "and only a few minor details need to be clarified. The executive committee is straightening out these points now."

But that was merely a public front—more deceptive fabricating by Lambeau. Clifford, Kelly and Calhoun remained vehemently opposed to Lambeau. And Curly was buying time for his next move. Behind the scenes, he was plotting to have his power restored, preferably by gaining financial control of a new for-profit Packer enterprise. Otherwise, he probably would need to leave Green Bay. Only one thing was certain. The only harmony that existed in the Packer organization came from the Lumberjack Band.

"Lambeau. . . had won an empty victory," *Press-Gazette* executive and Packer board member John Torinus wrote. "He had been confirmed for another two years as coach and general manager, but what Lambeau really wanted was the conversion of the corporation to a profit-making entity in which he and a few friends could in effect appropriate the franchise. The four men that he had mentioned at the committee meeting were ready, willing and able to subscribe the entire 200,000 shares of capital stock and take over ownership of the franchise."

\* \* \* \* \* \* \* \*

With the Green Bay hecklers a safe 900 miles away, Lambeau coached from the sideline on December 4 in Washington. When the Redskins kicked a field goal with less than two seconds left before halftime, Lambeau rushed the field, arguing that the kick had come after time expired. To no avail: Washington took a 13-0 lead into the locker room. Their ears singed, the officials gave Lambeau an unsportsmanlike-conduct penalty. Washington went on to shut out the Packers 30-0.

The defeat assured that the Packers would finish last for the first time in their history. From the moment in 1919 that an energetic young Lambeau had decided, at the urging of enterprising newspaperman George Whitney Calhoun, to start a football team three decades earlier, they had never hit rock-bottom in the standings. Until 1949.

On the train to Hershey, Pennsylvania, where the Packers would practice before their final game at Detroit, an angry Lambeau fined some of his players $500 "for eating pie," receiver Nolan Luhn said. "He didn't believe in eating pie after we lost. He took losing very hard. If we lost a game, he would get on his boat and go up the bay and and sit all day. You wouldn't see him at all on Monday. Never showed up. He wanted to win everything."

After the Redskin disaster, Lambeau waived end/defensive back Ted Cook and sent fullback Walt Schlinkman home to Green Bay due to a knee injury. That left the Packers with only 27 players on the roster. Only 24 were on the practice field in Hershey on Tuesday. Larry Craig (knee injury), Lou Ferry (ribs) and Ted Fritsch (intestinal flu) missed the practice, conducted by assistant coach Charley Brock.

Even Lambeau was missing. He had gone off to North Carolina to scout Art Weiner, an end who wound up being drafted by the New York Bulldogs 16th overall when the draft was held in January, one slot ahead of Packers draftee Tobin Rote, a quarterback from Rice. Considering that

Weiner only played for one year, while Rote had a productive 16-year career in professional football, that draft move turned out well.

Back in Green Bay, Packer fans were puzzled that Lambeau had cut Cook, who led the team in receptions and interceptions. The short answer, of course, was that the club was in precarious financial shape and trying to save every nickel. Lambeau also approached other players about taking pay cuts. Tackle Dick Wildung and quarterback Stan Heath turned him down.

On Friday, December 9, as the Packers were wrapping up practice in Hershey and preparing to move on to Detroit, Green Bay residents awoke to a 6 a.m. temperature of nine degrees below zero, tying it for the coldest spot in the nation.

By midday, though, it received some exceptionally warm news: The National Football League and the All-America Football Conference had agreed on peace terms. Faced with staggering financial losses, the AAFC was disbanding. Its three most prominent teams, the Cleveland Browns, San Francisco 49ers and Baltimore Colts, would join an unwieldy 13-team NFL. Green Bay, the city most likely to be trimmed if a more balanced 12-team circuit had been adopted, had survived.

"All those rumors that Green Bay was going to be dropped out of the league ought to be laid to rest now," Packers president Emil Fischer said. "Green Bay should be mighty proud to be part of this new league. It shows that the small town still is an important cog in the new machine."

In a further act of faith, Fischer was named president of the new league's National Conference, which wound up including the Chicago Bears, Green Bay, Detroit, the Los Angeles Rams, the New York Bulldogs, San Francisco 49ers and Baltimore Colts. The American Conference included Cleveland, the Chicago Cardinals, New York, Philadelphia, Pittsburgh and Washington.

"Now the work is just beginning," Lambeau said. "It's the greatest thing that ever happened to professional football. And for the Packers, nothing can be better. . . . it makes me the happiest I've been all season."

With the agreement, Green Bay football fans could breathe a sigh of relief. The city no longer had to worry about losing the Packers to merger intricacies. In addition, teams no longer would need to engage in bidding wars for players, which was especially critical to the community-owned Green Bay franchise. With plans for their $200,000 stock sale under way, the Packers would be on sound financial ground—and on their way to enjoying a championship team again. Their problems would be solved.

Or would they?

Green Bay still faced an uphill battle toward being stable financially and becoming a winning team again. The key figure in both issues was Curly Lambeau, who had become better at spending than winning.

Although Lambeau had won more NFL games than any other coach during the league's first three decades—and was among the nation's most prominent athletic celebrities—questions about his coaching ability were mounting.

Although he tried to mask it as a Wing T formation, he still basically ran the outmoded Notre Dame Box, which had been abandoned virtually everywhere for the T formation. And his tactic of inspiring his players through intimidation had become increasingly ineffective.

Most telling of all, he had become complacent—sloppy, really.

Ken Keuper, who had been a Green Bay halfback from 1945 to 1947 before finishing his career with the Giants in 1948, offered a telling reason why New York routed the Packers 30-10 in Milwaukee. "I naturally expected that Lambeau would be smart enough to change his offensive signals against us, rather than use the same ones with which I was thoroughly familiar," Keuper told an Elks Club banquet in Manitowoc on December 13, 1949. "But, no, there came the Packers up to the line with the quarterback calling the same signals that had been used for the past four years—and perhaps longer. Naturally I was able to tip off the Giants on most of the Green Bay plays, giving us a great advantage." Keuper called Lambeau's offense "outmoded by four or five years," with Green Bay sending out only two or three receivers when other teams used four or five.

Lambeau, it seemed, was being questioned at every turn. On the field. In the front office. And in the taverns and barber shops—wherever Packer fans gathered.

Curly wanted the freedom to operate the way he saw fit—the way he had operated before being reined in by committees. But restoring his authority was not going to happen. The organization no longer had the money to do that. And even if it did, Lambeau no longer had the organization's trust.

Although the club had announced a two-year extension for Lambeau to continue as coach and general manager, the details still needed to be worked out. And the devil would be in those details.

If Curly was running out of options in Green Bay, though, opportunities were opening up elsewhere.

## 52
## *"CARDINALS PREPARED TO PAY THE HIGHEST SALARY"*

In motion as usual, Lambeau left Green Bay on Thursday, December 15, for Los Angeles, where he could watch the Eagles and the Rams play for the 1949 NFL championship on Sunday, December 18— and sleep in his own Malibu bed, if he wanted.

Just before he left, an interesting announcement came out of Chicago. Cardinals coach Buddy Parker, fed up with front-office infighting, had quit on Monday, December 12, the day after the season ended.

Lambeau had used an embryonic AAFC team in Los Angeles for leverage in 1947. Would he find a way to use the Cardinals, who had a talented roster and a committed owner in nearby Chicago, for the 1950 season?

Like Lambeau, Parker wanted authority—and he thought he had earned it. Cardinals owner Violet Bidwill—who had presided over the club since her husband, Charlie, died of pneumonia in April 1947—declined to give Parker an answer.

"I wanted to learn whether I was to be a real head coach next season in full charge of players," he said. "Mrs. Bidwill wouldn't give me a direct answer. She said she wanted to wait and see. I've decided not to wait and see."

Parker had proven himself that fall. He and Phil Handler had been named co-coaches for the 1949 season. With Parker running the offense and Handler in charge of the defense, the Cardinals got off a messy 2-4 start. At that point, Handler moved to the front office and Parker became head coach. The team went 4-1-1 in its final six games, including a win and a tie against the division-champion Rams.

Parker was a well-known commodity on the South Side of Chicago. The folksy Texan had been a Cardinals assistant for five seasons and had been a fullback/linebacker for the team for seven seasons before that.

Most owners would be eager to move forward with results like Parker's. Vi Bidwill was not like most owners. She had recently remarried a longtime associate of her late husband. And her new husband, St. Louis businessman Walter Wolfner, was proving to be a meddlesome disaster.

When they were married on Wednesday, September 28, 1949. Irv Kupcinet, the *Chicago Sun-Times* columnist who had been an NFL referee after a brief pro quarterback career, described Wolfner as an "East St. Louis political and sports figure." Wolfner, who had a knack for annoying everyone in the Cardinals' organization, would take on a large role in the team's front office.

"We're not attempting to appraise the merits of Parker's surprise resignation," Kupcinet wrote, "but his timing certainly was bad—demanding a 'yes' or 'no' answer from Owner Vi Bidwill on his 1950 contract right after his team absorbed a 52-21 defeat by the Bears!"

Parker was the second Cardinals coach to walk away while seemingly at the top of his game in less than a year. Eleven months earlier, Jimmy Conzelman had resigned despite leading the Cardinals to the 1947 NFL championship and a loss in the 1948 NFL title game.

Keeping Conzelman might have been difficult. Dedicated to his third marriage, he had an 11-year-old son and diplomatically said he no longer wanted to move his family between his hometown of St. Louis and a football city. But the *Chicago Tribune* said Conzelman "could not see eye to eye with Mrs. Bidwill on problems involved in the direction of the club."

On top of the Cardinals' in-house politics, Conzelman had grown genuinely weary of football life. Spurning a reported $50,000 offer to coach the Redskins, he went back to St. Louis and took a full-time job with an advertising firm that he had been working for in the off-season.

Coming off the 1947 NFL championship and a loss in the 1948 title game, the Cardinals had taken a big step back in 1949. At 6-5-1, they had lost more regular-season games than they had in their two previous seasons (20-4). Vi Bidwill was in charge of an increasingly confused organization that seemed to be squandering its talented roster.

Losing Conzelman, who was 51 when he resigned, was one thing. He had been in the football spotlight since he had led the Rose-Bowl-winning Great Lakes Navy team along with George Halas and Paddy Driscoll in 1919.

Parker, on the other hand, was just 36 and eager to stay in coaching. "Guess I'll go back to Kemp, Texas, and peddle two-by-fours until I catch on with some other club," he said.

Parker was quickly hired as backfield coach of the Detroit Lions. After one year as an assistant, he moved up to head coach and won back-to-back NFL championships in 1952-53. After seven seasons in Detroit, he became the Steelers head coach for eight more years. He is one of only four NFL head coaches, along with George Seifert, Tom Coughlin and Mike Shanahan, who have won multiple championships but are not in the Pro Football Hall of Fame.

The day after Parker quit, Mrs. Bidwill told the *Chicago Daily News* on Tuesday, December 13, that she would spare no expense to hire a winner as the Cardinals' new coach. "The Cardinals are prepared to pay the highest salary in pro football to get a top-flight head coach for 1950. . . .This is big business. We're going to sign the best coach money can buy—[even] if we have to pay him the highest salary in the league."

Her comments made their way north on Wednesday in an *Associated Press* account carried by the *Green Bay Press-Gazette,* where they easily could have been read with interest by Curly Lambeau—if they were news to him.

Had Mrs. Bidwill given Buddy Parker the "wait-and-see" runaround, despite his second-half success, in hopes of making a splashier hire? Lambeau certainly would be that. And given the Cardinals' talented roster in nearby Chicago, the job just might be appealing to the NFL's most prominent coach if he found it impossible in Green Bay.

Would Lambeau be able to secure an offer from the Cardinals to get what he wanted from the Packers? That might have seemed far-fetched when Lambeau departed Green Bay and headed to California on December 15. The Packers without Lambeau was as unthinkable as the Bears without Halas.

But the discontent with Curly, combined with the Packers' financial crisis, had brought the unthinkable into play. Despite the Packer board's approval of a two-year extension, his situation remained in flux. He was determined to regain the power that the board of directors was unlikely to grant. And Lambeau's opponents were determined to see him gone.

With overnight temperatures dipping below zero in Green Bay when Lambeau departed for the West Coast, even loyal Packer fans might have been envious of Lambeau's "Gone Hollywood" lifestyle.

After watching the Rams and Eagles play for the NFL championship on December 18, Lambeau said he planned to scout players at the East-West Shrine game in San Francisco on December 31, followed by the Rose Bowl on New Year's Day between Ohio State and Cal.

In Green Bay, though, the Packer situation remained very cloudy.

# 53
## *WITH LAMBEAU, "A HOPELESS CAUSE"*

On the same December day that Lambeau headed West, Dr. Kelly, the team physician ousted by Lambeau, hinted at a gloomy Packer future as he submitted his resignation from the Packers' board of directors. Kelly had been on the board since its inception in 1922, when he, Joannes and Turnbull had been key organizers of the nonprofit that oversaw the football team.

"As everyone is aware, I was strenuously opposed to the renewal of E.L. Lambeau's contract as manager and coach of the Green Bay Packers," Kelly said in his letter of resignation. "My motive for opposing this renewal of contract was not from any personal feeling toward Mr. Lambeau, in spite of propaganda to the contrary; but was based upon my belief that a complete reorganization of the club was indicated at this time. I was supported in my position by only two other directors, and the vote of the board was practically unanimous in rejecting my ideas. . . . I think it is only fair that complete harmony in their ranks should prevail and that they should not in any way be hampered by my divergent ideas and views. Under the circumstances I feel I should resign. I wish them every success. It is with regret that I now sever all connection with this great community enterprise which I sponsored from its inception and which I have served to the best of my ability and at great personal sacrifice in various capacities for a period of 27 years. These capacities included that of a member of the board of directors, team physician, president, and as a member of the executive committee of the NFL. I consider it a privilege to have been permitted to render this service. Long live the Green Bay Packers!"

A week later, team attorney Jerry Clifford, who also had tried to oust Lambeau, sounded an even darker alarm, saying the Packers' situation was doomed if Lambeau remained at the helm. Clifford, who had steered the team through legal entanglements since 1929, argued against buying stock in the newest fundraising effort, saying that he would not advise "the people of Green Bay to pour another $100,000 into what looks like a hopeless cause. A complete reorganization of the club is necessary. We will lose as much money next year as we did this year. We will also lose on the field. The Bears, Rams and Lions all will beat us twice."

Clifford stopped short of resigning, but added, "Unless the present setup is changed, I shall have to resign as soon as I complete some legal matters I am now handling for the club. I cannot continue." Clifford reportedly felt betrayed when Joannes, the longtime Packer president who also had become a harsh critic of Lambeau, voted in favor of giving Lambeau a two-year contract extension.

While Joannes, Clifford and Calhoun—a trio that had been instrumental in keeping Green Bay's football team alive—continued to rail against what seemed to be a done deal—Lambeau's return—Lambeau also remained restless. He had been given a two-year extension, but neither side had agreed to the specifics of the deal.

That seemed apparent when Curly was one of the celebrities interviewed by comedian Bob Hope on a national radio broadcast during halftime of the NFL championship game in Los Angeles on Sunday, December 18.

"You're going to be back with the Packers again next season, aren't you, Curly? I see you have a new two-year contract," Hope said.

"You never know, Bob. You never know," Lambeau replied.

Ominously, a downpour dropped nearly two inches of rain on Los Angeles, making a sloppy mess of the Eagles-Rams championship meeting. Despite calls for the game to be postponed, commissioner Bert Bell had insisted that the game must go on. Disappointed fans stayed away in droves. Only 22,245 turned out at cavernous Memorial Coliseum, where more than 160,000 spectators had watched the Rams play the Bears (86,080) and Cardinals (74,673) during the regular season. Bell's decision enraged players on both teams, who believed they had missed out on a huge payday.

Led by 196 rushing yards from Steve Van Buren, the Eagles defeated the pass-oriented Rams 14-0 on the sloppy field. The Eagles' share was $1,090, the Rams was $789. That was about one-third of what they might have received if the game had been played in better weather.

Owners, coaches and players from both teams had pleaded with Bell to push back the game a week, giving competitive reasons but undoubtedly pondering the financial implications. Bell refused. Claiming he was ill, the commissioner had remained back home in Philadelphia, far removed from his critics.

The decision to play in monsoon-like conditions prompted *Los Angeles Daily News* sports editor Ned Cronin to write that Philadelphia, home of the Liberty Bell, had two bells with something in common: "They're both cracked."

While Lambeau's opponents continued to press for his removal, Lambeau also remained restless. He not only had failed to sign his new two-year extension; there apparently had been little meaningful discussion of the details.

Curly's demand to have his power restored had not been addressed. He also was quietly stepping up his effort to turn the Packers into a for-profit enterprise and was lining up investors to purchase the club.

Back in Green Bay, the executive committee, after deciding to take out a loan of up to $50,000 from the Kellogg Citizens National Bank, zeroed in on Lambeau's spending. It voted to examine a bill from the H.C. Prange department store and charge Lambeau for personal expenses that had been billed to the team. The executive committee also planned to give Lambeau a promissory note if it was unable to pay his salary.

This was a team that had lost $45,000 in 1949, and would have lost more than $80,000 if not for the Thanksgiving Day benefit game. For a team that had an average per-game cost of $30,000 to play a game, the debt was considerable. It was no wonder that Lambeau's expensive management style was under the microscope.

Many other teams in both leagues had lost money. Some of them had lost far more than the Packers. But they had wealthy owners who could grumble and pay their debts. As a community-owned team in a city that cherished its football team, the Green Bay club was in a unique position.

No one knew that better than Curly Lambeau. That's why, while the men who oversaw the team were feverishly trying to put the club on stable financial ground, The Man Who Invented the Green Bay Packers was immersed in his own very different plan: *To seize control of the team he had started in 1919.*

After the Packer board agreed to give him his two-year contract extension, team president Emil Fischer had gone to Florida—he annually took a long winter break at the Surf Club in Miami Beach—while Lambeau had gone to California. There had been no meaningful discussion of Lambeau's employment terms—perhaps because both knew that was unlikely to go well.

Curly wanted his team back. The problem was, it was not his team. For three decades, community support had allowed him to run it—to be the face and the force of the Green Bay Packers—bailing him out financially when hard times arose. But now, with the team on the brink of bankruptcy again, things had changed. The men who oversaw the Packers believed Lambeau had made the problems more acute through mismanagement. He had failed to keep up with the changes in pro football that were required to field a championship team. And he had spent recklessly, in the view of his critics.

\* \* \* \* \* \* \* \*

With the AAFC peace accord, the prospects for a flourishing NFL were great. But the Packers could only ride that wave by putting their house in order.

Green Bay loved Curly Lambeau for giving it a football team. He not only had kept a big-time team in a small town. He had won more games and more championships than any coach in the NFL. He and George Halas were pro-football patriarchs—the most important team leader of the NFL's formative decades.

But now, that football team had outgrown Curly Lambeau. In Chicago, Halas had scrimped and connived and sweated to maintain ownership of his team. He was in charge. Long after he was gone, his heirs would preside over a money-making franchise that left Bears fans frustrated but without the power to change things when the team under-achieved.

In Green Bay, things were different. Lambeau had let others handle the burden of keeping the Packers alive during their hardscrabble early years —during a depression, a bankruptcy and so many other threats that had made pro-football teams come and go. The Green Bay businessmen who had provided so much essential support to keep Lambeau's club alive had a voice.

Unlike the average Packer fan, the key insiders knew that the agreement to give Lambeau a two-year contract didn't really resolve anything in terms of who controlled the team. Lambeau would not be content to continue with his authority stripped. And the complete power he had enjoyed until 1947 would not be restored to a man who had presided over a team on the brink of financial ruin. Something had to give.

Knowing this, Lambeau and his allies had been working on an ambitious solution. Behind the scenes, he was working on a scheme in which four investors would each contribute $50,000 to buy the Packers and turn them into a privately owned team that could compete in the modern NFL. Lambeau would be in charge again. And if the team needed to move to Milwaukee or beyond—well, professional football had become a big business.

The investors were never identified publicly, but one of them almost certainly was Lambeau's friend, Vic McCormick, a wealthy Green Bay businessman who had inherited a family fortune that stemmed in part from the sale of a paper company sold to Charmin Paper, the brand that would become the toilet-tissue industry leader. At their meeting on August 8, 1949, Packer shareholders approved the transfer of a share of stock to McCormick from Jack Haslam, a first cousin of Lambeau's sister-in-law, Dorothy, who was married to his brother, Oliver Lambeau. At that same meeting, McCormick replaced Andrew Turnbull, who was retiring, on the Packer board.

Another likely investor was Turnbull, Lambeau's close friend and longtime supporter. The publisher and co-owner of the *Green Bay Press Gazette*, Turnbull had, in 1922, fulfilled his promise to bail out Curly and George Whitney Calhoun when they were at the end of their financial rope by leading the 1923 formation of the team's nonprofit community ownership.

A widower, Turnbull had retired and was moving to California, where he planned to remarry. Lambeau had been a pallbearer when Turnbull's wife, Susan, died from a heart problem in 1944. When Turnbull married a Los Angeles woman in the chambers of a Los Angeles Superior Court judge on Monday, April 18, 1949, Lambeau was his best man.

Turnbull was stepping down after 27 years on the Packers' executive committee and the board of directors. The only member of the Hungry Five that Lambeau had not alienated, Turnbull had been a central figure in the Packers' community-owned life.

Although the other two investors were not identified, Lambeau obviously would be a logical assumption. It's possible that the fourth investor could have been Don Hutson, who had become a thriving businessman after retiring from football. While lobbying for change after the disastrous 1949 season, Lambeau pushed for Hutson to be on the team's executive committee.

That said, Lambeau's plan to buy the Packers was a Hail Mary, whether he realized it or not. As the team's founder, he might have felt entitled to buy the team for its own good as well as personal gain. But the community leaders who had kept the team going for nearly three decades were entitled to the opinion that the Packers belonged to Green Bay. And they held the keys to the franchise, provided they could come up with a new financial plan.

Lambeau's plan to buy the Packers was not solely about restoring his power. That was his main goal, but he also had come to believe that a community-owned team no longer was viable. Professional football was becoming a big business. It was not surprising that Lambeau, who had started the Packers with an entrepreneurial enthusiasm, was looking for a modern solution. Virtually every professional football team was experiencing economic turmoil after World War II, due to the war between the NFL and the AAFC. The Packers were the last surviving community-owned major-sports team in America. It was reasonable for Lambeau to believe the team's unique situation had to change.

\* \* \* \* \* \* \* \*

With Lambeau in California and Fischer in Florida, no progress was made on Lambeau's contract extension. But there were hints that, as Lambeau had told Bob Hope, he might be parting ways with his creation.

In late December, Gene Ronzani, the Chicago Bears assistant who had been a star at Marquette before playing for the Bears, denied a report that he had been contacted by the Packers about their head-coaching job. The rumor apparently stemmed from an *Associated Press* digest of an interview with Ronzani that was boiled down to this in the *Rhinelander Daily News:* Ronzani "was on record [December 29] as `interested' in the head coaching job with the Green Bay Packers."

"I was not contacted by anybody from the Packers," said Ronzani, who was visiting relatives in his hometown of Iron Mountain, Michigan, 100 miles north of Green Bay. The inaccurate report, he said, must have stemmed from a conversation he had with *Iron Mountain News* sports editor Buck Erickson. "He wanted to know if I'd take the Packer job if it was offered to me," Ronzani said. "Naturally, I told Buck I'd be interested in any head coaching job. But I also told him that I've got a job with the Bears for life and it would take an appealing offer to move me from Chicago."

Despite all the denials, Ronzani, a football star from Michigan's Upper Peninsula with strong Wisconsin ties and the right NFL resume, looked like a good candidate if the Packers needed a coach to replace the legendary Lambeau. Thoughtful readers were left to wonder if it was true that "where there's smoke, there's fire."

# 54
## *LAMBEAU IN LIMBO*

"The man without a contract," as the *Press-Gazette* called Lambeau, was back in Green Bay at his Packer desk, contract or not, on January 10, 1950, sounding warnings about the future of the franchise if it did not restore his power to make decisions.

Although his contract had expired on December 31, Lambeau said at a press conference, "I am proceeding on the assumption that I will be here the next two years although I haven't heard a thing regarding a contract since the November meeting. It is my duty to prepare for the meetings in Philadelphia."

And then, in a clear effort to muster public support, Lambeau ridiculed his rivals—after saying that was not his intent.

"I don't want to criticize the committee or persons on it. . . but no group of men can get together once a week in the season for only an hour and a half, including lunch, and run a professional football team," Lambeau said. "The Packer franchise is sound. . . but I certainly can't feel too optimistic about the future if this thing is not run properly."

At one point, Lambeau said, "I am not a brilliant man but I certainly feel qualified to run our organization." It was a nice touch of humility for a man whose six NFL championships made him a hero among the citizens of Green Bay.

After lobbying for himself, Lambeau issued an urgent plea for giving the team a sound financial position. "We must sell stock," he said, noting that no action had been taken since the board recommended issuing $200,000 on November 30. Unspoken, of course, was that action also had not been taken on Lambeau's contract, which had been approved at the same time.

Lambeau then issued a strong hint that he understood how to get the Packers back on top—if they once again were on sound financial ground.

In the past, success went to the team with the best players, Lambeau said. With the player draft, he said, "all of us will have good teams. The teams with the best management will survive. . . disunity and nipping in the front office is bound to the hurt the team."

A few days later, on January 13, Lambeau pressed for a stock sale. Disagreements over the amount and type of stock were holding up the process, he said. One faction wanted to raise $50,000 rather than the approved $200,000. Opinions also were divided on whether to sell the stock in Green Bay or throughout Wisconsin. The key disagreement was whether the Packers should become a for-profit enterprise, with stockholders sharing in the revenue.

For the first time, Lambeau publicly put his cards on the table. As Torinus noted, he wanted to retake control of what he considered to be his football team. He had lined up four investors who would each put up $50,000. They would own the team and he would operate it. With that kind of financial stability, Lambeau would be able to build a championship team.

Casting aside the Packers' community ownership as a thing of the past, Lambeau now believed that a for-profit operation was essential to competing in the big-business world of the modern NFL. A privately-owned team would restore his power to operate the team independent of committee oversight—and give it the needed financial foundation for success.

He had been free to run the club as he saw fit until 1947. That system, he believed, had worked well. It had produced six championships and the NFL's most popular road attraction.

His plan to regain his authority contained major flaws, however. The Packers' board was not about to sell the team it had shepherded through so many lean times. And it was not about to restore the power that Lambeau was demanding. He had overstepped in the minds of even his mildest critics. The community-minded Packer supporters were not going to allow him to overstep again.

As the *Press-Gazette* said on January 13, "the main issue appears to be: Should Lambeau be given complete authority over the operations of the corporation?" On that question, the answer from the executive committee and the board of directors was an emphatic NO.

And for that reason, the assumption that Lambeau would continue to lead the Packers remained an unanswered question. The November 30 approval of a two-year contract merely extended the infighting.

Lambeau had decided that he could not run the team without authority that he wanted. And the board had decided that it would not grant that authority. The impasse was huge.

On the other hand, the thought of the Packers moving on from their founder, the man who had been the team's only leader for 31 years, was incomprehensible to many people in Green Bay. That's a big reason why there were so many conflicting stories floating around in December 1949 and January 1950.

While Lambeau was urging a plan that would allow him and his associates to buy the Packers, a report surfaced in the *Green Bay Press-Gazette* that the Los Angeles Rams were anxious to hire him. Was it true? Or was it a way for Curly to pressure the Packers board to see things his way? Difficult to say. But Lambeau had regularly manipulated media reports to suit his agenda. And one way or another, Rams co-owner Dan Reeves seemed to be aiding his narrative.

Publicly, Lambeau said "there was nothing to the report that he was interested in the job of general manager of the Los Angeles Rams," Art Daley told his *Press-Gazette* readers. "Information had come to Green Bay from a reliable source in NAFL circles [the NFL briefly used the cumbersome National American Football League name after absorbing the AAFC] that Reeves, the wealthy co-owner of the Rams, who retired recently as general manager of the club, called Lambeau his `favorite choice' for GM."

Lambeau coyly admitted that he had met with Reeves for "a number of conferences. . . [but] all of them had to do with problems in preparation for the league meetings in Philadelphia," to resolve some issues that would be on the agenda at the NFL's winter meetings in Philadelphia later in January. Lambeau said he also met with other club officials, including 49ers owner Anthony Morabito. "It's our plan to agree on as many matters as possible before getting to Philadelphia."

Although his contract had expired on December 31, Lambeau continued to play his role as a senior senator. He proceeded with his plan to represent Green Bay as usual at the NFL meetings. And the club's board of directors were on board with that. With club president Fischer going straight to Philadelphia from Florida, no negotiations were expected on Lambeau's contract until he and Fischer were together at the NFL meeting.

Clearly, though, the absence of a contract was contributing to speculation that he might end up elsewhere—and that Green Bay might have a new football boss. What wasn't clear was how much of that speculation was becoming a public bargaining tool.

Contract or not, Lambeau went to the Bellevue-Stratford Hotel in Philadelphia acting very much like an elder statesman. The Packers favored admitting Buffalo as a 14th team. The city had shown strong signs that it would support a team, and a 14th team would make scheduling games a much easier task. But Buffalo's application was rejected along with bids from Houston and Oakland/San Francisco.

When the draft was held on January 20 and 21, Lambeau made Clayton Tonnemaker, a center from Minnesota, the fourth pick overall in the draft. In the second round, he took quarterback Tobin Rote from Rice, followed by Gordy Soltau, an end from Minnesota, in the third round. All three went on to productive NFL careers, although Soltau spent his NFL career with the 49ers, who acquired him during his first training camp.

Lambeau dug in his heels against a proposal to have the Packers be the swing team, which would play each team once in the 13-team league. "We'll play two games with the Bears as long as I have two legs, two hands and a big mouth," he said.

Green Bay was placed in the Western Division with the Bears, preserving the historic and lucrative home-and-home series of the legendary franchises. Baltimore wound up as the swing team. The big loser, as it turned out, was Chicago's other team, the Cardinals, who were moved to the Eastern Division, where they would no longer play the Bears twice. Or the Packers twice, for that matter.

"It won't be too bad," said Cardinals president and general manger Ray Bennigsen, who expected the Cleveland Browns, who had won all four AAFC championships, to replace the Bears as a drawing card. "And we don't have to travel to Los Angeles. Financially, I'd say we'll do much better in 1950."

On that count, Bennigsen was overly optimistic. Playing the Bears only once a year would contribute to the decline that led to the Cardinals leaving Chicago in 1960.

Lambeau's other big campaign at the 1950 winter meetings in Philadelphia did not go as well. He had lobbied for the Packers, Detroit Lions and Baltimore Colts—the league's three weakest teams—to receive an extra draft pick in the second, third and fourth rounds. He also wanted the three tailenders to receive special considerations in the dispersal draft of players from the three disbanded AAFC teams in Buffalo, Chicago and Los Angeles. The lowly NFL New York Bulldogs were excluded because they were carving up the AAFC Yankees roster with the Giants. Lambeau's self-serving draft proposals were not accepted.

The most important development for the Green Bay Packers at the NFL's 1950 winter meetings went unreported. Behind the scenes, Lambeau and Packers president Emil Fischer made no progress regarding a contract for the club's unsigned leader.

Fischer flew in from Florida on Wednesday, January 18, the *Press-Gazette* said, and "went into a huddle. . . to go over Green Bay strategy in the secret [NAFL] meetings" scheduled to start the next morning. "Fischer and Lambeau will enter the meetings with an optimistic outlook. The chief reason, of course, is that the deadly cash war is over. Everything else seems minor by comparison."

However, the biggest development at the Philadelphia meetings, from Green Bay's standpoint, boiled down to this: Fischer and Lambeau finally were together to discuss the specifics of Lambeau's new two-year contract. And that conversation did not go well.

"Lambeau took one quick look at it, then tossed it back," *Milwaukee Journal* writer Oliver Kuechele reported a couple of weeks later. "It was a two-year contract all right, but it was not an extension of his old [agreement]. And it still left intact the galling authority of the executive committee and subcommittees."

## 55
### *DOWN GOES ROCKWOOD*

Lambeau and George Strickler headed west from Philadelphia at 5 p.m. on Monday, January 23, 1950, on the Broadway Limited. They were scheduled to arrive in Green Bay on Wednesday night. *Press-Gazette* writer Art Daley, who flew home, didn't beat them back to Green Bay by much, however, due to poor weather.

While the Green Bay coach and his trusted aide were traveling on Tuesday, yet another fable-like incident took place in the story of The Man Who Invented the Green Bay Packers.

Rockwood Lodge caught fire. The comprehensive facility—where the Packers could eat and sleep and practice football—had been one of Lambeau's many innovative ideas. But it had been a money-pit disaster for a team struggling to pay its bills.

While shocking, the fire also seemed. . . so convenient.

The two youngest children of caretaker Melvin Flagstead, at home because sleet and rain had canceled school, were playing with two neighbor children when they smelled smoke around 2 p.m. They yelled for their father, who found the attic in flames. Flagstead tried to extinguish the blaze, but was no match for the mounting inferno, which was fanned by wind gusts up to 25 miles per hour.

Flagstead broke a window, taking a three-inch gash on his left hand before he went out the window and jumped to safety. In what the *Press-Gazette* described as "a spectacular blaze," the wooden portion of the two-story lodge was engulfed in flames. Mrs. Flagstead fled in a house dress; the children, Danny, 12, and Sandra, 9, ran out into the snow without shoes.

An older daughter, Ellyn, 19, who was working in Green Bay, heard about the fire on the radio and raced to the scene. When she could not find her parents, she wept, believing they had died. The parents had left, though, to receive medical care for Mr. Flagstead's gashed hand.

A fire truck from Preble broke down on its way to the fire. A four-man crew from the Duquaine Lumber Company in New Franken arrived with a pumping unit, but didn't bother to use it. "It was no use," one of the lumbermen said. "Our job was to save the five adjacent cottages. But we didn't have to because the wind was in the other direction. As for the lodge itself, nothing could have been done to keep that fire down."

Packers secretary-treasurer Frank Jonet estimated that the blaze, which left only charred remnants of the lodge's stone walls, caused $50,000 damage, the amount the property was insured for.

It was the second major fire in the life of Curly Lambeau, who had lost his Green Bay house in a 1937 blaze, barely 10 miles down Highway 57. It would not be the last.

"I didn't set the Rockwood Lodge fire, but I was sure fanning it," said Packers halfback Tony Canadeo, who was among the crowd of 40 that came out to see the fire. Also watching the blaze was fullback Ted Fritsch, who said, "Well, I guess it's back to the Astor Hotel."

The cynical view naturally pointed toward arson. As Canadeo indicated, the timing was perfect for the Packers, a business desperately in need of cash. The insurance settlement on Rockwood, which had become an expensive boondoggle, would just about cover the team's operating deficit for the 1949 season.

"They torched it," Ken Kranz point-blank told *ESPN the Magazine* author David Fleming for an extensive 2013 piece, "How the Green Bay Packers averted financial ruin in a mysterious blaze of glory."

The problem is, there's no supporting evidence for arson. Kranz, a 21st-round pick in 1949 who appeared in seven games for the Packers that year, didn't have any proof. Nor did anyone else who subscribed to the Rockwood fire conspiracy theory. Although the fire looked convenient, there is no evidence of arson.

Cliff Christl, the Packers' official historian, categorically disputed that arson caused the fire. In stating his case, Christl argued that it was difficult to believe that an arsonist would put the Flagstead family at risk for an insurance settlement. Christl further argued that it would have been difficult for an arsonist to escape unnoticed. Behind the lodge was a 100-foot drop down a cliff to Green Bay. On the other sides, an arsonist would have needed to cover at least 100 yards of open space to get back to state Highway 57.

Melvin Flagstead blamed the fire on faulty wiring, and Christl agreed. Weeks earlier, a fire inspector had told Flagstead that bare wires outside a linen closet needed to be fixed, Flagstead's daughter, Ellyn, said in a 2007 interview with Christl.

In short, there is no proof of arson. However suspicious and convenient the fire was, the known facts point overwhelmingly toward an accident wrapped in a coincidence.

But there is no denying that the timing was remarkable. At the moment that Curly Lambeau's 31-year reign was ending, one of his visionary ideas, Rockwood Lodge, had become a charred ruin. It was another dramatic, almost mythical tale in the saga of The Man Who Invented the Green Bay Packers.

The flame was going out.

# 56
## *TAKING FLIGHT TO THE CARDINALS*

As the calendar moved through January 1950 with no contract for Curly Lambeau, there was more and more speculation that The Man Who Invented the Green Bay Packers really and truly might land with another team. Rumors about Lambeau joining the Rams in Los Angeles, where he spent so much time, had shifted to the Chicago Cardinals, whose owner, Vi Bidwill, had stated her intention to make a splashy hire.

By late January, Cardinals president Ray Bennigsen said he had narrowed his list to five coaching candidates. He reportedly was out of Chicago interviewing them on the last weekend in January.

Of the names being mentioned, the two most prominent ones were Lambeau and Clark Shaughnessy, who was still the Rams coach but was widely expected to be on his way out. The cantankerous Shaughnessy had just finished his second year as head coach of the Rams. He had just won the Western Division and lost to the Eagles in the 1949 championship game, which had been played in a downpour despite pleas from both teams to wait for better weather.

Despite the Rams' success, there was persistent speculation that Shaughnessy had fallen out of favor with Rams owner Dan Reeves and would not return. Shaughnessy's stopover in Chicago at the exact time the Cardinals were about to anoint their new coach added another layer to the speculation. Perhaps Shaughnessy thought he could use the Cardinals' supposed interest to solidify his position with Reeves, who had a habit of changing coaches.

Shaughnessy and Lambeau both suited Mrs. Bidwill's intention to hire a big-name coach at a big-time salary. They were polar opposites, though. Lambeau, 51, had spent his entire 31-year career—his entire adult life—with the Packers. Shaughnessy, 58, was nicknamed 'Hopalong Cassidy' because he changed jobs so often. He had done eight separate stints at six different colleges—everywhere from Tulane to Stanford to Maryland. And that did not include the times he had been an adviser to the NFL Bears and Redskins.

In another major difference, while Lambeau had stubbornly stuck to the single-wing/Notre Dame Box he had learned from Knute Rockne, Shaughnessy was an innovator who favored complex schemes. While head coach at the University of Chicago in the 1930s, Shaughnessy became an adviser to the Bears, helping Halas develop the T formation that made that made the Bears a powerhouse, highlighted by their 73-0 thrashing of Washington in the 1940 NFL championship game.

When the University of Chicago dropped football after the 1939 season, Shaughnessy moved on to Stanford in 1940. In Palo Alto, he added to his already-large reputation by guiding the school to the Rose Bowl in his first season. That earned Shag, as he was known, accolades as "the coach of destiny."

The Bears assistants and players who did not share Halas' fascination with Shaughnessy referred to him derisively as "the coach with 54 plays."

Decades later, longtime Bears assistant Hunk Anderson still seethed at the notion that Shaughnessy had anything to do with the Bears' legendary 73-0 rout of Washington in the 1940 championship game. In his 1976 autobiography, Anderson, who had become Notre Dame's coach after Rockne's death, called Shaughnessy "a charlatan" who had "a plagiaristic streak in him." and a gift for manipulating sportswriters.

"Sure enough, the writers gave Shaughnessy credit in almost equal terms with Halas for our victory," Anderson wrote in his autobiography, saying Shaughnessy merely sat on the Bears bench, watching the game only because his Stanford team had concluded its season. "Shaughnessy had nothing to do with the victory over the Redskins, and because there was no mention of the Bears' coaching staff of assistants, which had worked their butts off all year, we were grossly disappointed."

Even if Shaughnessy had not been involved directly with the 1940 championship game, though, his contribution to the Bears' installation of the T formation is accepted as groundbreaking. That said, Shaughnessy, who innovated defenses designed to stop the T formation while a Bears assistant in the 1950s, had a knack for rubbing people the wrong way. Along with Rams owner Reeves, Anderson clearly was among those people.

In 1943, when Hunk and Luke Johnsos were co-coaches of the Bears, Anderson locked Shaughnessy out of practice before the NFL championship game so that he couldn't see plays and take credit for them with Halas, who was in the Navy. In that game, the Bears defeated Washington 41-21.

Not subscribing to the predictions that he would be fired by Rams owner Reeves, Shaughnessy did not pursue the Cardinals job. But his name kept popping up for the job along with Lambeau's in January of 1950.

"The morning line on the Chicago Cardinals' new head coach held Clark Shaughnessy in the favorite's spot today," Harry Sheer wrote in the *Chicago Daily News* on Monday, January 31. Although Bennigsen had said a few days earlier that Shaughnessy was not a candidate, Sheer wrote, "things happens fast when football coaches are shopping. . . especially for such a fat salary as the Cardinals' vacancy provided."

"Sources on the West Coast have insisted since last Friday that the 58-year-old master of the 'T' will be the Cards' choice," Sheer reported. "Local sources hint just as strongly not to discount 'Curly' Lambeau of Green Bay."

Adding to the intrigue, Lambeau and Shaughnessy laughed off questions about the Cardinals job. And while both Bennigsen and Lambeau both denied they had talked, denials are standard procedure during coaching searches. Details of their Milwaukee meeting surfaced later.

On the weekend of January 28 and 29, Bennigsen "was out of the city. . . on his coaching mission," the *Chicago Tribune's* Edward Prell reported. "This was ample time for a round trip from Chicago to Green Bay, if such was necessary. Lambeau was reported absent from Green Bay yesterday as was his assistant, George Strickler. Lambeau, who organized the Packers as a sandlot team in 1919, does not have a formal contract with the club, but there has been evidence he is winning his fight against a faction which has been seeking to oust him."

What evidence? Chances are, that information came from Prell's former *Chicago Tribune* colleague, Strickler, who most likely was in Milwaukee for the Lambeau-Bennigsen discussion about the Cardinals job. If the maneuvering did not give Lambeau leverage in both Green Bay and Chicago, he certainly seemed to be trying.

On Monday, January 30, Art Daley, the *Press-Gazette's* top Packer writer, left the door open to a Lambeau exit. Under the headline, "Coffee Confab: Lambeau to Coach Cards, Scribes Say," he basically laid out the case for Curly to shock the football world. Although he noted that Bennigsen and Lambeau "both considered the report too ridiculous for comments," Daley basically ruled out all the candidates for the Cardinal job except Curly.

By Tuesday, January 31, the suspense was mounting. Longtime Packer loyalists might not have believed that Lambeau would leave Green Bay. But those who knew the inner workings of the community-owned club knew otherwise. Meanwhile, Chicago sportswriters were left to guess.

"One of the best kept sports secrets of the year has been the name of the new Chicago Cardinals football coach," an *Associated Press* account said on Tuesday, January 31, mentioning only Shaughnessy and Lambeau by name, but adding that a dozen others were possible.

"I haven't yet made up my mind, but on Wednesday I'll have the Cardinals' new coach with me at the press conference," Bennigsen said. "I am weighing one of my finalists against the other. I can go either way and be all right, but I want all day Tuesday to think about it."

That might not have been completely accurate, either. Lambeau confirmed later that he began talking seriously to the Cardinals on Sunday, January 29. He was in Milwaukee that weekend, a convenient midpoint for him and Bennigsen to meet.

More importantly, by Tuesday, January 31, Lambeau already was doing the unthinkable. He was making his exit from Green Bay. After composing his letter of resignation, most likely with the assistance of Strickler, Lambeau packed a bag for Chicago.

"It is apparent that there is a growing reluctance to alter the policies under which the corporation has operated the last several years," Lambeau wrote in his January 31 letter of resignation to Packers president Emil R. Fischer. "Unfortunately, I have not and cannot now subscribe to those policies. The difference of opinion, honest though it be, has brought about a dangerous disunity of purpose within the corporation, one which in my opinion threatens the existence of the club. No organization can survive divided against itself. Therefore I am resigning. . . . I take it with the deepest regrets. . . . One does not easily break away from something to which he has devoted 31 years. But I feel my decision is in the best interests of the Packers and the fans of Wisconsin, to whom the Packers belong."

Back in Miami Beach, Fischer reacted by saying Lambeau's departure "was not entirely unexpected." That was putting it mildly. Convinced that Lambeau was no longer fit to run the team because of his financial mismanagement and emboldened by the team's losing record, Lambeau's old friends on the Packers' board were glad to see him go.

"We've had two good breaks in Green Bay in the last two weeks. We lost Rockwood Lodge and we lost Lambeau," attorney Gerald Clifford said before a shareholders meeting on February 6. "If Lambeau had stayed here for two more years, we would have gone completely busted. We can now go ahead."

But how to proceed? Without The Man Who Invented the Green Bay Packers, the franchise was in uncharted waters. Its identity, its success, its ability to unite a community to do whatever it took to keep the team alive. . . all of them were wrapped up in one man. And now that man was gone.

"They grumbled about this and that," legendary New York sports columnist Red Smith, a Green Bay native, wrote about Lambeau's critics, "and their chief complaint was the silliest: Lambeau had moved his off-season residence from Green Bay to Malibu Beach, Calif.; he had thrown over his home town, no longer had any real identity with the city of his birth. As if that could have had any bearing on his qualifications for a job he had held thirty years."

Continuing, Smith said Lambeau "was the sole creator of the club without which Green Bay's fame would have been confined largely to men's rooms, where the town's name appears on those tin boxes that dispense paper towels."

Smith was among those questioning whether his tiny Green Bay hometown could keep its big-league franchise: "Perhaps their day is done. Maybe because of spiraling costs it never again will be possible for a small town to support a big team. If that is Green Bay's fundamental difficulty, Lambeau departure isn't going to remedy it."

Lambeau's name had been "synonymous with the Green Bay Packers for 31 seasons." the *Associated Press* account told the nation.

"We're through," said Buckets Goldenberg, a Packer star from 1933 to 1945. "I don't see how the Packers can last without him. He was the Packers."

To calm fears that the Packers could not survive in Green Bay without Lambeau, NFL commissioner Bert Bell told the *Press-Gazette* that "Green Bay will always have a place in the National Football League. I know I speak for the entire league when I say that."

Clifford, Joannes and Dr. Kelly, three formerly loyal supporters who had soured on Lambeau, had won. Curly's rampant free spending was gone. So was his plan to convert the Packers into a for-profit operation.

It was a wrenching departure, though, for Lambeau's many friends and supporters. They pointed to the good old days, not the Packers' current financial crisis.

As *Milwaukee Journal* sports editor Oliver Kuechle concluded, "Lambeau's organization [was] no longer fighting jealously against the big city rival on the field. . . [it was] fighting bitterly within itself. Something had to give. So Lambeau resigned and the era ended."

A *Chicago Tribune* writer dispatched to Green Bay reported that residents there "were not prepared for Lambeau's sudden resignation" and were stunned that "he had deserted the child he brought into being 31 years ago and had developed into a power in professional football."

\* \* \* \* \* \* \* \*

In a roundabout way, Lambeau's shocking departure from Green Bay greased the skids for Shaughnessy's exit from Los Angeles. After the Packers hired Gene Ronzani as their head coach, Ronzani asked Rams assistant Joe Stydahar, his former Bears teammate, to join his staff.

When Stydahar told Reeves he wanted to leave, Reeves asked for 48 hours. When Stydahar returned, Reeves told him, "Joe, you are the new head coach of the Los Angeles Rams." Stydahar was shocked.

"We have taken this drastic step," Reeves said, because of "internal friction" between Shaughnessy and "his assistants, players and others affiliated with the Rams." The "others" included Reeves, of course. The friction, Reeves said, contributed to the Rams finishing 2-3-2 in their final seven games after their 6-0 start. "Even the good soldier [star quarterback Bob] Waterfield bridled near the end of the 1949 season." Michael McCambridge wrote in his history of the NFL

Shaughnessy also was shocked—and bitter. And arrogant. "I can take any high school team in the country and beat Stydahar's Rams," he said.

Shaughnessy was a gifted football coach. Many people accept, for sound reasons, his legacy as a visionary who helped the Bears "thrill the nation," as their fight song says, with their T formation.

Contemporaries like Reeves and Hunk Anderson had a different impression, though. Shaughnessy never was a head coach again, except for one listless season at obscure Hawaii. After sitting out the 1950 season, Shaughnessy was hired by his unwavering friend, George Halas. He coached the Bears' defense skillfully from 1951 to 1962, where he mentored future Rams and Redskins coach George Allen. Not surprisingly, Hunk Anderson wrapped up an 11-year run as a Bears coach in 1950, just before "Shag" arrived.

Also leaving Green Bay for Chicago was George Strickler, who had ruffled many Packer feathers as Lambeau's skilled, but divisive publicity director. After resigning on February 4, Strickler would return as a writer and sports editor at the *Chicago Tribune.*

# PART FOUR:
# LIFE BEYOND GREEN BAY

## 57
### *A NEW BEGINNING IN THE WINDY CITY*

As Curly Lambeau and his California wife, Grace, rode the rails from Green Bay to Chicago on Tuesday, January 31, 1950, a flood of emotions and thoughts must have been going through The Man Who Invented the Green Bay Packers. Lambeau was 51 years old. He had spent the last 31 years—his entire adult life—dedicated to the Packers.

And now it was over.

He had fired one last shot—a Lincoln-esque remark that "No organization can survive divided against itself," a grand comment that bears the fingerprints of Strickler, the wordsmith who planted "Four Horsemen of Notre Dame" seed with Grantland Rice.

With his shocking resignation, Lambeau severed ties with the team he had founded—and guided to the highest heights before it went into a nose-dive. His doomed attempt to turn the Packers into a private, for-profit enterprise had not gotten far.

And now he would be coaching in the same city as his arch-rival and steadfast business partner, George Halas. Lambeau's Packer path and Halas' Bears stewardship, which had looked similar for decades, now were exposed as strikingly different.

Both men had been central to the NFL's birth and long struggle for survival. Both had operated two of the league's most successful teams for three decades. But when push came to shove, Halas was an owner. And Lambeau was an employee.

"Lambeau to Coach Chicago Cardinals. Leader of Packers For 31 Years Quits," the *Green Bay Press-Gazette* announced in a huge front-page headline on February 1.

"This does not mean the end of the Packers," team secretary-treasurer Frank Jonet said to reassure concerned Green Bay fans. "The Packers will definitely continue in Green Bay."

To further calm the fears of Packer fans, league commissioner Bert Bell emphatically said Lambeau's departure will have "no bearing on Green Bay staying in the NAFL." The *Press-Gazette* reached out to Bell "in a long distance telephone conversation" to put the damper on speculation that Lambeau was the key to keeping the Packers in Green Bay. "Green Bay will always have a place in the National American Football league," Bell said. "I know I speak for the entire league when I say that."

From the shakiest of beginnings, Lambeau had built a team that had reached the highest competitive heights—and made him rich and famous. Never mind that it had blown up for him at the start of his fourth Packer decade. Green Bay was where his heart, his friends and his Packers were. No new coaching job could compare with that.

And yet, he now was embarking on a very new chapter. He was being given a fresh start. True to her word, Cardinals owner Violet Bidwill had lured Lambeau with a top-dollar contract that paid $30,000 a year. Carving out a comfortable space for a football team that shared a city with George Halas' Bears would not be easy. But if there was a coach with the resume to take the Cardinals to those heights, Lambeau seemed to check the right boxes.

While the Cardinals had slipped to 6-5-1 in 1949, they had played in the NFL championship game the previous two years, winning the NFL title in 1947 and coming up short in 1948 despite an 11-1 regular season. This was a team that had talent. And unlike the cash-strapped Packers, the Cardinals had the resources to keep fielding a winning team—with the right management and coaching.

In another consoling thought, Lambeau and Grace would be living in Chicago, a city that had much to offer to a couple that liked to enjoy the finer things in life.

Soon after arriving in Chicago, they rented a Lake Shore Drive apartment with a majestic view of Lake Michigan. It was the same body of water, technically, as the one that brought timber into Green Bay and shipped that same timber out as paper products.

And yet, Chicago was as different as it could be from Lambeau's hometown. From their Gold Coast apartment, Curly and Grace were just steps away from Chicago's world famous eateries, renowned nightlife, high-end shopping and cultural landmarks. When they were dining out, Lambeau would be the new celebrity in town. He would be recognized, stared at—and yes, assessed based on what he accomplished with the Cardinals.

But it would be very different. In Green Bay, Lambeau had been embraced by a small community in countless ways. They were people he had grown up with, people who had been his classmates and neighbors. They had bought clothes and insurance from him when he worked off-season jobs. And most of all, they had put their passionate football faith in him as the founder and leader of the city's most beloved institution, its Packers.

They were invested in every way. They rooted for him and his team through the worst weather that northeastern Wisconsin had to offer. They had literally put their money where their mouth was, buying stock in this community-owned team, investing hard-earned dollars where the only return would be pride. They depended on him to show that their Packers, despite being from a small city, could whip teams from Chicago and New York.

In Chicago, there would not be that extreme level of civic passion. The Packers were a crusade. The Cardinals were a job.

And the techniques that had made Curly Lambeau a champion in Green Bay were no guarantee of future results. By 1950, many of Lambeau's offensive and defensive ideas were out-of-date. His passing schemes were no longer innovative. His leadership skills, which included threatening players when he could not inspire them, were not suited to a maturing NFL. And beating the bushes for talent was no longer a way to get ahead in an NFL that had embraced a player draft.

That said, it was not as if Lambeau had a choice. The Rockwood Lodge blaze summed up things succinctly. After three decades of leading the Packers in his hometown, Curly Lambeau had simply burned too many bridges.

\* \* \* \* \* \* \* \*

When he was introduced as the new coach of the Chicago Cardinals at the Blackstone Hotel on Wednesday, February 1, 1950, Curly Lambeau received a warm welcome.

That made perfect sense. He was the biggest name in NFL coaching. He had won the most games. With the possible exception of George Halas, he was the most recognizable coach—and an excellent promoter of pro football. He was an aging star, but still very much a star..

"Well, look who wind up as professional football opponents in Chicago—Curly Lambeau and George Halas! That's a twist that would have required a lot of digging by the imaginative writer of fiction," Lambeau's longtime friend, fellow Notre Damer Arch Ward, wrote in his *Chicago Tribune* column, "In the Wake of the News," the next morning.

Ward—who had painted a flattering portrait of Curly four years earlier in his popular, straightforwardly titled *The Green Bay Packers*—was an enthusiastic supporter of the Cardinals' new coach.

"Under Lambeau's direction, the Cardinals, for the only time in their up-and-down history, except for the last regime of Jimmy Conzelman, will enjoy the type of leadership necessary to sustained success," Ward said, adding, "Our association with Lambeau, which spans more than two decades, has been one of unbroken pleasantness."

That last remark conveniently overlooked Ward's key role in founding the All-America Football Conference, triggering the player payroll crisis that was a huge factor in ending Lambeau's reign in Green Bay.

Along with his two-year contract worth $30,000 a year—a very high-end salary for an NFL coach in 1950—Lambeau was named a team vice president as well as coach so that he could represent the Cardinals at league meetings.

"I am sure I can do a better job with the Cardinals than at Green Bay. You need harmony to win," Lambeau said, taking a jab at the Packers' board of directors, which had curbed his authority in an effort to keep the financially strapped franchise from going off of its financial rails.

"Lambeau will have a free hand and that's no idle statement," said team president Ray Bennigsen, adding, "I gave him my word I would draw up no sure-fire plays for him."

At first glance, it looked like a promising hire. Led by Elmer Angsman, Charley Trippi and Pat Harder, who all were among the NFL's top 10 rushers, the 1949 Cardinals had averaged 30 points a game. Only the NFL champion Eagles, who averaged 30.3 points a game, scored more.

Lambeau "comes into a town that for years has been dominated by the Bears in professional football," Ward noted. "It's a stern challenge. But the Belgian never was one to run away from a fight."

It was a flashy move by Violet Bidwill, the widow of Charles Bidwill—the businessman/attorney/race-horse owner son of a Chicago alderman who had bailed Halas out of a financial crisis in 1933. Violet, who had married St. Louis businessman Walter Wolfner after Bidwill had died of a pneumonia at 51 in 1947, seemed determined to keep the Cardinals jabbing back at the Bears in their battle for Chicago.

"I am extremely happy over this acquisition of the fiery ex-Packer coach," Violet Bidwill said when reached in Miami Beach, Florida, where she was vacationing. Her goal of hiring a big-time coach had been achieved.

The problem was, the Cardinals had acquired an NFL legend who seemed to be fading. He had won six championships while guiding the Notre Dame of professional football through countless threats to its survival. But that was in the past. Past performance was no guarantee of future results.

Curly Lambeau's bread-and-butter—innovative passing from a single-wing-style Notre Dame Box—was ancient history. He had taught the NFL the value of passing in the 1920s, an era when most teams were uninterested and clueless about throwing the ball. By 1950, when the T formation ingrained passing into the game, it was Lambeau who was behind the times.

In addition, he no longer was a master roster-builder who consistently outsmarted other teams when it came to spotting talent. When the NFL adopted a player draft in 1936, things changed. And while he was no longer as dedicated to scouting, other teams had improved greatly in that area. In short, roster-building now required different skills.

Lambeau's increasingly harsh motivational techniques—withholding players' pay, browbeating and blaming grown men with whom he had become more and more distant—also were out of step with the times. And now that he was no longer coaching in Green Bay, football was not as personal.

Hiring Curly Lambeau to coach the Cardinals in the same city as his storied rival, George Halas, might have looked like a shrewd move, especially with one of Lambeau's biggest cheerleaders, *Chicago Tribune* sports editor Arch Ward, on the scene. The Cardinals had gotten a headliner in Lambeau. And Curly had found a soft landing spot after crashing and burning in Green Bay.

But this was a marriage of convenience—not necessarily a path to championship football. Vi Bidwill saw a big-name coach—the NFL's winningest coach—with a gift for public relations. For Lambeau, the Cardinals were an opportunity to keep coaching—to continue battling with George Halas, and to prove his Green Bay enemies wrong.

On the bright side for devoted Packers fans, Lambeau's departure from Green Bay came two months after the NFL and the All-America Football Conference had ended their war. Under terms of the peace agreement, AAFC members Cleveland Browns, San Francisco 49ers and Baltimore Colts would join the NFL, which was briefly known as the National-American Football League.

With the NFL-AAFC war ended, Packer fans no longer had to fear the long-rumored scenarios in which the Green Bay franchise would be shifted to a larger market as part of a grand pro-football realignment plan.

In Philadelphia, NFL commissioner Bert Bell emphasized that point. After saying Green Bay "will always have a place" in the NFL, Bell reminded everyone that the Packers "were once the greatest drawing card in the league. . . . Green Bay has always been a great drawing power on the road and has done very well at Green Bay."

The NFL-AAFC accord ended the costly bidding war for players that had made it practically impossible for Lambeau to build a competitive roster, a key reason for his troubled demise from the franchise he had founded 30 years earlier.

Pro-football peace came too late, though, for Curly. Would he have been able keep the Packers competitive if salaries had not escalated? That's a complicated question, but probably not. The NFL draft, Curly's old-fashioned offensive scheme and the increased competition around the league dated the formula for success he had used to make Green Bay a perennial power. And the "dangerous disunity of purpose" that Lambeau mentioned in his resignation made it impossible for him to remain at the Packers' helm.

As a 51-year-old Lambeau went to work with the Chicago Cardinals, the real question remained. Was Lambeau still a championship-caliber coach? Arch Ward's cheerleading in the *Chicago Tribune* would encourage fans to go to Comiskey Park. To keep them coming, Lambeau would need to win.

After being introduced in Chicago on Wednesday, February 1, Lambeau returned to Green Bay on Friday, February 3, to clean out a desk filled with a lifetime of memories. Finding the franchise document he received from the NFL when Green Bay was readmitted to the league on June 24, 1922, he held it up for a photographer. "I never did get my $50 for that," he said.

Asked to pick his all-time Packer team, a jovial Lambeau ticked off a litany of fabled names and finished by saying, "And put me down for coach."

Lambeau took no further shots at Green Bay management, saying, "That's all water over the dam now," when asked to elaborate on his departure. "I hope the Packers are successful in every move they make," he said, adding that he had "no animosities" and noting that "everybody's wonderful."

But Lambeau, who had lobbied hard for the team to abandon its unique community ownership, hinted that he believed the Packers needed to adopt the private for-profit model that was the rule in professional sports if they were going to survive, saying, "They must operate in a big league manner."

If Curly Lambeau had gotten his way, the Packers might have ended up being a privately owned team playing in a domed stadium in Milwaukee. At various times, he advocated for not only private ownership, but the need, from a business standpoint, for football teams to play indoors in large cities.

It is one of the great ironies of his legacy. . . the team that Lambeau founded is still community-owned in a small town that celebrates playing outdoors on its legendary Frozen Tundra—in a stadium named for a man who had a very different vision.

As he packed up his things in Green Bay that weekend, Lambeau was making a monumental passage in his life. The 1950 season would be the first fall since he had played for Knute Rockne in 1918 when he wasn't leading the Packers into battle. But now, he needed to move on to arranging his affairs in Chicago.

An early priority was to convince quarterback Paul Christman not to retire. A key member of the "Million Dollar Backfield" that had come within one win of back-to-back NFL titles in 1947-48, Christman had said after the 1949 season that he was leaving the NFL to concentrate on his job as a salesman at Wilson Sporting Goods. After going 9-3 and 11-1 in the 1947 and 1948 regular seasons, the Cardinals' decline to 6-5-1 in 1949 probably made Christman's decision easier.

Lunch with Lambeau at the Balinese Room of the Blackstone Hotel on Tuesday, February 7, failed to sway Christman, an *Associated Press* wire story reported: "Earl (Curly) Lambeau, new coach of the Chicago Cardinals, is finding his persuasive powers dimming since he left the Green Bay Packers. Lambeau, who regularly used to talk famed Packer end Don Hutson out of 'retirement', yesterday was unable to coax Cardinal quarterback Paul Christman to shelve his plans to quit pro football. The 31-year old Christman told Lambeau he intends to make his retirement stick so he can devote full time to his sporting goods sales job. Jim Hardy is the only seasoned signal caller left on the Card roster. Lambeau will leave for the West coast tomorrow to contact several players on the Cardinals' 1950 draft list."

"Lambeau Picks up the Check, But Paul Turns His Down," a *Chicago Sun-Times* headline noted.

*Chicago Sun-Times* columnist Irv Kupcinet, a former NFL player and linesman, was not convinced. "You can make a neat wager that Paul Christman will be at quarterback for the Cardinals next fall. He's beginning to wilt (on his plan to retire) under the sweet talk of Curly Lambeau, new Card coach," *Kup's Column* reported on February 9.

Another priority for Lambeau was to complete his staff of three assistants. Staying on was Phil Handler, who had been a Cardinal coach since 1937, including three separate stints as head coach. Lambeau also added Billy Dewell, who had just retired as the Cardinals' all-time leader in pass receptions.

The key hire, though, was Cecil Isbell, who had cut short his standout career as a Packer passer to coach at his alma mater, Purdue. After being a Purdue assistant in 1943, Isbell was the Boilermakers' head coach for three years. He then was head coach of the Baltimore Colts, an All-America Conference team, in 1947-49.

Isbell had been very interested in succeeding Lambeau as the Packers' head coach. Apparently learning that he would not be getting the Green Bay job, Isbell agreed to join Lambeau as a Cardinals assistant on February 4, two days before the Packers introduced Ronzani, the former Bears player and assistant coach from the Upper Peninsula who had starred at Marquette.

Ronzani was a sound hire in many ways. His U.P. and Marquette heroics made him familiar in Green Bay, although his Bear roots made him a former enemy. He had not only been an assistant to Halas in Chicago. He also had been head coach of the Newark Bears, a minor-league team that Halas owned.

And while Isbell had been a star quarterback for the Packers, leading them to the 1939 NFL title and leading the league in passing two other years, his Lambeau connection might have been a negative in the eyes of a Packers board that was trying to move on.

By mid-February, Lambeau was back in Southern California, giving an interview to the *Los Angeles Times* "at his spacious Malibu Beach manse." Lambeau, the fourth husband of Grace, looked very comfortable in the home built by her second husband, in an accompanying photo, which showed a smiling Grace perched behind a happy Curly.

Lambeau "directed the Packers for 31 years and developed them into a big-business proposition," writer Frank Finch noted. "But second-guessers and snipers on the team's board of directors ultimately made Curly's position untenable, and so. . . he accepted the head coaching job with the Chicago Cardinals."

With the end of the AAFC-NFL war, Lambeau predicted that "pro football is headed for a long period of prosperity, and the Cardinals are going to go right along with the tide."

His departure from Green Bay had been wrenching. But there was a lot for him to be optimistic about. He had landed on his feet. . . a two-year contract at $30,000 a year, with a team that had won the NFL title and played in another championship game in the previous three seasons, in a big city that loved its sports teams.

What could possibly go wrong?

## 58
## *PACKER BOARD KEEPS A TIGHT GRIP*

On February 6, 1950, the same day that Gene Ronzani was introduced as coach, the Packers leadership announced a new fundraising campaign in which the team planned to sell 9,500 shares of stock at $25 per share, raising nearly $240,000. For a team that currently had less than $50,000 in the bank, including the $50,000 insurance settlement from the Rockwood Lodge fire that pulled the team from the brink of insolvency, this would be a huge infusion of cash.

The stock sale would give the Packers the kind of sound financial footing they needed to compete in the NFL—exactly what Lambeau had been striving for with his plan to take the team private and turn it into a for-profit enterprise that would attract big-dollar investors.

But the team's board, determined to avoid a repeat of Lambeau's excesses, ignored Curly's warnings that a football team could not be successful if its leader did not have the authority to make decisive moves. Ronzani not only lacked a roster capable of winning championships. Burdened by board members hovering over every move, his prospects for reviving the Packers were not promising.

With their new stock plan and the NFL's popularity growing rapidly in the prosperous 1950s, at least the Packers' financial situation would become stable—especially after city voters approved the construction of a new stadium that opened in 1956.

But neither Ronzani nor the next two coaches who succeeded him would lead Green Bay out of its doldrums. A return to championship glory would not happen until the Packers hired a man with Lambeau's gift for wielding power and winning—without being hamstrung by civilian oversight. Curly was right. No matter how well intentioned, no group of men could get together once a week for an hour and a half, including lunch, and run an NFL team.

# 59
## *PACKERS HONOR CURLY—AND BEAT HIM*

If there were any lingering animosities between Lambeau and the men who oversaw the Packers—and there undoubtedly were—they were put aside for the sake of box-office appeal. Curly brought the Cardinals to Green Bay on Wednesday, August 16, for their 1950 pre-season opener. It would be their only meeting that year. Under the NFL's new conference alignment, the Cardinals no longer were in the same division as their traditional rivals, the Bears and the Packers. Not having them as regular box-office attractions would be another obstacle for Lambeau.

Curly's first game as Chicago Cardinals coach attracted a crowd of 20,136 to Green Bay's City Stadium for an evening that began with a Lambeau love-in. The man who founded the Packers sounded genuinely moved when presented with a plaque bearing pictures of the six championship teams he coached.

"To say that I appreciate this plaque is putting it mildly," Curly Lambeau told the Packers' largest pre-season crowd of 1950. "It will always be. . . a staple remembrance of my 31 years here, and I will cherish it. I certainly want to thank whoever gave this plaque. And I want to take this opportunity to say something to you fans. For 31 years, you have given this team marvelous support. You deserve a team in the National league always and I certainly hope you always will have one."

Wisconsin Governor Oscar Rennebohm honored Lambeau by saying, "The Green Bay Packers have given to this state the finest and most advertising—and good advertising—it has had the last 20 years."

To keep Ronzani from feeling left out, Green Bay Mayor Dominic Olejniczak gave the Packers' new coach the key to the city. "With a little time," Ronzani said, "we hope to do the job for you that you expect—now and forever."

Earlier in the day, Lambeau was honored at a luncheon in which he received his award for being named to the Helms Foundation Football Hall of Fame along with three of his players—Don Hutson, Cal Hubbard and Clarke Hinkle. If Packers board members were uncomfortable with all of the adulation for Lambeau, they were soothed by the knowledge that the club had moved on.

And then, in the first game that the Packers played without Lambeau at the tiller, they defeated their founding father 17-14 despite being a 14-point underdog.

"They're playing like a college team," Notre Dame athletic director Moose Krause said after watching the fired-up Packers build a 17-7 halftime lead. Green Bay had been thrashed 38-7 a week earlier in its first pre-season game by the Cleveland Browns.

The *Green Bay Press-Gazette* gushed with the excitement of a Super Bowl: "Unleashing a tremendous wave of fight, fire and tenacity, the 1950 Green Bay Packers—once again the pro team with the college spirit—opened a new era in professional football lore by defeating Curly Lambeau and his Chicago Cardinals," Art Daley wrote. "The game, thrill-packed down to the last second, marked the turning point in Packer history. It was a strange twist in history but. . . a deliriously happy one."

It was entertaining and encouraging for Packer fans. And Green Bay would enjoy a few other moments. But in the end, the season would be a struggle. After a 2-1 start, the Packers would stumble to a 3-9 record in their first season without their founding father.

Jim Hardy had started at quarterback for the Cardinals. But when Hardy was not effective, Lambeau turned in the second quarter to Paul Christman, who quickly moved them to a touchdown that tied the game 7-7. Christman also threw an 11-yard touchdown to Charley Trippi in the third quarter. But the Cardinals, down 17-14, were unable to score again.

In February, Christman had rejected Lambeau's appeal and stuck by his plan to retire to sporting-goods sales. However, a week before the Cardinals opened their training camp in Beaver Dam, Wisconsin, on July 24, the team announced that the 32-year-old Christman, who held every Cardinals passing record, would not retire after all. "He's the 'old reliable' as far as we're concerned," Lambeau said, "and I think with Christman, Frank Tripucka and Jim Hardy on hand, we won't have to worry about passing this fall."

After being humbled in his hometown of Green Bay, Curly Lambeau quickly guided the Cardinals through three more exhibition losses—a four-game, 11-day odyssey that included stops in Des Moines, Los Angeles and Denver. They finally posted a 28-21 win in Chicago against the 49ers on September 1 in front of a crowd of 29,207 at Comiskey Park.

"We are far from the ball club we can be," Lambeau said. "There's a lot of room for improvement. . . . We played five games in 16 days and had no chance for drills which are vital. Now we have time to prepare for the Eagles."

The Cardinals played only one game in three weeks before their regular-season opener against the Philadelphia Eagles on September 24. With 13 teams in the NFL that year, someone sat out every Sunday. And Lambeau's Cardinals had drawn the first bye.

In a quick trip to Birmingham, Alabama, on Saturday, September 9, the Cardinals lost for the fifth time in their six exhibition games. After quickly jumping ahead 10-0, they stumbled 24-16 to the Detroit Lions, who had lost their first four pre-season contests. In the key footnote, it was the first Detroit win for quarterback Bobby Layne, a free-spirited Texan who would lead the Lions to three NFL championships.

Exhibition or not, Lambeau was furious at the blown lead against Detroit. At practice two days later at the University of Chicago on Monday, Lambeau, "fighting mad after an inexcusable collapse," blistered his players with a dressing-room tirade. "The cold facts were laid before them and their response was good," he said in the *Chicago Tribune*. "I'm sure they'll be thinking seriously about their profession from now on."

The 1-5 pre-season record was not the kind of start envisioned when the winningest coach in NFL history changed teams. They were only warmup games. But they often gave an indication of where a squad was headed. And they helped teams like the Cardinals build ticket-window appeal.

Although coaches generally would rather have their bye later in the season, Lambeau said he liked the idea of having an extra week to prepare for the season opener against the Eagles. He had not needed to travel far to scout them. Although they were the reigning NFL champions, the Eagles had already lost twice in Chicago, to the College All-Stars 17-7 and to the Bears 10-3 in an exhibition game. They also had been drilled 35-10 in their season opener in Philadelphia by the Cleveland Browns, the AAFC powerhouse playing its first NFL game, on September 16.

While the rest of the NFL opened its season, the Cardinals quietly went about practicing. On Tuesday before their Sunday opener, though, Lambeau left practice early, saying he had a stomach ailment but promising to be fine by Wednesday. "Lambeau's been working too hard," a team physician told reporters. The next day, Lambeau was back on the job, relieved that an electro-cardiogram had revealed no issues with his heart.

The big news, though, was that Lambeau had had a change of heart regarding Paul Christman. After urging the most accomplished passer in Cardinals history not to retire, Lambeau abandoned Christman on Thursday, September 21, three days before the season opener. He sold him to the Green Bay Packers for a small undisclosed amount.

Even Christman was surprised. After practicing with the Cardinals that morning, Christman received a call at 3:40 that afternoon at his suburban Park Ridge home from *Green Bay Press-Gazette* writer Art Daley, seeking a comment. "What? Me going to the Packers?" Christman said. "Well, I'm not the first player who heard it from other sources."

Just like that, Lambeau had given away his quarterback insurance policy. It reportedly happened under duress. The veteran quarterback and his new coach were not getting along. That wouldn't be surprising, considering that Christman seemed to be playing than better than Hardy, but Hardy remained the starter.

"The makings of a neat little rhubarb" involving Christman and "the feuding" Curly Lambeau "fizzled," the *Chicago Daily News* reported, adding that "Christman was shipped out because of differences with Lambeau."

"Lambeau explained the straight cash deal by pointing out that three veteran quarterbacks are too many," the *Chicago Tribune* said. Christman played along, denying reports of a rift with Lambeau by saying, "We got along fine." However, he did say, "The only thing I don't like about it is that not one Cardinal official has called me yet. I had to call them myself to find out what was happening after several newspapermen, including one from Green Bay, phoned me."

It's understandable that Lambeau liked Hardy. Not only was he five years younger than Christman. He had been among the NFL's top passers in 1948, but had been traded in September 1949 to the Cardinals for a first-round draft pick by the Rams, who preferred their All-Pro standout, Bob Waterfield, and their two young passers, Norm Van Brocklin and Bobby Thomason, who would go on to productive careers.

Although only 23, Tripucka also was an accomplished, promising young passer. He had gone 18-0-1 in 1947 and 1948 at Notre Dame, and had started four games for the Detroit Lions in 1949. Tripucka would go on to play for 15 years, including seven years in the Canadian Football League, before playing his final four years with the Denver Broncos.

That said, Lambeau's inability to make good use of Christman was the first of many soured relationships with talented players after he left the Packers. The game had changed; Curly had not. And turmoil would soon leave him desperate for a third quarterback.

Christman had a sharp mind. After his finishing as a player with the Packers in 1950, he went on to a distinguished career as a television broadcaster, working as the color commentator on American Football League games alongside Curt Gowdy in the 1960s. They worked the first Super Bowl together on NBC in 1967. In 1968 and 1969, he worked at CBS with Ray Scott. Christman died of a heart attack in 1970. He was only 51.

Failing to keep Christman happy and productive would prove to be a big Lambeau miscalculation. Between injuries and ineffective play, the Cardinals would have benefitted from a veteran quarterback who had recently won a championship. The problem was, the Lambeau who led the Cardinals was not as shrewd as the Lambeau who won championships in Green Bay.

Coaching systems were more complex, and Curly had not kept up. He also was no longer able to connect with his players, or perhaps even interested in that. Lambeau had inherited a Cardinals roster that, on paper, seemed capable of competing successfully in the NFL. On the field, though, the team looked very different.

# 60
## *CARDINALS DEBUT A DISASTER*

In his four decades as a coach and player, Curly was involved in many strange games. His debut as coach of the Chicago Cardinals might have been the weirdest of all.

When the NFL champion Philadelphia Eagles came to Comiskey Park on September 24, 1950, Lambeau had a perfect opportunity to elbow his way into a Chicago sports scene dominated by the Bears. A crowd of 24,914 showed up at Comiskey Park to see what Lambeau's Cardinals could do.

What they saw was a nightmare. Philadelphia crushed the Cardinals 45-7. Lambeau's quarterback, Jim Hardy, threw eight interceptions—an NFL record that's unlikely to ever be broken. It's difficult to imagine a scenario where a future quarterback would be left in a game long enough to throw that many interceptions.

In Hardy's defense, he was involved in a traffic accident on his way to the game. After waiting around at the crash site to file a police report, he had no time to warm up before the game. And that was just the beginning.

"I felt really low at halftime," Hardy said. "I can still remember sitting on a bench in the locker room with my head in my hands, thinking that nothing could be worse than three interceptions in one half. Little did I know I was to have five more."

Although the Cardinals trailed 31-0 at halftime, Lambeau didn't pull Hardy until early in the fourth quarter. When his replacement, 23-year-old Frank Tripucka, limped off the field with a knee injury after two plays, Hardy went right back in.

Just like that, Lambeau's premise for getting rid of Paul Christman made no sense. Three quarterbacks were too many, he had said—although the real reason seemed to be that they did not get along. Now, all of a sudden, he had a quarterback who had thrown eight interceptions, backed up by quarterback with a knee injury.

Meanwhile, just up the road in Milwaukee, Christman, in his Packer debut 48 hours after reporting to the team, threw a 21-yard touchdown. That was Green Bay's first score in a 35-21 victory over the Washington Redskins.

Even more troubling, while Lambeau was complaining about the Cardinals' lack of spirit. his successor, Gene Ronzani, was credited with restoring the Packers' spirit. "Green Bay has shown marvelous improvement," said Walter Halas, who was scouting the Packers for his brother, George.

After Redskins owner George Preston Marshall disrupted the postgame interviews of his coach, Herman Ball, by grumbling about the upset loss, he caught a train to Chicago, where he had a late dinner with Lambeau at the Blackstone Hotel. Under the heading "Saddest Sight in town," columnist Irv Kupcinet said, "The Cardinals' folderoo against the Philly Eagles will bring important repercussions." At least Lambeau's Cardinals had been a six-point underdog. Marshall's Redskins had been a 17-point favorite.

The reaction to Lambeau's Cardinal debut bordered on the cruel. "They never have been more inept, or as careless, or thoroughly outclassed as the Eagles outclassed them," Harry Sheer wrote in the *Chicago Daily News* the next day. "It was bad enough to draw loud and generous boos for the Big Red. . . the first of such nature in this writer's memory."

Describing the Cardinals' "complete lack of offense," Sheer said, "The Cards used five basic plays: The short, wild pass with no blocking; the long, wild pass with no blocking; the quickie over guard or tackle, ditto; the ancient Statue of Liberty, ditto; the end run, ditto."

Sheer stumbled on one count. He said the win was Philadelphia's first in Chicago since the Eagles joined the NFL in 1933. They actually had won once before, in 1938, in their 10 trips to play the Cardinals and the Bears. But his point was unscathed.

"We deserved to be booed," Lambeau told Sheer a day after the disaster. "I deserved to be booed, too. We looked lousy and there's no use denying it or trying to alibi. I don't intend to shift the blame on anybody. It's my fault. I'm the head coach and he's the only guy who should take the rap."

Lambeau vowed to motivate the Cardinals to play hard—his chief complaint—in their next game.

"Fining or firing somebody, or hiring new players, isn't the answer," he said. "We just haven't any spirit, any fight, or any desire. That's the big disappointment. . . . for next Monday night's date with Baltimore, we're going to build a fire under the Cardinals. When we get that, we'll click."

There would be no lineup changes, Lambeau said: "Not at this time. Our trouble is not with individuals. . . . it's the whole club. We'll stand pat and work on catching fire."

A day after taking the blame, however, Lambeau gave another interview a day later in which he hinted that something was lacking in his players.

"Any athlete, particularly a professional athlete, must have a desire to win," Lambeau said, pointing a finger at his players in a *Chicago Tribune* analysis on September 26. "He has to have the fire and the fight to get in there and battle. Football is not a parlor game. It is rough and tough and we have not approached those categories this season."

Lambeau at least shouldered a bit of the blame. He was no longer in a city where he was revered. As coach of the second team in the Second City, he had to be more subtle.

After repeating his high-road stance that "the fans had a right to boo me. I am the head coach," he added a comment that could have been sarcastic. "It probably was my fault that we were not blocking, that we were not protecting the passer, that the receivers were dropping the ball."

Just one game into the regular season, *Tribune* writer Harry Warren printed a vote of confidence from Cardinals president Ray Bennigsen. "Curly Lambeau is the boss," Bennigsen said in the same article. "One defeat is not going to knock any team out of the fight for the title."

Warren even reprinted a quote from team owner Violet Bidwill defending Lambeau after a troubling 31-7 exhibition loss to the Redskins in August, saying, "Curly Lambeau is in charge. . . . What he says goes. He can hire or fire anybody on the club."

Votes of confidence after one game? All in all, it was a miserable start in Chicago as the Green Bay legend began working on his tarnished coaching image with a new team.

"We may lose some more, but there will be no more of this," Lambeau vowed. "We'll go down swinging if we go down at all."

The next week, Lambeau's Cardinals bounced back, trouncing the struggling Baltimore Colts 55-13 to even their record at 1-1. They were upstaged, though, by the Packers, who shocked the Bears 31-21, and brought wide grins to Lambeau's Green Bay enemies.

Lambeau enjoyed the moment, encouraged by his team's 48-point second half after it had trailed 13-7 at the half. Never mind that Baltimore, which had come over from the AAFC, was a weak and precarious franchise that would disband at the end of 1950 after winning only two games in two seasons. Baltimore would be out of the NFL for two years, before the legendary Colts franchise that later moved to Indianapolis began play in 1953.

"It was just a matter of waking up," Lambeau said after Bob Shaw caught an NFL-record five touchdowns passes from feast-or-famine Hardy, the former USC star who shook off his boggling eight interceptions the previous week. "We knew the kids had the stuff. . . and I hope we still have it against the Bears. That defeat Halas took up at Green Bay isn't going to do us any good. They'll be twice as good."

Also troubling: Only 14,439 had ventured into Comiskey Park on Monday night, October 2, to see the Cardinals erupt against Baltimore. At least their victory set up a big turnout for Curly's first showdown as Cardinals coach against his longtime rival, George Halas.

"Everything looks different," *Chicago Daily News* writer Harry Sheer wrote, noting that a smiling "Curly Lambeau. . . now will be able to go home in daylight instead of sneaking in under cover of darkness."

\* \* \* \* \* \* \* \*

Up in Green Bay, Lambeau's successor, Gene Ronzani, also was savoring a big win. In his first game against his old boss, George Halas, Ronzani had guided the Packers to a stunning 31-21 upset of the Bears. Green Bay returned two of Johnny Lujack's four interceptions for touchdowns of 28 and 94 yards, and also scored on a 68-yard punt return. The fourth Packer TD came on a pass from Christman, the former Cardinals star whom Lambeau had talked out of retiring—and then sold to Green Bay.

"We were lucky, but that's what counts," said Ronzani, basking in a 2-1 start after a pair of surprising wins. "I'd rather be lucky than good."

The Packers' luck ran out the next week, when they lost 44-31 to the New York Yanks, a struggling franchise that would move to Dallas and finally resurface as the Baltimore Colts in 1953. Green Bay won only one more game in 1950, finishing with a 3-9 record in Ronzani's first season.

# 61
## *LOSING GAMES AND FANS*

After building high hopes with their trouncing of Baltimore, Lambeau and his Cardinals came back to soggy earth the following week. In Curly's first post-Packer meeting with longtime rival George Halas, Lambeau was defeated 27-6 on October 8, 1950. A crowd of 48,025 at Wrigley Field watched the muddy battle, enduring a steady rain that sometimes became a monsoon-like downpour.

Although roughed up on the scoreboard, Lambeau's Cardinals literally fought hard. "A slugging melee broke out in the third quarter when Charley Trippi, tackled by the Bears' Ed Cody, aimed a punch which raised a mouse over Ed's left eye," *Chicago Tribune* writer Edward Prell said. Apparently agreeing with Trippi, the officials gave the Bears a 15-yard penalty for roughness. The Bears wound up with 11 penalties for 92 yards, the Cardinals had three for 45. But the Bears rushed for 229 yards to the Cardinals' 66 yards.

Even in defeat, the Cardinals had gone down swinging—as Curly had promised.

The following week, the Cardinals opened an impressive 24-10 lead in the third quarter at Cleveland, but collapsed and lost 34-24 on October 15. The defeat was disappointing, but the start was encouraging against the Browns, who would add the 1950 NFL championship after winning all four AAFC titles the previous four years.

"I'm still convinced we have a winning ball club," Lambeau said after the Cardinals lost for the third time in their first four games. "[One] of these days when we all click together we'll really wallop somebody."

Browns owner Mickey McBride—outraged by an incident that left Cleveland's African-American tight end, Len Ford, with a broken jaw, cheekbone and nose—said he would ask NFL commissioner Bert Bell to order the Cardinals to pay Ford's salary and medical bills.

Lambeau replied that "Ford slugged anybody who blocked for our ballcarrier" adding, "On the play where Ford was injured, [Pat] Harder ducked a swing and then hit [Ford] with a hard shoulder block, which is legal."

The 6-foot-5, 245-pound Ford, described as a "giant Negro end" in the *Chicago Tribune,* recovered in time for the NFL championship game, when he made three huge tackles for loss as the Browns handled the Rams 30-28. A dominant defensive end in Cleveland from 1950 to 1957, Ford finished his Pro Football Hall of Fame career with Green Bay in 1958. By that time, alcohol troubles had reduced his effectiveness. He was kicked off the team before the final game.

Lambeau never knowingly had an African-American player on his roster during his 33 years as an NFL coach. It was later revealed, though, that Walter Jean, a Packer in 1925 and 1926, was a black athlete who passed for being Caucasian. The first acknowledged African-American Packer, offensive end Bob Mann, joined the team on November 25, 1950, and played the next day for Lambeau's successor, Gene Ronzani.

A week after losing to the Browns, the Cardinals got off to another fast start in Washington, opening a 38-14 halftime lead. Lambeau's team faded again at the end, but held on for a 38-28 win despite being shut out in the second half. Frank Tripucka, stepping in for Jim Hardy, who was sidelined by a broken finger, threw touchdowns of 65 and 81 yards.

Returning home on October 29, they beat the Giants, 17-3 to improve to 3-3 and build hopes that Lambeau would enjoy a strong first season as the Cardinals coach.

"We had a little defense of our own, didn't we?" a beaming Lambeau said after his Cardinals had knocked off the first-place Giants (4-2), who had brought the NFL's top-rated defense to Chicago. "We had everything—60-minute effort. That's what we've been waiting for."

Facing another tough matchup with the Browns, the Cardinals kept up the defense the next week, but struggled with the ball and lost 10-7. At least Lambeau's team had attracted a crowd of 38,456 to Comiskey Park, its biggest of the season. Three previous home games had failed to draw more than 25,000 fans, and the Cardinals admitted engaging in talks to play at Soldier Field in 1951.

The next week, Lambeau headed to New York for a rematch just two weeks after guiding the Cardinals to their 17-3 upset of the Giants. This time, it was New York's turn to pull off a shocker. Abandoning the T formation that had been stymied in Chicago, the Giants dusted off a single-wing attack and pounded the Cardinals 51-21. Held to 40 rushing yards two weeks earlier, New York rushed for 309 yards with its A formation, mustering its highest scoring total in 17 years.

"I didn't mean to use the A for more than the opening sequence of plays," said New York coach Steve Owen, who would guide the Giants to a 10-2 record and the 1950 NFL championship game. "But it worked and I left [it] in."

# 62
## *PONDERING TELEVISION*

The next day, Lambeau, who again had his defense primed to stop the Giants' T formation, admitted that Owen had outsmarted him. But what he really wanted to talk about was the drop in attendance at NFL games. Only 22,380 had ventured to the Polo Grounds for the Cardinals-Giants game—after only 23,964 had been at Comiskey Park for the same teams two weeks earlier. He also mentioned poor NFL attendance at other games, including the Giants' meeting with their key rival, the Redskins.

Lambeau said owners were to blame, for two reasons: One, he said the league needed to return to sending out its publicity from the media capitals of New York and Chicago rather than Philadelphia, where commissioner Bert Bell had moved league headquarters. Lambeau also called for a return to round-robin scheduling, where teams played everyone in the league, rather than the home-and-home division arrangement.

His most interesting comments to the New York Football Writers luncheon at Toots Shor's, however, came regarding television.

Television "definitely hurts football attendance," Lambeau said. "But it can't be blamed in our league because we don't have much of it—although in Los Angeles the Rams-Bears drew about 80,000 without TV in 1949 and 18,000 with TV this year."

That said, he predicted that a time might come when every NFL game would be televised because "the sponsors may offer so much money [that] we can't afford to do otherwise. Our entire picture may be changed and the stadium will become a studio, with television the chief source of revenue."

"Continued small attendance," he warned, "may compel us to seek revenue from that medium, which will result in even smaller turnouts."

Once again, Lambeau, who was often a forward-thinking innovator, foresaw how pervasive television would be in the future. But while he recognized the importance of televising games, his vision was not 20/20. His analysis strayed a bit from how the future actually played out. While television did become huge in revenue and influence, NFL fans still flocked to stadiums.

In that regard, Lambeau was not alone. George Halas, fearing that locally televised games would ruin ticket sales, and his business manager,

Rudy Custer, devised a 75-mile blackout area in the early 1950s. Halas convinced Bert Bell to use the 75-mile television blackout for all NFL home games. The policy remained in effect until 1973, when Congress barred blackouts for games that were sold out.

Seeing the vast potential, Halas also put together the first NFL television network, a collection of stations that beamed Bears games far beyond the Chicago area.

"George Halas was Roone Arledge before Roone Arledge was Roone Arledge," Halas biographer Jeff Davis wrote, comparing the Bears owner to the legendary television sports executive. "He was far ahead of the pack in his understanding of the medium's incredible potential."

Like Halas, Lambeau knew television would transform their game, and turn football into a vastly bigger business. Unlike Halas, Lambeau never put himself in position to reap those rewards by owning the Packers. Then again, only a wealthy man could have kept a team alive in Green Bay all of those years. In the early years, NFL pioneers like Halas and Lambeau were just trying to make ends meet.

With the Cardinals' next game in Philadelphia, Lambeau kept his team on the East Coast, practicing at the Westchester Country Club, outside of New York City. A popular private club with many celebrity members and a history of hosting golf tournaments, Westchester suited Lambeau's tastes well.

The Cardinals followed their Westchester week with a 14-10 upset win on November 19 over the Eagles, who had trounced them 45-7 in Lambeau's first game as Cardinals coach. After winning five of its first six games, Philadelphia would finish the season in a tailspin, losing its last four. But beating the Eagles was a step forward for Lambeau, a win in line with the expectations for his first season.

At 4-5, the Cardinals hoped to even their record in a Thanksgiving Day meeting with the Steelers, who also were 4-5. Instead, the inconsistent Cardinals lost 28-17 before a meager crowd of 11,622 on November 23 in Comiskey Park. A snowy 19-degree day held down attendance and lifted Pittsburgh's single wing. The Steelers, still clinging to the old Notre-Dame-style offense that Lambeau had long favored, had fashioned an old-school victory.

And Cardinals fans were already turning on their new coach, chanting, "Good-by, Lambeau!" Just 10 games into his Cardinals tenure, restless rooters already were giving up on him. It wasn't merely the losses.

The perception of his commitment and his strategic ability also were in question.

"When the Cards signed Lambeau I groaned. . . . he's seen his great days and can't come up with anything new," Cardinals fan Jack Landry wrote in the *Chicago Daily News'* Voice from the Grandstand column on November 29, 1950. "He has darn good material, 1,000 per cent better than he had at Green Bay. . . .When the Cards get a coaching staff that eats, drinks and sleeps football like the Bear staff (darn 'em, you have to admire 'em) then the Cards won't have to play to those small crowds."

Lambeau had been hired to win games and rally fans. He was failing at both. And he was already taking heavy fire.

"I doubt there will be any change on the South Side this year, but the chips will be down for Curly and his staff in '51," *Daily News* writer Harry Sheer replied, agreeing with Landry's assessment. "Furthermore, there will be plenty of new Cards. The Big Red has the largest payroll in the National Football League and is running one-two in coaches' salaries, so there is no alibi there. . . . the Lambeau offense shows lack of imagination, the defense a lack of preparation."

That was the gloomy assessment as the Cardinals prepared for their rematch with the Bears, who had already beaten their South Side rivals 27-6. With the unrest growing, the Cardinals gave their supporters something to cheer. They surprised the favored Bears 20-10 on December 3 before 31,919 shivering fans at Comiskey Park who braved gusty winds and temperatures in the 20s that felt much colder.

"The boys played good ball; fine ball," said Lambeau, giving his players the credit—and answering complaints that his schemes were too vanilla. "We didn't have any hidden weapons or special tricks."

The upset of the Bears gave Lambeau the satisfaction of spoiling the plans of his longtime rival Halas. The loss dropped the Bears into a tie with the Rams in the National Division, the forerunner of the Western Division. Both teams finished with 9-3 records. The Bears, who had been tracking for the NFL title game, then lost 24-14 in their playoff with the Rams. A huge turnout of 83,501 at the L.A. Coliseum eased Halas' pain. The Rams went on to lose the 1950 championship game 30-28 to the Browns in Cleveland on December 24.

Meanwhile, the Cardinals had hoped to even their record for 1950 in their final game at Pittsburgh. But they lost 28-7 to the Steelers on

December 10, and finished with a 5-7 mark. With two wins against Lambeau in the final three weeks, the Steelers managed to get to 6-6.

"This was a sort of shakedown cruise for me this season and I'm sure the Cards will do a lot better next year," Lambeau said.

No matter how he phrased it, his first season with the Cardinals had been a disappointment. The wins against the Bears and the Giants, two of the league's four top teams, showed that Chicago's South Side NFL team was capable enough. But the ugly opening loss to the Eagles; the rout against the Giants, a team they had just beaten, and a pair of late losses to the middling Steelers left Lambeau failing to live up to his considerable Chicago buildup. Also troubling, only two home games had drawn more than 30,000 to Comiskey Park—against the Browns (38,456) and the Bears (31,919).

Having been to the NFL championship game twice in the previous three years, Cardinals fans expected a winner. Curly Lambeau had not given that to them.

Cardinals owner Violet Bidwill had made good on her promise to spend freely for a coach and players. Lambeau received $30,000, a top-notch salary, while his three assistants divided $20,000. And the Cardinals payroll of about $240,000 was among the highest in the NFL, the *Chicago Sun-Times* reported on December 12, 1950.

Even after the Cardinals had surprised the Bears, Mrs. Bidwill found it necessary to answer "growing reports that Lambeau would never finish out his two-year pact" with an emphatic vote of confidence.

"Lambeau can have a contract for as long as he wants," she told *Chicago Daily News* writer Harry Sheer. "He knows all the tricks of the trade after more than 30 years in the business and as far as I'm concerned Lambeau rates right with George Halas as a top flight professional football coach."

In the same article, Lambeau predicted a "greatly improved team" next year. "I'll tell you bluntly that I haven't been satisfied with our coaching—and that includes me. At times we have looked very bad—and I'll take the rap for that. We didn't look like a well-coached team."

Addressing that concern, Lambeau dropped receivers coach Billy Dewell and made linebacking stalwart Buster Ramsey a player-coach responsible for the Cardinals defense. Ramsey was a good hire. After spending 1951 in his player-coach role under Lambeau, Ramsey became Detroit's defensive coordinator in 1952, helping the Lions win three NFL titles. Credited with developing the 4-3 defense and blitzing linebackers, Ramsey spent eight seasons in Detroit before becoming the Buffalo Bills' first head coach when the AFL began play in 1960.

For Lambeau and the Cardinals organization, the duel with the Bears for fans was difficult. Lambeau knew that would be a challenge when he agreed to be the Cardinals coach. With the Bears' history of success, and Halas' flair for publicity, the Bears had always occupied the top perch in Chicago.

The NFL's new conference alignment also dealt a serious body blow to the Cardinals. In absorbing the three AAFC teams for the 1950 season, the league had put the Cardinals in the American Conference, which would be renamed the Eastern Conference in 1953. Their two key rivals, the Bears and the Packers, were in the National/Western Conference.

Lambeau arrived in Chicago in the same season that the Cardinals had been shunted away from the Bears and the Packers. They would continue to play home-and-home with the Bears for two more years, but would meet only once beginning in 1953. The Cardinals also lost their attractive rivalry with the Packers. The teams did not meet in 1950 and would not play again until 1955.

Flexing his considerable muscle in league matters, Halas was maneuvering his crosstown rivals into a difficult corner. They would depart for St. Louis in 1960 and move on to Arizona in 1988.

Although the Cardinals were an original NFL team that traced its South Side roots to 1898, they worked out an arrangement to play at Northwestern's Dyche Stadium in north suburban Evanston in the late 1950s to bolster sagging attendance. But Halas blocked the move, producing a 28-year-old agreement he had signed with Charlie Bidwill in which the Cardinals agreed not to play north of Madison Street while the Bears would not venture south.

"That agreement wasn't worth the paper it was written on," Wolfner said when the team moved to St. Louis in 1960, "but [Bert] Bell gave it the force of law by stepping in and ruling that it was valid. If we had moved to Dyche Stadium, we wouldn't be leaving Chicago now."

In the long run, it made sense for the Cardinals to leave rather than be the second team in the Second City. That was also a big gain for the NFL's television situation.

Once again, Halas had combined a shrewd business sense with deft NFL politicking to keep the Bears flourishing. Meanwhile, Lambeau, who had lacked the front-office-management skills of his longtime rival, continued his effort to keep the Cardinals relevant despite being isolated by an NFL realignment that distanced them from the Bears and the Packers.

# 63
## *MORE FRONT-OFFICE TURMOIL*

Being the second team in the Second City was only one of the obstacles that Lambeau and the Cardinals faced. While Mrs. Bidwill's hiring of The Man Who Invented the Green Bay Packers was filled with good intentions, it was also filled with wrong assumptions.

Vi Bidwill and the mercurial Mr. Wolfner may have thought they were getting the coach who was not only the most well-known in NFL history, but also the best. They were only half-right.

Curly may have thought he was taking over a club where he would be free from front-office meddling—and free to coach in an era without a rival league trying to raid his roster. He was wrong on both counts.

Mrs. Bidwill had hired the most famous and most successful coach in NFL history. She also had hired a coach who was increasingly out of step with the modern NFL In short, the game that Lambeau had dominated had changed. It was, as his critics suggested, passing him by.

He could still tweak his old-fashioned schemes to occasionally surprise opponents. He could still pull a rabbit out of his motivational hat. He was still a legend, although a fading one. But day in and day out? He no longer was an upper-tier coach.

The new prototype coach for pro-football success was Paul Brown, who was in the midst of winning seven championships in 10 years with the Cleveland Browns—all four AAFC titles, and three more after the Browns joined the NFL. It's no wonder the team was named after him. Brown revolutionized scheme, organization and player procurement in ways that went beyond the old-school ideas of Curly Lambeau. Brown also was quick to hire black players, something Lambeau had never done in Green Bay and never did after he moved on.

With their upsets of the Bears and Giants, the Cardinals had shown hints of promise in Lambeau's first season. Freed from the budget crisis in Green Bay, it was reasonable to believe he could turn around the Cardinals, who were only two years removed from back-to-back NFL championship-game appearances.

The problem was, the Cardinals were immersed in their own version of front-office turmoil. While the Packers' were a house divided due to money problems that reined in Lambeau, the Cardinals' were a dysfunctional organization filled with infighting and intrigue.

Lambeau was the team's third coach in three years—or the fourth regime in three years, considering that Buddy Parker and Phil Handler started 1949 as co-coaches before Parker took sole leadership at mid-season.

Although Vi Bidwill was officially in charge, her new husband was stirring up all kinds of trouble with his meddling. Walter Wolfner "alienated everybody," George Halas biographer Jeff Davis concluded.

Wolfner drove away Buddy Parker, who happily left Chicago's South Side for Detroit, where he quickly won back-to-back NFL titles. Ray Bennigsen, who hired Lambeau, also would leave the Cardinals before Curly began his second season in Chicago, depriving Lambeau of the front-office support he had counted on.

Wolfner "just wrecked that franchise," longtime Chicago sportswriter Bill Gleason said. "Ray Bennigsen, the general manager, quit, as did coach Buddy Parker. It unraveled, and the players were dispersed."

Lambeau had to be aware of the reasons for Parker's departure. Perhaps he thought he could handle Wolfner's second-guessing with the aid of Vi Bidwill and Bennigsen, who emphatically gave their assurances that Curly would be in charge. At some level, it's also likely that Lambeau, who needed a soft landing spot from Green Bay, believed what he wanted to believe. At the very least, he was being given a huge salary and an enticing opportunity.

Whatever the mindset, Lambeau was entering a front-office minefield that was as complicated as the one he had left in Green Bay. With the Packers, he had created a big piece of the dysfunction; in Chicago, he simply parachuted into it.

That was the world that Lambeau was operating in as he started pondering his second season as the Cardinals coach. And yet, Lambeau emphatically insisted that the team's many voices were in harmony..

"Despite the chant of `So Long Curly' which used to arise automatically. . . when the Chicago Cardinals were behind, look for the durable Lambeau to remain at the Card helm next fall," an item in a national sports roundup column began. "Lambeau may not be solid with Windy City fans but he's well-liked by the club owners. Said Curly: `I've never had stronger support as a professional football coach than I received from the management of the Chicago Cardinals last year.'"

Lambeau—"a congenital liar" according to longtime *Green Bay Press-Gazette* writer Lee Remmel— could use dubious claims of harmony to dismiss the unrest swirling around the Cardinals organization. The reality, though, was very different.

In Green Bay, at least, Lambeau had been widely revered for founding a civic treasure. In Chicago, he needed to win games in order to win over a more sophisticated fan base that had recently enjoyed championship success. Cardinals fans sensed that their team was headed in the wrong direction.

"There were rumors that Wolfner was feuding with Lambeau, that Lambeau was feuding with assistant coach Phil Handler, and that very few members of the Cardinals' management were even on speaking terms." Joe Ziemba wrote in *When Football Was Football,* his history of the Cardinals. There was a lot of truth in those rumors.

Further undermining the team's chances of success, Lambeau's inability to connect with key players made a complicated situation even messier. Paul Christman, one member of the Million Dollar Backfield, already was gone. Others would soon follow.

\* \* \* \* \* \* \* \*

The NFL played its inaugural Pro Bowl, the first edition of the league's modern All-Star game, with great fanfare at the Coliseum in Los Angeles on January 14, 1951. Cowboy star Roy Rogers, "astride Trigger," headlined a "wild west" halftime show that featured more than 350 western riders. The halftime entertainment also included a square dance with "1,200 brilliantly garbed participants." In other words, the NFL was immersed in halftime extravaganzas long before the Super Bowl made halftime shows must-see events.

In a repeat of the NFL championship game coaching matchup, Cleveland's Paul Brown led the American stars past the National stars, coached by the Rams' Joe Stydahar, 28-27 before a crowd of 53,676.

"For individual brilliance, it equaled baseball's annual All-Star game," said Lambeau, identified as the dean of NFL coaches in the *Los Angeles Times*. "Never have I seen so many great players do so many things so well."

After the All-Star game, everyone headed to Chicago for the 1951 draft and winter meetings. One item on the docket was a close look at the tackle-eligible rule. Eagles coach Greasy Neale was furious after the Cardinals "completed a pass to an ineligible guard for [19] yards. And while the Eagles argued with the officials, Cardinal Coach Curly Lambeau lifted the guard from the lineup and covered him with a blanket on the bench. The officials couldn't find the player on the field." As a result, the completion was allowed.

The guard, Ed Bagdon, caught a shovel pass from running back Charley Trippi. The play turned a 10-yard loss into a 19-yard gain, helping the Cardinals upset the Eagles 14-10. The Hidden-Ball Trick was well-known to baseball. It took Curly Lambeau to come up with the The Hidden-Lineman Trick.

The key topic of the NFL's 1951 winter meetings quickly became divisional alignment, with George Halas lobbying for change. Moaning about the expense of traveling to Los Angeles and San Francisco, Halas proposed swapping divisions with Lambeau's Cardinals—which also would restore the Bears' home-and-home series with the popular Giants and Redskins.

In truth, Halas picked up $48,000 on his first trip to L.A., about $35,000 in San Francisco and $65,000 for the playoff game in Los Angeles, Art Daley said in the *Green Bay Press-Gazette*. "Money like that isn't available in the east often," Daley added.

Halas, who apparently didn't expect the West Coast paydays to be an annual event, was powerful enough to deadlock the league. Commissioner Bert Bell finally ruled that things would remain the same in 1951. Softening the blow for Halas, the Bears only faced the Rams and 49ers in Chicago that fall. So they had no expensive West Coast travel that year.

During the 1951 football draft, some concerns were expressed about whether the military draft, due to the Korean conflict, would impact the availability of players. While that affected a number of players, it didn't become the major issue it had been during World War II.

However, the peace agreement with the AAFC had not removed the threat of a rival league raiding NFL rosters. Canadian Football League teams, notably the Calgary Stampeders and Montreal Alouettes, were actively pursuing NFL stars, giving them an alternative to the newly merged pro circuit.

On April 4, 1951, *Chicago Sun-Times* columnist Irv Kupcinet reported from Palm Springs, California, where he was staying at the home of comedian Jack Benny, that he bumped into Cardinals quarterback Jim Hardy, who said "the Canadian League, which is trying to raid NFL rosters, has made him an attractive offer, as it has to Bob Waterfield, Tom Fears and Dick Hoerner of the L.A. Rams."

In a reversal almost as surprising as the eight interceptions he threw in Lambeau's first game as Cardinals coach, Hardy had bounced back to be named to the Pro Bowl, where he backed up starter Otto Graham, from the Browns. Although Hardy was tied for the league lead with 24 interceptions, his 17 touchdowns passes put him third.

A month later, Hardy was reportedly close to signing with the Calgary Stampeders. The always-interesting Hardy never did go to Canada. Instead of sticking with the Cardinals, though, he took a job as the Hoffman Television Network's director of athletics in Los Angeles. He began the 1951 season broadcasting junior-college games in his hometown, where he had led USC to a 25-0 rout of Tennessee in the 1945 Rose Bowl before being drafted eighth overall and joining the Los Angeles Rams in 1946.

But three other Cardinals did go to Calgary. Lambeau lost his star receiver, end Bob Shaw, who had led the NFL with 12 touchdown catches in 1950 and finished third, with 971 receiving yards. Also leaving the Cardinals for the Stampeders were center Bill Blackburn and tackle Jim Lipinski. Lambeau also was missing his leading rusher and place-kicker, Pat Harder, who had announced his retirement.

And so, as Lambeau prepared for his second Cardinals training camp at Lake Forest College in 1951, he was missing his top quarterback, his best receiver, his leading rusher and his place-kicker.

"Outside of that, we haven't got any tackles, no ends and one or two backs," lamented Cardinals scout Wally Cruice, who had also scouted for Lambeau in Green Bay.

The departure of Harder, the former University of Wisconsin star that Lambeau had wanted to bring to Green Bay, was especially difficult. Harder had led the NFL in scoring for three straight seasons in 1947-49. Only 28, he changed his mind and reported to the Cardinals' 1951 training camp on September 1. But something was going on behind the scenes. Lambeau traded him 19 days later to the Detroit Lions.

"I just didn't see eye to eye with the present Cardinals management," Harder told *Chicago Sun-Times* columnist Gene Kessler, who noted that "That was also [Detroit] Coach Parker's explanation for quitting the Cards."

Harder, who would help Detroit win the 1952 and 1953 NFL titles, was the second member of the Million Dollar Backfield to leave the Cardinals after not getting along with Lambeau. More disagreements with the team's 1947 championship stars would come.

In perhaps the most devastating blow to Curly's house of Cards, club president Ray Bennigsen, who had hired Lambeau, had resigned on July 12, a few weeks before training camp opened. A longtime business associate of the late Charlie Bidwill, Bennigsen had been a top executive of Bidwill's business empire, including the horse-racing-oriented Bentley-Murray Printing Company, the Hawthorne and Sportsman's Park race tracks and other businesses.

"There have been rumors of repeated disagreement between [Wolfner] and Bennigsen which Mrs. Bidwill was unable or unwilling to smooth over," the *Chicago Daily News* reported. And yet, "As far as is known, Wolfner has no official title, or connection, with the Bidwill estate or family."

With Bennigsen gone, Wolfner would be given the title of managing director. His meddling oversight now would be official. And Curly Lambeau would be without his biggest front-office ally.

## 64
## *CARDINAL SINS*

The Cardinals began the 1951 season, their second under Lambeau, exactly the way they had started their first campaign—with a pre-season game in Green Bay, where the Lambeau name would goose ticket sales. Exhibition games were not the easiest sell in those days in Green Bay. It was a small town that was used to winning. And the Packers, who had stumbled to a 3-9 season after their rousing 2-1 start, were not winning.

This was no mere exhibition game for Lambeau. The smug Cardinals had lost in Green Bay a year earlier. This time, Lambeau was taking nothing for granted. "Last year the Cardinals came to Green Bay obviously confident. Curly Lambeau, better than anyone else, knew his old club was on the floor, starting from scratch," longtime Lambeau-watcher Lloyd Larson wrote in the *Milwaukee Sentinel*. "Lambeau wasn't messing around this time. He wanted to make this the triumphant return he missed last time. The Cardinals looked like a ball club. They were ready."

Lambeau's squad led 14-7 heading into the fourth quarter before disaster struck. The Cardinals gave up 10 unanswered points on a 74-yard touchdown pass and a last-minute field goal to ruin Curly's homecoming 17-14 for the second straight year. Even the score was the same.

The comeback rewarded 16,168 Packer fans who "braved pre-game and first-quarter showers to witness the bitterly-contested non-conference struggle," Art Daley told *Press-Gazette* readers. "This particular bit of history was repeated," Larson said. "The Packers did it again."

In another indicator that Lambeau no longer was on top of coaching details, an unidentified Packer said the Cardinals' young quarterback, Frank Tripucka, "made the glaring mistake of maintaining a constant signal-call cadence" against Green Bay, the *Chicago Daily News* reported. "We timed ourselves to Tripucka's count," the Packer defender said, "and we were matching every rush the Cards made."

That was critical to stopping Lambeau's offense when it stalled at the 3 yardline on its first drive of the game. And without accomplished kicker Harder, who had forced a trade to Detroit, the Cardinals also missed three field goals.

Lacking a steady quarterback, Lambeau announced that Charley Trippi would start in place of Tripucka in the Cardinals' next game. Trippi was among the league's best halfbacks—one of the NFL's best players, really—an excellent all-around athlete who also had been a coveted major-league baseball prospect. But moving to quarterback was a a major change.

Trippi had an encouraging quarterback debut, completing 12 of 16 for 153 yards, throwing for one touchdown and running for another, in a 28-7 win. But that was against the New York Yanks, a team that would go 1-9-2 and fold at the end of season.

This was Lambeau's world in his second season in Chicago. Taking over a team that was only two years removed from the NFL championship game, he was reduced to using a halfback at quarterback. His Pro Bowl quarterback from the previous season had taken an obscure broadcasting job. He had lost a premier kicker due to discontent and a star receiver to Canada. The Cardinals still had some talented players, but they seemed to be in no danger of taking flight.

Lambeau's tumultuous second year in Chicago reached a crossroads very early in the season. His team lost two of its first three games, but the lone victory, against the Bears, had kindled hopes that the Cardinals could have a decent year. With their next two games against the winless Redskins (0-3) and Steelers (0-2-1), they seemed in position to build some momentum.

Curly tried to sound the alarm, countering speculation that "the South Siders should beat the hapless Redskins" by saying, "It may be tough getting our club up for this game. Washington was walloped 45-0 by the Browns last Sunday, but our scouts tell us the Redskins aren't that bad."

Instead of a positive stride, the trip to Washington on October 21, 1951, turned into a disastrous 7-3 loss. That listless performance set off another barrage of bickering.

"Before catching a train for Chicago, Walter Wolfner, managing director of the club and husband of Violet Bidwill Wolfner, confided to friends that 'this defeat will cost Lambeau his job,' " the *Chicago Sun-Times* reported under a headline that said "Lambeau On Way Out As Card Pilot?"

Oddly, Lambeau and the team flew back to Chicago, apart from Vi and Wolfner, who went by train. There would be no clearing of the air on the disappointing trip home.

Wolfner, the *Sun-Times* reported, was "critical of Lambeau's strategy against the 'Skins, particularly when quarterback Charley Trippi elected to pass instead of running with the ball after long drives carried the team to the Redskin 4 twice in the final period."

Even more galling, 37-year-old Slingin' Sammy Baugh, in his 15th NFL year and nearing the end of his Hall of Fame career, revealed that he threw a 48-yard touchdown despite lingering pain from a "shoulder injury incurred while roping steers at a rodeo last August."

In Lambeau's defense, the Cardinals were facing an emotionally fired-up team. Washington owner George Preston Marshall had fired head coach Herman Ball after the Redskins were routed by the Browns a week earlier. That left them playing with gusto in their first game under their popular interim coach, longtime Redskins back Dick Todd, who had gotten the job because George Halas was blocking Marshall's highly publicized first choice, Hunk Anderson.

Even though Hunk was out of football, working for a steel company in Detroit, he was still under contract until January 1 to the always-scheming Halas, who demanded standout tackle Paul Lipscomb from Washington in exchange for releasing Anderson. Marshall refused and made Todd his coach. Halas then said he would match Marshall's salary offer if Anderson would return as a Bears assistant.

Not only did the coaching turmoil fire up the Redskins. The Cardinals were down to one healthy quarterback, Trippi, the recently converted halfback. Frank Tripucka, who had been sharing the QB job with Trippi, had gone down with a shoulder injury in their previous game.

The crowd was so noisy that "The officials twice had to call time so that the Cardinals could hear [Trippi's] signals," the *Chicago Tribune* reported. Clearly, that was a kinder, gentler era in sports—a marked departure from home teams whipping up their fans to mayhem so that visiting teams can't hear.

"We lost, but we should have won," Lambeau said succinctly. The Redskins, he said, were "hotter than a firecracker." Beyond the coaching-change excitement, the Redskins were holding a Bill Dudley Day to honor their veteran star halfback. Before the game, Virginia Governor John Battle gave Dudley, who had played at the University of Virginia, "a silver service and the keys to a new Ford station wagon." An emotional Dudley fought back tears in his acceptance remarks.

To clear the air, Lambeau met with Wolfner on Tuesday at the Cardinals' office in Comiskey Park. Vi Bidwill and assistant coaches Handler and Isbell also attended.

"I didn't like Trippi's selection of plays when the Cards were near the Washington goal line," Wolfner said. "I suggested to Lambeau that hereafter he should send in plays for Trippi at opportune times."

Although Wolfner stood by his criticism of the two interceptions thrown by Trippi near the Washington goal line, he denied that the Washington loss would cost Lambeau his job. "I don't think firing the coach is the solution for the Cardinals," Wolfner said. "Curly may have made mistakes, but he's done a lot of good for the team. At the meeting today, I told him that it would be the coaches' responsibility to call the plays. In baseball the manager dictates the strategy, so why not in football? Paul Brown of the Cleveland club does a good job of it."

Lambeau could not have enjoyed being given a football lecture from know-it-all Wolfner. But he played along, saying, "It was good to have a meeting of minds. I'm sure it was beneficial to everyone."

Wolfner also said a decision on Lambeau and his assistant coaches, Isbell and Handler, would be made after the season, when their contracts expired. "Maybe they'll all be back next year, and maybe none of them will," Wolfner said. "I don't know. But if any changes are made, the men involved will get the news from me, not second-hand."

In an action that spoke much louder, though, the Cardinals announced that quarterback Jim Hardy had been lured out of retirement and would rejoin the team later that day. Acting on Lambeau's legitimate contention that he lacked a bonafide quarterback, Wolfner opened up the team checkbook.

"I couldn't afford to pass up the offer to go back to football," said Hardy, who was granted a leave from Hoffman Television. "It was awfully attractive financially."

The signing also gave the Cardinals a public relations advantage. Instead of *Wolfner and Lambeau clear the air*, the headline became, *Hardy to Return*.

The problem was, Lambeau's explanation that Trippi "was [calling plays] on his own" —an assumption amplified by Wolfner—infuriated Trippi, who felt he was being thrown under the bus by Lambeau.

"That isn't true. The Cardinal coaching staff called 90 percent of the plays against Washington," the halfback-turned-quarterback said. "I was pretty much on my own until the Cards reached the Washington 10 or 14-yard line. And then I got my instructions from the bench. . . . In the last series of plays. . . Lambeau called the first three plays. I called the fourth play. . . . If I make a mistake, I'll take full responsibility for it. But I don't like to be blamed for somebody else's doings."

Just like that, Lambeau had alienated a third member of the Million Dollar Backfield. Christman and Harder already were gone. Only Elmer Angsman had not voiced his discontent. And that would change when the time came.

Pointing a finger at Trippi was a clumsy move by Lambeau. He wasn't going to placate Wolfner, who was not the placating kind. And meanwhile, Curly had left Trippi, perhaps his best player, feeling betrayed. A gifted halfback, Trippi had agreed to become a raw quarterback. And now Lambeau was blaming him?

Lambeau tried to explain things away by saying he had been concentrating on the Cardinals' defense while Isbell, who was handling the offense, was responsible for sending in plays. After shifting the blame to Isbell, Lambeau said he would "have a lot more to say about what plays" were being called.

Trippi's eruption had overshadowed the clear-the-air meeting and the Hardy signing. To rekindle an air of harmony, the club made a public show of patching things up at practice on Thursday. Photographers snapped away as Lambeau and Trippi shook hands, with Wolfner looking on.

"It was only a misunderstanding," Lambeau said. "I feel better now. All we want to do now, Charley, is win!"

"Sure, that's right," a nodding Trippi said with a shrug.

# 65
## *TWO AND OUT*

As Halloween approached, in the middle of Curly Lambeau's second season as Cardinals coach, 14,773 dedicated fans ventured into Comiskey Park on October 28, 1951, to see them try to right their listing ship. For three quarters, all went well. And then, the previously hapless Steelers, who were trailing 14-7, erupted for three touchdowns to send Lambeau down to defeat 28-14.

For the second straight week, The Man Who Invented the Green Bay Packers had been shocked by a previously winless team.

"I have absolutely nothing to say," Cardinals managing director Walter Wolfner told reporters afterward. A week earlier, Wolfner reportedly had told friends the loss to the winless Redskins would "cost Lambeau his job." After this loss, Wolfner and his friends kept their mouths shut.

After a week in which Wolfner blamed Lambeau, who blamed quarterback Trippi and assistant coach Isbell, the finger-pointing Cardinals had sunk even lower. Jim Hardy, the quarterback brought out of retirement, threw five interceptions against the Steelers. Declarations that everyone was on the same page were no match for that.

After a week in which the Cardinals' troubles "centered around passing the buck," *Chicago Daily News* writer Jack Ryan playfully began his game story, " the trouble [was] simply passing."

Strangely, Lambeau's Cardinals had outgained all of their first five opponents while losing four of those five games. In Green Bay, he had built a legendary career, and a legendary franchise, by fielding innovative teams that combined spirit, cleverness and talent to find ways to win. In Chicago, Lambeau tarnished that legacy with a team that was deficient in all three categories and found ways to lose.

His dream of conquering Chicago—of out-dueling George Halas and proving his Green Bay detractors wrong—was looking more like a pipe-dream. A messy situation was becoming even messier. Denial or not, Wolfner's comment that the Cardinals' 7-3 loss in Washington in their fourth game would cost Lambeau his job was looking very accurate.

The tumult of that defeat started an irreversible downward spiral. After a week of bickering, the Cardinals managed only another humbling five-interception loss to the Steelers.

In their next game, the Cardinals cut down their interceptions against the NFL champion Browns, but lost four fumbles in a 34-17 defeat. Heading to the West Coast, they played the Rams to a 7-7 halftime tie but disappeared in the second half of a 45-21 blowout loss. They were 1-6. They had lost three more games since Walter Wolfner's seething criticism.

Then, when the Cardinals seemed to be the sorriest of teams, they erupted in San Francisco with a 27-21 win that wound up costing the 49ers the National/Western Conference title. The Cardinals reverted to form in their next game, losing 10-0 to the Giants. Even worse, only 11,892 showed up at Comiskey Park. Lambeau's team was losing money as well as games. This was not what Vi Bidwill and her new husband had bargained for.

The last straw came the following week. On December 2, Lambeau's squad fell behind 42-0 in a 49-28 loss to the Browns. With two games remaining in their 12-game season, the Cardinals were 2-8.

In a blunt interview, Wolfner, the team's managing director and the husband of the owner, carved up Lambeau. Although he stopped short of saying Curly would be fired, that was clearly where Wolfner was headed.

"Lambeau's made mistakes," Wolfner told *United Press* writer Ed Sainsbury in an interview that ran on sports pages everywhere. "They've been mistakes of omission and not commission. There have been things he could have cured, had he done something, but he didn't. We're not going to take any hasty action. We don't know what we're going to do. Curly's contract runs until February 1st, but the draft is in January and we'll know before then what we're going to do."

Clearly, Lambeau was not going to be renewing the lease on his plush Lake Shore Drive apartment, not with Walter Wolfner calling the Cardinals' shots. After marrying owner Violet Bidwill, Wolfner had forced out team president Ray Bennigsen, who had hired Lambeau. With two games left in the Cardinals' miserable 1951 season, Lambeau seemed certain to be next.

"There's no harmony among the coaches," Wolfner said, continuing his rant. "They're still at loggerheads most of the time, not speaking to each other sometimes. They've had the material. Why, with the players we've got on this team, they ought to be fighting for the championship. Paul Brown told me last Sunday, after he beat us, that the Cardinals were the best team the Browns faced. He said that if he coaches a team in the all-star game again, he's going to use six of our players on his first team. Look at the statistics of that Browns game. We outplayed them, ran them into the ground, in the second half. Fumbles cost us the game. It's been that way all season. It's just a combination of things wrong with the club."

Curly got the message. With two games left, rather than waiting to be fired, he resigned on Friday, December 7.

"I had heard Mr. Wolfner was going to act and I decided to beat him to the punch," Lambeau said, adding that he had planned to wait until the season was over, "but I just couldn't take it any longer."

"LAMBEAU QUITS; BLAMES CARDINAL OFFICE," the *Chicago Tribune* said in the same big, black type it had used when Bobby Thomson's dramatic home run had propelled the Giants into the World Series two months earlier.

The Tribune's two subheads said, `DON'T FIT INTO ORGANIZATION,' COACH STATES, and "Will Finish Last Two Games."

"Football success is about 50 physical and 50 percent emotional," Lambeau told his old friend, *Chicago Tribune* sports editor Arch Ward, at Lambeau's Gold Coast apartment. "A coach has little chance to build morale when management interferes with the normal relationship between him and his players. This is true particularly when the office manager thru inexperience has little knowledge of the problems that beset a coach."

In a complaint eerily similar to when he resigned from the Packers, Lambeau said, "No man can do a satisfactory job when constantly harassed by second guessers in the front office." In Chicago, Lambeau did not have to deal with the money problems that had led to his demise in Green Bay. But there was one major similarity: He no longer was winning. Or looking like a coach who was likely to win.

Wolfner fired back in a separate *Chicago Tribune* story, saying, "We have told Mr. Lambeau repeatedly that he was in charge of the team and we would stand back of any decisions he made. When reports of dissension in the coaching staff and among the players came up, we simply said: `Curly, you are the boss. You are at liberty to fire your assistant coaches and any players you have decided are not cooperating 100 percent.' When Lambeau asked us to get players for him, we always tried to sign the men he wanted."

The truth, of course, was somewhere in between. Wolfner was very much a meddling, heavy-handed manager. Lambeau's two predecessors, Jimmy Conzelman and Buddy Parker, also had resigned, in large part because they did not want to work for an interfering front office—and they had been far more successful than Curly. Ray Bennigsen, the general manager who hired Lambeau, also had quit rather than work for Wolfner.

Lambeau said he had decided in July to resign at the end of the season, not long after Bennigsen resigned. Bennigsen "knew where a coach's authority began and where it ended," Lambeau said. "That situation has not prevailed since his resignation and I simply can't work under the current setup and retain self respect."

Then again, Lambeau had left himself vulnerable to Wolfner's meddling by losing too many games in too many dispirited ways, and by losing players in too many unacceptable ways. Players know when coaching is not showing them the best way, and not working the right way. They know when a coach is throwing them under the bus.

Whether they didn't want to play for Wolfner or for Lambeau didn't matter. They didn't want to play for the Cardinals organization. That added up to unacceptable losses on the field and at the ticket window. The Cardinals had reportedly lost nearly $100,000 while floundering under Lambeau in 1951. By contrast, the Bears reported a $200,000 profit that season while posting a modest 7-5 record.

Lambeau vowed to work diligently until his contract expired on February 1, which meant he intended to coach the Cardinals in their final two games and preside over the 1952 draft on January 17 in New York.

"I'm going to try with every ounce of energy I possess to whip the Washington Redskins in Comiskey Park Sunday and the Bears in Wrigley Field a week from Sunday," he said. "I'll continue to fulfill my obligations to the club to the best of my ability until my contract expires or until I am relieved of command." In other words, Lambeau wanted to be paid the full amount that remained due on his $30,000-a-year contract.

Wolfner initially went along with Lambeau's plan to coach the final two games. But he quickly rescinded that, firing Lambeau and anointing the three assistant coaches to guide the Cardinals in their final two games. "This office has been under tremendous pressure from various sources, mostly from the fans, to relieve Mr. Lambeau of his duties," Wolfner said in another moment of buck-passing, an area where the Cardinals excelled. "We were hesitant in taking any such action as it is not the desire of this office to injure anyone. . . . [But] there has been a terrific lack of discipline on the ball club during Mr. Lambeau's tenure as head coach."

In its first game without Curly at the tiller, the team continued to chart the same course. Bill Dudley, who had inspired the Redskin victory in Washington that plunged the Cardinals into confusion, kicked a field goal with 15 seconds left to give the Redskins a 20-17 victory in Chicago. With one game left, the now-Lambeau-less Cardinals were 2-9.

Curly was among the few eyewitnesses. "Lambeau had announced his intention of paying his way into the park, but perhaps deciding the game would not be worth the price of admission, he flashed his National Football League pass to gain the right of way past the gate keepers," the *Chicago Tribune's* Harry Warren noted.

"The season's most minute crowd, a mere 9,459 turnout which included the ousted Lambeau, saw the Cards lose in the final 15 seconds of a game played on greasy soil and under dark skies," Jack Ryan told *Chicago Daily News* readers.

It was the Cardinals' smallest crowd in Comiskey Park since November 26, 1944. Lambeau also attended that game, a 35-20 Green Bay victory. It was the final regular-season game before the Packers defeated the Giants in New York to give him his sixth and final NFL championship.

The Cardinals went into frozen Wrigley Field a 10½ point underdog against the Bears, who needed a win to keep their hopes alive in the log-jammed National/Western Conference. When Detroit lost at San Francisco, all the Bears needed to do was beat the struggling Cardinals to pull into a tie with the Rams and force a conference playoff for the second straight year.

The Cardinals did not let that happen. Operating from a shotgun, Charley Trippi had a huge day, lifting the South Siders to a 24-14 upset. For the second straight year, the Cardinals had shattered Halas' post-season plans. With two of their five losses against the imploding Cardinals, the Bears (7-5) finished one game behind the Rams (8-4).

"At least we're city champs," Wolfner said with dark humor.

Continuing their puzzling season, the Cardinals had trailed the Bears 7-0 after a first half in which they used a T formation operated by Jim Hardy. In the second half, they lined up in a spread formation. With the temperature dipping to 1 below zero, Trippi ran for two touchdowns and passed for another.

"We worked on the formation all last week," said offensive assistant Cecil Isbell, who shared the coaching duties with Handler and Ramsey. "We didn't use the formation in the first half because we were just about holding our own. And another reason we weren't keen about using the formation in the first half was because the Bears could use the intermission to work out a defense for it."

Trippi was ejected in the final couple of minutes for taking a swing at Ed Sprinkle, a notoriously chippy Bear. "He's been hitting me when I'm down for the last five years," Trippi said. "So I just threw a punch at him." The Cardinals gave the game ball to Hardy, who had set up the Trippi surprise. Hardy quickly handed the ball to Trippi.

The sub-zero temperatures held the announced attendance to 15,805, but Bears officials said more than 30,000 tickets had been sold. Bundling up for the disappointing game were 75 former Bears, who warmed up at the team's annual homecoming party at the Edgewater Beach Hotel after the game. Clyde "Bulldog" Turner, nearing the end of his Hall of Fame career, was honored with a new car and other gifts.

The upset of the Cardinals was another indicator that Lambeau no longer was an elite coach. At that point, he had won more games than anyone in the league. And at one time, he had been an innovator and motivator. But with him gone, the Cardinals had used an inspired surprise attack to knock the Bears out of the championship hunt.

"I didn't want to play under Curly Lambeau," said Hardy, announcing that he would be back in 1952. "The fellows all like to play under men like Cecil Isbell and Phil Handler. They try a lot of new stuff."

Hardy was not alone in that sentiment. Bob Shaw, a star receiver, and Bill Blackburn, a top-notch center/linebacker, had gone to Canada. Fullback/place-kicker Pat Harder had forced a trade to Detroit. The combination of Wolfner and Lambeau wreaked havoc when it came to roster building.

At that point, Hardy didn't even know who would coach the Cardinals. A year earlier, he had explored playing in the Canadian Football League and had moved on to a job with a fledgling sports network rather than play for Lambeau. Only a big salary offer—a prorated $23,000—from Wolfner, who was trying to give Lambeau the quarterback he lacked, had lured Hardy out of retirement.

Meanwhile, the 53-year-old Lambeau seemed to be the man headed for retirement. For the last 33 years of his life, he had commanded a professional football team. He had spent autumns immersed in gridiron combat, and had spent the rest of the year acquiring and signing players, scheduling games, taking care of all the business that comes with putting together a football team.

He had grown rich and famous. Save for a few extra pounds—writers referred to him at times as "portly"—he still had the muscular physique of an athlete. He still had the dimples and charm that made women swoon.

He still had the curly hair that had given him his name as child. But now it was graying and a bit thinner. The lenses on his eyeglasses were getting thicker. The ever-present cigarettes he smoked on the sideline, and everywhere else, had probably taken a toll. And like many an old athlete, he did not bring the same enthusiasm to competition that once consumed him.

What he had was a wife who shared his love of California—and the bank account and real estate holdings to enjoy life.

The most famous and winningest coach of the NFL's first three decades would be mentioned for coaching opportunities early in 1952. But they would not materialize. Curly Lambeau did not ride off triumphant from his two-year Chicago Cardinal experiment. But he did seem to be riding off to a nice post-football life.

Then again, football was his life. And a man of his stature did not simply disappear.

# 66
## *MORE WOLFNER MACHINATIONS*

By the end of December, Lambeau was enjoying the sunshine in the Malibu home that Grace's second husband had built. Back in Chicago, his legacy of intrigue continued.

Cardinals managing director Walter Wolfner could not resist the opportunity to blame Lambeau for creating the dissension that ruined the Cardinals' season—and giving himself credit for smoothing things over. Lambeau had enticed rookies to sign by promising to pay them for exhibition games, Wolfner said, even though he and Lambeau had agreed not to pay them, which was standard practice in the NFL at that time. When the players pressed their demand to be paid, Wolfner said, "I met with [their] grievance committee and I succeeded in straightening out all of the athlete's problems."

That happened right before the Cardinals upset the Bears in their second regular-season games, Wolfner said. "After they won, they brought me the football and said I had overcome the dissension and was responsible for the victory."

Lambeau never publicly disputed that Wolfner tale, although he undoubtedly would have spun it differently if given the opportunity. Nothing was simple with Walter Wolfner running the Cardinals.

Meanwhile, Wolfner seemed to be pointing toward Curly's protege, Cecil Isbell, as the Cardinals' next head coach. "Right now he is my leading candidate," Wolfner said on December 18, just before leaving on a two-week vacation in Miami Beach.

The next day, though, Joe Kuharich abruptly resigned after leading the University of San Francisco to an undefeated season. While vacationing in Miami Beach, Wolfner met with four "big-time college coaches." Kuharich, a South Bend, Indiana, native who had played for the Cardinals after playing at Notre Dame, was among them.

Wolfner also met several times with Isbell, who was in South Florida to see his younger brother, Larry, play for Baylor in the Orange Bowl and "to inspect some newly acquired hotel holdings in Fort Lauderdale," the *Chicago Tribune* reported.

A few days after Wolfner called Isbell his frontrunner, halfback Elmer Angsman told the *Chicago Sun-Times* he would not play for the team if Isbell was the head coach. "And Charley Trippi won't play, either," Angsman added. The team's two offensive stars apparently believed they were under-used and misled by backfield assistant Isbell, who had been in charge of Lambeau's offense.

Beyond that, an unnamed Cardinal said Isbell undermined Lambeau, saying, "How can a fellow like Isbell, who was without a job, show the kind of attitude he did against Lambeau? Isbell, who quit his job as football coach at Purdue to become head coach of the now defunct Baltimore Colts, didn't have a job. What happened? Lambeau gave him a job as assistant. It is no secret that Isbell did not cooperate with Lambeau during the season."

In Los Angeles, Lambeau declined to unravel the mysterious rifts involving him, Isbell and disgruntled players, saying, "It's a long story and I'd rather not comment right now." Isbell at odds with Lambeau as well as Angsman and Trippi? Lambeau's 1951 Cardinals were an incredibly dysfunctional crew.

Undeterred, Wolfner forged ahead, continuing to call Isbell his No. 1 candidate, but adding, "That doesn't mean, though, that Isbell is going to get the job." Was Wolfner having second thoughts about hiring a coach that his two best players vocally opposed? That would make sense.

Wolfner gradually shifted, saying Isbell, Kuharich and two unnamed college coaches were his final four candidates. But the speculation turned increasingly toward Kuharich. When Kuharich finally was given the job on January 8, the opposition to Isbell from Angsman and Trippi seemed to be a key reason. Kuharich agreed to a two-year deal worth $15,000 a year, allowing Wolfner to save $15,000 compared to Lambeau's salary.

The North Side of Chicago also had its share of turmoil. Just four stellar seasons into his NFL career, quarterback Johnny Lujack was threatening to retire. "During the football season I am not able to devote any time to the insurance business and I intend to make it my life's work," Lujack said on the eve of his second straight Pro Bowl.

It was not an idle threat. Lujack, the Heisman Trophy winner from Notre Dame who seemed destined to be a Bears star for years, did retire. It was not about his desire to sell insurance, though. Lujack felt Halas had cheated him, reneging on their agreements for his signing bonus and later in contract negotiations. "I don't mind anybody being a hard negotiator," Lujack told Halas biographer Jeff Davis. "I just don't want to be cheated because of my inexperience."

The Bears maintained that Lujack, who had just turned 27, had retired because of injuries, but Lujack said he didn't want to play for Halas. Returning to Notre Dame as an assistant to Frank Leahy, he "developed the top Fighting Irish backfield quartet since the Four Horsemen," Davis wrote. When Leahy retired in 1954, he recommended that Notre Dame make Lujack head coach. Snubbed when the Irish hired Terry Brennan, Lujack moved to Davenport, Iowa, his wife's hometown, and joined her family's auto dealership business.

In the days before NFL players and coaches were paid boggling amounts of money, it was easier to walk away.

# 67
## *JOB RUMORS GALORE*

After Lambeau's two-year stint with the Cardinals ended badly, his name popped up for a variety of new NFL incarnations. His transition from Green Bay to the Chicago Cardinals had been swift and seamless. This time, when he was truly between jobs, his possible landing places seemed endless.

In one shocker, George Halas and Redskins owner George Preston Marshall were reported behind a move to make Lambeau the next commissioner of the NFL. *Milwaukee Journal* sports editor R.G. Lynch said Lambeau "is reported headed for the office as assistant to commissioner Bert Bell to be groomed as an eventual successor."

Citing Bell's poor health, Lynch said Bell "needs an assistant to take some of the work off his hands. Lambeau would make a good aide for Bell. He has the class for the job and an intimate knowledge of league problems, politics and personalities. The writer hears that the chief objection raised is that he might play favorites. Whoever thinks that does not know Lambeau. Once he got the commissioner's post and the power that goes with it, Curly would be an independent, fair and forceful league head, in the opinion of this observer."

Halas knocked down the report, calling it erroneous and saying, "This is the first time I've heard of it." Halas also discounted Lynch's evidence that Lambeau had spent a lot of time with NFL officials at the championship game in Los Angeles, saying that treasurer Danny Dhea and publicity man Joe Labrum were the only league officials at the game.

Arch Ward dismissed the report emphatically with one sentence in his *In the Wake of the News* column: "Reports emanating from Milwaukee that Curly Lambeau is being groomed for the post of commissioner of professional football yesterday were termed `asinine' by the one man who ought to know—Curly Lambeau."

Lambeau as NFL commissioner was far-fetched. Despite his high profile and innovative thoughts, the idea was outlandish in too many ways. His last two leadership positions had ended badly, for starters. Lynch evidently was fed some bad information, or came up with a shortsighted idea on his own.

The next possibility was also a reach—but at first glance, it seemed to make a bit of sense. Lambeau and boxing champion Jack Dempsey were said to be trying to buy the floundering New York Yanks franchise, which owner Ted Collins had sold back to the NFL. Lambeau and Dempsey had strong financial backing, prominent Detroit sportscaster Van Patrick told his WJR radio audience. An *Associated Press* article gave nationwide coverage to the report by Patrick, who did Lions and Tigers play-by-play after playing football at TCU with Sammy Baugh.

There was a bit of substance there. Lambeau seems to have been interested in being general manager or co-owner of the franchise, which was coveted by wealthy investors in Dallas and Baltimore. The problem was, the Jack Dempsey in the radio report was a Los Angeles broker by the same name, not the famous boxer.

"What's it all about?" the boxer said when asked about the report. In a comical twist, Dempsey and his business manager, Max Waxman, who was a Baltimore native, decided to look into buying the Yanks and bringing them to Waxman's hometown.

As it turned out, although Lambeau apparently made inquiries, he did not become involved. Nor did either of the Dempseys, the boxer or the broker. With the team overwhelmed by red ink, the NFL sold it in January to a Dallas group led by 32-year-old millionaire "textile tycoon" Giles Miller. When the Dallas Texans struggled in 1952—college football fans in Texas showed little interest in pro football—the franchise resurfaced as the Baltimore Colts in 1953.

Miller's group had Lambeau on its short list of general manager and coaching candidates, but he was not hired for either job. Jimmy Phelan, who wound up staying on as coach from the Yanks to the Texans, hired Isbell as his backfield assistant.

After leaving the Cardinals, Lambeau also had been mentioned as a candidate to coach the Eagles. But that job went to assistant Jim Trimble, leaving Lambeau tending to his chickens and cattle on the ranch that he and Grace had bought in Thousand Oaks, California. Despite that, The Man Who Invented the Green Bay Packers still remained interested in finding another NFL position.

While wintering in California, Lambeau was honored on March 6 by the Pasadena Sports Ambassadors for his contribution to pro football. The dinner event, which kept him in the public eye, was broadcast on armed forces radio. Lambeau also was photographed as one of the

"Sportsmen for Joe Holt," who was running for Congress in California's newly formed 22nd congressional district. Other Sportsmen for Holt included Cardinals quarterback Jim Hardy and a pair of Heisman Trophy winners, Rams halfback Glenn Davis and Les Horvath, who had moved on to dentistry after a brief NFL career.

In May, another report speculated that "if and when Tony Morabito, majority stockholder for the 49ers, sells out because of ill health, that his stock will be peddled to Curley Lambeau, one-time majordomo of pro football in Green Bay, Wis." That item, from *Valley Times* sports editor Claude Newman, was published on Lambeau's California turf.

Lambeau quickly denied that report, however, to another local sportswriter. "Curly Lambeau tells me there is absolutely nothing to the report that he may buy the San Francisco 49er franchise from the ailing Tony Morabito." *Los Angeles Mirror* sports editor Sid Ziff wrote.

Not giving up, Claude Newman ran another item, saying, "Former Packer Ernie Smith, who was an All-American at USC, 'hopes, as I predicted, Curley winds up buying the San Francisco 49ers.'"

Although he was now a Californian, Lambeau still was a regular visitor to northeastern Wisconsin. During the summer of 1952, he arrived in Green Bay on July 22 "to visit his mother and brothers." He "then headed for the Peninsula and some fishing." The Door County peninsula, a short drive from Green Bay, was becoming Lambeau's annual summer escape.

Lambeau also stopped in Chicago. On August 2, Arch Ward devoted a lengthy *Chicago Tribune* column to Lambeau's strategy for how the College All-Stars could defeat the NFL champion Rams in Soldier Field on August 15. "Develop a pass attack," Lambeau said in the August 2 column, giving Ward some good promotional material and reminding NFL teams that Lambeau was available. "Temporarily disassociated, for the first time in 34 years, from the sport he helped pioneer and develop," Ward wrote, "he therefore qualifies as a logical authority to present the professional coaches' viewpoint on football's greatest spectacle."

# 68
## *BACK IN THE SADDLE*

After his Wisconsin visit, Lambeau was back in California on August 14, chatting with his old friend and rival, Washington owner George Preston Marshall, during a Redskins practice at their Occidental College training camp.

When rookie quarterback Eddie LeBaron boomed a punt, Lambeau advised Marshall that LeBaron also would be a good place-kicker, saying, "Anybody who can punt like that can place-kick, too."

That led to Marshall and Lambeau agreeing that the NFL should eliminate kicking extra points. "It's automatic in pro football. It's meaningless," Lambeau said.

"Meaningless, all right," Marshall said. "A team marches down the field [and scores]. Everyone gets worked up.... Instead of getting right on with the game... everyone cools off [during the extra point]. If you wrote a play that way, you'd never see an opening night."

It was just two old warhorses shooting the breeze. In the two decades they had known each other, professional football had gone from an athletic sideshow dwarfed by college football and major league baseball to an immensely popular pastime and lucrative business on the verge of dazzling television success.

In 1936, when Lambeau's Packers met Marshall's Boston Redskins for the NFL championship, Marshall had moved the game to New York because Boston wasn't interested in his team. Even at the Polo Grounds, only 29,545 had showed up to see the league championship.

Now, 16 years later, a crowd of 88,110 would turn out at the Los Angeles Coliseum to see an exhibition game between the Redskins and the Rams a few days after Lambeau and Marshall chatted about extra points. Or was there more to their conversation?

Just before the kickoff, Washington coach Dick Todd gathered his team together in their dressing room and told them he had quit due to "interference" from Marshall. After serving as the Skins interim coach when Marshall fired Herman Ball three games into the 1951 season, the emotional Todd had been elevated for 1952.

"I told the players when I took over last year that either I would run the team my way or I wouldn't coach," said Todd, unable to go along with Marshall's order to cut five rookies after Washington's 35-0 loss in San

Francisco the previous Sunday. "It was a choice between being a man or a mouse.... I decided to be a man."

Immediately after the Redskins lost to the Rams 45-23 on Thursday night, August 21, Todd departed for his home in Crowell, Texas. He had wanted to leave sooner, but Marshall persuaded him to stick around until the game was over.

Suddenly, Curly Lambeau was on the short list of candidates to become the Redskins head coach. The very short list.

Lambeau had departed under pressure from the Green Bay Packers and the Chicago Cardinals, complaining loudly about front-office meddling. Now the Redskins job, where the coach had quit due to front-office meddling, was open.

Could there be a more perfect match?

Lambeau had visited the Redskins training camp at Occidental College several times while the team prepared for its pre-season games in San Francisco and Los Angeles—and was conveniently planning to be at the Redskins camp on the Monday after their Thursday night loss to the Rams.

The *Washington Evening Star* cautioned, however, that Lambeau "is embarked on a cattle and chicken raising program near [Los Angeles] and may not be in the market for a king-sized headache." This was only partially true. While Lambeau and his third wife, Grace, owned a ranch in Thousand Oaks, they had a staff handling the ranch.

Always a showman, Marshall announced that he would hold a press conference to introduce his new coach. The Washington owner even brought up four names, but declined to say if one of them was his choice. Along with Lambeau, he mentioned Hunk Anderson, whom he had tried to hire a year earlier, only to be stopped when George Halas brazenly demanded a top player as compensation; Greasy Neale, who had retired in 1950 from a distinguished run with the Eagles, and Red Strader, who had coached the New York Yanks in 1950.

Redskins assistant Jerry Neri, a longtime college coach in his first NFL training camp, had been a popular choice among the Redskins players to be their new head coach. But Marshall wanted no part of that, saying, "It'll be a pro, that's certain. I'm tired of fooling around with these amateurs. I'm interested in only one thing—getting a winner—and I don't care whose feet I step on to get it."

Clearly, all signs pointed toward Lambeau. He not only was one of the successful and well-known coaches in NFL history. He was a longtime friend of Marshall who had been hanging out with Marshall at practice. And like Marshall, he was a publicity-conscious sportsman who believed in the entertainment component of football.

The day after Todd quit, Marshall called Lambeau and and offered him the Redskins coaching job. Saying he was busy with his cattle and his chickens, Lambeau asked for time to think about it. By that night, though, Lambeau said he called Marshall back and accepted the job.

At least that's the story that the two fellow showmen gave to the press when Marshall introduced Lambeau as his new coach on Saturday. Considering that Todd told his assistants on Wednesday that he was going to quit, and that the Todd-Marshall friction had been building before that, it's possible Marshall had earlier conversations with Lambeau about taking a break from chickens and cattle to resume his pigskin duty.

"Curly and I have been in business for 21 years," Marshall said in introducing Lambeau on Saturday, August 23. "Nineteen of those years Curly ran a team in the National Football League called the Green Bay Packers—one of the most successful in the history of football, and a team that outdrew every team in professional football when I was first in it. . . . I hope Curly Lambeau stays with the Redskins as long as he stayed with the Green Bay Packers and I hope he does just half as well."

In Washington, a more recent memory was not as encouraging. "Curly Lambeau's appointment as Redskins' head coach won't cause any dancing in the streets by those who saw his Chicago Cardinals lose here," *Evening Star* sports editor Charles M. Egan wrote, recalling the game that left Cardinals boss Walter Wolfner saying the defeat would cost Lambeau his job.

While Lambeau had agreed to coach for two years, Marshall said, "that is only a statement between him and myself." In other words, there was to be no contract. Lambeau, who was very comfortable financially, seemed more interested in getting back into coaching than pondering a paycheck.

Although Curly had complained loudly about front-office interference after leaving the Packers and the Cardinals, he said Marshall's hands-on approach to his football team would not pose a problem.

"George's interference is constructive," Lambeau said. "It could be destructive. [But] For an owner to be interested in his team is a marvelous thing. From my experience with George I know I can talk to him and convince him of certain things. George will argue with you, but he'll go along with a coach who can convince him that his way is the right way."

Lambeau and Marshall had to do a quick turnabout when assistant coach Jerry Neri, a highly regarded college assistant who had just joined the

Redskins staff, quit to become an assistant at Yale, where he would be reunited with first-year coach Jordan Olivar, a friend he had worked with the previous nine years at Villanova and Loyola Marymount.

To replace Neri, they announced that Sammy Baugh, the passing pioneer who was entering his NFL-record 16th season, would be a player-coach. His top priority would be to mentor LeBaron, Washington's quarterback of the future. Baugh, who led the Redskins to two NFL championships, would retire after the 1952 season holding 13 NFL records as a quarterback, punter, and defensive back.

When Lambeau became the Redskins head coach, LeBaron was a 22-year-old rookie who had spent the previous two years in the Marines, mostly fighting in Korea. Washington had made him a 10th-round pick in 1950, when he was coming off a remarkable three-year run at the College of the Pacific.

Only 5-foot-9 and 168 pounds, he overcame his lack of size as a shrewd and agile leader that earned him nicknames such as the Little General, the Sorcerer's Apprentice and Supermouse. LeBaron was only 16 when he entered college. On a train from California to play Northwestern, a woman asked some of LeBaron's large teammates who they were. When they explained, she looked at Eddie and said, "How nice that you can take your son along on the trip."

The "son" led his team to an 11-0 record in 1949, playing safety and punting as well as quarterback. Pacific finished 10th in the final AP poll for 1949.

LeBaron bridged football eras in a remarkable way. In his first year at Pacific, he had played for 84-year-old Amos Alonzo Stagg, the college coaching legend who spent 14 years at Pacific after his 41 years at the University of Chicago. LeBaron would finish his career playing for the expansion-team Dallas Cowboys under Tom Landry, who was just embarking on his Hall of Fame career. Stagg first coached the University of Chicago in 1892. Landry finished his Cowboys career in 1988.

In between Stagg and Landry, LeBaron endured a couple of tempestuous seasons with another coaching legend: Curly Lambeau. During his 30-year Packer reign, Lambeau, the NFL's first 1,000-yard passer, had been known for clever offense. With the Chicago Cardinals, however, he had entrusted his offense to assistant Cecil Isbell, who had been his star quarterback in Green Bay. When Marshall hired him to coach the Redskins, Curly continued on the defensive side, despite his legacy as a passing pioneer who also liked surprise maneuvers.

"He was really a defensive coach," LeBaron said, "and at some point he turned the offense over to somebody else. In the two years Curly was with the Redskins, he probably didn't know more than ten offensive plays."

As he had done while coaching players like Johnny Blood and Cal Hubbard at Green Bay, Lambeau was willing, at times, to take strategic advice from knowledgable players, whether it was offense or defense. With Washington, Lambeau decided to alter the popular Oklahoma, or Eagle, defense, a 5-4 scheme that featured five linemen, including a middle guard. The 5-4 had become so effective at stopping the run that teams had turned to passing.

To counter that, Lambeau told middle guard Jim Ricca, "I think you're fast enough to drop back in a third-and-eight situation and almost become another linebacker."

When they tried it for a few days, Ricca said, "I'd see something and say, 'No, Coach. When that happens, we should do this.'" After a few days, Ricca said, Lambeau called him into his office and said, "You're upsetting me. You're saying things at practice and you're upsetting me because you're right. How do you know so much about this defense?"

Ricca replied that he had played at Georgetown for Mush Dubofsky, who literally wrote a book, *Everybody's Football*, which explained the four-man line. In the end, Ricca became a defensive tackle, not a linebacker, on defenses that used a four-man front.

Under Lambeau, Washington was adept at pass defense. It led the league in both 1952 and 1953. With Lambeau gone in 1954, Washington dropped to last in passing defense.

Lambeau had a dismal Redskin debut—an ugly 27-14 exhibition loss on Friday, September 5, in San Antonio to the lowly Dallas Texans. That team was the remnant of the New York Yanks, the franchise that Lambeau reportedly had been trying to buy. In the first half alone, three Washington touchdowns were wiped out by penalties.

"A good, sharp team doesn't get penalized in these situations," Lambeau said. "We lit a fire under them and had 'em going in that first half, but we wasted all our energy running up and down the field without scoring. That's no way to win ball games. I want more thinking on the field. I want everybody to know every assignment perfectly, offense and defense, and to carry it out properly. . . . I can't talk about all the things we have to do now, but it's plenty."

After flopping in Lambeau's debut, Washington moved on to its next game, against Green Bay in Kansas City on September 14. With Curly suddenly coaching the Redskins, an otherwise routine exhibition between struggling teams became an attraction: The Man Who Invented the Green Bay Packers would line up his new team against the Packers.

When the Redskins resumed practice in Kansas City, Lambeau held extra workouts to cut down the mistakes. He also announced that he would not hesitate to play rookies ahead of veterans if the newcomers were looking better. As part of his sweeping new "get-tough" policy, he announced fines for players late to practice and travel departures.

Lambeau also was greeted as a link to the past. It was a role he embraced. First he talked about the Kansas City Cowboys, who played in the NFL for a couple of seasons in the 1920s. As Curly recalled, the Cowboys drew a big crowd in New York, where their cowboy hats and boots intrigued New Yorkers.

A win over the Giants led to their demise, Lambeau said. The Giants had been so impressed, Curly told reporters, that they hired Kansas City coach Roy Andrews and many of his players, causing the team to fold in 1926. It wasn't quite as simple as that. The Giants acquired lineman Steve Owen, who had helped Kansas City beat them. Meanwhile, Andrews coached in Cleveland and Detroit the next two years before arriving in New York. But Lambeau never let details get in the way of a good story. And in this case, the details held a fair amount of truth.

Because both the Packers, who had been drubbed 38-7 by the Cardinals in Chicago, and the Skins were coming off bad games, Lambeau said he expected a pair of teams determined to play better. "Both our team and Green Bay played poorly the last time out and may be expected to bounce up. That should make it a great game," said Lambeau, who always had a ticket-selling pitch ready.

He also promised to use his best lineup, saying, "The time of experimentation is over." With that, Lambeau returned to Harry Gilmer just two weeks after announcing that rookie Eddie LeBaron was his man.

Quarterback change or not, it was the same old story for Lambeau against the Packers. Although Green Bay was the underdog, Lambeau's Redskins lost 13-7. Including his pre-season trips to Green Bay with the Cardinals, Lambeau was now 0 for 3 against the team he had guided for a remarkable 31 years.

And the Redskins were 0-4 in their 1952 pre-season games. Lambeau, who had presided over the last two losses, began pointing his finger at his players. Under a headline that began, "Bungling Redskins," Lambeau said, "We beat ourselves again today. Silly mistakes—penalties when they hurt—things like that beat us."

Meanwhile, as Washington moved on to its final pre-season game, against Detroit, owner Marshall cut a pair of players and claimed that the Redskins still had their most talented roster since 1942. If that was true, their opponents seemed to have upgraded even more effectively.

Washington finished its pre-season with a fifth straight loss, falling to the Detroit Lions 45-7 on September 20 in Norman, Oklahoma. A good crowd of up to 40,000 turned out to see the first professional game at the University of Oklahoma. Given the Sooners' record of 39-4 the previous four years, however, some cynics might have questioned whether the Lions and the Redskins were the first "professionals" to play there.

"The Lions rolled to a ridiculously easy 45-7 triumph," *Detroit Free Press* writer Bob Latshaw wrote. In the small world of the NFL, Lambeau was crushed by Buddy Parker, who had opted out as Cardinals coach two years earlier, opening the door for Curly there. Parker now presided over a juggernaut; Lambeau had gone in the opposite direction.

After the Detroit rout, Washington limped into Chicago to prepare for its regular-season opener against the Chicago Cardinals. For the second time in his four-game Redskin tenure, Curly Lambeau would be facing an opponent with whom he was intertwined. He had just suffered another loss to the Packers. Now he would have his first opportunity against the Cardinals, where his brief coaching run had ended badly.

The return to Chicago was an under-the-radar homecoming. Lambeau would not even see his old Notre Dame friend, Arch Ward. The *Chicago Tribune* sports editor was in Philadelphia, writing about the Marciano-Wolcott fight and doting on Notre Dame's highly anticipated opener at Penn. All 74,711 seats at Franklin Field had been bought by alumni and friends, with no public sale. Because of the interest, the NCAA television committee had agreed to allow the game to be televised in Philadelphia. But it said the Princeton-Columbia game, as scheduled, would be shown on the rest of the NBC network.

Although Lambeau, who had quit the Cardinals before Walter Wolfner could fire him, was tiptoeing back into Chicago, at least he had landed on his feet. The Redskins were not a very good team, but they were an NFL team. He was still in the game.

In a way, both Lambeau and the man who hired him, George Preston Marshall, were relics from an earlier NFL era. In the days when professional football was struggling to survive a depression and a world war, Lambeau and Marshall had been in the spotlight. They had put out teams that were successful on the field and at the ticket window.

But this was the beginning of a new era. By the end of the 1950s, television would beam professional football up to amazing heights.

Lambeau and Marshall realized it was coming. The Redskins-Cardinals game, a Monday night contest, would be televised live back to Washington. And Marshall had begun stringing together a network of stations to televise Redskins games far beyond Washington.

The question was, were the two old warhorses up to the task of fielding a football team good enough to capture the imagination of all those potential viewers?

\* \* \* \* \* \* \* \*

Washington's 0-5 pre-season campaign was a discouraging sign. Only the last three games had come on Lambeau's watch. But he had faced the weakest of the Redskins' opponents, and had been unable to show progress.

Was it any wonder that only 17,837 football fans were curious enough to show up at Comiskey Park on Monday, September 29, 1952, to see if Curly Lambeau could beat his old team?

To replace Lambeau, the Cardinals had hired Joe Kuharich, who had played at Notre Dame and for the Cardinals. Kuharich, coming off an unbeaten season at the University of San Francisco, was accompanied by his USF star, Ollie Matson, whom the Cardinals had drafted third overall. Matson, who was also a track star, had won two medals at the Olympics in Helsinki that summer before he integrated the Cardinals. However, even the lure of an African-American star on the heavily black South Side of Chicago failed to pump up the Cardinals' attendance that fall.

Although the Redskins were a two-touchdown underdog, they awoke from their pre-season doldrums and erupted for a 23-7 victory. "This is the biggest thrill I ever got out of football," said owner Marshall, casting aside the team's six NFL championship game appearances, including two NFL titles.

"You saw how hard we worked this week," said an exuberant Lambeau, who finally had notched his first Redskin victory. "I thought the boys did a wonderful job."

Seemingly with nothing up his sleeve, Lambeau pulled a surprise. After all the chatter about LeBaron and Gilmer, Lambeau turned to his aging player-coach, 38-year-old Sammy Baugh. The future Hall of Famer responded by completing 11 of his 15 passes, two of them for touchdowns, as the Redskins upset the injury-riddled Cardinals.

In the fourth quarter, the normally even-keeled Baugh was ejected for taking a few swings at 250-pound Cardinals lineman Don Joyce. "I was afraid to let go. No tellin' what he would have done if I'd turned him loose," Baugh said, claiming he was merely holding Joyce even though he was clearly punching. It was the first ejection of Baugh's NFL-record 16-year career.

Meanwhile, Gilmer rushed for 87 yards at halfback, leading a running game that piled up 196 yards to Chicago's 86. "I don't know whether their line was that good or ours was that bad," Kuharich said after his rough NFL coaching debut.

And this time, for a change, it was the opposing coach rather than Lambeau who was dealing with an insurrection. Kuharich defended using his star, Charley Trippi, sparingly due to a pulled thigh muscle. "We put him in for one series and he seemed a little hesitant, so we took him out," Kuharich said after Trippi rushed twice for two yards and was intercepted on his only passing attempt.

Some observers thought Kuharich was trying to keep Trippi healthy for the next game against the Bears. There was also speculation that Kuharich had angered Cardinal veterans by playing favorites with the six University of San Francisco players he had brought in. "The Cardinals have dissension, a deadly poison for any team," a Washington writer concluded after talking to Redskins who had been chatting with Cardinals at the practice field they shared during the week. Curly Lambeau was gone from the South Side of Chicago. Turmoil was not.

\* \* \* \* \* \* \* \*

Having handled the Cardinals, Lambeau quickly had another opportunity against the Packers. With the game just a short trip away in Milwaukee, the Redskins stayed in Chicago for practice. Curly even sounded excited to learn that Washington was a seven-point underdog against Green Bay, which had competed well in its 24-14 opening loss to the Bears.

"That's great," Lambeau said. "That's real good news and I hope they make 'em two-touchdown favorites. I want the other teams to be the favorites in every game this season, and most of them probably will be. I like my teams to be the underdog."

This was one of the many lessons Lambeau had learned from Knute Rockne. Once, while they were sitting at the Oliver Hotel in South Bend, "Rockne was asked to describe the kind of team he had," Rockne biographer

Ray Robinson wrote. "A grin crossed Rockne's face. 'It may be the best team I've ever had here,' he answered, 'but I'd never tell anyone that.' "

In a politically incorrect summation that reflected the times, the *Washington Star's* Redskin writer, Lewis F. Atchison, called this Packer game "the scalp [Lambeau] prized above all others in this year's race, for personal reasons."

Atchison went on to say, "It also figures to be one of the most important games in the Redskins' 16-year history in Washington. To come home with two league victories, after five exhibition defeats, would restore much of the club's shattered prestige, while a setback could be mighty painful at the box office."

The game also shaped up as critical, Atchison said, for Packers coach Gene Ronzani, "whose future with that club is reported to be dark at the moment." In other words, the stakes were unusually high for the second game of the season.

The problem was, Lambeau was concerned that his players were distracted by travel arrangements. The Redskins had been on the road for more than two months, since mid-July, when they they left Washington for training camp that opened at Occidental College in Los Angeles on July 25. After the Packer game in Milwaukee, they would fly to Washington at the end of a nearly three-month odyssey.

"All I've heard the last couple of days is, 'My car's in Indiana,' and 'Mine's in Ohio,' and 'How is your wife gonna make the trip?' " Lambeau said. "[The players'] minds are on autos and families, not the ballgame. And I don't like it. It's worse than being overconfident and it can lick us twice as fast."

Baugh, the team's quarterback and backfield coach, expressed concern that the Redskins had had a sloppy practice on Friday, which Lambeau called the best indicator of how a team would play on Sunday.

Their concerns came true. With rookie quarterback Babe Parilli leading the way, Green Bay handled the Redskins 35-20 on Sunday, October 5, 1952, before a meager 9,657 spectators at Marquette Stadium.

"The Packer team outplayed us and outgained us all the way. We were just outfought today. I have no alibis," said Lambeau, who fell to 0-4 against the team he started in 1919.

Although the Redskins had botched their opportunity to build momentum for their home opener, Lambeau disputed speculation that he and George Preston Marshall, an impatient, hands-on owner, "would inevitably clash," as *Press-Gazette* writer Lee Remmel put it. "Marshall is a wonderful man," Lambeau said. "He understands my problems and has been cooperative in every way."

Almost on cue, Marshall stepped into Lambeau's Ambassador Hotel room and voiced confidence in his longtime friend and rival, who was in his 34th season as a football mentor. "Don't try to sell us short yet. Mr. Lambeau's only had the club a little better than a month," Marshall said. "He has been handicapped by not being acquainted with personnel and by injuries. But he'll straighten those things out and, by November, I think we'll be able to take anybody in the league. I wouldn't be saying this unless I thought it was true and that's what I think."

Always opinionated, Marshall took a shot at the poor support for the Packers at Marquette Stadium.. "To me the biggest item of the day was that less than [10,000] people came to see the game," Marshall said. "If something isn't done, you'll have to play all your games in Green Bay."

Even the lure of seeing the Packers line up against the team's founder was not enough to excite Milwaukee fans, who were not nearly as supportive as Packer fans in Green Bay during lean times.

\* \* \* \* \* \* \* \*

Lambeau next turned his attention to his home debut as Washington coach against a familiar rival. For the second time in three weeks, he would be trying to beat the Cardinals.

The outlook of the two teams had changed dramatically in those two weeks. After their opening loss to Lambeau's Redskins, the Cardinals had seemed on the verge of collapse, with veteran stars resisting their unproven new coach. But running back Charley Trippi had gotten healthy—and gotten on the same wave length with rookie coach Joe Kuharich. While the Redskins were stumbling against the Packers, the Cardinals had shocked the Bears 21-10. All of a sudden, the Cardinals were the hot team and the Redskins were the team with a wobbly coach.

"Trippi's good, and this Matson showed great possibilities in our first game," Lambeau said. "But you can set up defenses for those fellows that will stop them some of the time. We can hold the Cardinals to a reasonable score if we carry out our assignments. Then it's up to our offense to get some points—a few more than the Cards—to win the game."

None of that happened. The Redskins played a listless game, losing 17-6 to the Cardinals and pretty much losing their fans and their coach in the process. Lambeau had feared that his players would be distracted by returning home after three months, and that seemed to be happening.

"The Redskins won no friends in the crowd of 24,600 who showed up at Griffith Stadium to welcome them home," Atchison concluded in the *Washington Star*. After the Cardinals, leading 7-6, scored 10 unanswered points in the fourth quarter, he said, "The slow, weary shuffle toward the exits eloquently expressed the spectators' fruition. It seemed to be the beginning of another losing season."

Putting the blame squarely on his players, Lambeau fashioned a conspiracy theory in which "the Redskins' hangdog spirit had been recognized around [the NFL] and would have to be eliminated before he could produce a winner. " For emphasis, he cut two players and threatened more changes to rub out the team's "second-division" attitude.

"The veteran coach charged certain players with refusing to work hard in practice and said others shirked contact work on the field," Atchison wrote. "Lambeau added, however, that the Redskins had enough material to produce a winner, if the club hustled and everyone gave his best. . . . Ironically, the players released today were two of the hardest workers on the squad but failed to measure up to Lambeau's expectations."

That was Lambeau. It was invariably somebody else's fault, and that was increasingly the case toward the end of his coaching career. Either the players weren't working hard enough, or weren't talented enough, or weren't listening enough. When the ranting about the players wasn't enough, it was front-office people who were the cause of the losing.

"After the game, Lambeau sat in his office brooding with two of his assistants. "The trouble is," he told a couple of writers, "my club just doesn't have enough fellows who want to win. . . badly enough."

After calling the tackling "terrible" and the blocking "terrible," Lambeau was asked what his team needed.

"A lot of hell-raising," he snapped.

After conferring with a few disappointed players, owner Marshall promised that things would get better: "By November we'll be a pretty good ball club. Right now, we're not good."

John Yonakor, a veteran Redskins tackle who had played on four straight championship teams with the Cleveland Browns, did not agree with Lambeau's claim that his team lacked a winning attitude.

"There's good *esprit de corps* on the Redskins," Yonakor said. "Damn it all, we don't have the depth of the Browns. When we have their depth, we'll win, too."

\* \* \* \* \* \* \* \*

In their next game, the Redskins found the determination that Lambeau had accused them of lacking. After blowing a 14-0 lead and trailing 17-14, Washington dug in and rallied for a 28-24 win at Pittsburgh on October 19, 1952. It helped that the winless Steelers were the kind of team that couldn't cope with success, either. But a win was a win. The Redskins were 2-2.

Much to the surprise of 22,605 spectators and the sportswriters in attendance, Pittsburgh coach Joe Bach sat Jack Spinks on the bench—after the 240-pound fullback from historically black Alcorn A&M had carried seven times for 48 yards, helping the Steelers nudge ahead of the Redskins.

"Yesterday's game was a comedy of errors—from the bench," *Pittsburgh Press* writer Pat Livingston wrote. "First of all, Bach yanked Spinks, the team's most effective ball carrier, and then in the fourth quarter he called for a quick kick on third down to set up the winning touchdown—for the Redskins."

Livingston disputed the coach's claim that Spinks came out due to a pulled leg muscle, saying that Spinks told him he injured the leg when he returned in the fourth quarter, long after Bach had benched him.

Did race have anything to do with his playing time? That subject did not come up. But fans and media continued to quiz and berate Bach for not sticking with Spinks. NFL teams were integrating slowly. Becoming comfortable with relying on their black players was an even slower process.

Spinks was the first African-American player drafted by the Steelers, and the first from Mississippi selected in the NFL draft. During his five-year NFL career, he played on the 1956 Giants championship team. He later coached at his alma mater, which became Alcorn State. The team's football stadium is named for him.

\* \* \* \* \* \* \* \*

Meanwhile, Lambeau took his Redskins back to Washington and started preparing for the monumental task of winning in Cleveland's Municipal Stadium, where the Browns had only lost three times in six years. At home and on the road, they were a dazzling 71-8-3. The Redskins were a three-touchdown underdog, a headline blared.

Always tinkering, Lambeau signed a guard, Knox Ramsey, and released a halfback, Neil Ferris. "The Redskins usually concentrate on shuffling the coaching staff, but Curly Lambeau, the fourth Washington coach in three years, is busy hiring and firing players," a *United Press* dispatch that was published nationwide reported. "He has made five changes within the last seven days." Ramsey had played for Lambeau with the Cardinals the previous season.

Complicating matters for Lambeau, legendary passer Sammy Baugh was sidelined by a hand injury, which meant that under-sized rookie Eddie LeBaron and Harry Gilmer, who divided time between halfback and quarterback, would be doing the throwing.

"We'll miss Sam, of course," Lambeau said. "But LeBaron is getting smoother and smarter, and Cleveland should be just another game for him." Lambeau dismissed reports that the Browns were vulnerable because of their many injuries. The key, he said, would be for his Redskins to be at their best.

"If we show the same spirit we displayed against the Cardinals in our opening game and against the Steelers last Sunday, and if we don't make too many mistakes, we can win," Lambeau said. "But if we play stupid football and pull too many boners, all the spirit in the world can't save us from defeat."

True to Lambeau's word, Washington played a stout game. The Redskins held a 13-6 lead at halftime and led 13-9 going into the fourth quarter. Even after Cleveland, which had been held to four Lou Groza field goals, took a 19-13 lead on a one-yard touchdown run by Otto Graham, Washington seemed poised to respond.

The Redskins moved the ball from their own 20 to the Browns 17 yardline. But Julie Rykovich fumbled, ending the hopes of three-touchdown-underdog Washington of pulling off a huge surprise. Cleveland ran out the clock, taking a safety to escape 19-15.

Since the Browns had entered the NFL in 1950, they had swept all four games against the Redskins. Noting this, some writers reminded Washington owner George Preston Marshall that he had predicted, during the NFL's war with the AAFC, that Browns players would soon be asking for jobs driving his laundry trucks. Marshall undoubtedly was aware that Browns owner Mickey McBride was employing his extra players as drivers at his Yellow Cab Company, a ploy that gave birth to the phrase Taxi Squad.

After this loss to Cleveland, though, Marshall was fuming rather than joking. "A couple of officials were out to get us and they did," he said.

"Some of the worst officiating I've ever seen," said Lambeau, joining Marshall in a chorus of griping. At the end of the game, Lambeau rushed at back judge Hinkey Haines, claiming the Redskins had time for one more play. Washington center Al Demao stepped in, preventing Lambeau from doing something he would regret.

Curly and Hinkey Haines were longtime rivals. After batting .160 as a reserve outfielder and pinch runner on the 1923 World-Series-winning Yankees, Haines played for six season on the NFL Giants and Staten Island Stapletons. The quarterback on the 1927 NFL champion Giants, Haines is the only athlete to play on World Series and NFL championship teams.

A transcript of the Lambeau-Haines conversation at the end of the Browns come-from-behind victory would make for interesting, profanity-laced reading.

Marshall and Lambeau reportedly planned to file a loud protest with NFL commissioner Bert Bell. Although they knew that wasn't going to change anything, complaining about officiating was something they could agree on. That would not always be the case.

\* \* \* \* \* \* \* \*

Next up on Washington's odd schedule was a rematch with the Steelers. Having played the Cardinals twice in three games, the Redskins now would do the same with Pittsburgh. And as with the Cardinals, the Steelers had scored an impressive victory in between Lambeau encounters by stopping the three-game winning streak of the Cardinals.

Once again, Lambeau's team was unable to win in Washington against a team it had recently beaten on the road. Following the Cardinals' lead, the Steelers beat the Redskins 24-23 on November 2.

Lambeau was said to be "at a loss to explain the slipshod football" that left him and 25,866 Washington fans frustrated. After giving up touchdowns on a blocked-field-goal return and a punt return to fall behind 24-9, the Redskins rallied for a safety and two touchdowns in the fourth quarter to come up one point short.

The defeat left the Redskins with a 2-4 record, tied with Pittsburgh for last place in the American Conference. In the whole NFL, only the Dallas Texans (0-6) had a worse record. And they would be regrouping a year later in Baltimore.

Marshall walked back his promise that the Redskins would be a good team by November. He did, however, stand by his coach.

"Curly will be back next year even if he doesn't win another game," the Washington owner said. "He's on his way with this team, but he'll need another year to finish the job—and we're going to finish it. The Redskins will be back on top in another year."

The slide continued for three more games, extending Washington's losing streak to six games and dropping the team's record to 2-8. But then, just as surprisingly, Lambeau's Redskins defeated the Giants and the Eagles in their final two games. The losses kept both teams from sharing the American Conference title with Cleveland and forcing a playoff.

"We've got the nucleus for a damned good team and we're going to have it," Lambeau said after Washington had defeated Philadelphia 27-21 in its final game on December 14 before 22,468 at its Griffith Stadium home. "It just proved we can beat the good ones," owner Marshall said. "We're on our way."

Sammy Baugh, one of the best quarterbacks of his or any other era, had just completed his NFL-record 16-year career. His successor, Eddie LeBaron, had just completed a promising first season in which he made the NFL's All-Rookie team. But whether LeBaron was capable of being a consistent winner remained an open question.

After appearing in the NFL championship game six times in 10 seasons, the Redskin franchise had gone seven seasons without even coming close to that kind of success. Only once in those seven seasons had Washington even won more games than it lost.

Championships continued to be the expectation of George Preston Marshall and his coach, Curly Lambeau. The question was, did they know how to get there?

Marshall's steadfast opposition to hiring African-American players greatly hindered Washington's ability to compete at the highest level. That deplorable stance was one of the many reasons he left a tarnished legacy despite a colorful, innovative career. Lambeau had not had a black player on any of his teams since the NFL started integrating after World War II. That might have helped him in Green Bay. It certainly would have enhanced the Cardinals' box-office appeal on the South Side of Chicago. As the Redskins coach, Lambeau occasionally expressed an interest in having talented black players. But he did not rock Marshall's boat.

Like the Redskins, Curly Lambeau had not known glory lately. Since winning his last championship in 1944, he had gone 34-56-1 in eight seasons with the Packers, Cardinals and Redskins. Before that, in the first 24 years of his career, his record had been 186-71-20. After averaging fewer than three losses for 24 years, Lambeau had averaged seven losses a season for the next eight years.

Curly's first season in Washington had ended on a high note, though, building hopes that he could be a coaching force in the NFL again. The final two wins, which spoiled the seasons of the Giants and the Eagles, were very encouraging.

"Each had a title chance until they met the Redskins in the final two games, and the 'Skins beat them both.. . . . Lambeau did a magnificent job of coaching and ought to be able to cash in next season," Washington-based *Los Angeles Times* columnist Bill Henry wrote before Christmas of 1952, already hyping the 1953 exhibition meeting between the Rams and the Redskins, a charity fund-raising contest sponsored by his newspaper.

Meanwhile, in Chicago, his successor with the Cardinals, Joe Kuharich, was cashiered on January 28 after just one season by managing director Walter Wolfner, Violet Bidwill's impetuous husband. Kuharich had gotten off to a great start, winning three of his first four games and prompting Wolfner to predict a championship. Then the Cardinals lost seven of their final eight, and Wolfner lost interest in Kuharich. Joe Stydahar was hired to replace him on January 29. And so, another shovel full of dirt was added to "the graveyard of coaches."

On Tuesday afternoon, December 16, barely 48 hours after the season ended, Lambeau departed for a three-week escape to California. After the 4-8 disappointment of 1952, he already was pondering the changes he had in mind for 1953. He would need a new assistant to replace player-coach Sammy Baugh, who was retiring. He also would be looking for quarterback depth and upgrades at other positions.

# 69
## *A SECOND TERM IN WASHINGTON*

Lambeau's first season in Washington had not gone well. But as the calendar turned from 1952 to 1953, Redskins owner Marshall, who was usually impatient, seemed hypnotized by old friend Lambeau. Still operating under their handshake agreement— Coaching contracts, the owner said, "aren't worth 15 cents."—Lambeau dug in on his off-season roster-building plans.

On the West Coast, Lambeau checked out Al Dorow, a former Michigan State passer who filled his need for quarterback depth, at the Poinsettia Bowl on December 20 in San Diego. Dorow had been drafted by Washington a year earlier, but was fulfilling his two-year military obligation playing for the Bolling Air Force Base Generals, conveniently located in Washington, D.C.

Despite a downpour that turned the field into a muddy mess, Dorow led Bolling to a 35-14 victory over the San Diego Naval Training Center. Lambeau must have liked what he saw. But he wouldn't see Dorow in a Redskin uniform until the 1954 training camp.

Lambeau also kept a close eye on the East-West Shrine game in San Francisco and the Rose Bowl. And he attended the Pro Bowl on January 10 at the Coliseum, where he stopped by the press box to chat with his many media friends.

By mid-January, he was back in Washington. Battling a serious flu bout, Curly went to Doctors Hospital on January 16 and remained there until January 20. While he was there, assistant Marvin Bass resigned to take a coaching job at North Carolina. Since player/coach Sammy Baugh was not returning, Lambeau now needed to fill two openings on his staff of three assistants.

Before the draft, Lambeau was quoted as saying he would be "delighted" to obtain the services of a black player like Tank Younger, an undrafted running back from Grambling who had joined the Rams in 1949. The first player from a historically black school to play in the NFL, Younger was named to four Pro Bowl teams.

But Redskins owner George Preston Marshall, whose legacy is steeped in racism, steadfastly opposed integrating his roster. Incredibly, Washington would not have a black player for another decade, 16 years after the Rams integrated the NFL after World War II.

"[Marshall] caved in, finally, when Interior Secretary Stewart Udall issued an ultimatum: Sign a black player or be denied use of the new 54,000-seat D.C. Stadium (later named RFK for Robert F. Kennedy) that the government had paid for, and to hell with the 30-year lease Marshall had signed," legendary *Washington Post* columnist Shirley Povich wrote. "Marshall's chief response was to make Ernie Davis, Syracuse's All-American running back, his No. 1 draft choice for 1962. Ernie Davis' response was: "I won't play for that S.O.B. He demanded to be traded and was, to Cleveland for all-pro halfback Bobby Mitchell, [one of three black players on the 1962 Redskins]. The Ernie Davis tale had a sad denouement; he developed cancer and died in 1963, never playing a down for Cleveland."

After all of his West Coast scouting, Lambeau took two players from nearby Maryland—All-America quarterback Jack Scarbath and defensive tackle Dick Modzelewski—with his first two picks at the NFL draft on January 22, 1953, at the Bellevue-Stratford Hotel in Philadelphia. They were good picks from a good team, which also included future Hall of Famer Stan Jones, a defensive tackle taken in the fifth round by the Bears. Maryland had won its first seven games, rising to second in the national rankings, beating Georgia and LSU before losing to Ole Miss and Alabama.

After the draft, Lambeau returned to California sunshine. Lambeau, one Southern California newspaper noted, "spends the off-season at his chicken ranch in Thousand Oaks, California."

On March 24, he was among the more than 600 attending a dinner at the Ambassador Hotel in Los Angeles to honor *Los Angeles Herald-Express* sportswriter George T. Davis, who was celebrating his 25th year in newspapering. "There are two types of columnists," Davis had once said. "The Gee Whiz writer and the Aw Nuts writer. A long time ago, I decided we had enough Aw Nuts writers."

Listing the many sports celebrities at the Davis dinner, *L.A. Times* columnist Dick Hyland mentioned Lambeau, "who knows more pro football than any other man in the game, including Paul Brown and George Halas." Despite Curly's faltering record on the field, his reputation remained strong.

His Thousand Oaks chicken ranch apparently in good hands, Lambeau returned to Washington on April 28 with George Preston Marshall and announced a deal to acquire halfback Paul Barry and guard Bill Lange from the Rams for Washington's third-round draft pick in 1954.

On Friday night, May 1, Curly and Marshall made the 15-mile trip to the University of Maryland to watch Scarbath and Modzelewski play in the school's Varsity-Alumni game. Scarbath, who wanted more money, remained unsigned.

While in Washington, Lambeau sharply criticized college football's decision to bar free substitution and return to iron-man football in which players played both offense and defense. "[It] will wreck John Public's interest in the game," he said. "And it's John Public who pays the freight. It's no good. It won't last." As an example, Lambeau mentioned Rams quarterback Norm Van Brocklin, the NFL's top passer in 1952. "The boy can't play defense at all and you guys can run faster than he can," Lambeau told reporters. "If the two-platoon system had not been in operation when Van Brocklin was at Oregon, we'd never have heard of him."

Lambeau was right, of course. It's unthinkable to imagine Johnny Unitas or Bart Starr, or Tom Brady or Peyton Manning, forced to play defense in the NFL. Brought back by NCAA rules makers in an effort to reduce the size of rosters and save money, the rules barring free substitution were gradually reduced over the next 11 years. By 1964, free substitution was unrestricted. As Lambeau had said, it produced a better game, which produced a bigger audience.

Departing Washington, Lambeau spent Mother's Day weekend in Green Bay visiting his mother, Mary, his son, Donald, and grandchildren, and two brothers and a sister.

After snubbing Marshall's initial offers, Scarbath, who had finished second in the Heisman Trophy voting to Oklahoma halfback Billy Vessels, finally agreed to terms on June 18. "Curly said Scarbath's wrangle over money with [Marshall] was a 'good sign' that the boy could think," the *Washington Star* reported.

To round out his coaching staff, Lambeau hired Larry Siemering and Bill Dudley. Siemering had been Eddie LeBaron's head coach at the University of the Pacific (1947-50). Dudley, a beloved Redskins halfback who had retired a year earlier, came back as a player/coach. A Pro Football Hall of Fame member, he is the only player to score touchdowns by rushing, passing, pass receiving, punt return, kickoff return, interception return and fumble return.

Herman Ball, the only assistant coach who returned in 1953 from Lambeau's first staff, went to the West Coast to discuss strategy with Curly in late June. Although LeBaron said Lambeau was focused on defense in Washington, Ball said most of their planning centered around offense, especially the passing game.

"After all, he was a pupil of Knute Rockne's. Curly's one of the most pass-conscious coaches in the league," Ball said, noting that Lambeau was the first NFL coach to pass from behind the goal.

"There are any number of reasons why I'm confident my team will be tougher," Lambeau said. "One of them is the fact that Eddie LeBaron has a year's pro experience under his belt and with Sammy Baugh gone, now is the boss of the whole show. This kid just can't miss being a great quarterback."

On July 3, Lambeau went to Gilmore Field in Los Angeles to see the Hollywood Stars, especially Dale Long, the Stars' 6-foot-4, 205-pound first baseman/outfielder. Lambeau had tried to sign him to play for the Packers in 1944, when Long was fresh out of high school.

"Man, not for me," Long recalled. "I went out to practice and I saw those monsters ripping the practice dummies out of their mooring. I thought I'd like baseball a lot better right then."

"You did the right thing," Lambeau told him even though Long, 27, would not establish himself as a big leaguer for two more years. "In football you'd be nearing the end. I'd say for nine out of ten boys who show talent in both football and baseball, it's wiser for them to choose baseball. In baseball, they have 10 years or more but in pro football, you generally go for only five. And less than that at times."

Again, Lambeau's assessment proved to be accurate. After an 11-year apprenticeship in the minors, Long finally reached the major leagues to stay in 1955, when he was 29. By the time he retired at age 37 in 1963, he had appeared in an All-Star game as a Pirate, won a World Series as a Yankee and become, as a Cub, the first left-handed catcher in the major leagues in 56 years.

Lambeau gathered his assistant coaches on July 20 to prepare for the start of training camp on July 27 at Occidental College in Los Angeles. Thirteen players who left Washington by train on July 23 were joined by 11 who boarded in Chicago, and seven more along the way.

When the Grand Canyon Limited finally arrived in Los Angeles on July 26, the *Los Angeles Times* noted, it was carrying a Redskin contingent of "31 large and burly citizens." Nineteen other players arrived on their own.

Many of the faces were either new or preparing to play new positions. "Lambeau has made more changes in personnel assignments than a new administration in Washington," the *Washington Star* Redskin writer Lewis F. Atchison noted on August 2, 1953.

Lambeau had unapologetically fashioned a team that emphasized size rather than speed. It had no breakaway offensive threats—and Lambeau seemed inclined to replace his best quarterback—small, but skilled and agile Eddie LeBaron—with his rookie quarterback, Maryland All-American Jack

Scarbath, who had a bigger body and a better arm, but would be learning on the job.

For the third straight pre-season, the Redskins opened with a pair of losses—to the 49ers in San Francisco and the Rams in Los Angeles. At least the 20-7 loss on August 19 to the Rams, which drew more than 80,000 each year, was a box-office hit against a perennial power.

"All in all, it wasn't a bad showing for a team admittedly not ready to play one as rugged and as far advanced as the Rams," Atchison concluded after speaking with Lambeau, who wasn't overly concerned with the setback. The Rams, after all, had started training camp July 13, two weeks earlier than the Redskins, and had played a pair of tuneups against military teams before playing Washington.

After the 7-0 loss to the 49ers on August 30, Lambeau's biggest concern was injured quarterbacks. LeBaron, the incumbent, was hobbled by a knee injury that would sideline him for Washington's next game, and possibly longer. That left rookie Scarbath playing while recovering from a fractured index finger on his throwing hand. Veteran halfback Harry Gilmer, who also played quarterback, was the next option.

Quarterback issues or not, Lambeau "blasted his men's failure to 'think,' and vowed to work them hard before their next game. "They thought they had a soft touch in the 49ers," Lambeau said. "I saw it coming and I tried to warn them, but they wouldn't listen to me. We lost the game through stupid mistakes—nothing else. And I don't mind telling you I'm burned up about it."

To fix the problem, the *Washington Star* reported, "Lambeau and his assistants spent most of yesterday discussing ways of getting the lead out of the squad's shoes. Curly complained that the team looked 'dead' on the field, and showed no appetite for the work,"

In the 21st Century, pre-season games in the NFL are primarily exhibitions in which players are trying to work on their timing or merely trying to earn a roster spot. Top players appear sparingly, or sit out. Ironically, pro football disdains the word "exhibition" in modern times.

In the mid-20th Century, though, when pre-season games were commonly known as exhibition games, they were generally more than that. Winning mattered more—to drum up ticket sales for the regular season, and for pride and bragging rights as well as roster spots. In the 1950s, a win was a win, pre-season or not, to a greater degree than it would be decades later.

When George Halas announced his retirement on January 24, 1955, for example, the *Chicago Tribune* credited him with 357 wins, more than any other coach, professional or college. Pop Warner, who had 313 college wins, and Amos Alonzo Stagg, who had 299 college wins, were second and third. Lambeau was fourth, with 255 wins.

At that point, however, Halas had 236 regular-season NFL wins in 29 years. The *Tribune* apparently gave him credit for 121 "exhibition" wins. Meanwhile, Lambeau had 226 regular-season NFL wins in his 33 years, so he seemed to have 29 "exhibition" wins. He actually won far more unofficial games—including 37 just from 1935-49, his last 15 years with the Packers.

It's difficult to say how the *Tribune* arrived at those win totals in 1955. It is clear, though, that non-league games had a higher value when Halas and Lambeau were trying to keep their franchises profitable by playing so-called exhibition games.

And so, when Curly Lambeau took his Redskins to Chicago immediately after their game in San Francisco, he was intent on winning the next game, exhibition or not. After some practice days in Chicago, Washington would play the Packers in Green Bay. Not only had his club failed to measure up in San Francisco; Lambeau now was going home to face the team he had founded on a dream and, according to the legend, on $500 from his packing-company boss.

Not that he needed to be reminded, but everyone was mentioning that Curly had lined up four times against the Packers since leaving Green Bay and had lost all four games.

In a pair of exhibition openers designed to attract a crowd, Lambeau had brought his Chicago Cardinals to Green Bay twice, in 1950 and 1951, and lost by identical 17-14 scores. After taking over the Redskins during training camp in 1952, he had lost a pre-season game against the Packers in Kansas City 13-7 and then lost to Green Bay in Milwaukee 35-20 in a regular-season meeting. Adding insult to injury, all four of Lambeau's losses had come against the man who followed him as Green Bay coach, Gene Ronzani.

Or, as the *Green Bay Press-Gazette* noted, "The burly Italian [who] succeeded the big Belgian at Green Bay's helm" in 1950 was 4-for-4 against The Man Who Invented the Green Bay Packers. "If you're superstitious, this means that Lambeau will have the law of averages on his side," the *Press-Gazette* said on Sept 5. Curly's chances of winning seemed to be more about talent and execution than superstition and the law of averages, though.

Surprisingly, this was the Redskins' first game in Green Bay since they had moved to Washington from Boston in 1937. The previous six regular-season meetings between the Packers and the Washington Redskins in Wisconsin had all taken place in Milwaukee. And while the teams regularly met in the pre-season, all of those games, except for one in Milwaukee, were played outside of Wisconsin.

After a few steamy days of practice in Chicago, Marshall, Lambeau and the rest of the Redskin party took a North Western train to Green Bay on Friday afternoon, September 4. Escaping the 100-degree heat in Chicago, they practiced at City Stadium that night. After practice, Lambeau "spent considerable time with his mother, Mrs. Marcel Lambeau."

Noting that this was his first trip to Green Bay since his Boston Redskins played there in 1932, Marshall held court with the media, anticipating a big year from Green Bay legend Curly Lambeau, his longtime friend and second-year coach. "I'm ashamed to say that we are carrying 43 players. Way too many," Marshall said, indicating with blustery hyperbole that "the excellent material has made it difficult for Coach Curly Lambeau to cut." Interviewed by Clair Stone on WBAY-TV, Marshall watched the Redskins practice at City Stadium, "had dinner at the Northland, sat around the lobby chatting with old friends, including former Packer line coach Tarz Taylor, and then spent a few hours at a supper club."

Washington general manager Dick McCann was impressed by the turnout to see Lambeau at the Redskins practice. "Curly had to take time out to shake hands with about 70 people —lots of his old friends. You know, coming back here, his home, must do something to a man. It gave me a lump in my throat."

That, of course, was a measure of how much The Man Who Invented the Green Bay Packers meant to the people of his home town. Never mind that Lambeau had left under acrimonious circumstances. He had given Green Bay the gift of football. And for that, he would always be revered.

Also pumped up for this game was Washington defensive tackle Paul Lipscomb. Undrafted out of Tennessee, he was signed by the sharp-eyed Lambeau in 1945 and was a five-year starter for the Packers before he was traded to Washington for offensive lineman Len Szafaryn.

"I'd rather win this one than a championship playoff. I'm gonna give 'em everything," said Lipscomb, who had a lot to give. He was named to the Pro Bowl in each of his first four seasons as a Redskin.

Lambeau also had a lot on the line. It was Washington's first-ever trip to Green Bay. He was trying to notch his first win against the Packers. He was giving rookie Jack Scarbath his first NFL start. And the Redskins were looking for their first win of the season.

Lambeau was especially animated during the game. Although 55 and in his 35th season leading a pro football team, he exhorted his team with "Let's get some zip! Let's get some life out there!" After a Packer first down, he shouted angrily, "What the hell's the matter with the defense on that side out there?"

One possible explanation for his nervous energy. Missing from Lambeau's sideline routine was his familiar cigarette, which he had traded for chewing gum during the game.

"Always a chain-smoker on the sidelines during his years here," the *Press-Gazette's* Lee Remmel noted, "Lambeau replaced the `weed' with chewing gum throughout Saturday night's contest. Asked for an explanation, he reported, `I quit smoking,' while flicking ashes from his cigarette." For this game, at least, he had abandoned his public chain-smoking sideline habit.

Led by Lipscomb and Scarbath, the Redskins gave Curly his first win in five tries against the Packers, 13-6, before a modest crowd of 16,425 at Green Bay's City Stadium on Saturday night, September 5, 1953. Bothered by the injured index finger on his throwing hand, Scarbath completed only 5 of 22 passes for 45 yards. But he ran three yards for the winning touchdown after putting Washington in scoring position with a 35-yard run. Halfback Harry Gilmer scored the Redskins' first touchdown on a 68-yard punt return.

"The boys got mad at themselves and played themselves a ball game. That's all there's to it," Lambeau said, singling out Lipscomb—``Paul had one of the best days I've seen him have in a long time."— and Scarbath: "He's only been with us since the All-Star game [on August 14]. I thought he did a great job for a rookie. And, do you know, he reported to us with a broken finger."

Although encouraged by the win, Lambeau downplayed the Redskins' potential. "Curly would not begin to speculate on a divisional title for his team in 1953. In fact, he indicated displeasure that anyone might voice such a thought. "We're definitely not talking championship this year," Curly declared, flatly. "We're talking it for '54. We don't have it yet but we could pester a lot of clubs—and I think we will."

The joy was short-lived. Washington followed its Packer win with a trio of losses in its final three pre-season games, finishing the exhibition season with a record of 1-5. The final loss, 9-3 to the Colts, a newly awarded franchise playing its first game in Baltimore, was especially discouraging. The Redskins had a boggling 10 turnovers.

"How can you win a game when you fumble six times. . . [and] they intercept four passes?" owner Marshall said. Lambeau rounded up the usual suspects—his players—saying, "Ever since we started training, they've been doping off in practice. Putting out on Sunday isn't enough."

Rookie quarterback Scarbath, who had the big arm and body preferred for NFL success, was struggling. And nimble little Eddie LeBaron, supposedly recovered from his knee injury, wasn't the answer, either.

"This is a pretty sad professional football squad that George Marshall and Curly Lambeau are bringing to town, perhaps the worst of all peacetime Redskin outfits," *Washington Star* columnist Francis Stann said glumly.

In their regular-season opener, though, the Redskins found a way, beating the Chicago Cardinals at Comiskey Park before just 16,055 spectators. Trailing 13-7 in the fourth quarter, Washington erupted for 17 points to win 24-13. "I love it," Lambeau said, happy to win although his team had given up 109 more yards than it had gained. "Let them have the statistics. Just give us the points."

The Redskins over-achieved again the next week, playing the favored Eagles to a 21-21 tie at Connie Mack Stadium on Friday night, October 2, despite being rocked by injuries and being outgained by nearly 100 yards,

That made the Skins 1-0-1 and built confidence. Lambeau signed end Fran "Pussyfoot" Polsfoot, a receiver he had drafted with the Cardinals. In Chicago, Polsfoot had had two big seasons for Lambeau, catching 95 passes, including 10 for touchdowns. Sidelined by a knee injury in 1952, Polsfoot was released by the Cardinals. Curly believed Polsfoot's surgically repaired knee was now healthy.

"Lambeau told [Washington] Touchdown Club members that he thinks the Redskins will be a championship contender because they should get better," the *Washington Star* reported. "It was a bold statement, made before the entire squad and coaching staff, but Curly has said it before and some folks are beginning to believe it."

Next came the Redskins' home opener. With 26,241 curious fans looking on at Griffith Stadium, Lambeau's squad handled the New York Giants 13-9. Jack Scarbath threw a 38-yard touchdown to give Washington an early 10-0 lead. But when Scarbath threw an interception that was returned 18 yards by Frank Gifford for a touchdown in the second quarter, Lambeau put in Eddie LeBaron to quarterback the second half, with instructions to keep the ball on the ground.

Neither the Giants nor the Cardinals were very good; they would combine for only four wins that fall. But how good were the Redskins? After their miserable 1-5 pre-season, the 2-0-1 start to the regular season, their best since 1946, had Washington wondering. The Redskins would play the Browns, a perennial power, in their fourth game. That would tell a lot.

"I saw every play of the Cleveland-Philadelphia game on television," Lambeau said, "and the Browns have a great team. They're simply great. But we'll show up for the game."

An eager crowd of 33,963 turned out on October 18, 1953, to see if Lambeau's squad could work more magic. They left Griffith Stadium disappointed. The Redskins were humbled by the Browns 30-14. "We tried to play it safe," an unnamed Redskin said. "We were too careful for our own good."

A curious newspaper headline blared, "Browns Convince Redskins Second Place Should Be Their Goal." Was Lambeau lowering his sights? His meandering post-game remarks seemed to indicate that. But then he abruptly seemed to say Washington could still win the division.

"It doesn't hurt too much to lose to a club like the Browns," he said.``They're great. . . . they've got it all. . . . Look, one defeat doesn't mean we won't be contenders. Cleveland will get beat once or twice, too. Maybe more. . . . They can get all get licked. They can all go over the hill in a big hurry. I've seen it happen. I've been in this game a long time."

In trying to give some good quotes, Lambeau had left some sportswriters scratching their heads. "When the group in Lambeau's office disbanded, one of the bystanders said to another, "When I first heard Curly talking I thought he said Cleveland was great and doesn't make any mistakes, and when I walked out I thought he said they could be beaten several times."

"That's right, said the other. "Puzzling, isn't it?"

A possible explanation: Curly was trying to downplay his team, the way he had learned from Knute Rockne. But his inclination to sell his team kept getting in the way.

There was no spinning, however, after the Skins' short trip to Baltimore ended in a 27-17 loss to the surprising Colts. "No comment," Lambeau said before using an explanation that would one day become a coaching cliche. "I won't have anything to say before Tuesday, after we've seen the pictures."

In their first season in Baltimore, the fledgling Colts had shown surprising muscle. With their win over Washington, they improved to 3-2. But then reality set in. They lost their last seven games.

By Tuesday, Lambeau's film session was forgotten. Everyone had moved on to the next challenge, a quick rematch with the Browns in Cleveland. With a roster decimated by injuries, Washington's prospects were not looking good. Lambeau's team gamely hung around, though, trailing by a mere 6-3 at halftime before stumbling to a 27-3 loss to the powerful Browns.

Burdened by a three-game losing streak and a lengthy injured list, the Redskins dug in and defeated the winless Cardinals 28-17. But it wasn't easy. Trailing 17-14 in the fourth quarter, Washington pulled away with a pair of short rushing touchdowns by Leon Heath. "We have a bunch of guys who won't quit," Lambeau said. "They played like old pros—strictly on guts."

That set up a meeting with Lambeau's ancient rival, George Halas, who brought his sagging Chicago Bears to Washington with only one win in their seven games. Unfortunately for Curly, the slumbering Bears awoke and knocked off the Redskins 27-24. Eddie Macon, the Bears' first black player, caught the game-winning touchdown, a 10-yard pass from George Blanda.

With the loss to the Bears (2-5-1), the Redskins (3-4-1) dropped into fourth place behind the unbeaten Browns (8-0), the Eagles (5-2-1) and the Steelers (4-4). That made their goal of finishing second to Cleveland, and earning the second-place consolation money that came with it, much more difficult. It was a frustrating day. Not only had the Bears looked beatable. Curly hated losing to Halas.

"We just got the pants whipped off of us," said Lambeau, who later launched into a detailed explanation for why his roster wasn't good enough. It boiled down to his players not being talented enough or being in good enough shape.

"I can't talk freely," he said. "I can't discuss what we need to replace this man and that man. But I'll say this: We've got a lot of correcting to do before we can become a winner. . . . [And] We're not in physical condition."

Asked if there was anything he could do about conditioning, "Lambeau didn't answer. He discarded a dark brown filter in his cigarette holder for a fresh one and lighted another smoke," *Washington Star* columnist Francis Stann said. In his later years, Lambeau had a reputation for letting his players get themselves into shape, rather than having a conditioning routine. Whether he was being lazy or trusting, the results translated into another sign of a coach in decline.

In another alibi/lament, Lambeau and Marshall also said Scarbath was held back by playing in the College All-Star game, which delayed their new quarterback's arrival at Redskins training camp. "The result is that he can't call plays like LeBaron," said a source "close to the inner circles of the Redskins."

"Lambeau is a strange man to interview after a losing game," Stann wrote. "You really don't interview him, you just wait in his office, watching him chain-smoke, and now and then he suddenly will pop up with a remark. Curly is one of those coaches who can't shrug off a defeat. He broods and takes it home with him and suffers for a week. Losing a ball game, even at this stage when it's evident the Redskins aren't going anywhere, is tragic to Lambeau."

In other words, Lambeau still had a fierce determination to win. But as players had been saying since his Packers teams began to decline after World War II, he no longer had the gift for building a winning team.

Although open to modern innovations like film study, he lamented his team's lack of conditioning instead of taking steps to address that. He was open to trying new offensive and defensive variations, but he still clung to many of his old ways.

And he was 55 years old. In future generations, that would put him in his prime. In Lambeau's era, that was old. Also, he had been overseeing pro football teams for 35 seasons. He not only was not going to muster the intensity of younger coaches. He now had a chicken-and-cattle ranch in Thousand Oaks among the many distractions in his life. And decades of heavy smoking could not have been good for his health. At that point, Lambeau may have still had the will to win. He simply no longer seemed able to win consistently.

Another major problem was that Marshall steadfastly refused to use black players. As *Washington Post* columnist Shirley Povich wrote, "the Redskins' colors are burgundy, gold and Caucasian." Marshall "bristled" at that notion, Povich said, but "For the 24 years when he was identified as the leading racist in the NFL, he simply stared down the criticism of his refusal to sign a black player. It was the only subject on which the voluble Marshall never expressed a public opinion, never resorted to a quip."

The example of Macon's game-winning touchdown for the Bears and the NFL's rising number of talented African-Americans failed to sway Marshall, who apparently opposed integrating the Redskins for what he considered business as well as racist reasons. He was trying to grow Washington's network of Southern television stations and the team's image as the South's pro football squad. The fight song his wife had written contained the line "Fight for Old Dixie," which was later changed to "Fight for Old D.C."

Before the 1953 draft, Lambeau had expressed a willingness to use black players like Tank Younger, an undrafted running back from Grambling who joined the Rams in 1949 and earned Pro Bowl honors four times. But that was a no-fly zone for Redskins owner Marshall. And Lambeau never did knowingly have a black player on his roster during his 35 years in the

NFL. Although African-Americans were not welcome in the NFL during most of Lambeau's career, that was no way to win in the integrated NFL of the 1950s.

\* \* \* \* \* \* \* \*

For Lambeau to whine and alibi after a loss was one thing. Berating and threatening his players after *a victory* took matters to another level. But that's what he did after the Redskins beat the Giants 24-21 on November 22, 1953.

At first glance, the game seems like it should have been a cause for celebration. Washington was on the road and considered the underdog. It had rallied back from a 14-0 halftime deficit to take a 24-14 lead before winning 24-21 in front of a meager 16,887 at the Polo Grounds. On top of that, injuries had left the Skins, the *Washington Star* said, "taped together like a 1914 flying machine."

And yet, the banner headline in the *Washington Star* the next day said, "Lambeau to Fire Some 'Loafing' Redskins as Morale Measure." Underneath that, a smaller headline said, "At Least 4 Men Are in Disfavor Despite Victory."

Rather than celebrate a win that kept Washington in the hunt for second place, Lambeau complained that "it isn't fair for injured players to carry the load while a few able-bodied teammates go along for the ride." In an era where the average NFL salary was less than $6,000, the $400 bonus that came with second place was a serious goal.

Lambeau declined to identify the four loafers he planned to fire. He gave an impassioned halftime speech that pumped up his team to rally against their longtime rivals from New York, who lost despite piling up eight more first downs and nearly 80 more yards.

"If I don't take action now, we won't have a ball club to play Pittsburgh next Sunday," Lambeau said in his curious rant. Was he genuinely concerned about loafers? Or was he trying to keep his team fired up with curious prodding?

Despite this apparent crisis, Lambeau left town for a speaking engagement in Charlotte, North Carolina, on Monday night, then referred the "loafing" matter to Washington general manager Dick McCann. Speaking at a Charlotte Quarterback Club dinner, Lambeau did not address his conspiracy theory about lazy players, which fit neatly into Washington of the early 1950s. On Capitol Hill, Senator Joe McCarthy—who was from

Appleton, just down the Fox Valley from Green Bay—was fist-pounding about Communists.

Lambeau did tell a story in Charlotte about "the greatest football player of them all," Don Hutson, who returned to a game after being knocked unconscious and caught a pair of touchdowns in the final three minutes to give Green Bay a 14-0 win. He wrapped up that tale with a "criticism of modern players: 'They quit too quickly.' "

It was a dramatic story, but the details were murky. Lambeau probably was referring to a game in Chicago in 1935 where Hutson caught two touchdowns in the final 3½ minutes for a stunning 17-14 Packer win. In Green Bay's only 14-0 win when Hutson was on the team, at Detroit in 1944, Hutson scored neither touchdown, and both came in the first half. But that was Curly—making his point, even if the facts were confused.

Meanwhile, a scene that could only happen in Green Bay was being played out. With two games left, the Packers' executive committee told Lambeau's successor, Gene Ronzani, he needed to resign or be fired. After Green Bay's Thanksgiving Day loss in Detroit 34-15, Ronzani resigned on November 27. The board appointed his assistants to lead the team for its two remaining games, at San Francisco and Los Angeles.

Ronzani, however, did not leave. He remained in his office from Friday until Tuesday morning, when the team boarded a train for San Francisco. The Packers, who wouldn't arrive until Thursday afternoon, flew to virtually all of their games at that point. But they went by train to the West Coast because Ronzani was afraid to fly over the Rocky Mountains.

Paying for his own ticket, Ronzani accompanied the Packers on the trip, his presence creating a unique distraction. Although barred from the Green Bay locker room before the game, Ronzani was taken to dinner after the game by his former players.

Dismissing the coach with two games to go didn't change Green Bay's losing ways. The fell to the 49ers 48-14 and to the Rams 33-17. Whatever the civilian businessmen in charge of the Packers had in mind by forcing Ronzani out early, all they had accomplished was creating a strange sideshow at the end of another disappointing season. They were wielding the power they had gained when Lambeau had left. But the Packers continued to be a floundering franchise.

In Washington, the Redskins were engaged in their own soap opera. While Lambeau was speaking in Charlotte, owner Marshall announced that fullback Chuck Drazenovich had been suspended for "improper attitude." A shocked Drazenovich heard about it from reporters after receiving treatment for a nagging knee injury from a doctor.

"I don't know what to say," said Drazenovich. "This really knocked me. Curly told me he wanted to see me Tuesday, but I didn't expect anything like this."

"I know nothing about the case, but I'll back up my coach," Marshall said.

The discontent with Drazenovich was curious. The NCAA heavyweight boxing champion in 1950 as well as a standout fullback at Penn State, he had played only sparingly since aggravating the knee injury in the fourth game of Washington's season. After he limped off the field in the first half at New York on Sunday, Lambeau told him he didn't need to return. But later, Curly said Drazenovich should have insisted on playing in the second half.

What was Curly thinking? It's possible he wanted to make an example of someone. He often did that. The Redskins, he said, were a divided squad, "the rough and ready group that wants to win, and the other group that wants to win, but not enough." He said he would never discipline an injured player without talking to the team's medical staff. But that seems to be what he did.

The whole incident seems to have been more about Lambeau than it was about Drazenovich, who apparently was caught in Curly's conspiracy theory about players who were not 100 percent committed to winning. If Drazenovich had privately questioned Lambeau's leadership, he wouldn't be the first dedicated player who didn't see eye to eye with The Man Who Invented the Green Bay Packers. There was no public mention of that, though.

When Lambeau finally met with Drazenovich on Wednesday after talking to his doctor, the coach reversed his field, reinstating Drazenovich. "I'll work like the dickens to get my knee in shape for Sunday," Drazenovich said, although it was not clear how he expected to do that.

Drazenovich, it turned out, was playing despite a serious knee injury. Five days after Washington's last game, he underwent knee surgery on December 18, hobbling on crutches through the holiday season. He originally injured the knee in a September exhibition against the Steelers and had been limited all season. Despite that, he was the only Redskin to receive an honorable mention on the official All-Pro team for 1953. He went on to play six more seasons with the Redskins, primarily as a middle linebacker, including four Pro Bowl seasons. After retiring, he was on the Redskins' radio broadcast team for four seasons. It was hardly the resume of a slacker.

In other words, why Lambeau decided to suspend Drazenovich is a bit of a mystery. Whatever the case, Lambeau got the victory he wanted when the Redskins went to Pittsburgh on Sunday, November 29. Led by Eddie LeBaron's first two touchdown passes of the season, they defeated the Steelers 17-9. LeBaron somehow had managed to play in Washington's first 10 games, starting five of them, without throwing a touchdown—for a coach who had pioneered passing in the NFL.

In a key moment, a field goal that would have given Pittsburgh a 12-7 lead was disallowed because the kicker failed to report to the referee when he entered the game. On the next play, Pittsburgh faked a field goal and threw a pass that came up short. The Steelers greatly missed their injured quarterback, future Chicago Bears executive Jim Finks.

Next up for for Washington was a visit from the Philadelphia Eagles, who were coming off an upset loss to the Giants. With another win, the Redskins could pull into a tie for second place with the Eagles in their quest for second-place money, about $400 a man.

As the Redskins prepared to play the Eagles on December 6, 1953, Washington's defense was receiving accolades for goal-line stands. In each of the previous five games, opponents had come up empty after notching first downs inside the 10 yardline.

"I suppose it's a combination of poor quarterbacking on the part of the opposition and tremendous spirit on the part of our line," Lambeau said.

Always a Barnum-like showman, Redskins owner Marshall added another of his pioneering halftime shows to lure spectators to Griffith Stadium. He also added to his racist legacy. "As an added attraction, a big minstrel show will be presented between halves. It is supposed to be as good as next Sunday's traditional Christmas program, usually the best production of the season," the *Washington Star* reported before the Eagles showdown. "But Curly isn't worried about minstrels or song and dance men. He wants points."

After the minstrels did their thing at halftime, the Redskins came up with a big performance. Despite being an underdog by at least one touchdown, Washington beat Philadelphia 10-0 on December 6, breaking a scoreless tie in the fourth quarter with a field goal and an interception. It was the first time in 127 games that the Eagles had not scored.

In a showdown filled with incentives, the victory assured the Redskins of their first winning season in five years and put them in position to reach their goal of earning their second-place bonus. All of a sudden, Lambeau looked like he had regained his coaching touch.

"Seven and four—that's what we want now," Curly said. "I told you at the beginning the season we'd win seven games and we will." With one game remaining, the Redskins and Eagles were tied for second place at 6-4-1. Given that the Eagles' final game was against the Cleveland Browns, who had won their first 11 games—and that the Redskins would be at home playing the Steelers, a team they had just beaten in Pittsburgh, Washington was in good position to achieve its goal of finishing alone in second place at 7-4-1.

And then, as Lambeau-coached teams had done often in his final NFL decade, Washington bumbled and stumbled. Before, during and after the game, it was a messy affair.

The day before the game, the Redskins angered the Steelers, calling the Pittsburgh hotel to say that halfback/kick returner Lynn Chandnois, Pittsburgh's leading breakaway threat, would not be allowed to play with the cast that was on his injured wrist. "It may have cost [Washington] the game," *Pittsburgh Press* writer Pat Livingston wrote. "The Steelers' coach was shocked, the players were furious."

When the referees inspected Chandnois' wrist, however, it was Lambeau and the Redskins who wound up being shocked. Chandnois had ordered trainer Mayo Donelli to cut the cast off of his wrist. Chandnois wound up running for 71 yards, leading all rushers. And every time Lambeau "came close enough to be insulted, the Steelers taunted him about his stand toward the injured Chandnois," Livingston said.

Entering the fourth quarter, Washington led 13-0 and still seemed set for the victory that Curly coveted. Even when Chandnois broke free for a 23-yard scoring run that cut the Redskins lead to 13-7, the crowd of 22,057 believed they were poised for victory.

Although Pittsburgh was moving the ball after that—seemingly closing in on a game-winning touchdown—the Washington defense had stopped the Steelers five times in fourth-and-one situations. Lambeau's defense did it again, heroically stopping the Steelers at the one-foot line to preserve Washington's 13-7 lead.

Eddie LeBaron then tried to direct the offense to some breathing room. That effort bogged down. Lambeau tried to send in end Gene Brito to tell LeBaron to quick-kick. But Brito didn't get on the field fast enough and had to race back to the bench.

Seeing room for a swing pass—it had been open on the previous play, a pitchout—LeBaron decided to try it. The Steelers defense was ready. Jack Butler stepped in, intercepting the pass at the 5 yardline and scooting into the end zone with the game-winning touchdown.

Washington's collective jaw dropped. The Redskins had blown a 13-0 fourth-quarter lead and had been dealt a devastating 14-13 loss.

On that one possession, the Redskins' whole world—especially Lambeau's world—turned upside down. LeBaron took responsibility for both the pitchout and the swing pass. Lambeau insisted that the Redskins didn't even have a swing pass in their playbook.

If, as LeBaron said later, Lambeau "didn't know more than ten offensive plays," Curly would have been winging it in a playbook controversy. But that never seemed to stop Curly Lambeau.

With that painful loss, the bottom also dropped out of LeBaron's future in Washington. All of a sudden, the Redskins were said to be prepared to draft another quarterback—and LeBaron's future in the Nation's Capital was in question. Lambeau had never truly embraced LeBaron as a quarterback who could win an NFL championship. Now he seemed certain that wasn't going to happen. "The [wrenching Pittsburgh loss] should change the Redskins' draft plans for 1954," Lewis Atchison told *Washington Star* readers.

That was Lambeau's pattern in his final coaching years. At the end of his Packer reign and during his coaching stints in Chicago and Washington, his teams would show flashes but would ultimately collapse. Along the way, he would have all kinds of public disputes with his best players. They would be neither well-coached nor have a unity of purpose. Considering that Lambeau had been a premier coach for 25 years, it was a frustrating and precipitous slide.

In Marshall, at least, Lambeau had an old friend who understood him. Curly had known and worked with the Redskins owner for 20 years, trying to build the scuffling NFL into the powerhouse it was on the verge of becoming. Lambeau also had socialized with Marshall and his wife, Corinne, to the point of revealing his most intimate feelings.

But now, things had gotten messy. On one December afternoon—in the final minutes of one frustrating fourth quarter—Lambeau's Redskins had gone from a team poised to finish its season upbeat—and looking forward to greater success in the next season—to a team in turmoil, a team that had suddenly lost direction.

On Sunday morning before the game, Lewis Atchison wrote in the *Washington Star* that "Lambeau's patched and revamped team had covered itself with glory in the long, uphill comeback march," and added that "Eddie LeBaron. . . is finishing out the string in a blaze of glory after a slow start."

By Monday morning, Atchison was concluding that neither LeBaron nor Lambeau were the answers for what was wrong with the Redskins:

"Owner George Marshall repeatedly has said the club doesn't need a quarterback, but he would have had a hard time proving it yesterday. . . [And] if it isn't a quarterback they need, then it should be a quicker sideline strategist." That was a dig at Lambeau's failed attempt to get Brito into the huddle so he could order LeBaron to quick-kick.

\* \* \* \* \* \* \* \*

Instead of the feel-good 7-4-1 finish that Lambeau wanted, the Redskins closed the ledger on 1953 with a 6-5-1 record, in third place and out of their $7,000 league bonus, roughly $400 per player.

Lambeau, though, was in a familiar place—bickering with one of his key players. At the end of his Packer run, he had feuded with kicker Ward Cuff, withholding Cuff's salary after absurdly accusing him of deliberately missing a crucial field goal. Cuff had replied by threatening bodily harm.

In his final year with the Chicago Cardinals, Lambeau had claimed that Charley Trippi had passed after being instructed to run, leading to a crushing Cardinals defeat. Refusing to be thrown under the bus, Trippi had angrily replied that the goal-line plays had come from the bench—although that apparently meant assistant coach Cecil Isbell rather than Lambeau.

And now, Eddie LeBaron was standing up to Lambeau, disputing his coach's criticism that LeBaron should have punted on third down rather than calling the pass play that resulted in that was intercepted for a touchdown that left Washington with a 14-13 loss to Philadelphia.

Under fire for his "$7,000 mistake," LeBaron insisted that none of the other 10 players in the huddle objected to the passing play. "I thought it was a perfect spot for a surprise pass," LeBaron said.

Lambeau countered that Charlie Justice, the target for LeBaron's pass, questioned the call. "Justice himself told me he checked LeBaron's call and suggested a quick kick," Lambeau said. "Anyway, Eddie should have called for a third down punt without even thinking. We've gone over that situation in quarterback meetings and he knows it's a standing order not to gamble under those circumstances."

Trying to soften the criticism, Lambeau said, "The little guy played a good game except for that one lousy call. I'd just as soon forget it happened and I know he would."

LeBaron would not forget the incident, however. And he soon would have an alternative to playing for the undependable Lambeau.

The dispute simmering, LeBaron headed to central California to see family, play golf and do some skiing. Meanwhile, Lambeau headed to Green

Bay for his own family visit. Arriving on Thursday, December 17, he spent a week in his hometown seeing his mother, Mary, his brothers, Ray and Ollie, and his son, Don, and their families.

The next day, Lambeau was photographed visiting his son, Don, Don's wife's and their three children, Barbara, 6, Mary, 5 and Jeff, 3. The *Press-Gazette* ran a family portrait of the group, with Jeff playfully grabbing a football from his grandfather. Before bouncing the grandchildren on his knee, Lambeau had breakfast at the home of his brother, Ray, where he talked football with *Press-Gazette* sports editor Art Daley.

"Green Bay is in my blood," Lambeau said. "This is where I was born. I can't help but want the Packers to prosper in the National League and see them become one of the top teams in the league again. . . . The Packers look like they've got the nucleus of a good team. '

That was a polite assessment. The Packers had just finished a 2-9-1 season. The team's executive committee had just forced out Gene Ronzani after four seasons, and was in the process of hiring a new coach. On January 7, Lisle Blackbourn became the third coach in the history of the Packers. Described as "likeable" in a *United Press* report, Blackbourn was hired away from Marquette, where he was "an unspectacular" 18-17-4 in four years.

It was not a splashy hire.

\* \* \* \* \* \* \* \*

Lambeau planned to fly to San Francisco on Christmas Day, 1953, to watch the East-West Shrine game and practice sessions, and look for future Redskins at both the Rose Bowl on New Year's Day and the East-West game on January 2.

Back in Los Angeles in early January, Lambeau was reported to be "doing the town. . . with his friend [Los Angeles restaurateur] Roy Harlow, and when Lambeau moaned that he needed a field goal and conversion expert, Harlow suggested [Wilbur] Snyder, who had a whale of a season kicking the ball through the uprights in the Canadian League."

"Don't be surprised," sports columnist Pete Kokon told readers of his "What's Cookin' with Kokon" column, "if you see Wilbur Snyder. . . in a Washington Redskins uniform."

That did not happen. Snyder, a Santa Monica native who had kicked for the Edmonton Eskimos in 1952 and 1953, was destined for a career as ``The World's Most Scientific Wrestler." But he did have a Green Bay football connection. He partnered with Dick Afflis, purchasing the

Indianapolis-based World Wrestling Association in the 1960s. After football, Afflis, a Packer lineman in 1951-54, became better known as Dick the Bruiser.

While Lambeau was checking out the East-West college all-stars, an important coaching hire that would impact the future of Lambeau and the Redskins came out of Canada. The Calgary Stampeders announced on January 1, 1954, that they had hired Lambeau's line coach, Larry Siemering, as their head coach. That raised the question of whether LeBaron would follow him. The quarterback had excelled for Siemering at College of the Pacific. Growing weary of Lambeau's mercurial ways, LeBaron now had an exit option.

To replace Siemering, Lambeau and Marshall hired Joe Kuharich, who had lasted only one season as the Chicago Cardinals coach. Kuharich, who had been Lambeau's successor in Chicago, had been an NFL scout in 1953 after being fired by Cardinals managing director Walter Wolfner at the end of the 1952 season.

"I think Eddie will be back with us," Lambeau said when he returned to Washington in late January to prepare for the NFL draft. "With LeBaron and Scarbath at quarterback we might be able to shift Al Dorow to halfback. That would give us a lot of power in our backfield."

Without LeBaron, Washington would be very green and very thin at quarterback. Scarbath had just wrapped up an inconsistent rookie season. Dorow, selected in the third round of the 1952 draft, would be a rookie in 1954 after two years of military service.

LeBaron proved Lambeau wrong on March 23, when he telephoned Marshall to say he was going to Calgary to play for Siemering. Two other Washington players, offensive tackle Don Campora, who had played at Pacific with LeBaron, and defensive end Gene Brito also went north to play for Siemering.

"That's the reason I went up there," LeBaron said later. "Curly was an old-timer. I got along fine with him at first, but after a while, he and I didn't see eye to eye. . . . At the end of that [1953] season, there were three of us who had a parting of the way with the Redskins. It was evident that Curly wasn't the kind of guy we wanted to play football for."

On one hand, Lambeau had never truly warmed up to LeBaron, who was too small and not strong-armed enough for his taste. On the other hand, with LeBaron gone, Washington's shaky quarterback situation got worse. And heading into the 1954 draft, Lambeau was not planning on losing LeBaron to Canada.

Marshall, who genuinely liked LeBaron, was disappointed, but said he would not take legal action to enforce the option on LeBaron's contract. Predicting that LeBaron would not like playing in Canada, Marshall left the door open for LeBaron to return, saying, "I'll always be glad to help him out in any way I can."

Although Lambeau spent most of his time in California after leaving the Packers, he made frequent trips to Green Bay and Door County, including a mid-June visit in 1954. Besides seeing his grandchildren and other relatives, "He spent part of the time in Door County fishing and boating," the *Press-Gazette* reported on Monday, June 14, the day Lambeau left "for his home in California, where the Redskins will launch training next month."

It's also likely that he was making some banking and investment maneuvers in preparation for resolving what would become a contentious divorce.

# 70
## *NO WIFE, NO TEAM*

The summer of 1954 was a tumultuous time for the 55-year-old Lambeau. On July 27, just as he was starting his third season as coach of the Washington Redskins, his third wife, Grace, filed for divorce in Santa Monica, California. Alleging "mental cruelty," Grace asked for "an accounting of funds and a court order restraining Lambeau from disposing of community property." In addition to his $50,000 annual income, Grace's attorney said, Lambeau owned the 200-acre Grajan Ranch near Oxnard, California, had an undetermined amount of cash in a Green Bay bank and "already has transferred substantial sums of community property." Married in July 1945, they had separated in March 1954.

Although not surprising given both of their marital histories—this was Grace's fourth marriage, and Curly's third—the divorce was a sad ending to a union that Lambeau had at one time described in precious terms. In 1946, he had called himself "the happiest man in the world" to Corinne Griffith, the wife of Redskins owner George Preston Marshall, and said, "I wouldn't do anything on earth to spoil this" marriage.

That proved to be impossible. Both Curly and Grace were physically attractive—a football hero and a beauty queen—and both were ambitious people who liked to live in grand style. Neither of them seemed able to stay content with married life, though.

Curly had bonded with Grace's daughter, Jane, a troubled child who became a schizophrenic requiring round-the-clock supervision. Born in 1933, Jane had been at the heart of a heated legal battle involving her and the five other grandchildren of William Garland, the railroad and real estate tycoon who was the father of Grace's second husband. When Jane was 4, a court ruling awarded an equal share of her grandfather's estate. It was worth about $500,000, money that would become important to a big spender like Grace. When Jane's father died, she and her mother also received a sizable trust fund. During Grace's marriage to Lambeau, the couple lived a glamorous, free-spending life. When their marriage soured, however, the caregivers that Jane needed for schizophrenia painted a grim picture.

"After Grace Garland's divorce from Gregory La Cava, she married this guy Curly Lambeau, who was a football coach from someplace in Wisconsin," said caregiver Ed Moses. "I saw a picture of him at the Malibu house—wide shoulders, a big guy probably. Looked like a real bullshitter. As soon as they got married, they started pissing away as much of Jane's money as they could. . . . When they split up there was a divorce settlement and he absconded with a good wad of property."

Moses had little sympathy, though, for Grace, saying she treated Jane badly. "Jane's mother was a hideous woman," he said. "Tough and opportunistic. She was very mercenary. . . . William Garland had left her all kinds of property, including some huge ranch in Thousand Oaks somewhere; it was beautiful acreage."

Grace still owned real estate after the divorce, but was short of money because it was tied up in trust funds, Moses said: "There was still plenty of money left, but it had been mismanaged. . . . Grace was real-estate poor. She had all this real estate, but not a lot of cash. . . . She couldn't go out and buy fur coats and do all the shit she wanted to do with her friends. . . only Jane's money was left. Grace Garland was mad as a wet hen because there was all that gold out there and she couldn't get her mitts on it."

\* \* \* \* \* \* \* \*

In the midst of his divorce strife, Lambeau had just started the Redskins training camp, which had a very early sense of urgency in those days. Washington's annual pre-season game against the Rams had become an extravaganza. A charity event sponsored by the *Los Angeles Times,* the game attracted crowds of more than 80,000 to the Coliseum each August. In Washington, by contrast, the Redskins needed four home crowds to attract that many people to their regular-season games.

The game was an especially big deal to Lambeau, who spent the off-season in Southern California, and to his boss, George Preston Marshall, who also indulged in California sunshine. From 1946 to 1962, the Redskins trained at Occidental College in Los Angeles, where Marshall's wife, a former silent film star, had a home. Like Lambeau, Marshall spent a lot of time in Southern California.

The Rams had won the three previous meetings with the Redskins. And Lambeau and Marshall were determined to change that. Convinced that the Rams had the edge because they traditionally started training camp earlier, Lambeau and Marshall moved the start of the Redskins' 1954 camp to July 19 and scheduled a tuneup with the Eleventh Naval District team in

San Diego. But that still did not level the practice field against the Rams, who opened a week earlier, on July 12, and played the New York Giants in Portland, Oregon, as well as the Fort Ord military team before meeting Washington.

And then there was this: The Rams had simply been a better team than the Redskins for several years. Washington had had only one winning season since 1945. The Rams, meanwhile, had played in the NFL championship game three times in the previous five years.

The trend continued in their 1954 meeting. The Rams roughed up Washington 27-7 before 79,813 spectators on Wednesday night, August 18, for the fourth straight year. Lambeau erupted, leaning hard on the excuse that the Rams, by opening their training camp so early, had an unfair advantage.

"I'm tired of getting licked like this," he said. "The game is too big to give the Rams an advantage—starting a week ahead of us and getting a good game under their belts to perfect their timing and coordination. I'm tired of it."

Owner George Preston Marshall joined in, demanding that NFL commissioner Bert Bell set a uniform starting date for training camp. Bell agreed, Marshall said, that it was a good idea. The Washington owner also objected to the Rams playing the Giants before playing the Redskins, saying that jeopardized the box office for a charity game that had raised about $1 million for the *Los Angeles Times* Boys Clubs.

Taking the conspiracy theory even further, Marshall expressed concern that the Rams would still have an edge even with a league-mandated starting date for training camp. "They have 27 players in this area," he said. "And nothing could prevent them from getting together on their own to work out."

Washington would find a solution in 1955 by opening against the 49ers in San Francisco while the Rams were playing the Steelers in Portland. The Redskins then beat the Rams for the first time in five years.

After the ranting of Lambeau and Marshall, the Redskins did not have to wait long for an opportunity to atone. Just three days later, on Saturday, August 21, they were to play the 49ers in Sacramento. Hardly sleeping after the Rams game, Lambeau was up at 5 a.m. on Thursday working on plans to have Washington ready for the Niners.

For all their grumbling about the Rams' scheduling advantages, though, Lambeau and Marshall had not done themselves any favors with the short turnaround between games. The 49ers not only had given themselves six days between games. Like the Rams, they were simply the better team.

San Francisco cruised to a 23-0 halftime lead and went on to win 30-7 before a crowd of 23,389 on Saturday, August 21, at Sacramento's Hughes Stadium. Despite an 8 p.m. kickoff, the temperature was in the mid-80s that night. Rookie running back John Henry Johnson scored the 49ers' first touchdown on a six-yard power run and set up their second score with a 51-yard burst to the 1 yardline.

"A super run, one of the greatest I've ever seen," Lambeau said. "At least seven Redskins should have brought him down." Johnson, who had finished his college career at Arizona State, would go on to a remarkable 13-year Hall of Fame career. Despite the obvious talent of Johnson and the many African-Americans that Washington encountered, Marshall would not integrate the Redskins until forced to do so in 1962.

A short turnaround had contributed to the Redskins' second loss in four days. Never mind that the Rams and 49ers were better teams and that these were so-called exhibition games. Nerve endings were frayed on the overworked, over-wrought Redskins. And their season had just begun.

\* \* \* \* \* \* \* \*

This was an especially rough time for George Preston Marshall. A hands-on owner in the mold of another mercurial owner named George, future New York Yankees boss George Steinbrenner, Marshall was miserable when his team lost. And determined to reverse his team's losing ways.

Returning to the Hotel Senator in Sacramento after Washington had been drubbed by San Francisco, Marshall encountered three players who were about to board an elevator. It was around midnight; he was not a happy man. His Redskins had just lost for the second time in four days. After a short night, they would be boarding a plane to Detroit, where the talented Lions would be favored to inflict more pain on Marshall's psyche.

The owner asked the players—defensive back Don Paul and ends Fran Polsfoot and Hugh "Bones" Taylor—why they were violating the team's midnight curfew. The players tried to explain that they were returning from the game, which had ended after 11 p.m. Marshall then asked the players what was in the bag they were carrying. They said they had some beer. Marshall informed them they were fined.

"Angry over the fines, the players called Lambeau out of the hotel cafe," where he insisted that, despite appearances, he was not drinking alcohol. "I'm interested in protecting my reputation," Lambeau told *Washington Post* writer Jack Walsh, "and I don't like to see the impression left with Washington fans that I was drinking last night. . . . I don't think it smart for the head man to be having a drink in the hotel bar where the team is quartered. . . . I went to that lounge to get a bite to eat. . . . No table was available so I stood near the bar when invited over by Jack Geyer, Los Angeles newspaperman, and his wife. I had a drink—a glass of of soda with ice and also I took three aspirin to help me get to sleep. Neither Marshall nor anyone else saw me having an alcoholic drink there."

Curly in a bar *not* having a drink after his team had gotten smacked around for the second time in four days? Seems a little far-fetched, especially coming from Lambeau, who was known for unabashedly spinning yarns. As longtime Packer writer Lee Remmel once told team historian Cliff Christl, Lambeau "was a congenital liar. He'd lie to your face and you knew he was lying and he'd still lie to your face and make you like it because he was so good at it." Not that it really matters whether he was having a drink. But it certainly would seem logical that alcohol was involved in what happened shortly after that.

While Lambeau was talking to the players in the lobby, Marshall approached and started berating Lambeau for the team's poor performance. its deplorable conditioning and whatever other dissatisfaction with his coach came to mind.

"I'm doing the best I can with what I've got," Lambeau said.

There would be variations on the exact details of the Lambeau-Marshall dustup. There generally were at critical moments in the life of The Man Who Invented the Green Bay Packers. It was clear, though, that the Redskins owner and his coach had reached a point of no return. Marshall had seen players with beer, especially after a humiliating loss. That set off a row between Marshall and Lambeau.

The incident was witnessed by three San Diego Padres baseball players—Al Lyons, Dick Sisler and Earl Rapp—who were in town for a Pacific Coast League series against the Sacramento Solons. "The argument rapidly became more heated," they told reporters. "Marshall attempted to jostle Lambeau, but was restrained by [Redskins general manager] Dick

McCann." Lambeau, who had won a boxing exhibition during his Notre Dame football days, shoved back and seemed poised to throw a haymaker, but McCann kept them separated them before the altercation escalated further.

"Come upstairs and we'll get this matter settled once and for all," Marshall told Lambeau.

At 10 the next morning, McCann announced that Lambeau had been fired and that assistant coach Joe Kuharich was Washington's new head coach.

"Forty Niner players expressed surprise that Lambeau had been fired," the *San Francisco Examiner* reported, "because as one put it: 'No coach could do anything with the players they had. They were easier than a high school team to handle.'"

Kuharich, 37, had been hired as line coach only 34 days earlier. The seventh Redskins head coach in 10 years, Kuharich also had followed Lambeau as coach of the Cardinals, who were led by their sixth coach in seven years. Clearly, both teams had impatient front offices.

Kuharich had lasted only one year with the Cardinals, another casualty of meddling managing director Walter Wolfner. Kuharich then spent the next season as an NFL scout and in private business. Lambeau had hired him in Washington as his line coach to replace Larry Siemering when Siemering left for Calgary. Marshall, who could be as inventive as Lambeau, later tried to spin the move by saying he and Lambeau always intended for Kuharich to be the next Washington coach when Lambeau retired.

With that, the Redskins departed for the Sacramento airport and their flight to Detroit—without their fired coach or their owner, who had a fear of flying.

After leaving Green Bay, Lambeau had found jobs. He had not found job security.

"I have no animosity," Lambeau said before heading back to his ranch in Thousand Oaks. "It was just an unfortunate thing. It's part of the game. After all, Marshall owns the club. I wish Joe well and I wish the team well. They're a good bunch and I think they can do it."

Washington also shed four players along with Lambeau. Marshall waived Polsfoot, linebacker Jack Cloud and rookie end Chuck Sitton. Paul, who had played for Curly on the Chicago Cardinals, simply quit, saying, "If Lambeau goes, I go."

The three players that Marshall cut never played in the NFL again. Paul was quickly traded on August 30 to Cleveland, where he played for five years, including three in which he was named to the Pro Bowl.

It was the second time in three seasons that Marshall had changed coaches during the pre-season. an odd time to make a coaching change. Lambeau had been hired on August 23, 1952, to replace Dick Todd, who resigned when Marshall insisted on releasing some players that Todd wanted to keep. Two years to the day, on August 23, 1954, Lambeau also was gone.

A few days later, White House reporters bumped into Frank Leahy, who was playing golf in Denver with on-vacation President Dwight D. Eisenhower. Since Leahy, who had resigned as Notre Dame coach for health reasons in January, was the highest profile football coach available in America, he was asked if he would be interested in coaching the Redskins. Leahy laughed heartily and said, "I think they already have a permanent coach in the person of George Marshall," adding that Marshall "is a good friend of mine."

"I am sorry it happened to Curly," Leahy said. "It must have been slightly embarrassing. However, from what I hear, Curly is pretty well fixed financially."

That was certainly true. Lambeau had angered the Packers' leadership with the way he handled the team's finances. When it came to his own bank account, however, he had been very shrewd.

# 71
## *COLLEGE ALL-STARS BECKON*

And so, just like that, Curly Lambeau, 56, was out of a job. For 35 autumns, he had led a professional football team into battle. Even as a 21-year-old on his honeymoon in August of 1919, he had, according to the legend, traveled around northeastern Wisconsin and the Upper Peninsula of Michigan, scheduling games. He had created the most unique franchise in professional sports, a community-owned team in a small town that became the standard of excellence in the National Football League, winning six of the league's first 25 championships and becoming America's most popular team. Following the lead of his college coach, Knute Rockne, Lambeau had created the Notre Dame of the NFL.

And now, he was out. A career that had begun over a beer with Green Bay newspaperman George Whitney Calhoun in 1919 had ended in an aborted shoving match with Redskins owner George Preston Marshall in 1954, triggered by some players drinking beer.

Lambeau grabbed a flight back to Burbank Airport, where he replied, "No comment," to a barrage of reporters' questions, finally saying, "I've got my future to look to. I suggest you can get anything you want from [Redskins general manager] Dick McCann at the Ft. Shelby Hotel in Detroit. I want time to think. I'm sure you will understand my position."

Lambeau did not refer reporters to Marshall, who was en route to Detroit by train. "Marshall," Lambeau said, "is afraid to fly."

Lambeau did not go immediately to his Thousand Oaks ranch. but "one of his hands" said he was expected to be there in a day or two. Nor did he go to the Malibu beach house he had lived in with his third wife, Grace. Since the couple had separated on March 25 and she had filed for divorce on July 27, he apparently stayed elsewhere in Los Angeles.

In just one month, he had become a man without a team or a wife.

Lambeau resurfaced in Washington on Friday, September 18, the day before the Redskins lost their sixth straight exhibition game, 49-14, to the Colts in Baltimore. While there, he met with Marshall to press his demand to be paid his entire 1954 salary, about $20,000. Lambeau also met with NFL commissioner Bert Bell in Philadelphia in his effort to be paid.

"Lambeau's two-year contract with the Redskins ended last August," Marshall said. "He did not have a verbal contract for 1954 although I had intended to keep him this season until that incident in the hotel lobby in Sacramento made it impossible for him to remain."

Why did two men who annually signed dozens of football players to contracts think they could operate indefinitely without a contract for one to coach the other's football team? It's a good question. Maybe they thought they would part amicably. Maybe they thought they could hustle each other, like friends in a poker game. Whatever they thought, it brought to mind a quote from movie maker Samuel Goldwyn: "A verbal contract isn't worth the paper it's written on."

Lambeau's argument: "No, I have no written agreement but I had an agreement the same as I did last season. And I certainly believe a big-time organization like the National Football League will make one of its clubs honor such an arrangement."

NFL commissioner Bert Bell agreed with Lambeau, Pittsburgh sportswriter Jack Sell wrote:. "The day of [Lambeau's] dismissal, NFL Commissioner Bert Bell happened to be in Pittsburgh, and told the *Post-Gazette* that Marshall would have to fork over."

Bell did not come to Lambeau's rescue. Eighteen months later, Lambeau was entangled in lawsuits with his attorney, Max E. Gilmore. After Gilmore sued Lambeau for $7,200 for divorce work and $501 for the salary dispute with Marshall, Lambeau counter-sued, asking $33,000, claiming that Gilmore botched the claim against the Redskins by accepting only one-third of the $20,000 Lambeau had been seeking

After pleading his salary case on the East Coast, Lambeau arrived in Green Bay on Wednesday, September 22, to visit his mother, brothers and son, and to watch the Packers play Pittsburgh in their season opener on Sunday, September 26. With Lisle Blackbourn making his debut as Green Bay coach and his predecessor, Gene Ronzani, on the other sideline as a Steelers assistant, the only three men who had served as head coach in Green Bay were present.

As Lambeau sat in the press box at City Stadium before the game began, a young press box attendant approached and asked, "Do you have a ticket, sir?" After pulling his ticket out of his pocket, The Man Who Invented the Green Bay Packers said, "This is the first time since I was a high school boy that I've watched the Packers without a coaching interest in the game."

Given that the Packers did not exist when he was in high school—even the NFL did not exist at that point—and that he had been employed by two opposing teams after his long run in Green Bay, that was absolutely true. That had to be a really strange moment for Lambeau. He had been a national celebrity for decades, and now he wasn't recognized at a Packer game. Professional football had been his life for the last 35 years. And even though he denied it, he still wanted to be a part of the game. His actions would prove that.

Although he told the *Green Bay Press-Gazette,* "I am not interested in a head coaching job in the National Football League," that was merely a man playing it coy. NFL teams clearly were not clamoring to hire him.

It also had to feel strange for Lambeau to watch Blackbourn, a middling college coach from a modest program at Marquette, direct the Packers against Walt Kiesling, a former assistant he had rudely dumped. Curly insisted that was not the case, saying, "I'm going to enjoy it. Let Kies and Lisle get the ulcers." His comment rang hollow. He had had his share of stomach problems, but had never let that stop him.

On a beautiful autumn day in northeastern Wisconsin, Lambeau watched a frenetic battle in which the Packers gave up 444 yards, nearly 200 more than they gained, but lost a 21-20 heartbreaker on a late 37-yard touchdown pass by Jim Finks, his third of the day. In other words, there was ulcer material for both coaches. And for all his protests, Curly Lambeau, who had thrived on stomach-churning football action his whole life, undoubtedly missed the feeling.

\* \* \* \* \* \* \* \*

After watching the Packers open an NFL season while in the unprecedented position of being a civilian, Lambeau apparently went back to his ranch in Thousand Oaks, California, to tend to his chickens and cattle.

Despite his insistence that he no longer was interested in coaching, actions spoke louder than words. In mid-October, less than two months after Marshall had fired him, Lambeau's name resurfaced as a candidate to coach the College All-Star team. In late November, the reports proved accurate. His old Notre Dame friend, *Chicago Tribune* sports editor Arch Ward, announced on November 22 that Curly would coach the 1955 College All-Stars against the NFL champion.

It was only one game, but that wasn't all bad. It would keep his name out there for when the inevitable NFL coaching changes happened. He would be able to keep his hand in football without being immersed in the intensity of coaching for months on end. And the All-Star game against the NFL champion was the kind of high-profile event that suited his taste for the spotlight.

That was especially true because the College All-Stars, who always had been led by college coaches, now would be under the direction of a distinguished NFL veteran. Lambeau would be a trailblazer in the blurring of the line between the college game, which had once ruled, and pro football, which had made dramatic gains in popularity. To explain the change, Ward said a poll of football fans had voted overwhelmingly for professional coaches "who knew the character of the opposition" to lead the college All-Stars. And Lambeau, "a name synonymous with professional football," was an ideal choice, Ward said.

Or, as another Lambeau friend, *Los Angeles Times* columnist Braven Dyer put it after Cleveland had won its sixth championship in nine years, Ward "thinks so highly of Lambeau that he has drafted the blue-eyed Belgian grid genius to teach the rah-rah All-Stars how to beat the Cleveland Browns next summer. This is the type of assignment which is calculated to drive a guy nuts, but if anybody can do it, Curly's the man."

He would turn 57 on April 9, about two months before training camp opened. He was no longer relentlessly energetic, but he still had the drive to win. He could muster his energy in bursts. He could still motivate players. And the spotlight of the College All-Star game, which attracted huge attention as the kickoff to another football season, would be a great motivator for him.

Lambeau would direct the offense, which was odd because he had delegated the offense to assistants when he was with the Cardinals and the Redskins. His old Notre Dame teammate and Bears rival Hunk Anderson was named line coach and chief of the college stars' defense. 'Ward designated Curly as the man in charge although we both got paid the same—$1,500," Anderson said in his autobiography. Other reports had Lambeau earning considerably more than $1,500. If Anderson had been misled, it would not be surprising. When it came to misleading people about salary figures, Lambeau was an old pro.

Lambeau promised to try and come up with a sharp passing attack, saying, "No All-Star squad ever is going to run effectively against the pro champions. They are too big, too mature and too experienced." It would be Lambeau's fourth appearance as a coach in the College All-Star game, which annually kicked off the football season in front of huge crowds at Chicago's Soldier Field. As Green Bay coach, he had won the 1940 and 1945 games after losing in 1937.

\* \* \* \* \* \* \* \*

Five weeks later, Lambeau made headlines of the wrong kind. "Curly Lambeau Denies Threats to Harm Wife," the *Los Angeles Times* said on December 30, 1954. A divorce hearing had turned ugly in Santa Monica

Superior Court. A *United Press* report carried the same message around the nation. "Lambeau Denies Threat to Wife," *Racine Journal Times* readers were told. In the *Green Bay Press-Gazette,* the headline said, "Lambeau Denies Threatening Wife With Bodily Harm." Denial or not, a dark side had surfaced. Conservative Green Bay had never been comfortable with aspects of Lambeau's personal life. And now it had gone from hometown whispers to national headlines.

"Lambeau denies that he threatened his wife with bodily harm should she seek her share of community property" the article said, after mentioning that "Mrs. Lambeau would forego her current expense claims" until the divorce went to trial. Major assets listed at the pre-trial hearing included the Malibu beach house, a 200-acre lemon grove in Ventura County and "a $150,000 ranch near Lake Sherwood," the Thousand Oaks chicken-and-cattle operation. Grace said the ranch was community property; Lambeau said it belonged to him alone.

* * * * * * * *

Bu the end of 1954, Lambeau's friends were promoting him for a job with the Los Angeles Rams, who were looking for a new coach. Hampton Pool—a talented coach who often rubbed people the wrong way—had resigned after three seasons on December 17 "for the good of the team" amid a cauldron of controversy, "a long-smouldering feud between Pool, his aides and his players," the *Los Angeles Times* said. Pool, who had been an end on the Bears championship teams of the early 1940s, had led the Rams to two good seasons before the turmoil of his third year. These types of NFL melodrama were hardly limited to clubs where Lambeau had coached.

Ignoring the campaign for Lambeau, Rams owner Dan Reeves went the opposite way. He hired University of Cincinnati coach Sid Gillman on January 25, hoping to find the next Paul Brown, who had gone directly from Ohio State to pro football championships.

Even then, Lambeau's friends saw an opportunity for him as the trusty assistant who could help an NFL novice like the 43-year-old Gillman. "Everyone likes Curly," Southern California native Ben Agajanian, a well traveled NFL place-kicker, told the *Long Beach Press-Telegram,* "and he likes football. Besides, he'd virtually do the job for nothing just to get back into the game. That should please the Rams."

"Curly Lambeau probably is the Rams' man who will provide the experience in the pro ranks by sort of running 'interference' for the man from Cincinnati," said another Lambeau friend, San Fernando *Valley Times* columnist Claude Newman.

No Rams offer developed. But Lambeau was still in demand as an authority on NFL prospects. He traveled to New York for the draft, which was held on January 27 and 28 at New York's Warwick Hotel.

Officially going over the candidates for his College All-Star team, Lambeau not only discussed that year's crop of players. He also put his finger on the reason that NFL teams were not excited about the talent they were seeing. The problem was, by clinging to the iron-man style in which players were required to play both offense and defense, he said, the college game was not developing pro-style players who excelled on one side of the ball.

"The reason for the absence of a lot of top talent is simple," Lambeau said. "Professional football is now feeling the effect of the collegiate single platoon rule." If the trend continued, Lambeau said, the NFL might cut back from its current 30-round draft to only 20 rounds.

\* \* \* \* \* \* \* \*

In another sign that time was passing, George Halas, Curly's longtime rival and business partner, announced his retirement from coaching, effective after the 1955 season.

Halas said he had decided two years earlier that he would retire if the Bears were playing well; he wanted to give his successor a team that could challenge for a championship. Coming off an 8-4 season in 1954, he felt the Bears would be solid contenders in 1956.

After another 8-4 finish in 1955, Halas, 60, gave the Bears coaching job to his old friend and longtime assistant, Paddy Driscoll, who actually was a few weeks older than Halas. Driscoll entered the world on January 11, 1895, followed by Halas on February 2. Driscoll, who had been a Bears assistant for 15 years, had head coaching experience, though. In 1920-22, he was player-coach of the Chicago Cardinals. His 34-year gap between NFL head-coaching assignments is a record unlikely to be broken.

In 1956, Driscoll would come oh-so-close, losing in the NFL championship game after a 9-2-1 campaign. But in Driscoll's second season, 1957, the Bears would falter to 5-7. And Halas would decide to return as coach in 1958. At age 63, nearly 40 years after he started the franchise, Papa Bear would be embarking on his fourth stint as the Bears coach.

That was the beauty of Halas' situation. Unlike Lambeau, George Halas was the owner. For nearly 30 years, they had stood shoulder to shoulder, two pillars in a league struggling for acceptance. If Halas was the NFL's most influential leader, Lambeau was not far behind.

In the end, though, their differences seemed bigger than their similarities. Lambeau had not paid the price of ownership, had not shouldered the financial stress of holding onto what had been a precarious business by himself. While Halas had clung tightly to the purse strings, Lambeau had relied on a legion of dedicated businessmen to mind the Packers' finances.

\* \* \* \* \* \* \* \*

In February, Lambeau and Hunk Anderson met in Chicago to go over their plans for the College All-Star game. At that point, they were focused on choosing the players they wanted. "We want the big, fast ones," Lambeau said. "We can't beat the Browns with small men."

Deviating from the single-platoon rule then being used in college, Lambeau wanted offensive and defensive specialists. "With the two platoon, everybody will have a good chance to play. . . and [will] work twice as hard to get in there."

He also planned to have fewer players on the roster, to avoid having players who, knowing they wouldn't play, were just along for the ride. Curly wanted everyone working hard.

For Lambeau, the College All-Star game was an opportunity to show all of his NFL friends that he could still coach—a chance to make his case for another NFL job. Although he publicly said he wasn't interested in coaching again, that didn't ring true. He spent a lot of time hanging out at NFL events—games, meetings, the draft. And his many media friends kept quoting him, and touting him as a coaching candidate who had seen and done it all.

While in Chicago, Lambeau and Hunk were guests on the Arch Ward Show, broadcast at 8:15 p.m. on WLS radio on Sunday, February 20. The *Tribune* promised that the show, sponsored by DeVry Technical Institute, would be especially interesting "if you want to learn how you can prepare. . . for a good technical career in the fast-growing, big opportunity fields of Television, Radio and Electronics."

\* \* \* \* \* \* \* \*

Back in Southern California in March, Lambeau made the usual rounds. He kept his name in the news, which helped his newspaper friends as well as his career prospects. Soon to be divorced, he was seen around town visiting with old friends and perhaps making new ones.

"Lambeau, stopping off at Rickey's Valley Inn for a steak brizzola, tells me that he would like to have Hampton Pool as one of his assistants for the College All-Star football team," Pete Kokon reported in his column, What's Cookin' with Kokon, in the San Fernando *Valley Times* on March 25, 1955.

Curly also spoke at the Van Nuys American Legion annual sports dinner on March 16, 1955, along with glamorous quarterback Bob Waterfield, who had retired after a stellar career with the Rams, and Don Paul, the defensive back who had left the Redskins in protest when Lambeau was fired.

In late April, Curly and Hunk added two accomplished assistants who were both former NFL coaches, Hamp Pool and Steve Owen, who had coached the Giants from 1930 to 1953. Pool had guided one of the NFL's best passing offenses. Owen, a defensive specialist, had split his eight meetings against Paul Brown while coaching the Giants.

Details of Lambeau's contentious divorce made headlines again on April 27. Newspapers around the nation described "a triple-threat legal action" in which Grace, 61, filed for divorce, seeking half of Lambeau's ranch in the Santa Monica Mountains, which she valued at $150,000. In the second prong, Lambeau, 57, countered that the 650-acre cattle and poultry ranch was not community property. With the couple and their attorneys in Superior Court in Santa Monica, Lambeau's lawyer made the third argument in the contentious divorce, claiming that Grace owed Curly $4,616, which he lent to her from 1946 through 1953.

The divorce was finally granted on June 6, 1955. "Mrs. Lambeau testified that the former professional football coach seldom took her out socially, was away frequently on unexplained absences and criticized her before friends," an *Associated Press* account that was printed everywhere reported.

Under the key terms of the settlement, Grace retained the Malibu beach house. That wasn't exactly a victory for Grace. It had been hers since her second husband, William Garland, died in 1940. She also kept title to a lemon grove in Ventura County, which also might have predated her July 16, 1945, marriage to Lambeau.

Grace also received "a half interest in an 840-acre ranch," the cattle and chicken enterprise in Thousand Oaks that allowed his newspaper friends to refer to Lambeau as a "country squire." For Grace, though, there was a catch to that, too.

"They had bought a great deal of undeveloped land together," Grace's daughter-in-law, Lila Hoyt, said. "Do you know where Lake Sherwood is out in Thousand Oaks? That would give you an indication of how he could persuade her to do things. He talked her into starting a chicken ranch out there. Yeah! For the sale of eggs! When they divorced, they divided that ranch in half, and his half was the one that was on the lakefront, with the buildings. I'm sure that it was profitable."

That's putting it mildly. Lake Sherwood is prime real estate less than 20 miles from Malibu and other Pacific Coast destinations—and less than 50 miles from downtown Los Angeles.

Making the whole divorce settlement even more murky, Grace had inherited a lot of the real estate, which had originally been acquired by her late husband, William Garland, or Garland's tycoon father.

"I don't know how he did it but she was crazy for him, and and he was a big tough son of a bitch," Jane's caregiver, Ed Moses, said. "I think Curly got half the money and he hooked on to all the land he could get his hands on—whatever it was that she had. He took her to the cleaners."

Considering how often Lambeau was mentioned on the sports pages of the Los Angeles area, it was surprising that his divorce received so little coverage. Even the *Los Angeles Times,* which frequently quoted Lambeau for football perspective, merely printed a four-paragraph wire story. And the *Valley Times,* his local daily, only printed one terse paragraph, taken from the *Associated Press:* "Mrs. Grace Garland Lambeau, 54, has been granted a divorce in Santa Monica from Earl L. (Curly) Lambeau, 55, former Green Bay Packers coach." Although she had aged well physically, Grace was actually 61 at that point; Curly was 57.

Then again, it wouldn't be surprising if his newspaper friends wanted to stay on Curly's good side. He was a legendary coach who was always willing to weigh in on football—whether assessing teams, players, rules changes, even college football. He was a good background source for coaching hires and other backroom rumors. And he was their charming friend. They were a part of Lambeau's Southern California Rat Pack, which included athletes, retired athletes, media and many other notables. As Lambeau once told a Green Bay writer, golf pals like Bing Crosby and Bob Hope were "just the guys next door" to him.

\* \* \* \* \* \* \* \*

With the divorce completed, Lambeau headed to the Midwest, where he would have his one-game season, guiding the College All-Stars against the Cleveland Browns, who had won their sixth championship in the nine years the team had existed—and lost in the championship game the other three years.

Although Lambeau's record after World War II suggested that his coaching skills had slipped precipitously, Browns coach Paul Brown said the All-Stars would be a tougher challenge with an old pro like Lambeau leading them.

"I do not want to minimize the ability of the college coaches who have handled the All-Star squads," Brown told Lambeau's old friend, *Chicago Tribune* writer George Strickler. "I have a very healthy respect for all of them. But there is a tremendous difference between pro football and college football. Curly Lambeau, Steve Owen, Hunk Anderson and Hamp Pool know that difference as well as anybody in football and we expect to run into an All-Star squad the like of which no other pro club has had to face."

Brown also realized how much this opportunity meant to Lambeau. "This will be the most thoroughly organized All-Star squad ever sent into the game. I know Lambeau and his assistants have been working for a couple of months now. This is a marked departure from other years.

"The manner in which they are picking their squad. . . indicates that they are not interested in a man's reputation or clippings, but his ability to work into this particular squad," Brown said, mentioning several players. "They're going to be pretty dangerous characters under Lambeau's guidance. . . . Frankly, however, I'm glad it's that way. . . . I'd much rather have trouble winning it. . . Football is competition and without competition there's no football."

When Lambeau arrived in Chicago on June 24, he welcomed running back Joe Heap, Notre Dame's leading scorer, to his All-Star roster. "Heap is tailor made for the pass attack Lambeau is expected to unleash," the *Tribune* reported, "against the world champion Cleveland Browns in football's greatest spectacle on Aug. 12 in Soldiers' field. He is a halfback who specializes in pass receiving."

"We've got to have offense," Lambeau said after meeting with assistants Hunk Anderson and Steve Owen at the Sheraton Hotel. "There is no defense in football like holding the ball."

Lambeau then headed north to see relatives in Green Bay and enjoy Door County, "relaxing a bit before the start of drills" at the All-Stars training camp at Northwestern University in Evanston in mid-July.

Curly told Arch Ward he turned down 49 requests from college coaches who wanted to join his All-Star staff. "They want to spend time in the All-Star camp to learn something for their own purposes," he said. "We want coaches who can help us whip the Browns."

Ward, however, was not destined to see his old Notre Dame friend, Curly Lambeau, try to work his magic against the mighty Browns. Just two days after that coaching item appeared, Ward died of a heart attack on July 9, 1955. He was 58. As the creator of baseball's All-Star game, the College All-Star game, the All-America Football Conference and many other innovative sporting events, he was the most prominent sports editor of a golden age for newspaper sports. In a measure of Ward's impact, baseball commissioner Ford Frick pushed back the starting time of the 1955 All Star game, to be played in Milwaukee, half an hour to allow baseball leaders to attend Ward's funeral in Chicago that morning.

"Sports, amateur and professional, have lost their best friend and staunchest supporter," Lambeau said. "His All-Star football game and All-America conference did more to bring about national acceptance of professional football than any other single factor. We will miss his guidance and encouragement in this year's All-Star camp."

Two weeks later, Lambeau opened training camp on Friday, July 22, at Northwestern University in Evanston with a roster of 47 College All-Stars. The All-Stars had trained at Purdue the previous two years. Lambeau also added former Green Bay running back Tony Canadeo, who had retired three years earlier, to his coaching staff.

A week into their drills, Lambeau, concerned about too much fumbling, spent the afternoon of Saturday, July 30, working on ball-handling and offensive assignments. He gave his players the next day off—the Cubs had invited them to be their guests at a doubleheader against the Phillies—but ordered everyone back to Evanston for a team meeting that night.

Although they were a two-touchdown underdog against Cleveland, the All-Stars were encouraged by their 9-6 edging of the Chicago Cardinals in a practice game on Friday, August 5. "The time has been short, but we'll be ready for the Browns," Lambeau said. "I think our scrimmage with the Cardinals gave the college boys a pretty good idea of what to expect from the pros—and what they have to do against the pros."

The All-Stars had lost four straight since 1950, when Iowa coach Eddie Anderson guided the college players to a 17-7 win over the Eagles, led by the passing of Eddie LeBaron.

"The All-Stars, who have 'gone pro' under E.L. 'Curly' Lambeau... could surprise," Bob Russell wrote in the *Chicago Daily News*. "But the Browns have been pros a long time. Football is their business and they know it well."

Although Arch Ward had succumbed to a heart attack a month earlier, his genius for publicity was carried on at the *Chicago Tribune*. Wilfrid Smith, the longtime sportswriter who succeeded Ward as sports editor, and George Strickler, Lambeau's good friend, kept the All-Star game in the public spotlight with daily stories.

The *Tribune* not only had detailed coverage of the Browns and the All-Stars. It also ran a Rockette-like photo of the Kilgore College Rangerettes, "a bevy of beauties from Kilgore, Tex.," who would entertain at halftime. The newspaper also announced that all governors attending a national governors' conference in Chicago would be their guests at the game. Frank Leahy, who had led Notre Dame to four national championships, was the master of ceremonies for the annual All-Star luncheon.

And although the All-Stars had outplayed the Cardinals 9-6 in their scrimmage, Strickler wrote that Lambeau had invited his players to "a private showing of a new horror picture" in the basement of Northwestern's Bobb Hall—the film of the scrimmage.

By Friday, August 12, when the game would finally be played, a sports-watching America had its gaze fixed on Chicago's Soldier Field. Sportswriters from around the nation had given the game a buildup worthy of a Super Bowl. That was not out of line. In the 1950s, the College All-Star game held that kind of stature. With its 8:30 p.m. kickoff, it would be nationally televised. *Tribune*-owned WGN-TV would show the game in Chicago.

Even the weather fell into line. "Clear skies and a stiff northeast wind off Lake Michigan made it a perfect night for football," Jack R. Griffin told readers of the *Chicago Sun-Times,* the *Tribune's* morning rival.

From the beginning, Lambeau's All-Stars showed that they were not awed by the NFL champions. After trailing 20-17 when the Rangerettes put on their halftime show, they pulled into a 20-20 tie in the third quarter. In the fourth quarter, the All-Stars took a 30-20 lead on a touchdown set up by an interception and their third field goal from 139-pound Ohio State kicker Tad Weed. Cleveland answered with an 80-yard touchdown drive, but could manage no more.

That gave Lambeau's All-Stars a 30-27 win before a crowd of 75,000 and a national television audience. It was the college players' first win in five seasons, and left them with a record of 7-13-2 in the history of the series.

The joyous collegians carried Weed and Notre Dame quarterback Ralph Guglielmi off the field. Weed had kicked three field goals. Guglielmi had completed 10 of 19 for 129 yards. "That was the greatest quarterbacking job I ever saw," said Lambeau, who had abandoned the traditional plan of using more quarterbacks. "I had to go all the way with him. . . and the other fellows understood."

For one glorious night, Lambeau was on top again. He had been determined to win—to show all of his NFL friends and other skeptics that he could still coach 'em up. Never mind that the Browns were playing without their peerless leader, Otto Graham, who had retired but would be persuaded to un-retire by the start of the regular season. Curly Lambeau once again was on top of the football world.

"E.L. (Curly) Lambeau this morning is the envy of every American football coach if you exclude, perhaps the Sing Sing coach who boasts he never has to worry about his stars graduating or alumni demanding he be fired," David Condon began the "In the Wake of the News" column, Arch Ward's old space. "Lambeau already has concluded an unbeaten season and now can rest up for the 1956 gridiron campaign, wherever it finds him [and football certainly is missing a bet if it doesn't try to find a top spot for the gray-haired founder of the Green Bay Packers!]"

"Spirit did it. The Boys won this one themselves," said Lambeau, a gracious and modest victor. "We felt all along that this squad had the proper attitude and the right morale as they drilled in 90 degree heat for two weeks without complaint." Lambeau said.

It was the kind of college spirit Lambeau had demanded when he was presiding over the Packer juggernaut he had guided to six of the NFL's first 25 championships. His stay at Notre Dame had been limited to one brief autumn. But he had learned the value of emotion from Rockne. It worked for coaching college All-Stars for one game, even if it was not practical for coaching an entire NFL season. The professional game was different after World War II. It was more business-like. And so was The Man Who Invented the Green Bay Packers.

The All-Stars' upset of the Cleveland Browns left media pundits urging NFL teams to hire Lambeau and his offensive assistant, former Rams coach Hamp Pool—and predicting that they would be hired. "Look for this: Lambeau and Pool form an ideal team. Lambeau as the front and head man, Pool in mapping strategy and taking a behind-the-scenes secondary role. It is safe to predict—indeed it appears as obvious—that they will be signed as a pair to fill the next NFL coaching vacancy. And when it happens, chances are that new NFL history will be made."

That opinion was written by *Los Angeles Evening Citizen* columnist Rube Samuelsen, in his Rube-Barbs column. It was, he said, "written on a

DC-7 United Mainliner, 19,000 feet above the cornfields of Nebraska" after a stifling week in New York and another in Chicago.

\* \* \* \* \* \* \* \*

Mixing football with the summer splendors of his native northeastern Wisconsin turf, Lambeau was at City Field in Green Bay on August 27, 1955, for the Packers' 16-14 exhibition loss to Pittsburgh. But if he expected to land another NFL coaching position based on his All-Star success, that telephone had not rung.

By the time he had returned to Southern California a month later, Lambeau denied being interested in a regular coaching job. None had materialized, anyway. "Curly Lambeau, the Old Pro among NFL coaches, says it was his swan song in football coaching when he mentored the College All-Stars to their thrilling victory over the Cleveland Browns." In the same article, *Valley Times* columnist Claude Newman reported that "Curly Lambeau had a narrow squeak the other night on the freeway near Agoura when his car hit a horse. Luckily, Curly says, he wasn't driving fast and escaped injury." Lambeau hitting a horse on the freeway? That must have led to a good yarn over a cocktail.

Lambeau continued to say he was not interested in coaching. He told *Valley Times* sportswriters Newman and Pete Kokon that he had turned down an offer to coach the College All-Stars again in 1956, although he wound up returning to that job. And he was a frequent press-box visitor to both college and pro games in Southern California in the fall of 1955.

He saw the Rams edge the Steelers 27-26 on October 2 from the Los Angeles Coliseum press box with his restaurateur friend, "sidekick" Roy Harlow, who said he was "looking for help for my `RAMS HORN' cafe when it opens next month." Meanwhile, Lambeau "praised Hamp Pool for the tremendous job he did" when the former Rams coach was his offensive assistant at the All-Star game.

A couple of weeks later, Curly watched 16th-ranked USC upset previously unbeaten sixth-ranked Wisconsin 33-21 on Friday night, October 14, before 75,162 in the L.A. Coliseum "They'll never get a Rose Bowl game as thrilling as that," Lambeau told Badger coach Ivy Williamson after the game.

Although he had told West Coast writers he had turned down a second campaign with the College All-Stars, Lambeau reversed his field on October 26, when he "assured officials of The *Chicago Tribune* Charities

Inc. that he had arranged his business affairs so that he again could head the staff of coaches."

The *Tribune's* sports section made the announcement by proclaiming, "LAMBEAU WILL COACH ALL-STARS IN 1956," with a banner headline. "Coaching the All-Stars was my greatest thrill in football," Lambeau said. "Maybe we won't do as well this time, but we'll give it the same effort. The 1955 squad had the desire to win. That's more than half the battle." Lambeau, the *Tribune* said, already had started preparing with a preliminary list of college seniors.

After watching UCLA crush Cal 47-0 at the Los Angeles Coliseum on October 29, Lambeau did not find any All-Star candidates from Pappy Waldorf's losing squad. "The alumni," he said, "just aren't beating the bushes for Pappy."

In November, Lambeau was a good neighbor to six families forced from their homes. When a stubborn brush fire burned 16,000 acres near the crest of Carlisle Canyon, southwest of Lake Sherwood, Curly allowed the displaced families to store their possessions at his chicken ranch.

On Friday, December 9, Lambeau paid a surprise visit to the Packers at the Green Hotel in Pasadena, where they were staying before playing the Rams on Sunday, December 11. After congratulating coach Lisle "Liz" Blackbourn on his 6-5 record, Lambeau said, "I'll be pulling for you to make it 7-5 Sunday."

Green Bay missed its goal, losing 31-17 in front of 90,535 to the Rams, who won the Western Division with an 8-3-1 record before losing the NFL championship to the Cleveland Browns. The Packers had given the Rams their first loss, 30-28, in Milwaukee on October 16 before a crowd of 26,960. The huge attendance difference drove home the widening gap between big-city teams and small-market Green Bay. That was an issue that would soon become a major issue in northeastern Wisconsin.

After beating the Rams for the NFL title, Cleveland coach Paul Brown mentioned that the Browns would have unfinished business with Lambeau and the College All-Stars the following August in Chicago. Under the headline "Coach, Champion Browns Vow Revenge on All-Stars," *Chicago Tribune* sports editor Wilfrid Smith put in an early plug for the Browns' rematch with Lambeau's collegiate squad.

Lambeau, who was in the Browns dressing room after they beat the Rams, talked to *Arizona Star* writer Lou Pavlovich about why Paul Brown was so successful. His explanation offered a glimpse into what Lambeau valued in his own coaching: "Paul Brown is great because he can round up material. He paces his club for the entire season. You'll notice that the

Browns are never outstanding early in the season. He doesn't go all out at the start. He is like a fighter, paces the team for the distance. He is one of the most clever men in football, mainly because of his pacing. Paul Brown will never have a team that is known as August or September champions. But they come through when it counts."

Brown's legacy goes much deeper than that. A thorough organizer who inaugurated many fundamentals of coaching, he stressed film study and classroom techniques, extensive scouting that included using intelligence tests, sending in plays with alternating players and gathering his team together in a hotel the night before games. But pacing his team? That might have been a by-product. But that was something Lambeau valued highly.

# 72
## *GREEN BAY NEEDS A STADIUM*

When the calendar turned to 1956, Lambeau was following his usual routine—scouting prospects at the East-West Shrine game in San Francisco and the Rose Bowl in Pasadena. Coaching the College All-Stars seemed to be a good fit for him. It kept him involved and gave him a chance for glory without an all-consuming effort.

It was at those West Coast games that Lambeau saw the two quarterbacks who would line up for his College All-Stars when they tried to make it two in a row against the Cleveland Browns. Earl Morrall helped Michigan State grind past UCLA 17-14 in the Rose Bowl. Held on January 2, 1956, because January 1 fell on a Sunday, that Rose Bowl was watched by 41.1 percent of Americans who had television sets at the time, making it the highest-rated college bowl game ever.

Two days earlier, Iowa QB Jerry Reichow, had led the East to a 29-6 rout of the West on December 31, 1955, in San Francisco. Reichow, who had earned no All-America honors, was named the most valuable player of the Shrine game. That was good enough for Lambeau.

When the NFL conducted the first three rounds of its 1956 draft in Philadelphia on November 28 to head off competition for the best college players from Canadian football teams, Reichow had not been selected. The Detroit Lions quickly corrected that oversight, making Reichow the top pick when the league went through its final 27 rounds at the Ambassador Hotel in Los Angeles on January 17 and 18, right after its Pro Bowl All-Star game.

A week after the Rose Bowl, the *Salt Lake Tribune* reported that Brigham Young boosters wanted Curly as their new football coach. Curly's response: "I'm out of football and intend to stay that way."

The BYU job, though, was hardly a measure of whether Lambeau wanted to return to football full-time. He was an NFL man who had been given the College All-Stars job because of his pro football background. And BYU was not USC.

After checking out the NFL draft in Los Angeles, Lambeau returned to northeastern Wisconsin in late January 1956 with two missions. One was to purchase a summer home in Door County. Although he initially seemed interested in Baileys Harbor, on the Lake Michigan side of the Door peninsula, he eventually settled on "a big mansion" in Fish Creek, on Green Bay. That description in the San Fernando *Valley Times,* most likely from Curly, was not an exaggeration.

The other mission: To join the campaign to build a new stadium for the Packers. Without it, Green Bay would be likely to lose its NFL team. For all of his expansive football thoughts and deeds, Curly probably had no idea the structure would give him enduring fame.

As the citizens of Green Bay pondered the future of the Packers. Lambeau had been gone six years, ousted by a combination of his own shortcomings and the growing pains of a National Football League that was on the verge of becoming a big business.

By shedding the twin budget crunches of Lambeau's spending and the costly war with the rival AAFC, the Packers had survived in Green Bay in 1950. But the financial strain on a publicly owned team in a small city had continued to mount.

"There is no use kidding ourselves," said Fred Leicht, chairman of the Packers' stadium committee. "We are doing more than deciding on a stadium. We are deciding whether we want to keep the Packers in Green Bay."

The Packers already were dividing their six home games evenly between Green Bay and Milwaukee, where County Stadium could accommodate 35,000 fans, 11,000 more than Green Bay's City Stadium. Even those capacities were modest. NFL teams playing in baseball parks could accommodate 50,000 or more fans. While the Packers had earned $261,000 in 1955 in gate receipts for their road games, Leicht said, visiting teams received only $161,000 for playing the Packers in Green Bay and Milwaukee. That imbalance made the Packers' NFL partners restless.

As the pressure mounted for Green Bay to build a modern stadium or lose the Packers, Lambeau did not hesitate to weigh in on the stadium question that had become critical to the Packers' future.

Three of the four stadium proposals were on the East Side site of the current City Stadium. Despite being from the East Side, Lambeau urged that the new stadium be built on the West Side, near the recently upgraded U.S. 41 highway. where it would be more accessible to Milwaukee and Fox Valley Packer fans.

It was not an idle issue. Although Fort Howard, on the West Side of the Fox River, had been annexed by Green Bay, on the East Side, in 1895, a rivalry continued. It played out in the intense competition between East and

West high schools. And in long-held biases by residents on both sides of the river.

"I've been visiting here since last Friday," Lambeau said on Wednesday, February 1, "and I've heard many arguments on which side of town it should be built. You know I'm an East Sider, strictly, but I firmly believe that a stadium on the West Side is the best answer to bigger attendance and easy access to the stadium. That super highway is a temptation for fans in Milwaukee, south of there and in the valley. Same for fans coming from the north and west."

The key question, though, was whether voters would approve a bond referendum. As much as Green Bay loved its Packers, John Borgenson, who headed up the Green Bay Association of Commerce, pointed out that Green Bay voters tended to be wary of bond issues. Based on their conservative political background, Borgenson said, "two-thirds [of voters] conceivably could vote no on any stadium proposal." He urged coming up with a bond issue that would draw unified support and "stand a chance of meeting public approval."

In February, the Green Bay City Council took steps toward putting a $960,000 bond referendum on the April 3 election ballot. Making the proposal even more palatable, the Packer organization would agree to pay $480,000 over a 20-year period.

On March 6, the City Council approved putting the bond referendum on the ballot. To enhance its chances, the question of where the stadium would be located was not mentioned. The cost of building a West Side stadium at Perkins Park was conveniently estimated at $950,450, "not including parking or lighting improvements," for a 32,000-seat stadium.

To drum up support for the bond issue, a pep rally was held at the Columbus Club, where the Packers had enjoyed exuberant victory dinners to celebrate championships, at 9:30 on Saturday morning March 31. A crowd of 1,000 attended, including 400 volunteers who would canvass the city before the election Tuesday to get the vote out.

Headlining the rally were ancient rivals George Halas and Curly Lambeau, plus a long list of Packer legends, including Don Hutson, Johnny Blood and Tony Canadeo. Angling for a bigger visitors' check, Halas had been trying to shift the Bears' trip north to Milwaukee.

Halas diplomatically laid out the financial reality that if the Packers did not have a larger stadium, other NFL teams would "look forward to playing at Green Bay with less enthusiasm," a polite way of saying the franchise was likely to move. "Buffalo," Halas said, "is ready to double-deck its 32,000-seat stadium at a cost of a million dollars if it can get a franchise."

To lure an NFL team, Minneapolis was building a stadium that would be attractive if Green Bay did not step up, Johnny Blood said. Metropolitan Stadium, which opened later in 1956, would become the home of the NFL Vikings and baseball Twins within five years.

On the other hand, Halas said, a new stadium would assure the Packers' future in Green Bay and increase "the Packers' potential for successful operation."

Mentioning the Bears' historic rivalry with the Packers, the Bears founder added, "I confess I have a deeper feeling of attachment for the Packers than any other club. Sometimes I wonder if there would be a Chicago Bears today if there had not been such a terrific rivalry, between the Packers and Bears since the early 1920's. I can say to you sincerely—just as sincerely as we hope to edge out the Packers in both games next fall – that the best way for you to guarantee the current and future success of the Packers is to build the new stadium—a place where your team can grow and flourish in the future, just as it has grown and flourished here in Green Bay from the earliest days of professional football."

Then it was Curly's turn. Six years earlier, he had left his hometown, essentially forced to abandon the Packer team he had founded and nurtured for three decades. Harsh words had been said on both sides. His critics had charged him with gross mismanagement; Lambeau had accused his critics of interference that made it impossible for him—or anyone—to operate the team.

But now, with the Packers facing another crisis, Lambeau, still beloved as The Man Who Invented the Green Bay Packers, had come to the franchise's aid in its time of need. His endorsement of a new stadium on the West Side was a large step toward overcoming the traditional East Side-West Side competition in the city.

The Packers franchise, Lambeau said, could be sold for a million dollars within 24 hours, "but who would want to throw away 35 years' work in 24 hours?"

Reciting the early struggles, Lambeau said, "Not two, three or four people were responsible for keeping the Packers alive in Green Bay. The people, the fans of Green Bay did it down through the years and I'm sure they'll continue to support the team and build a new stadium. . . . It makes no difference whether you are Packer fans or not—and who isn't in this town? A new stadium would benefit the entire city in different ways other than football."

Green Bay Mayor Otto Rachals noted that he had given out the key to the city many times to distinguished visitors and said, "Do you know what's printed on that key? Green Bay—Home of the Packers. Do we want to take it off the key?"

The citizens of Green Bay gave their answer on Tuesday, April 3. On the same day that tornadoes killed eight in central Wisconsin and claimed 22 more lives across Lake Michigan in Grand Rapids, more than 62 percent of registered Green Bay voters turned out for the primary. Of the 16,468 who cast ballots, 11,575 said yes to the bond issue that would finance their football team's new home.

"That's the greatest thing I've heard of in sports," NFL commissioner Bert Bell said. "A little town of 65,000 getting together and building a stadium for a big league football team! . . . It can only be done in one city in the world, and that's Green Bay."

"This means that the Packers will be able to compete as an equal with every other team in the National League," George Halas said. "This is one of the turning points in National League history." Even if the Packers frustrated the Bears on the field, they at least would boost the Bears' fortunes financially.

Also ecstatic was Packers' founder Curly Lambeau. He called the referendum approval "the greatest thing that ever happened in Green Bay. People all over the country were looking at Green Bay, including a lot of cities interested in the Packer franchise. But Green Bay has given its answer. The Packers' [franchise] is solid. And. . . no one person put this across. The fans of Green Bay did it."

Six years earlier, Lambeau had tried to buy back the franchise he had started, with an eye toward moving it to a larger city. But now, that was forgotten. The Packers were indeed in a position to remain a stable and competitive member of the National Football League.

The vote obviously was welcome news to Packers general manager Verne Lewellen, who had been a star on the team's three consecutive championships in 1929-31 as well as the Brown County district attorney

"I firmly believe the golden era is going to be the 1960's," Lewellen said. "We can look forward to crowds of 35,000 to 45,000 at our games here and those games will be witnessed by additional 50 to 100 millions of people on television. If our city has received publicity and advertising through the Packers in the last 30 years, can you imagine the type of publicity and advertising our city will receive in the 1960's?"

A golden era for the Packers in the 1960s? In 1956, no one could have known how true that phrase would become.

After helping secure the Packers' future with a new stadium, Lambeau returned to California for a few weeks. He was among the 1,000 guests who attended a testimonial dinner for *L.A. Times* sports editor Paul Zimmerman on May 16, 1956, at Frank Sennes' Moulin Rouge. Zimmerman received a Buick Century, a 3-D camera, a spinet piano and a round-trip ticket for Mrs. Zimmerman to accompany him to the Summer Olympics in Australia. It was not mentioned if the chicken for the dinner came from Curly's ranch.

A week later, Lambeau was back in Green Bay, "checking on the property he purchased recently in Door County." He apparently remained there, settling into his Fish Creek summer home and preparing to coach the 1956 College All-Star team. In mid-June, the *Chicago Tribune* listed the 51 players Lambeau had selected for the rematch against the Cleveland Browns.

# 73
## *THE SECOND TIME IS NOT A CHARM*

Lambeau left Door County in mid-July for downtown Chicago, where he huddled with his College All-Stars coaching staff at the Sheraton Hotel. The team opened training camp on July 19 at Northwestern, staying again at Bobb Hall on the Evanston campus. The staff included Hunk Anderson and Don Kindt on defense, and Hampton Pool, Tony Canadeo and Mike Michalske on offense. Lambeau also worked with the defense.

Signaling that he had no interest in being embarrassed again by Lambeau's All-Stars, Cleveland coach Paul Brown kept the four Browns' draft picks on Lambeau's squad in Ohio, forcing them to miss the start of All-Star camp.

"A cold war began building," George Strickler told *Chicago Tribune* readers, summing up the tension between Lambeau and Brown. "We were pathetic" in last year's 30-27 loss, Brown said. "We didn't have a winning attitude. We were full of ourselves and we showed it." Brown said he expected "a major player turnover this year. I have hopes that we have some young guys who are going to run some of the old ones out of business," Brown said. "If [a veteran] doesn't produce, he is through."

Hyping the game nicely, Strickler described Brown as bothered that Lambeau had taken four of his top rookies. That, however, was exactly what Curly was supposed to do. "Mr. Lambeau plucked four of our best guys," Brown said. "This, of course, gives him double advantage: First, the four youngsters will do a darned good job for the All-Stars, and secondly, we won't be able to use them against him."

On July 22, four days after they were due to report, "Warden Brown finally opened the gates of the Cleveland training institution, paroling his four All-Star prisoners into the custody of E.L. [Curly] Lambeau," *Chicago Tribune* writer Cooper Rollow said, mocking Brown's maneuver. And so, Preston Carpenter, Don Goss, Bob Moss and Larry Ross joined the All-Stars.

As the game—which would kick off the football season on Friday night, August 10—neared, Lambeau engaged in his own bit of gamesmanship. An *Associated Press* preview by Joe Mooshil splashed across the country with Lambeau refusing to give details about his offense, saying only that it would be different than the formula he used to shock the Browns 30-27 the previous year.

"I don't think we can surprise [Paul Brown]," Lambeau said. "But that's no reason to let him know what we're going to do. Cleveland will be a lot better this year, if for no other reason than we beat them last year. . . . it'll take a super effort to beat them." Oddsmakers agreed; the All-Stars were listed as a 9½-point underdog.

A year earlier, Lambeau had been hailed as a miracle worker who revived the College All-Star game by upsetting the Browns. In 1956, the question was, could he do it again?

The All-Stars' hopes took a serious hit on the fifth play of the game. Michigan State quarterback Earl Morrall, who had been directing an offense that was moving the ball effectively, left the game after being shaken up. "Disastrous," Lambeau said later. In the huddle after getting hammered, a foggy Morrall called for an "X-32 to the left." The All-Stars had no such play; a timeout was called and Iowa quarterback Jerry Reichow came in.

When the All-Stars resumed their drive at Cleveland's 34 yardline, Reichow dropped back and threw a long pass. In a make-or-break moment, the collegians' surprise move—a deep ball by a new quarterback—backfired. Reichow's throw was intercepted in the end zone. Cleveland then marched 80 yards for a 7-0 lead. Armed with the psychological edge as well as the better team, the Browns took care of their "unfinished business," rolling past the All-Stars 26-0 before 75,000 in Soldier Field.

Morrall, described as "groggy" after being hit, returned later in the game, but was ineffective. "I came out and sat on the bench. I couldn't remember our plays for a while,' he said. Neither Reichow, who was used primarily as a receiver in the NFL, nor Navy quarterback George Welsh, who went on to become the ACC's winningest coach at Virginia, was able to get the All-Stars offense going, either.

"They'll beat anyone they play if they play that way," Lambeau said after losing to Cleveland in their All-Star rematch. "If Morrall could have played all the way we would have made a better showing, but I don't think we could have beaten them. We just weren't as good as we were last year"

Lambeau, who had been a football hero after beating the Browns a year earlier, now was in the crosshairs. He was criticized for not having his team in shape, for not playing the right players, for saying the All-Stars could not have beaten the Browns. He not only lost a game. He lost respect.

Scheduled to be the principal speaker at a Meet-the-Lions dinner at the Sheraton-Cadillac Hotel in Detroit on Tuesday, August 14, Lambeau canceled by telegram. He apologized, but "insisted that the poor showing of the All Stars had nothing to with his inability to attend." With Lambeau, who frequently denied what seemed obvious, one never knew.

Even Lambeau's relationship with a long-ago former assistant, Steelers head coach Walt Kiesling, took a hit. When Pittsburgh's two College All-Stars, a pair of linemen who had played at 235 pounds at Purdue, reported at 255 pounds, Kiesling was "visibly disturbed," the *Pittsburgh Press* reported. "The condition in which [they] reported has soured the relationship between Kiesling and his ex-boss. . . .The Steeler All-Star players reported that Lambeau did very little to work his team into shape."

In Montgomery, Alabama, columnist Max Moseley wondered if using NFL coaches, which had been saluted a year earlier, might be scrapped. "There has been much criticism of the way coach Curly Lambeau handled the All-Stars," Moseley said. "Lambeau said that the All-Stars at their best could not have beaten the Browns. Incidentally, Lambeau is paid $11,000 and unlimited expenses to make the game a hit. They put it in his hands saying the college coaches weren't up to it. Another game like the one this year and it may go back to the college coaches."

Paid $11,000? Hunk Anderson had said he and Lambeau each received $1,500. Considering the amount of time Curly put in, and considering how important the game was for showcasing football and raising money for *Chicago Tribune* Charities, the higher figure seems plausible.

Lambeau, apparently finding respite with friends and family in Green Bay and at his grand new vacation home in Fish Creek, did venture into the press box to watch the Packers defeat the Giants in their exhibition home opener on August 25.

The 1956 season was the last in rickety old City Stadium. The Packers' modern new home would be ready by the fall of 1957. When the Packers played their last game in City Stadium against the 49ers on November 18, 1956, however, the spotlight was on George Whitney Calhoun rather than Lambeau, who already was back in California. A 15-minute halftime salute celebrated Calhoun's role as co-founder of the Packers.

"It was a fitting if long overdue tribute to the man who, with Curly Lambeau, conceived the Green Bay Packers," the *Press-Gazette* noted, "and whose unflagging enthusiasm through the years fanned the tiny spark. . . that became the wonder and delight of the sports world." It was also fitting, the newspaper noted, because City Stadium stood on land once owned by Calhoun's great grandfather, Daniel Whitney, a founder of Green Bay.

"Curly Lambeau has received most of the credit for the creation and development of the Green Bay Packers," the tribute said. "It is taking nothing from Lambeau, however, to insist that Cal deserves nearly equal credit. Without him there might never have been any Packers. . . . Curly got the spotlight, but Cal never cared. In fact, he wanted it that way."

Lambeau, who had enraged Calhoun by bringing in George Strickler as the Packers' publicity chief in 1947, did not participate in the Calhoun ceremonies. While Green Bay was closing the chapter on the stadium it had outgrown, The Man Who Invented the Green Bay Packers was enjoying California sunshine.

To head off Canadian raiders, the NFL again held the first four rounds of its 1957 draft on November 26, 1956, in Philadelphia. Finally winning the bonus-pick lottery that Lambeau helped create, Green Bay selected Paul Hornung, the Heisman Trophy winner from Notre Dame, with the first overall pick..

Lambeau joined the Packers, who stayed on the West Coast in between games in San Francisco and Los Angeles, for dinner on Wednesday, December 13, before they played the Rams on December 16. Praising the Hornung pick, Lambeau said he would play a big role when Lambeau led the College All-Stars for the third time in 1957. Lambeau was a big proponent of the bonus pick when it debuted in 1946. With previous winners ineligible, the lottery was down to Green Bay and the Chicago Cardinals when the Packers finally got their turn.

The Rams were struggling through their first losing season since moving from Cleveland to Los Angeles in 1946. They managed to beat Green Bay 49-21 in their 1956 finale, but wound up with a 4-8 record under second-year coach Sid Gillman.

With speculation swirling about the Rams' future, Curly Lambeau's name inevitably came up as a possible successor to general manager Tex Schramm—especially if owner Dan Reeves sold the team.

"Tex Schramm is through. Curly Lambeau becomes new general manager of the Los Angeles Rams. Sounds fantastic, doesn't it? But it could happen," Pete Kokon wrote in the *Valley Times*. "Of course, if Reeves goes [sells], so will Schramm, leaving the door open for a new general manager, and the name of Curly Lambeau has popped up more than once."

As it turned out, Reeves did not sell, but Schramm did leave in February 1957 for a high-paying job at CBS Sports. More interested in a marketing man than a football guru, Reeves hired a young Pete Rozelle as general manager in April. Rozelle, who had been the Rams publicist in 1952-55 before starting his own public relations firm, turned the Rams into a box-office success even though they continued to struggle on the field.

Although Lambeau professed to be uninterested in returning to the NFL, he kept being mentioned for jobs. Would his media friends have made those mentions without his consent? Perhaps. More likely, Lambeau at least had been consulted. Then again, when one of his sportswriter friends, *Milwaukee Journal* sports editor R.G. Lynch, had ambitiously speculated that Lambeau would succeed Bert Bell as NFL commissioner, Lambeau had called that report "asinine." And now Lambeau was being mentioned for the Rams' general manager job that went to Rozelle, who actually would be Bell's successor.

While watching the Packers and the Rams from the Los Angeles Coliseum press box, Lambeau was introduced by Rams broadcaster Bob Kelley, who also wrote a column for the *Long Beach Independent,* to UCLA quarterback Ronnie Knox, who had been selected 37th overall by the Bears with the final third-round pick in the draft. Lambeau urged Knox to play on the 1957 College All-Star team, saying, "It's a wonderful experience. No kid was ever sorry he played in the game."

"What does it pay?" said Knox's step-father, Harvey, who had a long history of meddling in Ronnie's football career, which included stops at three high schools—Beverly Hills, Inglewood and Santa Monica—plus two colleges. After leaving Cal, Knox's UCLA career was shortened by a Pacific Coast Conference suspension for accepting illegal payments. Unfazed, Knox went off to the Hamilton Tiger Cats in 1956, but quickly shifted to the Calgary Stampeders after Harvey demanded that the Ti-Cats play Ronnie for 30 minutes a game.

Another coach might have been wary. Lambeau was not just another coach. He had maneuvered to get Don Hutson. He had endured the whims of Johnny Blood. Handling players came with leading a team.

"Lambeau took his cigarette holder out of his mouth and smiled: 'Just figure that you work for nothing. Then anything over that is gravy,'" Kelley wrote.

Harvey did not like the sound of that. "The [All-Star] game's no good," he said. "He should be spending his time in the training camp of the club he's with."

Curly replied that the All-Star game had not hurt Rams halfback Ron Waller, who went to the Pro Bowl as a rookie. That seemed to soften up Harvey, but not completely. "All right, we'll think it over," the stage-managing father said. 'But remember, we're not amateurs. We like money."

As it turned out, Lambeau initially had Knox on his All-Star roster, but Knox began a six-month training tour with the California National Guard on March 1 and was unable to play. Although Lambeau had plenty of experience with quirky players, he apparently did not miss much in Knox's case. He joined the Bears in early September, but was suspended a month later for missing practices and team meetings. Alternating between a minor movie career—he had signed a 10-year contract with MGM—and three Canadian Football League teams, Knox only appeared in one game for the Bears. When he quit football for the last time in in 1959, Knox, 24, left the Toronto Argonauts, saying that football was "a game for animals." Knox said he planned to go to Europe and complete a novel.

When Lambeau released his 1957 College All-Star roster in June, he had included six Packer draft picks, led by Paul Hornung and Ron Kramer. Reached at his summer home in Fish Creek, Lambeau said he planned to play Kramer at end, explaining "he'd be good most anywhere but there's not enough time to change him from his college position."

## 74
## *THE ONLY CLASH OF GREEN BAY'S TWO TITANS*

It was not noted at the time. It was not significant at that point. But a symbolic passage occurred at the 1957 College All-Star game. Across the field from 59-year-old All-Star head coach Curly Lambeau stood Vince Lombardi, the New York Giants' 44-year-old offensive coordinator. It was the only time that The Man Who Invented the Green Bay Packers coached against the man who would take the Packers to dizzying heights. It was Lambeau's final appearance in a game involving NFL players—an understated passing of the torch.

But there they were, on Friday night, August 9, on the same rain-soaked Soldier Field along Chicago's lakefront: Lambeau, who had made Green Bay a football phenomenon by winning six championships in an era marked by the franchise's battle for survival. And Lombardi, who would restore the Packers to NFL glory by winning five championships during a magical golden age in which television turned the NFL into America's most popular spectator sport.

They had barely missed each other in 1954. While Lombardi was making his NFL debut coordinating the New York Giants' offense, Lambeau was making his dramatic NFL exit, fired after nearly coming to blows with Washington Redskins owner George Preston Marshall. They missed each other by two months. By the time that Lombardi's offense thrashed the Redskins 51-21 on October 24, Lambeau, who had been fired on August 22, had been reduced to arguing with Marshall about his severance pay, not football.

A thunderstorm wiped out the pre-game College All-Star extravaganza festivities, disappointing a drenched crowd of 75,000 that had gathered at Soldier Field. When the storm had relented enough for the game to be played, Chicago football fans, eager to see Lambeau's All-Stars pay back the Giants for embarrassing their Bears 47-7 in the 1956 NFL championship game, quickly took their seats. They used "slickers, umbrellas, newspapers and whatever other protection was handy, anxiously awaiting an All-Star rally," George Strickler wrote in the *Chicago Tribune*.

Lambeau had a remarkable collection of stars in 1957 The team included three players who would play prominent roles for Lombardi in Green Bay: Halfback Paul Hornung, from Notre Dame, end Ron Kramer (Michigan) and defensive tackle Henry Jordan (Virginia). Also on that team were many future NFL stars who would do battle with Lombardi's Green Bay teams: Cleveland Browns fullback Jim Brown, from Syracuse; 49ers quarterback John Brodie (Stanford), Kansas City Chiefs quarterback Len Dawson (Purdue), Baltimore Colts linebacker Don Shinnick, a UCLA quarterback; Bears defensive lineman Earl Leggett (LSU) and Dallas Cowboys linebacker Jerry Tubbs (Oklahoma).

New York end Ken McAfee caught a pair of touchdown passes from Charlie Conerly as Lombardi's Giants defeated Lambeau's All-Stars 22-12 on Chicago's rain-soaked lakefront. Frank Gifford, the Giants' star pass-receiving halfback, was credited with drawing the attention that allowed McAfee to get open.

Lambeau blamed the rain and "nothing but the rain" for the loss, insisting that he was not offering an alibi "but just stating a fact." But of course, he was offering an alibi. That was what he often did best—although this excuse was weak.

While it was true that Stanford quarterback John Brodie was expected to give the All-Stars a strong passing attack, Jim Brown led a group of running backs that looked promising regardless of the field conditions. And the Lombardi-coached Giants offense was able to pass despite the slippery field. The New York team was simply better.

"Our whole offense was geared to split-second timing and planned for a dry field," Lambeau said. "It just didn't work on the sloppy going. . . . I don't believe they were as superior to us as the score showed."

There was no question, though, that the All-Stars, who trailed 10-9 at the half, put up a much better fight than they had the previous year, when they lost 26-0. A 10½-point underdog, the All-Stars took an early 7-0 lead and wound up covering the spread. A late safety gave the Giants their final margin.

"I'd like a repeat performance on a dry field," Lambeau said. "We had to have a dry field to do anything. . . . We were a much stronger team this year. Brodie is a hell of a quarterback. I'd like to take 35 boys off this squad this year and really work with them. I think we'd hold our own in any league."

Purdue supporters were disappointed that their quarterback, Len Dawson, was the only All-Star who didn't play. Lambeau said he had plays designed for Dawson, but they wouldn't have worked in the wet weather. Dawson reportedly lost interest in training camp because he could see he wouldn't play much behind Brodie and Hornung. Dawson would finally have his chance to play against Lombardi as the Kansas City quarterback in the first Super Bowl.

Despite the loss, it was a decent showing for Lambeau, who had been ridiculed after his All-Stars were drubbed a year earlier.

Besides coaching against Lombardi, Curly also was marking another milestone that night. The only game in which he matched wits with Vince Lombardi also wound up being the last time Lambeau coached football at the highest level.

It was fitting that his coaching career should end with a game in the rain. In a way, that was how things had begun. When a downpour ruined the Packers' hopes for a good crowd and threatened their survival in 1922, his struggling franchise had been rescued by community fund-raising. That gave Lambeau the foundation to lead the Packers to the unique success that would make the team one of the most famous in American sports lore.

For Lambeau, though, the 1957 College All-Star game marked the end. He would pursue other jobs. But he would not lead another football team.

In 1958, Browns quarterback Otto Graham took the All-Star coaching reins from Lambeau. The *Chicago Tribune* announced Graham's hiring as major breaking news on December 3, 1957, in a banner headline, "NAME OTTO GRAHAM '58 ALL-STAR COACH, followed by a breathless subhead, "PRO FOOTBALL'S GREATEST QUARTERBACK TO DIRECT COLLEGIANS IN AUG. 15 GAME." When it came to promoting the College All-Star game, the *Tribune's* ink supply was vast.

The agreement apparently had been reached the previous spring, with Lambeau's knowledge and consent. Graham had begun his coaching career as a much-publicized assistant on Lambeau's 1957 All-Star staff. "GRAHAM JOINS ALL-STAR COACHING STAFF," the *Chicago Tribune,* always promoting its benefit game for the newspaper's charity arm, had proclaimed in another giant headline on May 14, 1957. It was the coaching debut for Graham, who said he hadn't thought about coaching until then. After leading the Cleveland Browns to four AAFC titles and three NFL titles, Graham had retired in 1955 to concentrate on his insurance business.

"When I retired from the Browns, I was asked to coach the College All-Stars by Wilfrid Smith, sports editor of the *Chicago Tribune*," Graham said. "I told him I had never coached anything in my life. We decided that I would be an assistant coach in 1957 before becoming head coach the next year. Curly Lambeau was the head coach, and he was an easygoing guy, not as well organized as Paul Brown. After that year there was no question in my mind. After working under Paul Brown, I knew I could coach. We beat the Lions in 1958 and everybody thought I was a genius. I knew it wasn't true, but I didn't argue."

Graham's meaning was clear. He had gained the knowledge he needed from Paul Brown, the coach of the future—not Curly Lambeau, the coach of the past.

It was also the last coaching assignment for Hunk Anderson, who had met Lambeau four decades earlier at Notre Dame in 1918 and played for him as one of the three college ringers against Racine in the game that got Green Bay booted out of the NFL.

Anderson voiced some strong views in his autobiography. One was an interesting suggestion for the College All-Star game. "I am of the opinion that perhaps an All-Star college team would have a better chance of winning if the format was changed for them to play an All-Star pro team instead of the champions," Anderson later wrote.

Matching two teams that had never worked together? It would have evened things out, in a way. But it would not have been practical, taking the best pros away from their teams during training camp. And the NFL, which originally had embraced the All-Star opportunity to promote itself against the more popular college game, no longer needed that kind of help.

Like Lambeau, Graham won his first game as All-Star coach, beating the Detroit Lions 35-19 in 1958, but then settled into the inevitable losing pattern. Graham wound up coaching the College All-Star team 10 times, and would win only once more, beating the Packers in 1963. He also coached the Coast Guard Academy team from 1959 to 1965 after being connected to the service academy by his suburban Cleveland neighbor, Yankees owner George Steinbrenner. Graham also coached the Washington Redskins from 1966 to 1968. He was followed by Lombardi and preceded by Lambeau, among others.

"Although Lambeau is retiring as head coach, he will not sever relations with the annual game conducted by the *Chicago Tribune* Charities Inc.," the *Tribune* said when it announced the Graham hiring. "He will serve in an advisory capacity to Graham, whom he selected as his assistant for last summer's game." If Lambeau ever wound up advising Graham, it was not noted, even in the *Tribune*.

Curiously for a story that received this much attention, there were no comments in the story, not even from Graham or Lambeau. Although the article described Graham as "Lambeau's choice" when he had been named offensive backfield coach for the 1957 game, Graham said the *Tribune's* sports editor, not Lambeau, had hired him.

It's unlikely that Lambeau cared about leaving the College All-Stars after three efforts. He might even have initiated his departure. The rousing upset of 1955 had not led to an NFL coaching or general manager job. The lopsided defeat of 1956 had brought ridicule. After the competitive loss of 1957, there wasn't really anything left for Curly to prove.

# 75
## *GREEN BAY BUILDS IT, AND THEY COME*

A month after Lambeau lost to the Giants and a thunderstorm in Chicago, The Man Who Invented the Green Bay Packers crossed another momentous threshold. His hometown celebrated the grand opening of the stadium that one day would bear his name. He had campaigned hard for this major stride and had been announced as a dignitary who would take his place alongside the politicians, Packer heroes and other celebrities marking the event.

It was a significant moment. Not only had Green Bay secured its NFL future. In an era where pro-football teams generally played in Major League baseball parks, the Packers' new stadium was the first built specifically for a pro-football tenant.

The month of September 1957 was filled with anticipation for the opening of the Packers' new stadium. The Chicago Bears, the natural foil for that September 29 opener, would be the opponent. The Bears even sponsored a float in the Saturday parade. So did the Detroit Lions and New York Giants. The parade, which featured 17 marching bands and more than 30 floats, attracted a crowd estimated at more than 70,000. When it came to the Packers, there was nothing small-town about Green Bay.

The parade started at the Walnut Street bridge and ended at old City Stadium, where a farewell program was held. The gala was attended by Miss America, Marilyn Van Derbur, but the star was James Arness, the popular Marshall Dillon of Gunsmoke television fame. "The program had to be halted several times because children from the stands kept coming onto the field and mobbing the actor," Packer historian Mark Beech wrote. "No one was arrested," the *Press-Gazette* said, "but neither was the field ever really cleared."

Miss America and Marshall Dillon were joined by for the opening game on Sunday by Vice-President Richard Nixon. That eclectic trio was backed up by many others, including Wisconsin Governor Vernon Thomson, NFL commissioner Bert Bell and Bears owner George Halas, whose team was coached by Paddy Driscoll that season.

Nixon praised Green Bay citizens for building the new City Stadium without federal funds. "In Washington, we are used to hearing requests for aid," he said. "It is in the great American tradition that you people did it all yourself. This is your team and your stadium."

A crowd of 32,125 filled the stadium for the inaugural game between the Packers and the Bears. That was 7,000 more people than had ever seen a Packer game in Green Bay.

Conspicuously absent was Curly Lambeau. He had planned to attend but cancelled at the last minute. Lambeau shared his thoughts in a telegram read by former Green Bay mayor Dominic Olejniczak, a Packers board member who soon would be team president.

"It's a great disappointment to me not to be able to return to Green Bay to be with you," Lambeau said. "The biggest little town in football is the only representative with a modern plant just for football. Long live the Packers."

Exactly what was behind Lambeau's absence is not clear. One never knew with Curly, although an illness makes sense. Even in his prime, Curly had his share of health issues. Whatever caused his absence, it is both strange and somehow appropriate that he would miss the dedication of the future Lambeau Field. The stadium would be the enduring tribute to the man who started it all, and yet became largely forgotten.

A week before the stadium opened, Lambeau's friend, *Milwaukee Journal* columnist Oliver Kuechle, nominated him for the honor that eventually would come his way. In a column entitled, "Miracles? Take a Look at Green Bay," he paid loving tribute to the city's dedication to its football team. After marveling that Green Bay was the first city to build a stadium for its NFL team, he said, "What a wonderful tribute it would be to him who contributed so much if some day Green Bay could see its way to call this field "Lambeau Field.' "

"No mention of Green Bay and professional football up there can be complete, can even be begun, without consideration of the man who started it all—Curly Lambeau," Kuechle wrote. "It was his idea in the summer of 1919 to organize a team; it was he who raised the money for the first team from a packing company and who most of all sweated through lean years that followed; it was he who coached the team for 31 years and who won those six championships—not only coached it but acted as general manager of the club."

Kuechle offered this take on Lambeau's departure: "Unfortunately, as pro football grew, jealousies cropped up within. Internal fights concerned themselves principally with personalities. Lambeau actually was ahead of his time in the things he wanted to do. But they clipped his wings, and a little weary he finally resigned. A lot of water has gone over the dam since he left; bitterness has been forgotten. And Green Bay has a stadium."

It was a sentiment that others had started mentioning, an idea shared by many longtime Packers fans. At that point, though, the Lambeau Field idea did not gain traction.

The first football game at the Packers' new home was as heartwarming as the buildup. Trailing 17-14 in the fourth quarter, Green Bay pulled out a 21-17 victory on Babe Parilli's second touchdown pass, a six-yard throw to Gary Knafelc.

The Bears, who had won the NFL's Western Division the previous year, outgained the Packers, who were coming off a 4-8 season that put them at the bottom of the Western Division. But Green Bay intercepted five Bears passes—four thrown by Ed Brown, and one by future Packer Zeke Bratkowski.

"The Green Bay Packers dedicated their swanky new million dollar football stadium today, and the Chicago Bears cooperated beautifully," Cooper Rollow told *Chicago Tribune* readers. "Almost as if the script had been written in Hollywood, the Bears wilted before Babe Parilli's passing in the fourth quarter to lose 21 to 17 and make this afternoon a rousing success for the partisan throng of 23,132."

Holding court at the Northland Hotel before boarding a train back to Chicago, second-year Bears coach Paddy Driscoll came up with analysis that Lambeau would have admired. "Parilli should have been tackled for a 15-yard loss on both of those touchdown passes. Our boys had him trapped both times but they missed their tackles. If Parilli is that hot all the time, you guys won't be where you were last year, that's for sure."

As it turned out, neither team enjoyed its 1957 season. The Bears stumbled to a 1-4 start and finished 5-7, prompting Halas to un-retire and resume coaching his team for the fourth time. Green Bay also struggled, compiling a 3-9 record that put fourth-year coach Lisle "Liz" Blackbourn on thin ice.

# PART FIVE:
# FROM EXILE TO RETIREMENT

## 76
### *EYING A RETURN*

Since 1950, the Packers had finished their seasons with games at Los Angeles and San Francisco. And Curly Lambeau had been a regular at their game against the Rams. He usually joined the team for dinner at least once before the game.

In 1957, though, Curly Lambeau missed his first Packer-Ram game in Los Angeles in years. He was "back in his old hometown, Green Bay, for the holidays," the *Press-Gazette* said. He arrived in Green Bay around December 10, 1957, from California "to spend the holidays with his mother, Mrs. Marcel Lambeau, and other relatives. He also will spend some time in his Fish Creek home."

But this was more than a "home for the holidays" visit. Curly also was interested in going home to the Packers. He had said it, in a way, by buying a huge house in Fish Creek. And while a return to coaching was unlikely—he was 59 now—a front-office position made a lot of sense—to him and his supporters.

Green Bay had not had a winning season in 10 years since 1947. In other words, the Packers had never had a winning season without their founder. Who better to restore the hallowed franchise, many Packers fans felt, than the man who created the team's success in the first place? The Packers had built a mystique fueled by winning championships. And Lambeau was the creator of that mystique.

While Lambeau said publicly that he enjoyed being retired, that was more about maintaining the proper public stance. The winds of change were blowing in Green Bay. And Lambeau wanted to return to a position of power with the Packers.

With their new stadium and the NFL's soaring television revenue, the Packers no longer had money worries. A team that was fighting for its financial life when Lambeau left eight years earlier expected to show a $50,000 profit, Lambeau's former punting star, general manager Verne Lewellen, had reported.

Now that the Packers were healthy financially, it made perfect sense to Curly Lambeau, who had laid the groundwork for NFL success, and his supporters that he should return. He was the only man who had led Green Bay to championship glory.

In the eight years since he had resigned under fire, the Packers had gone through the worst stretch in franchise history. The heavy-handed front-office oversight that had been adopted in the wake of Lambeau's abuses was not working. The overseers were businessmen, not professional football experts.

General manager Verne Lewellen "has to ask one of the subcommittees whether he can have an anchovy in his martini or an onion," *Milwaukee Journal* writer Oliver Kuechle said with an exaggeration that summed up the situation.

Green Bay was wrapping up another listless season in 1957. It would win only three of its 12 games. The rousing 21-17 upset of the Bears in the season-opening dedication of its new stadium only made things seem worse. The season, Liz Blackbourn's fourth as coach, fell far short of those opening-day expectations.

Complicating matters, the Packers needed to choose a new front-office leader. Team president Russ Bogda, a prominent Chevrolet dealer who had steered the team to its new stadium and financial stability, was dying of lung cancer.

A week after Lambeau arrived in Green Bay, Bogda submitted his resignation due to ill health at a December 17, 1957, meeting of the team's board of directors. The Lambeau supporters on the unwieldy 45-member board undoubtedly had kept him informed him about Bogda, who had undergone surgery the previous summer.

The next day, December 18, Lambeau met with team vice-president Lee Joannes, the former ardent supporter who had become a strident opponent, at the Joannes Brothers grocery office. Lambeau told Joannes he wanted to return as president and general manager at a salary of $15,000. "In outlining his plan for the team, Lambeau said he intended to oversee the expansion of television rights, cultivate the Milwaukee market, run the draft and serve as an advisor to the head coach and players. He even offered to work without a contract."

Joannes dutifully reported the details of Lambeau's offer to the team's executive committee at its December 23 meeting. The committee voted to "inform Mr. Lambeau that there was no opening with the Packers at this time." That was technically true because the board had not accepted Bogda's resignation. In addition, despite the team's failure to win, Verne Lewellen seemed to be firmly entrenched as general manager. If Green Bay had not won enough games on his watch, at least the team no longer had money worries.

Beyond not accepting Bogda's resignation, the board signaled its preference for a new leader by electing Dominic Olejniczak, one of the team's two vice-presidents, to the newly created position of executive vice-president. Olejniczak, a realtor who had been Green Bay's mayor in 1945-55, was designated to preside over the club until a new board and executive committee were elected at the annual meeting of stockholders in March.

As a further endorsement of Olejniczak, the other vice-president, Joannes, "resigned to leave the ascension of Olejniczak as a normal formality." While Packer president in 1930-47, Joannes initially had been a major Lambeau loyalist, but had soured on Lambeau and become a bitter opponent toward the end of his presidency. He was now making it clear that he vehemently opposed bringing back Lambeau. A large majority of the board shared that view.

A Lambeau return seemed remote. But The Man Who Invented the Green Bay Packers wanted a chance to revive the team. And given the team's mediocre play, there were people who thought that idea had merit. Lambeau had some supporters on the board, especially because he had expressed views encouraging to Milwaukee board members. He also had influential friends in the media. And many Green Bay fans still believed in the only man who had coached the Packers to glory.

At the December 23 meeting, it was revealed that Lambeau had offered "to help in any way he can to resolve differences which have recently split the executive committee," the *Milwaukee Journal* reported. As a result, "Rumors began to fly at once that Lambeau, who is in Green Bay for the holidays, might be the real dark horse in the fight for the permanent club presidency in March. Or the general managership in the very widening circle of internal controversy. Or the presidency and general managership both. Lambeau, who has lived in California for the last 15 years, bought a house in nearby Fish Creek a year ago and proposed to move back here."

An *Associated Press* report left people around the nation wondering on Christmas morning if Lambeau's return to the Packers was imminent. " Top Job May Be Given to Curly Lambeau—He's In Line to Head Green Bay Club," the *Cincinnati Enquirer* headline over the *AP* report said on December 25. In California, the *Pasadena Independent* ran a Christmas Day headline saying "Lambeau Looms as Next Boss of Green Bay." The story underneath was more cautious than the headline, however, reporting that the

*Milwaukee Journal* said Lambeau "has been mentioned in Green Bay as a dark horse candidate for club president, general manager or both."

Although the Packer leadership was making important decisions about who would direct the team, only 29 of the 45 members of the Board of Directors and 10 of the 13 members of the executive committee attended the December 23 meetings.

Retired Packer star Buckets Goldenberg, a board member who had opened a popular Milwaukee restaurant, blamed the Green Bay majority for trying to exclude dissenters. Goldenberg complained that he and several other directors from Milwaukee had planned to attend the Monday board meeting even though they had only been informed about it on the previous Friday. In a Sunday telephone conversation, Goldenberg said, Olejniczak told him he did not need to attend. "The whole thing was unbusinesslike and contradictory," he said. "We should have been up there and it wasn't entirely our fault that we weren't."

Goldenberg said he planned to "protest to the club's stockholders at their annual meeting in March the methods by which a small clique of Green Bay old-timers maintain their control. 'We're a bunch of strangers down here,' he said, referring to Milwaukee directors. 'We're window dressing for what they like to say is a Wisconsin operation, and which should be for the good of the club, but which is strictly Green Bay.' "

The *Milwaukee Journal* article said "Goldenberg has been a vocal critic of Packer management. At the San Francisco game [in Milwaukee on October 20] six weeks ago, he and Lee Joannes, vice-president of the club, got into a shouting argument in the stands."

The Packers' Milwaukee contingent was especially concerned about a proposal to play four of the team's six home games in Green Bay, leaving only two for Milwaukee, which had been hosting three games. Goldenberg not only was an advocate for continuing to play games in Milwaukee and assuring that board members from Wisconsin's largest city had a voice in team matters. He also was a strong supporter of bringing back Curly Lambeau, which was an unthinkable option to Joannes and his allies, who had a large majority on the board.

While no longer interested in coaching, Lambeau coveted a return to operating the Packer organization with the authority he had enjoyed for nearly 30 years. As president and general manager, he believed he could restore the team—and himself—to glory.

Lambeau's friend and rival, George Halas, operated the Bears as he saw fit in Chicago. Why not him in Green Bay? Both men had started their teams with big dreams—dreams that had become reality. The answer, of course, was that Halas owned the Bears, had fought and connived to keep his team financially viable as well as successful on the field. Lambeau had won games, but had largely left the money details to others.

With the Green Bay franchise on sound financial ground, Lambeau had convinced himself that he could guide the team back to championship glory. Lambeau's purchase of a home in Fish Creek, just up the peninsula from Green Bay, fit neatly into a plan to return from exile. So did his vocal campaigning for the new stadium the previous year. But now, he faced the difficult challenge of convincing others—especially men he had alienated—to bring him back.

Beyond choosing a new chief executive, the Packer leadership also needed at the end of 1957 to address the coaching situation. In his fourth season, Lisle "Liz" Blackbourn had won only three games (3-9). His four-year record was a dismal 17-31. When named as the Packers' interim leader on December 23, Olejniczak declined to enter into the growing discontent with Blackbourn. "We talked about a lot of things in general, but no action was taken," Olejniczak said. The Blackbourn question loomed large, though, at the next meeting, on January 6.

The new stadium and financial health had increased the pressure for success on the field—and the Packers had now gone a decade since their last winning season, in 1947.

The discontent with Blackbourn had increased as Green Bay stumbled through its 1957 season. After the Packers finished with a 27-20 loss at San Francisco on December 15, he remained on the job in early January. He still had a year to go on a contract worth $25,000, a sizable sum to a team trumpeting a $50,000 profit. Bur Green Bay had gotten accustomed to winning when Lambeau ran things. And new stadium or not, a small town used to winning could not be asked to buy tickets to a loser forever.

At its January 6 meeting, the team's executive committee acted swiftly, recommending that Blackbourn be dismissed and that assistant Ray "Scooter" McLean be offered the job for one year with a salary of $15,000. That meeting adjourned at 1:30 p.m. At 7 p.m. that night, a board meeting ratified the executive committee's recommendation.

"It was a complete surprise when they called me and told me," Blackbourn said the next day. That certainly seemed true. He had gone to Mobile, Alabama, to scout the Senior Bowl. "They said it was for the good of the Packers and that's what I was working for. I enjoyed my association and certainly wish them all kinds of luck. This is a wonderful break for Scooter." Green Bay would pay Blackbourn $25,000 not to coach in 1958.

Rumors that McLean, 42, was about to join the staff of Detroit Lions coach George Wilson—they had played together on the Bears before becoming coaches—apparently put a sense of urgency into the change. "The hope of the executive committee was that McLean would do for Green Bay what [Wilson] had done for Detroit," Packer historian Cliff Christl said. After eight years as a Detroit assistant, Wilson became the Lions head coach in 1957 and won the NFL championship.

McLean had been a Green Bay assistant for seven years when he became head coach in 1958. There were a lot of differences, though. The key, of course, was personnel. Detroit had won NFL titles in 1952 and 1953, and had played in the championship game in 1954, with Bobby Layne at quarterback. McLean took over a long-struggling Packer team.

Green Bay also was burdened by its cumbersome leadership, in which civic-minded amateurs were in charge. Blackbourn, who returned to coaching at Marquette after a year at Carroll College, blamed the same unwieldy oversight that Lambeau had complained about.

"My situation in Green Bay was bad, very bad," Blackbourn said years later. "I was only the coach, not the general manager, and I used to go to [the executive committee] every Monday noon. Sometimes they'd clap, sometimes they'd boo. I called them disciples because there were 12 of them."

Besides the example of George Wilson in Detroit, Scooter McLean had another thing going for him: Everyone agreed that he was a nice guy. Would that be enough to get the Green Bay Packers back on track? In the fall of 1958, they would find out.

\* \* \* \* \* \* \* \*

Russ Bogda died on February 22, 1958. He was only 46. He had been on the Packer board for 12 years and club president since 1953. It was a tragic loss for his family and his many friends, especially among the Packers' leadership. In uniting behind Olejniczak, though, they did stave off the turmoil of a contested decision for a team president.

Despite opposition from Milwaukee, the board voted on Monday, March 3, 1958, to play four games in Green Bay, trimming Milwaukee from three games to two. With its new stadium, Green Bay could accommodate 32,500 fans. While Milwaukee's County Stadium had 10,000 more seats for football, fans in Green Bay turned out more consistently than in Milwaukee, where attendance tended to fall off when the team was not doing well.

Rising expenses were putting pressure on the team to watch its budget closely, Lewellen said.

Amid these concerns, Lambeau's dark-horse campaign to return to the Packers remained shaky. But his supporters kept his name in the mix.

Refusing to accept the decision to reduce Milwaukee's home games, six Milwaukee area directors on the Packer board threatened on Friday, April 25, to quit if the team's leadership did not meet its three-point ultimatum at the annual meeting of the team's board of directors the following Monday. First, they wanted Milwaukee's third home game restored. Second, "Curly Lambeau must be considered for the general manager's post." And third, they demanded a second ballot for team president. In opposition to Olejniczak, the Milwaukee contingent planned to support insurance executive Max Murphy or Dr. Robert Cowles, who were both from Green Bay.

If the demands were not met, Goldenberg's group threatened to not only resign, but also to seek another NFL team. "Milwaukee is a good pro football town," Goldenberg said. "And if the Packers don't want anything to do with Milwaukee, you can bet there will be some negotiating for a pro franchise. . . . Like the [Chicago] Cardinals." Goldenberg had some leverage because the Cardinals, facing a losing battle for Chicago with the Bears, were shopping for a new home.

Besides having support from six of the seven Milwaukee directors, Goldenberg said Don Hutson, who now lived in Racine, stood behind the ultimatum.``We want better cooperation from Green Bay without the prevailing competitive feeling," Goldenberg said.

The dispute left Packer supporters bracing for "a battle between Green Bay and Milwaukee" at the annual meeting. The expected showdown never materialized, though, because Goldenberg ultimately had no leverage. Even though the Goldenberg and Hutson names carried weight, with only a half-dozen votes on a 45-member board, the former Packer star walked back his ultimatum, saying, "Everything's fine. I'm satisfied."

General manager Verne Lewellen explained that "The Milwaukee group advised the directors that statements in the two Milwaukee papers and the *Press-Gazette* were untrue as far as quoting Goldenberg were concerned. The Milwaukee group said "it was wholeheartedly behind the Packers. That was their entire attitude at the meeting. They said they would cooperate with us fully in promoting the games in Milwaukee. In fact, Buckets said he thought it was a good idea to play four games here and two in Milwaukee—on a one-year basis."

The bottom line was that Goldenberg had no power to back up his bluster. And further, the idea of considering Lambeau as president was so remote that it was not even dismissed publicly. As expected, Olejniczak was elected president. Lewellen offered the welcome news that 20,382 season tickets already had been sold for the four home games in Green Bay.

"In short, there was harmony instead of the expected war and bloodshed over Packer Power at this special spring meeting," the *Press-Gazette's* Art Daley concluded.

His Packer return thwarted, Lambeau continued to enjoy retirement in California and Door County. There was an effort in the spring of 1958 to honor him by renaming City Stadium "Curly Lambeau Stadium," columnist Arnie Hoffman wrote in the *Chippewa Herald-Telegram* in Chippewa Falls, Wisconsin. Citing the magazine "Proball," Hoffman said, "The move is already underway in the Green Bay area." Proball, edited by Lambeau's friend and supporter, Fritz Van, reflected the grass-roots appreciation for Curly. He was gone from directing the Packers. But he was not forgotten.

Lambeau had mysteriously been a late cancellation for the September 29, 1957, dedication of the stadium that one day would bear his name. He finally attended a Packer game at the new City Stadium on September 1, 1958, nearly a year after it opened. The pre-season Labor Day contest kicked off at 4:30 p.m.

"A very nice stadium," he said, taking a seat in the back row of the press box with three familiar faces who were scouting the game—Giants scout Jack LaVelle, a former Packer scout; Colts assistant coach Bob Shaw, who had been an end on the Cardinals when Curly coached in Chicago, and Redskins assistant Joe Tereshinski, an end when Curly coached Washington.

At that point, The Man Who Invented the Green Bay Packers had become just another face in the crowd.

# 77
## *"SOVIET" LEADERSHIP OF PACKERS?*

On the day that Curly Lambeau watched his first game at the stadium that would become Lambeau Field, Green Bay gave its new coach, Ray "Scooter" McLean, his first victory, 20-17, over the Philadelphia Eagles on Monday, September 1, 1958.

Although only an exhibition, "the game turned out to be another rough house encounter, sparked by numerous fistfights. Men were fighting for a pro football livelihood and they played for keeps," Art Daley told *Press-Gazette* readers.

Five days later, Green Bay defeated the Giants 41-20 in Boston, their second win in three exhibition games. At that point, the speedy hiring of popular assistant McLean to keep him in Green Bay looked shrewd.

Although the Packers lost their regular-season opener 34-20 to the Bears, George Halas called the Packers "the most improved team in our division" and predicted that Green Bay would finish with a better record than his Bears.

A 13-13 tie against the NFL champion Detroit Lions in their second game also seemed to be a good sign for the McLean hire, especially because the Packers stepped up despite some key injuries.

After that, though, a harsh reality set in. After two more losses, the Packers finally won their fifth game, against the struggling Eagles, who would win only two games that fall. During that October 26 adventure at rainy City Field, Babe Parilli threw four touchdowns to lead the Packers to a 38-14 fourth-quarter lead. They then held on for a 38-35 win.

"If you guys had blown this one," Packer vice-president and former president Lee Joannes reportedly joked after the Eagles game, `I would have gone home to get my shotgun and cleaned house but good."

For McLean, that was the high-water mark. Green Bay hit an unprecedented low the following Sunday, November 2, in Baltimore, losing to the Colts 56-0. From their tentative debut in 1953, the Colts had become a powerhouse on their way to winning the NFL title, beating the Giants 23-17 in overtime, a television classic that became known as "The Greatest NFL Game Ever Played." But the Colts' prowess did nothing to ease the hurt of the most one-sided loss in Green Bay history. Even the second-quarter departure of Baltimore quarterback Johnny Unitas with a rib injury did not stop the onslaught.

It was, the *Milwaukee Journal* said, "Green Bay's darkest two and a half hours in its 40 years of professional football. As the rain beat down and the lights shone through the gloom, Scooter McLean's Packers crumbled."

Afterward, McLean pulled a page from Lambeau's playbook, threatening to cut "some veteran players who have a defeatist attitude." Nothing worked, though. Green Bay lost its final seven games, finishing with a record of 1-10-1, the worst showing in franchise history.

Even the encouraging early tie with the Lions later would be tainted. "I swear [Lions quarterback] Bobby Layne was drunk that day," Art Daley told Packer historian Cliff Christl. "People say they saw Bobby Layne in the bar at the [Northland Hotel] before the game drinking. He was something else."

As the losses piled up, McLean's popularity declined. And Green Bay became the butt of jokes.

"The Packers were the most soft-bitten team in the league," Green Bay native Red Smith wrote in the *New York Herald-Tribune*. "They overwhelmed one, underwhelmed 10 and whelmed one."

*Milwaukee Journal* columnist Oliver Kuechle, the longtime confidante and supporter of Lambeau, did not miss opportunities to stump for The Man Who Invented the Green Bay Packers. That included taking shots at men like Joannes, who stood in the way of the growing clamor to bring back The Man Who Invented the Green Bay Packers.

A once ardent supporter of Lambeau, Joannes "first led the fight to clip Curly Lambeau's wings in the middle forties," Kuechle wrote on October 28, before the titanic loss at Baltimore. "Joannes [also] led the fight to get rid of [McLean's predecessor] Blackbourn, while Blackbourn was out of the city on a scouting mission, and Joannes who hired Scooter McLean as head coach. Not since these events transpired have the Packers won more games in a season than they have lost. There could be a connection."

As the losses piled up in the fall of 1958, Lambeau might have felt mixed feelings. On a pure pride level, it might have bothered him to see the team he had created and built into a perennial contender sink so low. At the same time, the continued struggles left open the possibility, however remote, that he might have an opportunity to return. He undoubtedly must have felt that he could have done better than one win. Every football fan in Green Bay probably felt that way.

What was abundantly clear was that Lambeau's appraisal shortly before he left the Packers in 1950 was absolutely true. A 45-member board of directors and a 13-member executive board was no way to run a football team successfully. Even a unique community-owned franchise needed a chain of command that could field a competitive team.

After the 56-0 debacle in Baltimore, Kuechle stumped for Lambeau while carving up the Packers' community leadership. "The day that the executive committee clipped Curly Lambeau of absolute authority in the mid-forties and substituted administration by soviet, that is the day the team's troubles began," he wrote, hinting that a Lambeau return would be a step in the right direction. "There hasn't been a winning season since. An executive committee of new blood, a new framework of club administration, are almost 'musts.' They must come first. Other things can be carried on from there. Sunday's game was just plain pathetic. The Packers aren't that bad. No pro club should ever be beaten, 56-0. And the principal trouble stems from within."

Administration by soviet? During the Cold War era, there could be no stronger indictment of an American institution.

That set off a newspaper war between Lambeau-backer Kuechle and Art Daley in the Packers-first *Press-Gazette*. "Trouble is, Arthur's boss, managing editor John Torinus, is a member of the [Packers'] executive committee," Kuechle said.

Disputing the notion of "soviet" leadership, Daley wrote that Kuechle that "has been on the Pack since he predicted back in the late forties that the Packers couldn't survive if Curly Lambeau left. This guy has done nothing since but hammer at the Packers' method of operation."

Kuechle responded to Daley's contention that the Packers had survived in Green Bay under their current leadership by saying that the surge in television revenue and the team's new stadium assured economic survival. "But have the Packers really 'survived' on the field? They have not. They haven't had a winning season—better than .500—since Lambeau left. They have the worst 10-year record in the league, the worst 10½ year record if you want to include the seven games played this year—37 victories, 88 defeats, two ties."

Addressing Daley's contention that Kuechle was distressed because "his direct pipeline inside the executive committee" —Max Murphy, who had resigned in protest—"dealt himself off the executive committee because of a stacked deck," Kuechle responded that Murphy had "never violated the confidence of the executive committee. That probably won't be believed by the soviet, but it's true."

Soviet! There was that ugly word, which was especially sensitive in the state of Wisconsin. Red Scare Senator Joe McCarthy was from Appleton, just down the Fox Valley from Green Bay.

There was no question, though, that the Packers were hurting. A few days after a 24-14 Thanksgiving loss to the now-struggling Lions that was regarded as a mistake-prone turkey of a game even in Detroit, Packer president Dominic Olejniczak "vigorously denied that any changes are being contemplated by the Packer executive committee."

Olejniczak was reacting to an *Associated Press* report that "There is mounting pressure among members of the Green Bay Packers' executive committee for a new general manager, as well as a new coach." Denial or not, general manager Verne Lewellen and coach Scooter McLean were in the crosshairs.

"Now comes the hunt for a scapegoat," Lambeau backer Kuechle wrote in the *Milwaukee Journal* as the Packers prepared to take their 1-8-1 record on their season-ending road trip to San Francisco and Los Angeles.

Kuechle threw his support behind Neenah realtor Hugh Strange, one of the Packers' 45 directors, who said the team's administration needed a complete overhaul. Strange publicly recommended reducing the size of the board and the executive committee, and combining the president and general manager positions.

"[Strange] was right," Kuechle said. "Cut the 45 to half or less. Why an unwieldy 45? They're mostly there for window dressing. Get rid of the 13 man executive committee. Why 13 except to let a few fellows throw out their chests around town? A small hard core of old-timers runs the executive committee anyway. Create a general manager's job of real authority. Let him run the show from the rising of the curtain to the falling. Let him be responsible to a compact executive committee (which doesn't meet every week) but let him have no interference. Get a top notch coach, pay him well, give him security. The Packers cannot be revived in a year or two. It took Weeb Ewbank five years to bring the Baltimore Colts to the top. The firing of coaches has solved nothing—and since Lambeau's last year, 1949, the Packers have had Ronzani, Blackbourn, McLean, and, if the *Associated Press* story of Tuesday is correct, will shortly have Mr. X. The Packers must be saved. Hunting for a scapegoat for what has happened this year won't save them. The real trouble lies deep and the sooner the executive committee realizes this, the sooner the Packers will be back. Why not reorganize the executive committee and start off fresh?"

# 78
## *"WE WANT CURLY!"*

Would the Packers actually try to move forward by turning to their hero from the past, Curly Lambeau? A day after Green Bay slipped to 1-9-1 with a 48-21 loss in San Francisco, that option gained some grass-roots support.

Two small businessmen from Green Lake, Wisconsin, gained national attention by launching a petition drive to bring back Lambeau as the Packers' coach. Contacted in Los Angeles by food-market owner Henry H. Eaton and restaurant owner Harry Norton, Lambeau said, "If it could be arranged, I'll be glad to come back." The details, however, were so fuzzy that a December 9, 1958, *Associated Press* report mistakenly put a Three Lakes dateline on the story, rather than Green Lake. One possible explanation: A wire-service rewrite man taking dictation from a far-off correspondent might have misheard the town name on a crackling telephone line.

"At least we're doing something," Eaton added. "Nobody else is doing anything. [The board] doesn't seem to be able to agree on anything or anyone. I don't know who else would work but Lambeau." Eaton said he and Norton were longtime Packer fans who are "fed up with the way things have been going."

From that little seed, a "Draft Curly" movement started to blossom. If it didn't necessarily have Lambeau's fingerprints on it, they weren't far removed. Lambeau's many supporters—men who had either played for him or written about him—were quietly, and sometimes not so quietly, stirring the desire for the return of The Man Who Invented the Green Bay Packers.

Even though his last years as Green Bay coach had been filled with frustration, the "We Want Curly" movement struck a chord. The Green Bay Packers were down. But the team's legacy of success was so embedded in the Lambeau name, its fan base was so devoted, that people rallied around an opportunity to voice support for Curly to lead the return to excellence.

The media noticed—and took interest. Speaking directly to an *Associated Press* writer from Milwaukee, Lambeau said he "might be interested in returning to the club under the right circumstances." Lambeau also said, "I have been contacted by individuals on the Board of Directors, but they were acting strictly as individuals and not speaking for the club."

There was a growing sentiment to blow up the "soviet" leadership among fans, media and on the board of directors. The question was, would Lambeau be restored to the throne? Or would a new Packer leader be chosen?

Out in Los Angeles, one of Lambeau's media friends helped him elaborate on the surge in interest. At 10:30 p.m. on Sunday, December 7, several hours after the Packers had fallen to the 49ers, he had been relaxing with Rams play-by-play broadcaster Bob Kelley, who also did a nightly sports show that "made as many people gnash their teeth as cheer," legendary *Los Angeles Times* columnist Jim Murray said. "But they listened. Even when I didn't agree with a bloody word he said I was entertained by the way Bob Kelley said it."

A triple threat, Kelley also wrote a column, "Bob Kelley Says," in two Long Beach newspapers, the *Press-Telegram* and the *Independent*. That was where Kelley wrote that he was relaxing with Curly at "a Valley restaurant when [Curly] was called to the phone." Given the hour, it's likely that bourbon and cigarettes were involved, rather than steak and potatoes.

"It's long distance, Mr. Lambeau," an excited waitress said. Curly shrugged and said, "Probably some of my cronies down in Palm Springs wanting me to settle a football bet."

When he returned, however, Lambeau said the call had been from Norton, the Green Lake restaurant owner. "Asked me if I wanted to coach the Packers. I told them I could hardly give an answer since they were not officials of the club—just fans."

Lambeau received a dozen more calls from enthusiastic Packer fans in the next 48 hours, followed by calls from *Associated Press* and *United Press* reporters.

Kelley, who had been "the Voice of the Rams" in Cleveland and moved with them to Los Angeles, went on to say that Curly was not truly interested: "Lambeau, I know, will never coach again—unless it's something like the one-shot deal he had with the College All-Stars."

Lambeau did not need the headache and did not need the money, Kelley said. "He's living the kind of life you and I would love," Kelley said, noting that Lambeau owned "a huge ranch in Thousand Oaks" and "maintained an apartment in Hollywood, all that a bachelor needs. His time is his own. He squires the dolls around Hollywood and the Valley. Or maybe he feels like a vacation in Palm Springs—he takes it. Or perhaps he wants to visit old friends in Wisconsin; he goes. . . Curly enjoys the type of life he's leading. Who wouldn't? Would he go back to the cold of Green Bay and attempt to rebuild the Packers? You know as well as I what the answer is. Wrong!"

Everything in Kelley's argument made sense—except for one thing. Lambeau did want to return to the Packers helm. He wasn't interested in the relentless grind of coaching. But the lure of running the Packers again—having a grand finish in Green Bay as president and general manager—was very attractive. Being forced out in 1950 had left a bad taste. If there was a groundswell of support that led to Lambeau being able to return, that would be irresistible to The Man Who Invented the Green Bay Packers.

Feigning disinterest fit right into the way Lambeau had often managed his media maneuvering. With an old friend like Kelley—who had casually mentioned that he had almost bought a half-share in Lambeau's ranch—the manipulation made perfect sense. Politicians regularly acted uninterested while cultivating a draft-me movement behind the scenes. It had helped put the current President, Dwight D. Eisenhower, in the White House.

A truer read on the situation came later that week, when Lambeau bumped into a group of Packers who were having drinks one night before their final game against the Rams. They were conveniently imbibing at the Ram's Horn, an Encino restaurant owned by another Lambeau drinking buddy, the flamboyant Roy Harlow, who also owned Roy Harlow's Pump Room, in Studio City. Kelley and a pair of Rams, Bob Waterfield and Don Paul, were involved in Harlow's restaurants. So it was no coincidence that Packers should end up quenching their thirst at the Ram's Horn along with Lambeau.

At least seven Packers—notably Paul Hornung, Ron Kramer, Forrest Gregg, Jim Taylor and Tom Bettis—had played for Lambeau's College All-Star teams. At that time, Lambeau and Halas were the winningest coaches in the NFL by a wide margin. They were still sixth and second, respectively, on that list as the NFL headed into its second century. Lambeau and Bill Belichick are the only coaches to win six championships. To young players in the late 1950s, Lambeau was an entrenched legend.

"We were [at the Ram's Horn] before the Los Angeles game, either Friday or Saturday night, and Curly comes in," Jerry Kramer recalled later. "It was Hornung, McGee, Jimmy [Taylor], myself. There were four, five, six of us, so we sit down with Curly at a booth and start having a few drinks. We're pretty excited to meet Curly. Curly was a symbol of success and achievement and those kinds of things from yesteryear. So we start talking to him about coming back. 'Any chance?' 'Hell, yes, I'd like to come back.' We think, 'Damn, Curly's coming back. He's a proven winner. He understands it. That would be pretty cool to have Curly Lambeau come back.'"

That said, Lambeau understood that it was wise to remain aloof. While he had many friends in Green Bay, he also had enemies on the team's board of directors. Acting disinterested would help him save face if his Hail-Mary bid to return to Green Bay did not work out. And so, his friend Kelley portrayed Lambeau as playing coy because that was the smart thing to do. Curly didn't need a job. And campaigning wouldn't go far. With influential enemies like Joannes, he was very much a longshot for returning to power in Green Bay. But if widespread support led to the ideal offer—the power to remake the Packers—that would be an opportunity he could not refuse. His friend Bob Kelley was playing along.

It was true that Curly was financially set. He had his ranch and "bachelor pad" in California, and a lovely summer home on the water in Door County. But he also had proclaimed in his high school yearbook, "When I get thru with athletics, I'm going out and conquer the rest of the world." He might not have grasped it at that time, but four decades later, the world he wanted to conquer was the world of professional football.

In Wisconsin, hundreds of "We want Lambeau" bumper stickers and window cards were popping up in Green Bay, courtesy of Fritz Van Duyse, an enterprising sportscaster reportedly selling them for four cents apiece. Van Duyse, who was known merely as Fritz Van, was the brother of Mary Jane Van Duyse, the young woman Lambeau would begin dating soon.

Meanwhile, three of Curly's former players, Pete Tinsley, Arnie Herber and Buckets Goldenberg, denied that they were involved in circulating petitions for their former coach. Goldenberg said he allowed the petitions to be circulated at his Milwaukee restaurant, "but I have no connection with them."

Goldenberg added that he would like to see Lambeau return as general manager. "I don't think he would want to come back as coach. I know for a fact he has not been approached. However, you couldn't find a better man. He is respected and he would give the Packers a lot of authority at league meetings."

Another log was added to the fire when an inaccurate report surfaced in the *Milwaukee Sentinel* on Thursday, December 11, that

Lambeau would be introduced as the Packers' GM on Monday, December 15—and that he would hire Kentucky coach Blanton Collier as the new Green Bay coach. "That's complete news to me," said Collier, a former assistant to Paul Brown in Cleveland.

By now, though, the grass-roots movement to bring back Lambeau was moving into high gear. Packer president Dominic Olejniczak, who had been hanged in effigy from a street light outside the Packer ticket office, stood firm, saying no decisions were scheduled to be made about the team's coaching and general manager jobs at the team's nest executive board meeting on Monday, December 15, 1958.

"McLean and Lewellen are not on the agenda," Olejniczak said. "There may be an announcement later in the week. The season is not over. It would be unfair to comment on personnel, players or otherwise at this time." Olejniczak also declined to comment on whether Packer management intended to contact Lambeau.

Apparently buoyed by the surge in support for him, Lambeau said it makes him "just sick [to see the Packers] floundering at the bottom" of the NFL. He then stated his conditions for returning to the Packers in an interview on Van's Green Bay WDUZ radio show. Speaking by telephone from Los Angeles, Lambeau said he was interested, but had not been contacted by anyone connected with the Packer executive committee or board.

"You know my heart is at Green Bay," he said, adding that he could turn around the team fairly quickly from the worst season in franchise history. "It can't be done in a year. . . but it can be done. I think there's a pretty good football team there and it wouldn't take much to make the team a winner."

"Let's put it this way," he said. "If I could be in a capacity where I had the authority to improve and correct situations that are necessary to make the Packers a power in the National [Football] League again, then I would return. If I had the same authority I had before December 1, 1947, I think I could do a job."

Keeping the momentum going, Lambeau stopped by the Packers' Los Angeles hotel before they played the Rams and gave a pep talk. "You're in an ideal spot for an upset," he told McLean. "They think they can murder you. I feel very strongly that if each one of your men does his job you can win Sunday. They're ready to be upset."

There was to be no upset. Green Bay lost 34-20. Its miserable 1-10-1 record left football fans in Wisconsin clamoring for change.

On Tuesday, two days after the final setback in Los Angeles, McLean told *Milwaukee Journal* writer Chuck Johnson, ``I have no alibis and no criticism of anyone," but added that he had no intention of resigning. "I'm letting nature take its course. If I worried about my future, I'd end up in the hospital." McLean, whose one-year contract expired on December 31, had to know, though, that he had virtually no chance of returning as Green Bay coach.

"Any time a professional club hits rock bottom, a change is inevitable," *Milwaukee Sentinel* writer Lloyd Larson said. "What form will it take? A good guess is that Ray (Scooter) McLean is a cinch to go after one year as head coach. It's more than possible that General Manager Verne Lewellen, too, will be a shakeup victim."

A day later, before he could be fired, McLean resigned on Wednesday, December 17, and took a job as backfield coach of the Detroit Lions.

Dismissing rumors suggesting Oklahoma coach Bud Wilkinson or Michigan State athletic director Biggie Munn might be coming to Green Bay, Larson said, "The only name really kicked around seriously is that of Curly Lambeau, who left the Bay nine years ago after a stormy final season. Surprisingly, Curly is said to have some support from the inside despite his record since quitting the Packers."

Support for Curly, however, seemed to be mainly among people not involved in the actual selection process. Lambeau's backers were media members and Packer fans who yearned for a return to the glory days. They did not have a vote, though. Lambeau supporters on the team's 45 board members and 13 executive committee members were clearly a small minority.

\* \* \* \* \* \* \* \*

While Lambeau seemed destined to remain in exile, his plan for reviving the team—the plan he had been harping about since he was forced out—was becoming the team's path forward. As McLean was exiting, club president Dominic Olejniczak announced a major restructuring on Tuesday, December 16, 1958.

Among the changes, the executive committee would be reduced from 13 to six members, and the posts of chairman of the board and second vice-president would be eliminated. The weekly executive committee meetings to review games, which had become excruciating for the head coach, also would be gone. A 45-member board of directors would remain the same, Olejniczak said, "because it was felt that the board constitutes a ready-made nucleus of top caliber, vitally interested men with executive ability immediately available for major actions and decisions."

Most significantly, Olejniczak said the club planned to hire a "general manager with complete responsibility for all phases of operation including coaching."

While his ideas for restoring Green Bay to football glory had gained acceptance, Lambeau certainly did not appear to be part of the plan. His transgressions had led to a curbing of his authority, and the authority of future general managers authority. There were still influential men, notably Lee Joannes, who would resist bringing back Lambeau with every tool they could use.

Beyond that, Lambeau's record as a coach and general manager since the Packers' last NFL title in 1944 did not suggest that he could build a championship-caliber organization. The game had changed. The way that Curly had won six NFL championships in 25 years bore very little resemblance to the way Paul Brown had won seven championships in 10 years after World War II.

In other words, while there was a groundswell of support for Lambeau among fans, media and players, that was not enough. Olejniczak and other team leaders were looking toward the future, not the past.

# 79
## *"THE SOVIET IS DEAD!"*

Under the headline, "The Soviet is Dead! Long Live the Packers!" Oliver Kuechle celebrated the plan to hire a football man to operate the Green Bay football team. "It took the Green Bay Packers 10 long years to find out a professional football team can't be run by committees and subcommittees. . . " he wrote. The executive committee's decision to "[strip] itself of the power and authority it took away from Curly Lambeau 10 years ago. . . came like a breath of fresh air to loyal and stifled Packer followers everywhere. . . . No more will an unwieldy and a bickering executive committee of 13 sit like a supreme soviet. The executive committee has been cut to six."

The executive committee, Kuechle said, was "scared stiff because a losing and rundown team [would] never be able to pay the $600,000 in rent it has promised the city it would over 20 or 25 years. It's scared stiff because, for the first time, it can look toward the horizon and envision Green Bay without a pro team if things continue as they are."

"It is not going to be as easy," Kuechle warned, "to find a topnotch man as the committee thinks. . . . They need pro experience. And just where is the ready old pro? That's the real tough part of the rub. Curly Lambeau? He's a strong possibility with all of the recent support built up for him but he is still a controversial figure in Green Bay and wants his own terms. Liz Blackbourn? He is one of the best men they could get but he is a controversial figure, too, with some of the old hard core. Eddie Kotal of the Rams? He knows the league inside out and once played for the Packers but he doesn't want to leave the coast. Tex Schramm, the former general manager of the Rams? He is with CBS now and happy. Nick Kerbawy, who did so much for the Lions as general manager a few years ago? He is getting $50,000 a year on a 20 year contract with the Zollner Manufacturing Co. Lewellen himself, who by Olejniczak's own words was little more than a figurehead while subcommittees did the job? He could do it—could have done it, if the soviet had only given him authority. But now? Old pros suggest themselves but try to get them. The big thing, the first big step forward in 10 years has been taken. There'll be front office reorganization. An executive committee that for years was assiduously trimming the wick on a lamp has finally decided to install electric lights. This column applauds."

On that same Wednesday, December 17, 1958, in a separate *Milwaukee Journal* story, Lambeau said Packer officials "have not contacted me, and I can't say what my answer would be. Actually I should not make any comment at all. Taking the job would depend on a lot of things. There are a lot of things to be considered, the authority a man would have, for instance."

For instance? Authority shaped up as the key factor. Unless Lambeau was given the decision-making power he held until 1947, a return would make no sense for either him or the citizen-executives that tried to oversee him. Chances are, Lambeau knew that the only way he was coming back was if public opinion forced the executive committee's hand. That was a very major long shot. On the other hand, there was no name more hallowed than "Lambeau" in Packer lore. As Jerry Kramer noted, even current Packers were excited about that prospect.

To nudge the team's leadership, Curly's supporters announced on Wednesday that a "We Want Lambeau" rally would be held on Friday night, December 19. In an ominous sign, though, the *Green Bay Press-Gazette*, which was closely aligned with the men in charge of the Packers, barely mentioned Lambeau's name amid the turmoil of McLean's resignation and the major restructuring of the team's administration.

When the *Press-Gazette* finally got around to the rally, it was under the headline, "Less Than 50 Attend `We Want Lambeau' Rally.' " The rally's organizers, led by Fritz Van, described the turnout at Pleasant View Hall as disappointing. Van, who had radio and magazine forums, was named chairman of the group. A *UPI* report said "75 turned out in icy weather to urge Lambeau to resume the helm of the floundering Packers."

Another rally was scheduled for Monday night, December 22, at the Riverside Ballroom. The group planned to have several former Packers and *Milwaukee Journal* sports editor Oliver Kuechle attend. A group of 200 attended the second Lambeau rally. They heard former Packer Pete Tinsley blame Packer defeats on easy living, predicting that "there would be less lipstick and beer for some of the Packers' high priced stars if Lambeau returns." Another former Packer, Wuert Engelmann, said, "There is no love lost between Lambeau and me, but nevertheless there is no question but that Curly Lambeau is the man to put the Packers back on their feet."

The next night, Tuesday, December 23, Curly arrived back in Green Bay "to spend Christmas with his mother" and other family members, including his brother, Raymond, who was terminally ill. "But, he added when pressed, he would be interested in a job as Packer general manager if it carried, as advertised during the recent administrative shakeup, 'absolute authority.'"

The Lambeau speculation cranked up to a new level with the news that Curly had met with Packer president Dominic Olejniczak late on Wednesday, December 24. According to Olejniczak's personal papers, the Packer president interviewed Lambeau for nearly two hours at the Northland Hotel on December 26, so it's possible the two men set up that interview on December 24.

In the notes of that meeting, Olejniczak said Lambeau indicated that " 'he would not coach himself but would be on top of the situation at all times,' working with coaches. talking trades and running the draft. Lambeau also said salary didn't matter. Paraphrasing him, Olejniczak wrote in his notes: 'Anything they want to pay—Does not have to work the rest of his life—Whatever the board wants to do—Just wants to help."

Near the end of their meeting, Lambeau asked, "Ole, tell me—have I got a chance?" There was no response in Olejniczak's notes.

After reading that Lambeau, former coach Liz Blackbourn and team scouting director Jack Vainisi had applied, former coach Gene Ronzani sent a letter to Olejniczak urging him not to hire any of them. "Curly bankrupt the Packers 3 times. Liz put the Packers in present position. Vainisi not enough weight—Frosty selfish and treacherous."

Lambeau knew he was not likely to be hired. He had burned too many bridges with men like Joannes. His record at the end of his Packer run, and with the Cardinals and Redskins, had been mediocre. And there were very real concerns about giving him the degree of authority that the next general manager would enjoy; he had abused that trust in the past.

And yet, Lambeau's public aloofness was mere posturing. He clearly, desperately, wanted the job. It wasn't about money; he would work for any amount. He wanted something that money he couldn't buy. An alpha male his entire life, Lambeau wanted a chance to be in charge again, to restore the Packers to their former glory—and restore his name. That opportunity was priceless—especially for a man who did not have a strong family foundation. He did not have a wife, he didn't seem especially close to one son and had no relationship with his other son. For all the glamour of his wealthy lifestyle, there was an undercurrent of loneliness..

Dismissing a *UPI* report that a meeting between him and a Packer official had "heightened speculation that Lambeau might return as general manager with absolute powers," Lambeau "flatly denied Friday night that he has held any secret meetings with Packers President Dominic Olejniczak concerning the position of general manager of the club."

Beyond the talk with Olejniczak, Lambeau said, "I haven't met with any member of the Packer front office and they haven't contacted me. Sure, I've expressed interest in the job, but that's all there is to it." Lambeau said his visit here was simply his annual holiday trip "to visit relatives. If I don't hear anything by Monday [December 29], I'm going home [to California] and forget about it."

# 80
## *LOMBARDI IN THE PACKERS' SIGHTS*

Olejniczak never showed any sign of considering Lambeau seriously. Their meeting seemed more of a courtesy interview, a show of respect for The Man Who Invented the Green Bay Packers. And a gesture to the people rallying for Lambeau's return.

A consensus builder as Green Bay mayor in 1945-55 and as a Packer official since 1950, Olejniczak already was diligently looking for the football man who would guide Green Bay's football forward, not backward.

His December 18 call to Paul Brown brought the recommendation of Blanton Collier, which prompted published speculation that Collier would coach and Lambeau would be general manager. But Olejniczak was merely making inquiries—casting a wide net to identify the best candidate.

Giants owner and general manager Wellington Mara called on December 19 to say he had two outstanding coordinators, Vince Lombardi and Tom Landry, who would make fine coaches. The Packer president talked to Lombardi by telephone on December 23, five days before the Giants met the Colts in their celebrated overtime NFL championship game. Olejniczak's notes indicated that Lombardi was very interested. Although he had turned down the Eagles job a year earlier, Green Bay was different. Lombardi planned to make decisions about his future after he coached in the Pro Bowl on January 11 in Los Angeles. As Eastern Division champion, Giants coach Jim Lee Howell and his staff oversaw the East's All-Stars.

Conducting a thorough and professional search, Olejniczak had many accomplished coaches on his list. San Francisco owner Tony Morabito called to recommend Forty Niners assistant Phil Bengtson. Olejniczak also looked at candidates from the college ranks, including Navy's Eddie Erdelatz, Michigan State's Biggie Munn, Northwestern's Are Parseghian and Iowa's Forest Evashevski. Also on his radar were former Browns quarterback Otto Graham and a pair of Canadian Football League coaches, Winnipeg's Bud Grant, a Superior, Wisconsin, native, and former Eagles coach Jim Trimble, of the Hamilton Tiger-Cats.

Meanwhile, hardcore Packer fans were growing impatient. On January 13, 1959, the American Legion Sullivan-Wallen Post No. 11, the designated beneficiary of the non-profit Packers, became so restless that it asked for the resignation of Olejniczak and every other team officer.

"The present committee has not demonstrated that it is capable of gaining and retaining the confidence of the community in the operation of the club," the post said. In its resolution, passed by a 23-9 vote, the post recommended that "some well known and public spirited individual such as Dr. R.L. Cowles replace the present president of the Packer Corp." Dr.

Cowles, a Packer board member, said he felt flattered "but I never have been and am not now a candidate for the presidency of the Packers."

This was a protest from one of the most dedicated segments of the Packers' fan base. Post 11 members routinely formed the color guard and worked many game-day jobs. Although only 32 of the nearly 800 post members had voted, Post 11 commander John N. Patton defended the resolution, saying, "This was not an overnight decision." A special Packer committee worked on it for two months, he said. In its attack, Post 11 identified itself as "a substantial stockholder in the Green Bay Packer Corp" and urged all stockholders to vote for change at the upcoming annual meeting.

Harry Norton and Henry Eaton, the Green Lake businessmen who were pushing for Lambeau's return, quickly endorsed the Post 11 call for the resignation of Olejniczak and all other officers. They said they presented 2,840 documents, with a minimum of 27 signatures each, to the Packers in early January urging that Lambeau be brought back as general manager and coach.

Although it demonstrated how frustrated Packer fans had become, none of the unrest affected Olejniczak, who had quietly and diligently been working to find the right football man to lead the Packers back to the top. By mid-January, he had zeroed in on his first choice, Evashevski, who flew to Green Bay for a face-to-face meeting on January 18 that went undetected in the media.

Drafting first overall, the Packers already had selected Iowa's All-America quarterback, Randy Duncan, when the NFL conducted the first four rounds of its draft on December 1 to thwart Canadian raiders. Duncan, who had led Iowa to a Rose Bowl victory, would have been a neat fit with his college coach.

Evashevski, 42, was offered a big increase from his package at Iowa, worth an estimated $40,000, but he turned it down. "I was committed to intercollegiate athletics and I had a longterm contract at Iowa," he explained later. In less then nine months, Evashevski headed in a different direction, announcing that he would retire from coaching and concentrate on being Iowa's athletic director. He coached two more seasons, stepping down after 1960.

As a result, Duncan never played in Green Bay. After dabbling in Canadian football with the British Columbia Lions, he quickly followed family tradition and became an attorney. "If [Evashevski] would have gone to Green Bay, I'm sure I would have gone too," Duncan said in 2009. "You have to remember, the Packers had only won one game in 1958. It wasn't a real popular situation at the time. Nobody could have seen what Lombardi would do. Being the No. 1 draft choice in the league wasn't what it was now. So basically it came down to money. I got more to play in Canada."

To make one last-ditch push for the Packer job, Lambeau returned to Wisconsin, arriving in Milwaukee on Friday night, January 23, and then moving on to Green Bay. Although a staunch Lambeau proponent, even *Milwaukee Journal* sports editor Oliver Kuechle predicted that Jim Trimble would be named to lead the franchise. Trimble dismissed the idea.

Amid reports from Milwaukee that Lombardi had emerged as the leading candidate, Lambeau had driven back from California, saying, "I'm closed up there now." He said he had bought a house in Green Bay, where he planned to live during the winter. In the summer, he would live at his Door County home. While he undoubtedly would have bought a Green Bay residence if rehired by the Packers, that purchase would depend on his Packer situation.

"I have no connection with those people," Lambeau said of the rally and other efforts on his behalf. "They did that on their own." Curly and his closest supporters might have encouraged the grass-roots support, though.

"I got especially interested in the general manager's job when the committee outlined its plans for that position," he said, "and I wired Ole [Olejniczak] my application for the job. I met with him for two hours here during the holidays. I like the new setup and it's certainly a step in the right direction." At least the next GM would be given the authority that Lambeau had been urging.

"I left here for unity's sake," he said. "I wouldn't be here right now talking this way if there was success by the method that caused me to leave."

If he returned, Lambeau said, "I wouldn't be interested in the coaching and I wouldn't interfere with the coaching. I don't think anybody can do as good a job as general manager and still coach in today's tough competition. The Browns have that setup, but [Paul Brown] has many excellent assistants."

As he had told Olejniczak, Lambeau said, "Salary is very secondary to me. Whatever the committee feels is proper. My only purpose is to build up the team." Asked if he planned to campaign for the job, Lambeau said, "I really don't know if I'll campaign for it. Think I'll wait and see."

But of course, he was already campaigning for it simply by expressing interest and encouraging, one way or another, the support of Packer fans who yearned for a return to Lambeau's championship days. Being realistic, though, he must have known it was not going to go his way. Only a massive "We Want Curly!" groundswell could change that. And that was going to require a miracle that was not going to happen.

With Evashevski out of the picture, a stealthy Olejniczak had turned his attention to Lombardi. There had been a preliminary telephone call in mid-December. In early January, Mara again called to tout Giants assistant Tom Landry. "Every time [Olejniczak] talked to Mara, he'd encourage him to hire Tom Landry, who also had applied," Packers vice-president Dick Bourguignon said. "[Olejniczak would] ask about Lombardi, and Mara would say, 'Landry is the man you want.' I remember Ole telling me, 'I think they're trying to hide [Lombardi].' He felt very strongly that he did not want to hire anyone or do anything until he talked to Vince."

Olejniczak arranged a face-to-face talk with Lombardi when the NFL completed its 1959 draft, reeling off 26 rounds on January 21 in Philadelphia. Five days later, Lombardi flew to Green Bay on January 26. Greeted by executive board members Bourguignon and Tony Canadeo, Lombardi was given a tour of the city. In meetings, he was offered a five-year contract at $36,000 a year, with incentives.

Finally, on Wednesday, January 28, Lombardi was named general manager and head coach. "A few die-hards apparently held out for Earl L. (Curly) Lambeau," the *Associated Press* report noted in the third paragraph of its Lombardi-hired story, "the club's founder and coach for the first 30 of their 40-year history."

Art Daley, the *Green Bay Press-Gazette's* longtime Packer writer, began his January 30th background piece on Lombardi with a two-word lead: "Who's that?" Maybe it was good, Daley said, that Lombardi was not widely known: "Packerland's lack of knowledge about Vince. . . kept this town from blowing an emotional gasket. When people get emotional over a new coach in this town, they mean just one thing—championship next season. We haven't heard the words yet, and that's just wonderful because Lombardi is no miracle man."

That assessment would change. Quickly.

Lombardi would be the Packers' fourth head coach in the last 10 years, a decade in which Green Bay had not had a winning record. The fifth coach in the Packers' 40-year history, Lombardi was hired to win Green Bay's first championship since 1944, which came at the end of a glorious 16-year run in which the Packers sat atop the National Football League six times.

It would become the most momentous decision in club history since Curly Lambeau and George Whitney Calhoun called a meeting at the *Press-Gazette* office in 1919 to organize a football team.

# 81
## *TWO LEGENDS, TWO DIFFERENT PATHS*

The two men were as different as night and day. Lambeau was a home-grown hero of Belgian descent whose star had ascended quickly in life. He had gone from high school hero to the leader of a pro-football team without missing a beat. In that simpler time, he had been a central player as well as coach and chief executive. He had quickly turned the Packers into a perennial power that was a national sensation—the Notre Dame of the NFL—when he was barely 30 years old. Along the way, he became a leading man, as handsome and glamorous as a Hollywood star. And he became financially secure.

When Lombardi arrived in Green Bay in January of 1959, he was a 45-year-old career assistant, a product of Brooklyn whose parents had emigrated from Italy. Curly had been winning NFL championships and hanging out with the most famous and beautiful people in America as a young man; Lombardi had been coaching a high school team, his only head-coaching experience before Green Bay. After that, he had been an assistant at nose-to-the-grindstone Army, finally advancing to the NFL as a Giants assistant when he was 41 in 1954.

When Lambeau was 33, he led the Packers to their third straight NFL title and was among the most prominent coaches in America's fledgling NFL. When Lombardi was 33, he was completing a stellar run at St. Cecilia, a Catholic high school in Englewood, New Jersey, and moving on to coach the freshman team at Fordham, his alma mater. He also coached the freshman basketball team.

Lombardi was a *cum laude* graduate of Fordham, where he had been a lineman, one of the Seven Blocks of Granite. Lambeau had spent only one football autumn at Notre Dame, in a season cut short by the Spanish Flu pandemic and World War I. A fullback playing alongside George Gipp, he had scored the first touchdown of Knute Rockne's coaching career.

Although highly regarded by NFL insiders—Colts owner Carroll Rosenbloom called Green Bay's hiring of Lombardi "probably the greatest coup in the history of professional football."—Lombardi had not been widely known when he accepted the assignment of restoring the Packers to glory.

During his many years of low-profile coaching, however, Lombardi had developed a philosophy that would resonate in the NFL and beyond. From the outset, there was no doubting Lombardi's style and success.

"It looks as though Green Bay beat Army to an outstanding coach," George Halas said.

"I've never been associated with a loser," he said at an introductory press luncheon at the Northland Hotel on Tuesday, February 3, 1959, "and I don't expect to be now. And, I want it understood that I'm in complete command here."

Lombardi had demanded and been given the authority that Lambeau knew was essential to success. When Curly had lost total authority after World War II, it had largely been his own doing. He had overstepped on budget, pushing the financially strapped team to the brink of bankruptcy. He had alienated many key supporters within the team's community leadership. And he had failed to cover up his transgressions by winning football games.

Ironically, while the hiring of Vince Lombardi signaled a new era in Packer history, it also marked the end of an era. Whatever hopes that Curly Lambeau had held for returning from exile to lead the team he had founded 40 years earlier were snuffed once and for all. No longer would Lambeau pursue football opportunities.

The Packers, once the darlings of a fledgling NFL under Lambeau, would go on to greater glory in the 1960s, a golden age for pro football. And Lombardi would replace Lambeau as the symbol of excellence in Packer and NFL lore.

"Today. . . the popular image of the history of the Green Bay Packers is more of a muddy, bloody Ray Nitschke calling out defensive signals against the Bears than it is a posed black-and-white portrait of Johnny Blood standing in front of a hedge," Packer historian Mark Beech concluded. "While the stadium being called Lambeau Field does force some acknowledgment of the Packers' distant past, it has not been able to prevent its namesake or his teams—and the stories of their glory and their struggle for survival —from being largely forgotten."

Lambeau would wistfully enjoy Lombardi's revival of the Packers. Thanks to Lambeau Field, his name would be remembered. His deeds would not.

# 82
## FULL RETIREMENT

On February 3, 1959, at virtually the same moment that Lombardi was pronouncing himself in complete command, Lambeau was preoccupied with a wrenching personal passage. His brother, Raymond, died shortly after noon in a Green Bay hospital after a lengthy illness.

Three years younger than Curly, Raymond, 58, had made his own successful way. In the early 1920s, Raymond had been secretary and treasurer of the Packers, and had gone on to a business career in Green Bay. A University of Wisconsin graduate, he had been at the time of his death the president of the Larsen Company, one of the Midwest's largest independent canneries, and a prominent member of many Green Bay civic organizations. Curly's son, Don, worked for him at the Larsen Company as an assistant traffic manager.

A month later, about 150 Packer stockholders approved some changes at their annual meeting that would shift authority to Lombardi and reduce the executive committee from 13 to seven members. They also were told that the club made a profit of $70,106, a $20,000 increase from the previous fiscal year. "I'm no magician," Lombardi said, "but we're going to win games somehow."

On Tuesday, April 28, the administrative operation of the clubs was officially shifted from the Packer executive committee to General Manager and Coach Vince Lombardi.

"The Packers have now entered a new era, which really isn't so new!" Art Daley wrote in the *Press-Gazette* on April 29. "While the changes seem revolutionary, the Packers headed in that direction when Curly Lambeau was leading the club in the late 1930s and up to the mid-1940s. The club shifted to an all-out democracy in 1950 after Lambeau resigned."

Daley's "democracy" was Kuechle's "soviet." But that was the difference between Packer-first Green Bay and win-first Milwaukee.

To rally fans behind their new coach, the Packers sent out form letters to season ticket holders with a personal message from Lombardi. "I hope and believe I can bring back the Packers along the path of glory that they knew so well," Lombardi said, invoking the team's championship past without mentioning Lambeau by name. "It was here that the greatest pro player of all time was fostered and developed. I speak, of course, of Don Hutson. I want you to understand I am no miracle maker; I have no rabbits in my hat; I have no illusions of grandeur, but with hard work, intelligent organization and good assistant coaches, success will not avoid the Packers for long."

Meanwhile, Lambeau, his last bid to return to Green Bay thwarted, took comfort in luxurious exile, enjoying California sunshine while waiting for balmier weather to return to his Door County summer place. But his shadow continued to loom large over the Packer team he had founded.

One obvious connection was Lombardi's coach at Fordham, Jim Crowley, who had been coached by Lambeau at Green Bay's East High School and steered by Curly to Notre Dame, where he became one of the famous Four Horsemen.

"Curly Lambeau was my coach back at Green Bay High," Crowley once told Grantland Rice, who created "The Four Horsemen" nickname. "He played with Gipp at Notre Dame in '18. We were State champions and when Curley mentioned Gipp and Notre Dame. . . well, I was on my way."

Another indelible connection: Lombardi's famous Packer Sweep had elements of the Notre Dame Box that Lambeau had relied on when his Packer teams were perennial powers.

"Not surprisingly, given that Lombardi played for Rockne disciple and former Notre Dame great Jim Crowley," Packer historian Cliff Christl wrote, "there were even some elements of Lambeau's supposedly outdated Notre Dame Box as his base offense. In fact, when Lombardi started coaching at St. Cecilia, he ran the Notre Dame Box as his base offense until Ed Doherty, former Boston College quarterback and later a head coach for 13 years at the collegiate level, introduced him to the T formation."

While Lombardi's Packer Sweep was run out of the T formation, a common thread with Lambeau's Notre Dame Box was that both required teamwork and execution—traits of well-coached teams. The Lombardi offense, often summed up as "Run to Daylight," had a large option component, similar to the Notre Dame Box. The difference was, in Lombardi's offense, a lone ball carrier exercised the option to cut or sweep wide, rather than flipping the ball to a teammate.

In another similarity, because both offenses required defenses to pay close attention to intricate running games, they opened up the passing attack. Lambeau's Packer teams featured quarterbacks like Arnie Herber and Cecil Isbell throwing to receivers like Hutson and Johnny Blood. Under

Lombardi, Bart Starr passed to Boyd Dowler, Carroll Dale and Max McGee.

It was also one more reminder that Green Bay, the Notre Dame of the NFL, traced its roots to Knute Rockne, who helped create the original Notre Dame mystique by catching passes in a shocking upset of Army, but relied on a difficult-to-defense running attack as the Irish coach.

While Lombardi was drawing up plans in the spring of 1959 to transform the slumbering Packers into an NFL champion, Lambeau was far removed from football. Although he had downsized his California real-estate holdings, he was never a fan of the Frozen Tundra. When it was cold in Wisconsin, he still could be found in Hollywood and Palm Springs, hanging out with his many pals in the sports and media worlds—and not lacking for female companionship.

Now in his 60s, Lambeau no longer was the svelte, powerfully built athletic adonis that women adored. His media friends diplomatically referred to him as portly if they mentioned his shape at all. The lenses on his glasses seemed to have gotten progressively thicker. And while he still had his hair, it was a silvery gray. But he still had vestiges of a football body. And he still was a glib charmer of both sportswriters and women.

And he seemed very accepting of the fact that his football career was over. He had made two last attempts to return to the Packers—when the team fired Liz Blackbourn after the 1957 season and when it turned to Lombardi after the 1958 disaster led by Scooter McLean.

Lombardi was the new man of the house that Lambeau built. Curly was knowledgeable enough to know that Lombardi was the right man to restore football glory in Green Bay. With the general manager reins in hand —the authority that Lambeau knew was essential—Lombardi was in an excellent position to be successful.

Football had been very, very good to Lambeau. He might have wanted one more go-round, as his campaigns to return to the Packers had indicated. But now, he seemed more focused on living well in retirement. And he had the means to do that.

While Lombardi was getting ready for his first Packer training camp, Lambeau was a judge at the 1959 Miss Wisconsin pageant on Saturday, June 27, in Fish Creek, his summer residence. The winner, Charlene Krause, 19, of Milwaukee, was chosen to participate in the Miss Universe pageant, to be held in Long Beach, California, in July. A crowd of more than 600 jammed the Gibraltar High School gym for the Fish Creek event.

The night before the pageant, a banquet was held at the C&C Supper Club for the contestants, chaperones and judges. Lambeau didn't even need to drive his trademark red Cadillac convertible there. The C&C, owned by one of his former Packers, Dick Weisgerber, was right around the corner from his large summer place on Cottage Row.

When Lombardi made his Green Bay coaching debut against George Halas and the Chicago Bears at City Stadium on September 27, 1959, Lambeau was in the press box, practically leading the cheers. The Bears held a 6-0 lead in the fourth quarter of a stout defensive battle, but Green Bay took a 7-6 lead on a five-yard touchdown run by Jim Taylor. With the Packers clinging to the lead with less than two minutes left, Lambeau stayed positive, telling anxious sportswriters, "Don't worry, we're going to win." Green Bay held on for a 9-6 win.

Any disappointment at being rebuffed in his effort to return to the team had been put aside. The Man Who Invented the Green Bay Packers was all about the team that wore Green and Gold.

Lambeau was also beaming in the press box as Green Bay cruised past Detroit 28-10 on October 4. With their 2-0 start, the Packers already had doubled their win total from the previous season. "This is the best I've seen Green Bay look in a long time," Lambeau said.

"If we win too many this year," Lombardi joked, "they'll expect too much next year."

The next week, in a showdown of the NFL's last two unbeaten teams, Green Bay reached a new height. Led by two touchdown passes from quarterback Lamar McHan and a rushing TD from Paul Hornung, who also kicked the extra points, the Packers edged San Francisco 21-20 on October 11 before their third straight sellout of 32,150 at City Stadium in Green Bay. It was Green Bay's first 3-0 start since 1944, when Lambeau won his sixth and final championship season. Football fans were becoming giddy in northeastern Wisconsin.

The NFL world was shocked and saddened, though, to learn that on that same day, commissioner Bert Bell died of a heart attack while watching the Steelers and the Eagles play in Philadelphia. Declining VIP treatment, Bell had bought his own ticket and was sitting with fans. He was 65.

In a tribute to Bell, Green Bay writer Art Daley recalled that around the time that Lambeau was leaving a Green Bay filled with financial problems that raised the question of whether a small city could keep its NFL team, "That's where Bert Bell stepped in and growled: 'There will always be a Green Bay in the National Football League.'"

Bell's death created a void not easily filled. With no obvious candidates to succeed him, Lambeau's *Los Angeles Times* friend, Braven Dyer, nominated the Packer founder, saying, "I don't have a vote but there are two gentleman of my acquaintance who could handle the NFL czar job adequately. The are Paul J. Schissler and Curley Lambeau."

Dyer's nominations were merely pats on the back. Neither Lambeau nor Schissler, a former coach and minor-league owner, was a serious candidate. With no obvious choice, NFL owners debated for seven days and went through 23 ballots before settling on Rams general manager Pete Rozelle, a 33-year-old marketing whiz.

"An excellent choice," Packer president Dominic Olejniczak said. "Pete is calm, young, smart, a good executive and he can grow right with the league." It was a spot-on description from the man who had brought Vince Lombardi to Green Bay.

Lambeau was in the press box for the fourth week when Green Bay — which was missing two of its top runners, Jim Taylor and Don McIlhenny, due to injury—was thrashed 45-6 by the Los Angeles Rams in Milwaukee County Stadium on October 18.

"I don't want to alibi but Paul Hornung and Lew Carpenter were our only halfbacks," said Lombardi, who had expressed pre-game injury concerns. "We'll be in better physical shape next week and there is no reason we can't bounce back... We better.'

Lambeau watched the Rams debacle with Roundy Coughlin, the folksy punctuation-optional columnist for Madison's *Wisconsin State Journal* who was a Lambeau golf buddy. "I sat next to Curly Lambeau down at the Packers game he lives in Green Bay now," Roundy wrote. "He was tough when he was coaching brother he won the titles and the ballgames and-how. They ain't been the same since."

Lambeau was less harsh, saying, "If the Packers had won today, they could have gone all the way. But they'll still win more than they lose."

Still finding their way in Lombardi's first season, the banged-up Packers continued to struggle, losing their next four games to fall to 3-5. Along the way, though, Lombardi did settle on a gem. When McHan, Lombardi's starting quarterback for his first six games in Green Bay, was sidelined by a minor leg injury, Bart Starr settled in at quarterback and went on to a legendary career. That reduced McHan—acquired from the Cardinals, who had made him the No. 2 pick in 1954 NFL draft—to a trivia question reminiscent of Wally Pipp losing his job to Lou Gehrig.

# 83
## *SCRATCHING HIS COACHING ITCH*

Retired from coaching, but still immersed in the game that had been his life's pursuit, Lambeau ventured out to watch the Vikings of Gibraltar High School in Fish Creek on Friday afternoons in the fall of 1959.

If he did not like what he saw, he was not alone. Gibraltar had not won a Peninsula Conference game in three years since September 29, 1956. It had a new coach, Patrick Spielman, who had only taken the job because that was a condition of being hired as the shop teacher. A gifted woodworker, he would go on to write more than 80 books on the subject and achieve wide renown in his chosen arena, which was not football. But in 1959, Pat Spielman was a 23-year-old with a wife and an infant son. He needed a job.

"During the games, my dad would hear this man hollering behind him," the son, Bob Spielman, said in an interview in July 2023 outside the Hat Head, the headwear store he owns in Fish Creek. "Finally after one game, this guy came up and said, `My name's Curly Lambeau and I think I can help you with your football team.' "

Lambeau came to practice soon after that. "He had a whole bunch of plays drawn up, which I still have," Bob Spielman said. Lambeau was assisted by Weisgerber, who had been a blocking back for Lambeau on the Packers from 1938 to 1942, with the exception of 1941. "In 1941, he sat out because Curly wouldn't give him a raise," Weisgerber's son, Rich, said in a July 2023 interview at his home in Baileys Harbor, near Fish Creek.

By 1959, Lambeau and Weisgerber had become close friends, their salary differences long forgotten. Lambeau took his meals and quenched his thirst at the C&C, the popular supper club that Weisgerber owned, right around the corner from his Fish Creek mansion on the waters of Green Bay. Many current and former Packers gathered at the C&C, which became an irresistible hangout.

"The C&C was a really hopping place," Packer historian Cliff Christl said. "It was a popular supper club that had a really lively bar business. You could hardly get in the place."

There was alway room for Curly, who liked to hold court there.

"He would always call me Marilyn," Dick Weisgerber's daughter, Judi Voight, who worked there as a teenager, said in a July 2023 interview.

"He said I looked like Marilyn Monroe. Oh, he was a ladies man. He was dapper. Very dapper."

Judi's husband of more than 60 years, Wayne Voight, was an outside linebacker and receiver on the Vikings high-school team that Lambeau had decided could use his help. "When I tell people Curly Lambeau was my coach, they think I'm giving them a line. But we learned a lot from him. It was interesting," Voight said, recalling a Lambeau tip. "I didn't realize you were supposed to turn the guy inside so the other linebackers could get him."

That was not Voight's first encounter with Lambeau. "The first time, I didn't even really know who Curly was," he said. "There was a TV man where we lived in Ellison Bay and I would go along with him." One day, the job was to put up a TV antenna on the steep pitched roof of Lambeau's mansion-like Cottage Row house. "I didn't know it was Curly's house," he said. "I've never been so scared in my life. We were up so high. I put my leg over to straddle the peak."

Weisgerber had helped connect the Packers legend with the struggling high school team, Gibraltar quarterback Dave Hubbard said: "Dick Weisgerber was aware that [Gibraltar] was going to have a young coach. Pat had played at one of the state schools but had never coached. So Dick got in touch with Curly and got things arranged."

Curly didn't take long to assume command. "We'd go over to Curly's house, three or four of us from the team and our young coach, Pat Spielman," Hubbard said in a 2024 interview with the author. "We were at his dining room, going over the offense and defense for the team. He showed us all the different plays, and what the defense should look like."

Pat Spielman often told his son that "Curly sort of took over. He came to practice once a week, then a little more. Then he'd come up in the middle of the day and say, 'Spielman, you have to get these kids out of school. We have to go practice these plays.'"

Lambeau was even more direct than that, Hubbard said. "Pat was at a high school reunion we had years later and he said, 'There's another piece of the story that you probably don't know. Curly used to call the high school principal, Tom Birmingham, and tell Tom that he wanted us excused from class so we could meet and study the plays. But Birmingham, he was a hard nut. He wouldn't give in.'"

The principal finally told coach Spielman, "You have to tell this Curly guy to back off," Bob Spielman said. "Because we can't have kids leaving school in the middle of the day for football practice."

Wayne Voight doesn't remember it exactly that way: "In those days, they didn't allow lay people to coach in high school. When the principal found out, he said, 'Those guys can't be here.'" Whatever the reason, Lambeau and Weisgerber were gone.

"Dad basically had to man up to Curly," Bob Spielman said. "Curly got so into it. My dad enjoyed it. He was amused, but also a little intimidated."

It is not reflected on Curly's official record, of course. But along with being bounced from the Packers, Cardinals and Redskins, he was ushered out by the Vikings. The *Gibraltar* Vikings.

Gibraltar finally won a game on October 23, 1959, beating Sevastopol 13-0 at its homecoming. By then, Lambeau was no longer involved. He had departed for the West Coast. When he heard the news, though, he probably took pride in the belief that his contribution, however brief, had brought the desired result.

# 84
## *ADMIRING LOMBARDI'S WORK*

After watching the first four games of Lombardi's 1959 Packer debut in person, Lambeau headed off to Los Angeles. He arrived in time to take in the Rams' 17-7 win over Detroit on October 25. 1959, at the Los Angeles Coliseum. At halftime, Lambeau did a national radio interview that sparked a flood of memories for a listener in Rochester, New York. The long-ago manager of the long-forgotten Rochester Jeffersons, a charter member of the NFL, Leo V. Lyons had been at the Hupmobile showroom in Canton, Ohio, with George Halas and the other founders of the NFL. Rochester competed in the NFL from 1920-25, including a trip to Green Bay in the Jeffersons' last NFL season.

"Lambeau coached the Packers. I managed the Jeffersons," Lyons said. "We had similar backgrounds. We played football on the sandlots in our youth (when we had cleats nailed on old shoes because of the lack of funds to buy regular football shoes). . . . The Jeffersons put up a good battle but lost, 33-13, chiefly because the Packers had a much stronger bench."

From nailing cleats onto old shoes to listening to Lambeau on a national radio hookup, Lyons' remembrance was a measure of how far Curly and the NFL had come.

By late November, Lambeau was enjoying life in Palm Springs, where he attended a party on November 20. "The James Hammond's handsome home on Hermosa was the focal point for a long list of guests Friday night, as the Hammonds held a house cooling party," the Palm Spring newspaper, the *Desert Sun,* noted, "before turning it over to the Sam Goldwyn's, who have leased it."

That Sunday, the Packers snapped their five-game losing streak, beating Washington 21-0 in Green Bay before playing their final three games on the road. After beating the Lions in Detroit, the Packers defeated the Rams 38-20 on December 6 in Los Angeles. A beaming Lambeau watched from the press box.

Lombardi and Rams coach Sid Gillman agreed that a pair of old-school option plays were the difference in the game. On both, Hornung, who had played quarterback at Notre Dame, took a handoff from Starr and passed to rookie receiver Boyd Dowler for touchdowns of 26 and 30 yards.

"It's not hard to cover," Gillman said grimly. "You not only watch the ball carrier but you look for receivers, too. . . . "The Packers are a lot better, but we're not playing good ball. . . . We have more cripples than we have healthy players."

Gillman sounded like a man who knew his five-year run as Rams coach was nearing an end. After a final-game loss to the Colts dropped the Rams to 2-10, Gillman was fired. He went on coach the Chargers, guiding them to five of the first six championship games in the fledgling American Football League.

The Rams hired Bob Waterfield, their former star quarterback, to succeed Gillman on January 12, 1960. Lambeau was quick to have some fun with his friend Waterfield, who also ran in the same crowd with restaurant owner Roy Harlow and broadcaster Bob Kelley.

Curly suggested a bold move: Pass on fourth down from punt formation. It was difficult to tell if he was kidding.

"We used to do it years ago at Green Bay," Lambeau said. "You don't do it deep in your own territory, of course. You've got to be up around midfield."

"Kind of risky, isn't it, Curly?" Waterfield said. The two went back and forth playfully like that for a while in a newspaper column by Kelley.

When Waterfield protested that modern teams covered potential receivers, Lambeau answered that a strong-armed punter could complete a throw to a receiver who flared out. When Waterfield said, "Name me some men in our league who can pass and punt," Lambeau replied, "Bob Waterfield could."

"But he isn't playing any more," Waterfield replied.

\* \* \* \* \* \* \* \*

After handling the Rams in Los Angeles, the Packers, led by a rapidly improving Bart Starr, had moved on to San Francisco, where they defeated the 49ers 36-14 on December 13. They finished their 1959 season with a 7-5 record that shredded pre-season predictions that they would lose a mountain of games and finish last again.

Reached in Palm Springs, Lambeau gave the Packers an enthusiastic review: "I saw the three games in Green Bay, one in Milwaukee and one in Los Angeles and they showed me plenty," Lambeau said. "I said after the opener when they beat the Bears that Green Bay would be hard to beat if they kept on playing like that. They have continued to play hard all the way. The team and coaching staff should be complimented and I'm glad to have this opportunity to congratulate them. . . It's been a long time, but the fans at home really have stuck with them. They certainly are loyal."

That loyalty was on display in all its shivering glory as Packer fans welcomed their team back from the West Coast with a homecoming celebration at Austin Straubel Field. A hearty crowd of 7,500 endured sleeting rain as the team landed at 9 p.m. Monday, an hour behind schedule.

Their United DC-6B charter, a four-propellor aircraft. was an eight-hour adventure, capped off by a low cloud ceiling that threatened to scratch their landing in Green Bay. "In that case, we'll just stop in Milwaukee, refuel and fly on to Bermuda," pilot Bud Smith, who lived in Green Bay, jokingly told his passengers.

"It would be a shame if we couldn't land—all those people waiting," Lombardi said before the team grew quiet for their landing. Delay aside, merely landing in Green Bay was a victory.

That kind of support for a team that finished tied for third in the six-team Western Division? Not many fan bases would brave an icy rain to welcome a 7-5 team. But as Lambeau noted, that was kind of loyalty that had allowed him and his civic-minded supporters to keep the team alive during precarious times.

After the players and coaches had been given Packer blankets, Mayor Roman P. Denissen presented Lombardi with a key to the city. "I know from the size of this crowd that you must all be as proud of this football team as we are," Lombardi said.

# 85
## *A PLAN TO HONOR LAMBEAU MEETS RESISTANCE*

Enthusiastically sensing that their team was at the dawn of a new golden age, some excited Packer fans started pushing for a way to honor their founder. Letters to the *Press-Gazette* editor suggested putting Lambeau's name on the new City Stadium.

Alderman Thomas Atkinson formally proposed on February 2, 1960, that City Stadium should become Lambeau Field or Lambeau Stadium. The proposal was sent to the Stadium Commission. In April, the Stadium Commission formed a committee to study the idea. "I just think we should pay Mr. Lambeau some tribute for founding the team and spending 30 years here, at least by dedicating the stadium in his honor," Atkinson said.

In May, the City Council endorsed a Stadium Commission proposal to honor Lambeau with a plaque instead of renaming the stadium. Although that was a very modest alternative, "The commission reported it had talked with Lambeau, who appreciated the consideration but who said his best memory would be the wonderful treatment he had received from the people of Green Bay and Packer fans from the area."

In a further watering down, the commission recommended that Lambeau merely be included on a stadium plaque it had been planning to honor past presidents of the Packers corporation. With that, the renaming of the stadium was scuttled. Instead, Curly would be included on the plaque, to be unveiled on November 13, 1960, when the Packers played their final game in Green Bay against the Dallas Cowboys, an expansion team making its NFL debut.

While Green Bay was pondering ways to honor him, Lambeau was enjoying himself in Palm Springs, where he was spending the winter. An avid golfer, Curly had stayed in a home at the San Jacinto Country Club, a new layout that had opened in 1959. Later, he bought a house at 1640 South Calle Rolph, not far from the center of town, which bustled with activity in the winter. Movie stars and others in the entertainment industry flocked to "The Desert," a convenient getaway from Los Angeles.

Lambeau also was a regular at O'Donnell Golf Club, where his former star, Don Hutson, also liked to tee it up. Hutson mainly played golf at the Thunderbird in Rancho Mirage, where he had a home.

On St. Patrick's Day in 1960, Lambeau was at the Riviera in Palm Springs, helping his friend, restaurateur Roy Harlow and his wife, Irene, celebrate their 25th anniversary. A posh and popular desert hot spot, the Riviera was a regular hangout for Frank Sinatra and his Rat Pack as well as the Lambeau-Harlow entourage. Opened in 1959, the Riviera was home to the Chi-Chi Club. After the COVID pandemic of 2020, the Riviera reopened as a Margaritaville resort hotel.

When Palm Springs became steamy in the spring, Lambeau returned to his over-sized Door County summer home, where he enjoyed his power boat, ironically named Lazy, and played golf and enjoyed cocktails with friends. When autumn arrived in 1960, he found a seat on the Packer bandwagon as a bonafide member of the media. WFRV-TV announced that it would air "Ask Curly Lambeau" every "Saturday nite at 10:15." Inviting viewers to mail in their questions, the station said, "Here's your chance to ask 'Mr. Football' himself, Curly Lambeau, questions about pro and college football, football history, the Packers and any football question you'd like answered."

Assisting Lambeau on the show was Mary Jane Van Duyse, the sister of Fritz Van. They had started dating after Fritz introduced them at the Nautical Inn in Sturgeon Bay earlier that year. Not only had Fritz, a broadcaster and Green Bay sports magazine publisher, stumped for Curly to be rehired by the Packers. Curly and another brother, Bob, often fished together on Green Bay. Lambeau also had struck up a friendship with their father, a Door County tavern owner who was roughly Curly's age. But Mary Jane was the key Van Duyse in Curly's life.

"They had a wonderful relationship," Mary Jane's niece, Alison Walker, said in a 2023 interview with the author. A Sturgeon Bay financial adviser, she cared for her Aunt Mary, who died in 2022 at 89. "She thought the world of him. They just had a lot of fun together. They were very close."

Lambeau was in the press box for the Packers' 1960 season opener against the Bears on September 25 at City Stadium. Green Bay led 7-0 at the half and was on top 14-0 in the fourth quarter. "You're seeing defense at its best. These are two of the greatest defenses I've ever seen," he said. Along with the capacity crowd of 32,150, he was disappointed, though, to see Green Bay surrender 17 fourth-quarter points and lose 17-14. It was the first loss in Green Bay under Lombardi for the Packers, who had swept their four games at City Stadium in 1959.

But Green Bay won its next four games to stay locked in a tight battle with Baltimore in the Western Division. Even after a loss to the Colts in Baltimore, the Packers remained tied with the Colts for the Western Division lead.

In keeping with their reputation for being the NFL team with college spirit, the Packers then held their homecoming on November 13 against the winless Dallas Cowboys. Nearly 60 former Packers were in Green Bay for the homecoming, which included a dinner at the Beaumont Hotel on Saturday night.

Curly went to the dinner, enjoying an evening with many of his former players. But at halftime on Sunday, for reasons unknown, he remained in the press box when the plaque honoring him and the six past presidents of the club was presented to the Stadium Commission.

Plaques were also presented honoring Don Hutson and Clarke Hinkle, who had recently been elected to the Wisconsin Sports Hall of Fame. Neither attended, although Hutson did cite a business obligation. Jug Earp, president of the Packer Alumni Association, introduced the Packer alums who were at the game.

And so, the first formal effort to call the Packers' home "Lambeau Field" had been reduced to a plaque. But Lambeau was able to enjoy a weekend with many of his former players. And enjoy the Packers' 41-7 rout of the expansion Cowboys, who were playing their first NFL season. Coached by Tom Landry, who had handled the defense when Lombardi was in charge of the New York Giants' offense, Dallas would soon become a key Packer rival.

A regular in the press box when the Packers played their early-season games in Green Bay, Lambeau was found in an odd place after the Packers defeated the Rams in Los Angeles on Saturday, December 17, 1960, to clinch their first division title since 1944. When a *Press-Gazette* reporter called for a comment, Lambeau was taking a shower at the Beaumont Hotel in Green Bay.

"I never doubted it," he said after toweling off. "I said all week we were going to win it all. And we will beat Philadelphia, too. The fans deserve a lot of credit. These fans in Green Bay deserve a championship. It's been a long time."

As the NFL championship game approached, Lambeau remained confident that the Packers would prevail against the Eagles in Philadelphia. Oddsmakers agreed, listing Green Bay as a 2½-point favorite.

"I definitely feel the Packers have an edge—and they're going to win," Lambeau told *Press-Gazette* writer Lee Remmel. "I base that on the fact that the field cannot be in good condition, because of the weather they've been having in Philadelphia, including both snow and rain. And any kind of off-track will favor the Packers." Lambeau not only was confident that Green Bay's superior running game would prevail over the Eagles' passing skill on a slick field. In addition, he said, "The Packers are a tougher team."

Philadelphia squeaked out a 17-13 win, though, edging Green Bay on Monday, December 26, 1960, despite being outgained by 105 yards and losing the turnover battle 3-1. "The Packers are the uncrowned 'world champions' of professional football—certainly in the eyes of Packerland. . . . The Packers did everything to the Eagles but beat them on the scoreboard," Art Daley wrote sunnily in the *Press-Gazette* from wintery Philadelphia.

By mid-January 1961, Curly was back in Palm Springs, accompanied by Mary Jane Van Duyse. They attended a pre-Pro Bowl party hosted by Roy and Irene Harlow at the Riviera Hotel. Since being introduced by Mary Jane's brother, Fritz, the previous summer, their relationship had blossomed.

Energetic, outgoing and ambitious, Mary Jane held a a variety of jobs. In addition to teaching baton twirling and being part of the Packers cheerleading program, she also worked as the self-described "weather girl" at a Green Bay television station and modeled clothes at Prange's department store.

# 86
## *BURNING DOWN THE HOUSE—AGAIN*

When spring turned to summer in Wisconsin, Lambeau was back in Door County, squiring Mary Jane around and enjoying his life of fishing on Green Bay, playing golf at the Peninsula State Park course and relaxing with his many friends.

On August 7, 1961, however, disaster struck. Lambeau left his Fish Creek home early for the 70-mile trip to Green Bay. On the way, he stopped in Sturgeon Bay to pick up Mary Jane, who was going to model clothes at Prange's department store, and her mother. Lambeau, who remained active in real estate and other financial dealings, planned to meet with his brother-in-law, attorney Francis Evrard, who was married to Lambeau's sister, Bea.

But Mary Jane was startled when Lambeau returned quickly to Prange's, "He came running and puffing in there and said, 'I've got to get home. My house is on fire.' " When Curly asked if they could find another ride home, Mary Jane's mother said, "Just go, Curly, we'll find a ride." They wound up returning to Sturgeon Bay by boat, Mary Jane said.

Fire departments throughout Door County responded to the blaze, which was reported at 10 a.m. It was no use. The rambling summer home, which had been named The Cedars, was a total loss. Firefighters contained the blaze, which had threatened neighboring homes. But even the large cedar trees that bordered the property caught fire.

The house had been built either in the 1860s or 1920, depending on original construction or later expansion. A sprawling six-bedroom summer home, it stood on eight-and-a-half acres along Cottage Row, a leafy lane overlooking the sparkling waters of Green Bay. Just south of the Fish Creek business district, it was an easy walk to the C&C Supper Club, the popular Lambeau hangout owned by former Packer Dick Weisgerber,.

"Curly was really upset," Mary Jane said. "He lost almost everything. By the time I got back that whole house had burned down."

Dick Weisgerber's 11-year-old son, Rich, was in the crowd that rushed over to watch the blaze. It threw off so much heat that no one ventured close. A couple of days later, Rich and a friend went poking around in the remains, basically a chimney foundation and rubble. "There was a big pile of melted silver," Rich said in a 2023 interview with the author. "He had two slot machines in the house."

The fire also destroyed Lambeau's method of payment for Rich, who mowed the lawn. "Every time I cut the grass, he gave me a picture—one of his old guys from the '20s and '30s," Rich said. "I was supposed to get more, but they were lost when his house burned down."

Rich put up the photos he had received on the wall at the Cornerstone, a pub he later owned in Baileys Harbor, across the peninsula from Fish Creek. "Johnny Blood's daughter came in one day," he said. After taking a look at the photo, she said, "That's not my dad's autograph."

Among the many things Lambeau lost were mementos and trophies from his football career, plus a draft of an autobiography he had begun. Suddenly homeless, Lambeau took up residence at Thorp's, an inn with cottages that was practically across the street.

For the second time in his tumultuous life, Lambeau's house had burned to the ground. In 1937, his newly acquired cottage near Green Bay had burned. A faulty chimney was blamed for the blaze, which came just days after he had separated from his second wife, who would give birth to a son four months later. No cause was publicly given for the 1961 fire that destroyed Lambeau's Fish Creek house. Counting the Rockwood Lodge fire that destroyed Lambeau's dedicated Packer practice facility, it was the third major blaze in his life.

Someone suggested that he turn his carriage house into a summer cottage. Embracing the idea, Lambeau renovated the carriage house into a stylish summer home that retained the character of it original purpose.

After winning all five of their pre-season games, the Packers were surprised by Detroit in their 1961 season opener, losing 17-13 in Milwaukee on September 17. From there, though, they went on a hot streak. By the time Lambeau went to Milwaukee on Thursday, October 26, to attend a testimonial dinner honoring his good friend, former Packer star Charles "Buckets" Goldenberg, Green Bay had reeled off five straight wins to lead the Western Division.

In a further statement, the Packers had won by an average margin of 28 points. No opponent had come closer than 20 points. And Green Bay had beaten Chicago 24-0, the first time it had shut out the Bears since 1935, when Goldenberg was in the third season of his stellar 13-year career.

"Never in my life have I seen an offensive line like the one operating for the Packers this year," Lambeau told the audience of 300. "That front line, especially from tackle to tackle, is really big and can move. This club is a powerhouse with unusual talent. Unless some unforeseen misfortune befalls this team, it should go all the way. Of course much depends, too, on how many players Uncle Sam takes away from Vince Lombardi—a great coach, by the way."

Lambeau was back in Milwaukee on Thursday, November 16, for Johnny Blood's induction into the Wisconsin Athletic Hall of Fame. Curly and Goldenberg unveiled Blood's plaque; Don Hutson read the text on the plaque. A crowd of nearly 1,000 attended the dinner, held at the Milwaukee Arena.

\* \* \* \* \* \* \* \*

Although Lambeau's campaign to be restored to power had failed when Lombardi was hired in 1959, that seemed like ancient history by the end of 1961. Lombardi had quickly and deftly turned the Packers into the kind of winner that Green Bay had grown accustomed to under Lambeau. Winning had brought harmony and smiles in Green Bay and around the state of Wisconsin.

That helps explain why so many ancient Packers were being honored. It was a joy to be associated with the Packers again. And everyone wanted in.

Lambeau seemed more and more comfortable in his role as the beloved, retired founder of the Packers. When 3,500 Packer fans turned out at the Brown County Arena on December 23. 1961, for a combination pep rally and Christmas party, Lambeau was among those asked to warm up the crowd.

Green Bay had just completed an 11-3 season, and was preparing to host the New York Giants in the 1961 NFL championship game. It was the Packers' best regular season since 1941, when Lambeau led them to a 10-1 record, but lost a playoff for the Western Division with the Bears, who also had gone 10-1.

When it was Lambeau's turn to speak, he relied on one of his favorite themes while saluting Lombardi and his players, saying, "You are going to beat the Giants if you show the spirit you showed during the past season. The Giants will not out-spirit the Packers."

Lombardi, of course, received the loudest cheers at the pep rally. "We express our gratitude for this party and the backing we have received," Lombardi said. "This proves this is a great place for the players to play football in and live in. . . . We should all be proud of this team because of its singleness of purpose, its dedication to winning."

Earlier that day, Lambeau received some personal Christmas cheer. He was named to the Wisconsin Athletic Hall of Fame. In 1961, two years before the NFL had opened its hall of fame, Wisconsin Athletic Hall of Fame was as good as it could get for Lambeau.

At first glance, it might seem odd that five of Lambeau's players had been selected before him: Hutson and Hinkle in 1951, Red Dunn (1957), Cub Buck (1955) and Johnny Blood (1960). Even Gus Dorais, the Chippewa Falls native who had made many coaching stops after famously throwing passes to Knute Rockne at Notre Dame, had gone into the Hall of Fame in 1955 despite leaving Wisconsin after high school.

But there was an easy explanation: The Wisconsin Athletic Hall of Fame, like the Baseball Hall of Fame, required athletes to be retired five years. Because Lambeau had coached the College All-Stars in 1957, officials even made a point of saying they had waived the five-year rule to let Curly in.

"That's the nicest Christmas present I ever received," Lambeau said. "I'm very happy and thrilled and, as I have said so many times in the past, I owe everything to the fans of Green Bay."

Three years earlier, Curly Lambeau had been a divider—either a revered or worn-out former king, trying to return from exile and regain the throne that would go to Vince Lombardi. Now, as Green Bay was ascending to the NFL greatness it had known when Lambeau was in charge, Curly seemed to bask in his role as the retired founder.

And with the balm of time, Green Bay football fans were choosing to remember the Lambeau who started the team and won a fistful of championships, rather then the Lambeau who was run out of town.

Three days before the Packers met the Giants for the 1961 NFL championship, Arthur Daley wrote in the *New York Times* that "Jean Nicolet founded Green Bay in 1634. Curly Lambeau founded the Packers in 1919. To the citizenry of that bosky Wisconsin metropolis there is almost unanimity of opinion about which is the more important date. If a vote were held this week, Lambeau would probably win by a landslide. The city is jumping so much that it has jostled Green Bay right off the map. Temporarily, at least, it is known by the cornball name of 'Titletown, USA.' Ugh!"

Speaking of cornball, in Daley's flowery tribute, *wooded* would not do when there was an opportunity to use the word *bosky*. The column was accompanied by a photo of Lambeau in his heyday, looking proud and menacing above a caption that read: "Curly Lambeau: *He invented the Green Bay Packers*"

Erudite New Yorkers were still mocking and marveling at Green Bay's football prowess—and its ability to endure and triumph over giant cities.

"If anyone rates credit for pro football's development and the million-dollar bonanza battle which will be fought here tomorrow, [Lambeau] is the man," Gene Ward added in the *New York Daily News*. "Through determination and dedication, he built the Packers into one of the bedrock organizations of the NFL. There isn't a man in the mob that turned out for the pre-game jamboree here tonight who wouldn't name him as one of the select few of whom the burgeoning sport owes the most."

Lambeau still had a reasonable number of curls, but they had gone silver, gray and white. He still had the dimples and full lips that had captivated women over the years, but his tough profile had been diminished by over-sized, dark-rimmed glasses that made him look more like a beardless Santa Claus than a fierce football man.

When the Packers took the field in Green Bay on December 31, 1961, they were playing a championship game in Green Bay for the first time. The Packers had won their first three titles before the NFL had figured out that championship games were a good idea. Two of Lambeau's other three titles had been won in New York. Milwaukee had hosted his only clincher in Wisconsin in 1939— to the outrage of Green Bay residents who had wanted the game played in their city.

And now, as Lambeau joined a paying crowd of 39,029, a record for Green Bay's City Stadium, to see if the Packers could add a seventh NFL title, he had no official role. Green Bay's football fortunes now rested on the sturdy shoulders of Vince Lombardi.

The Packers were a 3½-point favorite to defeat the Giants, the same New York franchise that Lambeau had won his last two titles against in 1939 and 1944. It was a blustery, winter day, with a wind chill that made the temperature feel cooler than the thermometer's 20 degrees.

"GREATEST SHOW IN FOOTBALL," the plain white lettering over a football clip told a national TV audience tuned in to flickering black-and-white screens. Announcer.Lindsay Nelson breathlessly said this was the first million-dollar game in pro football, with 40,000 tickets sold at $10 apiece, and $615,000 for TV rights.

"And to think that we once used to pass the hat to keep going," Lambeau told a wire-service reporter in the press box.

Representing Lambeau, in a way, was his girlfriend, Mary Jane Van Duyse, who twirled her baton and did cartwheels on camera for nearly two minutes while Nelson and his partner, Chris Schenkel, filled the pre-game air by talking about the "loving care" the field had received in snowy Green Bay.

Mary Jane wore tights and a sequined top, and had fluffy cuffs accenting her skilled hands. Moving gracefully and athletically through her fast-moving acrobatics, the national baton-twirling champion stayed warm with her energetic routine.

It was a championship moment for her, too. As a child, she had performed at a bar and dance hall owned by her father in Institute, near Sturgeon Bay. After Wilner Burke, from the Packers Lumberjack Band, noticed her, she joined the Packerettes in 1949, when she was 17. She became the team's majorette two years later, a spotlight she held from 1951 to 1966, When Vince Lombardi came to Green Bay, he asked her to form a cheerleading squad. A dedicated entertainer, she performed at halftime of the 1967 Ice Bowl NFL championship game when the temperature was 15-degrees below zero. By comparison, the 1961 game was balmy.

After their frustrating 17-13 loss to Philadelphia in the 1960 NFL championship game, the Packers were ready for the Giants in 1961. Green Bay erupted for 24 points in the second quarter and cruised to a 37-0 victory. The title, the first for the Packers without Lambeau at the helm, made it clear that Green Bay was entering a new golden era under Lombardi. In just his third season, he had won a championship with a previously bumbling team.

The *Press-Gazette,* which was not scheduled to publish on January 1 because it was a holiday, turned out a four-page Extra! to celebrate. Even though every word and photo was dedicated to the Packers, there was no mention of Lambeau. This was a time to celebrate the revival of the Packers, their exciting present rather than their glorious past.

But in the *Chicago Tribune,* David Condon led his "In the Wake of the News" column on January 1 with this tribute: "While watching yesterday's National Football league championship game, didn't you get the idea that the good folk of Green Bay, Wis., should be thankful for the many years of pioneer work done by E.L. (Curly) Lambeau and the hardy Packers of yesteryear?"

From across the Atlantic, in Madrid, Spain, Green Bay native Philip B. Sullivan, who had grown up adoring Lambeau's championship teams, congratulated "the Glorious Packer Team of 1961," but also urged "that some sort of tribute be given to Curly Lambeau. To my ear Lambeau Stadium is more euphonious than Municipal Stadium or even Packer Stadium."

Before Lombardi departed on a European vacation—first stop, Rome—Green Bay's new conquering hero attended the NFL's post-season meeting in early January in Miami, where he also emphasized the importance of Lambeau's contribution to the game and his hometown.

"The incident did not get any circulation," David Condon wrote in the *Chicago Tribune* on January 16, "but Coach Vince Lombardi of the Champion Green Bay Packers really stirred National Football league owners with his address on the final day of the circuit's meetings in Miami Beach. Vince's oration urged the naming of Curly Lambeau, long time Packer coach, to the league's Hall of Fame committee. Lombardi stressed Lambeau's great contribution to the game and to Green Bay."

# 87
## ONE HALL OF FAME AFTER ANOTHER

By the spring of 1962, the NFL was firming up its plans for a Pro Football Hall of Fame. The site would be Canton, Ohio, where the league famously held its first meeting in the legendary Hupmobile showroom. Groundbreaking was scheduled for August 11. The New York Giants and St. Louis Cardinals played that day in the first annual Pro Football Hall of Fame game.

Canton clearly was on Lambeau's mind when he was interviewed for a story marking the 40th anniversary of Green Bay being readmitted to the NFL in late June. After Lambeau used three college players in a non-league game against Racine at the end of the 1921 season, league president Joe Carr had revoked Green Bay's franchise. That set up the dubious yarn about Curly getting the franchise back for $50, aided by his friend Don Murphy, who supposedly sold his cream-colored Marmon roadster to fund the trip.

One possible explanation for Murphy being given credit, even in a discredited fable, is that he was a wealthy life-long friend of Lambeau who was actively involved in the early days of the Packers. After the family lumber mill burned down in Green Bay, Murphy went into the lumber business in Northern California. Like Lambeau, Murphy spent the winter in Palm Springs.

"We got the thing started," Murphy said in a 1965 interview, "and then it went over into the hands of the stockholders. . . . I moved out here in California and Curly kept on coaching."

The automobile sale was not the only disputed detail. Forty years later, possibly determined to add weight to the site of the Pro Football Hall of Fame, Lambeau insisted he had gone to Canton to regain his football franchise, even though the league clearly had met in Cleveland. "Well, Curly was there—he ought to know," a *Press-Gazette* reporter wrote in another example of Lambeau not letting the facts get in the way of a good story.

A couple of other notable developments took place at that 1922 NFL meeting, which was held at the Hollander Hotel in Cleveland, no matter what Lambeau said. For one: George Halas, who had led the Decatur Staleys to the 1921 championship, was granted a new franchise in Chicago for a team to be called the Bears. This was not surprising. After playing their first two games in Decatur, the 1921 Staleys had played their final 10 games at Cubs Park in Chicago. But now, the team belonged to Halas, not a starch company.

In addition, the league changed its name from American Professional Football Association to the National Football League. Halas had correctly argued that the cumbersome old name sounded too much like the American Association, a minor-league baseball operation.

It was pretty obvious that Lambeau would be among the inaugural inductees when the Pro Football Hall of Fame announced its first class. He and Halas stood out as pioneers who had founded, managed, coached and played for two of the NFL's flagship franchises for decades.

Before the Pro Football Hall of Fame opened in Canton, though, the Wisconsin Athletic Hall of Fame was the highest honor for Lambeau. And it intended to enshrine Curly with a flourish.

Departing from the previous year, when Johnny Blood and three others were inducted during a joint dinner at the Milwaukee Arena, the 1962 honorees each would be honored with dinners in their hometowns. Lambeau's gala was scheduled for the Green Bay Elks Club on Saturday, November 17, the night before the Packers played their homecoming game against the Baltimore Colts.

The date for Lambeau's Hall of Fame dinner was announced on Sunday, September 2, the day before the Packers played their only pre-season game in Green Bay, an exhibition "rematch" with the New York Giants, whom they had beaten in a frigid NFL championship game 246 days earlier.

When Lambeau's big night arrived, a sold-out crowd of 700 filled the Elks Club. Don Hutson was master of ceremonies. Longtime Lambeau rival Jimmy Conzelman, who had gone on to be a St. Louis advertising executive, was scheduled to be the featured speaker, but was unable to get out of Chicago due to airplane troubles.

Calling the record number of former Packers at the dinner "nothing but another tribute to Curly Lambeau," Lombardi said he felt honored to present Lambeau with his Hall of Fame certificate. "Curly Lambeau has a record that will hardly ever be equalled. The Packers have a proud, a great, tradition, one started by Curly Lambeau. For this proud tradition, we are thankful. This is one of the things that helps us to win."

In turn, Lambeau gushed back at Lombardi, saying, "I hope you win seven championships."

Pete Rozelle, the NFL's young commissioner, also paid tribute, telling the attendees, "Curly played a major part in building what we have in the NFL today. He will be remembered in the league for his tremendous efforts. All in the league know what Curly has done for the league in vision, determination and capability."

Still on top of his public-relations game, Lambeau accepted his award with humility and humor.

"Many times during my athletic and coaching career, I've been asked what has been my greatest thrill," Lambeau told the adoring crowd. "But I will have to say from the bottom of my heart that this is my greatest thrill."

And then, recalling the early days, Lambeau said, "At the end of our 1919 season each of us got $16. I was disappointed, too. I thought we'd get $20."

The next morning, the photo that would infuriate Lombardi—the shot of Lambeau and Lombardi shaking hands—ran prominently on the front page of the Sunday *Green Bay Press-Gazette.* The photo was taken on Saturday morning before the Lambeau love-in. Both men were beaming in front of rows of ominously empty seats at City Stadium—the Packers' legendary home that would soon be renamed, despite Lombardi's quiet resistance, Lambeau Field.

Lambeau was saluted at halftime by the capacity crowd of 38,669 at the stadium that would bear his name. Green Bay, which had won its first nine games, was an ambitious 16-point favorite against the Johnny-Unitas-led Baltimore Colts. The Packers, locked in a 10-10 halftime tie, fell behind 13-10, but rallied for a fourth-quarter touchdown and a 17-13 victory on November 18. That gave them a perfect 10-0 start in their bid for a second straight NFL title in 1962.

The Lions spoiled Green Bay's unbeaten record with a 26-14 win in Detroit on Thanksgiving Day, November 22. A few weeks later, Lambeau watched with pride from the Los Angeles Coliseum press box as Green Bay tried to lock up its third straight Western Division title. Early in their game, the Packers learned that they had clinched the division, thanks to the Bears' 3-0 upset of the Lions in Chicago. With the pressure off, Green Bay edged the Rams 20-17 for its 13th victory, eclipsing the team record of 12 regular-season wins by Lambeau's 1929 champions.

"Well, that's great. Three [conference] championships in a row," Lambeau said before heading to the Packers' dressing room, where he "congratulated Lombardi and all the players he could put his hands on."

In a rematch of the 1961 NFL championship, Green Bay again defeated the Giants 16-7 on December 30, 1962, but this time in New York, where Lambeau had won two of his NFL titles.

On January 29, 1963, Lambeau was among the 17 football men named to the inaugural class of the new Pro Football Hall of Fame. He was joined by three of his Packer stars: Don Hutson, Johnny Blood and Cal Hubbard. The four Green Bay honorees topped the list, one ahead of three Bears: George Halas, Red Grange and Bronko Nagurski.

Lambeau's friend and former boss, George Preston Marshall, and Redskin quarterback Sammy Baugh represented Washington. Giants owner Tim Mara and center Mel Hein were honored from New York. Also inducted were two former NFL leaders, president Joe F. Carr and commissioner Bert Bell, Cardinals star Ernie Nevers, Lions quarterback Dutch Clark, and 1920s pioneers Jim Thorpe and Pete "Fats" Henry.

Reaching for a local angle, the *Los Angeles Times* had led its Hall of Fame story with a headline saying that "two Southlanders"—USC assistant coach Mel Hein and Southern California resident Earl (Curly) Lambeau— "were among 17 men named Monday as charter members of the National Professional Football Hall of Fame." Hein had played his entire career with the New York Giants. Lambeau spent his winters in California, but was forever a son of Green Bay.

Blood, who had worked at his family's Minneapolis newspaper, found it amusing that a Los Angeles newspaper latched onto Lambeau. Blood was visiting Lambeau in California when they learned they were selected as charter members of the new Hall of Fame. "We had a ball together," Blood said. "Can you imagine the *Los Angeles Times* claiming him as a resident?"

Blood had one quibble with the 17 selections: "Verne Lewellen should have been in there in front of me and Hubbard. They missed a couple of guys but I guess you've got to be lucky as well as good."

Still a Packer and a vagabond, Blood said he had gone to the Rose Bowl to see Wisconsin play USC after "watching us win the championship out in little old New York. I just stayed out here."

To celebrate their Hall of Fame success, Blood said he took Lambeau out to dinner in Los Angeles "and we wound up at the Palmer

Hotel. Well, Curly was with me so I kind of guided things. In this place, in the Palmer, Chubby Checker was entertaining. He was there doing the Twist, when it first came out. Chubby put on a demonstration and then the nightclubbers got to do it. I didn't get up, but out there on the floor was Curly, doing the Twist. What a spectacle. Here was the guy who used to frown on me doing all that kind of stuff, and here I was watching from the sideline."

By that point in his life, Blood, who had been a notorious drinker, had sobered up—which made him less inclined to do the Twist. Lambeau, on the other hand, continued to enjoy being exuberant in his twilight years. Although Lambeau liked his bourbon, few people embraced alcohol with the zeal Blood had shown.

"I guess Curly was a human guy after all," Blood said. "He was not perfect, not an angel. But there weren't many angels in the pro league when I got there. I met a lot of good men there who had an angelic side and a devilish side. I'm sure a lot of them would say the same about me."

Back in Palm Springs, Lambeau continued to Twist, and found a new justification for his dance fever. "When it comes to exercise, twisting is better for me than golf," he told *Los Angeles Herald Examiner* columnist Bud Furillo.

Curly Lambeau doing the Twist for exercise? He may have gotten that thought from the Los Angeles Angels, the baseball team that held its spring training in Palm Springs. His comment came just a few days after *Desert Sun* columnist Bob Miller reported that "Curvy Candy Johnson, who appears nightly at the El Mirador, gave some of the [Angels] Twist lessons. The theory is (what rationalizing) that the dance will help keep Bill Rigney's players in condition, make them more supple and, oh, gad, 'keep their energy at peak levels.' " And so, Lambeau added a new activity to golf in the California desert and boating on Green Bay.

By the summer of 1963. he had completed a major project. After being devastated by the fire that leveled his Fish Creek summer home, he had turned the carriage house, which had escaped the blaze, into his new summer residence.

"Colorful Curly Lambeau, founder of the Packers and Green Bay's contribution to football's Hall of Fame, is undoubtedly its only member who sleeps in a remodeled horse stall and hangs his clothes on harness hooks," a *Press-Gazette* feature told readers.

"The summer home of this six-time National Football League pennant winner, a remodeled carriage house in Fish Creek, is as charmingly casual in appearance as its famous owner is in manner. Located on an eight-acre lot (about half the size of Monaco) it reflects the discriminating taste of a man who likes living the simple life—provided it is lived in absolute comfort. For a man who came up the hard way—Curley has it good."

Lambeau kept the interior of the structure largely intact. Two of the horse stalls were converted into "an attractively furnished bedroom and television room." The horses' water trough became a planter. The oat bin, he used as "a huge ashtray."

Wielding "a mean trowel," Lambeau built an outdoor barbecue pit. "The only meals he prepares are on this grill," the article said. The rest of the time, Lambeau ate at the C&C Club, owned by his friend, Dick Weisgerber, who played for the Packers in the late 1930s and early '40s. "I would always see him over there," Dick's son, Rich, said.

"Dick still kids Curly about the well-known Lambeau penchant for fining tardy players only (in most cases) to return the fine as a Christmas present," the 1963 article about Curly's carriage house said.

Although they were close friends in their later years, there was a time when money was not a joking matter. "In 1941, my dad sat out because Curly wouldn't give him a raise," Rich Weisgerber said. "He was a tyrant with his players when it came to money."

While "reluctant to discuss the past" in the article about his carriage house, Lambeau spoke freely about his winter life in Palm Springs, where he enjoyed playing golf with people like Bing Crosby, Bob Hope and former President Dwight Eisenhower, who were "just the guys next door" to him. And Curly probably was just one of the guys to men like Hope, Crosby and Eisenhower, who all admired athletic excellence.

While golf was his primary winter passion, boating on Green Bay was his favorite summer sport, the carriage house piece said. "Curly's yacht is named the 'Lazy,' . . . 'So people can feel as lazy and comfortable as I do."

The folksy article was accompanied by several photos of Lambeau enjoying life in his cozy carriage house. He was shown pointing to some framed mementos, stoking his antique pot-bellied stove and reading a *Sports Illustrated* featuring a cover photo of Paul Hornung, who had been suspended for gambling. "Every time I think about it, I see red," he said. "Hornung did not deserve the 'death penalty' of indefinite suspension. . . .

His bets were considered sporting bets—the kind many honorable citizens make."

Hornung, the Packers' charismatic star halfback, and Alex Karras, the Detroit Lions' outstanding defensive tackle, both sat out the 1963 season before being reinstated.

In a minor blow to Green Bay's "Titletown" claims, the Packers were surprised by the College All-Stars 20-17 on Friday night, August 2, in Chicago when the football season opened. The hero for the All-Stars was Wisconsin quarterback Ron Vander Kelen, who was born and raised in Preble, which would become a part of Green Bay in 1964. After throwing a 74-yard fourth-quarter touchdown to his Badger teammate, Pat Richter, Vander Kelen denied he had been motivated by his hometown Packers failing to draft him.

"There was nothing like that," he said. "I just want to play and do good. If it had been the Bears we were playing, I would have felt the same way." An undrafted free agent, Vander Kelen landed a spot on the Minnesota Vikings, where he backed up Fran Tarkenton for five seasons.

"We killed a dragon! How about that?" the college stars chanted joyously in their locker room. It was only the second All-Stars win over the NFL champion since Lambeau guided them to victory in 1955.

"We have no excuses, none whatsoever," Packers coach Lombardi said. "We just couldn't get going. The All-Stars were great. Much better than last year."

Lombardi would lead Green Bay into this high-profile kickoff to the football season three more times—and win all three by at least 17 points. There would be 12 more College All-Star games. This would be the last one, however, that went the All-Stars' way.

A month later, the National Football League turned its attention to the game that would replace the College All-Star game as the traditional start to a new season. On Sunday, September 8, Pittsburgh defeated Cleveland 16-7 in Canton, Ohio, in the Football Hall of Fame game.

A day earlier, NFL leaders gathered for what would become an annual tradition: Welcoming a new group into the Pro Football Hall of Fame. Canton, where the league had first taken shape in Ralph Hay's Hupmobile showroom, would become the NFL's version of Cooperstown, home of the Baseball Hall of Fame.

With 17 inductees spanning the first four decades of the NFL, the first Pro Football Hall of Fame class was remarkable in its size and accomplishment. The four Packer honorees—the most of any team—was a testament to Lambeau's immense contribution.

"Curly gave to America its most colorful team—the Green Bay Packers—when he put together the big team in the little town in 1919," Lambeau's presenter, Jim Crowley, told a gathering of 6,000 at Fawcett Stadium. "Even in retirement, he breaks coaching records—most Hall of Famers coached, Hutson, Blood and Hubbard."

Although never a Packer, Crowley was the perfect symbolic choice as Lambeau's presenter. Curly had coached him at East High, sent him on to Four Horsemen fame at Notre Dame. And then, presiding over the Seven Blocks of Granite at Fordham, Crowley had coached Lombardi, who would revive Green Bay's football fortunes.

"I am deeply grateful and very honored," Lambeau said in an acceptance speech described as `short and sweet' in the *Press-Gazette*. "Forty-one years ago, I came to Canton and got a franchise for $50. And the last time I heard, the Packers were very much in the league."

After being credited with "revolutionizing defensive football by being the game's first roving linebacker," Hubbard said modestly, "I'm in some pretty fast company today. I am proud and honored to be here."

Hutson's presenter, Cleveland Browns receiver Dante Lavelli, said, "Every good end is called another Don Hutson. . . . Then the years go by and Don is still up there—the greatest."

But Johnny Blood once again stole the show. In a seemingly odd coupling, he was presented by Supreme Court justice Byron "Whizzer" White, who had delayed his law career when Blood convinced him to join the Pittsburgh Steelers. They became lifelong friends.

"John was a magnificent performer," White said. "He was at his best when the going was toughest and that's proof of a great football player."

In his acceptance remarks, Blood also showed his gift for public speaking.

"When you stand in a place like this, you wonder, `How did I get here?' " Blood said. "You've got to have great luck and I had that kind of luck. But there is a lot more than luck. Some fine men took a chance and hired me—men like Ole Haugsrud, Curly Lambeau and Art Rooney."

Although Blood played for Haugsrud's accomplished but short-lived Duluth Eskimos and was improbably hired by Art Rooney to coach the Steelers, it was with Lambeau's Green Bay Packers that he earned his Hall of Fame credentials.

Showing his literary bent, Blood closed with a quote from his favorite poet, Kipling: "The tumult and shouting dies, the captains and the kings depart, still stands thine ancient sacrifice, and a humble and contrite heart."

Now 65, Lambeau spent the autumn of 1963 enjoying retirement. He was in the Pro Football Hall of Fame as well as the Wisconsin Athletic Hall of Fame. He had recovered from losing his house—for the second time—to a devastating fire and fashioned a cozy home in the carriage house that survived. He spent time with Mary Jane Van Duyse, the girlfriend who was half his age. And he followed the Packers.

"I fish almost every day," Lambeau told a reporter in the press box in Milwaukee while watching the Packers handle the Steelers 33-14 on November 3, 1963. "And with the weather turning cool I'll be heading for Palm Springs in California for the winter."

No longer an active participant, Lambeau was enthusiastic about the prospects for the football league he helped build. The early hand-to-mouth era, where teams scrambled to sell tickets, had been replaced by a surge in NFL interest. Not only were stadiums filled to the brim in the 1960s. Lambeau predicted even greater riches in the league's future.

"There's a new [era] just ahead," he said. "Pay TV will revolutionize pro football and pay all the bills. I have to admit that I enjoy being here in this nice, warm press box and meeting old friends like Art Rooney. But I'm sold on television. They do such a wonderful job with closeups to the huddles, on the sidelines, etc., that you can actually see more sitting at home than being in the stands. Pay TV is bound to come."

In one of the strange ironies of sports, while cold-weather games on the Frozen Tundra of Lambeau Field are embraced by Packer fans and old-fashioned football lovers everywhere, Lambeau himself fled wintry conditions whenever possible. Given the choice between freezing at the Ice Bowl and watching from his couch, he might have voted for the TV. He even tried having his substitutes wait in the warmth of the dressing room, using a sideline telephone to let them know when he needed them to come out and play.

Beyond his obvious dislike of chilly weather, he might have been scarred by the Packers' early struggles, in which foul weather meant poor attendance that threatened to bankrupt the team. And he often referenced how a slippery field hampered his players from being at their best.

Lambeau's friend and rival, George Halas, also had seen the television future. He had pioneered putting together a far-flung network of stations to air his Bears games, and protected his ticket sales by enacting a 70-mile television blackout.

If Lambeau had been envious, he now seemed content with the way his life had played out. Halas had built an empire that would be handed down in his family for generations. But Curly, who had not seemed interested in owning the Packers, had enjoyed a great run. He had avoided many of the business headaches that Halas endured. And if he had not reaped the same financial rewards as Halas, he had done very well for himself.

## 88
## *REUNION FOR KING CURLY AND HIS KNIGHTS*

Was Lambeau envious of the way George Halas continued to be a force in the NFL? Did he wistfully ponder what might have been if he had owned the Packers? Did he imagine what he might have accomplished if his many supporters had succeeded in restoring him to the helm of the Packers when Vince Lombardi was hired in 1959?

From time to time, perhaps. After Halas' Bears had defeated Lombardi's Packers 10-3 in their 1963 season opener, Lambeau showed a rare public down moment. The image was forever etched in the mind of longtime Packer executive Bob Harlan.

"The only thing I remember about the game was that as I was walking out of the press box, Curly Lambeau was standing there all by himself, kind of draped over the side of the stadium wall, looking like the season was finished," said Harlan, the Packers' president and CEO from 1989 to 2008. "He seemed like such a forlorn person. He was all by himself, and it was just like it was the last game of the playoffs and we had been eliminated. I'll never forget how terribly lonely he seemed standing there. And I'll always remember that."

Was Lambeau crushed by a Packer defeat? More likely, it had triggered a moment of reflection. Here he was, The Man Who Invented the Green Bay Packers, in a magnificent stadium filled with Packer fans. It was the kind of scenario only the boldest 21 year old would have imagined when he started a football team on a shoestring. And yet, it had moved far beyond him. Somehow, he had lost control of that team, that dream.

Or maybe his thoughts had moved on to his personal life, which had followed a similar pattern. There had been great highs, but also the ache of three failed marriages. He had countless friends and admirers, but might not have been close enough to anyone in a way that could erase the loneliness that he rarely acknowledged.

And yet, Lambeau enjoyed the balm of his considerable personal wealth, which allowed him to pursue his genuine passion for an active retirement. If he had not taken the same path as nose-to-the-grindstone George Halas, Curly Lambeau had never seemed completely dedicated to taking that path. His passions had been for adventure and glory. Halas had focused on the details of building a business empire. Lambeau had been too easily distracted, often detouring for immediate gratification.

Was that on the mind of a man who looked downcast and lonely to Bob Harlan after that season opener in 1963? Whatever caused Lambeau's post-game blues, the Bears' victory in the 1963 season opener turned out to be pivotal. Green Bay—playing without Paul Hornung, suspended for gambling that season—also lost to the Bears 26-7 in Chicago.

They were Green Bay's only two losses. Meanwhile, the Bears lost only once, in San Francisco, to win the Western Division. The Bears then defeated the New York Giants 14-10 in the NFL championship game. It was the eighth and final title for Halas as an owner, and his fifth as the Bears coach.

Rather than sulking, Green Bay came up with a true display of sportsmanship. It honored Halas with a testimonial dinner on April 13, 1964. A crowd of 700 filled the Elks Club—at $6 a plate—to pay tribute to the man who snuffed the Packers' hopes of winning a third straight NFL championship.

A dinner honoring a despised rival like Halas "is something that could only happen in Green Bay," Lombardi told the Elks Club crowd. "But I don't think George is convinced. I see he brought along his own food tasters," he added, pointing to a Bears contingent that included former Bears stars Sid Luckman and George Connor.

Playing along, the 69-year-old Halas solemnly said, "It is time to make an announcement. . . . I would like to take this opportunity to announce my retirement—" and paused for some stifled gasps. "—from the banquet circuit." The startled crowd responded with applause and laughter.

Absent from the third annual Elks Club Sports Night was Curly Lambeau, who also had missed the first testimonial, a salute to Lombardi on April 30, 1962. Lambeau had been scheduled to speak, but sent his regrets "because his mother, Mrs. Marcel Lambeau, is critically ill. Lambeau, at her bedside, sent 'his best to Vince. and to his old pupil,' principal speaker Jim Crowley, Emcee Tim Cohane announced early in the evening." Lambeau's mother, Mary, died after a six-month illness on September 17, 1962. She was 85.

Lambeau's absence from that 1962 banquet left an open link in a remarkable circle: Lambeau had coached Crowley at Green Bay East, steering him to Notre Dame and "Four Horsemen" fame. Crowley had gone on to coach at Fordham, where Vince Lombardi was one of his "Seven

Blocks of Granite" before becoming a coaching legend in Crowley's hometown.

In other words, Lambeau's protege had mentored Lombardi, who had come to Green Bay and restored the Packers to the traditional championship status. One does not have to be a Packer fan to appreciate the completeness of the team's fable-like history.

After featuring the sure-fire trio of Lombardi, Lambeau and Halas in its first three Sports Night dinners, the Elks Club came up with another winner in 1965: The six Green Bay heroes who were members of the first two Pro Football Hall of Fame classes gathered for a Packer love-in on April 26, 1965.

For that gala, Lambeau returned, accompanied by fellow charter Hall of Famers Don Hutson, Johnny Blood and Cal Hubbard, plus second-year inductees Clarke Hinkle and Mike Michalske.

When they gathered for a photo, they were just six old men in suits, smiling for the camera. To the untrained eye, they could have been a board of directors. To those who know their Packer lore, though, they were five wise old knights, gathered around King Curly, the man who brought them together to go out and conquer.

The exploits of Lombardi and his hallowed Packers—Hornung and Starr and Nitschke and so many others—have aged better. Lombardi's era is more recent than Lambeau's, and it can be watched on video. And for athletic football, modern heroes Brett Favre and Aaron Rodgers might be the shiniest knights in the Green and Gold kingdom.

But Lambeau and his colorful band established the Packer empire in Green Bay, and—against the odds—kept it there, enabling all the glory that their descendants achieved. And with Lambeau, Hutson, Blood, Hubbard, Hinkle and Michalske in one room together for one feast—no group could match the stories they must have told.

"These are the men who made the National Football League, who made it the great sport it is today and gave it its color," Vince Lombardi said before handing gold-plated helmet plaques to each of the six Packer legends. "Our present day players should be ever thankful to these men and those like them who gave them the game. . . and gave them the huge salaries we pay today."

While handing Lambeau his plaque, Lombardi said the NFL "owes him an eternal debt" after listing his accomplishments. Lombardi also made the crowd roar. Setting up a punchline by saying, "I did not realize that five

Hall of Famers played on one team," Lombardi said, "With all due respect to my friend Curly, I think I could have done a pretty good job of coaching these fellows myself."

When Lambeau's turn came, he returned the friendly needle. The previous season, when Green Bay had slipped to an 8-5-1 record, it had made only 30.8 percent of its field-goal attempts, low-lighted by a meager 4-for-23 on attempts of 30 yards or more. While paying tribute to Hinkle, Lambeau looked straight at Lombardi when he said Hinkle "could kick field goals from beyond 30 yards."

Lombardi showed his gap-toothed roasting humor with the other honorees, too. Noting that Hutson "has been called the greatest pro football player of all time," Lombardi said, "He's a man I'm proud to call my friend —even though he cheats a little on his handicap on the golf course."

Lombardi noted that Blood "was second only to Sammy Baugh in number of years in the NFL with 15," and added, "You can't find too much about him in the record book. But outside the record book, there's an awful lot."

All in all, it was a grand reunion and homecoming for Lambeau, who had driven back from another winter in California for this warm and fuzzy Elks Club salute to The Man Who Invented the Green Bay Packers and the five Hall of Famers who played for him.

And then, Curly Lambeau motored on to his Door Peninsula carriage house in Fish Creek. He planned to spend the summer there with his shiny new red Cadillac convertible, his latest power boat named *Lazy* and Mary Jane, the attractive young woman he was dating.

Life was good.

Six weeks later, on an early-summer evening, Lambeau drove down to Sturgeon Bay to take Mary Jane out to dinner. They never made it to dinner. On June 1, 1965, he was felled by a massive heart attack. He was 67.

Lambeau's death hit George Halas hard. The loss of his great friend and greatest rival moved the Bears founder to write a tribute that the *Associated Press* distributed around the nation.

"Life ends. Curly Lambeau is gone," Halas wrote. "Lambeau's death was a terrible shock. . . . He was one of the builders of the National Football League. Not only did he help by always fielding a team, but he was able to get financing to help others. . . Oh, yes, Lambeau forced me to make changes. In fact, he did such a great job with the Packers that the

Chicago Bears had to come up with something new. That's when we went to the T formation. . . . It's a great game and it'll get better. Let's thank the likes of Curly Lambeau."

In New York, NFL commissioner Pete Rozelle said, "Curly Lambeau was one of the true pioneers of the game. A great part of what the National Football League is today is directly traceable to him."

In Green Bay, Packer president Olejniczak said the city of Green Bay and the state of Wisconsin should be "eternally grateful to Curly. . . . we would not have professional football were it not for his untiring efforts and personal sacrifices. No man has made a greater contribution to the city, to the state or to the National Football League than Curly."

Lambeau's great friend and greatest player, Don Hutson, was "too broken up" to comment, his wife said in Racine. "Don and Curly were very close. He's gone to bed. This has hit him pretty hard."

# 89
## *LAST CONTROVERSY, LAST TRIUMPH*

How to honor The Man Who Invented the Green Bay Packers? His death sparked a renewed effort for Lambeau Field. That proposal also stirred a great debate. No one questioned that City Stadium was an uninspired name. There was no doubt that Earl Louis "Curly" Lambeau had started their beloved team. But some people could not get past the rough patches in his life. Would his death win them over?

Nearly 30 years earlier, *Milwaukee Sentinel* sports columnist Howard Purser wrote in 1937 that "Green Bay fans have started a movement to change the name of the city stadium to 'Lambeau field' as a tribute to the Packer coach."

There also had been Lambeau Field talk when Green Bay opened its new City Stadium in 1957, but that idea never went far. When Alderman Thomas Atkinson proposed that the stadium be renamed "in honor of the founder of the Green Bay Packers," the Green Bay Stadium Commission decided instead to place a plaque honoring Lambeau at the new stadium.

In a further change, the plaque also carried the names of the Packers' first six presidents. It was placed in November 1960 to the outer wall of the ticket office and later moved to the west side of the stadium. "It wasn't until Lambeau died that the suggestions to rename the stadium in his memory gained traction," Packers team historian Cliff Christl said. "Then the clamor built until officials had little choice but to stop stonewalling it."

Amid the mourning that followed Lambeau's death, the name change gained momentum from many corners. "I do think that our stadium or arena should be called by his name. This would be proper," Monsignor John Gehl of St. Francis Xavier Cathedral said in his eulogy at Lambeau's funeral on June 5, 1965.

In the days and weeks after the funeral, the subject of putting Curly Lambeau's name on the stadium continued to be a hot topic in the *Green Bay Press-Gazette* and virtually everywhere around the city and state.

A frequent writer to the newspaper, George Banta Jr., from nearby Menasha, said in a letter published June 6 that the name City Stadium "lacked color and interest" in pushing for Lambeau Field. Two days later, the Greater Green Bay Labor Council urged putting the Lambeau name on the stadium, saying that Lambeau "contributed more to the recognition of

Green Bay, both nationally and internationally, than any other native or adopted son."

On June 12, the Mike & Pen Club of Green Bay, a local sportswriters and sportscasters group, also called for Lambeau Stadium, saying, "Without the stamina of this man, building and coaching a football team, Green Bay would be just another location in the state of Wisconsin."

Two days after that, however, Mayor Donald Tilleman told the Green Bay Rotary Club that Lambeau's name should be relegated to the old City Stadium, where the Packers had played from 1925 to 1956. Some felt that was more appropriate because that stadium, which was still used for high school football, was where Lambeau had coached the team to glory.

The mayor was not the only prominent official who didn't want the Packers' home turf to be called Lambeau Field. Conspicuously absent from Curly's funeral was Lombardi, who was building his own Packer legend. Lombardi had been at an NFL meeting in New York the previous day. But so had Bears owner George Halas, who had flown to Green Bay to attend the funeral and serve as an honorary pallbearer. In Lombardi's absence, team president Dominic Olejniczak and defensive coach Phil Bengtson represented the team at the funeral of its founder.

"Curly Lambeau's death is a loss not only to Green Bay and the state of Wisconsin, but to all of professional football," Lombardi said, paying his respects from afar in a comment to the *Associated Press*.

Aside from the Lambeau Field issue, Lombardi had shown great respect and appreciation for Lambeau. Although Lombardi's absence from Curly's funeral raised eyebrows in Green Bay, the two great Packer leaders had been cordial outwardly. The night before a Packer game in Milwaukee, Mary Jane said she and Curly were having dinner at Pappy's, the restaurant owned by former Packer star Buckets Goldenberg. "In came Vince Lombardi," she said. "He and Marie came over and sat with us and talked. We had a real nice time."

Lombardi had taken over a slumbering franchise in 1959, a team that had won its sixth and final NFL title under Lambeau in 1944 and had not had a winning season since 1947. Questionable decisions by Lambeau exacerbated yet another budget crisis that threatened the team's existence, leading the Packers' board to rein in his power.

Demanding the decision-making authority that had been stripped from Lambeau in the late 1940s and that had hampered Lambeau's 1950s successors, Lombardi had been free to mold the team without the meddling of its nonprofit board members. He had quickly won NFL championships in 1961 and 1962. In 1965, the Packers were about to begin a run of three straight NFL titles that would anoint Lombardi as the greatest coach in league history.

The only other NFL coach to win three straight championships was... Curly Lambeau.

And while Lombardi paid his respects to Lambeau's accomplishments in his public comments, he seethed privately at the prospect of having his Packers play at Lambeau Field.

"He was diametrically opposed to it, no question about it," Lee Remmel, the longtime *Press-Gazette* sportswriter who later became the team's publicist and then its historian, told his successor as Packer historian, Cliff Christl. "Twice within my hearing, he inveighed against naming it Lambeau Field."

Similar to Lambeau's relationship with George Halas, he and Lombardi were friends on one level, and rivals on another. They were all football men. The game connected them to a gridiron fraternity. With Halas, Lambeau's rivalry involved winning games. With Lombardi, it was more a clash of egos.

In the 1960s, when Lombardi was presiding over a glorious time in Packers history, what he and Curly had in common as talented, take-charge football men who had won championships in tiny Green Bay meant very little. What mattered was that Lombardi didn't want to share the spotlight, especially with someone he didn't respect outside of football. They were very different personalities who just happened to be linked by their football epitaphs as the two great leaders of the beloved Green Bay Packers.

Lambeau was outgoing to the extreme, a sharp dresser and womanizer. "Curly was a ladies man," Harry Jacunski, a Packer from 1939 to 1944, said. "He actually competed with the players for some of the women in Green Bay."

Lambeau also angered his players at times by withholding their pay when he didn't like their effort. In addition, several key Packer executives found Lambeau's management style abrasive. At the end of his Green Bay run, they over-ruled his brash decision-making.

That said, he won more games, and more championships, than any coach in the NFL's first quarter-century. He still is the sixth winningest coach in the league's history and is tied for most NFL championships won. His Packers drew the biggest crowds in Chicago, New York and everywhere they played at a time when the NFL was struggling for survival. For all of his flaws, Lambeau and his rival, George Halas, were the most important team leaders of the NFL's precarious formative years.

"What a life this guy [Lambeau] had," Upton Bell, the son of Bert Bell, the NFL commissioner from 1946 to 1959, said in an interview with the author. "Whether he was a con artist, he was a great coach, a great player. He's in the Hall of Fame. He was a great liar. He was great in everything. He was the emperor of Green Bay. And yet, he probably wanted to be in Chicago or L.A., with the broads and booze and all the other stuff. On the other hand, he was brilliant. He could have been anything."

Lombardi, on the other hand, took a very different approach to women and life.

"We never dreamt that Vince would become a coach," said Alex Wojciechowicz, Lombardi's teammate at Fordham, where they were two of the "Seven Blocks of Granite," a famous set of linemen. "We all thought that he was going to be a priest."

Did Lombardi, a devout Catholic, despise Lambeau's womanizing, divorce-filled lifestyle? No doubt. Did he not respect Lambeau's coaching struggles at the end of his career? Probably. Did Lombardi have limits when it came to sharing Packer glory with its legendary founder? Yes. Did he prefer the idea of someday having the Lombardi name on the Packers' stadium? Any of these might explain Lombardi's disdain for Lambeau.

Were the mayor and other city officials aware of Lombardi's private disdain for Lambeau? Very likely.

The problem was, the photo of Lambeau and Lombardi shaking hands in the stadium was another log on the growing fire for turning City Stadium into Lambeau Field. To generations of Packer fans, Lambeau was, as the *New York Times* called him, The Man Who Invented the Green Bay Packers, who brought glory to northeastern Wisconsin, who made their small town stand tall.

The City Council tried to sidestep the issue on June 15, when it paid tribute to Lambeau in a resolution, but claimed that Curly didn't want his name on the stadium. The resolution said he had once told the Green Bay Stadium Commission, "Boys, I am glad that you didn't take any action on naming the new stadium after me. I never played there, had no part in building it, and it is my opinion that the new stadium belongs to the people who built it, the citizens of Green Bay."

That was not a good reason for keeping Lambeau's name off the Packers' home field, *Press-Gazette* sports columnist Len Wagner told his readers on June 17, 1965. If the city chose to merely honor Lambeau with a resolution "because he did not jump at the chance to have the stadium named after him," Wagner wrote, ". . . I am truly numb with shock."

A June 16 editorial in the *Press-Gazette* already had come out in favor of Curly Lambeau Field, saying, "Public sentiment in Green Bay, Northeastern Wisconsin and indeed all of Wisconsin appears to be strongly in favor of honoring the late Earl L. (Curly) Lambeau by renaming City Stadium in his honor."

The editorial said resistance in City Hall, which held the authority to make the change, apparently stemmed from the will of a local doctor, Del Marcelle, who had pledged his $230,000 estate to the city for the construction of a stadium—but only if the stadium was named for him.

That seemed to be a reach—particularly because the money wouldn't be available until Dr. Marcelle's four heirs had died. The editorial also noted that "it appears to be a fairly certain thing that the Packers will eventually pay the entire debt" for the stadium. Years later, a 1,750-seat Del Marcelle Stadium opened in 1979 for high school games.

"Any other name" than Lambeau Field, the newspaper editorial concluded, "would seem to be meaningless to the people of this community and in fact to the people of the United States where the names of Curly Lambeau, Green Bay and the Packers are known and associated from coast to coast."

Wagner, the *Press-Gazette* columnist, tried to bring the controversy into focus with a grass-roots approach the next day. He announced the result of a survey of 34 barber shops that was unscientific and sentimental, but also a sign of the times. "An overwhelming 23 said the idea of changing the name [to Lambeau Field] was heavily favored by their customers. Four others indicated that it was pretty much favored. Three said the pros and cons were evenly split. Four said that there had been too little discussion of it to establish an accurate sentiment."

Most telling, Wagner wrote that "there was not one [barber] that indicated the general feeling was against the proposed change." With full disclosure, Wagner said he wanted City Stadium renamed because "I feel, as the vast majority of Packer fans feel, that this is the only proper tribute available."

For several weeks after that, the clamor for Lambeau Field grew. On July 25, the *1965 Packer Yearbook* showing Lombardi and Lambeau together went on sale.

The next day, July 26, the seven members of a special citizens council appointed by the City Council unanimously recommended that Lambeau Field become the stadium name. Three of the seven men on the committee—Charley Brock, Arnie Herber and Andy Gram—had played for Lambeau. A fourth, newspaperman John Torinus, was a longtime Packer board member. The other three were from the Packer-centric media.

A week later, the Green Bay Stadium Commission joined in agreement with the Packers' Executive Committee and the citizens panel on the Lambeau Field question.

On Tuesday, August 3, "after eight weeks of avoiding a vote," the City Council adopted a resolution renaming the Packers' home Lambeau Field without debate, the *Press-Gazette* reported. "The only Council comment was the opinion of Ald. Francis Hessel that Lambeau Stadium would sound better than Lambeau Field on television," the newspaper noted. On that point, history has not been on Hessel's side.

It was official. City Stadium would become Lambeau Field.

The name of Curly Lambeau, who had been as important to the Green Bay Packers for their first 30 years as George Halas had been to the Chicago Bears, would live on forever.

# *EPILOGUE*

An ESPN ranking of NFL stadiums in 2020 placed Lambeau Field at the top. It cited Green Bay's long history of success, including the three NFL championships played there, and the Lambeau Leap, in which Packers jump up to celebrate touchdowns with their fans in the stands.

"If you're fortunate enough to walk through the tunnel at Lambeau Field, you will cross the same bricks that the likes of Bart Starr and Ray Nitschke crossed," Rob Demovsky wrote. "The same bricks that Brett Favre, Reggie White and Aaron Rodgers crossed. Throughout its various renovations and expansions, one thing has remained intact: history. It's why the Packers kept a strip of brick—embedded into the new concrete—from the original walkway to the field. Above it is a plaque that reads: `Proud generations of Green Bay Packers Players, World Champions a record 13 times, have run over this very concrete to Greatness.' It's enough to give you chills."

That is the legacy of Earl Louis "Curly" Lambeau.

It is a fitting tribute for the founder of a quaint small-town franchise that survived and thrived. As a player, he scored the first touchdown of Knute Rockne's career and was the NFL's first 1,000-yard passer. As a coach, he won six NFL titles and led a Green Bay franchise that became a national draw, putting fans in the seats at a time when the fledgling league was struggling to survive. More than a century after he began, he remains sixth on the all-time NFL wins list.

He took his Packers on a ground-breaking barnstorm trip to Hawaii. He made the Packers the first team in any sport to fly routinely to road games. He spoke of a future where domed stadiums and television would make football an immense, irresistible pastime long before those developments were feasible. He had the vision to see where spectator sports were headed.

Before Bud Lea became a sportswriter in Milwaukee, he grew up in Green Bay adoring the Packers in their Lambeau heyday. "Don Hutson was there. Clark Hinkle, Arnie Herber, Johnny Blood, Tony Canadeo," Lea wrote. "And there was Curly Lambeau. He stole the show. Lambeau was like nobody I had ever seen before. He was a fancy dresser. He marched up and down the sidelines with a cigarette dangling from his mouth. He was brash, assertive, colorful—the closest thing to royalty in Green Bay."

And yet, Curly Lambeau's legacy is more complex than his success as a glamorous football pathfinder. His melodramatic departure from Green Bay and his controversial personal life seem to have obscured his successes and tempered his legacy. He alienated some of his most important supporters, which led to his exile. Nor did his three marriages and many dalliances play well in his conservative and heavily Catholic hometown.

In addition, Vince Lombardi's joyous revival of the Packers in the 1960s, when the NFL was becoming an American obsession, further obscured the relatively ancient triumphs of Lambeau.

Despite that, the spotlight has been dimmed on the life of The Man Who Invented the Green Bay Packers, Lambeau Field remains a beacon to the past.

In yet another irony, the most famous game at Lambeau Field is filled with contradictions regarding Lambeau himself.

On Sunday, December 31, 1967, Green Bay defeated the Dallas Cowboys 21-17 in what has come to be known as the Ice Bowl. The temperature was 15 degrees below zero at kickoff, with a wind chill approaching 50 degrees below zero. NFL commissioner Pete Rozelle had considered pushing back the game for 24 hours. But he was told it would be even colder on Monday.

With 16 seconds left and the ball on the Cowboys two-foot line, quarterback Bart Starr famously tucked the ball and ran in for the game-winning touchdown behind right guard Jerry Kramer and center Ken Bowman. It was Lombardi's last home game as Green Bay coach.

When the Packers defeated the Oakland Raiders 33-14 two weeks later, that triumph was anti-climactic. Even the name of that game, the AFL-NFL World Championship, would change in time. It would become known as Super Bowl II.

That game, however, was played in a place Lambeau would have appreciated... Miami.

Because, while Lambeau Field is famous for cold-weather games, Lambeau the man was no fan of winter conditions. He not only fled Green Bay for California when the temperature dropped. He spoke admiringly of domed stadiums decades before they arrived, and sometimes kept his reserves warm in the dressing room, then called by sideline telephone when he needed them. If this was because the Packers frequently teetered on the verge of financial disaster when bad weather affected their attendance in the early years, that's understandable. Bad weather was the enemy in the early days.

While Lambeau didn't appreciate the foul weather that modern Packer fans have embraced, he also seemed poised to move the Packers to Milwaukee if his 1949 bid to buy the team had been successful. That was based on the belief that a modern football team needed a large fan base to be competitive and financially successful in a world where television was becoming as important as ticket sales.

In other words, Curly Lambeau was a man of vision for football's future. But he was also often shortsighted in his dealings with players and many of the most important people in his Packer support group. Which may explain why so many dedicated Packer fans know so little about their founding father.

The stadium that bears his name now is the anchor for Titletown, an entire neighborhood of businesses that have grown up around the Packers' home. That is something that would give Lambeau, an entrepreneur as well as a sportsman, great satisfaction if he were here to view it today.

While there were bumps in the road for The Man Who Invented the Green Bay Packers, it was a marvelous ride that set the foundation for the remarkable success his team enjoys today.

# *AUTHOR'S NOTE*

At his best, Curly Lambeau was a bold, brilliant and charismatic man. He defied the odds by creating a football team that is one of the most beloved in all of sports. He elevated his otherwise-modest hometown to dazzling heights. And he charmed men and women with his deeds and personality.

He also was a very complex man, with human flaws that do not reflect well under the harsh light of 21st century standards. Beyond that, his penchant for spinning the truth to suit his needs makes it difficult to reconstruct his tumultuous life.

That said, I found Monsieur Lambeau, as he was known due to his Belgian heritage, an irresistible subject. There may be a detail in question here or there; Curly spun a tangled web. But there is no doubt that Earl Louis Lambeau led a fascinating life—a life that created a football experience that brings thousands to the iconic stadium that bears his name and millions more to television screens on autumn Sundays.

He not only was a small-town pathfinder. He was grand-thinking innovator. He passed when others ran. He took player scouting to heights not known in his era. When others were content to ride trains, he put his team on planes. He put his Packers in a dedicated practice facility before anyone thought of that. He predicted that television would beam games everywhere—and said every team should play in a dome to spare fans the discomforts of foul weather.

In a 20th century where America embraced its teams in a rabid and relentless way, Curly Lambeau was in the upper echelon of sportsmen who made that happen. Flawed or not, his contributions were momentous, and he lived life large.

To understand Lambeau's many layers, I read newspapers wherever he worked, played and visited—especially the *Green Bay Press-Gazette,* but also newspapers in South Bend, Indiana; Chicago, Milwaukee, New York, Southern California, Washington and many other cities. I also read hundreds of books and magazine articles. The most important ones are contained in the Source Notes. I may post a complete bibliography online.

For help in telling his story, I would like to thank my friend, Packer historian Cliff Christl, who has spent a lifetime gathering research about the team that Lambeau started. His interviews, research and insights were invaluable. So was his guidance.

I would also like to express my appreciation to the people I interviewed, Upton Bell, who saw Curly and the NFL up-close as the precocious son of league commissioner Bert Bell; and the many Door County old-timers—especially Rich Weisgerber, Judi and Wayne Voight, Dave Hubbard and Bob Spielman—who shared Lambeau memories.

I would also like to thank Ed Sherman, Peter Christman and David Falk for their guidance and insight.

A special shout-out to Fort Raphael Publishing founder Kevin Theis and his Touchstone graphics whiz, Paul Stroili, who gave this book the look I envisioned.

Most of all, I would like to thank my wife, Liz, for her steadfast encouragement during a project that required time and patience. A ton of patience. Nothing happens without her.

Herb Gould
Sister Bay, Wisconsin

# SOURCE NOTES

**PART ONE: A DREAM BECOMES REALITY**
**CHAPTER ONE... *NO LOVE LOST***
Page
1   *In the spring of 1965*   Christl, Packers.Com, June 12, 2015.
1   *"A bear for exercise"*   *Green Bay Press-Gazette,* June 5, 1965.
1   *"He did give me a ring*   Christl, Packers.Com, June 12, 2015.
1   *Curly, who had arrived early*   Zimmerman, David. *Lambeau: The Man Behind the Mystique.* Hales Corners, Wisconsin: Eagle Books. 2003. p. 21.
2   *He had just had his annual*   *Green Bay Press-Gazette,* June 2, 1965.
3   *"He flat out refused*   *Green Bay Press-Gazette,* Jan. 15, 2007.
3   *Lombardi slammed down the telephone* Christl, Cliff. *Packers Heritage Trail: The Town, the Team, the Fans from Lambeau to Lombardi.* Stevens Point, Wisconsin: KCI Sports Publishing, 2017. p. 82.
3   *"In a rare acknowledgement of his oversized ego*   Maraniss, David. *When Pride Still Mattered: A Life of Vince Lombardi.* New York: Simon & Schuster, 1999. p. 388.
4   *"This guy did it all.*   Author interview with Upton Bell, Dec. 8, 2023.
4   *Oliver Griese, a huge Packer*   Fleming, David, "How the Green Bay Packers averted financial ruin in a mysterious blaze of glory," *ESPN the Magazine,* Sept. 19, 2013.

**CHAPTER TWO... *EARLY TIMES***
8   *"We had our railroad fare*   *Green Bay Press-Gazette,* Dec. 31, 1961.
9   *An immensely popular figure*   Ward, Arch. *The Green Bay Packers.* New York: G.P. Putnam's Sons, 1946. p. 92.
9   *Earl Louis Lambeau seems to have led*   Zimmerman, p. 30, and Christl, *Packers Heritage Trail,* p. 140.
9   *Curly's parents*   Christl, *Packers Heritage Trail,* p. 136, and Zimmerman, p. 29.
9   *Marcel had a rough-and-*   Christl, *Packers Heritage Trail,* p. 139-40.
10   *As an adult, Marcel matured*   Christl, *Packers Heritage Trail,* p. 138; Zimmerman, p. 31.
10   *"Oh, he was very handsome*   Christl, Packers.Com, June 12, 2015
10   *"Curly Lambeau," Griffith* Griffith, Corinne. *My Life with the Redskins.* New York: A.S. Barnes, 1947. p. 183.
10   *"Among the ladies*   Zimmerman, p. 122.
11   *"Always known as a sharp dresser*   Zimmerman, p. 122.

**CHAPTER THREE... *NOTRE DAME'S LONG-LASTING INFLUENCE***
13   *In the fall of 1916,*   *Green Bay Press-Gazette,* Nov., 11, 1962.
14   *"But there is one drawback,"*   Christl, Cliff. *The Greatest Story in Sports: Green Bay Packers 1919-2019.* Stevens Point, Wisconsin: KCI Sports Publishing, 2021, p. 23, and Sperber, Murray. *Shake Down the Thunder: The Creation of Notre Dame Football.* New York: Henry Holt, 1993, p. 50.
14   *Harper responded that*   Christl, *Greatest Story,* p. 23; Sperber, p. 50.

14    *Despite being expected*    *Green Bay Press-Gazette*, Oct. 23, 1917.
15    *A few days later, Lambeau* Green Bay *Press-Gazette*, Oct. 25, 1917.
16    *Officially, Harper was needed*    Rappoport, Ken. *Wake Up the Echoes: Notre Dame Football*. Huntsville, Alabama: Strode Publishers, 1975. p. 69, and Lefebvre, Jim, *Coach for a Nation: The Life and Times of Knute Rockne*, Minneapolis: Great Day Press, 2013, p. 206.
16    *Before leaving South Bend,*    Rappoport, p. 63.
17    *"That big fellow has surprised me,"*    *Chicago Sun-Times*, Feb. 4, 1950.
17    *"Rockne regards these two birds*    *Indianapolis Star*, Sept. 29, 1918.
18    *During their October lull, South Bend Tribune*, Oct. 18, 1918.
18    *To fill in the October schedule*    *South Bend News-Times*, Oct. 19, 1918.
18    *And so, Rockne's team*    *Nebraska State Journal*, Oct 27, 1918.
18    *"When their playing careers were over*    Littlewood, Thomas B. *Arch: A Promoter, Not a Poet. The Story of Arch Ward*. Ames: Iowa State University Press, 1990, p. 16.
19    *"Game Exceedingly Rough,*    *Indianapolis Star*, Nov. 10, 1918.
19    *At Purdue the next week,*    *Indianapolis Star*, Nov. 24, 1918.
19    *Five days later, Rockne took*    *Indianapolis Star*, Nov. 29, 1918.
19    *Taking advantage of freshman eligibility*    *Notre Dame Scholastic*, Dec. 21, 1918. http://archives.nd.edu/scholastic/
20    *The football season over, South Bend Tribune*, Dec. 14, 1918.
20    *The bout started off*    *South Bend Tribune*, Dec. 14, 1918.
20    *"I find my studies not very easy,"*    Christl, *Greatest Story*, p. 26.
21    *"He was a congenital liar,"*    Christl, *Packers Heritage Trail*, p. 29.
21    *That said, Remmel knew*    Christl, *Packers Heritage Trail*, p. 140.
21    *And so, the precise details* Christl, *Greatest Story*, p. 24.
22    *Despite that, Lambeau mailed a note*    Christl, *Greatest Story*, p. 24.
22    *In the second letter, Lambeau*    Christl, *Greatest Story*, p. 25.
23    *"The beginning of the 1919 season* Stuhldreher, Harry. *Knute Rockne, All American*. New York: Grosset & Dunlap, 1940, Originally published as *Knute Rockne: Man Builder* by MacRae-Smith, 1931, p. 143.
23    *Years later, Lambeau told*    *Green Bay Press-Gazette*, Nov. 11, 1962.
23    *In a strange coincidence,* Lefebvre, Jim, *Coach for a Nation: The Life and Times of Knute Rockne*, Minneapolis: Great Day Press, 2013, p. 237.
24    *And so Lambeau dropped out*    *South Bend Tribune*, Aug. 9, 1919.

**CHAPTER FOUR... *BIRTH OF A LEGENDARY TEAM***
25    *When Curly returned from South Bend*    Beech, Mark. *The People's Team: An Illustrated History of the Green Bay Packers*. Boston: Houghton, Mifflin, Harcourt, 2019, p. 19. quoting 1962 Sports Illustrated.
26    *"Cal knew Curly well*    Torinus, John B. *The Packer Legacy: An Inside Look*. Neshkoro, Wisconsin: Laranmark Press, 1982, p. 13.
27    *The next day, Aug. 16*    Zimmerman, p. 43.
28    *The next day, the newspaper*    *Green Bay Press-Gazette*, Sept. 6, 1919.
28    *Accompanying the report* *Green Bay Press-Gazette*, Sept. 15, 1919.
29    *The 1919 Packers*    profootballarchives.com/1919greenb.html
29    *"The game at Ishpeming*    Johnson, p. 43.

29   *Ishpeming's newspaper*   Ishpeming Historical Society website, http://www.ishhistsoc.com/Home_Tours/Copy of packvsish.html
30   *Fittingly, the name underscores*   translateojibwe.com/en/dictionary-ojibwe-english/ishpiming
30   *Even as a child, though,*   Arch Ward, p. 34.
30   *"I have great respect for Lambeau,"*   Don Hutson interview at PackersHallofFame/com
31   *The Packers also had to*   *Green Bay Press-Gazette,* Nov. 24, 1919.
32   *To commemorate that first*   *Green Bay Press-Gazette,* Dec. 6, 1919.
32   *For their efforts, according*   Arch Ward, p. 44.
33   *When nearly 40 people*   *Green Bay Press-Gazette,* Dec. 15, 1920, and Christl, *Greatest Story,* p. 58.
34   *"The great ones make enemies.*   Author interview with Upton Bell.
34   *"Everybody hated his guts*   Torinus, John B. *The Packer Legacy: An Inside Look.* Neshkoro, Wisconsin: Laranmark Press, 1982, p. 202.
35   *"I was fortunate in having a creative coach*   Whittingham, Richard. *What a Game They Played.* Lincoln: University of Nebraska Press, 2001, p. 125.
35   *"He was one of those rare coaches*   Cope, Myron. *The Game That Was: The Early Days of Pro Football.* New York: World Publishing, 1970, p. 98.

## CHAPTER FIVE... *LITTLE CITY, BIG LEAGUE FOOTBALL*
37   *Lambeau and Calhoun were determined*   Christl, Cliff. *The Greatest Story in Sports: Green Bay Packers 1919-2019.* Stevens Point, Wisconsin: KCI Sports Publishing, 2021, p. 59.
37   *On August 26, 1921,*   Christl, *Greatest Story,*, p. 51.
39   *In 2004, though, Hoeffel's grandson*   *Associated Press* article in *Sheboygan Press,* Jan. 10, 2004.
39   *Green Bay trailed 6-0*   Christl, *Packers Heritage Trail.* p. 118, and *Green Bay Press-Gazette,* Oct. 24, 1921.
39   *"Cushions went flying*   *Green Bay Press-Gazette,* Oct. 24, 1921.
40   *But this was a precarious time*   Christl, *Packers Heritage Trail.* p. 176.
40   *By 1926, after failed attempts*   Christl, *Packers Heritage Trail,* p. 178.
40   *"There is not a packing*   *New York Times,* Dec. 6, 1939, p. 37.
41   *"When the packing company folded,*   Johnson, Chuck. *The Green Bay Packers: Pro Football's Pioneer Team.* New York: Thomas Nelson, 1961, p. 48.
41   *As Lambeau once noted,*   Johnson, p. 140.

## CHAPTER SIX... *A FRANCHISE ON THE BRINK*
43   *"Seeing is believing*   *Green Bay Press-Gazette,* Nov. 6, 1922.
43   *"Halas' version of history*   Daly, Dan, and O'Donnell, Bob. *The Pro Football Chronicle.* New York: Collier Books/Macmillan Publishing, 1990, p. 13.
44   *The Pro Football Chronicle goes on*   Daly and O'Donnell, p. 14.
46   *Late in the 1921 season*   Anderson, Heartley (Hunk), with Emil Klosinski. *Notre Dame, Chicago Bears and "Hunk."* Los Angeles: Panoply Publications. 2014, p. 24.
47   *Rockne used the incident*   *Decatur Herald,* Dec. 29, 1921.

| | | |
|---|---|---|
| 47 | That stance had not stopped Rockne | Hickok, Ralph. *Vagabond Halfback: The Saga of Johnny Blood McNally*. Amazon, 2017, p. 48. |
| 48 | The same meeting in Cleveland | Willis, Chris. *Joe F. Carr: The Man Who Built the National Football League*. London: Scarecrow Press, 2010, p. 151. |
| 48 | "I lacked enthusiasm for our name," | Halas, George, with Gwen Morgan and Arthur Veysey, *Halas by Halas: The Autobiography of George Halas*. New York: McGraw-Hill, 1979, p. 91. |
| 49 | When Lambeau was cleaning out | *Green Bay Press-Gazette*, Feb. 4, 1950. |
| 49 | In addition, playing in Chicago | Anderson, with Klosinski, p. 64. |
| 50 | The conspiracy theory | *South Bend Tribune* and *Chicago Tribune*, Dec. 13, 1921; *Chicago Tribune*, Jan. 29, 1922. |
| 50 | In Ward's version, Curly told a friend | Ward, p. 54. |
| 51 | A few days later, the Philadelphia | *Philadelphia Inquirer*, Nov. 11, 1919.. |
| 52 | Forty years later, | *Green Bay Press-Gazette*, June 30, 1962. |
| 52 | Lambeau biographer David Zimmerman made the situation | Willis, p. 151. |
| 52 | There's no question that Murphy | Zimmerman, p. 62; Hurly & Murphy, p. 137; *Green Bay Press-Gazette*, April 16, 1921, and Jan. 17, 1922. |
| 54 | On the morning of the game | Johnson, p. 48; Christl, Greatest Story, p. 93. |
| 56 | "What a shame it would | *Green Bay Press-Gazette*, Nov. 27, 1922. |
| 56 | With Calhoun drumming up | *Green Bay Press-Gazette*, Dec. 8, 1922. |
| 56 | The committee eventually decided to sell | Packers.com, Stock & Financial History. |
| 56 | In another sign of stability | *Green Bay Press-Gazette*, Sept. 22, 1923. |

**CHAPTER SEVEN... *BIRTH OF A RIVALRY***

| | | |
|---|---|---|
| 61 | That 1921 meeting was the first | Christl, *Packers Heritage Trail*, p. 141. |
| 61 | After watching this scene | Christl, *Packers Heritage Trail*, p. 145. |
| 63 | "Green Bay in the '20s | Daly and O'Donnell, p. 107. |
| 63 | In one of the many colorful anecdotes | Daly and O'Donnell, p. 42. |
| 64 | Halas wasn't singling out Green Bay | Coenen, Craig R. *From Sandlots to the Super Bowl: The National Football League, 1920-1967*. Knoxville: University of Tennessee Press, 2005, p. 45. And profootballarchives.com statistics. |
| 64 | "Shake hands?" Lambeau once said. | Gulbrandsen, Don. *Green Bay Packers: The Complete Illustrated History*. Minneapolis: MVP Books, 2011, p. 17. |
| 65 | Two days before its season opener | Daly and O'Donnell, p. 10. |
| 67 | Lewellen was widely viewed | Christl, Packers.com. Feb. 22, 2018. |

**CHAPTER EIGHT... *THE CHAMPIONSHIP MYSTIQUE BEGINS***

| | | |
|---|---|---|
| 69 | "Curly felt the Packers | Ward, p. 90. |
| 69 | "He told the team, 'Trade me | Swain, Glenn. *Packers vs. Bears*. Los Angeles: Charles Publishing, 1996, p. 34. |
| 69 | It didn't hurt, of course, | DeVito, Carlo. *Wellington: The Maras, the Giants and the City of New York*. Chicago: Triumph Books, 2006, p. 49. |
| 70 | That said, as time went on, | Johnson, p. 53. |
| 70 | "Wild. Handsome. Unpredictable," | Zimmerman, p. 77. |
| 71 | Turning to his friend, | Hickok, p. 41. |
| 71 | The name stuck—to the point | Packers.com, March 26, 2015. |

| | | |
|---|---|---|
| 71 | *The 6-foot-1, 190-pound Blood* | Hickok, p. 139. |
| 71 | *"That's one reason I developed* | Hickok, p. 140. |
| 71 | *When Blood returned in 1935* | Hickok, p. 140. |
| 73 | *Lambeau need not have* | *Green Bay Press-Gazette,* Sept. 30, 1929. |
| 75 | *Calhoun also reported* | *Green Bay Press-Gazette,* Nov. 26, 1929. |
| 77 | *Gnashing his teeth* | Coenen, p. 25. |
| 77 | *And yet, owners could not resist* | Coenen, p. 92. |
| 78 | *In that account, Jorgensen* | Torinus, p. 202. |
| 78 | *"The weather was the greatest handicap,"* | *Green Bay Press-Gazette,* Dec. 16, 1929. |
| 79 | *Of course, Lambeau knew* | "When Piggly Wiggly Tried to Stick It to Wall Street," Slate.com, Feb. 8, 2021. |
| 79 | *After Memphis beat the undefeated NFL* | Coenen, p. 92. |
| 79 | *Rejecting NFL overtures* | *Chattanooga News,* Dec. 30, 1929, p. 9. |

**CHAPTER NINE... *ON TOP OF THE WORLD***

| | | |
|---|---|---|
| 81 | *"The reason the economy of Green Bay* | Christl, *The Greatest Story in Sports,* p. 128. |
| 82 | *"We had two offenses,"* | Vass, George. *George Halas and the Chicago Bears.* Chicago: Henry Regnery, 1971. p. 83. |
| 82 | *The October 5 game* | *Green Bay Press-Gazette,* Oct. 16, 1930. |
| 84 | *To accommodate fans* | *Green Bay Press-Gazette,* Nov. 8, 1930. |
| 87 | *"The Bays will leave* | *Green Bay Press-Gazette,* Nov. 18, 1930. |
| 88 | *Bystrom went on to* | *Green Bay Press-Gazette,* Nov. 18, 1930. |
| 88 | *Among the complaints* | *Green Bay Press-Gazette,* Nov. 24, 1930. |
| 89 | *Adding injury to insult,* | *Green Bay Press-Gazette,* Nov. 26, 1930. |
| 89 | *Lambeau and the Packers also were left to lament* | *Green Bay Press-Gazette,* Nov. 25, 1930, and Packers History website, https://packershistory.homestead.com/1930PACKERS/GAME10.html.\ |
| 90 | *"At the entrance, he pulled a Red Grange* | *Green Bay Press-Gazette,* Dec. 2, 1930. |
| 91 | *"Some of the guys* | Whittingham, p. 94. |
| 92 | *"One thing I do remember* | Whittingham, p. 94. |
| 92 | *"In my negotiations with Curly* | "Is that you up there, Johnny?" Gerald Holland, *Sports Illustrated,* Sept. 2, 1963. |
| 93 | *"I got along pretty well with Curly* | Whittingham, p. 39. |
| 93 | *Although Blood and Lambeau* | https://www.packers.com/history/hof/john-blood-mcnally |
| 93 | *"The Packers had a lot* | https://www.packers.com/history/hof/john-blood-mcnally |
| 93 | *"To be frank, Curly really didn't know* | Hickok, p. 84. |
| 94 | *While Hubbard didn't mince words* | Hickok, p. 85 |
| 94 | *The third member of Lambeau's* | Hickok, p. 85 |
| 94 | *"I remember a deal once* | Beech, p. 173. |
| 95 | *In later years, a sobered-up Blood returned* | "Is that you up there, Johnny?" Holland, *Sports Illustrated,* Sept. 2, 1963. |
| 95 | *He also coached the St. John's* | Hickok, p. 167. |

| | | |
|---|---|---|
| 95 | "I was going to fire him," | Jack Henry, *Pittsburgh Steelers Weekly*, 1979. |
| 96 | "Dr. Kelly said 'Curly' | *Green Bay Press-Gazette*, Dec. 16, 1930. |
| 96 | Years later, Dr. Kelly | Johnson, p. 92. |
| 97 | The next night, a crowd | *Green Bay Press-Gazette*, Dec. 17, 1930. |
| 97 | Not that the Packers needed | Daly and O'Donnell, p. 67. |
| 97 | Curly received a silver | *Green Bay Press-Gazette*, Dec. 17, 1930. |

**CHAPTER 10... *ROCKNE'S DEATH HITS HARD***

| | | |
|---|---|---|
| 100 | "Rock's death made me | Zimmerman, p. 93. |
| 100 | Privately, though, Rockne | Zimmerman, p. 93. |
| 100 | "Although Knute Rockne | *Green Bay Press-Gazette*, April 1, 1931. |

**CHAPTER 11... *THE THIRD TIME IS TRICKIER***

| | | |
|---|---|---|
| 101 | A group of influential | *Green Bay Press-Gazette*, Nov. 11, 1931. |
| 103 | At the league's schedule meeting | Willis, p. 275. |
| 103 | "We do not plan to put | *Green Bay Press-Gazette*, Dec. 4, 1931. |
| 103 | And then the ailing Packers | *Green Bay Press-Gazette*, Dec. 7, 1931. |
| 104 | "I don't see how a team | *Portsmouth Times*, Dec. 8, 1931. |
| 104 | "Several weeks ago | *Chicago Tribune*, Dec. 7, 1931. |
| 104 | Lambeau and Joannes steadfastly | *Portsmouth Times*, Dec. 8, 1931. |
| 104 | The Portsmouth Times also took up | *Portsmouth Times*, Dec. 8, 1931. |
| 106 | Calling themselves the Green Bay Pros | *Green Bay Press-Gazette*, Dec. 10, 1931. |

**CHAPTER 12... *THE MATH DOESN'T ADD UP***

108     *An hour after the game,*     Whittingham, p. 93.
108     *Michigan star Bill Hewitt*     Whittingham, p. 93.
108     *That assumes, of course,*     Pro Football Hall of Fame website, profootballhof.com/players/bill-hewitt/
108     *To cope with the decline*     https://packershistory.homestead.com/1932PACKERS.html
109     *Strange as it may sound*     Coenen, p. 96.
109     *Lambeau's rival, George Halas*     Coenen, p. 96.
110     *Meanwhile, in Chicago,*     Daly & O'Donnell, p. 13.
110     *Halas' tale of separation*     Vass, p. 96; Davis, Jeff. *Papa Bear: The Life and Legacy of George Halas*. New York: McGraw-Hill, 2005, p. 103.
110     *Halas was desperate.*     Halas, Morgan and Veysey, p. 148.
110     *At 11 a.m. on Aug. 9,*     Halas, Morgan and Veysey, p. 149.
112     *"By any ordinary method*     Hickok, p. 126; Gullickson, Denis J. *Vagabond Halfback: The Life and Times of Johnny Blood McNally*. Madison, Wisconsin: Trails Books, 2006, p. 138.
113     *In modern times, Green Bay*     thepostgame.com, Jeff Fedotin, Nov. 9, 2015.
115     *Any change that opened up football* Stan Grosshandler, *The Coffin Corner*, Pro Football Researchers Association, Vol. 8, No. 16, 1986.

**CHAPTER 13... *HAWAIIAN GETAWAY***

| | | |
|---|---|---|
| 117 | *To get the ball rolling,* | Hickok, p. 124. |
| 119 | *"John was going out with an entertainer* | Hickok, p. 127. |
| 119 | *"I could see Lambeau wasn't happy,"* | Hickok, p. 127. |
| 119 | *"To the tune of strumming* | Green Bay Press-Gazette, Dec. 22, 1932. |
| 123 | *Blood, who returned from a "flying* | Honolulu Advertiser, Jan. 4, 1933. |
| 124 | *Grange witnessed one of Blood's* | Whittingham, p. 23. |
| 124 | *Green Bay bounced back* | https://packershistory.homestead.com/1933PACKERS.html |

**PART TWO: FAME, FORTUNE—AND A DARK SIDE**

**CHAPTER 14. . . *FALLING FROM GRACE IN TOO MANY WAYS***

| | | |
|---|---|---|
| 125 | *The young woman, identified,* | Beech, p. 152. |
| 126 | *Curly finally married Copeland* | Waukegan News-Sun, June 27, 1935. |
| 126 | *"She said it wasn't* | Christl, Packers.Com, March 16, 2017. |
| 127 | *In the 1930s, Lambeau* | Christl, Greatest Story in Sports, p. 125. |
| 128 | *At a game two years earlier,* | Daly and O'Donnell, p. 53; Beech, p. 120. |
| 129 | *In contrast to his successful brother,* | Beech, p. 121. |
| 129 | *On September 20, 1931,* | Daly and O'Donnell, p. 53. |
| 129 | *When the case went to trial* | Beech, p. 121. |
| 129 | *To illustrate their point,* | Green Bay Press-Gazette, Feb. 15, 1933. |
| 129 | *Ordinarily, the Packers' liability* | The Morning News, Wilmington, Delaware, June 21, 1932. |
| 130 | *"When Judge Henry Graass* | Green Bay Press-Gazette, March 23, 1950. |
| 130 | *Team president Lee Joannes* | Green Bay Press-Gazette, Aug. 16, 1933 |
| 130 | *George Preston Marshall, the flamboyant* | Willis, p. 283. |
| 130 | *"Gentlemen, it's about time* | Daley, Arthur. Pro Football's Hall of Fame. New York: Tempo Books, 1963, p. 154. |
| 131 | *"The new rules are made* | Green Bay Press-Gazette, Feb. 27, 1933. |
| 131 | *On his way back to Green* | Green Bay Press-Gazette, Feb. 28, 1933. |
| 132 | *But Lambeau said* | Green Bay Press-Gazette, July 10, 1933. |
| 135 | *When Halas paid off* | Green Bay Press-Gazette, Nov. 20, 1933. |
| 135 | *"I don't like to be hauling* | New York Times, Nov.. 26, 1933. |
| 136 | *Ironically, the Fighting Irish* | Anderson, with Klosinski, p. 127 |
| 137 | *"Curly enjoyed the limelight* | Cameron, Steve, The Packers! Dallas: Taylor Publishing, 1996, p. 141. |
| 137 | *Calhoun's other great* | Green Bay Press-Gazette, Dec. 14, 1963. |
| 138 | *Always clever with words,* | Hickok, p. 134. |
| 138 | *At practice that Saturday,* | Hickok, p. 134. |
| 139 | *Not surprisingly, all the* | Green Bay Press-Gazette, Nov. 29, 1933. |
| 139 | *Two days before* | Green Bay Press-Gazette, Dec. 15, 1933. |
| 139 | *"Scratching those spectacular* | Green Bay Press-Gazette, Dec. 15, 1933. |

**CHAPTER 15. . . *PASSING FANCY***

| | | |
|---|---|---|
| 141 | *"Lambeau was one of the* | Christl, Greatest Story in Sports, p. 38. |
| 141 | *That seems to be the exaggeration* | Neft, Cohen and Korch, p. 49. |

142 *As Lambeau, who had been* Mathys Packer Hall of Fame bio, packers.com/history/hof/charlie-mathys

142 *Arnie Herber was more* Herber Packer Hall of Fame bio, packers.com/history/hof/arnie-herber

143 *Before the start of the 1929* Beech, p. 113; *Capital Times*, Oct. 20, 1969.

143 *Returning to Green Bay,* "Arnie Herber," Don Smith, *The Coffin Corner*, Pro Football Researchers Assn., Vol. 6, No. 7, 1984; Christl, *Greatest Story in Sports*, p. 144.

144 *Along with the rest* *Green Bay Press-Gazette*, Dec. 7, 1933.

145 *A day later, Lambeau spoke* *Green Bay Press-Gazette*, Dec. 4, 1934.

147 *Responding to the $10,000 fundraising* *Green Bay Press-Gazette*, Jan. 30, 1935.

## CHAPTER 16... *THE AGE OF HUTSON*

149 *In a 1944 article for Collier's* "The Wizard of Green Bay," Arthur Daley, *Collier's Magazine*, Nov. 25, 1944.

150 *No question, Hutson was* Packers.com, July 9, 2020.

150 *Another Bunyan-esque tale* Whittingham, p. 95.

151 *"Like the sailors, he had a lady* Stein, Jean, *West of Eden: An American Place*. New York: Random House, 2017, p. 156.

151 *Hired by Alabama in part* Barra, Allen. *The Last Coach: A Life of Paul "Bear" Bryant*. New York: W. W. Norton, 2005, p. 54.

152 *A few games into his senior* Barra, p. 64.

152 *While both were from Arkansas,* Barra, p. 20.

153 *"Coach Bryant said Lambeau's* Zimmerman, p. 124.

153 *In a sign of how football changed* Barra, p. 355.

154 *Lambeau, as a coach who* Whittingham, p. 121.

154 *"Finding the gates locked"* Swain, p. 67.

155 *Skeptics wondered* Whittingham, p. 122.

155 *Even before Hutson grabbed* Whittingham, p. 122.

155 *Both contracts supposedly* Willis, p. 339.

156 *"Unfortunately, through the lens* Christl, *Greatest Story*, p. 148

156 *As it turned out, Hutson* Christl, *Greatest Story*, p. 147.

156 *The only pass-catcher* Coenen, p. 97.

157 *In the 1970 oral history,* Cope, p. 145, and Beech, p. 137.

157 *However, in perhaps the best remembered* Whittingham, p. 122.

157 *Hutson actually signed* Christl, *Greatest Story*, p. 149.

## CHAPTER 17... *OUT OF BANKRUPTCY, INTO WINNING*

159 *Lambeau also put the Packers* packersuniforms.blogspot/com/p/uniform-timeline.html, Packers.com, July 19, 2018.

161 *Showing his usual flair* *Green Bay Press-Gazette*, Sept. 2, 1935.

161 *Cal Hubbard, who had been* *Green Bay Press-Gazette*, July 8, 1935.

162 *Hutson, who was under* *Green Bay Press-Gazette*, Sept. 16, 1935.

162 *When a streaking Blood* *Green Bay Press-Gazette*, Sept. 23, 1935.

164 *"Those paunchy Packers* *Green Bay Press-Gazette*, Jan. 25, 1936.

## CHAPTER 18... *SINGING THAT TITLE TUNE AGAIN*

# Notes

| | | |
|---|---|---|
| 165 | *The Herber Legend* | Don Smith, *The Coffin Corner*, Vol. 6, No. 7, 1984; |
| 165 | *Mr. Curly Lambeau wasn't* | *Green Bay Press-Gazette,* Sept. 30, 1936. |
| 166 | *"Curly himself became* | Stotts, Stuart, *Curly Lambeau: Building the Green Bay Packers.* Madison: Wisconsin Historical Society Press, 2007, p. 41. |
| 167 | *" 'Why do I get so* | Daley, p. 169. |
| 167 | *"I don't think Curly* | Cope, p. 108. |
| 167 | *"If you cash my check,* | Daley, p. 166. |
| 167 | *Hubbard, according to Daley,* | Daley, p. 166. |
| 168 | *"Curly got into the game* | *Green Bay Press-Gazette*, Nov. 18, 1929. |
| 169 | *"Just too bad that the Cardinals* | *Green Bay Press-Gazette,* Dec. 15, 1936. |
| 169 | *"Every man was working* | *Green Bay Press-Gazette,* Dec. 15, 1936. |
| 169 | *Lambeau's assertion that no* | Christl, *Greatest Story in Sports*, p. 148. |
| 171 | *"I like to play football* | *Green Bay Press-Gazette,* Dec. 15, 1936. |
| 171 | *Lambeau booked Green Bay* | *Green Bay Press-Gazette,* Dec. 17, 1936. |
| 172 | *Asked to break* | *Green Bay Press-Gazette,* Feb. 10, 1937; Hurly, Dr. James, and Murphy, Thomas. *Green Bay: A City and Its Team.* Green Bay: 2011; p. 186. |

## CHAPTER 19... *GROWING PAINS*

| | | |
|---|---|---|
| 173 | *"Our practice last night* | *Green Bay Press-Gazette,* Aug. 31, 1937. |
| 174 | *"We lost the game on* | *Chicago Tribune*, Sept. 2, 1937. |
| 174 | *The usually sympathetic* | *Green Bay Press-Gazette*, Sept. 2, 1937. |
| 175 | *"They were outhustled* | *Green Bay Press-Gazette*, Sept. 2, 1937. |
| 176 | *On Friday night, Sept. 24,* | *Green Bay Press-Gazette*, Sept. 25, 1937. |
| 177 | *On top of his broken marriage* | *Green Bay Press-Gazette*, Sept. 13, 1937. |
| 177 | *Green Bay added a seventh* | *Green Bay Press-Gazette*, Nov. 15, 1937. |
| 178 | *"This was easily the best* | *New York Times*, Nov. 22, 1937. |
| 178 | *For Lambeau, the season* | *Green Bay Press-Gazette*, Nov. 29, 1937. |
| 179 | *Lambeau gently directed* | *Green Bay Press-Gazette*, Dec. 1, 1937. |

## CHAPTER 20... *THE BEST IN THE WEST*

| | | |
|---|---|---|
| 181 | *If a playoff was needed* | *Milwaukee Journal,* Nov. 25, 1938. |
| 182 | *Noting that the Packers* | *Green Bay Press-Gazette*, Nov. 25, 1938. |
| 183 | *With a tip of the cap* | *Chicago Tribune*, Dec. 10, 1938. |
| 184 | *"I don't want to say this* | *Green Bay Press-Gazette*, Dec. 12, 1938. |
| 184 | *Stepping off the Milwaukee* | *Green Bay Press-Gazette*, Dec. 14, 1938. |
| 184 | *"Such rapid strides* | *Green Bay Press-Gazette*, Feb. 8, 1939. |
| 185 | *Lambeau's promise that* | *Green Bay Press-Gazette*, Dec. 15, 1938. |
| 186 | *Although the draft diminished* | *Green Bay Press-Gazette*, Jan. 16, 1939. |
| 187 | *"We were misinformed* | *Green Bay Press-Gazette*, May 10, 1939. |
| 187 | *"We were good,"* | *New York Times*, Feb. 22, 2003. |

## CHAPTER 21... *WORLD TRAVELER*

| | | |
|---|---|---|
| 189 | *Married, separated or divorced* | Stein, p. 156. |
| 189 | *Lambeau clearly enjoyed* | Christl, *Greatest Story in Sports*, p. 198. |
| 190 | *In late February,* | *Green Bay Press-Gazette*, Feb. 24, 1939. |
| 190 | *Other team executives* | *Pittsburgh Post-Gazette*, July 22, 1939. |
| 190 | *Although Lambeau's initial* | *Pittsburgh Press,* Aug. 5, 1945. |

| | | |
|---|---|---|
| 190 | On February 23, Curly | Green Bay Press-Gazette, Feb. 26, 1939. |
| 191 | While in New York | New York Times, March 6, 1939. |
| 191 | Donald would enlist in the Army | Beech, p. 154. |
| 192 | The Press-Gazette called | Green Bay Press-Gazette, April 12, 1939. |
| 192 | Sharing his European | Green Bay Press-Gazette, April 25, 1939. |
| 193 | "Having enjoyed a fine | Green Bay Press-Gazette, May 21, 1939. |
| 193 | "The loss of Mr. Carr | Chicago Tribune, May 21, 1939. |

**CHAPTER 22... *MILWAUKEE DEBATE HEATS UP***

| | | |
|---|---|---|
| 195 | Meanwhile, Johnny Blood, | Green Bay Press-Gazette, March 11, 1939. |
| 196 | "Lambeau regards it | Green Bay Press-Gazette, Sept. 2, 1939. |
| 196 | The Packers opened | Whittingham, p. 101. |
| 197 | "Despite the fact the Cardinals | Chicago Times,, Sept. 19, 1939. |
| 197 | Kupcinet was a busy man | Chicago Times,, Sept. 18, 1939. |
| 198 | "As the Packers looked | Green Bay Press-Gazette, Sept. 19, 1939. |
| 198 | Even though the Rams | Green Bay Press-Gazette, Sept. 26, 1939. |
| 198 | The ploy didn't work. | Green Bay Press-Gazette, Oct. 3, 1939. |
| 199 | Lambeau's former star, | Pittsburgh Sun-Telegraph, Oct. 3, 1939. |
| 199 | Blood's greatest legacy | Holland, Sports Illustrated, Sept. 2, 1963. |
| 199 | While Blood was departing | Green Bay Press-Gazette, Oct. 3, 1939. |
| 200 | With their backs to the wall, | Green Bay Press-Gazette, Nov. 6, 1939. |
| 200 | "Players came to blows | Chicago Tribune, Nov. 6, 1939. |
| 200 | "We can't lose a single | Green Bay Press-Gazette, Nov. 7, 1939. |
| 201 | "As Curly Lambeau's men | New York Times, Dec. 6, 1939. |
| 201 | The mania was so great | Green Bay Press-Gazette, Dec. 7, 1939. |
| 202 | "When the NFL forced | Coenen, p. 48. |
| 202 | "The strong resentment | Green Bay Press-Gazette, Dec. 7, 1939. |
| 203 | Even Milwaukee's State Fair | Milwaukee Sentinel, Dec. 6, 1939. |
| 204 | Putting aside their outrage, | Coenen, p. 49. |
| 204 | A blustery day | New York Times, Dec. 11, 1939. |
| 205 | Gracious to the extreme, | New York Times, Dec. 11, 1939. |
| 205 | "If the question of | Green Bay Press-Gazette, Dec. 11, 1939. |
| 205 | While Halas was obsessed | Green Bay Press-Gazette, Dec. 11, 1939. |
| 206 | To celebrate the 1939 | Green Bay Press-Gazette, Dec. 15, 1939. |
| 206 | "We have... a team | Green Bay Press-Gazette, Jan. 13, 1940. |
| 207 | Owen had a ready reply, | Green Bay Press-Gazette, Jan. 13, 1940. |
| 207 | When game day dawned, | Los Angeles Times, Jan. 15, 1940. |
| 207 | "It was just like | Green Bay Press-Gazette, Jan. 15, 1940. |
| 208 | Departing from his usual | Green Bay Press-Gazette, Jan. 18, 1940. |
| 208 | Before heading out | Green Bay Press-Gazette, Jan. 20, 1940. |
| 208 | "I can't put you on the spot | Green Bay Press-Gazette, Feb. 15, 1940. |

**CHAPTER 23... *A MESSY SECOND DIVORCE***

| | | |
|---|---|---|
| 209 | On March 25, 1940, Curly | Green Bay Press-Gazette, March 26, 1940. |
| 209 | Curly "alleged | Green Bay Press-Gazette, March 26, 1940. |
| 210 | "Herber ran into [Lambeau's] | Christl, The Greatest Story in Sports, p. 185. |

211   *After spending some early years*   Christl, *The Greatest Story in Sports,* p. 184; *Los Angles Times,* Jan. 27, 1987.
211   *Duryea told Cliff Christl*   Christl, *The Greatest Story in Sports,* p. 184.

## CHAPTER 24... *THE BEARS CLAW BACK*
213   *While Lambeau was single*   *Green Bay Press-Gazette,* June 3, 1940.
213   *In an effort to add depth*   *Green Bay Press-Gazette,* June 10, 1940.
215   *"We expected the All-Stars*   *Chicago Tribune,* Aug. 30, 1940.
215   *Another West Coast All-Star*   *Chicago Tribune,* Aug. 30, 1940.
215   *That day would have to wait.*   *Time Magazine,* Sept. 9, 1940.
215   *A teammate of Jackie Robinson*   *USA Today,* Feb. 14, 2016.
215   *An Ohio native, Jean divided*   Christl, Packers.Com, Jan. 28, 2016.
216   *Curly also used the game*   *Green Bay Press-Gazette,* Sept. 3, 1940.
216   *When the hated Chicago*   *Green Bay Press-Gazette,* Sept. 23, 1940.
217   *"Despite the size of the*   *Green Bay Press-Gazette,* Sept. 24, 1940.
218   *Later in the season,*   *New York Times,* Nov. 17, 1940.
218   *Lambeau took his lone*   *Green Bay Press-Gazette,* Sept. 26, 1940.
218   *Beyond the Cardinals'*   *Green Bay Press-Gazette,* Sept. 25, 1940.
218   *The Bears' hero was Bob Swisher*   *Chicago Tribune,* Nov. 4, 1940.

## CHAPTER 25... *FIRST IN FLIGHT*
221   *When the Douglas DC-3*   "How the DC-3 Revolutionized Air Travel," Kathleen Burke, *Smithsonian Magazine,* April 2013.
221   *Even Orville Wright*   Burke, *Smithsonian Magazine,* April 2013.
222   *At Chicago's Municipal*   *Green Bay Press-Gazette,* Nov. 15, 1940.
222   *"The men who make*   *Green Bay Press-Gazette,* Nov. 13, 1940.
222   *"The ponderous Packers*   *New York Times,* Nov. 15, 1940.
223   *Under the headline*   *New York Times,* Nov. 17, 1940.
224   *The Packers "were both*   *Green Bay Press-Gazette,* Nov. 19, 1940.
224   *"Yesterday the Packers ate*   *Green Bay Press-Gazette,* Nov. 19, 1940.
224   *Taking off from LaGuardia,*   *Green Bay Press-Gazette,* Nov. 19, 1940.
225   *For the return to Green Bay*   *Green Bay Press-Gazette,* Nov. 22, 1940.
225   *"None of the nervousness*   *Green Bay Press-Gazette,* Nov. 26, 1940.
225   *The only grumbling*   *Green Bay Press-Gazette,* Nov. 26, 1940.
226   *Despite the Bears' 7-3 loss*   Davis, p. 158.
226   *After that game, the Bears*   *Chicago Tribune,* Nov. 19, 1940.
226   *Amid the grumbling*   Page, Joseph S.; *Pro Football Championships Before the Super Bowl.* Jefferson, North Carolina: McFarland, 2011, p. 53.
226   *Halas, who saw*   Davis, p. 158.
227   *It was a day in which*   *Washington Post,* Dec. 7, 1940.

## CHAPTER 26... SHINING MOMENTS AS WAR CLOUDS GATHER
229  During training camp,    *Green Bay Press-Gazette*, Aug. 19, 1941.
230  The throng of Packer fans    *Green Bay Press-Gazette*, Sept. 29, 1941.
230  " `The game was a setup    *Chicago Tribune*, Nov. 3, 1941.
231  "Not one word about defense!"    *Chicago Tribune*, Nov. 3, 1941.
231  The game was a bonanza    *Chicago Tribune*, Nov. 3, 1941.
232  Halas declined to talk    *Chicago Tribune*, Nov. 3, 1941.
232  "We got cocky    *Chicago Tribune*, Nov. 3, 1941.

## CHAPTER 27... PEARL HARBOR AND A NEAR-SHOCKER
233  "That was the most absurd thing    *Chicago Sun*, Dec. 9, 1941.
234  With the Cardinals leading 17-14 at halftime,    Davis, p. 169.
234  "I didn't know what to do,"    *Halas by Halas*, p. 202.
234  Perhaps needing a diversion    *Chicago Tribune*, Dec. 12, 1941.
235  The players also were having    *Chicago Tribune*, Dec. 10, 1941.
235  "The Packers," Bears quarterback    *Chicago Tribune*, Dec. 10, 1941.
235  Amid boastful predictions    *Green Bay Press-Gazette*, Dec. 11, 1941.
235  Lambeau also disputed    *Chicago Sun*, Dec. 12, 1941.

## CHAPTER 28... AMERICA GOES TO WAR—THE NFL ADJUSTS
239  Returning home to Wisconsin,    *Green Bay Press-Gazette*, Jan. 24, 1942.
240  After detailing a Packer press release    *New York Times*, Aug. 29, 1942.
240  As it turned out, the Brooklyn    *New York Times*, Aug. 30, 1942.
240  Hutson "could pick your pocket    *Brooklyn Eagle*, Aug. 31, 1942.
240  Before the game, Lambeau,    *Baltimore Sun*, Sept. 8, 1942.
241  The flood of NFL players    *Green Bay Press-Gazette*, March 29, 1944; Christl, *Greatest Story in Sports*, p. 200
242  In Green Bay, 16 of the    *Green Bay Press-Gazette*, Sept. 25, 1942.
242  To help keep his roster stocked    *Appleton Post-Crescent*, Aug. 23, 1943.
242  The manpower shortage    Daly and O'Donnell, p. 101.
242  Under the headline, `No    *Green Bay Press-Gazette*, Sept. 15, 1942.
242  "The Packers," Lambeau    *Green Bay Press-Gazette*, Sept. 28, 1942.
243  By game day, interest    *Green Bay Press-Gazette*, Nov. 15, 1942.
243  "We had to gamble,"    *Green Bay Press-Gazette*, Nov. 17, 1942.

## CHAPTER 29... SOLDIERING ON
245  Having learned to be creative    *Chicago Tribune*, April 6, 1943.
246  "If we fold,    Vass, p. 154.
246  "Marshall's arguments    Vass, p. 154.
246  Halas led the chuckles    *Chicago Daily New*, April 10, 1943.
247  "Lambeau believes the rule    *Green Bay Press-Gazette*, April 23, 1943.
247  "In future years    *Green Bay Press-Gazette*, April 23, 1943.
248  "We had a good enough team    *Green Bay Press-Gazette*, Dec. 9, 1943.

## CHAPTER 30... A LAST HURRAH
249  "We've lost too many    *Green Bay Press-Gazette*, Sept. 25, 1943.
251  "The Giants are always tough," *Brooklyn Daily Eagle*, Nov. 20, 1944.

# Notes 633

| | | |
|---|---|---|
| 252 | "I am thoroughly burned | Green Bay Press-Gazette, Nov. 22, 1944. |
| 252 | One thing seemed clear. | Green Bay Press-Gazette, Nov. 22, 1944. |
| 253 | In departing from | Green Bay Press-Gazette, Dec. 16, 1943. |
| 253 | When Lambeau continued | Green Bay Press-Gazette, Dec. 1, 1944. |
| 254 | Isbell seemed destined | Beech, p. 161. |
| 254 | But that didn't ring true | Christl, The Greatest Story in Sports, p. 204. |
| 254 | Noting that Lambeau | Green Bay Press-Gazette, Dec. 16, 1944. |
| 254 | Green Bay Press-Gazette, Dec. 16, 1944. | |
| 255 | Lambeau wanted no part | Green Bay Press-Gazette, Nov. 24, 1944. |
| 256 | "Ted and I talked about that play | Beech, p. 163. |

## PART THREE: TURMOIL IN PACKERLAND

### CHAPTER 31... AN OLD FRIEND CREATES A NEW ENEMY

| | | |
|---|---|---|
| 259 | The man was Arch Ward, | Littlewood, p. 16. |
| 259 | Ward had left Dubuque | Littlewood, p. 23. |
| 260 | "So Ward agreed to use | Littlewood, p. 149. |
| 261 | "We owners were a tight little group," | Halas by Halas, p. 233. |
| 261 | "Arch could not bring | Littlewood, p. 151. |
| 261 | The disagreement fractured | Littlewood, p. 151. |
| 261 | "The rival league spoiled Eisenberg, John. *The League: How Five Rivals Created the NFL and Launched a Sports Empire*. New York: Basic Books, 2018, p. 225. | |
| 262 | Commissioner Elmer | Green Bay Press-Gazette, Dec. 19, 1944. |
| 262 | Meanwhile, War Mobilization Director | Press-Gazette, Dec. 26, 1944. |
| 263 | "There's plenty to do | Green Bay Press-Gazette, Dec. 21, 1944. |
| 263 | On January 10, the date set | New York Times, Jan. 11, 1945. |

### CHAPTER 32... BATTLES ON MANY FRONTS

| | | |
|---|---|---|
| 265 | The situation became more | Green Bay Press-Gazette, Feb. 22, 1945. |
| 265 | Like Red Smith before him, | Green Bay Press-Gazette, Feb. 22, 1945. |
| 266 | Trafton was yet another link | Halas by Halas, p. 149. |
| 266 | In 1920, when Decatur Halas by Halas, p. 64; and Don Smith, "George Trafton: The Toughest, Meanest and Most Ornery," *The Coffin Corner*, Vo. 7, No. 1, 1985, PFRA. | |
| 267 | After announcing on January 27 | Los Angeles Times, Jan. 31, 1945. |
| 268 | His first order of business | Los Angeles Times, Jan. 31, 1945. |
| 268 | "The war comes first, | Los Angeles Times, Jan. 31, 1945. |
| 268 | Lambeau also described | Seattle Star, Jan. 31, 1945. |
| 268 | By February 20, Lambeau | Green Bay Press-Gazette, Feb. 20, 1945. |
| 269 | "Curly Lambeau fears the NFL | Chicago Tribune, April 11, 1945. |
| 270 | Red Grange resigned | New York Times, June 1, 1945. |
| 270 | Although not interested Green Bay Press-Gazette and Associated Press, Aug. 20, 1945. | |

### CHAPTER 33... CHANGING OF THE GUARD

| | | |
|---|---|---|
| 271 | Club president Lee Joannes | Green Bay Press-Gazette, Aug. 10, 1945. |
| 271 | The plaque was presented | Green Bay Press-Gazette, Aug. 10, 1945. |

272   "I'm going to present Curly      *Associated Press*, Sept. 16, 1945.
273   "The Packers are playing possum  *Chicago Tribune*, Sept. 26, 1945.
273   While Curly closed               *Green Bay Press-Gazette*, Sept. 27, 1945.
273   Lambeau went along               *Green Bay Press-Gazette*, Sept. 27, 1945.
274   "It was old man Hutson,"         *Green Bay Press-Gazette*, Oct. 1, 1945.
274   "The Big Four reign              *Green Bay Press-Gazette*, Oct. 15, 1945.
274   Walsh's brother, Rams coach      *Green Bay Press-Gazette*, Oct. 15, 1945.
274   Lambeau pointed his usual        *Green Bay Press-Gazette*, Oct. 15, 1945.
275   Lambeau again blamed             *Green Bay Press-Gazette*, Nov. 13, 1945.
275   Walt Kiesling, the former        *Green Bay Press-Gazette*, Nov. 13, 1945.
276   Lambeau also announced           *Green Bay Press-Gazette*, Nov. 13, 1945.

**CHAPTER 34... *A NOVEMBER TO REMEMBER***
278   "There have been rumors    *Green Bay Press-Gazette*, Nov. 15, 1945.
278   "If we did not work        *Green Bay Press-Gazette*, Nov. 15, 1945.

**CHAPTER 35... *ANOTHER MATRIMONIAL CONTRACT***
281   Yet another momentous       *Chicago Tribune*, Nov. 6, 1945.
281   "Grace met Curly            Stein, p. 157.
281   It was the third marriage   Christl, *The Greatest Story in Sports*, p. 211.
282   When asked in Chicago       *Chicago Tribune*, Nov. 6, 1945.
282   Lambeau said he preferred       Neenah (Wisconsin) *News-Record, United Press*, Nov. 5, 1945.
282   The biggest headline Lambeau  *Oshkosh Northwestern*, Nov. 6, 1945.
282   ``Isbell was a master        *Chicago Daily News*, Nov. 6, 1945.
282   Of great interest in Chicago,  *Chicago Tribune*, Nov. 5 and 6, 1945.
283   Born Grace Nicholls          Christl, *The Greatest Story in Sports*, p. 211.
283   After five weeks of marriage,  *Los Angeles Times*, Nov. 23, 1932; .
283   By 1940, when La Cava     *Los Angeles Times*, April 12, May 2 and June 16, 1941; Christl, *The Greatest Story in Sports*, p. 211.
284   "This is the way to enjoy    *Los Angeles Times*, Dec. 18, 1945.
285   A friend and an admirer      Griffith, p. 183.
285   "Curly was gazing into the fire    Griffith, p. 184.
285   "Are you out of your mind?"   Griffith, p. 184.

**CHAPTER 36... *FROM WORLD WAR TO FOOTBALL WAR***
287   Back in Green Bay in late   *Green Bay Press-Gazette*, Jan. 25, 1946.
287   He also said he was pleased      *Green Bay Press-Gazette*, Jan. 25, 1946.
288   "I can hardly believe it,"   *Green Bay Press-Gazette*, April 23, 1946.
288   Fritsch's mother refused     *Green Bay Press-Gazette*, May 16, 1946.
288   After reporting to the Browns'  *Wisconsin State Journal*, Aug. 11, 1946.
288   The *Associated Press* reported   *Associated Press*, Aug. 11, 1946.

**CHAPTER 37... *ROCKWOOD BECOMES CURLY'S FOLLY***
290   "I've always had my mind   *Green Bay Press-Gazette*, May 25, 1946.
290   Rockwood Lodge was a cathedral-like    *Green Bay Press-Gazette*, Nov. 2, 1937.

# Notes

| | | |
|---|---|---|
| 290 | The main building had been | *Green Bay Press-Gazette*, July 31, 1944. |
| 291 | "I loved Rockwood Lodge," | Packers.com, Sept. 14, 2017. |
| 291 | "All the other camps I'd gone to | Author interview with Upton Bell. |
| 291 | "It seemed like a hell of an idea," | Poling, Jerry. *Downfield! Untold Stories of the Green Bay Packers*. Madison, Wisconsin: Prairie Oak Press, 1996, p. 178. |
| 291 | "It was built on a cliff | Christl, *The Greatest Story in Sports*, p. 218. |
| 292 | "The Rockwood Lodge purchase | Torinus, p. 60. |
| 292 | With the team isolated | *Green Bay Press-Gazette*, Aug. 14, 1946. |
| 292 | It was a hungry baby. | Christl, *The Greatest Story in Sports*, p. 218. |
| 292 | "Grace had threatened | *Green Bay Press-Gazette*, May 25, 1946. |
| 292 | "Expenses for equipping | Torinus, p. 60. |

## CHAPTER 38... AAFC HITS NFL IN THE WALLET

| | | |
|---|---|---|
| 295 | "All I know of new leagues | *Chicago Tribune,* April 21, 1945. |
| 295 | Answering Layden's dismissive remark | *Los Angeles Daily News* and *United Press,* Dec. 6, 1945. |
| 296 | Don Hutson, the Packers' | (Madison) *Wisconsin State Journal,* May 23, 1946. |
| 296 | That prompted Jimmy | (Madison) *Wisconsin State Journal,* May 23, 1946. |
| 296 | "The National League is no league | "The Grid is Hot," Stanley Frank, *Collier's Magazine,* Sept. 14, 1946. |
| 297 | For Cleveland, Ward brought | Littleton, p. 162. |

## CHAPTER 39... DEMANDING A THOROUGH EXPLANATION

| | | |
|---|---|---|
| 299 | After orchestrating the hoopla | *Green Bay Press-Gazette,* July 12, 1946. |
| 301 | "I am demanding a thorough | *Green Bay Press-Gazette,* Oct. 7, 1946. |
| 301 | "The most courageous guy | *Milwaukee Journal,* Oct. 9, 1946. |

## CHAPTER 40... A MODERN PASSING GAME?

| | | |
|---|---|---|
| 303 | Lambeau and Marshall | *Green Bay Press-Gazette,* Jan. 24, 1947. |
| 303 | The main point, | *Green Bay Press-Gazette,* Jan. 11, 1947. |
| 304 | The misfire on Case | *Los Angeles Times,* Feb. 12, 1947. |
| 304 | In his relentless quest | *Green Bay Press-Gazette,* Jan. 25, 1947. |

## CHAPTER 41... BITING THE HAND THAT FEEDS HIM

| | | |
|---|---|---|
| 306 | Before the 1945 season, | Christl, *The Greatest Story in Sports,* p. 219. |
| 306 | A year after being ousted, | Christl, *The Greatest Story in Sports,* p. 219. |
| 306 | On March 24, 1947, | Torinus, p. 29; Christl, *Greatest Story,* p. 222. |
| 306 | Calhoun could not have disagreed | Torinus, p. 29 |
| 306 | Calhoun resigned from his position | Christl, *Greatest Story,* p. 219. |
| 307 | Even after that, Calhoun | Torinus, p. 29. |
| 307 | Lambeau and Calhoun, | Christl, *The Greatest Story in Sports,* p. 220. |
| 307 | George Halas sent a floral | Beech, p. 242. |
| 308 | Atlas occupied the buildings | Beech, p. 185. |
| 309 | There has been debate | Christl, *The Greatest Story in Sports,* p. 94. |
| 309 | "While no longer as enthusiastic | Johnson, p. 89. |
| 309 | In this frosty and troubled | *Green Bay Press-Gazette,* July 26, 1947. |
| 310 | "Each sub-committees is | *Green Bay Press-Gazette,* July 29, 1947. |

| | | |
|---|---|---|
| 311 | "The Packers have a great | *Green Bay Press-Gazette*, Oct. 13, 1947. |
| 311 | Lambeau vowed to change | *Green Bay Press-Gazette*, Oct. 13, 1947. |

## CHAPTER 42... *OFF THE CUFF*

313     "Ward Cuff is Hero     UP, *Knoxville News-Sentinel,* Dec.. 12, 1938.
313     After playing in New York   *Green Bay Press-Gazette*, April 19, 1947.
314     By the time Cuff reached    "Remembering Ward Cuff, New York Giants All-Around Two-Way Star," Chris Willis, *NFL Football Journal*, March 7, 2022.
314     "We lost our own ball game.     *Green Bay Press-Gazette*, Nov. 3, 1947.
315     Riding the Milwaukee Road     *Green Bay Press-Gazette*, Nov. 3, 1947.
315     "Three or four times this year     *Chicago Tribune*, Nov. 10, 1947.
315     "We played a very good     *Green Bay Press-Gazette*, Nov. 10, 1947.
316     The press-box view     *Green Bay Press-Gazette*, Nov. 10, 1947.
316     Despite falling two games behind     *Green Bay Press-Gazette*, Nov. 10, 1947.
316     "I was warned before I went     Christl, Packers.com, June 21, 2018.
316     "A lot of the players     Christl, Packers.com, June 21, 2018.
317     By 1947, Cuff said, Lambeau     Christl, Packers.com, June 21, 2018.
317     For all the chatter     Christl, Packers.com, June 21, 2018.
317     Cuff's complaints were not merely    "Remembering Ward Cuff, New York Giants' All-Around Two-Way Star," Chris Willis, *NFL Football Journal*, March 7, 2022.
317     Evidently, he did not learn much     Christl, Packers.com, June 21, 2018.

## CHAPTER 43... *CARDINALS RULE*

320     As soon as a furious Lambeau     Christl, Packers.com, June 21, 2018.
321     "I've never in the history     *Green Bay Press-Gazette*, Nov. 17, 1947.
321     "We have got a good club,     *Green Bay Press-Gazette*, Nov. 17, 1947.
321     "He's gone," one player snarled, *Chicago Daily News*, Nov. 18, 1947.
321     "We knew," [said] tackle Chet     *Chicago Daily News*, Nov. 17, 1947.
321     Some wondered why Curly     *Chicago Sun,* Nov. 17, 1947.
321     "The answer: Cuff is supposed     *Chicago Times,* Nov. 17, 1947.
321     After the season ended,     Christl, Packers.com, June 21, 2018.

## CHAPTER 44... *THE GRIP KEEPS SLIPPING*

323     "Why didn't Lambeau     *Green Bay Press-Gazette*, Nov. 19, 1947.
323     Allouez, on Green Bay's southern     *Green Bay Press-Gazette*, Nov. 21, 1947.
323     That same day, A Personally     *Green Bay Press-Gazette*, Nov. 21, 1947.
324     Two of Fritsch's field goals     *Green Bay Press-Gazette*, Nov. 18, 1947.
324     "We should have won them     *Green Bay Press-Gazette*, Nov. 19, 1947.
324     Remembering that clever     *Green Bay Press-Gazette*, Nov. 19, 1947.
324     But that didn't change the fact     *Milwaukee Sentinel,* Nov. 19, 1947.
324     Years later, Cuff gave insight     Christl, Packers.com, June 21, 2018.

## CHAPTER 45... *AMID UNREST, LOS ANGELES RUMORS*

325     He dropped end Johnny Kovatch     Christl, *Greatest Story,* p. 224.
326     "It is based on unfounded facts,"     *Milwaukee Sentinel,* Dec. 16, 1947.
326     After Lambeau's denial,     *New York Daily News,* Dec. 17, 1947.
326     Adding to the mystery,     *New York Daily News,* Dec. 17, 1947.

| | | |
|---|---|---|
| 327 | *In an apparent effort to* | *Green Bay Press-Gazette*, Dec. 17, 1947. |
| 327 | *"How do I know Lambeau* | *Green Bay Press-Gazette*, Feb. 6, 1950. |
| 327 | *"He agreed to terms* | *Green Bay Press-Gazette*, Feb. 6, 1950. |
| 327 | *The scenario was eerily similar* | Sperber, p. 203. |
| 328 | *Lambeau would continue* | *New York Daily News*, Dec. 14, 1947. |

**CHAPTER 46... *PLANES AND TRAINS AND JUG GIRARD***

| | | |
|---|---|---|
| 329 | *After a brief Christmas* | *Green Bay Press-Gazette*, Dec. 30, 1947. |
| 330 | *Racing back to the West* | *Green Bay Press-Gazette*, Jan. 22, 1948. |

**CHAPTER 47...AN EXTREME MEASURE DOES NOT PAY OFF**

| | | |
|---|---|---|
| 331 | *"Set your watches back* | *Milwaukee Journal*, Sept. 19, 1948. |
| 331 | *"We are not as good as* | *Green Bay Press-Gazette*, Sept. 27, 1948. |
| 331 | *Lambeau was far less* | *Green Bay Press-Gazette*, Sept. 27, 1948. |
| 332 | *"I'm not feeling bad.* | *Green Bay Press-Gazette*, Oct. 11, 1948. |
| 333 | *"The Cardinals were league champions* | Johnson, p. 93. |
| 333 | *After reviewing the Cardinals* | *Milwaukee Journal*, Oct. 13, 1948. |
| 334 | *"Morale was at an all-time low,"* | Johnson, p. 94. |
| 334 | *"We thought we'd get the money* | Whittingham, p. 219. |
| 335 | *In the end, though, that* | *Green Bay Press-Gazette*, Nov. 15, 1948. |
| 335 | *Lambeau could find no* | *Green Bay Press-Gazette*, Nov. 15, 1948. |
| 335 | *An unnamed Packer said* | *Milwaukee Sentinel*, Nov. 16, 1948. |
| 335 | *"Green Bay fans don't* | *Green Bay Press-Gazette*, Nov. 15, 1948. |
| 336 | *"We've tried everything* | *Milwaukee Journal*, Nov. 21, 1948. |
| 336 | *To emphasize his point* | *Milwaukee Journal*, Nov. 22, 1948. |
| 336 | *Amid these splendid* | *Green Bay Press-Gazette*, Nov. 24, 1948. |
| 337 | *The season took another* | *Green Bay Press-Gazette*, Nov. 29, 1948. |
| 337 | *That ended "the most disastrous* | *Chicago Tribune*, Dec. 6, 1948. |
| 337 | *"All they need is a few* | *Green Bay Press-Gazette*, Dec. 6, 1948. |
| 338 | *"Although extremely disappointing* | *Green Bay Press-Gazette*, Dec. 7, 1948. |

**CHAPTER 48... *WAR AND RUMORS OF PEACE***

| | | |
|---|---|---|
| 339 | *"I think Stan will have a* | *Green Bay Press-Gazette*, Jan. 4, 1949. |
| 340 | *"Heath could throw the* | Christl, *The Greatest Story in Sports*, p. 224. |
| 340 | *To end the costly war,* | Christl, *The Greatest Story in Sports*, p. 229. |
| 340 | *Lambeau fired back* | *Green Bay Press-Gazette*, Oct. 27, 1948. |
| 340 | *Of far greater importance,* | *Green Bay Press-Gazette*, Jan. 21, 1949. |
| 341 | *Making light of the AAFC* | *Chicago Tribune*, Jan. 21, 1949. |
| 341 | *Speculation flared up,* | *Green Bay Press-Gazette*, Jan. 21, 1949. |
| 341 | *"Sooner or later, the top* | *Green Bay Press-Gazette*, Jan. 22, 1949. |

## CHAPTER 49...*A NEW COACHING STAFF*

343   *Overshadowed by all the*   *Green Bay Press-Gazette,* Jan. 20, 1949.
344   *"It will be a pleasure*   *Green Bay Press-Gazette,* Jan. 29, 1949.
344   *Snyder also explained*   *Los Angeles Mirror,,* Jan. 29, 1949.
344   *Facing a pivotal year,*   *Los Angeles Times,* May 1, 1949.
344   *"That is not true,"*   *Los Angeles Mirror,,* Jan. 29, 1949.
345   *Reached in Hollywood,*   *Green Bay Press-Gazette,* March 14, 1949.
345   *Although Lambeau insisted*   Christl, *The Greatest Story in Sports,* p. 233.
346   *"We are organizing chiefly*   *Green Bay Press-Gazette,* Feb. 8, 1949.
346   *Lambeau returned to Green Bay*   *Green Bay Press-Gazette,* April 1, 1949.
346   *Alumni club president Fee Klaus,*   *Green Bay Press-Gazette,* April 5, 1949.
346   *On Thursday, April 7,*   *Los Angeles Times,* April 8, 1949.
347   *A 25-year-old Wausau,*   *Green Bay Press-Gazette,* June 3, 1949.
347   *"Elroy Hirsch's decision*   *Milwaukee Journal,* July 31, 1949.
347   *"Hirsch is undoubtedly one*   Escondido, California, *Times Advocate,* July 26, 1949.
348   *Their Hirsch hopes*   *Green Bay Press-Gazette,* Aug. 1, 1949.
348   *The Green Bay Packer Alumni*   *Green Bay Press-Gazette,* Aug. 10 and 20, 1949.
348   *Quarterback Jack Jacobs*   *Green Bay Press-Gazette,* Aug. 22, 1949.
349   *"We played a team in*   *Green Bay Press-Gazette,* Aug. 22, 1949.
349   *Afterward, speaking in*   *Green Bay Press-Gazette,* Sept. 26, 1949.
349   *Outwardly, Lambeau also*   *Green Bay Press-Gazette,* Sept. 26, 1949.
349   *Many years later, Roger Skaletski*   Christl, *Greatest Story,* p. 234.
350   *"Under this arrangement*   *Green Bay Press-Gazette,* Sept. 30, 1949.
350   *"Curly Lambeau, founder*   *Milwaukee Sentinel,* Oct. 1, 1949.
350   *The official front-office*   *Milwaukee Sentinel,* Oct. 1, 1949.
351   *"It was a complete surprise*   *Green Bay Press-Gazette,* Sept. 30, 1949.
351   *Or three more surprised*   Christl, *The Greatest Story in Sports,* p. 235.
351   *Two days after Lambeau's*   *Green Bay Press-Gazette,* Oct. 3, 1949.
352   *"Get out the band,*   *Green Bay Press-Gazette,* Oct. 8, 1949.
352   *When Daley had been hired*   Beech, p. 180.
352   *Fritsch made a pair*   *Chicago Tribune,* Oct. 8, 1949.
352   *Far removed from angry*   Christl, *The Greatest Story in Sports,* p. 236.
352   *That afternoon, Lambeau*   Christl, *The Greatest Story in Sports,* p. 236.
353   *Playing at night after*   *Green Bay Press-Gazette,* Oct. 10, 1949.
353   *By mid-October, Lambeau*   *Milwaukee Journal,* Oct. 18, 1949.
353   *To encourage Packer fans*   *Green Bay Press-Gazette,* Oct. 13, 1949.
353   *Lambeau and his sagging team*   Christl, *Greatest Story,* p. 236.
353   *On that Sunday,*   *Green Bay Press-Gazette,* Oct. 24, 1949.
354   *Returning to Green Bay,*   *Green Bay Press-Gazette,* Oct. 28, 1949.

## CHAPTER 50. . . *A $50,000 DRIVE TO SAVE THE PACKERS*

357   *Green Bay was a 14½-point*   Boyle, Robert H., "The Brain That Gave Us the Point Spread," *Sports Illustrated,* March 19, 1986.
357   *"Open $50,000 Drive*   *Green Bay Press-Gazette,* Nov. 14, 1949.
358   *Although many Packer fans*   Christl, *The Greatest Story in Sports,* p. 240.

| | | |
|---|---|---|
| 358 | *"It would not be necessary* | *Green Bay Press-Gazette,* Nov. 14, 1949. |
| 358 | *A proponent of the negotiated* | *Green Bay Press-Gazette,* Nov.. 14, 1949. |
| 359 | *In addition to hawking* | *Green Bay Press-Gazette,* Nov. 23, 1949. |
| 359 | *After the meeting, club* | *Green Bay Press-Gazette,* Nov. 21, 1949. |
| 360 | *Lambeau also knocked* | *Idaho State Journal, UP,* Nov. 21, 1949. |
| 361 | *"The differences among them* | *Milwaukee Journal,* Nov. 22, 1949. |
| 363 | *A dozen members of the* | *Green Bay Press-Gazette,* Nov. 25, 1949. |
| 363 | *Team president Emil* | *Green Bay Press-Gazette,* Nov. 25, 1949. |
| 363 | *Milwaukee Sentinel columnist* | *Milwaukee Sentinel,* Nov. 26, 1949. |
| 364 | *To further inspire the team* | *Green Bay Press-Gazette,* Nov. 28, 1949. |
| 364 | *It lacked the emotion* | *Green Bay Press-Gazette,* Nov. 28, 1949. |

## CHAPTER 51... *THE GREAT LAMBEAU DEBATE*

| | | |
|---|---|---|
| 365 | *As Green Bay lost for the eighth* | *Chicago Tribune,* Nov. 29, 1949. |
| 365 | *"If Curly Lambeau is retained,"* | *Milwaukee Journal,* Nov. 30, 1949. |
| 367 | *The board also approved* | *Green Bay Press-Gazette,* Dec. 1, 1949. |
| 367 | *The day after the showdown,* | *Green Bay Press-Gazette,* Dec. 2, 1949. |
| 367 | *"Lambeau... had won an empty* | Torinus, p. 63. |
| 368 | *On the train to Hershey,* | Zimmerman, p. 178. |
| 369 | *"All those rumors that Green* | *Green Bay Press-Gazette,* Dec. 9, 1949. |
| 369 | *"Now the work is just* | *Green Bay Press-Gazette,* Dec. 10, 1949. |
| 370 | *Ken Keuper, who had* | *Green Bay Press-Gazette,* Dec. 14, 1949. |

## CHAPTER 52... *"CARDINALS PREPARED TO PAY THE HIGHEST SALARY"*

| | | |
|---|---|---|
| 371 | *Just before he left* | *Chicago Tribune,* Dec. 13, 1949. |
| 371 | *"I wanted to learn* | *Chicago Tribune,* Dec. 13, 1949. |
| 372 | *When they were married* | *Chicago Sun-Times,* Sept. 29, 1949; *Chicago Daily News,* July 12, 1951. |
| 372 | *"We're not attempting* | *Chicago Sun-Times,* Dec. 13, 1949. |
| 372 | *Keeping Conzelman might have* | *Chicago Tribune,* Dec. 13, 1949. |
| 372 | *Parker, on the other hand,* | *Chicago Tribune,* Dec. 12, 1949. |
| 373 | *The day after Parker quit,* | *Chicago Daily News,* Dec. 13, 1949. |

## CHAPTER 53... *WITH LAMBEAU, "A HOPELESS CAUSE"*

| | | |
|---|---|---|
| 375 | *"As everyone is aware,* | *Green Bay Press-Gazette,* Dec. 15, 1949. |
| 375 | *A week later, team attorney* | *Green Bay Press-Gazette,* Dec. 22, 1949. |
| 376 | *"You never know, Bob.* | *Green Bay Press-Gazette,* Dec. 19, 1949. |
| 376 | *The decision to play* | *Los Angeles Daily News,* Dec. 19, 1949. |
| 377 | *Back in Green Bay,* | Christl, *The Greatest Story in Sports,* p. 247. |
| 378 | *The investors were never identified* | *Green Bay Press-Gazette,* Aug. 9, 1949; Christl, *The Greatest Story in Sports,* p. 233. |
| 379 | *A widower, Turnbull had retired* | *Los Angeles Times,* Apr 19, 1949. |
| 380 | *In late December, Gene* | *Green Bay Press-Gazette,* Dec. 29, 1949. |
| 380 | *"I was not contacted* | *Green Bay Press-Gazette,* Dec. 29, 1949. |

## CHAPTER 54... *LAMBEAU IN LIMBO*

| | | |
|---|---|---|
| 381 | *"The man without a contract,"* | *Green Bay Press-Gazette,* Jan. 10, 1950. |

| | | |
|---|---|---|
| 381 | In the past, success | Green Bay Press-Gazette, Jan. 10, 1950. |
| 383 | Publicly, Lambeau said | Green Bay Press-Gazette, Jan. 11, 1950. |
| 383 | Lambeau coyly admitted | Green Bay Press-Gazette, Jan. 11, 1950. |
| 384 | Lambeau dug in his heels | Green Bay Press-Gazette, Jan. 20, 1950. |
| 384 | "It won't be too bad," | Chicago Daily News, Jan. 24, 1950. |
| 385 | Fischer flew in from Florida | Green Bay Press-Gazette, Jan. 18, 1950. |
| 385 | "Lambeau took one quick look | Milwaukee Journal, Feb. 2, 1950. |

### CHAPTER 55.... *DOWN GOES ROCKWOOD*

387 Rockwood Lodge caught fire.  Green Bay Press-Gazette, Jan. 25, 1950.
387 Flagstead broke a window,  Green Bay Press-Gazette, Jan. 25, 1950.
387 An older daughter,  Green Bay Press-Gazette, Jan. 25, 1950.
387 A fire truck from Treble  Green Bay Press-Gazette, Jan. 25, 1950; Beech, p. 188.
388 Packers secretary-treasurer  Green Bay Press-Gazette, Jan. 25, 1950.
388 "I didn't set the Rockwood  Green Bay Press-Gazette, Feb. 13, 1950, and Jan. 25, 1950.
388 "They torched it,"  Fleming, David, "How the Green Bay Packers averted financial ruin in a mysterious blaze of glory," *ESPN the Magazine*, Sept. 19, 2013.
388 Cliff Christl, the Packers' official  Christl, *The Greatest Story in Sports*, p. 257 and 259.

### CHAPTER 56.... *TAKING FLIGHT TO THE CARDINALS*

392 When the University of Chicago  Chicago Sun-Times, Jan. 30, 1950.
392 Decades later, longtime Bears  Anderson, with Klosinski, p. 163-164.
392 In 1943, when Hunk  Anderson, with Klosinski, p. 191.
393 On the weekend of January 28  Chicago Tribune Jan. 31, 1950.
393 "One of the best kept  Green Bay Press-Gazette, Jan. 31, 1950.
394 "I haven't yet made up  Green Bay Press-Gazette, Jan. 31, 1950.
394 "It is apparent that there  Green Bay Press-Gazette, Feb. 1, 1950.
394 Back in Miami  New York Times, Associated Press, Feb. 2, 1950.
394 "We've had two good  Christl, *Greatest Story*, p. 266; Zimmerman, p. 204.
394 "They grumbled about this  Lancaster New Era/New York Herald Tribune, Feb. 3, 1950.
395 Lambeau's name had been  Associated Press, Feb. 2, 1950.
395 "We're through,"  Milwaukee Journal, Feb. 2, 1950.
395 To calm fears  Green Bay Press-Gazette, Feb. 2, 1950.
395 As Milwaukee Journal sports editor  Zimmerman, p. 205.
395 A Chicago Tribune writer  Chicago Tribune Feb. 2, 1950.
396 When Stydahar told Reeves  McCambridge, p. 67.
396 "We have taken this drastic  McCambridge, p. 67.
396 Shaughnessy also was shocked  *Associated Press, Knoxville Journal*, Feb. 19, 1950

# Notes

**PART FOUR: LIFE BEYOND GREEN BAY**

**CHAPTER 57.... *A NEW BEGINNING IN THE WINDY CITY***
397  "This does not mean the end  *Green Bay Press-Gazette,* Feb. 1, 1950.
397  To further calm the fears  *Green Bay Press-Gazette,* Feb. 2, 1950.
400  "I am sure I can do a better job  *Chicago Tribune* Feb. 2, 1950.
400  "Lambeau will have a free hand  *Chicago Tribune* Feb. 2, 1950.
400  Lambeau "comes into a town  *Chicago Tribune* Feb. 2, 1950.
400  "I am extremely happy  *Green Bay Press-Gazette,* Feb. 1, 1950; Ziemba, Joe. *When Football Was Football.* Chicago: Triumph Books, 1993, p. 368..
401  In Philadelphia, NFL  *Green Bay Press-Gazette,* Feb. 2, 1950.
402  After being introduced  *Green Bay Press-Gazette,* Feb. 4, 1950.
402  Asked to pick  *Green Bay Press-Gazette,* Feb. 4, 1950.
402  Lambeau took no further  *Green Bay Press-Gazette,* Feb. 4, 1950.
40   Lunch with Lambeau  *Green Bay Press-Gazette,* Feb. 8, 1950.
403  "Lambeau Picks up the Check,  *Chicago Sun-Times,* Feb. 8, 1950.
403  Chicago Sun-Times Columnist  *Chicago Sun-Times,* Feb. 9, 1950.
404  By mid-February, Lambeau  *Los Angeles Times,* Feb. 19, 1950.
404  Lambeau "directed the Packers  *Los Angeles Times,* Feb. 19, 1950.

**CHAPTER 58....*PACKER BOARD KEEPS A TIGHT GRIP***
405  On Feb. 6, 1950,  *Green Bay Press-Gazette,* Feb. 7, 1950.

**CHAPTER 59....*PACKERS HONOR CURLY—AND THEN BEAT HIM***
407  "To say that I appreciate  *Green Bay Press-Gazette,* Aug. 17, 1950.
407  Wisconsin Governor Oscar  *Green Bay Press-Gazette,* Aug. 17, 1950.
407  To keep Ronzani from feeling  *Green Bay Press-Gazette,* Aug. 17, 1950.
408  "They're playing like a college team,"  *Chicago Tribune,* Aug. 17, 1950.
408  In February, Christman had  *Chicago Sun-Times,* July 16, 1950.
408  "We are far from the ball club  *Chicago Tribune,* Sept. 5, 1950.
409  Exhibition or not, Lambeau  *Chicago Tribune,* Sept. 12, 1950.
409  While the rest of the NFL  *Chicago Sun-Times, Sept. 20, 1950; Chicago Tribune,* Sept. 22, 1950.
410  Even Christman was  *Green Bay Press-Gazette,* Sept. 22, 1950.
410  "The makings of a neat little  *Chicago Daily News,* Sept. 22, 1950.
410  "Lambeau explained the straight  *Chicago Tribune* and *Chicago Daily News,* Sept. 22, 1950.

**CHAPTER 60....*CARDINALS DEBUT A DISASTER***
413  "I felt really low at halftime  Nash, Bruce, and Zullo, Allan. *The Football Hall of Shame.* New York: Pocket Books, 1986, p. 67.
414  Even more troubling,  *Green Bay Press-Gazette,* Sept. 25, 1950.
414  After Redskins owner  *Chicago Sun-Times,* Sept. 26, 1950.
414  The reaction to Lambeau's  *Chicago Daily News,* Sept. 25, 1950.
414  "We deserved to be booed,"  *Chicago Daily News,* Sept. 26, 1950.
415  "Any athlete, particularly  *Chicago Tribune,* Sept. 26, 1950.
415  After repeating his high-road  *Chicago Tribune,* Sept. 26, 1950.

| | | |
|---|---|---|
| 415 | *Just one game into* | *Chicago Tribune,* Sept. 26, 1950. |
| 416 | "*It was just a matter* | *Chicago Daily News,* Oct. 3, 1950. |
| 416 | "*Everything looks different,"* | *Chicago Daily News,* Oct. 3, 1950. |
| 416 | "*We were lucky,* | *Green Bay Press-Gazette,* Oct. 2, 1950. |

## CHAPTER 61.... *LOSING GAMES AND FANS*

| | | |
|---|---|---|
| 417 | *Although roughed up* | *Chicago Tribune,* Oct. 9, 1950. |
| 417 | "*I'm still convinced* | *Chicago Daily News,* Oct. 17, 1950. |
| 417 | *Lambeau replied that* | *Chicago Sun-Times,* Oct. 24, 1950. |
| 417 | *The 6-foot-5, 245-pound Ford,* | *Chicago Tribune,* Dec. 25, 1950. |
| 418 | "*We had a little defense* | *Chicago Daily News,* Oct. 30, 1950. |
| 418 | "*I didn't mean to use* | *New York Times,* Nov. 14, 1950. |

## CHAPTER 62.... *PONDERING TELEVISION*

| | | |
|---|---|---|
| 419 | *Television "definitely hurts* | *New York Daily News,* Nov. 14, 1950. |
| 419 | *That said, he predicted* | *New York Daily News,* Nov. 14, 1950. |
| 419 | "*Continued small attendance,"* | *New York Times,* Nov. 14, 1950. |
| 419 | *In that regard, Lambeau was* | Davis, p. 259 |
| 420 | *Seeing the vast potential,* | Davis, p. 259 |
| 420 | "*George Halas was Roone Arledge* | Davis, p. 260 |
| 420 | *And Cardinals fans were* | *Chicago Tribune,* Nov. 24, 1950. |
| 421 | "*When the Cards signed* | *Chicago Daily News,* Nov. 29, 1950. |
| 421 | "*I doubt there will be any* | *Chicago Daily News,* Nov. 29, 1950. |
| 421 | "*The boys played good* | *Chicago Sun-Times,* Dec. 4, 1950. |
| 422 | "*This was a sort of shakedown* | *Chicago Sun-Times,* Dec. 10, 1950. |
| 422 | "*Lambeau can have a contract* | *Chicago Daily News,* Dec. 6, 1950. |
| 422 | *In the same article,* | *Chicago Daily News,* Dec. 6, 1950. |
| 423 | "*That agreement wasn't worth* | Olsen, Jack, "The Unhappiest Millionaire: Walter Wolfner Sadly Leads His Football Cardinals Out of Chicago and Into Prosperity," *Sports Illustrated,* April 4, 1960. |

## CHAPTER 63.... *MORE FRONT-OFFICE TURMOIL*

| | | |
|---|---|---|
| 426 | *Although Vi Bidwill* | Davis, p. 231. |
| 426 | *Wolfner "just wrecked* | Davis, p. 231. |
| 426 | "*Despite the chant of* | *Los Angeles Daily News,* Jan. 19, 1951. |
| 427 | "*There were rumors* | Ziemba, p. 371. |
| 427 | *The NFL played its inaugural* | *Los Angeles Daily News,* Jan. 13, 1951. |
| 427 | "*For individual brilliance,* | *Los Angeles Times,* Jan. 16, 1951. |
| 427 | *After the All-Star* | AP, *Lancaster Sunday News,* Jan. 19, 1951. |
| 428 | *In truth, Halas picked up* | *Green Bay Press-Gazette,* Jan. 20, 1951. |
| 428 | *On April 4, 1951,* | *Chicago Sun-Times,* April 4, 1951. |
| 429 | "*Outside of that, we haven't* | *Green Bay Press-Gazette,* Aug. 13, 1951. |
| 429 | "*I just didn't see eye to eye* | *Chicago Sun-Times,* Sept. 26, 1951. |
| 430 | "*There have been rumors* | *Chicago Daily News,* July 12, 1951. |

## CHAPTER 64... *CARDINAL SINS*

| | | |
|---|---|---|
| 431 | *This was no mere exhibition* | *Milwaukee Sentinel,* Aug. 28, 1951. |

| | | |
|---|---|---|
| 431 | *Lambeau's squad led 14-7* | *Green Bay Press-Gazette*, Aug. 27, 1951. |
| 431 | *In another indicator that* | *Chicago Daily News*, Aug. 27, 1951. |
| 432 | *Curly tried to sound* | *Chicago Sun-Times*, Oct. 17, 1951. |
| 432 | *"Before catching a train* | *Chicago Sun-Times*, Oct. 22, 1951. |
| 433 | *Even more galling,* | *Chicago Sun-Times*, Oct. 22, 1951. |
| 433 | *Even though Hunk was* | *Green Bay Press-Gazette*, Oct. 24, 1951. |
| 433 | *Not only did the coaching* | *Chicago Tribune*, Oct. 22, 1951. |
| 433 | *"We lost, but we should* | *Washington Evening Star*, Oct. 22, 1951. |
| 434 | *"I didn't like Trippi's* | *Chicago Sun-Times*, Oct. 24, 1951. |
| 434 | Although Wolfner stood by | *Chicago Tribune*, Oct. 24, 1951. |
| 434 | *Lambeau could not* | *Chicago Tribune*, Oct. 24, 1951. |
| 434 | *Wolfner also said a decision* | *Chicago Sun-Times*, Oct. 24, 1951. |
| 434 | *"I couldn't afford to pass* | *Los Angeles Times*, Oct. 24, 1951. |
| 434 | *The problem was,* | *Chicago Sun-Times*, Oct. 25, 1951. |
| 434 | *"That isn't true.* | *Chicago Sun-Times*, Oct. 25, 1951. |
| 435 | *Lambeau tried to explain* | *Chicago Sun-Times*, Oct. 26, 1951. |
| 435 | *"Sure, that's right,"* | *Chicago Tribune*, Oct. 26, 1951. |

**CHAPTER 65... *TWO AND OUT***

| | | |
|---|---|---|
| 437 | *"I have absolutely nothing* | *Chicago Sun-Times*, Oct. 29, 1951. |
| 437 | *After a week in which* | *Chicago Daily News*, Oct. 29, 1951. |
| 438 | *"Lambeau's made mistakes,"* | UP, *Green Bay Press-Gazette,,* Dec. 5, 1951. |
| 439 | *"I had heard Mr. Wolfner* | *Chicago Sun-Times*, Dec. 8, 1951. |
| 439 | *"LAMBEAU QUITS* | *Chicago Tribune*, Dec. 8, 1951. |
| 439 | *In a complaint eerily* | UP, *Green Bay Press-Gazette,,* Dec. 8, 1951. |
| 439 | *Wolfner fired back* | *Chicago Tribune*, Dec. 8, 1951. |
| 440 | *Lambeau said he decided* | *Chicago Tribune*, Dec. 8, 1951. |
| 440 | *Lambeau vowed to work* | *Chicago Tribune*, Dec. 8, 1951. |
| 440 | *Wolfner initially went* | *Chicago Sun-Times*, Dec. 9, 1951. |
| 441 | *Curly was among the few* | *Chicago Tribune*, Dec. 10, 1951. |
| 441 | *"The season's most minute* | *Chicago Daily News*, Dec. 10, 1951. |
| 441 | *"We worked on the formation* | *Chicago Sun-Times*, Dec. 17, 1951. |
| 442 | *The sub-zero temperatures* | *Chicago Sun-Times*, Dec. 17, 1951. |
| 442 | *"I didn't want to play* | *Chicago Daily News*, Dec. 17, 1951. |

**CHAPTER 66... *MORE WOLFNER MACHINATIONS***

| | | |
|---|---|---|
| 445 | *That happened right before* | *Chicago Sun-Times*, Dec. 19, 1951. |
| 445 | *The next day, though,* | *Chicago Tribune*, Dec. 21, 1951. |
| 445 | *Wolfner also met* | *Chicago Tribune*, Dec. 18, 1951. |
| 445 | *A few days after Wolfner* | *Chicago Sun-Times*, Dec. 22, 1951. |
| 446 | *Beyond that, an unnamed Cardinal* | *Chicago Tribune*, Dec. 22, 1951. |
| 446 | *In Los Angeles, Lambeau* | *Los Angeles Times*, Dec. 30, 1951. |
| 446 | *Undeterred, Wolfner forged* | *Chicago Sun-Times*, Dec. 29, 1951. |
| 446 | *The North Side of Chicago* | *Los Angeles Times*, Jan. 8, 1952. |
| 446 | *It was not an idle threat.* | Davis, p. 237. |
| 447 | *The Bears maintained that Lujack* | Davis, p. 240. |

## CHAPTER 67... *JOB RUMORS GALORE*

449      *In one shocker,*    *Green Bay Press-Gazette,* Jan. 8, 1952.
449      *Citing Bell's poor health,*    *Green Bay Press-Gazette,* Jan. 8, 1952.
449      *Halas knocked down the*    *Green Bay Press-Gazette,* Jan. 8, 1952.
449      *Arch Ward dismissed the report*    *Chicago Tribune* Jan. 9, 1952.
450      *The next possibility was*    AP, *Wisconsin State Journal,* Jan. 10, 1952.
450      *"What's it all about?"*    *Baltimore Sun,* Jan. 12, 1952.
450      *While wintering in California,*    *Green Bay Press-Gazette,* Feb. 28, 1952; *Valley Times,* May 8, 1952.
451      *In May, another report speculated*    *Valley Times,* May 22, 1952.
451      *Lambeau quickly denied*    *Los Angeles Mirror,* May 30, 1952.
451      *Not giving up, Claude Newman*    *Valley Times,* June 3, 1952.
451      *Although he now was a*    *Green Bay Press-Gazette,* July 23, 1952.
451      *Lambeau also stopped in Chicago.*    *Chicago Tribune,* Aug. 2, 1952.

## CHAPTER 68... *BACK IN THE SADDLE*

453      *When rookie quarterback*    *Los Angeles Times,* Aug. 15, 1952.
453      *"I told the players*    *Washington Evening Star,* Aug. 22, 1952.
454      *The Washington Evening Star*    *Washington Evening Star,* Aug. 22, 1952.
454      *Redskins assistant Jerry Neri*    *Washington Evening Star,* Aug. 23, 1952.
455      *"Curly and I have been*    *Washington Evening Star,* Aug. 24, 1952.
455      *In Washington, a more recent*    *Washington Evening Star,* Aug. 24, 1952.
455      *While Lambeau had agreed*    *Washington Evening Star,* Aug. 24, 1952.
456      *Only 5-foot-9 and 168 pounds,*    Leuthner, Stuart. *Iron Men: Bucko, Crazylegs and the Boys Recall the Golden Day of Professional Football.* New York: Doubleday, 1988, p. 107.
457      *"He was really a defensive coach,"* Leuthner, p. 111.
457      *To counter that, Lambeau*    Leuthner, p. 31.
457      *"A good, sharp team doesn't*    *Washington Evening Star,* Sept. 6, 1952.
458      *A win over the Giants*    *Kansas City Star,* Sept. 9, 1952.
458      *Because both the Packers,*    *Kansas City Star,* Sept. 9, 1952.
458      *He also promised to*    *Washington Evening Star,* Sept. 15, 1952.
459      *"The Lions rolled*    *Detroit Free Press,* Sept. 22, 1952.
459      *The return to Chicago*    *Chicago Tribune,* Sept. 26, 1952.
460      *Although the Redskins*    *Washington Evening Star,* Sept. 30, 1952.
461      *Some observers thought*    *Washington Evening Star,* Oct. 1, 1952.
461      *"That's great," Lambeau said*    *Washington Evening Star,* Oct. 5, 1952.
461      *This was one of the many*    Robinson, Ray, *Rockne of Notre Dame: The Making of a Football Legend.* New York: Oxford University Press, 1999, p. 239.
462      *In a politically incorrect*    *Washington Evening Star,* Oct. 5, 1952.
462      *The game also shaped up*    *Washington Evening Star,* Oct. 5, 1952.
462      *"All I've heard the last*    *Washington Evening Star,* Oct. 4, 1952.
462      *Although the Redskins had*    *Green Bay Press-Gazette,* Oct. 6, 1952.
463      *Almost on cue, Marshall*    *Green Bay Press-Gazette,* Oct. 6, 1952.
463      *Always opinionated, Marshall*    *Green Bay Press-Gazette,* Oct. 6, 1952.
463      *"Trippi's good, and this*    *Washington Evening Star,* Oct. 9, 1952.
464      *"The Redskins won no friends*    *Washington Evening Star,* Oct. 13, 1952.

# Notes 645

| | | |
|---|---|---|
| 464 | "The veteran coach charged | Washington Evening Star, Oct. 13, 1952. |
| 464 | After conferring with | Washington Evening Star, Oct. 13, 1952. |
| 464 | "There's good esprit de corps | Washington Evening Star, Oct. 13, 1952. |
| 465 | "Yesterday's game was | Pittsburgh Press, Oct. 20, 1952. |
| 465 | Meanwhile, Lambeau took | Washington Evening Star, Oct. 26, 1952. |
| 465 | Always tinkering, Lambeau | UP, Oshkosh Northwestern,, Oct. 21, 1952. |
| 466 | "We'll miss Sam, | Washington Evening Star, Oct. 26, 1952. |
| 466 | "If we show the same spirit | Washington Evening Star, Oct. 26, 1952. |
| 466 | "Some of the worst officiating | Washington Evening Star, Oct. 27, 1952. |
| 467 | "Curly will be back | Washington Evening Star, Nov. 4, 1952. |
| 468 | "We've got the nucleus | Washington Evening Star, Dec. 15, 1952. |
| 469 | "Each had a title chance | Los Angeles Times, Dec. 20, 1952. |
| 469 | On Tuesday afternoon, | Washington Evening Star, Dec. 16, 1952 |

**CHAPTER 69... *A SECOND TERM IN WASHINGTON***

| | | |
|---|---|---|
| 471 | Lambeau's first season | Washington Evening Star, Dec. 16, 1952. |
| 471 | Lambeau also kept a close eye | Los Angeles Times, Jan. 11, 1953. |
| 471 | By mid-January, he was | Washington Evening Star, Jan. 20, 1953. |
| 471 | Before the draft, Lambeau | Pittsburgh Courier, Jan. 17, 1953. |
| 472 | "[Marshall] caved in, finally, | Redskins: A History of Washington's Team, |

By the Washington Post. Washington Post Books: Washington, D.C., p. 17.

| | | |
|---|---|---|
| 472 | After the draft, Lambeau | South Gate Daily Press-Tribune, March 27, 1953. |
| 472 | On March 24, he was | Los Angeles Evening Citizen News, March 24, 1953. |
| 472 | Listing the many sports | Los Angeles Times, March 29, 1953. |
| 472 | On Friday night, May 1, | Washington Evening Star, April 30, 1953. |
| 473 | While in Washington, | AP, Cedar Rapids Gazette, May 3, 1953. |
| 473 | Departing Washington | Green Bay Press-Gazette, May 11, 1953. |
| 473 | After snubbing Marshall's | Washington Evening Star, June 18, 1953. |
| 474 | "There are any number | Los Angeles Times, June 14, 1953. |
| 474 | "Man, not for me," | Los Angeles Evening Citizen News, July 6, 1953. |
| 474 | When the Grand Canyon | Los Angeles Times, July 26, 1953. |
| 475 | Quarterback issues or not, | Washington Evening Star, Aug. 31, 1953. |
| 475 | To fix the problem, | Washington Evening Star, Sept. 1, 1953. |
| 475 | When George Halas announced | Chicago Tribune, Jan. 25, 1955. |
| 477 | After a few steamy days | Green Bay Press-Gazette, Sept. 3, 1953. |
| 477 | Noting that this was | Green Bay Press-Gazette, Sept. 5, 1953. |
| 477 | "I'd rather win this | Washington Evening Star, Sept. 5, 1953. |
| 477 | Lambeau was especially | Green Bay Press-Gazette, Sept. 8, 1953. |
| 478 | "Always a chain-smoker | Green Bay Press-Gazette, Sept. 8, 1953. |
| 478 | "The boys got mad | Washington Evening Star, Sept. 8, 1953. |
| 478 | "How can you win | Washington Evening Star, Sept. 21, 1953. |
| 479 | "Lambeau told [Washington] | Washington Evening Star, Oct. 6, 1953. |
| 480 | "I saw every play | Washington Evening Star, Oct. 12, 1953. |
| 480 | A curious newspaper | Washington Evening Star, Oct. 19, 1953. |
| 480 | There was no spinning, | Washington Evening Star, Oct. 28, 1953. |
| 481 | Burdened by a three-game | Washington Evening Star, Nov. 9, 1953. |
| 481 | "I can't talk freely," | Washington Evening Star, Nov. 16, 1953. |

| | | |
|---|---|---|
| 482 | Another major problem | *Redskins: A History of Washington's Team*, p. 17. |
| 483 | At first glance, the game | *Washington Evening Star*, Nov. 23, 1953. |
| 484 | Lambeau did tell a story | *Charlotte Observer,*, Nov. 24, 1953. |
| 485 | "I don't know what to | *Washington Evening Star*, Nov. 24, 1953. |
| 485 | What was Curly thinking? | *Washington Evening Star*, Nov. 25, 1953. |
| 485 | When Lambeau finally | *Washington Evening Star*, Nov. 26, 1953. |
| 486 | In a key moment, a field | *Washington Evening Star*, Nov. 30, 1953. |
| 486 | "I suppose it's a combination | *Washington Evening Star*, Dec. 4, 1953. |
| 486 | Always a Barnum-like | *Washington Evening Star*, Dec. 6, 1953. |
| 487 | "Seven and four | *Washington Evening Star*, Dec. 7, 1953. |
| 487 | The day before the game, | *Pittsburgh Press*, Dec. 14, 1953. |
| 487 | When the referees inspected | *Pittsburgh Press*, Dec. 14, 1953. |
| 488 | If, as LeBaron said later | Leuthner, p. 111. |
| 488 | With that painful loss, | *Washington Evening Star*, Dec. 14, 1953. |
| 488 | On Sunday morning | *Washington Evening Star*, Dec. 13, 1953. |
| 488 | By Monday morning, | *Washington Evening Star*, Dec. 14, 1953. |
| 489 | Under fire for his "$7,000 | UP, *Fresno Bee*, Dec. 15, 1953. |
| 489 | Lambeau countered | United Press, *Fresno Bee*, Dec. 15, 1953. |
| 489 | Trying to soften the criticism | United Press, *Monongahela Daily Republican*, Dec. 15, 1953. |
| 490 | The next day, Lambeau | *Green Bay Press-Gazette*, Dec. 18, 1953. |
| 490 | Back in Los Angeles | *Valley Times*, Jan. 14, 1954. |
| 491 | "I think Eddie will be back | *Washington Evening Star*, Jan. 25, 1954. |
| 491 | "That's the reason I went up there," | Leuthner, p. 111. |
| 492 | Although Lambeau spent | *Green Bay Press-Gazette*, June 15, 1954. |

## CHAPTER 70... *NO WIFE, NO TEAM*

| | | |
|---|---|---|
| 493 | The summer of 1954 | *Green Bay Press-Gazette*, July 28, 1954. |
| 493 | Although not surprising | Griffith, p. 184. |
| 493 | "After Grace Garland's divorce | Stein, p. 156. |
| 494 | Moses had little sympathy, | Stein, p. 153. |
| 494 | Grace still owned real estate | Stein, p. 157. |
| 495 | "I'm tired of getting licked | *Washington Evening Star*, Aug. 19, 1954. |
| 495 | Owner George Preston | *Washington Evening Star*, Aug. 20, 1954. |
| 496 | "A super run, | *Los Angeles Times*, Sept. 8, 1954. |
| 496 | The owner asked the players | *Los Angeles Times*, Aug. 24, 1954. |
| 497 | "Angry over the fines, | *Los Angeles Times*, Aug. 24, 1954, and *Washington Post*, Sept. 20, 1954. |
| 497 | Curly in a bar | Christl, *Packers Heritage Trail*, p. 29. |
| 497 | "I'm doing the best I can | *Sacramento Bee*, Aug. 24, 1954. |
| 497 | The incident was witnessed | *Los Angeles Times*, *San Francisco Examiner*, *Sacramento Bee*, Aug. 23, 1954. |
| 498 | "Forty Niner players | *San Francisco Examiner,*, Aug. 23, 1954. |
| 498 | "I have no animosity," | *Los Angeles Times*, Aug. 23, 1954. |
| 498 | Washington also shed | *Washington Evening Star*, Aug. 23, 1954. |
| 499 | A few days later, | *Washington Evening Star*, *Washington Post* Aug. 26, 1954. |

## CHAPTER 71... *COLLEGE ALL-STARS BECKON*

| | | |
|---|---|---|
| 501 | *Lambeau grabbed a flight* | *Los Angeles Mirror,* Aug. 23, 1954. |
| 501 | "*Lambeau's two-year contract* | *Washington Evening Star,*, Sept. 20, 1954. |
| 502 | *Lambeau's argument:* | *Pittsburgh Post-Gazette,* Oct. 1, 1954. |
| 502 | *NFL commissioner Bert Bell* | *Pittsburgh Post-Gazette,* Oct. 1, 1954. |
| 502 | *Bell did not come* | Associated Press, *Chicago Tribune, St. Louis Globe-Democrat,* March 22, 1956. |
| 502 | *As Lambeau sat in the press* | *Pittsburgh Post-Gazette,* Oct. 1, 1954. |
| 503 | *Although he told the Green* | *Green Bay Press-Gazette,* Sept. 23, 1954. |
| 503 | *It also had to feel strange* | *Pittsburgh Post-Gazette,* Sept. 23, 1954. |
| 503 | *Despite his insistence* | *Los Angeles Mirror,* Oct. 16, 1954; *Chicago Tribune,* Nov. 23, 1954. |
| 503 | *That was especially true* | *Chicago Tribune,* Nov. 23, 1954. |
| 504 | *Or, as another Lambeau friend,* | *Los Angeles Times,* Jan. 26, 1955. |
| 504 | *Lambeau would direct* | Anderson, with Klosinski, p. 198. |
| 505 | "*Lambeau denies that he* | *Los Angeles Times,* Dec. 30, 1954. |
| 505 | *By the end of 1954,* | *Los Angeles Times,* Dec. 18, 1954. |
| 505 | *Even then, Lambeau's* | *Long Beach Press-Telegram,* Jan. 28, 1955. |
| 505 | "*Curly Lambeau probably is* | *Valley Times,* Jan. 27, 1955. |
| 506 | "*The reason for the absence* | *Los Angeles Times,* Jan. 27, 1955. |
| 507 | *In February, Lambeau and Hunk* | *Chicago Tribune,* Feb. 11, 1955. |
| 508 | "*Lambeau, stopping off at Rickey's* | *Valley Times,* March 25, 1955. |
| 508 | *In late April, Curly and Hunk* | Associated Press, *Wausau Herald,* April 26, 1955 and *Chicago Tribune,* April 28, 1955. |
| 508 | *Details of Lambeau's* | Associated Press, *Sheboygan Press,* April 28, 1955. |
| 508 | *The divorce was finally* | AP, *Janesville Gazette,* June 7, 1955. |
| 509 | "*They had bought a great deal* | Stein, p. 157. |
| 509 | "*I don't know how he did it* | Stein, p. 156. |
| 509 | *Considering how often Lambeau* | *Valley Times,* June 7, 1955. |
| 509 | *Then again, it wouldn't be* | *Green Bay Press-Gazette,* July 14, 1963. |
| 510 | "*I do not want to minimize* | *Chicago Tribune,* July 7, 1955. |
| 510 | *When Lambeau arrived in Chicago* | *Chicago Tribune,* June 24, 1955. |
| 510 | "*We've got to have offense,"* | *Chicago Tribune,* June 25, 1955. |
| 510 | *Lambeau then headed north* | *Green Bay Press-Gazette,* June 28, 1955. |
| 510 | *Curly told Arch Ward* | *Chicago Tribune,* July 7, 1955. |
| 511 | *Ward, however, was not destined* | *Chicago Tribune,* July 10, 1955. |
| 511 | "*Sports, amateur and professional,* | *Chicago Tribune,* July 11, 1955. |
| 511 | *A week into their drills,* | *Chicago Tribune,* July 31, 1955. |
| 511 | *Although they were* | Associated Press, *Nashville Banner,* Aug. 11, 1955. |
| 511 | "*The All-Stars, who have* | *Chicago Daily News,* Aug. 9, 1955. |
| 512 | *The Tribune not only had* | *Chicago Tribune,* July 31 and Aug. 7, 1955. |
| 512 | *Even the weather fell into line.* | *Chicago Sun-Times,* Aug. 13, 1955. |
| 512 | *The joyous collegians carried* | *Chicago Daily News,* Aug. 13, 1955. |
| 513 | "*E.L. (Curly) Lambeau this morning* | *Chicago Tribune,* Aug. 13, 1955. |
| 513 | "*Spirit did it.* | *Chicago Tribune,* Aug. 13, 1955. |
| 513 | *The All-Stars' upset* | *Los Angeles Evening Citizen,* Aug. 16, 1955. |
| 514 | *By the time he had returned* | *Valley Times,* Oct. 1, 1955. |

| | | |
|---|---|---|
| 514 | *Lambeau continued to say* | *Valley Times,* Oct. 1 and Oct. 5, 1955. |
| 514 | *He saw the Rams edge the Steelers* | *Valley Times,* Oct. 5, 1955. |
| 514 | *A couple of weeks later,* | *Los Angeles Times,* Oct. 15, 1955. |
| 514 | *Although he had told West Coast* | *Chicago Tribune,* Oct. 27, 1955. |
| 515 | *After watching UCLA crush* | *Long Beach Independent,* Oct. 31, 1955. |
| 515 | *In November, Lambeau was* | *L.A. Evening Citizen,* Nov. 10, 1955. |
| 515 | *On Friday, December 9* | *Green Bay Press-Gazette,* Dec. 10, 1955. |
| 515 | *After beating the Rams* | *Chicago Tribune,* Dec. 28, 1955. |
| 515 | *Lambeau, who was in the Browns* | *Arizona Star,* Jan. 1, 1956. |

**CHAPTER 72.... *GREEN BAY NEEDS A STADIUM***

| | | |
|---|---|---|
| 341 | *It was at those West Coast* | *Los Angeles Times,* Dec. 29, 1988. |
| 517 | *A week after the Rose Bowl,* | *Salt Lake Tribune, Star,* Jan. 10, 1956. |
| 517 | *After checking out the NFL draft* | *Valley Times,* Oct. 20, 1956. |
| 518 | *"There is no use kidding* | *Green Bay Press-Gazette,* Jan. 12, 1955. |
| 519 | *"I've been visiting here* | *Green Bay Press-Gazette,* Feb. 2, 1956. |
| 519 | *The key question, though,* | *Green Bay Press-Gazette,* Jan. 5, 1956 |
| 519 | *In February, the Green* | *Green Bay Press-Gazette,* Feb. 10 and 22, 1956 |
| 519 | *On March 6, the City Council* | *Green Bay Press-Gazette,* March 7, 1956. |
| 519 | *Halas diplomatically laid out* | *Green Bay Press-Gazette,* April 2, 1956. |
| 520 | *To lure an NFL team,* | *Green Bay Press-Gazette,* April 2, 1956. |
| 520 | *Mentioning the Bears' historic* | *Green Bay Press-Gazette,* March 31, 1956. |
| 520 | *The Packers franchise,* | AP, *Racine Journal-Times,* April 1, 1956. |
| 520 | *Reciting the early struggles,* | *Green Bay Press-Gazette,* March 31, 1956. |
| 521 | *The citizens of Green Bay* | *Green Bay Press-Gazette,* April 4, 1956. |
| 521 | *"That's the greatest thing* | *Green Bay Press-Gazette,* April 4, 1956. |
| 521 | *"This means that the Packers* | *Green Bay Press-Gazette,* April 4, 1956. |
| 521 | *Also ecstatic was Packers'* | *Green Bay Press-Gazette,* April 4, 1956. |
| 521 | *"I firmly believe the golden* | *Green Bay Press-Gazette,* April 3, 1956. |
| 522 | *After helping secure* | *Los Angeles Times,* May 17, 1956. |
| 522 | *A week later, Lambeau* | *Green Bay Press-Gazette,* May 23 1956, and *Chicago Tribune,* June 16, 1956. |

**CHAPTER 73.... *THE SECOND TIME IS NOT A CHARM***

| | | |
|---|---|---|
| 523 | *"A cold war began building,"* | *Chicago Tribune,* July 21, 1956. |
| 523 | *On July 22, four days after* | *Chicago Tribune,* July 23, 1956. |
| 523 | *As the game—which would* | AP, *Sioux Falls Argue-Leader,* Aug. 5, 1956. |
| 524 | *The All-Stars' hopes took* | *Detroit Free Press,* Aug. 15, 1956. |
| 524 | *Morrall, described as "groggy"* | *Chicago Tribune,* Aug. 11, 1956. |
| 524 | *"They'll beat anyone* | AP, *Arizona Daily Star,* Aug. 11, 1956. |
| 525 | *Scheduled to be the principal* | *Detroit Free Press,* Aug. 14, 1956. |
| 525 | *Even Lambeau's relationship* | *Pittsburgh Press,* Aug. 30, 1956. |
| 525 | *In Montgomery, Alabama,* | *Montgomery Advertiser,* Aug. 17, 1956. |
| 526 | *"Curly Lambeau has received* | *Green Bay Press-Gazette,* Nov. 19, 1956. |
| 526 | *"Tex Schramm is through.* | *Valley Times,* Dec. 5, 1956. |
| 527 | *As it turned out, Reeves* | MacCambridge, Michael. *America's Game: The Epic Story of How Pro Football Captured a Nation.* New York: Anchor Books, 2005, p.144. |

| | | |
|---|---|---|
| 527 | While watching the Packers | *Long Beach Independent,* Dec 18, 1956. |
| 528 | "Lambeau took his cigarette | *Long Beach Independent,* Dec 18, 1956. |

## CHAPTER 74.... *THE ONLY CLASH OF PACKERS' TWO TITANS*

| | | |
|---|---|---|
| 529 | A thunderstorm wiped out | *Chicago Tribune,* Aug. 10, 1957. |
| 530 | Lambeau blamed the rain | UP, Hastings (Neb.) *Daily Tribune,* Aug. 10, 1957. |
| 530 | "I'd like a repeat performance | *Indianapolis News,* Aug. 10, 1957. |
| 531 | "When I retired from the Browns, | Leuthner, *Iron Men,* p. 98. |
| 531 | Anderson voiced some strong | Anderson, with Klosinski, p. 201. |
| 532 | "Although Lambeau is retiring | *Chicago Tribune,* Dec. 3, 1957. |

## CHAPTER 75.... *GREEN BAY BUILDS IT. AND THEY COME.*

533    The parade started    Beech, p. 209, *Milwaukee Sentinel,* Sept. 22, 1957, *Green Bay Press-Gazette,* Sept. 30, 1957.
533    Nixon praised Green Bay    *Green Bay Press-Gazette,* Sept. 30, 1957.
534    A week before the stadium    *Milwaukee Journal,* Sept. 21, 1957.
535    "The Green Bay Packers dedicated    *Chicago Tribune,* Sept. 30, 1957.
535    Holding court at the Northland    *Green Bay Press-Gazette,* Sept. 30, 1957.

## PART FIVE: FROM EXILE TO RETIREMENT

## CHAPTER 76.... *EYING A RETURN*

537    In 1957, though, Curly    *Green Bay Press-Gazette,* Dec. 11 and 13, 1957.
538    General manager Verne Lewellen    Christl, *Greatest Story,* p. 300.
538    The next day, December 18,    Christl, *Greatest Story,* p. 324.
539    As a further endorsement    *Green Bay Press-Gazette,* Dec. 24, 1957.
539    At the December 23 meeting,    *Milwaukee Journal* and *Milwaukee Sentinel,* Dec. 24, 1957.
541    Beyond choosing a new    AP, *Stevens Point Journal,* Dec. 24, 1957.
541    "It was a complete surprise    *Green Bay Press-Gazette,* Jan. 7, 1958.
542    Rumors that McLean,    Christl, *Greatest Story,* p. 323.
542    "My situation in Green Bay    Christl, *Greatest Story,* p. 320.
542    Russ Bogda died    *Green Bay Press-Gazette,* March 13, 1958.
543    Refusing to accept    *Green Bay Press-Gazette,* Associated Press, *Wausau Daily Herald,* April 26, 1958.
543    Besides having support    *Green Bay Press-Gazette,* April 29, 1958.
544    "In short, there was harmony    *Green Bay Press-Gazette,* April 29, 1958.
544    His Packer return thwarted,    *Chippewa (Falls, Wisconsin) Herald-Telegram,* July 15, 1958.
544    "A very nice stadium,"    *Green Bay Press-Gazette,* Sept. 2, 1958.

## CHAPTER 77...."SOVIET`` LEADERSHIP OF PACKERS?

545    Although only an exhibition,    *Green Bay Press-Gazette,* Sept. 2, 1958.
545    Although the Packers    *Green Bay Press-Gazette,* Sept. 29, 1958.
545    "If you guys had blown    *Milwaukee Journal,* Oct. 28, 1958.
546    It was, the Milwaukee Journal    *Milwaukee Journal,* Nov. 3, 1958.
546    Afterward, McLean pulled a    *Milwaukee Journal,* Nov. 4, 1958.

546   Even the encouraging early tie     Christl, *Greatest Story*, p. 324.
546   "The Packers were the most     Christl, *Greatest Story*, p. 325.
546   A once ardent supporter    *Milwaukee Journal*, Oct. 28, 1958.
547   After the 56-0 debacle     *Milwaukee Journal*, Nov. 4, 1958.
547   Disputing the notion of "soviet"    *Milwaukee Journal*, Nov. 11, 1958.
548   There was no question,    *Green Bay Press-Gazette*, Dec. 2, 1958.
548   "[Strange] was right.    *Milwaukee Journal*, Dec. 3, 1958.

## CHAPTER 78.... *"WE WANT CURLY!"*
549   Two small businessmen    AP, *Green Bay Press-Gazette*, Dec. 9, 1958.
549   The media noticed    AP, *Wisconsin State Journal,*, Dec. 9, 1958.
550   "It's long distance,    *Long Beach Independent*, Dec. 10, 1958.
551   "We were [at the Ram's Horn]    Christl, *Greatest Story*, p. 330.
552   Meanwhile, three of Curly's    United Press International, *Portage Daily Register and Democrat*, Dec. 12, 1958.
552   Another log was added    *Milwaukee Sentinel*, Dec. 12, 1958.
553   "McLean and Lewellen    Associated Press, *La Crosse Tribune,*, Dec. 14, 1958.
553   Apparently buoyed    UPI, *Eau Claire Leader-Telegram*, Dec. 14, 1958.
553   "Let's put it this way,"    UPI,, *Eau Claire Leader-Telegram*, Dec. 14, 1958.
553   Keeping the momentum going, *Milwaukee newspapers*, Dec. 14, 1958.
554   "Any time a professional club    *Milwaukee Sentinel*, Dec. 16, 1958.
554   Dismissing rumors suggesting    *Milwaukee Sentinel*, Dec. 16, 1958.
555   Among the changes,    AP, *Racine Journal Times*, Dec. 17, 1958.
555   Most significantly, Olejniczak    UPI, *Portage Daily Register*, Dec. 17, 1958.

## CHAPTER 79.... *"THE SOVIET IS DEAD!"*
557   Under the headline, "The Soviet    *Milwaukee Journal*, Dec. 17, 1958.
558   On that same Wednesday,    *Milwaukee Journal*, Dec. 17, 1958.
558   Another rally was scheduled    *Green Bay Press-Gazette* and *United Press International/Terre Haute Tribune*, Dec. 23, 1958.
559   The next night, Tuesday,    AP, *Marshfield News-Herald*, Dec. 24, 1958.
559   The Lambeau speculation    UPI, *Valley Times*, Dec. 25, 1958; Christl, *Greatest Story*, p. 331.
559   In the notes of that meeting,    Christl, *Greatest Story*, p. 331.
559   After reading that Lambeau,    Christl, *Greatest Story*, p. 332.

## CHAPTER 80 .... *LOMBARDI IN THE PACKERS' SIGHTS*
561   Conducting a thorough    *Green Bay Press-Gazette*, Jan. 14, 1959.
562   Harry Norton and Henry Eaton,    *Green Bay Press-Gazette*, Jan. 15, 1959.
562   As a result, Duncan    *Milwaukee Journal-Sentinel*, May 5, 2009.
563   Amid reports from Milwaukee    *Green Bay Press-Gazette*, Jan. 26, 1959.
563   With Evashevski out    Christl, Packers.com, March 22, 2018.

## CHAPTER 81 .... *TWO LEGENDS, TWO DIFFERENT PATHS*
565   Although highly regarded    Christl, *Greatest Story*, p. 340; *Pro!* program magazine, Aug. 20, 1976.
566   "It looks as though Green Bay    *Chicago Tribune*, Jan. 30, 1959.

566    "I've never been associated    Green Bay Press-Gazette, Milwaukee Sentinel, Feb. 4, 1959.
566    "Today. . . the popular image    Beech, p. 243.

## CHAPTER 82 .... FULL RETIREMENT
567    A month later, about 150    Associated Press, Milwaukee newspapers, March 2, 1959, La Crosse Tribune, March 3, 1959.
567    To rally fans    Associated Press, Racine Journal-Times, March 24, 1959.
568    "Curly Lambeau was my coach    Rice, Grantland, The Tumult and the Shouting: My Life in Sport. New York: A.S. Barnes, 1954, p. 179.
568    "Not surprisingly, given that Lombardi    Christl, Greatest Story, p. 341.
569    While Lombardi was getting    Green Bay Press-Gazette, June 29, 1959.
570    When Lombardi made    Green Bay Press-Gazette, Sept. 30, 1959.
570    Lambeau was also beaming    Green Bay Press-Gazette, Oct. 5, 1959.
570    In a tribute to Bell,    Green Bay Press-Gazette, Oct. 15, 1959.
571    Bell's death created a void    Los Angeles Times, Oct. 17, 1959.
571    "An excellent choice,"    Green Bay Press-Gazette, Jan. 27, 1960
571    "I don't want to alibi    Minneapolis Star, Oct. 19, 1959.
571    Lambeau watched the Rams    Wisconsin State Journal, Oct. 22, 1959.
571    Lambeau was less harsh,    Minneapolis Star, Oct. 19, 1959.

## CHAPTER 83 .... SCRATCHING HIS COACHING ITCH
The information for this chapter comes from interviews conducted by the author with Door County residents in Fish Creek and Bailey's Harbor in July 2023 and July 2024. It also includes an author interview with Cliff Christl in July 2023.

## CHAPTER 84 .... ADMIRING LOMBARDI'S WORK
577    "Lambeau coached the Packers.    Rochester (New York) Democrat and Chronicle, Nov., 1959.
577    By late November, Lambeau    Palm Springs Desert Sun, Nov. 24, 1959.
578    "It's not hard to cover,"    Los Angeles Times, Dec. 7, 1959.
578    Curly suggested a bold move:    Long Beach Independent, Jan. 17, 1960.
578    Reached in Palm Springs,    Green Bay Press-Gazette, Dec. 14, 1959.
579    Their United DC-6B    Green Bay Press-Gazette, Dec. 15, 1959.

## CHAPTER 85 .... A PLAN TO HONOR LAMBEAU MEETS RESISTANCE
581    Alderman Thomas Atkinson    Green Bay Press-Gazette, Feb. 3 and April 14, 1960.
581    In a further watering down,    Green Bay Press-Gazette, May 4, 1960.
581    While Green Bay was pondering    Palm Springs Desert Sun, June 2, 1965.
581    Lambeau also was a regular    Palm Springs Desert Sun, Nov. 13 and Dec. 31, 1960.
582    On St. Patrick's Day    Valley Times, March 18, 1960.
582    Lambeau was in the press    Green Bay Press-Gazette, Sept. 26, 1960.
583    Curly went to the dinner,    Green Bay Press-Gazette, Nov. 14, 1960.
583    A regular in the press box    Green Bay Press-Gazette, Dec. 18, 1960.
584    "I definitely feel the Packers    Green Bay Press-Gazette, Dec. 23, 1960.

584    Philadelphia squeaked out Green Bay Press-Gazette, Dec. 27, 1960.

## CHAPTER 86 .... BURNING DOWN THE HOUSE—AGAIN

585    But Mary Jane was startled    Christl, Packers.com, June 12, 2015.
586    "Never in my life    AP, Green Bay Press-Gazette, Oct. 27, 1961.
587    When it was Lambeau's turn    Green Bay Press-Gazette, Dec. 24, 1961.
588    Earlier that day, Lambeau    La Crosse Tribune, Dec. 24, 1961.
588    "That's the nicest Christmas    Green Bay Press-Gazette, Dec. 24, 1961.
588    Three days before the Packers    New York Times, Dec. 28, 1961.
589    "If anyone rates credit    New York Daily News, Dec. 31, 1961.
590    "And to think that we    UPI, Pasadena Independent, Jan. 1, 1962.
590    But in the Chicago Tribune,    Chicago Tribune,, Jan. 1, 1962.
591    From across the Atlantic    Green Bay Press-Gazette, Jan. 10, 1962.
591    "The incident did not get    Chicago Tribune,, Jan. 16, 1962.

## CHAPTER 87 .... ONE HALL OF FAME AFTER ANOTHER

593    "We got the thing started,"    Palm Springs Desert Sun,, Oct. 27, 1965.
593    The automobile sale was not    Green Bay Press-Gazette, June 30, 1962.
594    When Lambeau's big night    Green Bay Press-Gazette, Nov. 18, 1962.
595    "Many times during my    Green Bay Press-Gazette, Nov. 18, 1962.
596    "Well, that's great.    Green Bay Press-Gazette, Dec. 18, 1962.
596    Reaching for a local angle,    Los Angeles Times, Jan. 29, 1963.
596    Blood, who had worked    Green Bay Press-Gazette, Dec. 18, 1962.
596    To celebrate their Hall of Fame    Whittingham, p. 41.
597    "I guess Curly was a human guy    Whittingham, p. 41.
597    Back in Palm Springs,    Appleton Post-Crescent, March 31, 1963.
597    Curly Lambeau doing the Twist    Desert Sun, March 27, 1963.
597    "Colorful Curly Lambeau,    Green Bay Press-Gazette, July 14, 1963.
599    "There was nothing like that,"    Green Bay Press-Gazette, Aug. 3, 1963.
599    "We have no excuses,    Chicago Tribune Aug. 3, 1963.
600    "Curly gave to America    Green Bay Press-Gazette, Sept. 8, 1963.
600    "I am deeply grateful    Green Bay Press-Gazette, Sept. 8, 1963.
600    "John was a magnificent    Green Bay Press-Gazette, Sept. 8, 1963.
601    "I fish almost every day,"    Pittsburgh Post-Gazette, Nov. 7, 1963.
601    "There's a new [era]    Pittsburgh Post-Gazette, Nov. 7, 1963.
601    In one of the strange ironies    Pittsburgh Post-Gazette, Nov. 7, 1963.

## CHAPTER 88 .... REUNION FOR KING CURLY AND HIS KNIGHTS

603    "The only thing I remember    D'Amato, Gary, and Christl, Cliff. Mudbaths & Bloodbaths: The Inside Story of the Bears-Packers Rivalry. Madison, Wisconsin: Prairie Oak Press, 1997, p. 43.
604    Rather than sulking,    Chicago Tribune April 14, 1964.
604    Absent from the third annual    Green Bay Press-Gazette, May 1, 1962.
605    "These are the men who    Green Bay Press-Gazette, April 27, 1965.
605    While handing Lambeau    Green Bay Press-Gazette, Associated Press, Waukesha Daily Freeman, April 27, 1965.
606    When Lambeau's turn    AP, Waukesha Daily Freeman, April 27, 1965.

| | | |
|---|---|---|
| 606 | "*Life ends. Curly Lambeau is* | *Green Bay Press-Gazette,* June 2, 1965. |

## CHAPTER 89 .... *LAST CONTROVERSY, LAST TRIUMPH*

| | | |
|---|---|---|
| 609 | *Nearly 30 years earlier,* | Christl, Packers.com, June 1, 2017. |
| 609 | *Amid the mourning* | *Green Bay Press-Gazette,* June 6, 1965. |
| 610 | *"Curly Lambeau's death* | AP, *Sheboygan Press,* June 3, 1965. Beech, p. 242. |
| 610 | *Aside from the Lambeau Field* | Christl, Packers.Com, June 12, 2015. |
| 611 | *"He was diametrically opposed* | Christl, *Packers Heritage Trail.* p. 181. |
| 611 | *Lambeau was outgoing* | Zimmerman, p. 122. |
| 612 | *"What a life this guy* | author interview with Upton Bell, Dec. 2023. |
| 612 | *"We never dreamt* | Whittingham, p. 157. |
| 612 | *The problem was, the photo* | *New York Times,* Dec. 28, 1961. |
| 613 | *"Any other name"* | Green Bay *Press-Gazette,* June 16, 1965. |
| 613 | *Wagner, the Press-Gazette* | *Green Bay Press-Gazette,* June 17, 1965. |
| 613 | *Most telling,* | *Green Bay Press-Gazette,* June 17, 1965. |
| 614 | *On Tuesday, August 3* | *Green Bay Press-Gazette,* Aug. 4, 1965. |

## *EPILOGUE*

| | | |
|---|---|---|
| 615 | "*If you're fortunate enough* | ESPN.com, Sept 16, 2020. |
| 615 | *Before Bud Lea became* | *Milwaukee Journal-Sentinel,* June 19, 2003. |

*INDEX*

**A**
Acme Packing Company, 34, 37, 40, 48, 271, 308
All-America Football Conference (AAFC), 34, 257, 262, 268, 270-71, 277, 287-89, 295-97, 299, 303-04, 310, 320, 325-27, 329-30, 337-41, 343-45, 347, 358, 366, 369, 371, 378-79, 383-84, 399, 401, 404, 409, 415, 471, 423, 425, 427, 466, 511, 518, 531,
American Professional Football Association (APFA), 34, 37-39, 40, 47-48, 50, 51, 56, 59, 594
Anderson, Hunk, 17, 46, 49, 136, 243, 249, 273, 392, 396, 433, 454, 504, 507, 510, 523, 525, 531
Atchison, Lewis F., 462, 464, 474-75, 488

**B**
Barra, Allan, 152-53
Baugh, Sammy, 131, 174-75, 178-79, 210, 216, 219, 227, 229, 254, 269, 282, 300, 303-04, 433, 450, 456, 460-62, 466, 468-69, 471, 474, 596, 606
Beech, Mark, 129, 533, 566
Bell, Bert, 51, 177, 182, 287-88, 291, 301, 340, 376, 395, 397, 401, 417, 419-20, 423, 428, 449, 467, 495, 501-02, 521, 527, 532, 570, 596, 612
Bell, Upton, 4-5, 11, 34, 62, 72, 291, 612
Bellevue Park, 57, 64
Beloit Fairies, 31-33, 38
Bennigsen, Ray, 384, 391-94, 400, 415, 426, 430, 438-40
Bent, Willard, 128-29, 132, 134, 209
Bidwill, Charlie, 260, 319, 424, 430
Bidwill, Violet, 371-73, 391, 398, 400-01, 415, 422-23, 425-26, 430, 432-33, 438, 469
Blackbourn, Lisle, 490, 502-03, 515, 535, 538, 541-42, 546, 548, 557, 559, 569
Blood, Johnny, 30, 63, 70-71, 75, 78-79, 82, 85, 89-95, 99, 112, 117-124, 133, 137-38, 160-2, 165-66, 169, 172, 177, 190, 195, 198-99, 216, 265, 276, 313, 362-63, 457, 519-20, 527, 566, 568, 586-88, 594, 595-97, 600-01, 605-06, 615
Bogda, Russ, 538-39, 542
Brock, Charley, 185-86, 203, 343, 346, 351, 354, 368, 614

Brown, Paul, 34-35, 288, 297, 425, 427, 434, 438, 472, 505, 508, 510, 515-6, 523-24, 531, 553, 555, 561, 563
Bryant, Paul "Bear", 152-53, 348
Buck, Howard "Cub", 38, 55, 59, 588
Bystrom, Arthur, 74, 83, 86, 88, 102, 133

**C**
C&C Supper Club, 2, 570, 573, 585, 598
Calhoun, George Whitney, 7-8, 14, 25-28, 31-33, 37, 39, 41, 44, 50, 53-56, 58, 61, 72, 75-76, 88-91, 96, 134, 137, 139, 147, 292, 306-09, 346, 366-68, 376, 379, 501, 525-26, 564
Canadeo, Tony, 2, 128, 214, 229, 285, 300, 310, 334-35, 349, 356, 363, 388, 511, 519, 523, 564, 615 Carr, Joe F., 43, 48, 52-53, 77-79, 96, 103-05, 107, 113-14, 155, 165, 182, 193-94, 260, 593, 596
Chamberlain, George, 44
Chance, Frank, 44
Chicago Bears, 8-9, 19, 21, 33, 41, 43-46, 49-50, 53-54, 61, 63-67, 69, 72-74, 76, 79-87, 90, 93, 95-96, 102-05, 108-15, 118, 122, 127, 131-36, 138-39, 141-42. 144-45, 147, 149-50, 154, 160, 162-63, 165-66, 169, 171, 175, 177-82, 195, 197-200, 205, 207, 208, 213, 216-19, 223-24, 226-27, 229-37, 239-44, 246, 248-51, 257, 259, 266-67, 269, 273-75, 278, 281-82, 286, 289, 291, 295-96, 300-03, 310-11, 314-17, 319, 321, 323, 325, 328, 331-32, 335-36, 340, 343, 345, 349, 351-53, 357-58, 363, 369, 372-73, 375-76, 378, 380, 384, 391-92, 396-98, 400, 403, 407, 409, 413-17, 419-25, 428, 432-33, 440-42, 445-47, 461, 463, 472, 481-82, 486, 504-06, 519-21, 527-30, 533-35, 538, 540-43, 545, 566, 570, 578, 582, 586-87, 594-96, 599, 602, 603-04, 606-07, 610, 614
Chicago Cardinals, 9, 19, 54, 59, 67, 73-74, 79, 82-83, 86-87, 101-02, 105, 109, 113, 123, 131, 134, 142-43, 145, 161-64, 168-69, 171, 175, 177, 179-80, 191, 195-97, 199, 218-19, 230, 233-34, 241-42, 246, 255, 260, 262, 274, 291, 301, 310-11, 313, 313-16, 319-21, 323, 325, 331-35, 337-38, 351-53, 359, 369, 371-3, 376, 384, 391-94, 397-404, 407-51, 454-56,

# Index 655

458-61, 463-64, 466-69, 476, 479, 481, 489, 491, 498, 504, 506, 511-12, 526, 543-44, 559, 572, 575, 593, 596
Christl, Cliff, 22, 38, 66, 71, 99, 125-26, 142, 150, 156, 189, 210-11, 216, 254, 349, 388, 497, 542, 546, 568, 573, 609, 611
Christman, Paul, 319-20, 332, 402-03, 408, 410-11, 413, 416, 427, 435
City Stadium, Green Bay, 8, 10, 73-74, 82, 84, 128-29, 134, 146, 165, 182, 192, 195, 197-99, 201, 216, 230, 242, 249-50, 274, 310, 331-32, 345-46, 348-49, 351, 357, 362, 407, 477-78, 502, 518, 525-26, 533, 544, 570, 581-83, 589, 595, 609-10, 612-14.
Clair, Emmett, 34, 37-38, 47-48
Clair, John M., 34, 37-38, 47-48
Clark, Dutch, 114-15, 596
Clifford, Gerald, 68, 96, 129, 135, 147, 157-58, 308-09, 354-55, 361, 366-67, 375-76, 394-95
College All-Star Game, 45, 160, 162-63, 171-75, 177-78, 187, 195-96, 205, 213-14, 216, 229, 240, 260, 272-73, 348-49, 409, 451, 481, 503-04, 506-08, 511-15, 517, 522-29, 531-32, 550-51, 588, 599
Comiskey Park, 54, 86, 168, 218, 233-34, 319-20, 332, 363, 365, 402, 408, 413, 416, 418-22, 433, 437-38, 440-41, 460, 479
Comp, Irv, 254, 256, 275, 300, 335, 339
Condon, David, 513, 590-91
Conover, Larry, 183, 185-86, 190
Conzelman, Jimmy, 19, 310-11, 319, 321, 337, 372, 399, 439, 594
Coolidge, Calvin, 226
Copeland, Billie / Copeland, Billie John *see Sue Lambeau*
Coughlin, Roundy, 207, 571
Craig, Larry, 183, 185, 199, 349, 368
Crowley, Jim, 33, 45, 67, 100, 152, 187, 191, 297-97, 568, 600, 604
Cuddy, Jack, 113, 254
Cuff, Ward, 291, 313-17, 320-24, 332, 489

## D

Daley, Art (*Green Bay Press Gazette* writer), 3, 247, 252, 254, 303, 323-24, 329, 341, 345, 348, 351-53, 359, 362, 383, 387, 393, 408, 410, 428, 431, 490, 544-7, 564, 567, 570, 584

Daley, Arthur J. (*New York Times* writer), 74, 149-50, 167-68, 178, 204, 222-3, 252-53, 588-89
Daly, Dan, 44, 63
Dalton, Jack, 33-34
Demovsky, Rob, 615
Dempsey, Jack, 100, 127, 450
Detroit Lions, 72, 94, 144-45, 163-64, 171, 177, 181-82, 199-200, 225, 230-31, 241, 246, 274-76, 314, 325, 332, 334, 354, 372, 375, 384, 409-10, 422, 429, 450, 459, 496, 517, 525, 531-33, 542, 545-46, 548, 554, 557, 577, 595-96, 599
Dilweg, Lavvie, 67-68, 78, 84, 89, 129, 170, 255, 362-63
Door County, 1, 10, 213, 215, 337, 451, 492, 510, 517, 522-23, 544, 552, 563, 568, 582, 585, 607
Dorais, Gus, 15, 18, 33, 47, 174-75, 214, 259, 588
Drazenovich, Chuck, 484-6
Driscoll, Paddy, 19, 59, 142, 372, 506, 533, 535
Duluth Eskimos, 117, 278, 343, 600
Duncan, Randy, 562
Dunn, Red, 30, 67, 75, 82, 85, 88. 142-43, 255, 588
Duryea, Earl Louis, 211
Dyer, Braven, 284, 326, 504, 571

## E

Earp, Jug, 65, 89, 363, 583
East-West Shrine Game, 91, 107, 127, 151-52, 154, 185, 239, 262, 329, 339, 373, 471, 490-91, 517 Eaton, Henry H., 549, 562
Ebbets Field, 102, 240, 295, 352
Eisenhower, Dwight D., 499, 551, 598
Evashevski, Forest, 561-63

## F

Feathers, Beattie, 150, 162, 213, 363
Fischer, Emil, 40, 308-09, 327, 339, 351, 353-59, 361, 363, 366-67, 369, 377, 380, 383, 385, 394
Fish Creek, Wisconsin, 1-2, 10, 518, 522, 525, 528, 537, 539, 541, 569-70, 573, 585-86, 597-98, 606
Fortmann, Danny, 109, 229, 236
Frankford Yellow Jackets, 73-76, 82, 86-87, 89-90, 107

Fritsch, Ted, 242, 256, 288, 300, 317, 321, 323-24, 332, 351-52, 368, 388

**G**

Gantenbein, Milt, 99, 166, 171, 177, 184-85
Garland, Grace *see Grace Garland Lambeau*
Garland, Jane, 283, 346-47, 493-94, 509
Gavin, Fritz, 141
Gibraltar High School, 570, 573-75
Gillman, Sid, 505, 526, 577-78
Gipp, George, 17-19, 23, 29, 46, 51, 218, 324, 364, 565, 568
Girard, Earl "Jug", 329, 330, 338, 358, 363
Goldberg, Marshall, 218, 234, 319
Goldenberg, Charles ``Buckets'', 115, 215, 276, 395, 540, 543-44, 552, 586-87, 610
Goodnight, Clyde, 275, 282, 291, 304, 350
Gordon, Lou, 169, 174
Graass, Henry, 130, 132, 135, 209
Graham, Otto, 297, 429, 466, 513, 531-32, 561
Grange, Red, 68, 70, 85-86, 88, 90, 108, 114, 123-24, 154, 226, 266-67, 269, 596
Griese, Oliver, 4
Griffith, Corinne, 10, 284-86, 488, 493
Grove, Roger, 123, 125, 161
Gutowski, Ace, 164, 231

**H**

Hagemeister Park, 15, 27-29, 33, 37-40, 55, 57, 271
Halas, Frank, 61
Halas, George, 2, 4, 5, 7, 9, 19, 21, 37-38, 41, 43-46, 48-50, 54-55, 58-61, 63-64, 73, 76, 79-82, 85, 88, 93, 109-11, 113, 118, 128, 131-32, 134-37, 141, 145, 147-49, 153, 156-57, 165-66, 169, 171, 177-78, 193, 197-99, 205, 215-17, 226-39, 241, 243, 245-47, 249, 255, 259-61, 267, 273, 275, 278, 289, 295, 300, 302, 305-07, 311, 315, 328, 331, 340-41, 345-46, 349, 351, 372-73, 378, 391-92, 396-401, 403, 414, 416-17, 419-23, 426, 428, 433, 437, 441, 446-47, 449, 454, 472, 475-76, 481, 506-07, 519-21, 533, 535, 540-41, 545, 551, 566, 570, 577, 593-94, 596, 602-06, 610-12, 614
Halas, Walter, 414
Harder, Pat, 314, 319-20, 400, 417, 429-31, 435, 442
Hardy, Jim, 403, 408, 410, 413, 416, 418, 429, 434-37, 441-42, 451
Harlow, Roy, 490, 514, 551, 578, 582, 584
Harper, Jesse, 14-20
Heath, Stan, 338-40, 344, 358, 363, 369
Heinz, W.C., 3
Herber, Arnie, 30, 63, 123, 142-44, 156, 161-63, 165-66, 171-72, 174-75, 179, 181, 184, 199, 207-11, 215, 250, 255, 313, 363, 552, 568, 614-15
Herber, Mary Jane, 81
Hewitt, Bill, 108, 133, 182-83
Hickok, Ralph, 93-94, 117, 119, 138
Hinkle, Clarke, 35, 91-92, 107-08, 117, 150, 161, 163, 166-67, 170, 174, 196, 198-99, 200, 203, 226, 229-30, 235, 237, 313, 407, 583, 588, 605-06, 615
Hirsch, Elroy, 347-48, 350
Hoeffel, Joe, 13, 34, 38-39, 59-60, 65
Hornung, Paul, 526, 528-30, 551, 570-71, 577, 598-99, 604-05
Horrigan, Joe, 38-39
Hoyt, Lyla, 151, 189, 281, 509
Hubbard, Cal, 69-70, 72, 79, 85, 92-94, 138, 160-161, 167, 317, 407, 457, 596, 600, 605
Hubbard, Dave, 574
Hungry Five, 147, 158, 309, 361, 379
Hunter, Scott, 153
Hutson, Don, 30, 34-35, 45, 71, 92-93, 149-57, 159-60, 162-66, 177, 181, 183, 186, 199, 203, 205-06, 213-15, 217-19, 222, 229-30, 235, 240, 242-44, 247, 251-56, 265, 272-76, 296, 299-300, 304, 313, 316-17, 331, 339, 343, 348, 350, 358, 362-63, 379, 403, 407, 484, 519, 527, 543, 568, 582-83, 587-88, 594, 596, 600, 605-07, 615

**I**

Indian Packing Co., 14-15, 25, 27-28, 33, 37, 40, 43, 60, 130, 192, 308
Isbell, Cecil, 30, 157, 181, 198, 203, 205-06, 210, 214, 222, 229-30, 235, 240, 242-44, 251-54, 269, 282, 300, 304,

# Index

338-40, 403, 433-35, 437, 441-42, 445-46, 450, 456, 489, 568
Ishpeming, Michigan, 29-30, 33, 267

**J**

Jacobs, Jack, 303, 314-15, 320, 339, 344, 348-49, 351
Jacunski, Harry, 187, 205, 611
Jean, Walter, 215, 418
Joannes, Lee, 56, 96, 104-06, 130, 133, 135, 145-47, 157-58, 182, 201, 257, 261, 271, 307-09, 346, 355, 361, 366, 375-76, 395, 538-40, 545-46, 552, 555, 559
Johnson, Chuck, 29, 38, 41, 55, 309, 554
Johnsos, Luke, 96, 133, 243, 249, 273-74, 392
Johnston, Janice, 10
Jones, Ralph, 82, 84, 86, 96, 132
Jonet, Frank, 130, 146-47, 309, 359, 388, 397
Jorgensen, Bud, 34, 77-78, 87, 335

**K**

Kelley, Bob, 527-28, 550-52, 578
Kelly, Dr. William Webber, 56, 96, 144, 147, 157-58, 271-72, 306-09, 355, 361, 366-67, 375, 395
Kelly, Shipwreck, 155
Kennedy, John F., 198-99
Kennedy, Merna, 124
Kessler, Gene, 429
Keuper, Ken, 346, 370
Kieran, John, 135-37, 191-92, 223, 240
Kiesling, Walt, 198, 265, 267, 275, 315, 331, 343, 350, 503, 525
Kinnick, Nile, 214-15
Kittell, John, 56, 309
Klaus, Fee, 346, 363
Knox, Ronnie, 527-28
Kramer, Jerry, 551, 558, 616
Kramer, Ron, 528-29, 551
Kuechle, Oliver, 70, 144-45, 359, 361, 365-66, 395, 534, 538, 546-48, 557-58, 563, 567
Kuharich, Joe, 445-46, 460-61, 463, 469, 491, 498
Kupcinet, Irv, 165, 197-98, 237, 372, 403, 414, 428

**L**

Lambeau Evrard, Beatrice (sister), 349

Lambeau, Donald (son), 60, 126, 191, 473, 490, 567
Lambeau, Earl Louis II (son), *see Earl Louis Duryea*
Lambeau, Grace (*Nicholls Garland*, third wife), 189, 281-85, 287, 292, 299, 327, 329, 339, 344, 349, 353, 397-98, 404, 445, 450, 454, 493-94, 501, 505, 508-09
Lambeau, Marcel (father), 9-10, 25, 33, 37-38, 129, 192
Lambeau, Mary (Mrs. Marcel, mother), 9, 451, 473, 477, 490, 502, 537, 558, 604
Lambeau, Marguerite Van Kessel (first wife), 15, 20, 22, 25, 27, 60, 72-73, 126, 132, 151, 189
Lambeau, Oliver (brother), 379, 490
Lambeau, Raymond (brother), 490, 559, 567
Lambeau, Susan, (*Billie John/Billie Sue Copeland*, second wife), 125-26, 151, 159, 176, 189, 209-11
Landry, Tom, 456, 561, 563-64, 583
Larson, Lloyd, 363, 431, 554
Layden, Elmer, 152, 245, 257, 260, 262, 287, 295, 297
Lea, Bud, 615
Leahy, Frank, 447, 499, 512
LeBaron, Eddie, 453, 456-58, 460, 466, 468, 473-75, 479, 481, 486-89, 491-92, 511
Lee, Bill, 154-55, 205, 218
Lewellen, Verne, 66-67, 70, 74-76, 84-85, 89, 121, 136, 163, 362-63, 521, 537-38, 543-44, 548, 553-54, 557, 596
Lindheimer, Ben, 297, 326-27
Lipscomb, Paul, 433, 477-78
Lombardi, Vince, 1, 3-4, 7, 15, 33-35, 62, 72, 105, 112, 127-28, 167, 187, 529-30, 532, 561-71, 577, 579, 583, 587-91, 594-96, 599-600, 603-06, 610-12, 614, 616
Long, Dale, 474
Luckman, Sid, 67, 149, 197, 200, 210, 216-17, 229, 234-36, 239, 243-44, 250, 254, 256, 269, 282, 300, 304, 343, 604
Lujack, Johnny, 349, 416, 446-47

**M**

Mara, Tim, 204-05, 246, 269, 295, 596
Mara, Wellington, 70, 246, 269, 295, 561, 563-64

Marshall, George Preston, 10, 107, 130-31, 133-34, 165, 178, 215, 226, 240-41, 245-46, 260, 263, 272, 284-85, 303, 414, 433, 449, 453-56, 459-60, 462-64, 466-68, 471-73, 477-79, 481-82, 484-86, 488-89, 491-99, 501-03, 529, 596
Mathys, Charlie, 65, 142
Matson, Ollie, 460, 463
Maxwelton Braes, 337
McAfee, George, 217, 234-35, 239
McCann, Dick, 477, 483, 498, 501
McGlynn, Stoney, 142, 195, 203
McLean, Ray "Scooter", 243, 541-42, 545-46, 548, 553-54, 558, 569
McNeil, Charles K (point spread inventor), 357
Memphis Tigers, 77-79
Michalske, Mike, 69-70, 72, 94, 99, 108, 123, 523, 605
Molenda, Bo, 72, 75, 85, 143, 331, 343
Morabito, Tony, 297, 383, 451, 561
Morrall, Earl, 517, 524
Murphy, Don, 50-53, 593
Murphy, Neil, 33

**N**
Nagurski, Bronko, 67, 96, 114, 132, 267, 59
Nesser, Al, 47
Nevers, Ernie, 73, 86, 101-02, 108, 117, 123, 278, 596
New York Giants, 9, 68-69, 72, 74-75, 82-84, 86-92, 95-97, 102, 107, 109, 111, 127, 131, 133-35, 137-39, 144-45, 168, 178-79, 181-85, 191, 195-96, 198, 200-201, 204-07, 216-17, 219, 221, 223-24, 233-34, 237, 240, 242, 244, 246, 249-51, 253-56, 262-63, 269-70, 274, 276, 286, 289, 291, 295-96, 302, 313, 317, 325, 331, 333, 336, 344, 346, 352-53, 357, 370, 384, 418-19, 422, 425, 428, 438-39, 441, 458, 465, 467-68, 479, 483, 486, 495, 508, 525, 529-30, 533, 544-45, 561, 563, 565, 583, 587-90, 593-94, 596, 604
Nixon, Richard, 533
Northland Hotel, 64, 179, 205, 213, 230, 349-50, 352, 357, 359, 477, 535, 546, 559, 566
Norton, Harry, 549-50, 562
Notre Dame, 7-8, 14-25, 29-30, 33-34, 37, 44-47, 49-50, 60, 67, 69, 82-83, 89, 92-93, 99-101, 121-22, 135-37, 142-43, 151-52, 154, 159, 168, 171, 173-74, 183, 187, 200, 204-05, 210, 213-14, 218, 236, 242, 248, 252, 257, 259-60, 266, 275, 281, 296-97, 299, 303-05, 311, 317, 328-29, 353, 363, 370, 391-92, 397, 399-400, 408, 410, 420, 445-47, 459-60, 498-99, 501, 503-04, 511-13, 526, 529, 531, 565, 568-69, 577, 588, 600, 604

**O**
O'Donnell, Bob, 44, 63
Olejniczak, Dominic, 407, 534, 539-44, 548, 553-55, 557, 559-64, 571, 607, 610
Owen, Steve, 191, 206, 254, 313, 418-19, 458, 508, 510

**P**
Parilli, Babe, 462, 535, 545
Parker, Buddy, 371-73, 426, 429, 439, 459
Parsons, Louella, 281-83
Paul, Don, 496, 508, 551
Peck, Frank, 25, 37, 57
Polo Grounds, 51, 74, 83, 88, 91, 102, 111, 137, 165, 178, 181, 183, 196, 204, 249-50, 256, 263, 271, 302-03, 325, 352-53, 419, 453, 483
Pool, Hampton, 505, 508, 510, 513-14, 523
Portsmouth Spartans, 8, 60, 72, 77, 83-84, 87, 89, 96-97, 101-106, 109, 111-12, 114-15, 117-18, 127, 131-35, 144-46
Powers, Jimmy, 178, 296
Pro Bowl, 205-06, 427, 429, 432, 446, 471, 477, 482, 485, 499, 517, 528, 561, 584
Pro Football Hall of Fame, 19, 38, 67, 70, 85, 93, 142, 198, 266, 307, 363, 373, 418, 473, 593-94, 596, 599, 601, 605

**R**
Ray, Buford ``Baby,'' 200, 225
Reagan, Ronald, 23, 218
Reeves, Dan, 260, 284, 287, 383, 391-92, 396, 505, 526-27
Remmel, Lee, 13, 21, 23, 38, 127, 307, 314, 335, 363, 427, 461-62, 478, 497, 584, 611
Rice, Grantland, 45, 397, 568
Rock Island Independents, 40, 46, 56, 61, 65, 147, 266-67, 310

# Index

Rockne, Knute, 7-8, 15-20, 22-25, 30, 33, 35, 45-47, 49, 69, 83, 99-100, 136, 143, 151-52, 174, 198, 214, 218, 252, 259-60, 297, 305, 327-28, 364, 391-92, 402, 461, 473, 480, 501, 513, 565, 568-69, 588, 615
Rockwood Lodge, 289-93, 299, 306, 325, 348, 354, 358-59, 361, 365, 387-89, 394, 399, 405, 586
Rollow, Cooper, 523, 535
Ronzani, Gene, 380, 396, 403, 405, 407, 414, 416, 418, 462, 476, 484, 490, 502, 548, 559
Rooney, Art, 95, 161, 190, 245, 600-601
Roosevelt, Franklin D., 52, 107, 236
Roosevelt Hotel, 281-82
Rose Bowl, 19, 51, 107, 127, 151-55, 185, 214, 239, 262, 284, 303, 339, 372-73, 392, 429, 471, 490, 514, 517, 562, 596
Rozelle, Pete, 527, 571, 595, 607, 616
Rudolph, Jack, 26-7, 137
Ryan, Willard ``Big Bill,'' 28, 31, 34

**S**

Schneider, Val, 26
Schneidman, Herm, 125, 210
Schramm, Tex, 526-27, 557
Shaughnessy, Clark, 347, 391-93, 396
Sheer, Harry, 321, 392-3, 414, 416, 421-22
Skaletski, Roger, 349
Smith, Red (assistant coach), 205, 218, 243, 251-55, 265
Smith, Red (newspaper columnist), 41, 252, 394-95, 546
Smith, Wilfrid, 85-87, 512, 515, 531
Snyder, Bob, 340, 343-44, 346, 348-49, 351, 353-54
Sperber, Murray, 22
Spielman, Bob, 573-75
Spielman, Patrick, 573-75
Spinks, Jack, 465
Stagg, Amos Alonzo, 100, 456, 476
Sternaman, Dutch, 43-44, 55, 73, 79, 81-82, 110-11, 132, 267, 328
Strickler, George, 45, 162, 183, 200, 213, 215, 226, 241, 306-07, 345-46, 350, 359, 361, 387, 393-94, 396-97, 510, 512, 523, 526, 529
Stuhldreher, Harry, 23, 152, 329
Stydahar, Joe, 229, 236, 396, 427, 469

**T**

Thomas, Frank, 45, 151, 153
Tilleman, Don, 5, 610
Tinsley, Pete, 282, 552, 558
Todd, Dick, 433, 453-55, 499
Topping, Dan, 263, 269-70, 295-96, 329, 340
Torinus, John, 26, 78, 292, 306, 367, 382, 547, 614
Trafton, George, 249, 257, 265-67, 274-76
Trippi, Charley, 319, 332, 400, 408, 417, 428, 431-35, 437, 441-42, 446, 461, 463, 489
Tripucka, Frank, 408, 410, 413, 418, 431, 433
Turnbull, Andrew, 8, 55-56, 97, 118, 147, 158, 268, 309, 345, 352, 361, 375, 379

**V**

Vandeveld, Patricia, 126
Van Duys, Francis, 2
Van Duyse, Fritz, 544, 552, 558, 582, 584
Van Duyse, Mary Jane, 1-2, 10, 552, 582, 584-5, 590, 601, 606, 610
Van Kessel, Marguerite, *see Lambeau, Marguerite*
Voight, Judi Weisgerber, 573-74
Voight, Wayne, 574-75

**W**

Walter, John, 175, 200, 216, 224-25
Ward, Arch, 9, 18, 21, 25, 30, 32, 38, 45, 50, 52, 69, 147, 171, 205, 240, 259, 261-62, 270, 272, 295-97, 299, 309, 399-401, 439, 449, 451, 459, 503-04, 507, 510-13
Washington, Kenny, 215
Waterfield, Bob, 274-75, 301, 333, 339-40, 343, 396, 410, 429, 508, 551, 578
Weisgerber, Dick, 2, 203-04, 570, 573-75, 585, 598
Weisgerber, Rich, 203, 573, 585, 598
White, Byron "Whizzer," 198, 600
Whittingham, Richard, 35, 91, 157
Wildung, Dick, 291, 369
Willis, Chris, 48, 67, 85, 103, 155
Wisconsin Athletic Hall of Fame, 2-3, 587-88, 594, 601
Wisconsin, University of, 8, 13-14, 17, 22, 24, 38, 55, 59, 99, 142-43, 166, 314, 320, 329, 339, 347, 429, 514, 567, 596, 599

Wolfner, Walter, 371, 400, 423, 425-27, 430, 432-35, 437-42, 445-46, 455, 459, 469, 491, 498
Wright, Orville, 221
Wrigley Field, 41, 64, 76, 83-84, 87, 90, 96, 101-03, 110, 113, 118, 124, 134, 139, 163, 177, 179, 199, 218-19, 230, 233, 235, 237, 243, 249, 275, 315-16, 319, 335, 357, 417, 440-41

**Z**
Zabel, George ``Zip,'' 31
Zimmerman, David, 11, 50, 52

www.ingramcontent.com/pod-product-compliance
Lightning Source LLC
Chambersburg PA
CBHW022220090526
44585CB00013BB/444